Handbook of Online Learning

2ND EDITION

Handbook of Online Learning

2ND EDITION

EDITORS

Kjell Erik Rudestam
Fielding Graduate University

Judith Schoenholtz-Read
Fielding Graduate University

Los Angeles | London | New Delhi
Singapore | Washington DC

For information:

SAGE Publications, Inc.
2455 Teller Road
Thousand Oaks, California 91320
E-mail: order@sagepub.com

SAGE Publications India Pvt. Ltd.
B 1/I 1 Mohan Cooperative Industrial Area
Mathura Road, New Delhi 110 044
India

SAGE Publications Ltd.
1 Oliver's Yard
55 City Road
London EC1Y 1SP
United Kingdom

SAGE Publications Asia-Pacific Pte. Ltd.
33 Pekin Street #02-01
Far East Square
Singapore 048763

Printed in the United States of America.

Library of Congress Cataloging-in-Publication Data

Handbook of online learning / edited by Kjell Erik Rudestam, Judith Schoenholtz-Read.—2nd ed.
    p. cm.
Includes bibliographical references and index.
ISBN 978-1-4129-6103-5 (pbk. : acid-free paper)
    1. Education, Higher—Computer-assisted instruction—Handbooks, manuals, etc. 2. Internet in education—Handbooks, manuals, etc. 3. Employees—Training of—Computer-assisted instruction—Handbooks, manuals, etc. I. Rudestam, Kjell Erik. II. Schoenholtz-Read, Judith.

LB2395.7.H23 2009
378.1′7344678—dc22   2009008632

This book is printed on acid-free paper.

09 10 11 12 13   10 9 8 7 6 5 4 3 2 1

Acquisitions Editor:	Diane McDaniel
Editorial Assistant:	Ashley Conlon
Production Editor:	Karen Wiley
Copy Editor:	Renee Willers
Typesetter:	C&M Digitals (P) Ltd.
Proofreader:	Wendy Jo Dymond
Indexer:	Julie Grayson
Cover Designer:	Gail Buschman
Marketing Manager:	Stephanie Adams

Brief Contents

Part II. Implementation of Online Learning

Detailed Contents

Preface

In the 7 years since the first edition of the *Handbook of Online Learning* was published, innovations in computer technology and the Internet have expanded exponentially and their impact on the quantity and quality of online learning has been dramatic. Online programs that were just beginning are now well established in many classroom-based universities and organizations. We represented one of the few graduate universities with a long history in distance and online learning. Now we are members of a very large community of higher education institutions that rely on virtual classrooms to deliver at least a portion of their education and training curricula. During this time, many of our values, beliefs, and concerns have remained constant. We continue to believe that education and training thrive in an intimate learning community that supports academic rigor. We maintain that technology must serve learning needs rather than the other way around. At the same time, we have welcomed the institutionalization of online learning and the availability of a burgeoning conceptual and applied literature represented by a wellspring of new books and journals in the field. We view technology and the Internet as innovative forces that interact with pedagogy in potentially creative ways. As such, we assert the need for best practices to support the development and maintenance of high-quality, innovative online programs and courses.

As we have become more expert about how to work in virtual space so have our students, faculty, and administrative colleagues. Our experience continues to convince us that online learning can serve students from diverse locations around the globe and engage them in productive, exciting, and satisfying learning communities. We recognize that the vast array of available learning platforms and Internet resources can be overwhelming to faculty and administrators seeking to design and launch online programs. We have become more sensitive to the barriers to adopting new technology and networked approaches to learning, as well as to the frequent resistance by administrators and faculty in employing new teaching methods. This handbook builds on our experiences and also picks up where the previous edition left off. We hope we have captured the progress and possibilities that lie ahead and provide a useful roadmap for navigation.

As before, our primary goal in this edition of the handbook is to clarify and illustrate theories of online learning and pedagogical implications of teaching and training in online environments and virtual worlds. A second goal is to provide practical guidance and best practices to educators and trainers who teach and administer online courses and programs.

In this edition, we have included several new authors who are highly respected, knowledgeable contributors to current topics within the online education landscape. For example, we have included eleven new chapters addressing such important areas of interest as globalization, emergent technologies, virtual libraries, and accreditation of online programs and institutions. In addition, the eight chapters which are retained from the previous edition are all significantly revised and updated. We are extremely grateful to our contributors for their dedication and commitment to the field of online learning. Their chapters reflect their passion and enthusiasm for teaching in the virtual environment. One of their most important lessons is to remind us that students learn most when they can be collaborators in their educational experiences. As well, our students continue to inspire us and serve as our first source of innovation.

On a more personal basis, this project was supported by the love and commitment of our life partners, Jan Rudestam and David Read, who graciously endured our numerous phone calls and absences. Our dear friends and colleagues at Fielding Graduate University also deserve our appreciation for their ongoing support and wisdom. We want to acknowledge one another as well. We worked as coeditors while one of us resided in Santa Barbara, California, and the other in Vancouver, British Columbia, reinforcing our belief that the Internet can effectively support long-distance writing projects.

We sometimes take for granted the exceptional services and encouragement provided by members of the Sage Publications family of editors and staff. In this case we deeply appreciate the contributions of James Brace-Thompson and Lisa Shaw, our chief editors, for their encouragement and ongoing enthusiasm for our work; our editorial assistant, Ashley Conlon; our production editor, Karen Wiley; our copy editor, Renee Willers; and the Sage staff. We would also like to acknowledge and thank the reviewers of this edition: Chris Dede, Harvard University; Carol Watson, Indiana University; Pamela Whitehouse, West Virginia University; Jeffrey Alejandro, East Carolina University; and Jody Clarke, Harvard University.

Chapter 1

The Flourishing of Adult Online Education

An Overview

Kjell Erik Rudestam

Judith Schoenholtz-Read

What is important is to keep learning, to enjoy challenge, and to tolerate ambiguity. In the end there are no certain answers.

—Matina Horner

The primary purpose of this handbook is to clarify the conceptual issues that underlie effective online teaching and to offer practical guidance to educators and trainers who plan to establish or teach in a virtual environment (VE). The chapters in the book are written by experts in the field who share their experiences and suggestions for working effectively in this medium. If there is one central tenet to this handbook, it is this: The adoption of the online environment as the teaching vehicle of the future in higher education and corporate training demands a reexamination of our core beliefs about pedagogy and how students learn. It challenges us to find new ways to evaluate learning and to confront the professional and ethical issues that emerge from working in this new environment. It forces us to figure out how to use rapidly changing technologies to enhance learning. Although the transfer of classroom-based learning into cyberspace at first appeared to be deceptively simple, we have discovered that doing so without an appreciation for the nuances and implications of learning online ignores not only its potential but also the inevitable realities of entering it. Before we tackle a discussion of the pedagogy itself, as well as significant changes that have emerged in recent years, we need to provide a context for this educational revolution.

A Brief History of Early Computer-Assisted and Web-Based Instruction

The history of computer-assisted instruction, which first attempted to use timesharing computers during the 1960s, is clearly described by Harasim and her colleagues (Harasim, Hiltz, Teles, & Turoff, 1995). Communication took place over dumb terminals connected to mainframe computers or dial-up telephone lines. In 1969, the U.S. government experimented with dedicated telephone lines for data exchange by constructing the ARPANET (Advanced Research Projects Agency Network) to connect researchers with remote computer centers to share resources. It was not long before these researchers wanted to exchange messages with one another about their projects. The electronic mail (e-mail) function was born and became immensely popular. Other communication networks (e.g., USENET, BITNET, CSNET) followed, still predominantly connecting researchers and scientists. Eventually, the Internet, a global network of networks, supplanted these individual efforts.

Murray Turoff is given credit for designing the first computer conferencing system in 1970 (Hiltz & Turoff, 1993). Today, of course, there are many conferencing systems available that support discussion as well as a myriad of more sophisticated features. Bulletin boards, a common space for posting messages over the computer, were developed during the late 1970s (Sterling, 1992) but did not proliferate until a decade later. Both of these functions are at the heart of the implementation of computer networks for training and education. Computer conferencing systems were applied to course activity in higher education during the 1980s and remain a prominent feature of online education today. All of these variants have found their way into higher education in the public and private sectors.

Distance Learning Terminology

One of the difficulties in obtaining a clear sense of the literature on online learning is the multiplicity of terms used to describe the phenomenon. Commonly employed terms include *distance learning, distributed learning, online learning, computer-mediated learning,* and *e-learning.*

Some educational institutions conceived their mandate as training students who are geographically dispersed from one another and from the institutions themselves. They represent what has historically been known as *distance education.* According to the U.S. Congress for Technology Assessment, distance education refers to the "linking of a teacher and students in several geographic locations via technology that allows for interaction" (Daniel & Stevens, 1998, p. 162). However, many distance learning institutions that have come to adopt a strong online presence were functioning prior to the Internet by relying on individually directed study, mail, telephone, and/or infrequent residential sessions for contact between students and instructors.

One example is the United Kingdom's Open University, which initiated use of computer conferencing as a small adjunct to a large multimedia course (Harasim et al., 1995). Course tutors held discussion groups in closed conferences with relatively small numbers of students. Interestingly, the computer conferencing forum that was open to all students and tutors purely for socializing purposes generated the most traffic and became the most productive workspace. This unanticipated outcome, as we shall see, has had significant implications for practitioners of online education. Another example, with which we are more personally acquainted and which serves as the source of much of our experience with online teaching, is the Fielding Graduate University based in Santa Barbara, California. Fielding, as is true for a few other academic institutions such as the Union Graduate School, Empire State College, and the University Without Walls, established a distance education model many years ago to provide an educational opportunity for a group of geographically dispersed, adult, mid-career professionals who could not easily give up their family and work responsibilities to move to a campus-based institution for a lengthy period of time. Today, Fielding offers graduate degree programs in clinical psychology, human and organizational behavior, and educational leadership. Each program has its own unique blend of online and face-to-face seminars and tutorial experiences. In many cases, students take courses as asynchronous and/or synchronous online seminars. A few of the chapters in this handbook illustrate the ways in which these online programs and courses are structured and taught.

As indicated above, adherence to a distance model of training does not necessarily imply the adoption of an online teaching environment. Because the term distance education has traditionally implied delivery of instruction or course materials over a distance, educators who support a model of education that emphasizes student initiated access to learning resources have recommended the use of the term distributed learning or flexible learning rather than distance learning to refer to new forms of online learning (Carr-Chellman & Duchastel, 2000). Distance education institutions have not necessarily embraced online learning, but when they have done so, the transition to a communication-based technology has often gone more smoothly because of the overlap of values and skills required to succeed in the virtual setting. As described later in this chapter, other distance education programs have been established solely online.

Perhaps the favored term in the literature today for designating courses and programs offered over the Internet is e-learning. E-learning has been defined by the Instructional Technology Council as "the process of extending learning or delivering instructional materials to remote sites via the Internet, intranet/extranet, audio, video, satellite broadcast, interactive

TV, and CD-ROM" (Holsapple & Lee-Post, 2006, p. 2). Nonetheless, the term that most accurately describes the contemporary trend of incorporating distance technology and the Internet into the educational process is *blended learning*. Blended learning refers to an amalgamation of face-to-face learning and online learning. The other term that is frequently used in this context is *hybrid learning*, again referring to the possibility of combining face-to-face and online modalities, either within the same course or across courses or programs within the same institution.

A predictable risk in the face-to-face educational environment is a disproportionate focus and responsibility on the teacher, whereas a common risk in the online environment is lack of structure and organizational coherence because the objective is for students to become self-directed (Garrison & Vaughn, 2008). In our experience, some topics or courses are taught most efficaciously in a face-to-face format, while others are more suited to an online format. The combination of both formats within the same course or program allows for capitalizing on the advantages of each approach. Moreover, the availability of both formats allows for sensitivity to the diverse learning styles and needs of different students.

Osguthorpe and Graham (2003) have argued that the rationale for adopting a blended system is that it allows for pedagogical richness, access to knowledge, social interaction, personal agency, cost-effectiveness, and ease of revision. In a 2003 survey, 80% of undergraduate and graduate higher education institutions were found to be offering blended learning courses (Arabasz & Baker, 2003). Perhaps one reason for the burgeoning popularity of the hybrid model is that the current generation of students moves effortlessly between face-to-face and online environments; they were weaned on the Internet, and the online milieu serves as a second family (Taffel, 2000) for them. At the same, Garrison and Vaughan (2008) have pointed out that although this generation of students is very open to computer-mediated education and value social interactions and collaborative learning, they also view the instructor as a critical element of the learning experience and are apprehensive that technology will reduce communication between students and faculty. These authors believe that a "tipping point" has been reached for the dominance of blended learning in higher education and that the roots of this movement are technological, financial, and pedagogical. We concur.

Current Status of Online Learning Programs

Nearly every institution of higher learning has incorporated or intends to incorporate some aspects of online technology into its curriculum delivery system. The way in which online technology becomes operationalized, however, differs significantly among institutions. At this time, there appear to be three major forms of computer-networked technology, or Internet-based learning, in education: 1) Web facilitated with less than 30% of the content online—this is a face-to-face course that has moved online with the help of a course management system (CMS), 2) a blended or hybrid course that uses both face-to-face and substantial online content, and 3) a fully online course with most of the content online (Allen & Seaman, 2006). Each of these options can be seen in traditional educational institutions and corporate training programs.

Some institutions were created after the advent of the Internet, and many of them were designed to offer classes, programs, and degrees exclusively online. While many of these programs have closed, others are incredibly successful in the marketplace. Smith and Mitry (2008) have been particularly vocal in terms of questioning the integrity of some selected for-profit institutions that are drawn to computer-based learning solely for cost advantages and are willing to sacrifice educational quality by, for example, hiring underqualified faculty as instructors or facilitators of their online courses. In a more general sense, it is our impression that organizations that gravitate to the online environment exclusively for financial reasons are apt to be disappointed. As Levy (2005) has put it, some proponents of online learning have focused on accessing a greater number of students rather than on serving current students in a better way.

Market Issues and Demographics

Hanna and Associates (2000) cited consumer demand as the key factor creating new forms of distance learning. The demand comes from the need for, and interest in, increased student access, lifelong learning, and professional and work-related training. Drucker (1999) highlighted the need for knowledge workers of the future to have the ability to update their skills quickly and to take responsibility for their learning. In part due to changing demographics, the globalization of the workforce, and the aging and increasing professionalization of the population, adult students are returning to school, driven by their own developmental interests and by the requirements of their employers. The pressure to respond to the desire for just-in-time learning is a powerful force for change. Some institutions are more capable of responding than others, and new approaches to learning continue to emerge.

According to the Sloane Consortium's annual surveys on the state of online learning in the United States, the enormous growth in online enrollments has begun to stabilize but will continue at a higher level than traditional classroom-based enrollments (Allen & Seaman, 2005; Allen & Seaman, 2007). The number of online students increased at an annual rate of 9.6%, whereas the classroom-based enrollments increased by only 1.5%. This difference is expected to continue. The results of the Sloane 2007 survey indicate that about 35% of higher education institutions have three quarters of the online enrollments (Allen & Seaman, 2007). If we look at the type of institutions with the largest numbers of online students, the 2-year associate colleges have the highest level of engagement in online learning (62%). Masters or doctoral research institutions have lower rates of engagement, followed by the baccalaureate schools. The smallest private colleges and universities are the least engaged in online learning. In total, online students comprise about 20% of all students (Allen & Seaman, 2007). These figures suggest that the future bodes well for online enrollments. However, it is unlikely that many new institutions will enter the field.

Corporate universities are growing faster than higher education (Hearn, 2001; Urdan & Weggen, 2000). These "universities" focus on educating their employees to improve the quality of the globally distributed workforce and to maintain the corporate culture. Corporate training programs have used learning management systems (LMS) or more recently, content management tools and blended formats. In a 2008 survey conducted by the American Society for Training and Development's (ASTD) Learning Circuits (Learning Circuits, 2008), companies reported using e-learning for training in business skills, task specific skills, desktop applications, and regulatory and compliance issues. Reported problems with e-learning were related to cost and employee buy-in, technical competency, and time commitment. Some corporate universities have partnered with traditional universities to offer online degree opportunities to employees. For example, United Health developed United Health Learning Institute in collaboration with Renselaer Polytechnic Institute to offer degree programs to employees. As well, the U.S. military provided over 50 online degree programs to more than 30,000 service men and women through the American Public University System and the American Military University in 2008 (www.apus.edu). However, not all institutions have joined the Internet bandwagon. The Sloane Consortium (Allen & Seaman, 2007) found that smaller public colleges and universities tend not to have online learning as part of their strategic plans. Perhaps this is due to the continuing perception among their faculty that online learning is not as effective as classroom-based learning. Resistance to online teaching has been attributed to faculty lack of confidence, feelings of loss, and lack of awareness of and training in new approaches (Panitz & Panitz, 1998). Others fear for the demise of the university as we know it. Talbott (1998) cited the apprehension of faculty who are currently at the center of traditional teaching and learning models and who anticipate a loss of status and power. Noble (1999), for example, argued that higher education is being commercialized and that teaching is becoming a commodity that steals the faculty's control, knowledge, skill, and livelihood.

Fears have morphed into other issues. Students entrenched in the digital society have changing expectations about the relationship between learning and technology. Successful operation of new technology can lead to a greater sense of knowledge and efficacy, but failure can evoke feelings of stupidity and ineptitude. There are also built-in paradoxes to the technology itself. What seems radically new and innovative one day becomes old and obsolete the next day. What appears to provide remarkable savings in efficiency and cost-effective service can inefficiently consume huge amounts of time and attention. Naïve expectations that online learning is financially rewarding have been disappointed. What is experienced as fulfilling can easily become a craving for more and better technology. The interface of technology with pedagogy gives rise to complex struggles. What has the potential for assimilating and joining people together on any number of topics and experiences can easily lead to feelings of loneliness and isolation.

University administrators attribute the growth of their online programs to student demand. Online programs increase access to education for students who are nontraditional and are unable to attend classroom-based environments. This fulfills a significant mission for many institutions. Online programs have also grown to meet the need for increased continuing and professional education, increased retention and degree completion, and accessibility for new students outside their catchment areas (Allen & Seaman, 2007). At the same time there are significant barriers to the development of online programs and courses. These are perceived by administrators to be related to (1) faculty resistance to online programs and courses, (2) increased time and effort for faculty, (3) increased needs for student focus and discipline, (4) high costs of online programs, (5) issues with retention, and (6) employers' negativity (Allen & Seaman, 2007). It is interesting to note that faculty's need to learn new technologies is not mentioned as a barrier. However, online learning is not seen as a cost savings approach to education since it requires a large investment in infrastructure and support. Rather than shifting to entirely new pedagogies applicable to fully online programs, blended programs integrate more traditional learning methods with new approaches. In a survey of chief academic officers, Allen, Seaman, and Garrett (2006) found that contrary to beliefs about the appeal of blended courses and programs, the picture is complex and difficult to research. Apparently, blended courses are not identified separately from classroom-based classes. If we look across disciplines, there are more blended programs than online programs, with the highest number of blended programs in the areas of business and information technology. Although baccalaureate programs have fewer online courses, they have many more blended courses. Doctoral and masters programs tend to have a high number of both blended and online courses. When consumers are asked about blended versus online learning, they are favorable to both, with 80% of students indicating positive interest (Allen et al., 2006). They suggest that that their findings point to high acceptance of online and blended models as compared to the traditional classroom approach. They indicate that when students select programs, they are more interested in factors such as reputation, learning model, location, transfer policy, and price and are less concerned about whether the program is online or blended compared to classroom based. Essentially, the institution's or organization's mission strongly influences the level and structure of the commitment to online education.

The Players: Current Online Learning Environments

Online learning takes place within a variety of educational learning environments, from the traditional distance learning universities to e-learning for-profit. What follows is our categorization of the dominant players in the online teaching profession today.

Nonprofit traditional distance learning universities. Traditional distance learning schools have ventured into the online environment and brought with them the values and educational philosophies of their traditional distance environments. Some have attempted to replicate their models in other countries. The United Kingdom's Open University has entered the U.S. market with an MBA program for students without BA degrees (www.open.ac.uk). Canada's Athabasca University began as a correspondence program in 1972 and now offers several online graduate degree programs (www.athabasca.ca).

Other traditional learning distance learning institutions have expanded directly into the online market. For example, Fielding Graduate University, which began in 1974, offers masters and doctoral programs that combine face-to-face and distance modalities as well as programs that are entirely online. The university is accredited by the Western Association of Universities and Colleges, and its doctoral program in clinical psychology is the only blended program to be accredited by the Committee on Accreditation of the American Psychological Association (www.fielding.edu).

Traditional nonprofit universities. Large traditional public universities have the highest number of online degree and certificate programs as well as courses across a wide range of disciplines. There are examples of traditional universities developing entirely new entities for their online programs, such as the formation of Cardean University and Ellis College of New York Institute of Technology. Some of the elite universities, including Columbia and Northwestern, have formed for-profit businesses by partnering with online learning companies to offer online courses. Some efforts have failed, such as NYU Online and Cornell University's ECornell, which had to be reorganized. Many universities have applied corporate practices to their online efforts. One successful example is Steven's Institute of Technology's WebCampus. In the last 6 years, Stephens, with 10,000 undergraduate and graduate students, has collaborated with Beijing Institute of Technology to offer a masters program in IT and plans to expand to other Chinese universities. This is an example of the international potential for collaboration and transfer of learning (Skaare, 2006). In an open source effort, Massachusetts Institute of Technology (MIT) offers free online courses through MIT's OpenCourseWare site and has at least a million hits per month. The courses are posted by MIT professors who offer their work to the public through the Web site.

Military online universities. The Department of Defense (DOD) has two online universities to provide continuing education and professional training as well as degree programs primarily to military personnel and DOD civilian employees. The DOD standards for online learning are maintained through SCORM (Shareable Content Reference Model), a collection of standards and specifications for Web-based e-learning to help maintain reusable learning content. SCORM defines how learning is sequenced in learning modules and is part of the Advanced Distributed Learning Initiative. The SCORM framework is being adopted by learning systems worldwide so that learning content can be easily transferred to any learning platform. Other universities, such as Park University, collaborate with the military online programs.

For-profit universities. The University of Phoenix is the largest and most financially successful for-profit university that has both campus-based and online programs. University of Phoenix Online offers BA and MA programs as well as corporate certificate programs. Jones International, founded in 1995, is an exclusively online university with students located in 57 countries. The school is accredited by the North Central Association of Colleges and Schools and offers undergraduate and graduate degrees. Other for-profit schools that offer graduate degrees online include Strayer University Online, DeVry's Keller School of Management, Capella University, Argosy University, and Walden University.

For-profit e-learning organizations. Beginning in 1998, Kaplan Learning Systems, in conjunction with the *Washington Post,* developed Kaplan University and Kaplan College Online offering degrees and certificates. It partners with the University of Alabama to provide library services and is accredited by the North Central Association of Colleges and Schools. Another large for-profit company, Sylvan Learning Systems, has consolidated some of the important players in the online market by acquiring Walden University, National Technology University, and Canter (a program for teacher's professional development). Sylvan collaborates with the University of California to facilitate their development of online programs and has a similar arrangement with the University of Liverpool to develop their online capabilities (Garrett & Verbik, 2004).

Corporate online universities. Many major corporations have developed corporate universities with online components. It is common practice for the corporate universities to work collaboratively with for-profit learning organizations. Numerous e-learning organizations provide contracted services as consultants or providers to corporate universities. The Corporate University Xchange (www.CUX.com) provides information for corporate university organizers, including a newsletter, e-news (*Corp U Journal*), Webinars, survey research, and an annual conference. Examples of corporate universities include Motorola University, Daimler Chrysler University Online, McDonald's Hamburger University, EMC University, General Motors University, NCR University, Shell Open University, and Vanguard University. Cisco provides Cisco Networking Academies, which has served 153,000 employees worldwide (Morrison & Meister, 2001).

Online learning digital content resources and open sources. A sample of online organizations and Web sites that provide support for research, content, and collaboration for online learning indicates there is a wealth of support and rapid expansion of Web-based resources. A well-developed effort to support the online learning environment is the Sloane Foundation's Asynchronous Learning Network, which has promoted asynchronous (anytime and anywhere) learning since 1994, holds an annual conference, and has a Web site (www.aln.org) containing research and educational resources. Another nonprofit online learning venture is IMS Global Learning Consortium. Established in 1996, the membership organization publishes research and provides conferences to examine how technology can enhance Internet-supported learning with an effort to promulgate best practices and standards. Other efforts include the Online University Consortium, which publishes the results of their assessment of online universities who submit their programs for evaluation. In the corporate training arena, Corporate University Xchange partners with University of North Carolina to enhance the relationship between industry leaders in information technology and education by publishing a newsletter, research, and conferences. Online learning information resources such as ASTD's *Learning Circuits* publish e-learning news and research. Multimedia Educational Resource for Learning and Online Teaching (MERLOT) provides a Web site for peer-reviewed, online course material and discussion. Topics cover most disciplines and include tutorials, lectures, simulations, and hypertext books. Online distance and e-learning journals, many of which are peer-reviewed, provide a rich source of easily accessible research. Blogs such as *e-learningpundit,* wikis, and virtual reality sites provide a new generation of e-learning possibilities.

Along with the enormous growth and competition in online educational ventures, we have already witnessed the demise and consolidation of some online learning schools. Future developments will continue to be influenced by an institution's or organization's mission, commitment of leadership, desire to improve access, administration and faculty beliefs that online education is equal to or better than traditional education as well as an impetus toward creativity and collaboration.

Pedagogical Implications of Online Learning

Seven years ago we began this handbook by recognizing that the technological wonder of the Internet was spawning a rapid and inevitable surge in online education. We were awed by the way in which technological innovation had demolished traditional institutional boundaries to expertise and knowledge, citing Drucker's (1999) observation that the Internet had given everyone who seeks information access to resources once held within the ivory tower. In turn, we were curious about the pedagogical implications of online learning and acutely concerned that participants in distance education were merely trying to move the traditional classroom approach to teaching into the online environment without fully considering the advantages and limitations of the medium.

Online teaching developed from advances in communication technology, not from innovative changes in pedagogy (Rudestam, 2004). This fact has had profound implications for identifying a suitable place for technology in training and education. Generally speaking, educational institutions that offer courses online have done so within the context of their dominant pedagogical principles and historical attitudes toward education. When those principles emphasize the authoritative expertise of the instructor who disseminates knowledge and information to relatively passive students using lectures supported by audiovisual aids, the virtual classroom is likely to consist of instructional materials presented to the students in the form of lecturettes, either in real time or in archived video form. Using learning management tools, measures of competence might involve responding to a set of exam questions or writing a term paper and e-mailing it to the professor. The professor evaluates the material and provides some feedback, and the student receives a grade in the course. Thus, reliance on a prevailing educational paradigm means that face-to-face instructional practices (and distance learning by correspondence) are now being replicated in a new medium. However, we maintained that this might not be the best and most effective use of the online environment.

We argued that optimal use of the electronic environment for teaching classes necessitates a shift in pedagogy and moreover, that the Internet as a medium for teaching and learning requires epistemological changes that are worthy of consideration (Rudestam & Schoenholtz-Read, 2002). This perspective to education represented our own experience at Fielding

Graduate University and was reflected in most of the chapters of the first edition of the *Handbook of Online Learning: Innovations in Higher Education and Corporate Training.*

We continue to endorse Schrage's (1990) observation that "technology is really a medium for creating productive environments" (p. 67). Thus, technologies can be effective if they are designed to empower student engagement with the learning process and collaboration. Sherry Turkle (1995), among the most visionary thinkers regarding the impact of technology on the psyche, noted that a single person working alone on the computer can work through identity issues regarding control and mastery; once the computer is used as a communication medium, the control offered by the computer can be transformed into generating collaboration and intimacy.

The Internet has exposed people to a huge variety of opinions, values, personalities, and conventions from an ever-increasing number of people from diverse backgrounds and affiliations. In cyberspace, the self is readily constructed in diverse ways, and students readily form different opinions and interpretations regarding the same reading material and com- mentaries. This perspective stands at odds with the traditional model of education, dubbed by Freire (1985) as the nutritionist model (and by Dabbagh, 2000, as the instructivist approach), which arranges its participants hierarchically dependent on their status as authors of knowledge. The hierarchy starts with the authority of the knowledge creators in a field (esteemed scientists and scholars who hold the truth that students need to discover and assimilate), moves to those who design curricula for students to master, and ends with teachers who dispense the goodies to hungry students who are expected to consume them. According to Gergen (1995), the nutritionist perspective does not fit well with how knowledge is actually generated. Education, he suggests, must abandon the task of discovering universal authoritative knowledge and move to giving teachers more authority about what to teach. And education must proceed within a dialogic relationship between students and teachers. As W. B. Yeats put it, "Education is not the filling of a bucket, but the lighting of a fire."

There is reason to believe that there has been a greater commitment to constructivist pedagogy within the world of online learning during the past decade. Many leaders in the field reflect this orientation. Adams and Morgan (2007) noted that the first generation of online learning was technology driven, whereas the current generation focuses on "soft skills" and pedagogy. The first-generation approach, with its emphasis on faculty being in control and students learning specific content with the aim of passing tests, lends itself to delivering expert knowledge, especially in situations where there are right and wrong answers. The second-generation approach places the learner in control of goal setting and negotiating meanings with others while participating in learning activities. It emphasizes the exploration of ideas and integrating theory with practice and application. Alonso, Lopez, Manrique, and Viñes (2005) describe the pedagogical shift inspired by the Internet as a shift from teaching to learning, a shift which is particularly well suited to adult learning in context. They noted that one of the contributions of social constructivist theory in education is "anchored instruction"—that is, students organizing their explorations around an anchor, which might be a case study or a theme or an applied problem. Others such as Chen (2007) have described how an increasingly constructivist approach to instructional design principles over the past several years is reflected in a combination of active learners challenged by complex real-world problems using continuous assessment of progress and outcomes.

Future Issues in Online Learning: Pedagogy

Consistent with this depiction is one of John Seely Brown's (2008) predictions for the future of online learning: an increase in learning by doing and a decrease in learning about. In practical terms, this means that the focus on traditional instructional design is apt to decline and be replaced by authoring tools designed by and suited to the increasing computer sophistication of current young adults, by allowing them to locate and take advantage of their own learning resources. This distinction is reminiscent of what in networking terminology is called *pull* technology versus *push* technology. With push technology, there is often information overload because senders are responsible for sending messages; with pull technology, the recipient requests what he or she wants to receive. With a pull type of communication, it is like going from "drinking from a fire hose . . . to directing a fine water fountain stream" (Doucette, 1998, p. 26). We have seen this shift in the world of home entertainment and education with the availability of TiVo, Kindle, and other forms of on-demand audio-visual media products. Similarly, computer applications such as Moodle allow graduate education content to be highly individualized and available on request by the active learner.

Now that the pedagogy is catching up with the technology, we can anticipate another significant leap in online education, this one ushered in by Web 2.0, the more recent evolution of the Internet, and by the so-called open resources movement. As Brown and Adler (2008) have recently noted, the distinction between producers of Internet content and consumers of Internet content is gradually being eroded. A well-known example of this theme is Wikipedia, a kind of open source software that allows anyone, anywhere, to contribute to the current state of knowledge being assimilated by this highly accessible, diverse, and comprehensive online encyclopedia. The sharp demarcation between the creation of knowledge and the dissemination of knowledge (by universities) is being eradicated so that learning is becoming truly democratized through the rapid proliferation of Web 2.0 software. This is very different from the learning management software, which has dominated online learning for the past several years. Such software has been predicated on the concept that knowledge products are something to be administered and controlled and financially supported by tuition dollars from captive students who are in residence somewhere (Nagy & Bigum, 2007). As Nagy and Bigum point out, the intellectual property issues involved in cocreated knowledge are mind-boggling. How will the intellectual contributions of future knowledge creators be protected? How will they be remunerated for their work? And most importantly, what incentives will assure the continued production of quality scholarship in a digital environment?

It is well-known that the British Open University system has been a global leader in online education. A recent interview with leaders from that organization clarifies that an initial focus on the quality of instructional materials and an attendant focus on responsive student support services were instrumental in the rapid growth of their distance education programs (Katz, 2008). The system still prospers. At this point, more than 200,000 students are being served by the Open University, facilitated by between 7000 and 8000 part-time tutors. The leaders note that technological innovations on the horizon, such as 3G technology, are making it much easier to network students across locales to engage in joint learning tasks. They also point to Second Life and other distributed virtual communities as representative of the new wave of Web 2.0 distributed learning. Second Life is a three dimensional virtual world owned and operated by its several million residents (Hargis, 2008). Second Life captures the essence of new generation experiential learning: dynamic experimentation with a variety of learning tools and educational content, simulations that allow for testing new ideas and practicing new skills, community building, and networking with a diverse set of learners. According to the Second Life Web site (www.secondlife.com), "In Second Life you can create anything you can imagine with powerful, highly flexible building tools, using geometric primitives and a simple, intuitive interface. Building is easy to learn, yet robust enough to inspire creativity."

In sum, the trajectory of distance learning environments has moved from the relatively passive to the increasingly active and interactive. Web 2.0 implies a shift from traditional software to Internet services (Bray, 2007), which supports a parallel paradigm shift from traditional learning to digitized formats of learning. The technological possibilities include the opportunity for students to design their own content as well as to rely on social software that allows for one-to-one communication (e-mail, instant messaging), one-to-many communication (Web pages, blogs), and many-to-many communication (wikis and blikis) (Kesim & Agaoglu, 2007). Where Web 1.0 had Britannica Online, Web 2.0 has Wikipedia; Web 1.0 had personal Web sites, Web 2.0 has blogging; Web 1.0 had content management systems, Web 2.0 has Wikis, Web 1.0 had directories, Web 2.0 has tagging (Kesim & Agaoglu). Technological trends of the near future may include the following (Punnie & Cabrera, 2006, p. 23):

- more widespread broadband Internet access, including peer-to-peer file sharing and always on features;
- Web logs and blogs as information and communication sources;
- podcasting as a generator of mobile learning;
- short message services (SMS) and multimedia messaging services (MMS) as new content providers and for information sharing; and
- open source software and content in place of institutional software and content.

As Brown (Brown & Adler, 2008) saw it, the most profound contribution of the Internet is in the arena of social engagement and access to other people rather than to information—how to learn rather than what to learn. The emphasis on the social matrix of education is supported by studies such as one by Light (2001), which concluded that student success in higher education was determined more by the opportunity to participate in study groups than by the teaching style of the instructor.

Future Issues: Different Models for Different Settings

We do not want to give the impression that small-group collaboration is the only viable approach to online education. As data and experiences from online educational initiatives are collected from diverse cultures and sectors around the globe, it becomes clear that not one form of online learning fits all consumers. Martin, Massy, and Clarke (2003), for instance, have studied the *absorptive capacity* for online learning in organizations. Absorptive capacity, in this context, refers to the factors that govern how "organizations have different capacities for acquiring, assimilating, transforming, and exploiting knowledge on e-learning" (Martin et al., 2003, p. 230). Martin et al. have generated a host of propositions that promote receptivity to penetration and use of online learning based on their assessment of individual and cultural variables. Interestingly, they see more rationally based models of learning, represented by the cognitive and behavioral approaches that they view as more common in the United States, as lending themselves more easily to the adoption of online learning than the constructivist models of education more commonly found in Europe. They believe that the relative receptivity to e-learning in the United States is rooted in the short-term perspective, closely connected information infrastructure, and vertical, individualistic culture of

Northern American business. As such, they foresee that a more constructivist model of e-learning that embraces a high level of social interactivity would be more compatible with online training initiatives in many other parts of the world. Thus, one dichotomy that deserves our attention is the distinction between knowledge as a product or commodity in the marketplace versus knowledge as a social practice, heavily influenced by context and active engagement. Both types of philosophical perspectives can currently be found in online education, with turmoil at the intersection.

Another take on the influence of cultural factors in online learning can be found in a variety of studies comparing student experiences from different countries (Rutherford & Kerr, 2008). One frequently cited variable is the difference between high-context and low-context learning cultures (Morse, 2003). Cultures differ in their relationship to authority, individualism versus collectivism, masculinity versus femininity, and tolerance of uncertainty and ambiguity, among other things (Hofstede & Hofstede, 2005). High-context learning emphasizes the authority and wisdom of teachers, formality of methods, and a focus on assessments and examinations, whereas low-context learning emphasizes learning outcomes, deep learning and personal skill development, and informal teacher–student interactions. The implication is that online pedagogy may also need to be tempered to meet the expectations of diverse students in order to promote positive educational outcomes.

Future Issues: Synchronous Versus Asynchronous Approaches

The respective advantages and disadvantages of online and face-to-face learning are moderated by the form and quality of each modality. One key dimension that discriminates the current use of the online environment is the synchronous versus asynchronous nature of the course. Historically, synchronous and asynchronous e-learning models have been matched against one another. Traditional classroom teaching, of course, is real time and synchronous instructional technology probably originated with closed-circuit television on college campuses in the middle of the 20th century (Johnson, 2006). Asynchronous instruction, on the other hand, has its roots with the pioneers of distance education. Each approach has its own advantages and disadvantages. The anywhere-anytime feature of the asynchronous format allows for more flexible scheduling. According to its proponents, it also encourages more thoughtful and reflective learner participation as well as the opportunity to preserve and archive entire conversations and courses. The synchronous format offers greater spontaneity and more social interactions, but it is more likely to suffer from technology breakdowns and networking problems. Leaders within the education community who resonate with a constructivist approach to learning have clearly favored the asynchronous model with its "richer, more inclusive types of interchange" (Dede & Kremer, 1999). Trainers in the organizational sector have also elected asynchronous approaches, ranging from PowerPoint slides to simulations with creative graphics (Welsh, Wanberg, Brown, & Simmering, 2003). Studies have also found that asynchronous discussion leads to equal or superior student satisfaction (Johnson, 2006).

Within a blended learning paradigm there is ample place for both synchronous and asynchronous learning modalities. In the recent past, chat rooms and synchronous conferencing systems were generally relegated to serve a supplemental function in online courses in the form of socializing (virtual cafes), peer support, and virtual office hours (Branon & Essex, 2001). Everything has changed, however, with the advent of social software and groupware that facilitate real-time collaboration and problem solving. Park and Bonk (2007) report the results of a small ASTD study, which found that 86% of 145 survey participants intended to incorporate synchronous technology into their future online courses. No doubt the current generation of students in higher education is not as threatened by technological bells and whistles as previous students, nor as resistant as a previous generation of educators and trainers to dive into new Internet-based accessories.

On the other hand, changes in online technology and pedagogy need to consider the opinions and sensibilities of faculty and trainers who are charged with implementing them. The DialogPLUS project, described by Davis and Fill (2007), describes a joint venture in blended learning among major universities including Pennsylvania State University, University of California at Santa Barbara, University of Leeds, and University of South Hampton. Early on, the institutions sponsoring the project agreed that the teachers needed to have ownership of the way it evolved in order to be successful. For example, relying on reusable learning objects contributed by commercial content providers, as opposed to educational content produced by faculty participating in the program, reduced local ownership and commitment. Another potential problem was restraining instructors from taking advantage of creative new learning approaches by saddling them with outmoded hardware and software. This is the flip side of previous observations that the field of online learning has been characterized by juxtaposing new technology and old pedagogy (Levy, 2005).

Future Issues: Best Practices

We have now had sufficient time to generate any number of benchmarks and best practices for online education from the perspective of students, teachers, and administrators. The authors of the chapters in this handbook have contributed their observations and recommendations to this status report. Other available sources include benchmarks for success provided by the Institute for Higher Education Policy (2000), best practices for evaluating online faculty (Tobin, 2004), relationships between interactions and learning in online environments (Swan, 2004), success factors for online learning and institutional change (White, 2007), principles of online course design and teaching (Garrison & Vaughan, 2008), online business education practices (Grandzol & Grandzol, 2006), and regional accreditation (Loane, 2001; Swail & Kampits, 2001). Among these contributors lie the seeds for the future of online learning.

It is likely that education and training programs of the future will increasingly customize learning to take advantage of individual needs and learning styles and combine the best elements of classroom education and technology. Increasing consideration needs to be given to what method of teaching is best for what type of student for what subject matter under what circumstances. The modality depends, moreover, on the desired learning goals and outcomes. The dissemination of highly structured basic content might not require much discussion and may be suitable for a teacher-focused approach. Content that is heavily value laden may be more appropriate for peer discussion. It is up to educators to blend teaching modalities and methods in ways that match student needs and capacities to create optimal learning outcomes. The distinctions between campus-based learning and distributed learning, between classroom-based education and Internet-based education, will no doubt continue to erode.

An ongoing challenge for the future of distributed education is to meet the needs and values of individual institutions while serving the high market demand for lifelong learning worldwide. Educational institutions that are motivated to revisit their missions and integrate the appropriate technologies with their pedagogy will become more competitive in the educational marketplace. One recent survey of emerging technologies that are apt to have the greatest impact on the delivery of online education in the near future found that reusable content objects, wireless technology, and peer-to-peer collaborative tools were at the forefront (Bonk, Kim, & Zeng, 2005). Other noteworthy technologies include digital libraries, simulations and games, assistive technology, and digital portfolios.

Yet, almost all advocates of online learning agree that technology should never drive educational needs, but educational needs should determine the appropriate use of technology. The same survey cited above found that the most highly predicted pedagogical techniques for the online future in higher education were group problem solving, collaborative tasks and problem-based learning (Bonk et al., 2005). This suggests that even in a significantly decentralized learning environment abetted by the wonders of 21st century information technology, the power of human relationships and the wisdom of the learning group can be mobilized.

Introduction to the Chapters in the Book

Part I of the revised handbook explores a wide range of issues relating to changing philosophies and theories of online learning. In "Presence in Teleland," Gary Fontaine and Grace Chun offer an update of Fontaine's chapter on the ecology of the virtual world from the perspective of the academic traveler. The authors focus on the importance of having a sense of presence in the online classroom and how that sense of presence can be fostered to generate significant learning outcomes. They build on our understanding of the phenomenology of space and help us think about ways in which to create and nurture virtual spaces to make them conducive to learning. The revised chapter offers a summary of research drawn from a community of inquiry model describing how students can create a sense of online community to enhance their learning. Throughout the chapter the authors help keep us current about both synchronous and asynchronous course ecologies.

The following revised chapter is by Jeremy J. Shapiro and Shelley K. Hughes and titled "The Challenges of Culture and Community in Online Academic Environments." The authors discuss the complex task of building and managing an online learning community given the diverse motives, styles, and preferences of the participants and the realities of computer mediated communication. They expose the technocultural paradigms and social norms that undergird the virtual community and its classrooms. The updated chapter offers forms of information literacy that make learning communities safe environments for students, faculties, and administrators in a decade challenged by the rampant use of innovations such as iPods, cellphones, Webcams, Web 2.0 social networking sites, wikis, and blogs. Shapiro and Hughes adopt a neohumanist paradigm (Hirschheim & Klein, 1989) to address these issues. The rapid speed of change in educational technologies that provide the foundation and vehicle for online learning are captured in Robin Mason and Frank Rennie's chapter on "Evolving Technologies." The Web 2.0 tools that are currently available emphasize what Mason labels as the *convergence* occurring in distributed education: the integration of synchronous and asynchronous communication and the integration of face-to-face and distance education into blended learning, all provided by the pervasiveness of the World Wide Web. After a solid foundation describing the evolutionary process, Mason and Rennie go into considerable detail in examining six popular Web 2.0 tools: blogs, wikis, podcasting, e-portfolios, social networking, and Second Life. The strengths and limitations of each tool are addressed, followed by issues for both students and teachers pertaining to their adoption.

Pierre-Léonard Harvey has taken on the task of providing a conceptual framework for future generations of educational delivery systems in the chapter "Applying Social Systems Thinking and Community Informatics Thinking in Education: Building Efficient Online Learning Design Culture in Universities." He recognizes that technological innovation is proceeding exceeding rapidly in the online world but that epistemological and theoretical principles must also be applied to innovation in system design. This ambitious chapter explores the philosophical underpinnings of design theory and opts for a perspective that is systemic, constructivist, and transformational. His approach to an online learning community and a community supported collaborative learning community is indebted to the contributions of Bela Banathy. Harvey describes a free open source socioconstructivist virtual community of social designers (FOSSVCSD) charged with building an online learning system. As an example he describes the experience of educators at the University of Quebec in Montreal with the open source Moodle community. Harvey concludes by proposing a comprehensive research agenda for the social system design community.

Bernard Luskin and James Hirsen predict an expansive future for online education in their chapter "Media Psychology Controls the Mouse That Roars." They document the rapid growth of online learning and argue that it is being fueled by persistent market forces. Lifelong learning is in demand, the costs of campus-based education are skyrocketing, and an eager world provides a fertile ground for educational entrepreneurs and nontraditional institutions, resulting in a rapidly growing market for online education. Meanwhile, Luskin and Hirsen point out the role that the relatively new field of media psychology can play in the years ahead in contributing to an understanding of the human learning experience online at the interface between technology and psychology.

Janet Poley takes us from the local context to the global scale of e-learning in her chapter "Globalization in Online Learning." This chapter addresses global trends, challenges, and opportunities in online learning and gives us an up-to-date overview of what is taking place on the forefront of Internet-enabled learning throughout the world. Poley reminds us that the digital divide is still very real so that many people, especially in the poorer countries of Africa and Asia, have no access to quality learning resources and opportunities. She reminds us of the moral and practical challenge to bring online connectivity to all underserved regions and highlights programs and institutions that are committed to expanding connectivity to the underserved. The open source grassroots movement is a particularly swift and powerful force in this endeavor. With the global expansion of online learning comes pedagogical changes, especially in the learner-centered, collaborative, contextual direction previously described in this section. Finally, we are reminded that care must be exercised to assure that the global community is offered content and method that are consistent with their own cultures and not dominated by Western content as in previous periods of educational colonization.

Yolanda Gayol covers an ambitiously large territory in her review of the status of research on online education. She positions her review within the context of a historical overview of the area. Gayol comes from the field of distance education, but she recognizes that one of the challenges in reviewing the research literature in this field is its fractured representation by many different communities of practice using very different terminologies. Wisely focusing on meta-analyses, Gayol decries the overrepresentation of descriptive, atheoretical research studies. She divides her review into research on learning, teaching, and outcomes. A significant trend, noted by several of our authors, is the emergence of Web 2.0, e-research, and open-systems models of learning.

The final chapter in the first section is a scholarly updating of "Uncertain Frontiers: Exploring Ethical Dimensions of Online Learning" by Dorothy Agger-Gupta. Agger-Gupta illustrates how difficult it is to discern the ethical nature of our actions in the VE. We are in relatively uncharted territory when we consider how to understand the appropriate rules and norms of behavior in the virtual world. Emerging ethical dilemmas in the 21st century include questions concerning online community, authorship and ownership of online text, identity, privacy, secrecy, power, and dominance. The author takes us on a tour of alternate perspectives on ethical beliefs and values and draws upon these perspectives to consider specific ethical dilemmas in online learning. She argues persuasively that professional ethical principles for online educators need to change and highlights the unanswered questions influencing the nature of online living and learning communities that need to be addressed in the digital era.

The second part of the book moves from theory to practice. The first section addresses the implementation of online learning in terms of programs and courses. Program implementation, be it online or bricks-and-mortar, requires a vision and a road map. In the first chapter, "Revisiting the Design and Delivery of an Interactive Online Graduate Program," revised and updated from the previous edition, Judith Stevens-Long and Charles Crowell refer to a model master's program in organizational management to describe the power of peer-to-peer, small-group, problem-based interactions in the online learning environment. The authors guide the reader through the steps to develop and manage online courses using a learner-centered pedagogy. The chapter concludes with a discussion of how the group process theory of Wilfred Bion lends itself to understanding the development and dynamics of online classes, including the meta-learning that takes place in addition to the absorption of academic content.

Barclay Hudson exemplifies the unusual creativity he brings to online teaching in an updated chapter titled "Candlepower: The Intimate Flow of Online Collaborative Learning." Hudson explains that, contrary to common belief, the online classroom can be an intensely intimate and collaborative learning environment. He argues that modern complexity theory, with its emphasis on self-organizing capacities, nonlinear systems, and nondeterministic outcomes, serves as an apt metaphor and explanatory theory for generating online collaborative critical thinking. The chapter includes many useful recommendations and exercises (i.e., candlepower) for the online facilitator to draw upon to establish an appropriate level of group trust to optimize collaborative critical thinking.

The next chapter, by Kay Wijekumar, is titled "Designing and Developing Web-Based Intelligent Tutoring Systems: A Step-by-Step Approach With Practical Applications." Intelligent tutoring systems have demonstrated significant success in improving learning outcomes by incorporating modeling, interactive practice tasks, assessment, and feedback. Wijekumar notes that the perceived complexity of intelligent learning systems has retarded their use in the online learning environment. However, recent advances such as the Web 2.0 and virtual reality environments have expanded the range of technologies available for enhancing learning. Wijekumar has developed and herein describes in great detail a four step model called 4M (multimedia, motivation, metacognition, and memory) that enables the creation and application of intelligent tutoring systems to the virtual classroom. In the example described in this chapter, the model employs expert performance, interactive activities, and feedback to increase writing skills among K through 12 students. The principles and techniques, however, are equally applicable to higher education and corporate settings and a wide variety of academic and professional skills.

The corporate learning environment has not been neglected in terms of taking advantage of technological change in online education. Bruce LaRue and Stephanie Galindo's updated chapter, "Synthesizing Higher Education and Corporate Learning Strategies," proposes that rapid technological change profoundly affects both the university and the corporation. LaRue and Galindo focus on the ongoing expansion of "knowledge work" and argue that successful adaptation to increasingly dispersed organizations necessitates a "heightened level of epistemological development." They point to the rise of flexible, networked corporations and "communities of practice" and propose a set of core competencies drawn from higher education to serve knowledge workers of the future. The 4-plex model of networked learning is a tool for corporate trainers in multinational companies that provide a practical link between the corporation and the university.

The final chapter in the programs and courses section is written by Jenny Edwards and Sue Marquis Gordon and is titled "Teaching Action Research at a Distance." The authors offer a very practical overview of how action research, which is itself a form of applied research that serves as a powerful change agent in academic or corporate organizations, lends itself to the online environment. They begin by proposing three different models of teaching action research, differing in their (combination) levels of didactic versus experiential emphases, and go on to provide examples of each model. In concert with most authors in this volume, Edwards and Gordon opt for an approach that involves considerable small-group interaction among students and faculty. They conclude with specific recommendations for instructors who may be interested in taking on this teaching challenge.

The second section of Part II focuses on issues pertaining to faculty and students in the virtual classroom. These two chapters are written by experienced online instructors and trainers and are complementary contributions to further our understanding of faculty and student needs appropriate to succeeding in online courses. The first, by Rena M. Palloff and Keith Pratt, is an updated and revised version of "Beyond the Looking Glass: What Faculty and Students Need to Be Successful Online," which appeared in the first edition of this handbook. Palloff and Pratt make it clear that not everyone is suited for online teaching or learning. For instance, charisma and content expertise, highly valued in face-to-face teaching, may be less important than having social presence in an online environment, where a learner-focused introvert can shine. The authors use their extensive experience in training online instructors to describe what makes a good online teacher and the components that would represent an optimal faculty development program for preparing instructors for this challenge. An important element in orienting faculty is assimilating a pedagogy that emphasizes the changing nature of faculty–student relationships represented by the principles of active learning, interactivity, and collaboration.

The second chapter, "Teaching Professionals to Be Effective Online Facilitators and Instructors: Lessons From Hard-Won Experience," by Leni Wildflower, argues for creating a framework for optimal online learning by subordinating technology to educational needs. Wildflower's chapter presents a number of practical suggestions for selecting the best, as opposed to the most ornate, software, designing an online course, setting norms and boundaries for students, defining confidentiality, facilitating dialogue, providing feedback, managing conflict, sustaining motivation, and providing record-keeping and organization. Her experience in designing an online program in Evidence Based Coaching at Fielding Graduate University is used to illustrate many of these principles and techniques.

The final section of the book addresses administrative and support structures relating to the successful implementation of online courses and programs. The first chapter, by Anna DiStefano and Judy Witt, is titled "Leadership and Management of Online Learning Environments in Universities." The chapter is written from the perspective of high-level administrators at Fielding Graduate University, a distributed academic institution employing a blended learning model of education. Educational administrators who are interested in initiating or expanding an institutional presence in online education will appreciate the guidelines described in this chapter. The authors stress the importance of aligning institutional mission, values, and organizational culture with new online proposals. It is very easy to underestimate both internal and external barriers and factors, including institutional capacity, technological capacity and support, administrative structures, academic governance, faculty roles, student engagement and orientation, educational outcomes, and marketing and recruitment. DiStefano and Witt share their experience and wisdom with regard to the factors that need to be considered to move forward in online programming. They consider both the idea of going it alone as an educational institution and the option of finding, assessing, and managing partnerships and strategic alliances. Finally, they provide the reader with alternative resources to support the development process.

As a companion piece, Ralph Wolff, President and Executive Director of the Senior College Commission of the Western Association of States and Colleges, has contributed an immensely helpful chapter on "Accrediting Online Institutions and Programs: Quality Assurance or Bureaucratic Hurdle?" Wolff offers an insider's perspective and succeeds in clarifying and humanizing what many indeed regard as a bureaucratic hurdle. He notes that all regional accreditation agencies today are receptive to accrediting online programs and then highlights "problems associated with gaining accreditation of online programs and institutions, and ways to address them." Each set of principles and best practices that is described is accompanied by one or more practice tips. He includes coverage of the following areas of concern: relationship of online program or course to the mission of the institution, links to institutional planning, curriculum development and oversight, faculty qualifications, student evaluations and outcomes, and admissions requirements.

The final chapter addresses an often overlooked implication of establishing online courses or programs: How can students and faculty have access to suitable library resources if a physical library is not readily available to them? Stefan Kramer, a research librarian with significant experience in this area, discusses this and related issues in "Virtual Libraries in Online Learning." Kramer provides a detailed, immensely practical overview of what is variously known as online, digital, or virtual libraries and reference methods. He discusses instructional services, such as Web-based instruction and synchronous and asynchronous search strategies, as well as the content of virtual libraries, including electronic journals, digitally formatted articles, e-books, digital images, and aggregator databases. The chapter also offers guidance on how to obtain access to online information as well as content that a particular library may not own. The field of library science is preparing for a future in which the Internet is becoming the universal content delivery and access channel. Moreover, virtual libraries are also becoming repositories of fragile and difficult to access resource materials. Kramer captures the excitement of how learning resource materials can be accessed and retrieved efficiently and sensitively in an open access age of online education.

References

Adams, J., & Morgan, G. (2007). "Second generation" e-learning: Characteristics and design principles for supporting management soft-skills development. *International Journal on E-Learning, 6*(2), 157–185.

Allen, E. I., & Seaman, J. (2005). *Growing by degrees: Online education in the United States, 2005.* Available from http://www.aln.org/publications/survey/pdf/growing_by_degrees.pdf

Allen, E.I., & Seaman, J. (2006). *Making the grade: Online education in the United States, 2006.* Available from http://www.aln.org/publications/survey/pdf/Making_the_Grade.pdf

Allen, E. I., & Seaman, J. (2007). *Online nation: Five years of growth in online learning.* Needham, MA: Sloan-C. Available from http://www.sloanconsortium.org/publications/ survey/pdf/online_nation.pdf

Allen, E. I., Seaman, J., & Garrett, R. (2006). *Blending in: The extent and promise of blended education in the United States.* Available from http://www.sloanconsortium.org/publications/survey/pdf/Blending_In.pdf

Alonso, F., Lopez, G., Manrique, D., & Viñes, J. M. (2005). An instructional model for Web-based e-learning education with a blended learning process approach. *British Journal of Educational Technology, 36 (2),* 217–235.

Arabasz, H. G., & Baker, M. B. (2003, March). *Evolving campus support models for e-learning courses.* Boulder, CO: EDUCAUSE Center for Applied Research Bulletin. Retrieved from http://www.educause.edu/ir/library/pdf/ecar_so/ers/ERS0303/EKF0303.pdf

Bonk, C. J., Kim, K., & Zeng, T. (2005). Future directions of blended learning in higher education and workplace learning settings. In C. J. Bonk, C. R. Graham, J. Cross, & M. G. Moore (Eds.), *The handbook of blended learning: Global perspectives, local designs* (pp. 550–568). San Francisco: Pfeiffer.

Branon, R. F., & Essex, C. (2001). Synchronous and asynchronous communication tools in distance education: A survey of instructors. *TechTrends, 45*(1), 36–42.

Bray, T. (2007). *Not 2.0?* Retrieved June 24, 2007, from http://radar.oreilly.com/archives/2005/08/not-20.html

Brown, J. S. (2008). Interview: Speaking personally—With John Seely Brown. *American Journal of Distance Education, 22,* 57–62.

Brown, J. S., & Adler, R. P. (2008, January/February). Minds on fire: Open education, the long tail and learning 2.0. *EDUCAUSE Review,* 17–32.

Carr-Chellman, A. A., & Duchastel, P. (2000). The ideal online course. *British Journal of Educational Technology, 31,* 229–241.

Chen, S. (2007). Instructional design strategies for intensive online courses: An objectivist-constructivist blended approach. *Journal of Interactive Online Learning, 6*(1), 72–86.

Dabbagh, N. H. (2000). The challenges of interfacing between face-to-face and online instruction. *TechTrends, 44*(6), 37–42.

Daniel, J., & Stevens, A. (1998). The success stories: The use of technology in "out-of-school education." In C. de M. Moura Castro (Ed.), *Education in the information age* (pp. 156–167). New York: Inter-American Development Bank.

Davis, H. C., & Fill, K. (2007). Embedding blended learning in a university's teaching culture: Experiences and reflections. *British Journal of Educational Technology, 38*(5), 817–828.

Dede, C., & Kremer, A. (1999). Increasing students' participation via multiple interactive media. *Inventio, I.* Retrieved March 1, 2005, from http://www.doit.gmu.edu/Archives/feb98/dede_1.htm

Doucette, N. (1998). Relieving information overlaod. *Rough Notes, 141*(2), 26–27.

Drucker, P. F. (1999). *Management challenges for the 21st century.* New York: Harper Business.

Freire, P. (1985). *The politics of education.* South Hadley, MA: Bergin & Garvey.

Garrett, R. & Verbik, L. (2004). Sylvan buys K.I.T. and strikes ten year deal with University of Liverpool. *The Observatory on borderless higher education.* Retrieved June 18, 2008, from http://www.uol.ohecampus.com/presscoverage/2004/Observatory_08_04_04.pdf

Garrison, D. R., & Vaughan, N. D. (2008). *Blended learning in education: Frameworks, principles, and guidelines.* San Francisco: Jossey-Bass.

Gergen, K. (1995). *Technology and the transformation of the pedagogical project.* Retrieved July 1, 2001, from http://www.swarthmore.edu/socsci/kgergen1/text12.html

Grandzol, J. R., & Grandzol, C. J. (2006). Best practices for online business education. *The International Review of Research in Open and Distance Learning, 7.* Retrieved September 3, 2008, from http://www.irrodl.org/index.php/irrodl/article/view/246/475

Hanna, D. E., & Associates (2000). *Higher education in an era of digital competition: Choice and challenges.* Madison, WI: Atwood.

Harasim, L., Hiltz, S. R., Teles, L., & Turoff, M. (1995). *Learning networks.* Cambridge: MIT Press.

Hargis, J. (2008). A Second Life for distance learning. *Turkish Online Journal of Distance Education, 9*(2), 57–63.

Hearn, D. R. (2001). *Education in the workplace: An examination of corporate university models.* Retrieved June 10, 2008, from http://www.newfoundations.com/OrgTheory/Hearn721.html

Hiltz, S. R., & Turoff, M. (1993). *The network nation: Human communication via computer* (2nd ed.). Reading, MA: Addison-Wesley.

Hirschheim, R., & Klein, H. K. (1989). Four paradigms of information systems development. *Communications of the ACM, 32*(10), 1199–1215

Hofstede, G. H., & Hofstede, G. J. (2005). *Cultures and organizations: Software of the mind.* New York: McGraw-Hill.

Holsapple, C. W., & Lee-Post, A. (2006). Defining, assessing, and promoting e-learning success: An information systems perspective. *Decisions Sciences Journal of Innovative Education, 4*(1), 67–85.

Institute for Higher Education Policy. (2000, April). *Quality on the line: Benchmarks for success in Internet-based distance education.* Washington, DC: Author. Retrieved from http://www.ihep.org/assets/files/publications/m-r/ Qualityon theline.pdf

Johnson, G. M. (2006) Synchronous and asynchronous text-based CMC in educational context: A review of recent research. *Techtrends, 50*(4), 46–53.

Katz, R. N. (2008). Open to change: An interview with leaders of the Open University. *EDUCAUSE Review,* pp. 1–3.

Kesim, E., & Agaoglu, E. (2007). A paradigm shift in distance education: Web 2.0 and social software. *Turkish Online Journal of Distance Education, 8*(3), 66–75.

Learning Circuits. (2008). [Online survey]. Retrieved June 17, 2008, from http:// www.learningcircuits.org/0308_tends.html

Levy, J. (2005). Envision the future of e-learning. *CIO Canada, 13*(2), 2. Retrieved September 3, 2008, from http://www.educause.edu/ers0506

Light, R. J. (2001). *Making the most of college: Students speak their minds.* Cambridge, MA: Harvard University Press.

Loane, S. (2001). *Distance Education and Accreditation.* Washington, DC: ERIC Clearinghouse on Higher Education (ERIC Document Reproduction Service No. ED464525).

Martin, G., Massy, J., & Clarke, T. (2003). When absorptive capacity meets institutions and (e)learners: Adopting, diffusing and exploiting e-learning in organizations. *International Journal of Training and Development, 7*(4), 228–244.

Morrison, J. L., & Meister, J. C. (2001). *E-learning in the corporate university: An interview with Jeanne Meister. The Technology Source.* Archives at the University of North Carolina. Retrieved June 18, 2008, from http://technology source.org/article/elearning_in_the _corporate_university

Morse, K. (2003). Does one size fit all? Exploring asynchronous learning in a multicultural environment. *Journal of Asynchronous Learning Networks, 7*(1), 37–55.

Nagy, J., & Bigum, C. (2007). Bounded and unbounded knowledge: Teaching and learning in a Web 2 world. *Turkish Online Journal of Distance Education, 8*(3), 76–86.

Noble, D. F. (1999). Digital diploma mills; The automation of higher education. *First Monday, 3*(1). Retrieved July 1, 2001, from http://www.firstmonday .dk/issues/issue3_1noble

Osguthorpe, R. T., & Graham, C. R. (2003). Blended learning environments: Definitions and directions. *The Quarterly Review of Distance Education, 4*(3), 227–233.

Panitz, T., & Panitz, P. (1998). Encouraging the use of collaborative education in higher education. In J. F. Forest (Ed.), *University teaching: International perspectives.* New York: Garland.

Park, Y. J., & Bonk, C. J. (2007). Synchronous learning experiences: Distance and residential learners' perspectives in a blended graduate course. *Journal of Interactive Online Learning, 6*(3), 245–264.

Punnie, Y., & Cabrera, M. (2006, March). *The future of ICT and learning in the knowledge society. Report on a joint DG JRC-DG EAC workshop.* Seville, Spain: European Commission Joint Research Center.

Rudestam, K. E. (2004). Distributed education and the role of online learning in training professional psychologists. *Professional Psychology: Research and Practice, 35*(4), 427–432.

Rudestam, K. E., & Schoenholtz-Read, J. (2002). The coming of age in adult online education. In K. E. Rudestam & J. Schoenholtz-Read (Eds.), *Handbook of online learning* (pp. 2–28). Thousand Oaks, CA: Sage.

Rutherford, A. G., & Kerr, B. (2008). An inclusive approach to online learning environments. *Turkish Online Journal of Distance Education, 9*(2), 1–19.

Schrage, M. (1990). *Shared minds: The new technologies of collaboration.* New York: Randome House.

Skaare, R. (2006). In line with online success: The Stevens Institute of Technology/WebCampus Stevens. *Corporate University XChange.* Retrieved from http://www.corpu.com/news/writings/2006-stevens.asp

Smith, D. E., & Mitry, D. J. (2008, January/February). Investigation of higher education: The real costs and quality of online programs. *Journal of Education for Business 83*, 147–152.

Sterling, B. (1992). *The hacker crackdown: Law and disorder on the electronic frontier.* New York: Bantam Books.

Swail, W. S., & Kampits, E. (2001). Distance education & accreditation—Riding a tide of opportunity. *New Directions in Higher Education, 113*, 35–48.

Swan, K. (2004). *Relationships between interactions and learning in online environments.* Needham, MA: Sloan-C.

Taffel, R. (2000). *The second family.* New York: St. Martin's Griffin.

Talbott, A. (1998, October). Who is killing higher education? Or is it suicide? *Netfuture,* p. 15.

Tobin, T. J. (2004). Best practices for administrative evaluation of online faculty. *Online Journal of Distance Learning.* Retrieved April 2, 2009, from http://www.westga.edu/~distance/ojdla/summer72/tobin72.html

Turkle, S. (1995). *Life on the screen: Identity in the age of the Internet.* New York: Simon & Schuster.

Urdan, T. A., & Weggen, C. C. (2000). *Corporate e-learning: Exploring a new frontier.* Retrieved April 2, 2009, from http://www.spectrainteractive.com/pdfs/CorporateELearingHamrecht.pdf

Welsh, E. T., Wanberg, C. R., Brown, K. G., & Simmering, M. J. (2003). E-learning: Emerging uses, empirical results and future directions. *International Journal of Training and Development, 7*(4), 245–258.

White, S. (2007). Critical success factors for e-learning and institutional change—Some organizational perspectives on campus-wide e-learning. *British Journal of Educational Technology, 38*(5), 840–850.

Part I

Changing Philosophies and Theories of Online Learning

Presence in Teleland

Chapter 2

Gary Fontaine

Grace Chun

We all have journeyed to many "strange lands" over the years, miles, and technologies. Coauthor Gary has taught traditional face-to-face (f2f) courses and training workshops for over 30 years. Over the last decade, however, many of his academic and professional journeys have been to Teleland. He has taught there f2f using the added support of asynchronous communication technology (at the University of Hawaii using e-mail and various Web forums). He has taught courses in which there was a combination of f2f and distant participants using synchronous communication technology (the Hawaii Interactive Telecommunication System based on interactive video). Typically, the distant participants in these courses were in several different remote classrooms. And he has taught courses with solely distant participants using asynchronous technology. In these latter courses, the participants were not only distant from him but also distant from each other without any real classrooms as such (the Fielding Graduate University's program in Organization Management and Development). Often both the participants and he were mobile, traveling throughout the world on business during the course. Strange lands for sure! Coauthor Grace's career, on the other hand, has emerged more recently in an academic world spanning both China and the United States and blending both f2f and online courses. Her graduate research (at the University of Hawaii) has focused specifically on the challenges in the latter. This chapter describes some of what we have learned thus far from these journeys to Teleland—both from a growing body of research on it and from our own experience in Teleland. Whereas in a chapter such as this there is always the temptation to provide lists of "dos" and "don'ts," we believe it is way too early to identify such with a great deal of certainty—we still need to understand the basic research increasingly available as the backdrop to understanding our personal experiences and designing our courses.

The Challenges Faced in Strange Lands Anywhere

Gary's professional focus has primarily been on helping people to deal effectively with more literal strange lands they encounter on real journeys to other companies, cultures, and countries as part of business, diplomacy, service delivery, technology transfer, and education. But a strange land is a new or changing ecology, including those associated with the use of new technologies. These journeys to Teleland present the same three key challenges to success (Fontaine, 2000, 2006). The first challenge is coping with the physical and psychological reaction to the strangeness itself—*ecoshock*. The symptoms of ecoshock can include frustration, fatigue, clumsiness, anxiety, paranoia, depression, irritability, and rigid thinking that interfere with adjustment and performance. In strange lands, the ecology changes, the appropriateness of normal or habitual ways of doing tasks becomes problematic, and we are faced with the second challenge—developing and implementing strategies to complete the tasks essential for living and working in these new ecologies. With respect specifically to the cultural confrontations with which Gary has most frequently worked—given that we expect and are skilled in doing things one way and those in a strange land expect and are skilled in doing them in another way, how are we going to do them well together? Do we continue do them our way, try to adopt their way, compromise, or develop some new way? We return to this challenge shortly. The third challenge is to maintain the motivation to continue in spite of inevitable frustration, fatigue, ecoshock, and poorer than desired task performance. In our own experience, this challenge is the most important of all because it takes time for ecoshock to diminish and for new strategies and skills to be developed and practiced in order to get tasks done.

Gary has previously suggested that, rather than selecting specific strategies based on what has typically been our way, their way, or a compromise, the second challenge requires a more generic strategy of accommodation. With accommodation these—or frequently other—specific strategies are selected based on what is most appropriate to the new task ecology. He has referred to them as *microcultures* (MCs) to emphasize that they most commonly are shared perceptions for completing specific tasks (Fontaine, 1989, 2000, 2006). MCs specify how task participants are to negotiate, communicate, teach, make decisions, supervise, delegate, lead, appraise performance, manage, plan, conduct meetings, resolve conflicts, and form, maintain, and dissolve relationships. They specify the meaning of a contract, a treaty, a policy, or an agreement in terms of time, responsibilities, and comprehensiveness. They are bare bones cultures in that they typically include only the minimal number of shared perceptions required for getting the task done acceptably for all parties concerned. In our case, an MC would specify how a particular course in Teleland is to be conducted by the participating teachers, students, and relevant others. To be optimally effective, the course must be accommodated to the task ecology in which the participants are interacting. This ecology includes the characteristics of the participants (their knowledge and skills, national and organizational cultures, personalities, relationships to one another, objectives, and expectations), characteristics of the course itself (purpose, novelty, difficulty, and requirements), and characteristics of the broader organizational context (facilities, resources, communication technologies, course duration, time and time zones, travel, administrative support). Developing and using MCs is the optimal strategy for effectiveness in strange lands in contexts ranging from international business (Fontaine, 2006; Hofner-Saphiere, 1996) to diplomacy (Kimmel, 1989). It is the optimal strategy for teaching in the new and rapidly changing ecologies of Teleland as well.

To some degree, participants (whether global assignees or teachers and students in Teleland) can prepare in advance for the ecology they will encounter through some form of training or orientation. However, as noted in the previous paragraph that the development and use of MCs typically require knowledge of the task ecology at a level of detail far in excess of what is available in advance. To a significant degree, participants must assess what is necessary in terms of these or other characteristics, identify a broad range of possible options for dealing with them, and select the most desirable options to constitute an MC all on the spot. The key skill in doing it on the spot is effective use of *a sense of presence*—the experience we all commonly have in strange lands anywhere in which we have a heightened awareness of everything around us (Fontaine, 2000, 2008). It is an important part of the street smarts we need to succeed or survive there.

A Sense of Presence

If one were to ask people in (or returning from) strange lands about their experiences, they often report a feeling of immediacy and a broad awareness of everything around them. They report that everything to them is real and vivid, and they feel very alive. They describe clarity of perception and responsivity to the world (Fontaine, 1993, 2008). The totality of the experience constitutes this state of mind called a sense of presence. It is a state in which we are psychologically present in the immediate task situation and are broadly aware of a range of ecological characteristics of it—rather than attending narrowly to a few selected characteristics or to events occurring in other times or places. When engaged in familiar tasks at home, we are often much less than 100% present psychologically. Our minds may be occupied by extraneous events so that we are not "tuned in" to the ecology of the immediate task. Because so many tasks at home are routine and predictable, we can get by on being less present. The relatively stable, familiar ecology allows general rules for completing various categories of tasks to develop. We need not stay alert for variations in the ecology between successive occurrences of a task. Each task can be successfully completed by applying these habitual rules.

But in strange lands, life and work are not so routine. Because the new ecologies are unfamiliar, we must be aware of a much broader range of ecological characteristics; we do not know which are going to be important. Because so many of them are unpredictable, we rarely have the opportunity for adequate planning. Because they change so often, we need to monitor them continuously. Because there is always the danger—particularly at times of stress or frustration—of falling back on habits from home, we need to monitor our own behavior as well. To be effective in strange lands, we need to be nearly 100% involved, 100% present!

Purposeful attention involves focusing narrowly on a selected set of characteristics of a task ecology, usually those previously found to have been essential for completing the task (e.g., the teacher's PowerPoint presentation). *Presence* involves a broader focus that is more likely to include other potentially relevant characteristics of an ecology (e.g., what the teacher is wearing, which words are chosen, who is looking at whom, the reaction of other students). Presence is less purposeful. It is stimulated by novelty, something like an orientation reflex. Attention is the optimal mode for learning in the familiar task contexts of home; a sense of presence is the optimal mode in contexts that are new, diverse, or changing—strange lands. The key skill for doing things in strange lands is to use the opportunity provided by our typically higher sense of presence to develop the MCs we need to perform effectively.

Presence in Teleland

For most participants (students and often faculty), each course in Teleland presents an ecology that is new and different from traditional f2f courses—a strange land. Typically, each is unique relative to other Teleland courses in terms of content, technologies, participant characteristics, and so forth. O'Hara-Devereaux and Johansen (1994) present a useful taxonomy of general ecologies of Teleland and the support technologies we find in them:

- *same time–same place* (blackboard, flip charts, video, PowerPoint or other computer projections; traditional classrooms),

- *same time–different place* (synchronous technologies—voice communication, video conferencing, chat rooms, Webcams; dispersed classrooms),

- *different time–same place* (workstations, bulletin boards, voice mail; team workrooms), and

- *different time–different place* (asynchronous technologies—e-mail, voice mail, text messaging, Web forums, computer conferencing, shared databases, blogs, wikis; dispersed personal, and perhaps mobile, learning sites).

As in any other strange land, in Teleland participants need to develop strategies for meeting course objectives that are accommodated to the particular course. Important ecological characteristics often are those associated with teaching versus training versus facilitating courses, working with undergraduates versus advanced students (graduates, professionals, managers, and executives), dealing with cultural diversity both domestically and globally, dealing with different course topics and content, working with different communication technologies and software, accommodating students differentially experienced with it, and working with varying degrees of administrative support and—sometimes—administrative, student, or faculty resistance. As in any strange land, there is no simple recipe for success, no universal best way. Part of the skill of being effective is learning to make those accommodations quickly and well. As with other journeys, some planning can be done in advance, particularly in terms of developing course architecture. But as with other journeys, doing it well requires skill in the use of presence.

Although in his own work Gary has used a sense of presence (Fontaine, 1989, 2006) to describe the state of being psychologically present in the situation in which one is physically present, he adopted the term from mentor and colleague Bill Uttal (1989), who was conducting early research on teleoperator systems (the remote operation of undersea recovery and extraterrestrial exploration vehicles). Uttal, and others, were somewhat ironically using the term *a sense of remote presence* to describe the experience of being present someplace else (in the remote vehicle being navigated) and were interested principally in the degree to which the experience enhances the operator's performance. The experiential characteristics (e.g., spatial presence, involvement, and realness), however, have been found to be similar to Gary's own work in intercultural and global f2f encounters (Mantovani & Riva, 1999; Schubert, Friedmann, & Regenbrecht, 1999). Subsequently, the terms *a sense of presence*, *telepresence*, and *virtual presence* (Lombard & Ditton, 1997; Riva, Davide, & Ijsselsteijn, 2002) have all been used to refer to the perception that any mediated experience (e.g., virtual environments [VEs], training simulations, distance education, computer-mediated collaboration, videoconferencing, home theater, high-definition television, and some amusement park rides) is not mediated—the experience that we are really there, somewhere. In the case of virtual presence, it is the experience of being somewhere that does not really exist at all outside the computer! The somewheres of interest in this chapter, of course, are the classrooms of Teleland. To keep from getting lost in a maze of terminology, we use the term *a sense of presence* to refer to all of the above.

Lombard and Ditton (1997) defined presence as "an illusion that a mediated experience is not mediated" (p. 1). It includes the characteristics of *realism, transportation* ("you are there" or "it is here" or "we are together in a shared space"), and *immersion* ("involved, absorbed, engaged, engrossed"). Witmer and Singer (1988) defined it as "the subjective experience of being in one place or environment, even when one is physically situated in another.

As applied to a virtual environment (VE), presence refers to experiencing the computer-generated environment rather than the actual physical locale" (p. 225). Much of the theory, research, and application of work on a sense of presence is accessible online at www.presence-research.org. In this chapter, we try to distill that work with the most implications for online education. In both Gary's own work and that of researchers in Teleland, a sense of presence is conceptualized as a characteristic of the psychological experience of the participant rather than of the medium. Thus, it is differentiated from the concept of *social presence* (Short, Williams, & Christie, 1976), defined as a subjective quality of the communication medium that reflects its capacity to transmit cues about facial expression, direction of looking, posture, dress, and other nonverbal cues that are key to effective communication. Whereas a sense of presence refers to the state of mind of being in a particular place (proximal, remote, or virtual), social presence is a perceived capacity of the medium to convey these cues. Social presence does not necessarily entail an experience of actually being there. We believe, however, that these concepts are interdependent in many types of mediated communication and increasing one will enhance the other. Because of that both are addressed through this chapter.

The Effects of Having Presence in Teleland

Research on a sense of presence in all contexts—mediated or not—is still largely in the embryonic stage, and many of the presumed effects are based largely on anecdotal evidence. In Teleland, much of the research that has been done has focused on same time–different place ecologies supported by audio, video, sometimes tactile, and VE technologies. The effects of interest have been both individual and group learning and performance. There is mounting evidence that an enhanced sense of presence improves both as well as other variables related to performance in distance education (Riva et al., 2002). Some of these latter include arousal (Heeter, 1995; Lombard, Grabe, Reich, Campanella, & Ditton, 1995), enjoyment (Heeter, 1995), involvement (Heeter, 1995), persuasion (Kim, 1996), memory (Ditton, 1997), and motivation to complete the task (Whitelock, Romano, Jelfs, & Brna, 2000). Involvement, in particular, is likely to be key in both same time–different place and different time–different place ecologies, in part to overcome the distracting effects of the technologies used, an issue discussed later. Research has also found positive relationships between the social presence of a learning environment and students' satisfaction (Gunawardena & Zittle, 1997), degree of interactivity (Tu & McIsaac, 2002), formation of interpersonal relationships (Walther & Burgoon, 1992), depth of online discussion (Polhemus, Shil, & Swan, 2001), and affective learning (Kearney, Plax, & Wendt-Wasco, 1985). The lack of social presence may lead to frustration, a critical attitude toward the teacher's effectiveness, and a lower level of affective learning (Hample & Dallinger, 1995).

In journeys to the intercultural and international strange lands that have served as Gary's professional focus, heightened presence appears to occur naturally as a consequence of the novelty encountered. The skill is to make use of it to define the necessary, possible, and desirable, as described earlier. In Teleland, however, because of distance and the obtrusiveness of media, the sense of presence required for optimal performance may more frequently need to be created—or at least nurtured and supported. Thus, in journeys to Teleland, we have an additional presence-related challenge.

Precipitants of Presence in Teleland

A variety of conditions appear to nurture a sense of presence in mediated contexts, and a selection of those most likely relevant to teaching in Teleland is presented next.

Media characteristics. The more completely and consistently all senses are stimulated, the greater the presence (Witmer & Singer, 1998). Clearly presentation of both visual and audio stimuli is important (Lombard & Ditton, 1997; Whitelock et al., 2000). Given that, however, visual display characteristics (when available) appear to have the most impact. These characteristics include image quality, size, and viewing distance; proportion of a user's visual field occupied by an image; motion, color, and dimensionality). Hendrix and Barfield (1996), for example, found that presence was higher when head tracking and stereoscopic cues were provided to participants and when the visual display represented a 50- or 90-degree geometric field of view rather than a 10-degree field. Important audio characteristics include quality (frequency range, variations in loudness, and distortion in sound reproduction) and dimensionality. Gilkey and Weisenberger (1995) stress that "Background auditory stimulation may be useful or even critical for achieving a full sense of presence" (p. 364). Lombard and Ditton suggest that "adding the smells of food, flowers, or the air at a beach or in a rain forest to the corresponding images and sounds seems likely to enhance a sense of presence" (p. 17), as interestingly, do surprises (e.g., video clips running in picture frames in VE displays or pop-up help guides). Fencott (1999) stresses that "cues and surprises in VEs work together, supporting each other and thus the virtuality they inhabit by seeking to both establish fidelity and catch and retain the attention of the visitor and thus maintain presence" (p. 4). We will return specifically to the role of surprises in the online classroom later in this chapter. In general, the more the above cues support scene realism, consistency with the objective world, and environmental richness, the greater the presence (Witmer & Singer, 1998).

Most computer-mediated communication (CMC) learning environments, including those in online learning, typically have fewer visual or audio channels available than in those just described, and thus, the nonverbal cues that are crucial to conveying meaning and building relationships are diminished. Therefore, other techniques are needed to create an environment in which people feel at ease in communicating. Practitioners have found that social presence can be enhanced by strategically using text-based message tools such as emoticons, providing frequent feedback, sharing personal stories and experiences, and using humor (Aragon, 2003). Studies have also found that adding supplemental media such as cell phone text messaging can increase the capacity for social presence in the environment (DuVall, Powell, Hodge, & Ellis, 2007). They emphasize that "the key to success in online learning involves using strategies that facilitate communication and enhance social presence among online learners, not just applying the newest technologies" (p. 24).

Orientation and movement in space. The more the observer can perceive self-movement and the movement of other people or objects relative to the self, the greater the presence (Witmer & Singer, 1998). Likewise, it is greater the more the participants can modify their viewpoint to change what they see or hear or when kinesthetic cues are provided that the participants bodies are actually moving in physical space during a mediated experience (e.g., vibrating theater seats to enhance the illusion that the viewers are experiencing an earthquake; Lombard & Ditton, 1997) and haptic cues (touch or force-feedback) are present as participants encounter other people or objects (Ho, Basdogan, Slater, Durlach, & Srinivasan, 1998).

Freedom from distractions. Both isolation (the degree to which participants are isolated from their physical surroundings) and selective attention (participants' ability to focus on the task stimuli and ignore distractions) facilitate presence. Conversely, interface awareness produced by "unnatural, clumsy, artifact-laden interface devices that interfere with the direct and effortless interpretation of and interaction with a remote or virtual environment diminish presence" (Witmer & Singer, 1998, p. 230; see also Schubert et al., 1999). Lombard and Ditton (1997) likewise suggest that "the medium should not be obvious or obtrusive—it should not draw attention to itself and remind the media user that she/he is having a mediated experience" (p. 19).

Degree of control, interaction, and exploration. The more control participants have over the task environment and their interactions with it, the greater the presence (Schubert et al., 1999; Welch, Blackmon, Liu, Mellers, & Stark, 1996; Witmer & Singer, 1998). Stimuli should be responsive to input by the participants, and noticeable delays between input and reaction diminish presence. Presence is enhanced if the mode of interaction with the environment is natural or well practiced as opposed to artificial or new. Lombard and Ditton (1997) noted, "Most writers have either implicitly assumed or explicitly suggested that a major or even the primary cause of presence is the ability to interact with a mediated environment"

(p. 19). They suggest that the degree to which a medium is interactive depends on a) the number of inputs from the user that the medium accepts, b) the number of characteristics of the mediated presentation or experience that can be modified by the user, c) the range of change possible in each characteristic of the mediated presentation or experience, d) the degree of correspondence between the type of user input and the type of medium response, and e) the speed with which the medium responds to user inputs. With respect to the latter, Heeter (1995) noted, "When forced to choose between responsiveness to motion and resolution of images, virtual environment developers are choosing responsiveness as the more important factor" (p. 203).

Nature of the task or activity. The nature of the task or activity (e.g., motor vs. cognitive, learning vs. performance, individual vs. group) is likely to affect the experience of presence, as is the importance, meaningfulness, interest value, and past experience with it (Lombard & Ditton, 1997; Witmer & Singer, 1998). Gary's own work strongly suggests that task novelty or unpredictability in the unfolding of events is a key precipitant of presence (Fontaine, 1993), although there is recent evidence that in some contexts predictability and contiguity with expectations may enhance presence (McGreevy, 1994). Clearly, much research and model development is necessary. The earlier mentioned findings with respect to the role of surprises could also be included here. Schubert et al. (1999) found that drama ("the extent to which the environment presents a strong story line, is self-contained, [and] has its own dynamic, and unfolding sequence of events" [p. 4]) also contributes to presence.

The number of participants and copresence. Lombard and Ditton (1997) suggested that, at least up to a point, the greater the number of participants, the greater the presence experienced. The issue as to whether there is some optimal number is still largely unexplored, although Rovai (2001) suggested that in an asynchronous learning environment, a student–instructor ratio should be no higher than 30 to 1. In our experience, however, that ratio is very optimistic. For example, the rule of thumb for the graduate students in the Fielding Graduate University's program in Organization Management and Development is more like 15 or 18 to 1. A key, of course, is the degree to which each participant is aware of the presence of others in the task or activity. This awareness of being and interacting with others has sometimes been called a sense of copresence (Couch, 1989). Generally, the more participants are aware of the presence of others and that those others are reciprocating that awareness, the higher the sense of presence (J. Anderson, Ashraf, Douther, & Jack, 2000; Kaltenbrunner & Huxor, 2000; Steed & Slater, 1998; Thie & van Wijk, 1998), particularly when interactions with them are possible (Schubert et al., 1999). Several studies have examined the variables contributing to the sense of copresence (J. Anderson, et al., 2000; Durlach & Slater, 2000; Ho et al., 1998).

Trait and state characteristics of the participants. There are likely to be individual and cultural differences associated with the experience of presence in Teleland. Some participants might be both more willing and able to experience presence than others (Thie & van Wijk, 1998). Lombard and Ditton (1997) suggested that "the identical media form and content might generate a sense of presence in one media user and not in another, or might generate presence in the same user on one occasion but not another one" (p. 22). Willingness to suspend disbelief can facilitate getting into the experience and overlooking obtrusiveness of the media. Those unfamiliar with technology might be less distracted by its workings than those closely acquainted with it. More prior experience may lead to more habitual use of media controls and habituation to its distractions and, thus, facilitate presence. Lombard and Ditton also suggest that the participants' preferred representational system (visual, auditory, or kinesthetic), cognitive style, the degree to which they screen complex stimuli, their level of sensation seeking, their need to overcome loneliness, and their mood can have an effect. Mantovani and Riva (1999) suggested that both the meaning of presence and the experience of it is related to the participants' culture. Rovai (2003), too, has found that the communicator styles differ significantly across personality styles among online students and suggests that online teachers should vary their teaching methods and assignments so that "no learning styles are totally disadvantage across an entire course" (p. 361).

Tu and McIsaac (2002) argued that people's perceptions of CMC technology are based on their culture background, their particular situation, their previous experiences, and their psychological attitude. Gary has elsewhere pointed out that until very recently online environments have tended to be very task orientated. For American students, and those from other individualist cultures, "The team begins with the task, ends with the task and does very little other than the task" (Fontaine, 2002, p. 125). This is something of a problem for those from more collectivist cultures in which building relationships is an essential part of doing tasks. Grace has found, for example, that Chinese international students experience a lower level of social presence than American students in online learning environments (Chun, 2008). Chinese students had different expectations from their American student counterparts, particularly in terms of quickness of feedback and importance of social relationships. With more limited English-language skills, they also needed to continually strive to "save face." Lack of awareness of, and responsivity to, these differing expectations and needs by online teachers and other participants produced a higher level of frustration and anxiety in the Chinese students.

Student Sense of Community

Research over the last decade within a community of inquiry model has found that students' sense of community in a learning environment sustains productive discourse and enhances learning (T. Anderson, Rourke, Garrison, & Archer, 2001). That sense of community involves goal-directed collaborative interaction, trust, and mutual support. Shea, Li, and Pickett (2006) have studied the role that teaching presence has in the development of sense of community for both f2f and online learners (the term *presence* clearly is very popular these days; we apologize for any consequent confusion!). In the community of inquiry model, high teaching presence is defined as student perception that the teacher is providing *effective course design* (e.g., setting curriculum, effective use of available media), *facilitating productive discourse* (e.g., identifying areas of agreement-disagreement, helping to reach consensus, prompting discussion), and *providing direct instruction* (e.g., presenting content, asking questions, focusing and summarizing discussion). In a large study of f2f and online learners, Shea et al. found that high teaching presence was associated with a greater sense of classroom community for both types of learner. Of the components of teaching presence, *directed facilitation* (a combination of facilitating productive discourse and direct instruction) had a larger impact than course design, though the latter was still important. Shea et al. conclude that "a strong and active presence on the part of the instructor—one in which she or he actively guides and orchestrates the discourse—is related both to students' sense of connectedness and learning" (p. 14).

Clearly, there are likely to be significant cultural differences in just what students' perceive to be high teaching presence. For example, online courses tend to promote student-centered learning; teachers post the learning material and expect students to learn by themselves. Students from some cultures may have difficulty with that. Education in Asian countries tends to be teacher oriented (Zhan, 1995). Aubrey (1991) found that Asian, Middle Eastern, and African students reported that they had been trained to sit quietly in lecture-type classrooms and take verbatim notes to be memorized in preparation for exams that are usually given only once or twice a year. Tu (2001) reported that in an online learning environment Chinese students might not be aware that the role of the teacher is as facilitator rather than as lecturer and that learning is expected to occur during interaction among students and through self-discovery. In Grace's research, Chinese students reported that "it is hard to learn all material by myself" and "I think I can get more from the teacher in a real class" (Chun, 2008). Asian students generally might feel frustrated not receiving clear or frequent opinions and explanations from their teachers. She found, for example, that 72% of Chinese students believed that the response time to their messages exceeded their expected limits, while only 53% American students felt so (which is still a lot!); 45% of Chinese students expected a response within 8 hours, but none of the American students did (Chun, 2008). Thompson and Heng (2005) also found that Chinese students expected feedback sooner. Tu (2001) stressed that when the response time exceeds expected limits, the level of social presence is diminished and that such "silence" is commonly interpreted as a negative response—"Why didn't the teacher answer my e-mail? Because I am not a good student?"

Building relationships with teachers and other students can be another challenge for those from different cultures. For example, most Asian cultures are high in *power distance* (Hofstede, 1986). In a high power distance culture, the teacher is viewed with absolute respect and admiration. Thus, building relationships with teachers and receiving affirmation from them are crucial for Asian students' self-confidence. Providing opportunities for such relationship building is key to teaching presence in this cultural context, and not having such may negatively impact the perceived presence and satisfaction of any student from a relatively high power distance academic culture (Tu & McIssac, 2002).

Grace had experiences in two recent online graduate courses that reflect both general student responses and those more culturally based. In the first course, the professor met f2f with students in the first class session to build relationships and assign them to teams and projects. However, once the course moved into its online format, she did not give any feedback for several weeks after the completed projects were posted. The latency in the feedback caused all students to feel a loss of connection and community and produced consequent distrust, frustration, and anxiety. The professor in the other course did not meet f2f at all but laid out a very clear syllabus, schedule, and academic learning goals. However, without the opportunity for relationship building, the learning environment quickly became very cold, particularly for the Asian students, and they felt uncomfortable communicating. One Chinese student stated,

> After awhile, I totally lost learning motivation from this class. I didn't even know if our instructor is a real person or not. Besides her name, I know nothing about her and I don't think she is interested in knowing anything about me. I could not build any relationship with her and this made me feel extremely frustrated. Sometimes, I felt like I was communicating with a machine, or maybe I was learning from software designed for this class! (Chun, 2008, p. 45).

Nurturing Presence in Online Education

Developing and delivering a good course anywhere—at home or in Teleland—requires putting it together in a nurturing ecology that consists of talented, motivated participants (teachers, students, resource persons) with appropriate texts, multimedia, and technological resources, and administrative support. As noted earlier, doing all this in today's world, in which many of the ecological characteristics are new or changing, requires building MCs accommodated to each for a particular course at a particular time. There are no recipes here—few well-marked highways—at least not yet. The theme of this chapter has been that optimizing a sense of presence is a valuable objective in these strange lands of Teleland. A growing body of research suggests such, and our own experiences teaching and learning in Teleland convinces us of the fact. As Gristock (1998) asserted, in effective geographically dispersed teams (which online courses must be) knowledge exchange must be "supported by the development of a *sense of telepresence . . .* and *telecommunity* between members . . . , at least for as long as the duration of the exchange" (italics added; p. 3). Tammelin (1998) reinforced the point specifically for online education. As we just saw, Shea et al. (2006) stress the importance of directed facilitation and course design. The task, then, is to draw upon as many clues or tools as we can from research and experience to help us design and deliver the particular course to which our journey takes us. We next examine some of those applicable to synchronous and asynchronous course ecologies. We emphasize the latter because, in our view, asynchronous ecologies are likely to be most accommodating to the needs of education, training, and collaboration in a global world.

Synchronous Course Ecologies

Synchronous course ecologies in Teleland can involve same time–different place classrooms connected by interactive audio and video or combinations of those with a same time–same place f2f classroom (the teacher presents to physically proximal as well as dispersed sites in real time through broadcast, cable, or wireless). Both may also be supported by phone, mail, e-mail, or Web connections with electronic whiteboards, chat rooms and video. There have been both heavy investments and significant improvements in supportive technology for this ecology, much of which is likely to influence the level of presence experienced. The course architecture (e.g., syllabi, lectures, texts, assignments, evaluations, and media) and the degree to which that architecture is accommodated to the ecology of the specific course significantly affect the success of that course. Among the ecological necessities for a course to be effective are that (a) participants be always (or nearly so) physically present in a classroom (somewhere) that can support the appropriate media technologies, (b) they be roughly on the same daily schedule, and (c) they be in proximal time zones. It is also useful for them to have similar backgrounds in terms of course prerequisites and preparation and the same primary language and culture.

The research reviewed earlier and our experiences suggest that in this ecology, the keys to an optimal sense of presence are as follows:

- a ratio of high realness and intensity of audio, video, and other display characteristics to distractions associated with the media-computer technology used to produce the displays and

- a ratio of high interactivity between participants in different sites to those same distractions.

In other words, if we can absorb participants in the scene through sensory integrity and interpersonal interactions, then they will forget about the medium through which all this is occurring. Strangely, an analogy to skin diving comes to mind! When Gary dives at home in Hawaii where there is relatively little to see in terms of varied marine flora and fauna compared to other tropical seas (because of isolation many fewer species have made it there than elsewhere in the Indo Pacific), he typically becomes distracted and irritated by the "fog" on his face mask. He constantly finds himself spitting on the glass to keep it clear. When he dives in the lagoon in front of his cottage in the Philippines where there are always new and intriguing sights, he loses awareness of the mask and the face plate altogether and becomes absorbed in the scene—same mask, same spit, different show!

The audio and video characteristics reviewed earlier can all play a role in nurturing presence in synchronous courses, including image quality and size; viewing distance; proportion of a user's visual field; motion and color; audio frequency range; and variations in loudness, distortion, and dimensionality. To the degree possible, teachers need the best of each as budgets support. In our experience, however, the keys to optimizing presence are big video monitors (consume as much of the field of vision as possible), cameras and monitors that allow participants (certainly the teacher) to perceive self-movement and to modify their viewpoints to change what they see or hear, and real-time audio feedback. Monitors—however many—that make up a very small percentage of the visual field both diminish telepresence and interfere with presence in the proximal f2f classroom (if there is one). The situation is exacerbated since the image size and depth of field of monitors—at least those we have had available—generally resolve remote classrooms into some "big heads" of front-row students, with those in back coming through at best as Lilliputians who raise from time to time what appear to be hands (we may wonder, "Are they asking a question? Or is that just lint on the camera?").

Although the availability of several monitors displaying different viewpoints (including overhead or other graphic material) can be initially disorienting (especially if there are several dispersed sites), the freedom to select what to see can certainly enhance a sense of presence. Strangely, this seems particularly true if one can see oneself on one or more monitors as well. There is an interesting parallel here to some of Gary's own work in strange lands that suggests that our sense of presence is enhanced if we perceive that others are attending to us!

Real-time video and audio feedback—consistent across sites—is also key. Even relatively short delays—3 to 5 seconds—can be a problem. Gary can recall one class in which a couple of the dispersed sites were real time and the other was slow screen video and real-time audio. If he saw a student in the latter classroom raise her hand, he would wonder, "When did she do that and in response to what?" Or if he heard her say something with exclamation or inquiry, he would turn to look at her in his monitor only to find her still smiling and content—yet to be struck by whatever was to lead to her query! He might then wonder suddenly if the comment was delivered instead by somebody else in one of the other classes—and in a panic look around to other monitors. And gee, as Lombard and Ditton (1997) suggested, either the scent of her perfume or a breath of fresh air from the window near her would help with presence a bit, too.

A particular challenge in this ecology is handling the audio. It is technically difficult to pick up every student everywhere equally well without everyone having his or her own microphone. So then the problem becomes everybody talking over everyone else! Thus on-off buttons are used to synchronize input. But it is distracting for all but the very experienced to remember to press a button before speaking and then again when finished (remember two-way radios?). The obtrusiveness of the technology can be devastating to presence—people are attending to their buttons and not present either here or there! And what if they forget to turn off the button, then turn with a joke or obscenity to your neighbor! Researchers at the Ontario Telepresence Project at the University of Toronto have designed fascinating collaboration environments using unobtrusive computer and media technology to heighten the sense of telepresence (Buxton, 1997). These latter technologies have been integrated in a manner that is ecologically valid in terms of participant "social conventions and mores of architectural location-distance-function relationships" (Buxton, 1997, p. 372). Desks, computers, and imaging devices become one physically and functionally integrated entity. The office or classroom door serves input functions—as a mouse or keyboard might—to indicate to colleagues the availability of the occupant for discourse!

Same time–different place collaborative virtual environments (CVEs) have been developed for computer supported cooperative work such as meetings or classes (Frecon, 1998; Steed & Slater, 1998). Some use avatar representations of participants as they interact with one another in a electronic team rooms that mimic the characteristics of physical ones. Frecon (1998, pp. 10–11) describes how these rooms support peripheral awareness (of what other participants are doing to promote coordination), provide for the possibility of chance encounters, offer natural metaphors by mapping participants' understanding of the real world onto virtual counterparts, and provide persistence in recognition that cooperation happens over long periods and involves results from a series of interrelated events. Rooms offer standard collaboration tools such as whiteboards, flip charts, overhead projectors, handouts, and models or prototypes viewable by all. Frecon notes that teams usually elect a room as theirs and that members seem naturally drawn toward their room. Research is examining the requirements for nurturing both effective communication and presence in this state-of-art synchronous ecology (J. Anderson et al., 2000; Rauthenberg, Kauff, & Graffunder, 2000; Riva et al., 2002).

Another common component of synchronous course ecologies is online chatting. Participants can communicate at the same time in different places through software such as MSN, Google Talk, AIM (AOL Instant Messenger), or text message through cell phones. Although participants cannot experience the vividness of more visual or graphic components through such text-based media, they can enhance awareness of another persons and building relationships with them. However, online synchronous discussions may present special difficulties for participants whose primary language is other than that of the discourse. In online synchronous discussions, the pace is rapid and topics change frequently. It is challenging for second-language participants to follow the flow of the discussion. Further, they may fear that their poorer quality writing will leave a bad impression on the instructor and refrain from frequent participation. For example, in order to save face, Asian students may take more time than their American counterparts in reading and writing and polishing messages (Tu, 2001). By the time they post, most likely the topic has changed. Thus, they feel left out of the discussion and are discouraged to enter future ones.

There are a number of other issues introduced earlier that are likely to be key for maximizing presence in this course ecology; determining the optimal number of sites and participants are two. But more research and practical experience with them are needed prior to suggesting their impact with confidence. There are yet many shortcomings of this rapidly developing technology. Again, we believe the key to optimizing presence is to absorb the participants in the scene—wherever that is—through the vibrancy of the presentation, resource media used, or interpersonal interactions between participants. The more this can be done, the more unobtrusive the medium becomes.

Asynchronous Course Ecologies

Asynchronous course ecologies in Teleland involve different time-different place activities in which participants typically access a Web site when it is appropriate or convenient to do so and only for as long as it remains so. Their classroom is a desktop or notebook computer with Internet access, and they may move from job to home to airport to hotel as participants' lives and work dictate. The same may be true for teachers as well as students. Typically, most or all participants are physically isolated from one another by time zone and distance. The primary medium for interaction is some form of *groupware* or forum software, though that may be supplemented again by phone, cell phone, chat, instant messaging, mail, e-mail, or intermittent scheduled or unscheduled f2f contact. DuVall et al. (2007) found that text messaging (or texting)—long popular in Asia and Europe and more recently in North America accompanying the enormous expansion in the use of cell phones—can help engender the sense of immediacy associated with enhanced presence in university courses.

An asynchronous ecology requires groupware that is closely accommodated to course requirements (e.g., access to resources, written assignments, group discussions or projects, feedback), a sufficiently high capacity and dependable server, reliable Internet service provider, high-speed access, adequate computer capacity, and participant computer skill. In this ecology, participants need not be fully in synchrony in terms of course background or preparation (they can "make up" work when off-line). They do not have to have the same primary language (they can work on wording off-line) or be from the same culture (they can consider, and if necessary, get assistance with intercultural issues off-line). A Chinese student in Grace's research noted that "as an introvert, it gives me time to formulate my thoughts and not be intimidated by someone's strong f2f presence, use of verbal cues or tonality"; another noted that "the sense of being shy is not there. You don't have to be shy in speaking up" (Chun, 2008, p. 47).

Generally, she found the asynchronous ecology enhanced the Chinese students' learning experience because they felt freer to express themselves. This ecology also allows for timely silences or absences—built-in pauses in communication—so important for absorption and integration of material, creativity, stress reduction and deepening connections with ourselves and others (Rubin, 2000; Waterworth & Waterworth, 2000). It is particularly well suited to education or training for busy students and professionals in our global world. And it is an ecology in which a sense of presence, again, appears to play a key role in performance (Mania & Chalmers, 2000).

Whereas the burden of nurturing a sense of presence in synchronous ecologies is on the sophistication of technology support, the burden in asynchronous ones is much more on groupware and participant skill. The material reviewed above and the authors' experiences suggest that in these ecologies the keys to an optimal sense of presence are as follows:

- high psychological texture for people, settings, worktables, and assignments;
- high interactivity among an optimal combination of number of participants and tasks and the responsivity of those participants; and
- high meaningfulness and an optimal mixture of predictability, surprise and drama of course content and activities that foster a merging of proximal and dispersed settings into one place.

To the degree these criteria are met, participants' perceptual worlds are altered such that the "here and now" expands to include the "there and then"!

In the asynchronous course ecologies of Teleland, architecture remains important for supporting course objectives, although components may be somewhat different (groupware forums with topics, replies, and meeting areas against a backdrop of office, home or park replace proximal and distal classrooms and video-audio media). But in these ecologies, optimizing presence requires going beyond architecture to "interior decorating" the site by spraying texture on all its surfaces, for it is that texture built in the mental image each participant has of this world that replaces the realness and intensity of the transmitted visual and audio images in synchronous ecologies.

The participants in an asynchronous course must furnish and decorate the site—even to the wallpaper—themselves. It does not come with a technology package. They must provide as much texture as possible. This texture can come in the form of the recall of previous f2f interactions among participants; shared experience online in previous courses or the academic program itself; shared experience with the server, the syllabus, course assignments, or texts; or continuing reflections on ongoing world or local events. Metacommunication (communicating about course communication) and communication aimed at building a context of shared experience, expanding interpersonal familiarity and relationships, reducing conflict, providing support and encouragement—and sometimes humor and perspective—all can be valuable to texturing this dispersed world to the point that it can be seamlessly integrated into the proximal one. Exchanging small talk or stories of travels, vacations, celebrations, sorrows, hopes, and fears can help merge the worlds together and nurture the important sense of community described earlier (Shea et al., 2006).

Tammelin (1998) described the inclusion of informal discussion rooms or "cafés." In his own asynchronous courses, Gary typically has a "sTrANgE laNDs Roadside Inn" or "bAbbiE's bAr" (named after the author of the research methods text used [Babbie, 2002]). These bars, cafés, or their counterparts can provide "taste," "smell," and "favorite food and drink" (indeed, Gary sometimes get the impression that participants do mix a real drink or prepare real food as they are sitting at home or office posting their messages). These places provide a bulletin board for course announcements, a table to argue across, an opportunity for social comparison, a voice to console, some space to chat in, a forum to share a joke with, a hall to scream in, or a seam to talk (to anyone) between time zones! They are by no means the only part of the architecture with texture. Assignment areas, work areas, links, and so forth can be textured as well, but the texture of a sTrANgE laNDs Roadside Inn after a semester of occupancy is real indeed—at least as much as the bar down the street!

Although the explicit purposes of these informal rooms are as indicated above, their primary (albeit implicit) purpose should be to pull the participants out of their different worlds and into a shared place for awhile—to enhance their sense of presence. Tammelin (1998) stressed likewise: "The main purpose of the café conference was to establish a space where the participants could demonstrate their own social presence and sense the presence of the other participants" (pp. 5–6). The techniques Gary has used for doing so, consistent with the earlier review of the characteristics nurturing presence, can involve presenting participants through topic postings with *novelty* ("The moonrise"—the description of a bloodred moon rising from out of the black Sibuyan Sea one evening before Gary went online), *surprises* ("A bolt from out of the blue"—an account of Gary being hit by lightning from a clear blue sky while strolling along the beach drinking coffee in the morning, again just before going online), opportunities for *chance encounters* with important people ("A word from our Program Director"—the director of our graduate program visited our bar to dialogue about program changes), and *drama* ("The murder"—a traveler found naked and dead on a nearby beach!)—all this in a course on global assignments or, perhaps, research methodology. But, of course, to be credible they must all be true! Typically, the other course participants (the students) also make major contributions to this presence-nurturing effort as they post topics from their current lives about the death of a father, the sickness of a child, a marriage, a coup d'etat at home in Kathmandu, the chaos following a nearby explosion in the Green Zone in Baghdad, or the promotion to the new job of organizational televangelist.

And these postings cannot simply be scripted and reproduced from semester to semester. Doing so nearly always "shows" to the participants. Rather, the trick is for the teacher to maintain a high sense of presence while participating in the course as well so that the topics flow from real experience and are accommodated to needs stemming from the personalities, experiences, and culture of that particular class. To the degree that we have been successful in evidencing this sense of presence we have variously attributed it our dealing with new, highly talented students; dealing with the rapid growth and change of our fields; dealing with new Teleland technologies; and dealing with other new, strange lands, we may be encountering as we teach the courses. With respect to the latter, for example, Gary has often been on the road while maintaining a presence in his class from Internet cafés or via his notebook and a variety of tenuous Internet connections. Again, strange lands indeed!

The appendix illustrates a sample course architecture from a recent asynchronous course on "Global & Intercultural Strategies & Skills" that Gary taught for the middle- and upper-level managers in the Fielding program mentioned earlier. It presents the topics (with the number of postings-replies) that are associated with the course syllabus, assignments, the sTrANgE laNDs Roadside Inn, the introduction to that inn, and resource and work folders.

Including in the forum, a guest participant (a program administrator or an outside resource person) with whom participants have had previous f2f contact has a particularly strong effect in weaving proximal and dispersed realities together. If individual courses can be housed within a broader programmatic ecology that arranges at least occasional f2f interaction, then texture is further enhanced. If those f2f interactions can also include husbands or wives or bosses or workmates, texture is enhanced even more and the dispersed and proximal realities are integrated further in a web of the present. A student in one of Tammelin's cafés noted,

> I feel that at least a few group meetings face to face are needed to create a certain atmosphere. A course where several communication channels are used is very different from a course where only for example e-mail would be used to communicate between the participants. If you never see what the

others really look like, it somehow makes it all much more distant and so there will not be the same kind of a connection. (Tammelin, 1998, p. 8)

Another key to optimizing presence is just the right amount of interaction between teacher and students and between students and students to keep this world going. Too little input or responsivity and most participants will fade—or be drawn—into other worlds; too much input inhibits student interaction, and a real but strange world is transformed into a series of Internet lectures or teacher–student dialogues. Note that the key to the timing of interactivity in these asynchronous ecologies is not immediacy (the different time–different place ecology does not support that) but sufficiency. When participants go online, there must be relevant and timely messages for them, and they must have confidence that responses to those messages, or new ones, will be equally timely to the recipients in the not-too-distant future. Participants need a sense of copresence. They need to feel that someone is really there—that if they cannot catch him or her in this forum topic today, they can catch him or her in the bar tomorrow. That is necessary to support the reality that participants share a present. As indicated previously, maintaining that flow requires some optimal combination of number of participants, task communication requirements, and participant responsivity. Our guess is that at this point in our understanding of Teleland, identifying and maintaining that flow is much more an interpersonal art than a science, or perhaps, mostly good luck. We remember those courses in which the optimal levels were obtained, and we forget—and hopefully our students forgive us for—the course that fell short!

In asynchronous ecologies, distractions from texture or interactivity can inhibit the sense of presence. Intrusions from bosses or coworkers at the office or from spouses or children or pets at home can force Teleland back into a distant reality. Even in an ecology that is based on asynchronous technologies, it can be tempting—but often dangerous—to provide supplementary synchronous ones. For example, if a given participant is not responding quickly to a forum posting, there can be the temptation to actually telephone! But if the phone rings and rings and rings or if he or she is there but busy with other things, then the illusion of sharing presence in a course reality can be shattered. The difficulty of trying to use phone (or other synchronous technologies) to supplement asynchronous technologies can have an impact on presence analogous to the earlier mentioned distracting effect of pushing buttons to sequence audio input in synchronous ecologies.

Asynchronous ecologies place a greater burden on psychologically constructing a broadened sense of place than being provided with a media enhanced awareness of one. Developing and/or maintaining a sense of presence in asynchronous ecologies may then require greater sustained effort and thus motivation on the part of participants. Although there may be several motives for participants to take such courses, the meaningfulness of either the message (the course content) or the medium (distance education) to professional goals is likely to be key to nurturing presence. In other words, in synchronous ecologies, presence may be high or not based primarily on the quality of the visual/auditory display, distractions, or interactions without much effort required on the part of participants. In fact, if similarities to work on presence in real strange lands hold true, focusing attention on having presence may have the contrary effect of dissipating it. But in asynchronous ecologies, such effort may be required; it is an ecology that does not naturally produce a sense of presence, so it must be constructed and nurtured—with care.

Finally, in asynchronous course ecologies our rich imaginations are by necessity prompted to paint images of people, places, and events beyond the immediate ones. The sense of presence thus created may well surpass that achieved in synchronous ecologies which rely so significantly on the image quality and transparency of the support technology—both still somewhat problematic in most courses in Teleland today. Our minds are still better than our monitors!

So Where Are We, Really?

Sense of presence, telepresence, copresence, social presence, teaching presence all are terms referred to in this chapter, all with related but differentiable meanings. Biocca (1997) said,

> The compelling sense of presence in virtual environments is unstable. At best it is fleeting. Like a voice interrupting a daydream in the imaginal environment, presence in the virtual environment can be interrupted by sensory cues from the physical environment and imperfections in the inter-face (Slater & Ush, 1993; Kim & Bocca, 1997).
>
> At one point in time, users can be said to feel as if they are physically present in only one of three places: . . . the *physical environment,* the *virtual environment,* or the *imaginal environment.* (pp. 15–16, italics added)

It appears that the chief concern in synchronous course ecologies is telepresence or remote presence in the sense that has evolved in research on teleoperator systems. Much remains to be learned, however, especially about how different types of tasks in classrooms affect presence and its antecedents.

In asynchronous ecologies, however, the state of mind appears more akin to virtual presence or a sense of being present in a place that isn't. But there is a place! On closer examination, a sense of presence in asynchronous ecologies may actually be something like that "old" unmediated (recall that it is the mind not the media that appears critical here) presence in strange lands akin to travel abroad. Only it is a very strange land, indeed; it is here, there, and moving. The tentacles of the immediate present extend from the here and now to several "theres" and "thens." It is like expanding a sense of presence to include many selected distal places and times. As Mantovani and Riva (1999) stated, "The validity of presence does not consist of simply reproducing the conditions of physical presence but in constructing environments in which *actors may function in an ecologically valid way*" (p. 545, italics added). That is, our presence is where we *interact*, not necessarily where we physically are!

In today's world, we in fact need to maintain multiple presences. Lipnack and Stamps (2000) stressed, "In cyberspace, people do not have to desert old places in order to access new ones. You can simultaneously be in numerous online places, joining new groups while weaning yourself from old ones" (p. 105). Similarly, Kaltenbrunner and Huxor (2000) noted that online collaboration requires the following: "One has *a variety of presences.* One can be both in a physical office and engaged in a telephone conversation: in this situation where is ones' presence? It seems to be in both 'places' at once" (p. 2, italics added). Certainly, online education is centered on just that kind of collaborative work. Both teachers and students need to maintain multiple presences in a variety of courses, teams, and activities—both f2f and dispersed. To be optimally successful, then, any given virtual classroom must be competitive in nurturing its share of our presence in Teleland.

APPENDIX

Sample Course Architecture and Introduction to the sTrANgE laNDs Roadside Inn for OMD604 Global & Intercultural Strategies & Skills *(Number of postings in parentheses)*

Discussions and Documents

OUR SYLLABUS, TEAM MEMBERS AND ASSIGNMENT SCHEDULE (7)

Our sTrANgE laNDs Roadside Inn (330)

Our sTrANgE laNDs Roadside Inn. This is a place to exchange our concerns, worries, suggestions, encouragement and support appropriate to getting tasks done effectively in this course. It's a place to share stories of the strange lands we visit—and live in, or just a place to drop in for a chat with one another as we explore lands together in this course, the OMD program, our jobs, and our lives. While I regularly peruse other topics, I will stop by here frequently for a break, new ideas, drinks and "pupus," and companionship. And a chance encounter. You all are invited to do likewise. We NEVER close

CRITICAL INCIDENT Assignment (119)

CULTURAL SELF-ASSESSMENT Assignment (146)

PERSONAL CASE STUDY Assignment (99)

FINAL TEAM HANDBOOKS (60)

Document and Work Folders

RESOURCES FOR THE ROAD (9)

TEAM CRIMSON Worktable (18)

TEAM ORANGE Worktable (106)

TEAM TEAL Worktable (195)

References

Anderson, J., Ashraf, N., Douther, C., & Jack, M. (2000). *A participatory design study of user requirements for a shared virtual meeting space.* Paper presented at the Presence 2000: 3rd International Workshop on Presence conference, Delft, The Netherlands.

Anderson, T., Rourke, L., Garrison, D. R., & Archer, W. (2001). Assessing teaching presence in a computer conferencing context. *Journal of Asynchronous Learning Networks, 5*(2), 1–17.

Aragon, S. R. (2003). Creating social presence in online environments. *New Directions for Adult and Continuing Education, 2003*(100), 57–68.

Aubrey, R. (1991). International students on campus: A challenge for counselors, medical providers, and clinicians. *Smith College Studies in Social Work, 62,* 20–33.

Babbie, E. (2002). *The basics of social research.* New York: Wadsworth.

Biocca, F. (1997). The "cyborg's dilemma" progressive embodiment in virtual environments. *Journal of Computer-Mediated Communication, 3*(2). Retrieved from http://jcmc.indiana.edu/vol3/issue2/biocca2.html

Buxton, W. (1997). Living in augmented reality: Ubiquitous media and reactive environments. In K. Finn, A. Sellen, & S. Wilber (Eds.), *Video mediated communication* (pp. 363–384). Hillsdale, NJ: Lawrence Erlbaum.

Chun, F. Y. G. (2008). *Social presence differences between Chinese and American students in text-base online learning environments.* Unpublished master's thesis, University of Hawaii.

Couch, C. J. (1989). *Social processes and relationships: A formal approach.* New York: General Hall.

Ditton, T. B. (1997). *The unintentional blending of direct experience and mediated experience: The role of enhanced versus limited television presentation.* Unpublished doctoral dissertation, Temple University.

Durlach, N., & Slater, M. (2000). Presence in shared virtual environments and virtual togetherness. *Presence: Teleoperators and Virtual Environments, 9*(2), 214–217.

DuVall, J. B., Powell, E. H., Hodge, E. & Ellis, M. (2007). Text messaging to improve social presence in online learning. *EDUCAUSE Quarterly, 30*(3). Retrieved from http://connect.educause.edu/Library/EDUCAUSE+Quarterly/TextMessaging toImproveSoc/44833

Fencott, P. C. (1999). *Presence and the content of virtual environments.* Extended abstract presented at the 2nd International Workshop of Presence, University of Essex, Colchester, Essex, UK.

Fontaine, G. (1989). *Managing international assignments: The strategy for success.* Englewood Cliffs, NJ: Prentice Hall.

Fontaine, G. (1993). The experience of a sense of presence in intercultural and international encounters. *Presence: Teleoperators and Virtual Environments, 1*(4), 1–9.

Fontaine, G. (2000). Skills for successful international assignments to, from, and within Asia and the Pacific: Implications for preparation, support, and training. In U. C. V. Haley (Ed.), *Strategic management in the Asia Pacific: Harnessing regional and organization change for competitive advantage* (pp. 327–345). Oxford, UK: Butterworth-Heinemann.

Fontaine, G. (2002). Teams in Teleland: Working effectively in geographically dispersed teams "in" the Asia Pacific. *Team Performance Management, 8*(5/6), 122–133.

Fontaine, G. (2006). *Successfully meeting the three challenges of all international assignments.* Retrieved from http://ebooks.ebookmall.com/ebook/225098-ebook.htm

Fontaine, G. (2008). *Presence in strange lands.* Retrieved from http://ebooks.ebookmall.com/ebook/277757-ebook.htm

Frecon, E. (1998). Actively supporting collaborative work. *ACCENTS Common European Newsletter, 3*(2). Retrieved from http://homes.esat.kuleuven.be/~konijn/accents8.htm

Gilkey, R. H., & Weisenberger, J. M. (1995). The sense of presence for the suddenly deafened adult: Implications for virtual environments. *Presence, 4*(4), 364–386

Gristock, J. J. (1998). *Organizational virtuality.* British Telecom Presence Workshop, BT Labs, Ipswich, UK. Retrieved from http://www.cs.ucl.ac.uk/staff/m.slater/BTWorkshop

Gunawardena, C. N., & Zittle, F. J. (1997). Social presence as a predictor of satisfaction within a computer-mediated conferencing environment. *American Journal of Distance Education, 11*(3), 8–26.

Hample, D., & Dallinger, J. M. (1995). A Lewinian perspective on taking conflict personally: Revision, refinement, and validation of the instrument. *Communication Quarterly, 43*, 297–319.

Heeter, C. (1995). Communication research on consumer VR. In F. Biocca & M. R. Levy (Eds.), *Communication in the age of virtual reality* (pp. 191–218). Hillsdale, NJ: Lawrence Erlbaum.

Hendrix, C., & Barfield, W. (1996). Presence within virtual environments as a function of visual display parameters. *Presence, 5*(3), 290–301.

Ho, C., Basdogan, C., Slater, M., Durlach, N., & Srinivasan, M. A. (1998). *An experiment on the influence of haptic communication on the sense of being together.* British Telecom Presence Workshop, BT Labs, Ipswich, UK.

Hofner-Saphiere, D. M. (1996). Productive behaviors of global business teams. *International Journal of Intercultural Relations, 20*(2), 227–259.

Hofstede, G. (1986). Cultural differences in teaching and learning. *International Journal of Intercultural Relations, 10,* 301–320.

Kaltenbrunner, M. F. H., & Huxor, A. (2000). *Multiple presence through auditory bots in virtual environments.* Paper presented at Presence 2000: 3rd International Workshop on Presence Delft, the Netherlands. Retrieved from http://yuri.at/marvin/delft

Kearney, P., Plax, T., & Wendt-Wasco, N. (1985). Teacher immediacy for effective learning in divergent college classes. *Communication Quarterly, 3*(1), 61–74.

Kim, T. (1996). *Effects of presence on memory and persuasion.* Unpublished doctoral dissertation, University of North Carolina, Chapel Hill.

Kimmel, P. R. (1989). *International negotiation an intercultural exploration: Toward cultural understanding.* Washington, DC: U. S. Institute of Peace.

Lipnack, J., & Stamps, J. (2000). *Virtual teams: People working across boundaries with technology.* New York: Wiley.

Lombard, M., & Ditton, T. (1997). At the heart of it all: The concept of telepresence. *Journal of Computer-Mediated Communication, 3*(2), 1–39.

Lombard, M., Grabe, M. E., Reich, R. D., Campanella, C. M., & Ditton, T. B. (1995). *Big TVs, little TVs: The role of screen size in viewer responses to point-of-view movement.* Paper presented to the Mass Communication division at the annual conference of the International Communication Association, Albuquerque, NM.

Mania, K., & Chalmers, A. (2000). *A user-centered methodology for investigating presence and task performance.* Paper presented at the Presence2000: 3rd International Workshop on Presence conference, Delft, The Netherlands.

Mantovani, G., & Riva, G. (1999). Real presence: How different ontologies generate different criteria for presence, telepresence, and virtual presence. *Presence: Teleoperators and Virtual Environments, 8*(5), 538–548.

McGreevy, M. W. (1994, May). *An ethnographic object-oriented analysis of explorer presence in a volcanic terrain environment* (NASA TM-108823). Moffett Field, CA: NASA.

O'Hara-Devereaux, M., & Johansen, R. (1994). *Global work: Bridging distance, culture and time.* San Francisco: Jossey-Bass.

Polhemus, L., Shil, L. F., & Swan, K. (2001, April). *Virtual interactivity: The representation of social presence in an online discussion.* Paper presented at the annual meeting of American Education Research Association, Seattle, WA.

Rauthenberg, S., Kauff, P., & Graffunder, A. (2000). *A realtime implementation of a shared virtual environment system using today's consumer technology in connection with the MPEG-4 standard.* Paper presented at the Presence2000: 3rd International Workshop on Presence conference. Delft, The Netherlands.

Riva, G., Davide, F., & Ijsselsteijn, W. A. (2002). *Being there: Concepts, effects and measurements of user presence in synthetic environments.* Amsterdam: IOS Press.

Rovai, A. P. (2001). Building and sustaining community in asynchronous learning network. *The Internet and Higher Education, 3,* 285–297.

Rovai, A. P. (2003). The relationship of communicator style, personality-based learning style, and classroom community among online graduate students. *The Internet and Higher Education, 6,* 347–363.

Rubin, A. L. (2000). *The power of silence: Using technology to create free structure in organizations.* Unpublished MA thesis, The Fielding Institute, Santa Barbara, CA.

Shea, P., Li, C. S., & Pickett, A. (2006). A study of teaching presence and student sense of learning community in fully online and Web-enhanced college courses. *The Internet and Higher Education, 9*(3), 175–190.

Short, J., Williams, E., & Christie, B. (1976*). The social psychology of telecommunications.* New York: Wiley.

Schubert, T., Friedmann, F., & Regenbrecht, H. (1999). *Decomposing the sense of presence: Factor analytic insights.* Extended abstract presented at the 2nd International Workshop of Presence, University of Essex, Colchester, Essex, UK.

Steed, A., & Slater, M. (1998). Studies of the behaviour of small groups of users in CVEs. *ACCENTS Common European Newsletter, 3*(2). Retrieved from http://homes.esat.kuleuven.be/~konijn/accents8.htm

Tammelin, M. (1998). From telepresence to social presence: The role of presence in a network-based learning environment. In S. Tella (Ed.), *Aspects of media education: Strategic imperatives in the information age* (Media Education Publications No. 8., pp. 219–231). Helsinki, Finland: Media Education Centre, Department of Teacher Education, University of Helsinki. Retrieved from http://www.hkkk.fi/~tammelin/MEP8.tammelin.html

Thie, S., & van Wijk, J. (1998). *A general theory on presence: Experimental evaluation of social virtual presence in a decision making task.* Paper presented at British Telecom Presence Workshop, BT Labs, Ipswich, UK.

Thompson, L., & Heng, Y. K. (2005). Chinese graduate students' experiences and attitudes toward online learning. *Education Media International, 42*(1), 33–37.

Tu, C. H. (2001). How Chinese perceive social presence: An examination of interaction in online learning environment [Electronic version]. *Education Media International, 38*(1), 45–60. Available at http://www.tandf.co.uk/journals

Tu, C. H., & McIsaac, M. (2002). The relationship of social presence and interaction in online classes. *The American Journal of Distance Education, 16*(3), 131–150.

Uttal, W. R. (1989). Teleoperators. *Scientific American, 261*(6), 124–129.

Walther, J. B., & Burgoon, J. K. (1992). Interpersonal effects in computer-mediated interaction: A relational perspective. *Communication Research, 19*(1), 52–90.

Waterworth, E. L., & Waterworth, J. A. (2000). *Using a telescope in the cave: Presence and absence in educational VR.* Paper presented at the Presence 2000: 3rd International Workshop on Presence conference, Delft, The Netherlands.

Welch, R. B., Blackmon, T. T., Liu, A., Mellers, B. A., & Stark, L. W. (1996). The effects of Pictorial Realism, Delay of Visual Feedback, and Observer Interactivity on the Subjective Sense of Presence. *Presence, 5*(3), 274–289.

Whitelock, D., Romano, D., Jelfs, A., & Brna, P. (2000). Perfect presence: What does this mean for the design of virtual learning environments. *Education and Information Technologies, 5*(4), 277–289.

Witmer, B. G., & Singer, M. J. (1998). Measuring presence in virtual environments: A presence questionnaire. *Presence, 7*(3), 225–240.

Zhan, C. Y. (1995). Evaluation of ethic education: The review and breakthrough of concept. *Education and Information Research 2.* Education Information Bureau, Taiwan.

Chapter 3

The Challenges of Culture and Community in Online Academic Environments

Jeremy J. Shapiro

Shelley K. Hughes

In a social world increasingly shaped by algorithms, the mechanical procedures that computers are so good at carrying out, there is no algorithm for building culture and community in online academic and educational environments. For better or worse, it requires the ongoing monitoring and analysis of the fabric of institutional life in which social and technological threads are woven together in complex, concrete, unrepeatable, and sometimes confusing and contradictory ways. The combination of several trends has brought about a situation where, both in the larger society and in academic environments, one can no longer take for granted what it means to have community or a common culture: trends such as rapidly changing technologies; changes in higher education, such as the increasing number of adult and returning students in colleges and universities, the spread of corporate education, and the trend toward the convergence of education, business, and entertainment; and major social and cultural changes, such as the globalization of the economy, the informatization of work, and the increasingly multicultural environment. Students, faculty, and administrators come together with a multiplicity of beliefs and values about what kind of culture, what kind of community, is real, desirable, or possible. Consequently, culture and community cannot simply be presumed; they also cannot be built or developed in one fell swoop, but can only be built as an ongoing process. This process, moreover, will in general be not smooth, but bumpy.

Over the past 20 years, information technologies have continued to be introduced at a dizzying pace into the larger society as well as into educational environments, usually with unpredictable effects and unintended consequences. Even with a single technology, there is a well-known "cultural lag" (Ogburn, 1964) between its introduction and cultural adaptation to it. But over the past decade in particular, before such adaptations have even attained coherence and stability, new technological innovations have intervened, setting off new adaptation processes. The Web site, the cell phone, the iPod, the Webcam, Web 2.0 social networking sites such as Facebook and MySpace, Wikpedia and wikis in general, blogs, YouTube, social tagging sites—each has generated new forms of communication, of social connection, and of information acquisition and sharing, both in society at large and in higher education in particular. By the time courses migrated to Web sites, and course and learning management systems were developed to make possible the location of courses on Web sites, the iPod brought about the use of podcasting, the spread of cell phones made it desirable to deliver information to the cell phone, the wiki introduced widespread collaborative content creation, Webcams and Internet-based videoconferencing enabled new depths of connection across distances, and social networking sites and software such as Facebook strengthened the bonds of social networks that stretch beyond the confines of institutions.

It seems certain that these innovations herald a transformation of education, one that John Seeley Brown and Richard P. Adler have named Learning 2.0. In their words,

> We now need a new approach to learning—one characterized by a *demand-pull* rather than the traditional *supply-push* mode of building up an inventory of knowledge in students' heads. Demand-pull learning shifts the focus to enabling participation in flows of action, where the focus is both on "learning to be" through enculturation into a practice as well as on collateral learning. The demand-pull approach is based on providing students with access to rich (sometimes virtual) learning communities built around a practice. It is passion-based learning, motivated by the student either wanting to become a member of a particular community of practice or just wanting to learn about, make, or perform something. (Brown & Adler, 2008, p. 30)

This corresponds to Henry Jenkins's claim (2006) that user and citizen and audience creation, transformation, and participation in content and information associated with these technologies represent a democratization of culture.

At the same, the educational forms and practices that these developments will both lead to and require are not yet clear. Web 2.0 was only labeled as a distinctive phenomenon and modality in 2004. It is clear that social networks and user involvement in the creation and categorization of information are here to stay. In the meantime, the educational environment is in flux. As an EDUCAUSE publication said in its analysis of the social networking service Ning,

> The flipside of the flexibility of social networks is that the norms and expectations for how such tools should work continue to evolve. Putting almost total control into the hands of users encourages experimentation and innovation, but such a dynamic landscape leaves most social networks in a near-constant state of change, with no clear model of organization and function that will best suit a particular community. Ning touts the ability for users to join many different social networks, which, despite its obvious benefits, also adds to the growing burden of managing involvement in multiple personal networks and keeping track of perhaps dozens or hundreds of "friends" across networks. (EDUCAUSE Learning Initiative, 2008, p. 2)

In this dynamic but volatile environment, it is too soon to be able to lay down general guidelines for building culture and community, especially when it involves, for educational institutions, an overlap between some forms and structures that have been around for a millennium and others that have come into being in the past 5 years and between individuals and groups of widely divergent cultural backgrounds, belief systems, and values. This situation provides a strong rationale for the dynamic, emergent, and participatory neohumanist approach to information systems development that will be discussed below.

This situation of multiple and sometimes radically conflicting values and beliefs implies that the individuals who come together to build culture and community, either online or off-line, will be doing so with rather different conceptions of what culture and community are, what forms of culture and community should exist in an academic or educational environment, what values should underlie them, and what norms should govern them. Furthermore, because divergent paradigms govern the theory and practice of information systems development (see, for example, Hirschheim & Klein, 1989), there is no value-neutral or purely administrative or technical way of building culture and community. This lack is the weakness of the otherwise helpful literature that already exists on this subject (Kim, 2000; Palloff & Pratt, 1999; Rheingold, 2000). Although containing useful technical and practical tips, the literature tends to assume that people already know or that there already is a consensus about what community is and that people just need to be wise or astute in making it happen. It assumes consensus on how one goes about creating and interacting with an information system. But in an academic environment that for 2 decades has been the site of the so-called culture wars, how could it be simple to develop culture? In a society in which there are profound ideological differences about the nature and value of community—and in which these differences mark students and faculty at schools—how could one even know what to aim at in building online community? The technological environment is relatively new, changes constantly, and directly affects how people communicate and interact, often in ways that are not well understood. How can these not fully understood, not fully controllable communication tools be used constructively to help develop culture and community in such a conflicted or at least turbulent context? And when those who work with information systems come from orientations as different as engineering and community organizing, as business and academia, how can one lay down neutral rules for improving the human dimension of an online environment?

Humans Hard-Wired for Face-to-Face?

The authors share in the visible, broad energy, and enthusiasm of many individuals, universities, corporations, government agencies, and cultural commentators for the development of computer-mediated communication (CMC) and its extension into many domains of life—from education through telecommuting and commerce to intimate relationships—and the proliferation and frequent success of such communication in these domains. At the same time, human beings are often impaired with regard to their ability to interact naturally in the text-, image-, and multimedia-based computer-network spaces that are still the predominant form of online environment. There are reasons to think that humans may be neurologically hard-wired for face-to-face interaction in which bodily and emotional communication are the infrastructure, or at least the constant context, of verbal communication. This has been so forcefully, compactly, and eloquently stated by Jonathan Turner (2000) that we quote him in full:

> At the behavioral level, the evidence [for the disposition of our brain toward face-to-face interaction] is clear each and every time humans interact: ritualized openings, repairs, and closings of encounters; extensive use of body positioning and countenance to communicate meanings; and heavy reliance upon facial gestures and voice intonations to communicate emotional states. When any of these signals is missing or is produced in an inappropriate way, interaction becomes strained, even if a constant flow of instrumental verbal chatter continues. For language alone, without an accompanying array of nonverbal, emotional clues first used by our hominid ancestors to strengthen social bonds, cannot sustain the flow of an interaction. Without the more primal, visually based language of emotions, interaction becomes problematic along several fronts: individuals are not

sure how to frame the encounter in terms of what is to be included and excluded; they are not sure of the relevant norms and other cultural systems to be employed; they are not sure of what resources, especially the intrinsic ones so essential to interaction, are to be exchanged; they are not sure if they are really a part of the ongoing flow of interaction; they are not sure if they can trust others to do what they are supposed to do; they are not sure if they can predict the response of others; and they are not sure if they can even presume that they subjectively experience the situation with others in similar ways. (p. 121)

All of the problems identified by Turner are no strangers to online environments and can turn into obstacles to effective communication and to a sense of being part of a community.

Because people depend on emotional, bodily communication, conducting effective, humane, and fulfilling communication in online environments would be challenging even against a stable background of beliefs about and orientations toward culture and community in the larger society. Those involved would need to work in an ongoing way to maintain the flow of interaction so that it was interpersonally inclusive and made people feel visible, recognized, and understood. In face-to-face interaction, much of this work is done intuitively and habitually using methods into which people have been socialized. Consequently, people are often not even aware that it is being done. The need to engage in deliberate and conscious work becomes clear when certain kinds of differences or breaches occur. As Turner (2000) reminded us, "If there is disagreement over relevant cultural symbols, over understandings about the social structural demography, positions, or ties, and over meeting transactional needs, then interaction soon disintegrates, arousing potentially disassociative emotions like anger, fear, and sadness" (p. 152). Even in face-to-face contexts, considerable effort may need to be extended to maintain or restore understanding and community in the face of such disagreement.

When considering that academic environments are likely to contain or generate such disagreements and that online academic environments are marked by the absence of some of the social and emotional resources upon which people have come to rely face-to-face, then building culture and community online can be demanding. If there is any level of interpersonal or cultural diversity, difference, or conflict, which can lead to gaps in understanding, then our work, as people familiarly say, is cut out for us. It is true that the incorporation of multimedia tools, such as video-conferencing and Webcams, provide more presence and sense of face-to-face contact, more interpersonal information and cues, than purely text-based environments, and it is conceivable that in the long run they may make possible the incorporation of "the more primal, visually based language of emotions" of which Turner spoke (2000, p. 121). There is also some reason to think that generations that have grown up with the newer technologies as a constant, taken-for-granted background may not be hard-wired for face-to-face communication and may not have the impediments to mutual understanding that are familiar to the first-generation inhabitants of the online environment. Nevertheless, there is currently still a big gap between the richness of face-to-face communication and that mediated by computers and networks, especially for those accessing a network with a low-bandwidth connection.

Of course, not every online setting is fraught with disintegrative tendencies or is a communicational headache. Computer-mediated courses, discussions, and public spaces are thriving everywhere. But in the words of the Internet guru of online or virtual community, Rheingold (n.d.), "All online social systems are challenged by human social foibles and technological bugs that tend to split groups apart" (sect. 23). That is why those responsible for online educational settings and those who participate in them need to be aware of the issues mentioned, take them into consideration in the design and structuring of these settings, and have some experience or orientation to dealing with typical communication and technical problems and some methods for responding to them. They also need to pay attention to these issues in an ongoing way, both to maintain constructive interaction and to be able to engage in activities of reflection and problem solving when misunderstandings or difficulties arise. This is especially true because, as has long been noted by participants and observers, communicational or cultural misunderstandings in online interaction sometimes develop in a significantly nonlinear fashion. From what seems like one moment to the next, a slight misunderstanding can turn into a flare-up of anger. The posting of one message that is not responded to can lead to the individual posting it feeling totally unrecognized or ostracized. If this chapter focuses especially on understanding communicational problems and gaps or breaches in community, it is because it is there that reflection, action, and intervention can make the most difference in building culture and community online.

There are two principal levels at which it is possible to focus on cultural and community issues: that of the individual class, course, or seminar and that of the larger institutional environment within which it (usually) resides. A course is a little microcommunity of its own, with its own distinctive culture, and educators are beginning to realize that online education is not primarily about course delivery or content delivery, but about creating learning environments or learning communities in which content delivery is just one component. This means attending to the course as a learning community. Usually a course is embedded in an academic institution or a corporation with its own culture, and aspects of the institutional culture that have nothing to do with course content, such as drinking on campus at a college or employee motivation in a corporation, have a major effect on the individual learner and the immediate learning environment. The university or corporation is, in turn, part of the larger social environment, with its distinctive culture, or usually cultures, which affects the institution and the individual course in many ways. This means attending to trends and tensions in both the institutional culture and its social context as part of shaping benign learning environments. In the perspective from which the present authors view information systems and educational environments, which are laid out briefly below, the microcontext (in this case, the course, class, or seminar) and the macrocontext (the institution as well as the larger social environment) are seen as intertwined and interdependent. Hence, the focus here is not on courses per se, but rather on learning environments.

A Paradigm for Information Systems Development

The present authors intentionally adopt what Hirschheim and Klein (1989), in their categorization of paradigms used in the development of information systems, called the neohumanist paradigm, according to which the systems developer proceeds "from within, by improving human understanding and the rationality of human action through emancipation of suppressed interests and liberation from unwarranted natural and social [and we would add technical] constraints" (p. 1210). The present approach emphasizes

- the perspective of a person who is part of and engaged with the situation, mindful of her or his own experience and role, and aiming at human betterment;
- the nature, importance, and logic of procedures for arriving at genuine, unforced mutual understanding, at rational, unforced consensus, and at norms that derive from that understanding and consensus—what this approach refers to as *communicative rationality* (Habermas, 1984);
- the recognition that this logic of mutual understanding and rational consensus differs from the logic of control, efficiency, and predictability (technical-strategic rationality): each is legitimate in its own domain, but problems arise when one is applied to the other, especially when the world of mutual understanding and shared experience is colonized by the principles of control, efficiency, and predictability;
- the interlocking of communication structures with visible and invisible power structures as well as with the structure of work and technology so that improving communication has technical and political implications, and changes in technology and power have communicative implications;
- affirming egalitarian and democratic values, looking at the potential in a situation for increased freedom, happiness, and justice, and sustaining utopian ideals;

- paying attention to what is historically and culturally unique about the situation being analyzed and recognizing that the broadest social and historical trends and tensions, such as the globalization of the economy, are present in even the smallest of human interactions;

- using a systemic approach, with special attention to a system's internal contradictions, especially those between what is espoused and what is practiced and between visible and invisible power structures;

- exposing unequal power relations and revealing that what is put forward as the common good may really serve special interests; and

- finding ways to undo or weaken distorted communication, illegitimate power, and repression and to counteract the closing off of possibilities for communication (i.e., encouraging noise to break socially structured silences).

This paradigm seems particularly suited to the shift occurring at many institutions toward learner-centered education. Whether driven by a philosophical commitment to the autonomy of the individual or the market-driven orientation toward the customer, the learner- or student-centered approach implies taking seriously students' perspective on their own learning and its environment and, to whatever extent possible, fitting the environment to their needs rather than fitting them to the environment. Because the neohumanist paradigm takes seriously all points of view within the system, including learners', rather than regarding it just as input to be managed, it fits with this educational approach. Ironically, though, because graduate education is increasingly driven by the demands of workplace relevance—more than 50% of all graduate students in the United States are now in the workforce—it is sometimes the students themselves who bring the criteria of productivity, efficiency, and output into education and who experience themselves as having not enough time for humanistically oriented exploration.

The neohumanist paradigm advocates and encourages a particular mode of critical, creative, and reflective engagement with one's own institutional and informational environment. It asserts that educators, administrators, and systems developers do not build or create community and culture. Rather, they work with the community and culture that is there to make it more rational, meaningful, productive, satisfying, humane, democratic, and, in education, enhancing of learning. At certain points and in certain situations, they may need to take leadership and initiative, but in general, they need to act as particularly responsible and effective members of the environments that they inhabit. This sometimes means articulating needs and interests that are located in them, but are not expressed, and this sometimes involves making proposals or taking actions. In the neohumanist paradigm, however, one is always working within a human-technical environment rather than doing something to it.

Its principles are not a set of mechanical procedures to be applied to an online educational setting, but rather guidelines to be interpreted creatively by actors or members who inhabit it. As Rheingold (n.d.) wrote, "Communities can't be manufactured, but you can design the conditions under which they are most likely to emerge, and encourage their growth when they do" (sect. 20).

In applying the neohumanist paradigm to building culture and community, it is useful to be aware of some of the concepts and tools that have been developed to capture cultural preferences and differences about fundamental cultural and social issues (e.g., Hofstede, 1997; Parsons, 1977; Slater, 1976). These define dimensions or axes along which cultures vary. Each culture embodies a preference for a specific point along these axes, although not every individual within a culture prefers the same point as the general or average norm or preference of his or her culture. This approach helps people see, articulate, and work with cultural differences within or among groups. It also means recognizing that some of these differences are genuinely antagonistic or mutually exclusive. This does not mean, however, that a group cannot work out a method or perspective that enables individuals with different values to coexist or cooperate.

The educator or administrator working with an online culture may want to ask about herself or himself, about a specific group (class, seminar), about the online community as a whole, and about different individuals or interest groups within it, "Where am I (is it, is he or she, is his or her cultural background) located along the following dimensions or axes?"

hierarchy ⟷	equality
community ⟷	competition
engagement ⟷	detachment
dependence ⟷	independence
risk taking ⟷	risk avoidance
masculinity ⟷	femininity
emotionality ⟷	emotional neutrality
short-term orientation ⟷	long-term orientation
universalism ⟷	particularism
majority ⟷	minority
task orientation ⟷	process orientation
self-disclosure ⟷	self-concealment
structure ⟷	structurelessness

Although these do not exhaust the dimensions of difference students identified as affecting groups and organizations, they are particularly useful for working with online communities. Simply by formulating the differences and preferences that exist within a community, the educator or facilitator can enhance mutual understanding by making comprehensible and discussable differences that were neither. Negotiating the tensions between the ends of these axes can be challenging for administrators with responsibility for the organization of an online environment. For example, Shirky (2003), in his "A Group Is Its Own Worst Enemy," pointed out that online groups tend to sabotage themselves, driven by a set of processes first identified by the psychoanalyst Wilfred Bion in his pioneering work with and on groups. Online groups move in the direction of structurelessness and of people running amok in a way that can defeat the purposes for which the group was formed, and unless administrators provide structure and limits, a group can self-destruct. How to defend the group from its members while maintaining the value of openness and academic freedom is an ongoing task, and a challenging one.

It is also useful to draw from the approach to design and habitat represented by the work of Alexander et al. (1977). Being sensitized to the ways in which the built environment shapes experience and life is particularly valuable for work in online environments for two reasons. First, many of the familiar guideposts of the physical world are missing. In this cyberspace, moreover, computer and network tools play the role of physical objects in physical space: as markers of boundaries, as resources, as shapers of attention, as stimuli, as obstacles, and as creators of closeness or distance.

Pervasive Social Trends

Central to the neohumanist paradigm is the notion that even the smallest social unit is also a microcosm of the larger society. There is a tendency among technophiles and naive commentators to consider online environments as though they were self-contained. In this view, they can also serve as oases or refuges, somehow immunized against the rest of the world, an attitude symbolized in the famous *New Yorker* cartoon (Mankoff, 2000, p. 68) of the dog sitting in front of a computer and saying to another dog, "On the Internet, nobody knows you're a dog." As Wellman and Gulia (1999) pointed out about this approach,

> Much of the analysis that does exist is parochial. It almost always treats the Internet as an isolated social phenomenon without taking into account how interactions on the Net fit with other aspects of people's lives. The Net is only one of many ways in which the same people may interact. It is not a separate reality. People bring to their on-line interactions such baggage as

their gender, stage in the life-cycle, cultural milieu, socioeconomic status, and off-line connections with others. (p. 170)

Through this baggage—through people's involvement in multiple social worlds and networks—it is only natural that important social and cultural issues and tensions migrate from the larger society into online environments. Of course, there are places in cyberspace where some individuals go to escape from some of the limitations of their everyday social identities, where they can assume alternate identities, act out different gender roles, and so on (Dery, 1996; Turkle, 1995). And many individuals in text-based online environments, where they are not seen physically and communicate only via text, have had experiences of being temporarily liberated from social constraints in the sorts of communication or interaction in which they have engaged (an experience that may vanish when videoconferencing over the Internet becomes more widespread). Nevertheless, most available research (see, for example, Smith & Kollock, 1999) shows that existing social differentiations, such as those of race and power, persist in online communities. And it makes sense that in the online educational environments in which students and faculty participate in a substantial way, they would be there with major aspects of their preexisting selves, including identities, social-group memberships, backgrounds, biases, and so on.

As Polanyi (1966) has pointed out with regard to tools in general, it is natural that, in the early stages of their utilization, the physical and technical features with which people interact are in the foreground of awareness. As tool use becomes habitual, these features fade into unawareness, and instead, their intended uses and objective purposes become more prominent. In the early phases of computer and network use, their technical surfaces may obscure the human relationships that they mediate, and they are perceived as technology. As they become increasingly transparent to the user, their human and social context and impact become more prominent and visible. This is well symbolized by another *New Yorker* cartoon (Mankoff, 2000, p. 58), which depicts a man and woman saying firmly to a bespectacled boy in their living room, "We're neither software nor hardware. We're your parents."

There are a few core, complex social and cultural issues of the present that inevitably shape the nature of culture and community in any particular online academic or educational environment and make them into contested fields and concepts. Tensions, divergences, confusions, and conflicts in online communities often arise around these core issues from the larger society. Because they are pervasive in the larger society, and globally, not merely in a particular nation, they can be expected to surface in any academic community, virtual or physical. They will be familiar to most readers, both personally and intellectually. Some of them overlap and intertwine. And because they are fundamental contradictions, or sources of conflict and tension in society, they come with no easy resolution: They may be dilemmas to be lived rather than problems to be solved, at least in the short run (Farson, 1996). The core issues are as follows:

Multiculturalism—Meaning here not only the awareness and validation of individuals with different racial, ethnic, cultural, and gender backgrounds, but also the question whether and to what extent any particular cultural or group background should be privileged or taken for granted as normative either epistemologically (e.g., in the role given to the culture of dead White European males) or as the basis for the communicative and cultural norms of the educational environment

The extension of the principles of instrumental, strategic, and technical rationality—Of means-ends thinking, control, productivity, efficiency, predictability, quantifiability, and profit—that govern business, bureaucracy, and technology to areas of life that have been organized around principles of communicative rationality, that is, of mutual understanding, shared culture and experience, and personal expression and, in higher education, of the pursuit of knowledge and cultural creation. This is what Habermas (1988) referred to as the issue of the system versus the lifeworld or the colonization of the lifeworld. This tension affects both the nature and quality of academic community as well as the value and goals ascribed to learning. It governs the extent to which education and learning should be subordinated to instrumental, business, technical, and credentialist considerations or should be open ended, exploratory, and humanistic—whether they should be fundamentally oriented toward skill enhancement and problem solving for the workplace or should encourage goals and aspirations that transcend it. As has been already pointed out, the large number of graduate students who are in the workforce often come to their university programs with a set of business- or work-related goals that moves the issue of system versus lifeworld squarely into the everyday reality of higher education.

The relative weight assigned to individualism on the one hand and collectivism or community on the other—Slater (1976) pointed out that individuals and cultures need both autonomy and dependence, individuality and community, and that particular cultures may be weighted more toward one or the other pole. American culture, for example, is so focused on individualism and autonomy to the exclusion of interdependence and embeddedness that it can become a pursuit of loneliness. Furthermore, as Bourdieu (1998) argued, currently, the world as a whole, through the global extension of the logic of the market to all provinces of social life, is being subjected to "a program of the methodical destruction of collectives," in which the individual as economic actor is given pride of place over collectives, communities, associations, and groups. This has implications for individualistic versus collaborative models of learning and for the norms that govern action and discourse in the educational environment.

Locating, maintaining, and overstepping boundaries—The major net effect of computer and network technology on all aspects of human life—personal, interpersonal, organizational, community, political, social—is the elimination and redrawing of boundaries: between private and public; work, family, and personal; intra- and interorganizational and national. The relevant phenomena are too well known, widespread, manifold, and multiform to be reviewed here. A common thread that runs through all of them is the dissolution of what used to be considered natural boundaries, whether of an individual's private life, a class or course, or an institution. Increasingly, as already mentioned, individuals are members of multiple, disparate, but overlapping social networks. This has a number of implications and raises questions without easy answers: Who are the actual members of a group? Where is an individual located? To whom should norms or rules apply, and how can they be enforced? Where should the informational or attentional boundaries of an activity be drawn? For example, currently on college campuses, there is controversy about the use of laptops and mobile phones in classrooms because students, while attending a class, are also surfing the Web and sending and receiving text and instant messages—that is, they are not only in the classroom, but they are also at the same time in their personal networks of friends or family and in their Facebook or MySpace or other networks and in various intellectual or information domains accessible on the Web. The technology has eliminated the boundary previously constituted by the classroom. Should they limit their attention to what goes on in the classroom? Should the activities planned for a class or course exclude those other domains and networks or recognize and include their reality? Does a university consist of its enrolled students and employed faculty and staff or also all of the people who access its resources via the Web? What sorts of community are possible and desirable in a world of multiple, simultaneously present group membership? These questions are thrown up by technology and are bound to become more insistent. But the technology provides no answers.

Technogenerations and their cultural differences—For present purposes, a technogeneration can be thought of as an age group whose modus vivendi is so shaped by particular technological tools that its members develop distinctive ways of learning, thinking, communicating, expressing, and defining themselves that do not easily interoperate, to use a technical computer term, with those of prior and successive technogenerations. The age range of a technogeneration is shaped by the lifespan of the technology or technologies that condition its modus vivendi. So a technogeneration may last for 500 years or for only 5. Since educational environments consist almost entirely of the creation, transmission, and acquisition of information, the cohabitation and interaction in one single educational setting of different technogenerations with different practices, habits, and assumptions about the production, transmission, and acquisition of information can create its own kind of cultural tensions and misunderstandings. And designing or supporting an environment that will accommodate multiple technogenerations is not only a technical challenge—"How can we support multimedia streaming and file exchange on the bandwidth of our network?"—but also an educational one—"How can we design a course that will satisfy readers of books, readers of Web pages, and listeners to podcasts?"—and a social one—"How can we facilitate a discussion that includes both those who take e-mail as the fundamental vehicle of communication and those for whom instant messaging plays that role?"

How the educator or administrator relates to these issues—or to a context in which these issues are active—will have a major impact on the culture of the online educational environment.

The Case of the Inflammatory E-Mail

As pointed out at the beginning, building culture and community online involves analyzing and monitoring in detail the fabric of institutional life. It is in this spirit, and with the larger context in mind, that we take up an e-mail brouhaha in an online academic environment in which an e-mail message was experienced by some members as inflammatory and set off a variety of interactions that were conflictual, confusing, and emotional for a number of those involved. Although e-mail is by now one of the older computer-network tools used in higher education, it is still widely used, even though there is reason to think that for some younger users, text messaging via mobile phones is replacing e-mail as the default method of communicating. And while the incident discussed does not by any means raise all of the larger issues about culture and community in online environments that have been mentioned, it is instructive nevertheless regarding some of them, regardless of the particular technology or communication medium being used. For example, some of the same issues and conflicts, such as about the existence and common understanding of social norms, manifest themselves in such environments as Wikipedia and LiveJournal (Fono & Raynes-Goldie, 2006). It should be mentioned that the incident discussed here occurred in our own environment, and we were involved both as participants and as observers.

About 10 days before the November 2000 U.S. presidential election, a faculty member sent an e-mail message to the faculty and student e-mail lists of the graduate program in which he teaches stating his reasons for believing that people who were political Greens should vote for

Democratic candidate Al Gore rather than for Green candidate Ralph Nader. All told, the initial message went to about 400 students and faculty. This message led to a flurry of e-mail messages, several dozen over the next several days, many of them angry or excited, several of which accused him of violating an implicit ethical code regarding faculty behavior toward students. Some of these messages, in turn, were also sent to the faculty and students of another, equally large graduate program, which increased the number of people who entered the melee. The faculty member who initiated the exchange felt so offended by the angry responses to his message, which he experienced as "hate mail," that he announced that he would resign from the institution (this decision was later rescinded after a cooling-off period). Some students were so distressed about some of the messages that they received in the course of the fracas that they requested to be removed from mailing lists that are part of the administrative infrastructure of the institution. The spreading of distress eventually led to the temporary suspension of the mailing lists entirely.

With a few exceptions, the messages were not about political issues of the Presidential campaign. They were primarily about issues central to culture and community in an online environment, such as the cultural norms that are to govern it, its definition of the boundaries between private and public, and its information structure.

Of course, every example has its own specific qualities that make it what it is and resist generalization. As local background of the case at hand, it is useful to know that all of the several hundred students in each of several graduate programs were automatically added to program wide e-mail lists that are used only occasionally and in a limited way. These lists differ from many Internet e-mail lists in that their members do not join it voluntarily but were added by the institution's administrative staff and removed when they either graduate or drop out. Thus, they were a captive audience, even though that is not part of the local definition of the situation and is usually not relevant since the list is used infrequently. At the time when the incident occurred, there were between half a dozen and a dozen messages per list per month. Communication designed for a list of 400 students clearly differs from that in an online seminar of eight.

Typical messages to the list included administrative announcements, requests for bibliographical information, faculty or administrative requests for student input or interest regarding intellectual or administrative projects, a faculty member notifying the program of a change in e-mail address, or an administrative assistant informing students that a faculty member's computer is down and therefore would not be able to communicate for several days. On entering the program, students were encouraged not to use these mailing lists for personal discussions or for communications that would be of interest or relevance to only a small subset of the student body and instead to use online bulletin boards (forums) or more narrow group mailing lists for this purpose. Some typical messages from one of the lists should give a sense of what list members regarded as normal or acceptable communication:

> Please pardon the intrusion. I am looking for realistic novels about men at midlife, either making the passage or later reflecting on it. An example of the genre might be Wallace Stegner's last two—*Crossing to Safety* and *The Spectator Bird*. Your suggestions would be appreciated.

> Faculty member Harrison Smerdyakov is alive and well after knee surgery and receiving messages at 702/555–0226. He will not be up on e-mail until August 21st. Thanks.

> I highly recommend *Butterfly*, an independent film that was recently released (Spanish with American subtitles). It is about freeing the human spirit from oppression and reminded me in many ways of our school.

> Enjoy,
> Rosa Vorian, student
> P.S. I also posted this message on the program forum in case anyone would like to discuss further.

A typical e-mail sequence on one of these lists was a query sent out by a faculty member to students soliciting input about the program's research training, several subsequent messages from faculty and students containing ideas and suggestions in response, and finally a message from the initial faculty member saying that she had initiated an online forum (bulletin board) conversation about this so that those interested could continue the discussion while keeping those not interested from receiving unwanted e-mail.

As background, one also ought to know that the student body consisted of adult professionals who have decided to pursue the doctoral degree, in programs with a very substantial online component as well as occasional face-to-face contact, while continuing to live and work in their usual environments and social contexts. Importantly, as is increasingly characteristic of members of online communities and social networks, many of them were also members of other online environments, groups, or social networks, which means that neither their personal identity nor social behavior nor CMC was defined principally by either this particular e-mail list or this particular social group, the graduate program in which they are students. Thus, they are what people all are becoming, according to Wellman, a preeminent scholar of technologically mediated social networks: "limited liability members of several partial communities rather than fully committed members of one all-embracing community" (Wellman & Hampton, 1999, p. 650).

GMOTL: Get Me Off This List!

The first issue was visible in the well-known hysterical Internet positive-feedback-loop "get me off this list" phenomenon (for which the present authors coined the acronym GMOTL). In this phenomenon, inexperienced individuals do not know how to unsubscribe from a list. They then send urgent or impassioned messages to other list members rather than to the list manager software asking to be removed from the list, which leads other inexperienced members to "reply all" to these messages, which result in list members receiving more unwanted messages, which in turn sets off even more desperate and often angry requests to be removed from the list and other angry responses, sometimes reducing communication to a rather primitive level. For those who may have never experienced GMOTL, here is an example from the situation under discussion:

> Please take me off the list!!!!
> Please take me off the list!!!
> PLEASE take me off the list!!!
> Thank you and have a nice day.
> Zorena Livingston

A sample response in this case (capitals in the original):

> DEAR ALL, MUCH WORSE THAN POLITICAL E-MAILS ON THE LIST ARE THE COUNTLESS RESPONSES TO THAT INCIDENT. ALL YOU COMMENTERS PLEASE MAKE SURE THAT YOU DON'T SEND YOUR COMMENTS TO ME. I AM NOT INTERESTED TO HEAR ANYTHING OF ANY SORT ABOUT ANYTHING. CLEAR? THANKS.

This example points both to the way in which participants in CMC can exhibit greater emotional volatility than they do in face-to-face communication (Wellman & Hampton, 1999) and to the impact of individuals' computer literacy on the tone and substance of their communication: People's unfamiliarity with a medium or difficulty in navigating in it can affect their experience of the medium and the nature of their social interaction. In the event, the positive feedback loop, which produced an amplification both in the number of GMOTL messages and the intensity of their emotions, led to something unheard of at this institution: the temporary suspension of the e-mail lists in order to prevent further escalation and distress. It should be noted that, given the way the lists were set up, the procedure for unsubscribing from them was not generally known or easily visible and was almost never used. This apparent "no exit" situation surely added to or caused the intensity of members' receiving unwanted messages. Since this situation had occurred infrequently in the past—and because the institution wanted all students to be available via an e-mail list for essential administrative communication—administrators did not immediately come forth with the standard response in Internet environments, which is to point people to the procedure for leaving the list. In the Internet as a whole, GMOTL and users' frustration about it have become so widespread that the headers of many e-mail lists include a link that one can click on to unsubscribe.

GMOTL is an excellent starting point for consideration of problems in online community and culture: first, because of the way in which human communication and technology, in their intertwinement, can be at cross-purposes with one another and, second, because this clash can have wide-ranging emotional and interpersonal consequences. It is probable that most of those wanting to unsubscribe from the mailing list were trying to do the responsible thing in asking to be removed from it. However, because they did not do so in the technically appropriate way, they provoked a widening pool of emotional distress. Correspondingly, the recipients of the messages, instead of responding to them as technical problems, mistook them as personal offenses or inappropriate behavior deserving of blame or outrage. That these interchanges could generate such intense reactions points to some of the unusual qualities of online environments.

Cultural Norms and Technocultural Paradigms

The second issue was discussion of the appropriateness of sending political messages on or to this e-mail list—in other words, of the cultural norms of the list. Furthermore, since a significant portion of the institutional life of this graduate program occurs through CMC, discussion of the norms of the mailing list was immediately also a discussion of the norms of the academic community. So one student wrote,

> I would like to go on record as being vehemently opposed to any students using this school for their own political agenda. I find it offensive, inappropriate, and downright tacky! I am here to further my education, and I resent receiving e-mails from anyone that have absolutely nothing to do with the school per se. I also feel that the faculty should have some kind of policy against any person attempting to capitalize on students with his or her politicking!

While another replied,

> I think that a university e-mail account is the most appropriate place to get political information—especially a university that deals with psychology and human organizations. What could be more "political"? What a terrific way to make the connections between individual effort and social policy and change; in a practical way so that we can all contribute to improving our lives through political action.

At this university, as in many online environments, participants may not have explicitly negotiated or contracted about either the communicational norms and ground rules or more importantly, about the root values and beliefs that are to govern it. In this particular academic environment, as in many others, there are fundamental disagreements about the nature of the academic community itself and of the boundaries between private and public and between educational and social or political matters.

Of course, differences about social norms, values, and boundaries exist in many human groups. But current information technologies raise special issues because implicit norms are built into them, at least as users experience them and conceive of them. When one participant wrote, "Perhaps there are those that feel that their e-mail boxes are akin to private property, to which they are only willing to permit entry to those they approve of," he was surfacing the important fact that technical tools are not merely neutral conveniences but rather are embedded in cultural and social meanings that shape how they appear to the users. People may all have e-mail boxes or accounts, but if one thinks of his or hers as private property and another thinks of his or hers as a public communication vehicle, they are not using the same tools. Rather, the same tools appear within different technocultural paradigms. A technocultural paradigm "is not discernible in the intrinsic features of technology and transcends particular actors . . . [Technocultural paradigms] provide model uses, designs, and implementations to a community of decision-makers" (Mowshowitz, 1985, p. 105).

Everyday language misleads people. In the everyday language of both contemporary culture in general and of information technology professionals in particular, people are surrounded or confronted by a multiplicity of neutral technical tools and objects—computers, modems, network cables, software applications, cellular phones, and so on—which they use and of which they are mere users. As Mowshowitz (1985) shows, however, what exists is almost always a tool plus a technocultural paradigm, taken together. Moreover, there can be divergent paradigms for the same tools. Thus, discourse about the technology and its uses needs to be deconstructed to reveal the paradigm, the taken-for-granted cultural and social meanings, that are attached to the tools and objects, that always shape their meaning for actual human beings, and that can easily lead to conflict and misunderstanding because of the differences between them.

Meta-Issues

The third issue—really a set of issues—was visible in an ongoing metadiscussion of where and how to conduct such a political discussion about the election in the online environment. As in most institutions, here the online environment is actually an assemblage of a variety of technological resources, which in current practice range from e-mail lists and newsgroups through bulletin boards and Web-based groupware and course management systems to synchronous media such as chat, whiteboard, and videoconferencing and integration with Web 2.0 technologies and social networking sites. An online environment is not a simple unity, but a complex one. Sometimes, a single online course will use a combination of media and communication tools, and a member of an institution with a significant online component is likely to be part of several online subenvironments within the same institution, not to mention other online environments and online social networks that are not housed within the institution. Just as a face-to-face community consists of multiple institutions with their own norms—the norms of communication at work are different from those at home, which in turn are different from those in bars, restaurants, and places of entertainment—so online communities operate according to different norms in their different computer-mediated spaces. Different media or computer tools, partly by convention or tradition and partly because of their intrinsic features, seem to favor or disfavor particular kinds of communication and interpersonal ties. What is appropriate in an e-mail sent to a few individuals may be inappropriate in a message sent via e-mail to a group or mailing list, and what is appropriate to any e-mail context may seem inappropriate in a public, Web-based forum or bulletin board or on a Facebook page, and vice versa.

When one combines this consideration with the fact that participants in CMC sometimes also interact with their CMC partners face-to-face in other contexts, creating or even identifying the relevant cultural and social norms can be a complex matter. It has often been observed that participating in multiple online environments contributes to the formation—or at least the manifestation—of multiple identities or personalities corresponding to these different environments (Turkle, 1995). This is clearly correlated with the way in which different computer- and network-mediated environments are also different cultures, with their own norms, symbols, values, rituals, and practices. Accordingly, resolving issues about culture and community requires metacommunication about both cultural differences and about the appropriate uses of the technologies, which themselves affect these differences. It may also involve dealing with the special character of collisions among the multiple personalities generated by these complex, multidimensional environments and among the diverse norms of different parts of the same institution. For example, sometimes, individuals who have had frequent or intense exchanges in a Web-based discussion group or via e-mail—who might even consider themselves friends or intimates in those contexts—will find themselves in the same face-to-face environment and not even acknowledge each other's existence, as though their intimacy online had no bearing on their face-to-face relationship. This can be distressing when one person expects such acknowledgment and the other does not provide it. The first person can feel rejected or that something is wrong because of expecting that the relationship in one domain will extend to another, while the second is oblivious of any problem, simply because of not sharing that expectation. People can be confused about the appropriate sort of language (e.g., polite or familiar) to use in an interaction because of having used language in one domain that does not seem to transfer naturally to another. Hence, in online environments, it is important to surface, articulate, and discuss these expectations and any conflicts that exist with regard to norms and the definition of roles.

In the context that has been discussed, the metacommunicative discussion had three foci: the ability to delete messages, the use of e-mail lists versus Web-based discussion forums, and, perhaps most peculiar but also most important, whether such metacommunication should take place at all.

To Delete or Not to Delete: Who's in Control?

As an instance of how fine grained technological issues become, and how they impact upon human interaction, the issue of the deleteability of messages is illuminating. A principal source of contention—and of emotional outbursts—in the controversy about the use of a general e-mail list for political messages was that, to some members of the community, the fact that they received unwanted messages at all made them feel persecuted, while to others the fact that anyone can easily delete any message that he or she receives means that by definition there can be no problem of unwanted messages. In the words of one participant,

> For those that don't like the topic or tone, I suggest the delete button. Having an e-mail address will always open you up to some level of communication you don't like/approve/want. However, e-mail, unlike the phone, is a window on the world, and the world is not always neat and orderly.

This message points to the subtle ways in which cultural and community issues are subtly interwoven with matters of computer literacy in particular and information literacy generally (Shapiro & Hughes, 1996). It is probable that some students receiving messages from the e-mail list felt either that they did not know how to easily or automatically delete them or that they were obligated to read them so that for them the receipt of messages constituted a burden in a way that did not hold for the more experienced (or more cynical). In computer-mediated environments, the same environment, the same phenomena, and the same issues appear quite differently to people with different levels of technical skill and familiarity. A person who is learning to drive an automobile may experience a street as a chaotic and dangerous environment with automobiles and pedestrians flying toward her or him in unpredictable, uncontrollable, and frightening ways, whereas an experienced driver may perceive the same street as a calm and ordered environment. Just so, a new user of particular software or a new member of a particular computer-mediated environment may perceive herself or himself as beset by a large number of chaotic and disturbing stimuli requiring attention and response, whereas an experienced user or member may have a greater subjective sense of control induced by the skills to bring about such control. That is why, in the present case, a technically astute faculty member even sent out instructions as to how students could create an e-mail filter that would delete all unwanted messages automatically with the hope that this would bring about the sense of control that some experienced as missing.

It is likely that greater familiarity with e-mail software, and a greater sense of autonomy with it or control over it, would have solved the problem of unwanted e-mail messages for some people. It would not, however, resolve the tension between opposing values about whether the world is, or should be, neat and orderly. One person's neat and orderly is another person's messy and chaotic, and when one considers the interplay of personal and cultural values—for there are cultural as well as personal differences in conceptions of order and chaos, public and private, open and closed, and so on—one can begin to grasp one of the challenges of building culture and community in an online educational environment.

There are also multiple layers of cultural lag with regard to the methods people adopt to handle different communication vehicles. For example, an individual who has habituated herself or himself to receiving and throwing out physical, paper junk mail delivered by the postal service without emotion may not have developed the same emotional neutrality about getting junk e-mail. In addition, of course, the subjective meaning of different media may differ for different people. E-mail, because it arrives on one's computer, may be experienced as more inside of one's private space than postal mail. To someone else, postal mail may seem more private because the address is handwritten and stamp has been physically canceled.

In a culture that is in the course of technological change, which reaches different individuals at different moments in time, there is also a sort of life-historical cultural lag with regard to different individuals who are at different points in the process of adapting to a new technology and assimilating it into their lives. Partly in accordance with the phases identified by Rogers's (1995) theory of the diffusion of innovation and partly because of life-historical and social accidents, one individual may be just learning a new technology while another is already abandoning it for a subsequent one or just worn out from its use. In the world today, there are people who are just beginning to use e-mail in their leisure time and experiencing the excitement of connecting with long-lost and distant friends and relatives while others have been using it for decades for work and spend each day trying desperately to cope with literally hundreds of messages upon which their professional future or financial security depends. People who were part of the early, noncommercial phase of the

Internet may be despondent about its commercialization, while others have no conception of that phase. With this diversity of background, experience, and orientation, the members of an online community may be separated by vast differences that are not easily visible in public communication but are also forcefully shape individuals' experience of what is going on in that environment and what it means to them. As mentioned above, this sort of difference exists not only among individuals but also among techno-generations. Entire groups take for granted particular technologies and the practices, assumptions, and norms that cluster around them.

The issue of the deleteability of messages also points to a deep and important consequence of the extension of information and communication technologies into daily life, one that has scarcely received adequate treatment in either popular or scholarly literature: the breakdown of communication barriers and the elimination of silence. In an article in the *New York Times,* Thomas Friedman (1999) predicted that the major social problem for developed nations in the 21st century would be "overconnectedness," an anxiety that will result when "everyone will be able to be connected all the time, everywhere" (p. 17). Friedman pointed out that "time and distance provide buffers and breathing space in our lives, and when you eliminate both you eliminate some very important cushions" (p. 17). He went on to point out that "the boundary between work and play disappears." Perhaps the major difficulty in analyzing developments and prescribing methods and solutions in online education is precisely one of cultural lag: Many enthusiastic educators, software developers, and other leaders in the field had their initial experiences of online learning and developed their enthusiasm for it at a time of minimal connectedness. Thus, they are often thinking about it within the attitude of bringing connection to the unconnected, when, by the time that their programs and software are set up and their advertising copy written, they may be confronting a population of the overconnected who already have mental calluses from the barrage of digitized information they receive from multiple sources on a daily, hourly, or even minute-by-minute basis and no longer have the enthusiasm and pioneering orientation of the innovators and leaders in the field.

Finding the Right Place

Another focus of the metadiscussion was moving the discussion to a Web-based online forum. To some people, there is a significant difference between two sorts of messages: those that one receives automatically and as it were involuntarily via e-mail and are stored in one's own e-mail box on one's own computer and those that are posted and stored in a public place on a Web site, which one must travel to in order to read them. As

Messerschmitt (1999) pointed out, one task of configuring CMC for a group is finding the right balance between push and pull information because push information, which arrives relatively uncontrolled, is invasive, while pull information, such as notices on a Web page that one has to go to, can be overlooked and requires more attention and conscious activity on the individual's part. There are differences both in how they are experienced and in how the norms governing them are perceived. To some, an unwanted e-mail message is an invasion of privacy and would be more appropriate in a public place where privacy is not expected. To others, the very fact of having to go to a Web site makes such supposedly public messages de facto nonpublic by virtue of the arbitrariness of whether people actually see them or not. To them, it is precisely by going to everyone on an e-mail list that these messages become public. As a participant remarked in the present case,

> Someone suggested moving this to the community issue board. Some may gasp at this, but I admit publicly that I rarely if ever check that board and I would have missed this discussion. Please, for my sake, don't move it to obscurity. It will die after a couple of posts by the same small group that frequents the boards most often. At least out here in public, there seems to be more of an opportunity for us "lurkers" to throw in the odd comment.

To some, in other words, the repeated proposal by others to relieve those who felt persecuted by moving the discussion to an online forum—which is the cultural norm for handling such issues in this particular academic environment—was really a way to kill the discussion, to remove it from the public realm. Thus, the most mundane and operational technical solutions or policies can be seen to have social and political agendas or implications. Within this same group of people, some defined e-mail as public and bulletin boards as private. For others, precisely the reverse was true.

Furthermore, the meaning and value of the public sphere in higher education generally and in online academic environments in particular is itself controversial, partly because of the issue of individualism versus collectivism that was discussed above. Is the public realm—for example, an online forum or bulletin board or chat space or e-mail list—merely a place for individuals to pursue their own individual and instrumental goals? Or is it a place for the building of group or institutional understandings, discourse, culture, and norms? Do individuals in online educational environments have responsibilities to the group or community of which they are a part, to a public that is larger and broader than they are, or does the public realm exist only to help individuals pursue their own private purposes?

These questions can arise in some form in any social group. But as suggested above, a radical impact of current information and communication technologies on society, culture, politics, and personal life at present is precisely their redefining the lived experience of public and private and the radical dislocation of the boundary between them. In a world in which it is impossible to sit in a doctor's office or café without listening to someone else's conversation on a cellular phone, in which more than half of all businesses read their employees' e-mail, in which individuals are having sexual intercourse in their own home and broadcasting their activities to millions of viewers over the Internet, in which it is possible to steal someone's identity via technological means and impersonate her or him remotely, centuries-old meanings of private and public are being fundamentally recast. The very conceptions of public and private are in crisis. Under these circumstances, it is quite unlikely that any collection of individuals will enter a group, class, or community with identical experiences, definitions, and values regarding them.

In the actual situation being analyzed, two solutions were adopted to the problem of experiencing public messages as an invasion of privacy or personal space (partly in consequence of our suggestions and direct involvement): first, an admonition to use Web forums for messages to the whole community and, second, the creation of additional, separate, opt-in and opt-out mailing lists for each graduate program, not for the delivery of administrative messages but rather only for those students and faculty who were both interested in public discussion and willing to delete unwanted messages. Because of the way in which the evolution of culture is itself part of the hermeneutics of culture—that is, because new developments make people reinterpret the past and even experience it differently in retrospect—an interesting sidelight on the entire incident was cast by the development of the new, separate mailing lists. They came into existence under different conditions and with a different contract, or set of shared understandings, on the part of their subscribers. For one thing, membership was by voluntary self-subscription. In addition, those who joined did so with an explicit belief in the value of public discussion and an explicit understanding that individuals would delete unwanted messages rather than complain about them. And they knew that they could unsubscribe if and when they wished, especially because, following current Internet practice, each message from the new list ended with instructions as to how to unsubscribe. Not only did these repeated brief instructions give people an easy exit from the list, but they also had a quasi-ethical subtext: that the individual subscriber was on this list of his or her own free choice and that what happened there was his or her own responsibility.

Metacommunication and Double Binds

Perhaps the most striking metacommunicative feature of the e-mail flurry set off by the political message was the extent to which the most vocal and emphatic messages, those that were written in imperative sentences and uppercase type, seemed directed more against those who were discussing the propriety of political discussion than those who were engaging in it—indeed against the legitimacy of reflecting or metacommunicating at all—for once the initial message (about voting for Gore rather than Nader) had been sent, there were in fact only one or two more about the election itself. The articulate, thought-out messages were, regardless of their position, about the nature of academic community and the appropriateness of political discussion. In other words, they were metacommunicative in nature. It is known, from a long-standing intellectual and research tradition originating in Gregory Bateson's double-bind theory (Bateson, 1972; Sluzki & Ransom, 1976; Watzlawick, Beavin, & Jackson, 1967), that the solution of interpersonal problems is directly bound up with the possibility of communicating about them (i.e., metacomunication) just as the impossibility or prohibition of communicating about them leads to stasis and alienation in a group or psychosis in the individual as a way of managing irresolvable conflicts. The most virulent messages here were not about receiving political propaganda. Rather, they followed immediately, and seemed to be responses to, messages discussing the norms of the e-mail list itself. This was particularly true of the above mentioned *"I AM NOT INTERESTED TO HEAR ANYTHING OF ANY SORT ABOUT ANYTHING,"* which was addressed not only to the list but also to the two individuals who had written the most articulate arguments for and against discussing political issues on the list. In other words, they appeared to express the attitude, "I do not want to be a member of a group that discusses or publicly reflects on the norms of the group itself."

Taken to its logical conclusion, such an orientation traps those who hold it in the very predicament they are trying to escape because they have no means of reflecting on the situation and considering alternatives, options, and solutions. And in this situation, that is precisely what happened to some participants, indeed to those who chose the simplest, most obvious technological solution, by hitting the "reply all" button. Like the sorcerer's apprentice, a person set off a vicious cycle of an increasing number of unwanted messages, bringing about the very thing that he or she wanted to escape. The consequences of this extreme antimetacommunicative, antireflective attitude show clearly why metacommunication and reflection are so important in building culture and community in online educational environments. Perhaps because currently most online communication is denuded of the indirect, nonverbal metacommunication that is so prominent in face-to-face communication, it is particularly prone to misunderstanding and miscommunication and thereby requires more intentional, explicit, and articulate metacommunication. This is, as has been so often pointed out, why online communicators sometimes resort to emoticons (i.e., graphic representations of human faces smiling, frowning, etc.) to function as nonlinguistic metacommunicative devices. It would be a rather important consequence of CMC if its very limitations led to a compensatory flourishing of metacommunication.

Yet, people cannot be forced to reflect or metacommunicate. Rather, they can only be shown the impact of not doing so. This impact, moreover, will differ depending on the meaning of the particular limited-liability environment to the individual, which will not be the same for different individuals. Therefore, people cannot assume an equal interest in metacommunication on the part of all members of an online group. They need to think themselves into the situation of the person who does not wish to metacommunicate. In an intimate relationship or in psychotherapy, this unwillingness may be regarded as a defense mechanism. However, in an online community of diverse individuals of different social backgrounds, it may mean something quite different. It is conceivable that the person who wrote *"I AM NOT INTERESTED TO HEAR ANYTHING OF ANY SORT ABOUT ANYTHING"* is an individual with a family who is under financial stress, is working two jobs, and is in graduate school to receive a credential that will alleviate her or his situation, with a predominantly instrumental and credentialist approach to getting a degree. For this person, the activities of a community that discusses large issues in an open-ended way, indeed anything other than taking and passing courses, may seem like a luxury that is beyond her or his possibilities. They may strike her or him as the pastime of idle rich students, flaunting their freedom to indulge in such activities. Or the student may come from a family or cultural background in which metacommunication was taboo. The point here is that the neohumanist perspective involves understanding all of the positions in the situation, not just the ones who the neohumanist prefers.

The Information Structure of the Online Environment

Finally, the fourth issue to surface in the vortex of e-mail communication about the incident was the information structure of the online community itself, that is, how in a community of geographically far-flung individuals with different levels of involvement in the community and its technology one could even find out what the norms and ground rules actually are. As someone asked in an e-mail,

> I wonder if there is, somewhere, a posting that specifies the uses to which the student/faculty mailing lists can be put to. If so, then we who are on those lists should abide by those guidelines as though they were a contract for our inclusion on those lists. I do not know if such guidelines exist, and if they do, I obviously do not know where to find them. If someone does, would they kindly either reproduce and add them to this mailing, or at least send out the url so we can check them out.

Regardless of how involving an online educational environment may be, its normative structure can sometimes seem either opaque or invisible, even when embodied in written rules and guidelines that are posted in known places, as in the environment referred to here. The reasons for this are worthy of detailed consideration and research. Noted here is that people both navigate through Web sites at their own will and import into one environment assumptions and norms that are derived from others. This can make it easy for the norms, even when explicit, to slip by the participants. Since there is no standard format or structure for an online environment, there is no standard place for the location or display of its norms, even if they have been formulated. Those who remember their ancient history will know what a decisive step it was in the evolution of civilization when the laws of the city were first written down—chipped into walls, such as the ones still visible in the Cretan town of Gortyn—so that in matters of dispute, people could go down to the wall and read the laws themselves.

In recent years, the FAQ (frequently asked questions) document has begun to take on some of that function in computer- and network-mediated environments, even though FAQs (or "How Do I" documents) are still largely technical in content. What is needed is something like a FANQ (frequently asked normative questions) or FASQ (frequently asked social questions) in a publicly identified place, and such documents are rarely to be found. Wikipedia is unusual in having an explicit statement of policies and guidelines (http://en.wikipedia.org/wiki/Help:Contents/Policies_and_guidelines) that govern not only the content of the encyclopedia, but also the communication among editors (and, of course, on Wikipedia, anyone who wants to be is automatically an editor), including such values and practices as assuming good faith, civility and etiquette, consensus, the avoidance of personal attacks, and methods for resolving disputes. On Wikipedia, these norms are both discussed and strictly enforced, and any member of the community has the right to revise or delete other users' content if it does not conform to the norms. Wikipedia is, however, a special case in that it is devoted to creating and maintaining a product that conforms to standards from the surrounding culture about what an encyclopedia is supposed to be, for example, objective and neutral.

A more common way in which normative information is provided is as a part of formal or legal policy documents, such as the terms of service or terms of use documents that users must agree to explicitly or implicitly in order to use particular services or sites. However, these are often formulated with an eye to possible future legal protection or litigation and thus are mandated, rather than arrived at by or open to public discussion, and are designed primarily to prevent crimes or to prevent legal liability on the part of the network service or site. Facebook's "Terms of Use" (http://www.facebook.com/terms.php), for example, include both a section on "User Conduct," which includes the prescription that a user may not "intimidate or harass another," and a link to "Content Code of Conduct" (http://www.facebook.com/codeofconduct.php), which tells users that they "may not post or share Content that is obscene, pornographic or sexually explicit, graphic or gratuitous violence, makes threats of any kind or that intimidates, harasses, or bullies anyone, is derogatory, demeaning, malicious, defamatory, abusive, offensive or hateful." Primarily, however, it is focused on crime prevention and legal liability issues. Some social networking sites have FAQs about how to deal with specific social problems. For example, MySpace's FAQ page (http://www.myspace.com/index.cfm?fuseaction=misc.faq) gives operational answers to such questions as "Someone on MySpace is bugging/harassing/threatening me—what can I do about it?" and "I am a parent who needs help with my teen's profile. How do I address this issue?" But neither Facebook nor MySpace have a general statement of positive norms that are to govern communication among members of the site (e.g., civility): nothing that looks like a frequently asked normative questions document.

Even a FANQ, however, presupposes a subjective orientation toward finding out the norms and taking them into account in one's behavior. How many people read the terms of service of networking sites, the privacy policies of the companies from whom they buy on the Internet, or the legal and copyright stipulations that appear on their screens when they install software? For many people, cyberspace is still their personal Wild West of liberation from social constraints, or at least the social constraints that operate in their noncyber environment. Although this may be truer of people who have not grown up in online environments, in recent years, there has been public discussion of the ways in which young people may jeopardize their future careers by writing things in social networking sites that may be looked at as problematic by future employers, given that anything written or posted on the Web may be visible and accessible forever. In any case, this issue focuses people's attention on the special need not only to clarify and articulate the norms of the online educational environment, but also to then make them visible and public in adequate ways. In the situation of the inflammatory e-mail, we did in fact create and send out a message trying to articulate the norms of this particular institutional and online culture and pointing to existing documents available online that set out the sort of norms and guidelines that were being requested.

The fact that, in this case, there actually were such guidelines already available online, although their locations were not generally known, points to another important matter. Individuals in any particular online environment will have been there for different lengths of time and with different histories, which are sometimes less visible online than in face-to-face groups or communities. These differences in history make for different stocks of knowledge (Schutz, 1970), which in turn create important differences in how the online environment is perceived, experienced, and known and how people interact in it. In face-to-face communities, people have a sense of when people enter the community and leave it, who is a newcomer and who an old-timer, and so on, and this knowledge becomes associated with people's perception of even the physical appearances of others. In Japan, small children in their first year of school wear specially colored clothing so that people who see a child dressed this way on the street will know that this child may need some special attention or help getting across a street, finding her or his way, and so on. Although these kinds of differences can be visible and can be made known in online groups, they may not be, and consequently, knowledge that could be shared may not be. The very assumption of equality that has been hailed as a virtue in online interactions can also efface relevant history and differences, the knowledge of which could make interactions more cooperative and result in communicating information that otherwise remains invisible.

Some Tentative Lessons

In general, information literacy and computer literacy are defined as competences that inhere—or should inhere—in an individual in order to serve her or his goals. A few years ago we developed an expanded and now widely used conception of information literacy as consisting of seven dimensions (Kirk, 2000; Shapiro & Hughes, 1996): tool literacy, resource literacy, social-structural literacy, research literacy, publishing literacy, emerging technology literacy, and critical literacy. At the time, it was recommended that education for information literacy focus on all of these dimensions. Now that an increasing portion of an increasing number of lives is spent in online social networks and environments, it is becoming clear that this and other conceptions of information literacy are deficient through neglect of a vital competence area, that of communication, interaction, and interpersonal behavior in the world of cyberspace. This eighth dimension of information literacy could be called online community literacy or, following Habermas's notion of communicative competence (Habermas, 1970, 1984), online communicative competence.

The notion of communicative competence in general, in Habermas's sense, denotes individuals' ability to construct interpersonal, intersubjective relationships of shared meaning and understanding through their communicative acts in the dimensions of defining a shared objective reality, acting according to interpersonally valid norms, and expressing their own subjective reality. Competent communication includes what Schutz (1970), in line with Mead's notion of the construction of the self through communication, called the *reciprocity of perspectives*, that is individuals' ability to relativize their own perspective in relation to that of the person(s) with whom they communicate. Through the reciprocity of perspectives, the individual recognizes that, just as a partner in communication is an other to her or him, part of the periphery of one's own self-centered world, she or he is an other to that partner, a peripheral person in the partner's self-centered world. Maintaining the reciprocity of perspectives in communication requires communication partners to continuously adjust their egocentric perspective to take account of the other's. Indeed, it requires a synthesis that incorporates and transcends both: When I sit across from you, not only do I know implicitly that what is to my left is to your right, I also know implicitly that neither of these directions is absolute. They are always relative to someone.

In online environments, communicative competence involves recognizing that, in CMC, interpersonal actions are mediated by the computer and network structures and tools though which they take place: that the processes of constructing an interpersonal world as well as the world that is constructed are affected and shaped by those structures and tools. Competent communication in face-to-face situations involves awareness both of context and of impact. For all communication has an implied reference to the context in which it takes place and some kind of acknowledgement of the way in which that context enters into what is communicated. This includes the famous sociological concept of the definition of the situation, in which communicators define and experience themselves as sharing a context. Competent communication also involves the awareness of impact—that precisely through my communication and action I am affecting those with whom I communicate. Indeed, being competent in this way is part of what we mean and assume in thinking of someone to be rational, adult, and sane. Nevertheless, it is possible to be communicatively competent in general—that is, to be a rational, sane, adult person in the general social world—without being able to translate this ability into competence within online environments. Thus, a generally rational, sane adult may not automatically know how to be so in cyberspace (just as it is said of some rational, sane adults who learn how to drive that they are a terror at the wheel). Conversely, of course, it is possible to master computer communication tools without being communicatively competent in this interpersonal sense. That is why it makes sense to identify online communicative competence as a separate dimension or skill area and to concentrate on it educationally: to focus on the intersection of communicative competence and computer and network tool use as an area for development in both individuals and groups. This domain poses additional challenges when it includes young people who are not yet adult as defined by the surrounding culture and who are in the process of evolving into (it is to be hoped) rational, sane adults but who are still trying out the necessary competences and groping toward maturity, responsibility, and interpersonal awareness.

Developing online communicative competence is shaped by social, cultural, psychological, and technical factors. It cannot be taught like a technical skill or an aggregate of information. It is quite likely that particular cultural and social environments may be more or less favorable to it. It may be, for example, that a culture such as that of the United States that emphasizes the individual over the community and, as Slater (1976) argued, is pathologically individualistic to the point of denying individuals' interdependence, may make it harder for individuals to become communicatively competent online or literate with regard to community membership. Nevertheless, in orientation programs for new students and in courses in computer and information literacy, it would be wise for educators to spend time focusing on online communicative competence, which goes well beyond Netiquette. It would also be useful to devote some time to it in online courses, as well as to prepare FANQ and FASQ documents and make them available in known places.

Over and above these specific educational activities, how can the neohumanist, emancipatory, or critical information-systems developer, educator, or administrator contribute to the development of community literacy and online communicative competence in her or his environment? Central to this role is aiming at and modeling a particular sort of metacommunication—an ideal rational discourse in which all of the technical, social, cultural, value, and psychological interests at play in the situation, as well as the technology through which they are shaped and mediated—would be represented and articulated in a reflective process (a notion clearly derived from Habermas's theory of communicative rationality). In this process, mutual understanding and reflection would also make possible shifts in people's positions, views, and interpreted needs, such that a new, genuine consensus and a new configuration of the system could be arrived at. The neohumanist actor must aim at such a discourse, even if it is impossible, while understanding and trying to educate the community about why it is impossible in the particular situation. He or she should try to act in a way that best mediates between the constraining and enabling factors to move the system in the direction of such a state, choosing from a repertoire of possible actions and techniques to create this movement: educational and informational comments and documents, policy proposals, process comments, humor, alliances, conspiracies, assistance to individuals, negotiations, psychological and cultural interpretations, imaginative and innovative actions, surrealist, or absurd gestures. In any actual situation, power structures and inequalities, patterns of distorted communication, psychological deformations, and skill deficits may severely curtail what can be done. But there is almost always something that can be done.

References

Alexander, C., Ishikawa, S., Silverstein, M., Jacobson, M., Fiksdahl-King, I., & Angel, S. (1977). *A pattern language: Towns, building, construction.* New York: Oxford University Press.

Bateson, G. (1972). *Steps to an ecology of mind.* New York: Ballantine Books.

Bourdieu, P. (1998). The essence of neoliberalism. *Le Monde Diplomatique.* Retrieved from http://mondediplo.com/1998/12/08bourdieu

Brown, J. S., & Adler, R. P. (2008). Minds on fire: Open education, the long tail, and learning 2.0. *EDUCAUSE Review, 43*(1), 16–32.

Dery, M. (1996). *Escape velocity: Cyberculture at the end of the century.* New York: Grove Press.

EDUCAUSE Learning Initiative. (2008). *7 things you should know about Ning.* Retrieved May 30, 2008, from http://net.EDUCAUSE.edu/ir/library/pdf/ELI7036.pdf

Farson, R. (1996). *Management of the absurd: Paradoxes in leadership.* New York: Simon & Schuster.

Fono, D., & Raynes-Goldie, K. (2006). Hyperfriends and beyond: Friendship and social norms on LiveJournal. In M. Consalvo & C. Haythornthwaite (Eds.), *Internet research annual: Vol. 4. Selected papers from the Association of Internet Researchers Conference.* New York: Peter Lang.

Friedman, T. L. (1999, Aug 10). The Y2K social disease. *New York Times,* p. 17.

Habermas, J. (1970). Toward a theory of communicative competence. In H. P. Dreitzel (Ed.), *Recent sociology* (No. 2, pp. 114–148). New York: Macmillan.

Habermas, J. (1984). *The theory of communicative action:* Vol. 1. *Reasons and the rationalization of society* (T. McCarthy, Trans.). Boston: Beacon Press.

Habermas, J. (1988). *The theory of communicative action:* Vol. 2. *Lifeworld and system: A critique of functionalist reason* (T. McCarthy, Trans.). Boston: Beacon Press.

Hirschheim, R., & Klein, H. K. (1989). Four paradigms of information systems development. *Communications of the ACM, 32*(10), 1199–1215.

Hofstede, G. H. (1997). *Cultures and organizations: Software of the mind* (Rev. ed.). New York: McGraw-Hill.

Jenkins, H. (2006). *Convergence culture: Where old and new media collide.* New York: New York University Press.

Kim, A. J. (2000). *Community building on the Web: Secret strategies for successful online communities.* Berkeley, CA: Peachpit Press.

Kirk, T. G., Jr. (2000). *Information literacy in a nutshell: Basic information for academic administrators and faculty.* Retrieved June 22, 2001, from http://www.ala.org/acrl/nili/whatis.html

Mankoff, R. (Ed.). (2000). *The* New Yorker *book of technology cartoons.* Princeton, NJ: Bloomberg Press.

Messerschmitt, D. G. (1999). *Networked applications: A guide to the new computing infrastructure.* San Francisco: Morgan Kaufmann.

Mowshowitz, A. (1985). On the social relations of computers. *Human Systems Management, 5,* 99–110.

Ogburn, W. F. (1964). *On culture and social change.* Chicago: University of Chicago Press.

Parsons, T. (1977). *The evolution of societies.* Englewood Cliffs, NJ: Prentice Hall.

Palloff, R. M., & Pratt, K. (1999). *Building learning communities in cyberspace: Effective strategies for the online classroom.* San Francisco: Jossey-Bass.

Polanyi, M. (1966). *The tacit dimension.* Garden City, NJ: Doubleday.

Rheingold, H. (n.d.). *The art of hosting good conversations online.* Retrieved November 18, 2000, from http://www.rheingold.com/texts/artonlinehost.html

Rheingold, H. (2000). *The virtual community: Homesteading on the electronic frontier.* (Rev. ed.). Cambridge: MIT Press.

Rogers, E. M. (1995). *Diffusion of innovations* (4th ed.). New York: Free Press.

Schutz, A. (1970). *On phenomenology and social relations: Selected writings.* Chicago: University of Chicago Press.

Shapiro, J. J., & Hughes, S. K. (1996). Information literacy—Technical skill or liberal art? Enlightenment proposals for a new curriculum. *EDUCOM Review, 31*(2), 31–35.

Shirky, C. (2003). *A group is its own worst enemy.* Retrieved June 1, 2008, from http://shirky.com/writings/group_enemy.html

Slater, P. (1976). *The pursuit of loneliness: American culture at the breaking point* (Rev. ed.). Boston: Beacon Press.

Sluzki, C. E., & Ransom, D. C. (1976). *Double bind: The foundation of the communicational approach to the family.* New York: Grune & Stratton.

Smith, M. A., & Kollock, P. (Eds.). (1999). *Communities in cyberspace.* New York: Routledge.

Turkle, S. (1995). *Life on the screen: Identity in the age of the Internet.* New York: Simon & Schuster.

Turner, J. H. (2000). *On the origins of human emotions: A sociological inquiry into the evolution of human affect.* Stanford, CA: Stanford University Press.

Watzlawick, P., Beavin, J. H., & Jackson, D. D. (1967). *The pragmatics of human communication: A study of interactional patterns, pathologies, and paradoxes.* New York: W. W. Norton.

Wellman, B., & Gulia, M. (1999). Virtual communities as communities: Net surfers don't ride alone. In M. A. Smith & P. Kollock (Eds.), *Communities in cyberspace* (pp. 167–194). London: Routledge.

Wellman, B., & Hampton, K. (1999). Living networked on and offline. *Contemporary Sociology, 28*(6), 648–654.

Chapter 4

Evolving Technologies

Robin Mason

Frank Rennie

Web 2.0 and Evolving Technologies

One of the acknowledged truisms of educational technology is that technology evolves much more rapidly than the willingness of teachers, learners, and educational institutions to exploit those technologies for learning. In short, there is usually a long lag time between the appearance of a new technology and its eventual widespread adoption for educational purposes. Educational authorities are often reluctant to invest in buying hardware and software that will be out of date before the teachers have really begun to make good use of it. A vicious circle can develop whereby educators wait for the next evolution of the software or hardware to become available, but the next version is rapidly followed by another which may be incompatible with the previous. This is particularly true with respect to the technologies underpinning distributed education, where over the last 20 years information and communication technologies have evolved very rapidly. However, on the whole, the early adopters among educators at the postcompulsory level have been quick to apply each new refinement to improve the quality of distributed learning and to increase access and enhance the online learning environment for the benefit of distributed learners.

The evolution of technologies for distributed learning is characterized by convergence: Stand-alone systems have converged onto the

---

Note: This chapter draws on material from *The E-Learning Handbook: Social Networking for Higher Education*, by R. Mason and F. Rennie (2008), Abbingdon, Oxon, UK: Routledge.

Web; the distinct technologies for synchronous and asynchronous communication have blurred into each other; the separate teaching modes of face-to-face and distance education have also converged with the evolution of technology such that the most common mode is now blended learning.

This chapter considers the impact of Web 2.0 technologies as an evolution of online learning. It focuses on how to use a wide range of existing tools, which are currently popular with students for leisure and social activities, and how to integrate them into formal courses for learning.

Web 2.0 Tools

The various tools to be considered in this chapter are all part of what has been called Web 2.0 (O'Reilly, 2005). The underlying practice of Web 2.0 tools is that of harnessing collective intelligence. As users add new content and new sites, they are connected through hyperlinking so that other users discover the content and link to it, thus the Web grows organically as a reflection of the collective activity of the users.

Examples of social software with relevance to education are as follows:

- Wikipedia, an online encyclopedia, in which the content is created and edited entirely by users;

- folksonomy sites such as del.icio.us and Flickr in which users tag with keywords their photos or other content entries, thus developing a form of collaborative categorization of sites using the kind of associations that the brain uses rather than rigid, preordained categories;

- blogging, a form of online diary, which adds a whole new dynamism to what was in Web 1.0, the personal home page;

- RSS (which stands for Really Simple Syndication or Rich Site Summary) is a family of Web feed formats used to publish frequently updated digital content, such as blogs, news feeds or podcasts;

- podcasting is a media file that is distributed over the Internet using syndication feeds for playback on mobile devices and personal computers;

- e-portfolios, which encourage students to take ownership of their learning through creating a dynamic, reflective, multimedia record of their achievements; and

- real-time audio and shared screen tools for multiway discussions.

The Web has always supported some forms of social interaction, for example, computer conferencing, e-mail and listservs. The level of social interaction they afford has become an established component of distance and even campus-based education. What has changed with Web 2.0 is the popularity of social networking sites, which Boyd claimed, have three defining characteristics:

1. *Profile.* A profile includes an identifiable handle (either the person's name or nickname), information about that person (e.g., age, sex, location, interests, etc.). Most profiles also include a photograph and information about last login. Profiles have unique URLs that can be visited directly and updated.

2. *Traversable, publicly articulated social network.* Participants have the ability to list other profiles as friends or contacts or as some equivalent. This generates a social network graph that may be directed (attention network type of social network where friendship does not have to be confirmed) or undirected (where the other person must accept friendship). This articulated social network is displayed on an individual's profile for all other users to view. Each node contains a link to the profile of the other person so that individuals can traverse the network through friends of friends of friends. . . .

3. *Semipersistent public comments.* Participants can leave comments (or testimonials, guestbook messages, etc.) on others' profiles for everyone to see. These comments are semipersistent in that they are not ephemeral, but they may disappear over some period of time or upon removal. These comments are typically reverse-chronological in display. Because of these comments, profiles are a combination of an individual's self-expression and what others say about that individual. (Boyd, 2006, para. 3)

These three attributes do not immediately suggest an educational use. Furthermore, the question needs to be asked, "Do students want their much used tools to be used for education as well as leisure activity?" More recently, the term *people power* on the Web has been noted in relation to the success of blogging, user reviews, and photo sharing (C. Anderson, 2006), and observers speak of a gift culture on the Web whereby users contribute as much as they take. Examples include YouTube, MySpace, and Flickr. The primary focus in social networking is participation, not publishing, which was the primary feature of Web 1.0 activity. Bloch (n.d.) linked Web 2.0, mashups, and social networking as "all intertwined in the brave new Internet, the so-called second phase of the evolution of the online world" (para. 1). The essence of social networking is that the users generate the content. This has potentially profound implications for education.

User-Generated Content

The theoretical benefits of user-generated content in education are fairly obvious:

- Users have the tools to actively engage in the construction of their experience rather than merely absorb existing content passively.

- Content will be continually refreshed by the users rather than require expensive expert input.

- Many of the new tools support collaborative work, thereby allowing users to develop the skills of working in teams.

- Shared community spaces and intergroup communications are a massive part of what excites young people and therefore should contribute to users' persistence and motivation to learn.

However, these benefits assume a transition between entertainment and education that has never in the past been an obvious or straightforward one. The early champions of educational television had a difficult time persuading learners that this entertaining (but passive) medium could be a tool for active and demanding education. Similarly, how will current users of computer games, blogging, podcasting, and folksonomies be convinced that they can use their favorite tools for getting a degree? O'Reilly (2005) suggested that we look at what commercial organizations are doing:

> One of the key lessons of the Web 2.0 era is this: *Users add value.* But only a small percentage of users will go to the trouble of adding value to your application via explicit means. Therefore, Web 2.0 companies *set inclusive defaults for aggregating user data and building value as a side-effect of ordinary use of the application.* As noted above, they build systems that get better the more people use them. . . .
>
> This architectural insight may also be more central to the success of open source software than the more frequently cited appeal to volunteerism. The architecture of the internet, and the World Wide Web, as well as of open source software projects like Linux, Apache, and Perl, is such that users pursuing their own "selfish" interests build collective value as an automatic byproduct. Each of these projects has a small core, well-defined extension mechanisms, and an approach that lets any well-behaved component be added by anyone, growing the outer layers of what Larry Wall, the creator of Perl, refers to as "the onion." In other words, these technologies demonstrate network effects, simply through the way that they have been designed ("The Architecture of Participation" [sidebar]).

What is the comparable onion in relation to education? Could it be high-quality course design? Through appropriate course design, we can help learners pursue their selfish interests of passing the course, while at the same time adding value to the learning of other students.

Another way of looking at user-generated content, and one that is possibly less contentious, is to see it as a network. In a recent report from Futurelab, Rudd, Sutch, and Facer (2006) argued that

> the network is now the fundamental underpinning structure of social organisation—that it is in and through networks—both real and virtual—that life is lived in the 21st century. This perspective is also advocated by social commentators such as Demos, who argue that networks are the "most important organisational form of our time," and that, by harnessing what they describe as "network logic," the ways we view the world and the tools we use for navigating and understanding it, will change significantly. The ability to understand how to join and build these networks, the tools for doing so and the purpose, intention, rules and protocols that regulate use and communications, therefore, become increasingly important skills. This concept of the "network society" calls into question what it means to be "educated" today—what new skills, what new ways of working and learning, what new knowledge and skills will be required to operate in and through these networks? It requires us to ask whether our current education system, premised not upon networks but upon individualised acquisition of content and skills, is likely to support the development of the competencies needed to flourish in such environments. (p. 4)

The wise use of Web 2.0 technologies in education addresses this call for students to develop 21st century skills. Blogging, wikis, e-portfolios, and social networks are all excellent tools for allowing learners to clarify concepts, establish meaningful links and relationships, and test their mental models. Furthermore, they provide a public forum in which the cumulative process of concept formation, refinement, application, and revision is fully visible to student peers and teachers. By providing a comprehensive record of how concepts take form through multiple clusters of knowledge, such media can promote more complex and lasting retention of course ideas among students (Boettcher, 2007).

What Are the Limitations?

Critics of user-created content refer to a breakdown in the traditional place of expertise, authority, and scholarly input. They express concerns about trust, reliability, and believability in relation to the move away from the printed word to the more ephemeral digital word (Poster, 1990). The Web contains a plethora of unauthenticated, unfiltered information, and most students lack the critical skills to penetrate this mass of undifferentiated material. In short, traditional notions of quality in higher education seem to be abandoned in the move to Web 2.0 learning.

Another line of criticism is that course designers who use these technologies are merely pandering to the Net generation, a pandering which is not in their best interests. Carlson (2005) noted that "not everyone agrees that Millennials are so different from their predecessors, or that, even if they are different, educational techniques should change accordingly." These critics feel that new technologies encourage a short attention span and lead students to demand immediate answers rather than thinking for themselves.

Furthermore, if content is created by users on different systems (e.g., podcasts, blogs, wikis, chat systems, and other social networking software), then it can be difficult to keep track of where everything is and to access it with ease, both for the users and for the casual visitor. This in turn calls for new tools to help users search and integrate across content that may be quite fragmented.

Other commentators question whether social networking has real learning value and point to the superficiality of this informal mode of learning. Learning from Web sites and online discussion groups is very different from the orientation of formal courses, where stress is laid on learning step-by-step, just in case one needs it later or for the exam. By contrast, informal learning is just-in-time and just the amount necessary to put to immediate use. However, Kapp (2006) argued that

> we can contemplate whether "real" learning happens with Web 2.0 tech-
> nologies, we can be philosophical about the value of informal learning ver-
> sus formal learning, we can tout the virtues of "collective wisdom" but in the
> end . . . none of that matters.

What matters is that students are already using Web 2.0 technologies comfortably and effectively. If instructors (over 30) do not figure out how to effectively use these tools to help the younger generation learn what they need to be successful in our baby boomer–run companies, government agencies, and other large organizations, then learning and development will be irrelevant. Conducting traditional classroom lectures for these gamers is not going to cut it and neither is our multiple-choice question, e-learning module format. We need to stop bad mouthing Web 2.0 or eLearning 2.0 and start using these technologies or be passed up by the digital natives, as Prensky called them (Kapp, 2006).

Others of the same persuasion apply the dictum, "If you can't beat them, help them." They focus on developing critical thinking skills, analysis of the content of Web sites, and peer commenting on student assignments. In a similar way, Cross (2007) took a positive stance toward integrating informal learning and Web 2.0 and described an approach that has implications for the role of the teacher:

> Because the design of informal learning ecosystems is analogous to land-
> scape design, I will call the environment of informal learning a learnscape.

A landscape designer's goal is to conceptualize a harmonious, unified, pleasing garden that makes the most of the site at hand. A learnscaper strives to create a learning environment that increases the organization's longevity and health, and the individual learner's happiness and well-being. Gardeners don't control plants; managers don't control people. Gardeners and managers have influence but not absolute authority. They can't make a plant fit into the landscape or a person fit into a team. A learnscape is a learning ecology. It's learning without borders. ("Learnscaping," para. 2)

In short, designing challenging and rich learning environments that employ Web 2.0 technologies is the way forward.

Studies of Student Behavior

The predictions that students who have grown up with digital media will learn differently and demand a more engaging form of education have led to a number of studies and surveys of student attitudes, behaviors, and uses of technology. A study by Oblinger and Oblinger (2005) talked about millennials, those born since 1982, whose learning characteristics are defined as follows:

- ability to multitask rather than single task;
- preference to learn from pictures, sound, and video rather than text; and
- preference for interactive and networked activities rather than independent and individual study.

However these characteristics have the following disadvantages:

- shorter attention spans or choosing not to pay attention,
- lack of reflection,
- relatively poor text literacy, and
- a cavalier attitude to quality of sources.

Millennials could be described as having hypertext minds, craving interactivity, easily reading visual images, possessing good visual-spatial skills, and having the ability to parallel process. They will prefer learning in teams, will seek to engage with problems, and will enjoy experiential forms of learning. Another study of millennials by Raines (2002) listed similar characteristics:

- skilled at teamwork,
- techno savvy,

- preference for structure,
- desire for entertainment and excitement, and
- biased toward experiential activities.

Two European reports, one from Germany (Veen, 2003) and the other from Hungary (Karpati, 2002) both largely confirmed the description of millennials outlined in the Oblingers' (2005) study. The German report refers to millennials as Homo Zappiens because of their habit of using remote controls, and it outlines four characteristics:

- scanning skills,
- multitasking,
- processing interrupted information flows, and
- nonlinear learning.

Not all of these skills, whether positive or negative, can be attributed to social networking, although a number of online gaming sites have Web 2.0 characteristics.

An extensive study in the United Kingdom of largely preuniversity students' use of online technologies (Livingstone & Bober, 2005) had some sobering conclusions:

- Young people lack key skills in evaluating online content, and few have been taught how to judge the reliability of online information.
- Most online communication is with local friends.
- Nearly one quarter of the sample admitted to copying something from the Internet and passing it off as their own.

The researchers note, however, that the opportunities and risks of these technologies go hand in hand, and the more users experience the one, the more they experience the other.

Beyond Constructivist Theory

Many researchers consider that course design based on constructivist theories of learning is highly compatible with the use of Web 2.0 tools. Constructivist curricula favor an open-ended, negotiable approach that structures activities so that students have opportunities to collaboratively negotiate knowledge and to contextualize learning within an emergent situation. This reflects the two tenets of constructivism:

1. that learning is an active process of constructing knowledge rather than acquiring it and

2. that instruction is a process of supporting that construction rather than of communicating knowledge. (Duffy & Cunningham, 1996, p. 171)

Through the provision of activities for students to direct their own learning, the designer acknowledges the students' need for autonomy in the learning process in order to construct their own understanding. The provision of realistic or authentic contexts for learning is the basis for many constructivist learning environments, as the purpose is to stimulate learners to relate their thinking to actual practice.

Communication through the learning environment is a key feature of constructivist design, especially where the students are geographically isolated. It is through dialogue in chat rooms, commenting on blogs, collaborating through wikis, self-expression through e-portfolios, and so on that students are able to develop as members of their learning community, to create shared understandings, and to challenge and to question the key issues of their area of study.

Learners are considered to be distributed, multidimensional participants in a sociocultural process. This concept moves away from the idea that learning is effective when one internalizes knowledge toward one that involves a connection with communities and a pattern of participation in community. It should not be a lonely act of a single person, but a matter of being "initiated into the practices of a community, of moving from legitimate peripheral participation to centripetal participation in the actions of a learning community" (Duffy & Cunningham, 1996, p. 181).

Learners in a constructivist environment need to be active and interactive, and Web 2.0 software is inherently participative. Web 2.0 is where anyone can not only take information down from it, but also create content and upload to it. In this respect, the Web is not simply a one-way means of obtaining knowledge, but a place where one interacts with the materials and annotate and contribute to the content. Such sites frequently display other Web 2.0 characteristics such as automated access through RSS feeds and ability to find related materials through tagging and other social networking devices (Stevens, 2006).

Nevertheless, other educators are beginning to look beyond constructivism and to associate it with Web 1.0 thinking. For example, Siemens (2004) claimed that Web 2.0 technologies have changed the learning landscape such that the three pillars of learning theory (behaviorism, cognivitism, and constructivism) are no longer adequate for describing the world in which we now are learning:

Constructivism suggests that learners create knowledge as they attempt to understand their experiences (Driscoll, 2000, p. 376). Behaviorism and cognitivism view knowledge as external to the learner and the learning process as the act of internalizing knowledge. Constructivism assumes that learners are not empty vessels to be filled with knowledge. Instead, learners are actively attempting to create meaning. Learners often select and pursue their own learning. Constructivist principles acknowledge that real-life learning is messy and complex. Classrooms which emulate the "fuzziness" of this learning will be more effective in preparing learners for life-long learning. ("Background," para. 6)

Learning theories are concerned with the actual process of learning, not with the value of what is being learned. In a networked world, the very manner of information that we acquire is worth exploring. The need to evaluate the worthiness of learning something is a metaskill that is applied before the learning itself begins. When knowledge is subject to paucity, the process of assessing worthiness is assumed to be intrinsic to learning. When knowledge is abundant, the rapid evaluation of knowledge is important. Additional concerns arise from the rapid increase in information. In today's environment, action is often needed without personal learning—that is, we need to act by drawing information outside of our primary knowledge. The ability to synthesize and recognize connections and patterns is a valuable skill (Siemens, 2004).

Siemens posited, instead, a theory he calls connectivism, whose principles he defined as follows:

- Learning and knowledge rests in diversity of opinions.
- Learning is a process of connecting specialized nodes or information sources.
- Learning may reside in nonhuman appliances.
- Capacity to know more is more critical than what is currently known
- Nurturing and maintaining connections is needed to facilitate continual learning.
- Ability to see connections between fields, ideas, and concepts is a core skill.
- Currency (accurate, up-to-date knowledge) is the intent of all connectivist learning activities.
- Decision making is itself a learning process. Choosing what to learn and the meaning of incoming information is seen through the lens of a shifting reality. Although there is a right answer now, it may be wrong tomorrow due to alterations in the information climate affecting the decision. ("Connectivism," para. 4)

Connectivism as a theory presents a model of learning that reflects a society in which learning is no longer a personal, individualistic activity. It acknowledges the fact that the ways people learn and function are altered when new tools are used. Siemens (2004) was critical of educators for being slow to recognize both the impact of new learning tools and the environmental changes in what it means to learn. Connectivism is his theoretical foundation for the learning skills and tasks needed for learners to flourish in a digital era.

Yet Another Trend . . .

The popularity of a wide range of social software, particularly with young people, has led many educators to think that this practice and enthusiasm could be turned to educational use. It could be argued that the roots of social networking are not a paradigm shift from what went before but a growth or development from previous practice and theory.

Of course, there have been other media that educators were convinced could transform teaching and learning:

- Television and then videoconferencing were going to render most ordinary lecturers redundant, as every student would have easy access to outstanding lecturers, with resulting cost savings.

- Computer-based training was going to allow learners to work at their own pace, by practicing as often as necessary and receiving programmed feedback from the ever-patient computer.

- Artificial intelligence was going to provide a truly responsive tutor that would understand the student's misunderstandings and respond appropriately.

- Asynchronous computer conferencing was going to support global education in which students from different time zones around the world could take courses from prestigious universities without having to leave home or work.

The list could go on. Educational hype has a long and resilient history of jumping on the latest technology as the means of making education better, cheaper, more available, or more responsive. Is social networking going to be any different? The answer is probably not, but this may be the wrong question. Ignoring social and technological trends is not the way forward for educators anymore than is chasing after every new movement because it is new. If a university were to issue each student with a slate and chalk, it would be ludicrous, but equally ludicrous is expecting all students on all courses to benefit from keeping a blog or from creating multimedia items in their e-portfolio; this is not a sensible way forward either. What this chapter is advocating is an open mind to the possibility that using some form of social software could be beneficial in most courses, given imaginative course design. The emphasis is squarely on how to use social software creatively, not on any assumption that these tools are predisposed to improving education, reducing costs, or widening participation or any future priorities of higher education. These are merely tools; however, as we know, man is a tool-using animal!

Specific Tools

In this section of the chapter, a range of Web 2.0 tools are discussed and their advantages and disadvantages outlined. In all, six of the most popular Web 2.0 tools are included: blogs, wikis, podcasting, e-portfolios, social networking, and Second Life.

1. Blogs (Web Logs)

A blog (short for Web log) is a type of Web page that is simple to create and to disseminate and that is used as a form of online journal. Already, there are millions of users (bloggers). Some blogs take the form of regular diary entries that are posted in reverse chronological order (newest at the top) and deal with the enthusiasms of the user who will combine personal opinions with links to other related Web sites, blogs, and other online articles. The ability for other users to leave comments on blog messages means that themed discussions can be built up very quickly, and supporting information (other Web articles, images, etc.) can be shared with people who have similar interests. There are a variety of different services available on the Web that enable people to set up their own blog, and although some use hosted software (located at another location on the Internet), while others require people to install the software on their own computer, they are all basically very similar. Due to their simplicity of use and their flexibility, blogs have become a very fast-growing feature of educational establishments, corporate businesses, and the public sector, for example, news media sources such as the online *Guardian.*

Blogging offers opportunities to extend discussion beyond the classroom, or it can add value to the online community in blended and distance learning courses. The immediacy of blogging encourages a fresh approach to sharing information. Although some blog spots can simply be a rant on a personal soap-box issue, most are genuinely interactive sites where like-minded users can share information and ideas. The many-to-many mode provides a learning framework that allows bloggers to acquire information quickly and to report on what they have learned. This can easily be used by tutors to both extend the subject matter and to reinforce key learning points. As with other digital media available over the Internet, the challenge is to somehow separate the useful information in the background noise of tens of thousands of self-publicizing blog sites. In order to try to minimize unhelpful blog messages (or just plain vandalism), some institutions have established blog sites that are open only to registered members (students and staff) of that institution, but this may be argued as being counterproductive in seeking to engage with the global learning community, while still not being able to ensure the quality of the posted messages.

Strengths of the Resource

- As personal, even reflective online journals, blogs can encourage the skills of writing and self-expression. New resources and ideas can be added to the discussion for sharing and further feedback, so blogs make it easy to access new resources quickly.

- A general strength is the ability to make connections with experts and opinions outside the classroom or institutional circle, and though this requires a level of trust and openness, supporting evidence can be included to contribute to the construction of a themed archive of information. This leads to the ability to categorize learning and relate it to the experience of the individual, encouraging the learner to contextualize and personalize the learning activities in ways that strengthen learning and build confidence.

- The ability to request automatic feedback information when users link to their blog (trackback) allows blog authors to keep a record of who is accessing and/or referring to their blogs and to receive some acknowledgement of the value of their blog site.

- Potential benefits are that blogs can be used to promote critical and analytical thinking on chosen topics and that the combination of individual working and social interaction can induce critical self-reflection in a rich learning environment.

Potential Disadvantages

- Although extensively used in education, there are mixed views about the added-value effectiveness of the medium to enhance learning over other forms of electronic communication.

- Most blog spaces are public, even when contained within the firewall of a single institution, and this may discourage less confident students from contributing to the blog, much less using it to think aloud and expose their thoughts to scrutiny.

- Although a strength of the blog is its immediacy, this also means that any lack of attention in maintaining a regular flow of messages may lead to the abandonment of the blog by readers and therefore by contributors.

- Detractors of blogs and other online fora maintain that being unseen makes it easier for students to become lurkers that are not engaging with the learning community, but careful attention to the tutor moderation of the discussion can alleviate this problem to a large extent.

- Similarly, although the lack of technical confidence in using new software can be addressed through careful induction training for new students, as can concerns about the development of writing skills, there needs to be a strong motivation on the part of users to want to communicate and exchange ideas. This need requires thoughtful course design.

Key Points for Effective Practice

1. Start your own blog related to your own course or subject area. Start small, but without regular entries, your readers will quickly tire and move somewhere else if you allow too much time to elapse before the next entry.

2. Give your students a list of some active blog sites and get them to look at other blogs before they start to post their own comments so that they get a feel for the medium.

3. Ask each student to start their own blog about a subject that interests them and is relevant to their course. It may be more efficient to provide them with their own blog site and to ask them to maintain it.

4. Setting formative or graded assessments that require students to read (and comment upon) each others' blog sites and summarize the issues can be a good way to focus the learners' attention on the essentials.

2. Wikis

A wiki is a collaborative, Web-based site for sharing text and other resources. The significant feature of wikis is their open editing function that allows users to jointly create the resource. The information on a wiki can be edited by any and all users, but it can be controlled by allowing or denying password access. Superficially, a wiki may appear not dissimilar to any other Web page, but the ease with which the wiki Web pages can be edited means that the application is much more versatile than a conventional static Web page. The medium deliberately encourages participation in the joint creation of content, and this may be either by revising existing text or by adding links to other Web pages (within the wiki or to external Web sites) to extend the information provided. Through the participation of many authors constantly adding and revising information, the wiki can be effectively self-policed to reduce misinformation through inaccuracy or malicious intent. The rapid growth of Wikipedia, the free, online, multilingual encyclopedia, has helped to popularize wikis as an effective tool for generating and sharing large amounts of complex knowledge. The wiki has given real substance to the shift of the Web toward Web 2.0—that is, toward an online environment in which users are encouraged to contribute and interact with other users rather than be the passive recipient of static information. Another Web 2.0 characteristic of wikis is that they encourage a different attitude to information: Whereas print suggests that information is fixed and authoritative, wikis create an environment in which information is seen to be fluid and flexible and, even more importantly, communally constructed and owned.

Wikis allow asynchronous peer-to-peer interaction, and with the convergence of digital media, a wiki can include images and sound as well as text. There are several crucial aspects of wikis that would seem to make them ideal for use in an educational environment. First, wikis are subject driven rather than time driven and can be adopted as repositories of information on specialist areas of interest, for example, an academic course, a research group, or a corporate organization with participating workers scattered across the globe. The fundamental premise of wiki construction is a belief in the shared construction of knowledge, and this is consistent with a constructivist pedagogy and a focus on encouraging learner-centered content rather than on the oracle of tutor generated content that students are expected to read and digest. Wikis are very flexible in being able to adapt the way in which information is organized so that new pages can be added, the layout changed, and sections deleted by interacting to a common consensus. Most wikis will allow users to compare the current version of the text with previous versions to refine the text and also will enable each amendment or addition to be traced to individual users. This ability facilitates wikis being used to build collaborative projects, while still enabling the contribution of individual students to be credited.

Because of their potential for dispersing disinformation, wikis offer an ideal opportunity for educators to help students gain the skills to differentiate and make their own judgments regarding the accuracy of information.

Strengths of the Resource

- Wikis enable the users to generate Web pages easily and to alter or amend the text in collaboration with peers in order to create a mutually agreed version that is commonly accessible. Information is not fixed (as in print) but is flexible and changeable to meet the needs of the community of users.

- Wikis can be closed (i.e., only an agreed group of users can change the text) or open (i.e., allowing any registered password holder to change text).

- Generally, a wiki requires very little technical skill or training to use it effectively, which allows the users to concentrate on the contents and the context rather than being distracted by the technology.

- The resource encourages users to work in groups, to develop peer-to-peer generation of information, and to contextualize knowledge by linking text to other relevant resources.

- The ease and accessibility of the resource encourages wikis to be utilized for building common agendas, problem solving, brainstorming, and creating complex reference lists of hyperlinked information.

- The medium is ideal for creating group cohesiveness and commonly agreed definitions or information sources among online communities.

- Wikis allow the structured organization of resources as well as asynchronous editing and participation by geographically distributed users and can link with other digital resources including image repositories and e-portfolios.

Potential Disadvantages

- Some critics have argued that the ease of access to wiki editing and the unmonitored open environment may lead to a very low level of content and no contextual relevance.

- There has been an extended debate relating to the lack of accuracy of wiki content, but educators have argued the importance of using the opportunities of this medium to educate learners to make their own judgments regarding the accuracy of information.

- The potential complexity of a site that has many authors requires care in the construction of the navigation to ensure that users are able to locate and extend the information in a systematic manner and without repetition.

Key Points for Effective Practice

1. Although wikis lend then themselves to collaborative writing by groups of users, this ability requires you to have a clear focus and an element of self-discipline. This ability has several points of advantage over traditional forms of writing, including the ability to trace comments and feedback from other users and simple linking with other digital sources of knowledge.

2. As with other forms of educational resource, a little bit of pre-planning and some clear guidelines on its use, can really help students to make the best use of the resource. The flexibility of the wiki can allow users to create some effective, dynamic knowledge bases and to share these widely for further comment, and these can range from the trivial (a shopping list or to-do list) to the complex (a personal e-portfolio or the activities of an interdisciplinary research group.

3. One particularly valuable use of a wikis is for a group to think about how information is organized, especially in a large or complex area, and to consider how to present it in small, hyperlinked chunks.

3. Podcasting

A podcast is an audio file that can be downloaded and listened to either on an iPod or MP3 player for mobile study or a computer or laptop for location-based study. Video podcasts (sometimes shortened to vidcast or vodcast) are also possible and useful for referring to visual material or for accompanying PowerPoint slides. A blogcast is a blend of two tools: blogging and podcasting. The blog contains associated text and makes the podcast indexable by search engines. The term podcasting is a combination of iPod (Apple Computer's portable media player) and broadcasting. As with the term radio, podcasting can refer to either the content or the process. Anyone with access to the Internet and the capability of playing audio files on a computer or any portable media device can listen to podcasts.

The most exciting challenge that podcasting represents is the empowering of students to create content and take part in authentic learning projects. In other words, students can be active learners, not passive consumers of information. There are uses of podcasting for assessment, as part of e-portfolios and as collaborative projects. For example, students can conduct oral histories and create podcasts that are then used to present their work. Other examples involve students creating reports, historical interpretations, or scientific narratives.

Universities can make podcasts of special lectures, cross-cultural exchanges, guest speeches, or other events and make them widely available to students. A number of institutions are using podcasts of all lectures as a way of providing access for certain kinds of disabled students and incidentally, for all students as a method of review or access to missed lectures. For distance or distributed institutions, podcasting offers a way of providing a richer environment than text for remote students. The ready availability of podcasts on the Internet provides a resource for teachers to add global perspectives to their teaching through adding podcasts to their reading lists.

Strengths of the Resource

- It provides the ability to listen to material multiple times.
- It allows flexibility and portability (when and where to listen).
- Audio resources for blind and distance education students exist.
- There are varied opportunities for student-generated content.
- There is a relatively low-cost, low-barrier tool for both students and teachers.
- It is ideal for short preclass listening segments, for example, to address students' preconceptions.
- It has a good use of dead time while travelling or even walking between classes.

Compared to written text, the spoken word can influence both cognition (adding clarity and meaning) and motivation (by conveying directly a sense of the person creating those words). Audio is an extremely powerful medium for conveying feelings, attitudes, and atmosphere.

Listening to an iPod or similar device in public is now common practice and hence socially acceptable. These devices have a tremendous consumer appeal that works to their advantage, particularly for younger students who may be impatient with traditional forms of teaching and learning. For distance education students, the strength of podcasting lies in the potency of voice communication, which cuts through the dense text of the Internet and offers a human connection. Tutors, professors, and librarians have already begun using podcasting for myriad training and learning situations, for example, podcasts of academic journal digests and vodcasts demonstrating how to use software and operating systems.

Potential Disadvantages

- The shortcomings of audio in general appear to be in the area of providing complex and/or detailed information that needs to be heavily processed, logically deconstructed, committed to memory, or otherwise requires a great deal of concentration.
- It is not as good at conveying detail and facts in that we do not remember facts and figures from audio as easily as general opinions and arguments.
- Unlike text, audio is hard to browse and hence is a less efficient use of study time than text.
- Copyright is a potential issue if podcasts are available outside institutional firewalls. Searchability is also potentially problematic as numbers of podcasts increase. Likewise, where will podcasts be archived and by whom?

- In higher education, podcasting has been widely identified with recording lectures and then uploading them as podcasts. Unfortunately, this single use of podcasting in higher education has seemed to define its identity. This perspective needs to be changed quickly; otherwise, podcasting will become just another dissemination medium.

- If a transcript of the podcast is called for—and it usually is, both for deaf students and for students who request it for easier access or review—then the workload for preparing a podcast is increased.

Key Points for Effective Practice

1. A podcast must be professional and compelling—not the equivalent of shaky home videos. Nevertheless, good podcasting is about the message and the content, not the technology, which should be transparent.

2. Podcasts are great for conveying passion, personality, and a limited amount of content. Use text instead if there is a lot of material to cover.

3. Like all technologies, podcasting should supplement and enhance, not replace. The aim should be to more deeply engage the student with the concepts of the course, not to convey basic course material.

4. Tips for keeping the learners' attention include alternating speakers, surprising turns in the conversation, changing the pace, and relating the topic to learners' experience.

5. Devise relevant, authentic and fun projects for students to make their own podcasts. Integrate with assessment if possible.

4. E-Portfolios

E-portfolios are electronic collections of documents and other objects that support individual claims for what has been learned or achieved. In higher education, e-portfolios can be used at course, program, or institutional level. There is still lack of clarity about whether the term e-portfolio refers to the software, a particular presentation of the content, or all of the content.

The primary challenge is in engaging students to maintain their e-portfolio. This challenge is partly because of the tension between institutional control and student ownership of the e-portfolio. When the institution hosts the software and insists on its use for either assessment or accreditation, the student does not take ownership of the process. The challenge then is for course designers to find a way of integrating the use of the e-portfolio into the course, to motivate learners in maintaining them, and to support them in understanding the value of reflection.

E-portfolio software is still immature: There are a few proprietary systems, but many institutions are developing their own software, sometimes using open source approaches.

Strengths of the Resource

- At an individual level, e-portfolios could become a portable, lifelong record of achievements, and hence, there would be many advantages for individuals in maintaining them. Not only would they contain a certified record of educational qualifications, but also they would be a comprehensive resource on which to draw for job interviews and promotions.

- At a course level, e-portfolios can provide a strong impetus for students to take ownership of their learning. Given appropriate course design, e-portfolios encourage reflection on learning and hence a deeper approach to learning in which learners relate new material to concepts with which they are already familiar.

- At an institutional or program level, e-portfolios are ideal for encouraging students to set their own goals. The role of the teacher is to monitor students' progress toward the goals and to advise on strategies and resources that would help students meet their goals. The e-portfolio provides the focus for reviewing and discussing student work as well as the record of progress toward the goals.

- Through peer- and self-assessment, e-portfolios can also be used to help students develop generic skills, such as reflective and critical thinking, the ability to evaluate and provide thoughtful responses to different points of view, and the capacity to assess their own work as well as that of their peers.

- As a presentation tool, e-portfolios provide the opportunity for students to make a selection of their work for specific purposes, for example, a class presentation or job interview. E-portfolio software allows different levels of access, so for example, users can make some parts available only to themselves, other parts accessible by their teacher, and yet others open to their classmates or the Internet generally.

- E-portfolios can also be used for group work, and there is no impediment technically to a group e-portfolio. The reflective element of e-portfolios bears some resemblance to blogging, and e-portfolios can contain podcasts as evidence of learning. In short, there is convergence among many types of social networking.

Potential Disadvantages

- The communication element of e-portfolios begins to blur the boundary with a virtual learning environment and hence cause confusion or overlap in trying to establish a central discussion area.

- If an institution uses e-portfolios primarily for assessment and accountability, students soon cease to engage with e-portfolios as a life-long learning tool and view it purely as a course or degree requirement.

- Even so, teachers often need to be persistent, skilled, and dedicated to develop reflective practices in their students. E-portfolios can all too easily be used as a dumping ground for odd bits of multimedia and other course work without the student engaging with the issue of what constitutes evidence of learning.

- Because e-portfolio development on a technical level is still imma-ture, there is a major problem with compatibility, as students change institutions, graduate, and move to employment. Will e-portfolios be held by the individual or by the institution? What happens as systems develop over time? It is hard to imagine that e-portfolios can really be a lifelong learning tool either at a technical or a personal level, given the speed of technical advance. Yet, this is how their full poten-tial will eventually be reached.

Key Points for Effective Practice

1. Use formative or iterative assignments with comments from the teacher and peers.

2. Relate reflective activities to the learning outcomes of the course and prompt students to think further about issues and consider other perspectives.

3. Provide examples of reflective writing so that students understand what reflection means in an academic context and build activities around them.

4. Make it fun by giving students the tools to control the look and feel of their e-portfolio (and templates for those without the relevant skills).

5. Integrate the e-portfolio with the users' online workspace to encour-age regular updating and seamless moving from course to portfolio.

6. Provide scaffolding, advice, and resources on what constitutes evidence of learning.

5. Social Networking Sites Such as MySpace and Facebook

Social networking sites have become incredibly popular with young people almost overnight. They offer an interactive, user-submitted network of friends, personal profiles, blogs, groups, photos, music, and videos internationally. There are many such sites, some more specialized than others and some much more popular than others. MySpace is a popular, general social network that allows members to set up unique personal profiles that can be linked together through networks of friends. MySpace members can view each others' profiles, communicate with old friends and meet new friends on the service, share photos, post journals and comments, and describe their interests. Facebook is another network that was originally developed for college and university students, but it has since been made available to anyone with an e-mail address. People may then select to join one or more participating networks, such as a high school, place of employment, or geographic region. At the time of writing, Facebook had just become the number one site for photos, ahead of public sites such as Flickr, and is the sixth most-visited site in the United States.

Bulletins are posts that are posted onto a bulletin board for everyone on a user's friends list to see. Bulletins can be useful for notifying an entire, but usually a portion of, a friend's list (depending on how many friends are added) without resorting to messaging users individually. Some users choose to use bulletins as a service for delivering chain messages about, for example, politics, religion, or anything else. They have also become the primary attack point for phishing. Bulletins are deleted after 10 days. Some systems offer a groups feature, which allows a group of users to share a common page and message board. Groups can be created by anybody, and the moderator of the group can choose new members to join or to approve or deny requests to join.

Users can browse profiles by age, interests, subjects being studied, or names of friends. Then private messages can be exchanged or public notices left on their profile. In most cases, users are allowed to customize their user profile pages by entering HTML into such areas as "About Me," "I'd Like to Meet," and "Interests." Videos and Flash-based content can be included this way. Users also have the option of adding music to their profile pages.

The rationale for using social networking in education is that teachers have a responsibility to give students skills in how to cope with virtual relationships and to understand what friendship means in the new social culture that has been created by the Web 2.0 environment. It is a well-known fact that the social areas of forums used in higher education receive more messages and visits than the educational conferences. Since the introduction of educational forums in the 1990s, educators have begun to realize that social communication is an important aspect of learning.

Another rationale for the use of social networking in education is the opportunity it provides for student creativity, both in self-presentation through profiles and in artistic presentation through photos and music additions to their profiles. In short, the use of social networking in education is an acknowledgement of the social change this phenomenon has spawned. As with the social forums in educational conferencing, networking sites give students the feeling of belonging and the chance to explore their own identity.

Strengths of the Resource

- As with other Web 2.0 tools, ease of use explains much of their success. Social networking is an asynchronous tool and has many of the same advantages as educational forums: allows flexible access and keeps a written record of communications. With social networking, virtual connections often lead to real, face-to-face connections.

- Many observers claim that these types of networks are ingrained in Internet practice now and are here to stay, though the formats will change. The essence of them is the idea of joining online communities and being able to participate in them.

Potential Disadvantages

- The volatility of the youthful user base means that social network sites are unusually vulnerable to the next new thing. As quickly as users flock to one trendy Internet site, they can just as quickly move on to another, with no advance warning. Already, there is evidence of this in the rise of Facebook compared to MySpace.

- On a more serious note, there is evidence of teachers and employers viewing the profile of a student or prospective employee and seeing a very different persona than the one expected, a difference which has had negative consequences.

- There are also access issues due to the pages being designed by users with little HTML experience. (HTML is a language used to create Web pages. A Web client interprets HTML and displays documents and graphics accordingly.) A large proportion of pages do not satisfy the criteria for valid HTML or CSS (Cascading Style Sheets) laid down by the World Wide Web Consortium. (CSS is a style sheet language used to describe the presentation of a document written in a markup language.) Poorly formatted code can cause accessibility problems for those using software such as screen readers. They can also freeze up Web browsers due to malformed CSS coding, or as a result of users placing many high-bandwidth objects such as videos, graphics, and Flash in their profiles (sometimes multiple videos and soundfiles are automatically played at the same time when a profile loads).

- Finally, social networking has become an addictive pastime for many young people, as they keep monitoring their site for new activity or comments. Students even do this during lectures and seminars, a practice that has led at least one American university to ban laptops in the classroom.

Key Points for Effective Practice

1. Rather than blocking students from using social networking in the classroom, teach them how to discern when, where, and for what purpose technology may be appropriate or inappropriate.

2. Offer opportunities for students to discriminate content on social network sites, not to accept profiles at face value, and to realize that others—marketeers, university authorities, police, and so on—can and do access profiles as well as peers.

3. Provide opportunities for discussion about profiles—how to construct them and what it means to present oneself online.

6. Second Life

First opened to the public in 2003 and designed by Linden Lab in California, Second Life is a 3-D multi-user virtual environment. It is a user-defined world, owned by its residents, in which people explore, communicate, and do business. Well over 7 million people around the globe inhabit Second Life. More surprisingly, Second Life supports a fully integrated marketplace in which millions of U.S. dollars a month are transacted. The residents create their own virtual goods and services, retaining the intellectual property rights on their virtual goods and services.

Given these components, it would not appear to have significant educational potential. However, the ease with which users generate content appears to be a particular draw for Second Life in a range of educational projects, especially business and marketing programs. Each user creates an avatar and personalizes it to represent him or her in this virtual world. Avatars walk, fly, and gesture and may resemble the user's real-world appearance or may appear very different. They can communicate by chat, by sharing files and documents, and by eventually voice teleconference. This kind of virtual presence helps the development of community, especially for distance education. Second Life is not a game. It has no goal, and most resources are not restricted. Characters move through space or breathe water, and they never age or die. Massively multi-user virtual environments such as Second Life are a new type of collaborative workspace.

Adepts are convinced of the future applications of this first example of a mass market virtual reality. In fact, many see Second Life as taking Web 2.0 into Web 3.0 or even Web 3.D!

Second Life provides a unique and flexible environment for educators interested in distance learning, computer-supported cooperative work, simulation, new media studies, and corporate training. Using Second Life as a supplement to traditional classroom environments also provides new opportunities for enriching existing curricula. For distance education, Second Life offers an opportunity to weave in real-time activities.

Besides improving the quality of distance learning, educators are finding that Second Life is a good way to introduce international perspectives. Students from around the world can join in discussions and work on team projects. Unlike online forums, students in Second Life cannot lurk. Their presence is visible to all. The quality of interaction in Second Life is what distinguishes it from online forums and online games—it does not replace face-to-face communication, but it is more engaging than text-based communication.

Second Life provides an opportunity to use simulation in a safe environment to enhance experiential learning, allowing individuals to practice skills, try new ideas, and learn from their mistakes. The ability to prepare for similar real-world experiences by using Second Life as a simulation has unlimited potential! Many predict that real and virtual worlds will merge, and we will become used to the metaverse as a part of everyday life. More and more people will work in virtual worlds. Instead of frustrating hours in traffic jams to reach the workplace, work will take place in a virtual office, perhaps located on the other side of the world.

Strengths of the Resource

- The wide availability, global reach, and low barrier to entry are the essential qualities that make it a useful educational tool.

- It offers opportunities to use simulation, and the immersion experience is very powerful.

- Private islands provide the ability to create secure intranet spaces with restricted membership for students and faculty, or islands can open up to be accessible to everyone in Second Life.

- Second Life has a Help Island, and there are volunteer mentors there to help students navigate, change their avatar's appearance, learn how to build, and so on.

Potential Disadvantages

- Although Second Life is relatively easy to use, without a solid foundation, students can struggle while trying to learn the navigational skills necessary to complete assignments. Frustration can lead to disengagement, and then it is hard to encourage students to reengage.

- The benefit of being entirely user-driven has the disadvantage that it depends entirely on users to make it a learning experience. It is essentially a blank space.

- At the moment, Second Life supports only text chat. Many residents interested in serious business and educational applications consider the lack of a native voice chat system a significant disadvantage and use Skype conferences to talk to other avatars. (Skype is an Internet telephony service provider that offers free calling between computers and low-cost calling to regular telephones.)

- Although Second Life is a great first step in virtual world building, the environment looks cartoonish, and there are rendering artifacts due to the need to balance realism with bandwidth and computing resources. Adepts predict that in a few years, computer-generated virtual worlds for end users will have photorealistic visual quality.

- The appropriateness of some Second Life content for students is an issue. As with the Web itself, there is a range of seedy activity available to users: gambling, stripping, and virtual prostitution are easy to find if one looks for them. Partly because of that, Linden Lab has set up a teen version of the world known as Teen Second Life.

Key Points for Effective Practice

1. Use the many available tutorials and Second Life support materials to help students become proficient users.

2. Second Life provides an opportunity to think outside the box, to practice the true constructivist principles, and to empower students to learn rather than to be taught.

Constraints

Perhaps the most significant factor that will constrain the development of Web 2.0 for education is the degree of unresearched, overblown, and unsubstantiated claims currently being made about the effect that these tools will have on education in general and on young learners in particular. So much Web 2.0 literature focuses on the potential of these tools to

- provide anytime, anywhere learning;
- allow students to become publishers, teachers, and creators;
- give access to vast amounts of content;
- increase students' opportunities to interact with other students, teachers, and experts; and
- extend learning to the traditionally excluded, to the disabled, and to the global community.

The list goes on, and most of these potentialities are perfectly accurate. The more relevant issue is whether any are being actualized! Just because the tools allow these facilities is no guarantee that they are wanted or desirable or without other insuperable barriers.

The kind of enthusiasm that Web 2.0 has generated is not unique; in fact, it is common to most social initiatives, particularly those related to education. The problem is that it creates unreasonable expectations and an inevitable backlash. Already, people have seen many commentators objecting to the very category Web 2.0, by downplaying its importance and innovatory qualities. Whether it is new, different, or merely evolutionary, what the Web was originally meant to be, or all of these, the fact is that it is a force to be reckoned with in education. This requires research, experimentation, and an open, but not a gung-ho, attitude.

Issues for Students

Although many commentators have written about the readiness of the young to use Web 2.0 tools and the effects this readiness is having on their perceptions of learning (e.g., Oblinger & Oblinger, 2005; Prensky, 2001a, 2001b), there is also evidence that some students do not welcome e-learning, much less the use of Web 2.0 tools for education. Although this preference may well change with time, it will probably take considerably longer than the enthusiasts assume. Kirkwood and Price (2005), for instance, noted that online access remains problematic for some students and access from work or public machines is frequently not adequate for the kinds of online activities that Web 2.0 tools require. They noted that

- Access to Information and Communications Technologies (ICT) is rarely ideal and unrestricted: Learners often need to share computing and communication facilities with others. Course design should reflect this and not be overdependent upon ICT.

- Getting access to and downloading remote resources can be very time consuming when working via a dial-up network: In certain circumstances such activities will not be sanctioned. (p. 271)

These researchers point to another student issue: the blurring of the distinction between full-time and part-time study, such that many of the constraints that used to be unique to part-time, distance students are now faced by those ostensibly engaged in full-time study—namely, combining employment with study (Kirkwood & Price, 2005, p. 258). This means that lack of time and the need for flexible study patterns are major considerations for course designers.

The degree to which young learners are using Web 2.0 tools masks another student issue: The need to provide training for those, possibly a small minority, who are not skilled in the use of a range of software that might be used in formal courses. This creates problems for course design in that it is necessary to cater for novices as well as to provide stimulating and challenging activities for the very experienced users. In terms of the kind of training required, there are further headaches: Novices (whether students or tutors) want personalized, just-in-time training opportunities, not formalized, standardized courses at a time convenient to the providing institution. Despite the fact that commentators have been predicting for nearly 20 years that training will no longer be required as software becomes more intuitive and more widely used, every evaluation study still cites training as a continuing requirement (e.g., Weyers, Adamson, & Murie, 2004).

Related to technology training is the need for training in information literacy. Recent research in a Horizon Report noted that

> Contrary to the conventional wisdom, the information literacy skills of new students are not improving as the post-1993 Internet boomlet enters college. At the same time, in a sea of user-created content, collaborative work, and instant access to information of varying quality, the skills of critical thinking, research, and evaluation are increasingly required to make sense of the world. (New Media Consortium and EDUCAUSE Learning Initiative, 2007, p. 4)

Guinee and Eagleton (2006) have observed students taking notes from online sources and have discovered that they tend to copy large blocks of text rather than paraphrase for future reference. When they come to use the material, they have lost track of the distinction between their own words and material copied from other sources. Furthermore, they do not assess the quality of the ideas copied, nor do they try to produce a synthesis from the materials they have copied. In short, they have the technical skills to find, cut, and paste information but not the pedagogical literacy skills to make it their own.

Several studies seem to indicate that students want only a moderate amount of new learning tools to be used in formal courses (e.g., Kvavik & Caruso, 2005) and that most students are very strategic in their use of these tools. For example, Kear (2004) found that

> students will participate in a discussion forum if they see sufficient benefits for the time invested—and there are different kinds of benefits for different students. Some students will only take part if the course assessment gives them marks for doing so. Some will take part because they gain information and help from others, which supports their learning. Others value interaction for its own sake, and gain support and motivation from other students in the forum. (p. 162)

Students continue to value face-to-face teaching, though it is unclear whether they simply say this in response to questionnaires, regardless of whether they actually attend, or whether they equate face-to-face with value for money, or whether they are suspicious of online forms of learning. Course design must, therefore, address two aspects of the student perspective:

1. The need to keep the student workload very much in mind—there is evidence that overloaded courses lead to surface-level learning, and activities and online interaction are much more time-consuming than is usually acknowledged.

2. The need to plan every aspect of the course for strategic learners— that is, every element must deliver learning value for time spent.

These are both difficult elements to judge accurately when designing a course, as there is a large unpredictable element in online learning. Having the honesty to admit that some element has not worked, as well as the perceptiveness and resources to change it, are the best ways of approaching the problem.

Reflection as a Learned Skill

The expanding use of e-portfolios and blogging in higher education has uncovered another shortcoming of many students: the misunderstanding of, or inability to, reflect on their learning. Yet, the practice of reflection has become a prominent tool for learning in recent years. One definition of it is the following:

> Reflection is a form of mental processing that we use to fulfill a purpose or to achieve some anticipated outcome. It is applied to gain a better understanding of relatively complicated or unstructured ideas and is largely based on the reprocessing of knowledge, understanding and possibly emotions that we already possess. (Moon, 2005, p. 1)

Successful uses of e-portfolios in higher education inevitably ascribe a key role to reflection in the design of the course. As the definition suggests, structuring the practice of reflection transforms it into a learning experience. For example, the teacher may provide prompts to help students connect their reading with the core issues of the course. The affective dimension of reflection is also an important part of the process and one with which students may well need guidance. They may need encouragement to use the first person in their reflective writing and to acknowledge the significance of feelings in the learning process.

One effective way of structuring reflective activities is to relate them to the learning objectives of the course. Documents, project plans, and an annotated bibliography might also be organized around the objectives along with the reflective pieces of work. Frequent feedback may be required to prompt students to think further about issues and to consider other perspectives.

Reflection is not something to be carried out only at the end of an activity or learning experience. Reflection should be a continuous process throughout the study period. At the beginning of a course, it is useful for students to reflect on what they do not know, what they would like to learn, and how they want to go about it. Students might then work in small groups to identify useful resources to address their knowledge gaps. They might also form larger discussion groups to evaluate the resources they have found. Students might be required to keep a learning journal throughout the course in which they record their thoughts, observations, feelings, and questions. It is up to the teacher or tutor to direct students' attention to other resources or to further questions. This process is facilitated by e-portfolio software, which allows the student to share parts or all of the growing portfolio with named people.

Many students will need help in understanding what reflection means in an academic context. For this reason, it is useful to provide examples of reflective writing and to build an activity around them by asking students to evaluate what learning is being gained through the reflective process. One of the barriers to learning through reflection is that students rely on formulaic responses to reflection exercises. This may be prevented by studying examples of authentic reflection and by the teacher referring to the examples if students appear to be floundering.

Issues for Teachers

Ever since the introduction of online learning in the early 1990s, there have been reports about the ways in which technology changes faculty roles because it changes their workload and responsibilities. The change is usually regarded as more work for the same pay and recognition. This perception on the part of teachers has four related elements: workload, promotion, skills, and intellectual property rights.

Workload

Parker's (2003) analysis of over 100 articles concluded that it is intrinsic rewards that motivate most teachers to develop innovatory, online elements in their courses: personal satisfaction, flexible scheduling, and reaching nontraditional students. Using new technologies and developing new ideas also enter the equation. Maguire's (2005) study showed that if the necessary extrinsic rewards are offered, for example, decreased workload, release time, stipends, and technology support, then the usual barriers are more easily overcome.

Workload and time requirements are difficult to measure, a difficulty which perhaps explains contradictory evidence from studies claiming that moving to online teaching takes more time and those which show that it does not. Sammons and Ruth (2007) concluded that

> time requirements are difficult to measure, as they are dependent on the subject, number of students, instructor skills, type of technologies used in the course, and course quality, but the clear finding is that for most full timers the conversion to online mode is a significant user of previously discretionary time. Regardless of whether the workload actually increases, certainly the pace of work and the working style change. The time spent teaching online may not actually be greater, but the "chunking" or flow of tasks online is different. ("The 24/7 Professor," para. 3)

Nevertheless, there is some evidence that the amount of interaction with students actually increases. Because of the individualized nature of e-mail communication, interactions are more numerous and personalized than in many traditional courses (AAUP, 2002). For some faculty, the increase in student-teacher interaction may be viewed as a disincentive: for others, it acts as an incentive.

Faculty also complain about changes in the scale of their teaching, and this is linked to government- and university-level policies and pushes to save money. They often report increasing staff workloads, first-year transition problems, and problems arising from the increasing diversity of students. Although generally critical of pushes for flexible delivery through the use of Internet-based technologies, these new modes of delivery are acknowledged as the most obvious way to deal with the larger student numbers. However, many faculty members continue to express reservations about more flexible modes because although they are an obvious response to larger student numbers, they are not viewed as solutions to problems caused by these large numbers. They fear that online solutions will diminish community involvement on campus, personal contact, self-development, and one-to-one contact.

Promotion

The traditional processes of recognition and promotion act as a barrier to faculty venturing into the Web 2.0 environment. The 2007 *Horizon Report* noted that

> Academic review and faculty rewards are increasingly out of sync with new forms of scholarship. The trends toward digital expressions of scholarship and more interdisciplinary and collaborative work continue to move away from the standards of traditional peer-reviewed paper publication. New

forms of peer review are emerging, but existing academic practices of specialization and long-honored notions of academic status are persistent barriers to the adoption of new approaches. Given the pace of change, the academy will grow more out of step with how scholarship is actually conducted until constraints imposed by traditional tenure and promotion processes are eased. (New Media Consortium & EDUCAUSE Learning Initiative, 2007, p. 4)

Related to the issue of promotion is the perception that using these tools will de-professionalize the faculty role. As content is increasingly available online and particularly in open-content sites (see, for example, the Open Learn Web site by the Open University, http://www.open.ac.uk/openlearn/home.php), some academics see their traditional role as content experts being undermined. Chisholm (2006) noted that

Faculty who use commercial course management software become almost invisible . . . this invisibility contributes to the illusion that the twenty-first century instructor is a generic, easily replaceable part in a larger Automated Education Machine. ("Product Delivery," para. 8)

Instead of seeing Web 2.0 tools as an opportunity, instructors see it as a threat to their traditional ways of working, to their well-established view of their curriculum and their notions of teaching and learning. They perceive that their role as teachers will be diminished as the role of technology increases, even though most studies suggest that the role of the teacher will change but not necessarily diminish. Although it is true that the nature of the interaction with students becomes computer mediated, the quality of interaction often improves—moving from question and answer to genuine discussion and debate.

Skills

Lack of the necessary skills to use Web 2.0 and other online tools is a recurring theme in the literature on inhibitors to innovation in education. There are two aspects of this skill shortage: lack of experience with the technology and lack of understanding about how to use it for learning. Many teachers are worried about developing online courses on their own time with few institutional resources. Without assistance from instructional designers or graphic designers, faculty may feel that the task is too daunting (O'Quinn & Corry, 2002). Wilson (2001) found that faculty frequently expressed inhibitions about not possessing the necessary and progressive technological savvy or having the requisite technical support for themselves.

Technical skills need to be offered by the institution, although they may best be acquired through personal practice, collegial interaction, or one-to-one sessions with friends. The same applies to pedagogical skills, which include the following:

- Online community building: Academics have to learn how to welcome, encourage, support, and control students in an online environment. They also have to encourage intraclass participation (e.g., introducing and connecting students).

- Designing online activities: Academics need to be able to design learning activities that can effectively be carried out online.

- Discussion forum: There is a wide range of skills to learn to facilitate an effective online discussion. These include discussion activity design and set-up, discussion introduction and close-down, discussion moderation, and assessment of contributions.

- Information literacy: Academics have to develop skills to help students find and manage information. (McSporran & Young, 2004, "Online Pedagogical Skills")

Academics have always seen themselves as content experts not media experts. Online learning is increasingly demanding a different set of skills.

Intellectual Property Rights

Many faculty members see the move from face-to-face teaching to online learning as a loss of their rights over their teaching material. Open content initiatives by universities are an obvious example, but even material posted in the institutional virtual learning environment may be considered the property of that institution. Chisholm (2006) noted that

> Teachers can lose their intellectual property when they upload course materials to course-management programs. In a 2000 article published in the *Atlantic Monthly*, Eyal Press and Jennifer Washburn reveal that many teachers who develop courses on WebCT and similar systems lose the rights to their material after they post it, thereby enabling the vendor or the university to sell the material to an online school or to hire an adjunct to "redeliver" the same material for considerably less money. Many universities have rewritten their faculty handbooks or intellectual property agreements so that the university or the course-management system owns the course material. Their doing so is part of a larger effort to turn faculty work into a currency that retains its value long after a teacher graduates or is laid off. ("Product Delivery," para. 5)

Chisholm (2006) argued that faculty who knowingly or unknowingly give up ownership of their course materials contribute to the erosion of intellectual freedom and that when individual course material is distributed to others as part of a standardized curriculum initiative, that freedom is compromised. Furthermore, distance education courses are often treated by universities like inventions, with the result that the university treats them more like items for which they own the patent and for which they will return a portion of the royalties to the faculty member. This is in contrast to the traditional classroom where the faculty members have the full rights to publish their materials and all royalties return to the faculty member (Estabrook, 1999).

These perceptions and attitudes are clearly at odds with the social changes happening on the Web regarding what is often called the gift culture, the notions of user-generated content and the evidence from research on socially constructed knowledge.

Implications

The beginning of this chapter asked the question about whether students actually want their courses to use Web 2.0 tools. A number of studies have begun to tackle this question by asking students what technologies they currently use for their study (Conole, de Laat, Darby, & Dillon, 2006) and how much technology they want to see used on courses (Kvavik & Caruso, 2005). The evidence from these and other studies is that students are definitely using a wide range of tools, for example, mobile devices, social bookmarking, Google, and so on, and they do want a moderate amount of information technology to be used in their courses. However, because the number of academics engaging thoroughly with Web 2.0 tools and designing courses that embed these technologies (rather than using them peripherally or using them in Web 1.0 ways) is so few, it is still too early to say whether students in general would welcome learning through these tools rather than merely using them as peripheral support tools.

Obviously, it would be foolish to throw away centuries of structured knowledge-building in a headlong rush to adopt social networking practices. Clearly, there is a place and role for knowledge to be organized for the learner by others with acknowledged expertise. Newcomers to a knowledge domain will find it more efficient to access a structured resource than to try to grapple with multiple representations arising from social shaping. Finding the balance between the two extremes is the art of the teacher!

There is considerable argument over whether Web 2.0 tools are a revolution or merely an evolution. I will not add to the debate, as it seems irrelevant to my purpose here. What instructors need to understand is how people can learn in this environment and how they as course designers can enhance learning through the right tools and applications.

The key points suggested are as follows:

1. Instructors need to trust the power of peer learning and the importance of self-expression as vehicles for developing the kinds of process skills that are of increasing value in a socially networked world.

2. The learning process is more important and more lasting than the recollection of any particular content and hence should be

given more significance in course design than the transfer of information.

3. The art of course design is to capture the essence of the informal uses of Web 2.0 tools while introducing structure and direction into students' engagement with them.

4. Passing control of learning to learners will be a challenging and threatening request for many lecturers and most institutions. This is where the essential feature of social networking conflicts with educational practice.

5. Changes to existing courses require maintaining a balance among different kinds of learning opportunities.

The Educational Future of Web 2.0

P. Anderson (2007) suggested three elements of current Web 2.0 practice that look to have a profound impact on education in the future. The first of these is the notion of the wisdom of crowds, or the power of groups. This emergence of online social networking communities could create a significant threat to universities as the traditional repositories of wisdom and knowledge creation. P. Anderson's (2007) corollary to this possibility is that the issue of online identity and privacy will increasingly become the focus of tension and acrimony. The rise of blogs particularly is already beginning to affect journalism and newspaper circulation. How will universities be affected by the wisdom of the crowd rather than the wisdom of the expert?

P. Anderson's (2007) second prediction is that the growth of user-generated content will increase the rise of the amateur and the culture of "do it yourself" (p. 53). These two will also challenge the status of the academy as the elite source of knowledge. P. Anderson (2007) said that "These challenges may not be as profound as some of the more ardent proponents of Web 2.0 indicate, but there will be serious challenges none the less" (p. 53).

Finally, P. Anderson (2007) predicted that there will be profound intellectual property debates over the ownership of the huge amounts of data that Web 2.0 is generating, along with new tools for aggregating and processing it.

All of these futures point to a large-scale transformation toward a more participatory form of learning, where teachers and learners share the teaching and learning roles, where information is found in blogs and wikis, controlled through RSS feeds and connected through social networking sites. The participatory culture is empowering, and while the tools will change, the genie of participation will be reluctant to go back into the teacher-centered bottle of traditional education.

References

AAUP (American Association of University Professors) Special Committee on Distance Education and Intellectual Property Issues. (2002). *Suggestions and guidelines: Sample language for institutional policies and contract language.* Retrieved December 29, 2008, from American Association of University Professors Web site: http://www.aaup.org/AAUP/issues/DE/sampleDE.htm

Anderson, C. (2006, July). People power. *Wired Magazine, 14*(7). Retrieved December 29, 2008, from http://www.wired.com/wired/archive/14.07/people.html

Anderson, P. (2007). *What is Web 2.0? Ideas, technologies and implications for education* (TechWatch report). Retrieved December 29, 2008, from http://www.jisc.ac.uk/publications/publications/twweb2.aspx

Bloch, M. (n.d.). *Web 2.0, mashups and social networking—What is it all about?* Retrieved December 29, 2008, from http://www.tamingthebeast.net/articles6/web2-mashups-social-network.htm

Boettcher, J. (2007). Ten core principles for designing effective learning environments: Insights from brain research and pedagogical theory. *Innovate Journal of Online Education, 3*(3). Retrieved December 29, 2008, from http://innovateonline.info/index.php?view=issue&id=18

Boyd, D. (2006). *Social network sites: My definition.* Retrieved December 29, 2008, from http://www.zephoria.org/thoughts/archives/2006/11/10/social_network_1.html

Carlson, S. (2005, October). The Net generation goes to college [Electronic version]. *The Chronicle of Higher Education 54*(7) p. 34A. Retrieved December 29, 2008, from http://chronicle.com/free/v52/i07/07a03401.htm

Chisholm, J. (2006). Pleasure and danger in online teaching and learning. *Academe Online, 92*(6). Retrieved December 29, 2008, from http://www.aaup.org/AAUP/pubsres/academe/2006/ND/Feat/chis.htm

Conole, G., de Laat, M., Darby, J. & Dillon, T. (2006). *An in-depth case study of students' experiences of e-learning—How is learning changing? Final report of the JISC-funded LXP Learning Experiences Study project.* Available at http://www.jisc.ac.uk

Cross, J. (2007). *Designing a Web-based learning ecology.* Retrieved December 29, 2008, from http://informl.com/?p=697#more-697

Duffy, T. M., & Cunningham, D. J. (1996). Constructivism: Implications for the design and delivery of instruction. In D. H. Jonassen (Ed.), *Handbook of research for educational communications and technology* (pp. 170–198). New York: Macmillan Library Reference.

Estabrook, L. (1999, April 10). *New forms of distance education: Opportunities for students, threats to institutions.* Presentation at the Association of College and Research Libraries National Conference, Detroit, MI.

Guinee, K., & Eagleton, M. (2006). Spinning straw into gold: Transforming information into knowledge during web-based research. *English Journal, 95*(4), 46–52.

Kapp, K. (2006). *Gadgets, games and gizmos: Informal learning at Nick.com.* Retrieved December 29, 2008, from http://karlkapp.blogspot.com

Karpati, A. (2002). *Net generation.* Retrieved December 29, 2008, from http://www.elearningeuropa.info/directory/index.php?page=doc&doc_id=1573&doclng=6

Kear, K. (2004). Peer learning using asynchronous discussion systems in distance education. *Open Learning, 19*(2), 151–164.

Kirkwood, A., & Price, L. (2005). Learners and learning in the twenty-first century: What do we know about students' attitudes towards and experiences of information and communication technologies that will help us design courses? *Studies in Higher Education, 30*(3), 257–274.

Kvavik, R., & Caruso, J. (2005). *ECAR study of students and information technology, 2005: Convenience, connection, control, and learning.* Boulder, CO: EDUCAUSE. Retrieved December 29, 2008, from http://www.EDUCAUSE .edu/ir/library/pdf/ers0506/rs/ERS0506w.pdf

Livingstone, S., & Bober, M. (2005). *UK children go online.* Retrieved December 29, 2008, from http://www.york.ac.uk/res/e-society/projects/1.htm

Maguire, L. (2005). Literature review—Faculty participation in online distance education: Barriers and motivators. *Online Journal of Distance Learning Administration, 8*(1). Retrieved December 29, 2008, from http://www.westga .edu/%7Edistance/ojdla/spring81/maguire81.pdf

McSporran, M., & Young, S. (2004, November) Critical skills for online teaching. *Bulletin of Applied Computing and Information Technology, 2*(3). Retrieved December 29, 2008, from http://www.naccq.ac.nz/bacit/0203/ 2004McSporran_OnlineSkills.htm

Moon, J. (2005). Learning through reflection. *Higher Education Academy Guide for Busy Academics* (no. 4). Retrieved December 29, 2008, from http://www.heacademy .ac.uk/resources/detail/id69_guide_for_busy_academics_no4_moon

New Media Consortium and the EDUCAUSE Learning Initiative. (2007). *The Horizon report, 2007 edition.* Retrieved December 29, 2008, from http://www.nmc.org/horizon/2007/report

Oblinger, D., & Oblinger, J. (Eds.). (2005). *Educating the Net generation.* Boulder, CO: Educause. Retrieved December 29, 2008, from http://www.EDUCAUSE .edu/Books/635

O'Quinn, L., & Corry, M. (2002). Factors that deter faculty from participating in distance education. *Online Journal of Distance Learning Administration, 5*(4). Retrieved December 29, 2008, from http://www.westga.edu/~distance/ojdla/ winter54/Quinn54.htm

O'Reilly, T. (2005). *What is Web 2.0: Design patterns and business models for the next generation of software.* Retrieved December 29, 2008, from http://www.oreillynet.com/pub/a/oreilly/tim/news/2005/09/30/what-is-web-20.html?page=1

Parker, A. (2003). Motivation and incentives for distance faculty. *Online Journal of Distance Learning Administration, 6*(3). Retrieved December 29, 2008, from http://www.westga.edu/~distance/ojdla/fall63/parker63.htm

Poster, M. (1990). *The mode of information: Poststructuralism and social contexts.* Cambridge, UK: Polity Press.

Prensky, M. (2001a). Digital natives, digital immigrants. *On the Horizon, 9*(5), 1–6.

Prensky, M. (2001b). Digital natives, digital immigrants, part 2: Do they really think differently? *On the Horizon, 9*(6), 1–6.

Raines, C. (2002). *Generations at work: Managing millennials.* Retrieved December 29, 2008, from http://www.generationsatwork.com/articles/millenials.htm

Rudd, T., Sutch, D., & Facer, K. (2006) Opening education: Towards new learning networks. *Futurelab.* Retrieved December 29, 2008, http://www.futurelab

.org.uk/resources/publications-reports-articles/opening-education-reports/
Opening-Education-Report121

Sammons, M., & Ruth, S. (2007). The invisible professor and the future of virtual faculty. *International Journal of Technology and Distance Education, 4*(1). Retrieved December 29, 2008, from http://www.itdl.org/Journal/Jan_07/article01.htm

Siemens, G. (2004, December 12). *Connectivism: A learning theory for the digital age.* Retrieved December 29, 2008, from http://www.elearnspace.org/Articles/connectivism.htm

Stevens, V. (2006). Revisiting multiliteracies in collaborative learning environments: Impact on teacher professional development. *Teaching English as a Second Language, 10*(2). Retrieved December 29, 2008, from http://www-writing.berkeley.edu/TESL-EJ/ej38/int.html

Veen, W. (2003). A new force for change: Homo Zappiens. *The Learning Citizen, 7.* Retrieved December 29, 2008, from http://www.friends-partners.org/GLOSAS/Global_University/Global%20University%20System/The%20Learning%20Citizen/LCCN_Newsletter_N7.pdf

Weyers, J., Adamson, M., & Murie, D. (2004). *2004 student e-learning survey, University of Dundee.* Retrieved December 29, 2008, from http://www.dundee.ac.uk/learning/dol/ELS_final_report.pdf

Wilson, C. (2001). Faculty attitudes about distance learning. *EDUCAUSE Quarterly, 2.* Retrieved December 29, 2008, from http://www.EDUCAUSE.edu/ir/library/pdf/eqm0128.pdf

Chapter 5

Applying Social Systems Thinking and Community Informatics Thinking in Education

Building Efficient Online Learning Design Culture in Universities

Pierre-Léonard Harvey

The viability and relevance of the educational profession will be judged based on the extent to which we spearhead the evolution of education, place ourselves in the service of transforming education, and help create just systems of learning and development for future generations. We now realize that systems design is a missing inquiry in education. Confronted with "new societal realities" and new educational requirements of a rapidly changing world, people look to the professional education community for guidance in the design of their educational systems. This expectation confronts us with the challenge to individually and collectively acquire systems thinking and develop competence in systems design and practice. Education creates the future, and there is no more important task and no more noble calling than participating in the creation.

—Bela Banathy (2000a, 2000b)

T he purpose of the online learning community and the computer supported collaborative learning community (CSCL) is to challenge our understanding of how visions, epistemologies, theories, systems thinking, and design thinking and practices are interrelated (Harvey, 2006a) and to contribute to an ecosystemic, evolutive, and socioconstructivist learning perspective within information and communication technologies (Frielick 2004; Laszlo, 2001).

Online learning and CSCL do not have an adequate transformational, conceptual, and practical framework to formally and systematically consider new learning spaces designed for reforming our education system. Stagnation in education cannot be explained by a shortage of theories about online learning on a microlevel (class or course level) or on an individual level (mind and cognition), but rather by a lack of models for sustainable growth and change on the mesolevel (virtual communities of practice) and the macrolevel (social systems, learning networks, and educational ecosystem) (Cavallo, 2004). Too many traditional approaches in instructional design are being used, usage which prevents larger-scale projects from emerging. Furthermore, instructional design theories of human learning are too exclusively based on a classroom learning experience. The behavioral, organizational, and psychological approaches serve only a small part of the entire learning experience. Therefore, we must explore complex models of growth in several domains related to many fields of lifelong learning activities in a broader sociocultural context (Fischer, 2007). Moreover, the importance and relevance of social software, communityware, and community informatics design in education is underestimated (Anderson 2004; Barab, Kling, & Gray, 2004; Bieber, McFall, Rice, & Gurstein, 2008). Yet, they are present in so many aspects of the online lives of our students and our own professional environment. Social software such as blogs, wikis, time-sharing environment, collaborative filters, tagging, and communityware (e.g., del.icio.us, YouTube, MySpace, SecondLife, LinkedIn and other tools) are increasingly becoming part of the design of an online environment.

Contemporary research treats the communities of practice and virtual communities of learning as important objects in social system design theories and sociotechnical design fields (Dron, 2007). Thus, we must reconsider how our learning design strategies apply to worldwide collaborative learning platforms such as Moodle. The resulting online ecosystem and interactions between large numbers of actors with new roles in the process of online learning design should be investigated through suitable social and cultural lenses. I suggest some key principles and terms taken from social constructivism (or sociocultural theory) (Bonk & Cunnigham, 1998) and integrate them with social software design principles (Dron, 2007) as applied to open software online learning environments conceived as a social system: the approach of community informatics design (Bourgeois & Horam, 2007; Harvey, 2005, 2006a).

It appears that traditional online learning design is often indicative of the learning field's reluctance to change (Siemens, 2005). In spite of radical new learning opportunities created by social system design, evolutionary learning communities (Laszlo, 2001), collaborative technologies, and participative culture in which learners act as designers of their own knowledge building communities (Fischer, 2006), online learning and CSCL are still largely based on design theories created during the early 1900s to 1960s. Meanwhile, the environment in which we are immersed has evolved dramatically. Media and technology have changed. The whole social ecosystem has been altered by new worlds of experience. The world is now connected, networked, internetworked, and we cannot continue to rely on the old static methodologies used to foster learning and educational requirements and translate them into online learning, (Fallman, 2003; Fisher et al., 2007; Fox, 2002; Haythornthwaite et al., 2007; Jenlink, 2001). We are facing a colossal evolution where sequential learning development and the waterfall model borrowed from software and engineering system sciences remain strangely outdated. Society is becoming a highly independent social system, therefore, it is our responsibility and challenge to orient and give a sense of ethics to our future. As Banathy pointed out in his seminal book, *Designing Social System in a Changing World* (1996),

> These changes touch the lives of every person, family, community, and nation and define the future of humanity. However, we are entering the twenty first century with organizations designed during the nineteenth. Improvement or restructuring of existing systems, based on the design of the industrial machine age, does not work anymore. Only a radical and fundamental change of perspectives and purposes, and the redesign of our organizations and social systems, will satisfy the new realities and requirements of our era. (p. 1)

Moreover, the significance of design thinking and systems thinking for the design of online learning and CSCL has gained much recognition in recent years. In comparison to design thinking (Owen, 2008), scholarly discussion about systems thinking has a much longer history and includes multiple and divergent perspectives. In this chapter, I propose a new approach for learning design and online learning design, the community informatics design approach based on Banathy's social system view, to provide a broader conceptual framework for online learning in the 21st century, and to elaborate new possibilities of fostering a design culture through the movement of open source virtual communities of learning (or knowledge-building communities).

In an effort to make the movement more concrete, I present the implementation of an online learning collaborative design environment that is manifested in the domain of free-open source software environment: the Moodle platform. Two examples are presented, including the Moodle community of multiperspectives designers that we have implemented at University of Quebec in Montreal (Fusaro, 2005). Moodle proposes the base for the emergence, development, management, and design of an evolutionary online learning environment by taking a spontaneous learner-centered, socioconstructivist, and sociocultural view of knowledge management in collaborative online learning communities via new social computing learning tools and design across multiple users and stakeholders. Therefore, the CSCL communities of learners and designers-users are good examples of evolutionary learning communities (Laszlo, 2001; Norman & Porter, 2007; Pettenatti & Cigognini, 2007; Scardamalia & Bereiter, 1994) that can act as drivers of invention and innovation dedicated to radically transform online education (Smith & Brown, 2006). They can contribute to the evolution of public understanding of online learning, and furthermore, they can mobilize and engage people to develop their own personal and collective skills in designing creative online learning systems in the information society.

Research and practice in online learning and CSCL are inherently transdisciplinary, requiring collaboration between those who design technology and a broad range of communities of practice in the public, private, and university spheres who seek to understand the nature and use of social system design in learning environments and their organizational effects. Enabling, establishing, and maintaining this transdisciplinary research (Nicolescu, 1996), particularly given the longitudinal character of the research involved, requires us to move forward in a coordinated manner to enable design learning and to build effective online learning environments in the future. In the last section of the chapter, I outline an online learning design research agenda for the years to come.

This effort is built upon my participation in community informatics since the beginning of the Rheingold appeal for research in this field at the end of the 1980s. During the last 15 years, I have also participated in online learning research and have identified many relevant concepts in design thinking, computer mediated communication, and related disciplines such as human computer interaction and distance education. In the last decade, the research in this field has focused on open source computer aided design in the Laboratoire de communautique appliquée of the University of Quebec in Montreal. More recently, I had the opportunity to contribute to the Moodle Committee of the University of Quebec in Montreal, Canada. The successful implementation of the Moodle platform in my own institution and my participation in that experience have led to a few reflections about the role of universities in the knowledge society beyond their walls and their traditional roles in research and training.

From Socially Designed Learning to Socially Designed Thinking and Community Informatics

Systems thinking has played a critical role in the historical development of instructional technology since the beginning of the 1990s. Unfortunately, the instructional models that adopt systems thinking were once widely recognized in the online learning and CSCL context and reflect first order cybernetics and sequential instructional design with a few feedback loops. Despite the positive recognition of its value to education and training online, the essence of systems thinking is reduced to a systematic view (and not a systemic view), greatly distorting its true spirit. Although socioconstructivist learning, blended learning, and situated learning gain more attention in the open source movement and in the instructional design communities of users-designers such as the Moodlers' socioconstructivist community of practice, the way systems thinking has been interpreted and applied in online learning until recently can be challenged. At the fundamental level, one of the main challenges is to cultivate communities of practice of user-designer system thinkers for online learning design (Stephan, 2006; Taylor et al., 2004; Warfield, 1976, 1990; Ye & Fisher, 2007). That is to say, we must build a design culture to foster future online learning design.

Banathy (1996) has enumerated several definitions of design from various design disciplines such as architecture, artistic fields, software engineering, and communication. He discovered that design is practiced by many professions in various ways and is applied in very different contexts. Cross (1974, 1984) claimed that design is an important and unique mode of culture, like science culture and humanities culture, and that the sociocultural aspect of design is receiving more and more attention in the instructional design community. Banathy is probably the best-known scholar to interpret Cross's thinking about design culture. Banathy stated, 30 years after Jay Forrester (1971), that it is important to build a design culture by cultivating the general public's collective design competence. In this regard, the Moodlers' open source community has been extended not only to designing learning resources but also to cultivate design thinking and systems thinking on a scale never before seen. We have at our disposal a unique, distributed technology of intelligence for leveraging design thinking and the culture of our universities and learning society. Therefore, we will indicate how universities and the open source movement can engage learners and large virtual communities of learners in envisioning the future of their learning systems and systemically designing their own online learning environments. The massive innovation of a self-organized, open source design culture such as Moodle and the informatics communities of users-designers represents the next future social learning revolution. I now focus on Banathy's social system thinking and briefly draw on Senge's (1990) systems thinking and Engeström's (1987) activity theory to explore a possible foundation for community informatics design and its relevance in open source social system design to online learning in the service of massive innovation.

Experimenting With Collaborative Online Social System Design: A New Approach to Socioconstructivist Virtual Communities of Social Designers

The Internet and particularly the Web open source movement continue to support the emergence and growth of communities of practice and more and more virtual communities of designers. Free open source socioconstructivist virtual communities of social designers (FOSSVCSD) are attracting a lot of attention in educational communities as best practices in learning objects, resources, and design artifacts shared by both learners and instructors. The socioconstructivist foundation on which they are built continues to influence teaching and learning, content quality, and CSCL tools in many projects around the world (Mor, Tholander, & Holmberg, 2005). These CSCL environments can be studied within the fields of collaborative human-computer interaction as the computer-supported cooperative work (CSCW) domain and through the lens of community informatics design (Bieber et al., 2007; Cavallo, 2004; de Moor, 2005; Fischer, 2006, 2007; Gurstein, 2003; Harvey, 1995, 2004a, 2006b; Rheingold, 1993).

Over the next few years, the cooperative-collaborative aspect of learning and knowing in FOSSVCSD will keep drawing the attention of community informatics designers as they are pioneering and challenging social system design theories and methodologies in large sociotechnical systems. The socioconstructivist view of community informatics theory of learning in the CSCL environment shows that people construct knowledge by self-designing their online learning environment. This CSCL view of community informatics is very different from the analysis of cooperation through the eyes of content analysis or the semiotic perspective of discourse analysis that have dominated computer-mediated communication (CMC) research since the beginning of the 1990s. The focus has passed from the electronic discourse of the learner to the broader social context of cosocial system design (Engeström, 1987), trying to discover the ways different interactional patterns of knowing are enabled across multiple sites. Community informatics designers are among the first designers to integrate social system design and sociotechnical perspectives to enable participants in online communities in the service of learning. Some of them propose the term *supporting enabling communities* (Bieber et al., 2007), where collaborative designs guide the analysis, pattern of participation, and principles of knowledge appropriation among people and members of designing and learning communities.

According to the writings of Orlikowski (2002, as cited in Falin, 2007), it is relatively safe to say that although *designerly knowing*[1] is often the kind of knowing inseparable from the knower; it is not developed in isolation. Designerly knowing does not limit itself within organizational boundaries either. The process of designing is itself a social practice of learning to design. It is in fact the social practice that is essential to building designerly knowing. Interdependence between the individual (i.e., the designer) and the social practice (i.e., of designing) can be seen as the basis for knowing in practice (Billett, 2001). Engagement in the practice of designing is essentially social—the participation of individual designers in the community of practice is indispensable for the development of competence. Engagement in the practice of designing is not the only active process generating designerly knowing. In design practice, the task sets the directions for the expertise of the designer to reach. Design competence constitutes much more than skills and knowing how to design. Many of the domains of knowledge in design tasks are understood through interaction and then constituted and reconstituted over time and across contexts through design practice (Norman, 2007; Rasmussen, 2003; Reigeluth, 1995; Reigeluth, Banathy, & Olson, 1993).

Designerly knowing is developed and cultivated in communities like Moodle's FOSSVCSD around social practices and social system design activities in the larger social system. Open source communities generate specialized knowledge that can be utilized in applications for instructional design. These often intangible social processes that are part of the construction of designerly knowing are related to the core concepts of the community informatics field (Gurstein, 2000, 2003) such as virtual communities and community-building (Harvey, 1993; Rheingold, 1993), communautique (Harvey, 1993, 1996), knowledge-building communities (Scardamalia & Bereiter, 1994), reflexive communities (Fischer, 2006), communities of practice (Wenger, 1998), and communities of creation (Fischer, 2006). These shared practices can be identified at different levels of social engagement, for example, at the level of individuals, virtual teams, organizations, and, finally, at the sociocultural level and the level of large evolutionary learning communities, as illustrated in Figure 5.1.

The informatics community proposes that the understanding and learning experiences developed through designers' engagement in social practices in various contexts and at different levels of social commitment evolves into designerly knowing. We have already seen the collaborative platforms and emergent tools of the social Web (social computing). The interpretation of design practice and the construction of designerly knowing fundamentally as social activity resembles current perspectives on user studies, where the focus has turned to interactive environments and human systems (cf. Buchanan, 2001). If we consider users of design products to be situated in social and cultural environments that affect their product experience, we see designers practicing design in similar environments. This view of design practice is also congruent with the view of design as a discipline that integrates knowledge for practical action (Buchanan, 2001, p. 19).

Designerly creativity and innovation can be encouraged and enabled, but not deliberately produced or manipulated. What seems to be crucial to the development of designerly knowing is its nature as a social and active process transcending and expanding both personal and organizational limits. Sudden insights or illuminations that are essential to innovation may be grounded in a combination of knowing and understanding from various social actions. The diverse social practices in which the designer participates, both on a personal level and a professional level, may be important references in design practice and serve as notable bases for the growth of designerly knowing.

The Community Informatics Design Framework for Online Learning Based on Banathy's Social Systems Design

Banathy maintains that a system's view enables us to explore and characterize the system of our interest, its environment, and its components and parts. In the context of online learning, we can acquire a systemic view by integrating systems concepts and principles in our instructional thinking and designing and learning to use them in representing and building our socioconstructivist online learning space. This new way of thinking enables us to explore, understand, and describe characteristics of online learning systems operating at several interconnected levels: individual, group, communities of practices, organizational, institutional, administrative, instructional, and evolutionary (as can be seen in Figure 5.1). The levels include the following:

- relationships, interactions, and mutual interdependencies of online learning systems operating at those levels within universities or the larger educational system;

- relationships, interactions, and information-matter-energy exchanges between online learning systems and their environment;

- purposes, goals, and boundaries of online learning systems as those emerge from the observation of the relationship between, and mutual interdependence of, the open source online learning community (OSOLC) and the university system;

- the dynamics of interactions, relationships, and patterns of design and connectedness between socioconstructivist communities of practice; and

- systems processes, that is, the evolution of the online learning system as a living and knowing system through design and transformational changes that are manifested in the system and evolutionary environments over time and space.

During the past 2 decades, Banathy has applied systems thinking and the systems view in human systems and social systems. As a result, we now have at our disposal a large range of systems models and methods that enable us to work creatively and successfully with different socioconstructivist and systemic approaches to online learning. Following Banathy's approach, we can organize these models and methods in four complementary domains of inquiry:

1. the systemic analysis and description of online learning systems by the application of three models: the systems environment (the context of communities of designers), functions-structure (goals, functions, components and their relational arrangements), and process-behavioral models (activity planning, activity transformational input for use in the systemic engagement of the designer in a common ground activity, guiding operations, validation, adjustment and redesign);

2. systems design and comprehensive design inquiry with the use of approaches such as sociotechnical design, community informatics design methodology for building communities of practice, and CSCL tools appropriate to a specific OSOLC;

3. implementation of the design of the OSOLC by systems development and institutionalization of best practices and solutions; and

4. systems management and the management of change through design practice and configuration design.

Figure 5.1 depicts the socioconstructivist arrangement of the four complementary domains of online learning organizational inquiry. In the middle of the diagram is the integrating cluster; in the center, the core ideas and values, the best practices, and the organizing perspectives that constitute the foundation for both the development of the inquiry approach and the collective decisions taking from the course of the inquiry. Of special interest to Moodlers' communities of open source designers is the description and analysis of the online learning system and social system design as a disciplined inquiry that may be a unique opportunity for the building of truly systemic online learning in education (Ama, 2006). The four dimensions help us to think about education online as a systems inquiry based on five interrelated domains: ontology, epistemology, theory, methodology, and applications (Figure 5.2).

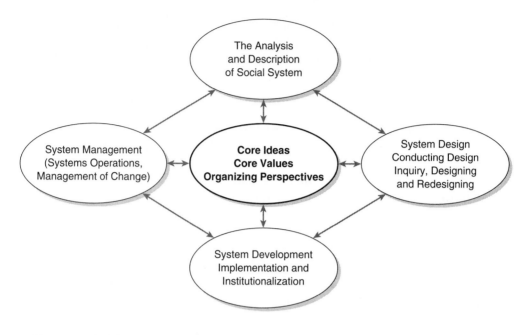

The center of the figure is an integrating cluster. In this cluster, we articulate sets of core values and organizing perspectives that collectivity guide our inquiry. The four domains of inquiry are recursive relationships which mutually affect each other. Each domain can become the source of initiating and activating an inquiry process in the field of online learning.

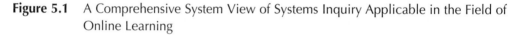

Figure 5.1   A Comprehensive System View of Systems Inquiry Applicable in the Field of Online Learning

SOURCE: Adapted from Banathy (2000a).

There are five domains in systemic inquiry dedicated to online learning. Systemic knowledge is formed from an integration of the social system's ontology (pluralist open object, project process) in the center of the diagram, the philosophy of socioconstructivism, and the theory of online learning instructional design, while methodology and applications form systemic activities dedicated to online learning space design. Ontology is concerned with a systems view of education in the online environment, shifting from a view of online learning as static and linear instructional design to a view of online learning as a living, free, open system, recognizing the primacy of an organizing relationship process over a programmatic curriculum such as computer-based training. Ontology is intimately linked with epistemology and with two domains of inquiry: (a) the evolutionary process of change within the online learning design space to generate knowledge about how system thinking and design thinking patterns change the way we learn and know by participating in the online environment and (b) the axiological dimension of social systems like Moodle's open source online learning platform that brings to the foreground ethical (justice, equity, community, citizenship and democracy, intellectual rights), and aesthetic qualities of the hypermedia virtual environment.

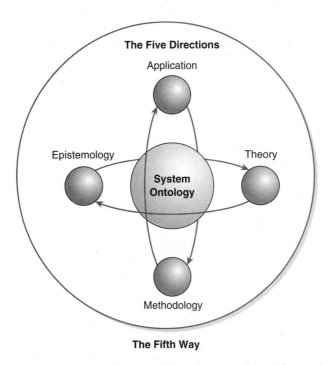

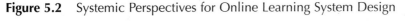

There are five domains in systemic inquiry. Systemic knowledge is formed from an integration of ontology, epistemology, and theory, while methodology and application from systemic action. Systemic ontology is the base of these aspects.

Figure 5.2   Systemic Perspectives for Online Learning System Design

SOURCE: Adapted from Banathy (2000a).

Systems theory integrates interrelated concepts and principles that apply to systemic evolutionary processes of online learning as a human activity system (Ackoff & Emery, 1972; Argyris & Shön, 1982; Checkland & Scholes, 2001; Harvey, 2004a; Harvey & Lemire, 2001; Jenlink & Reigeluth, 2000; Warfield, 1976, 1990). It seeks to offer general and praxeological principles coming from many disciplines (social system, communication, instructional design, community informatics, among others) that explain and foster the analysis and design of social practices, design activities, and communicative action in the online learning environment.

Systems methodology has two fields of inquiry: a) the study of methods by which value added knowledge and social capital are created and generated through learning community of design and b) the description of CSCL and community informatics design strategies, social Web-based and social computing tools, methods, intellectual technologies and models used to design online learning inquiry systems, as well as those used for the sociocultural animation process in relation to the activity of designing a complex project such as building and integrating an open source learning management systems (LMS) in a university. The applications refer to the sociodynamic interaction and translation of ontology, epistemology, theory, and methodology into social practices through design activity and a social systems inquiry process.

What is important for users-designers is that no single model can provide our university online learning platforms with a true representation of an optimal online education. The knowledge base of instructional design for online learning encompasses behaviorism, cognitivism, sociocultural and situated theory, social constructivism, constructionism, and even critical theory and postmodernism. It also integrates various disciplines, views, and concepts of social system design, knowledge management, computer mediated communication, community informatics design, and activity theory. When socioconstructivist philosophy and the distributed and situated view of online learning gain more attention, instructional designers are expected to design with more comprehensive and timely understanding of users' needs, requirements, and feedback. They are also expected to create socially rich environments to designerly codesign new situations for knowing and learning. Although reviewing the evolutionary trends in instructional design, Li (2000) found that different orientations of instructional design imply different design philosophies and methodologies. Online learning design inspired by Banathy's systems view represents a paradigm shift with the confluence of many important dimensions: the confluence of Web-based collaborative technologies, continued advances in digital memorizing, processing and new media, an the ongoing multi-practices approach to socioconstructivist design or open source software and learning design (Koohang & Harman, 2005). Several dimensions, orientations, perspectives, and disciplines in social system design or in designing a human activity system like a CSCL open source platform represent a future-creating discipline inquiry. This representation (the image, the rich picture, or the metaphor) can be found in Figure 5.3. It helps the designer community to transcend the present state of learning structures in the institution to explore new models for building an online social learning system (Ackoff & Emery, 1972; Checkland, 1981; Checkland & Scholes, 1990; Nadler, 1981; Nelson, 1993) and to discover important design principles to serve as guidelines in seeking solutions and envisioning the creation of the first representation of the system.

The socioconstructivist approach (the resulting integration-translation of different disciplines and domains; Banathy, 2000b) to online learning should explore the open source metaphor (image) to extend the systemic power of social design inside and outside the university. The social systems approach to online learning shows that the importance of universities in the knowledge society is beyond their traditional instructional role in society, especially in the fast growing context of the OSOLC of designers. The open source movement is rooted in the social constructivist movement, and the social constructivist movement is itself based on the pragmatism and instrumentalism drawn from Dewey's theory of understanding when applied to the online learning context. The use of open source and participative design communities as metaphor for online

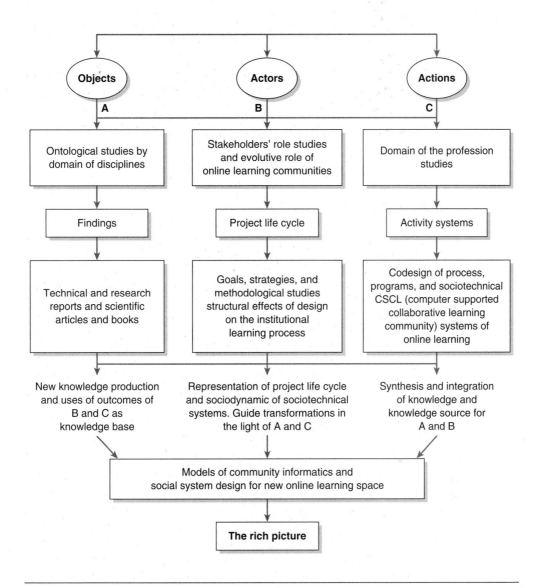

Figure 5.3   A Relational Framework of Three Modes of Disciplined Inquiry and its Application

learning and as a motivating rich picture of new instructional design practices for the design of better online learning platforms represents the next big shift in online learning.

In the last section of this chapter, I offer a few arguments in support of the preceding statement. For now, I examine the process model of the new online social learning system resulting from the representations, choices, and decisions that have been made between different theories, models, and practices (the shared representation or the rich picture coming from the exercise conducted with the support of the framework of three modes of disciplined inquiry). In other words, I describe how to design the system based on the rich picture of Banathy's working model (we can use a diagrammatic model or conceptual mapping to derive a useful representation of an online learning model). Purpose, process, interaction, integration, and emergence are important dimensions in the way we understand social system design. Furthermore, we should think of our university online learning systems at four levels: the online learning social system must serve the purpose of its institution, its members, the larger social system's communities of which it is part, and the international and networked communities in which it is embedded on the Internet.

Following Banathy's definition of a human activity system, I propose a characterization of an open source online learning system as a human activity system or as a social system (interchangeably). A FOSSVCSD is a sociotechnical community of users-designers and technological and material resources organized into a whole system in order to build an online learning system. The users-designers in the online learning system are affected by being in the system, and by their participation in the design system as they affect the system. Users-designers in the system select and carry out activities—individually and collectively—that enable them to attain the development of a whole emergent online learning system.

The FOSSVCSD maintains sets of relations—sustained through time—among the people who are in the system. Emerging models for mobilizing resources and the maintenance of these relations is of fundamental importance. The process by which these relationships are maintained is the system's regulation—the rules of the game—and the limits within which these rules can be sustained are the conditions of the system's stability through time. It is here where commitment (to shared purpose) and engagement (to carry out activities) play an important role and also where the open source community produced a new common ground model of empowerment for learning, an approach focusing on pull creating platforms. FOSSVCSDs are open to their environment and interact with university members and the larger local, regional, national, and international communities. They depend on it. One can say that FOSSVCSDs contribute to the creation of a whole network of learning design activity shared social practices. The nature of their relationship with the environment is one of mutual interdependence. They also sustain themselves through their internal relations and internal integration. Thus, while I view the FOSSVCSD as a whole, I also consider them as part of, and embedded in, their social networked environment. I can now discuss the development of an online learning systems view through a FOSSVCSD.

The observation and analysis of various online learning socioconstructivist-oriented platforms have allowed us to recognize some characteristics that are common to all platforms. Once we have identified and described a set of concepts that are common to the platform as a social system and have observed and discovered certain relationships among them, we can construct general systems principles for online learning. Thus, a social system principle emerges from an interaction-integration of interrelated

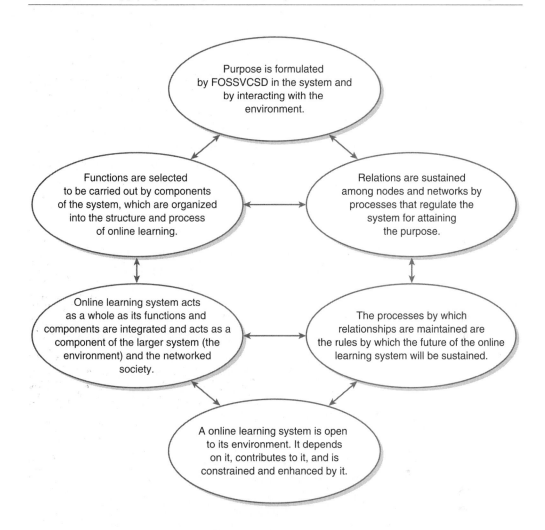

Purpose, process, interaction, integration, and emergence are important dimensions in understanding the online learning system. Furthermore, we should think about and define human activity systems always at three levels:

1) An online learning system serves the purposes of its various cybercommunities of learners-designers.

2) It serves the purposes of its members.

3) It serves its environment of the larger system in which it is embedded: virtual campus and the networked society.

Figure 5.4   A Social System Model of Online Learning Systems as Designed by Free Open Source Socioconstructivist Virtual Community of Social Designers (FOSSVCSD)

SOURCE: Adapted from Banathy (2000a).

concepts. Next, we are in a position to look for relationships among principles and to organize related principles into conceptual schemes that systemicists called systems models. The process of starting from observation and arriving at the construction of systems models constitutes the first stage of developing a systems view based on Banathy's work (see Figure 5.4).

Concepts and principles that are manifested in social systems can be organized into general models of social systems. These models then can be transformed into the context of specific social systems. In systems research, we develop models that represent one or more classes of systems. The more classes of systems a model represents, the more comprehensive or generalizable the model is. Our present examination focuses on a single class of systems—social systems or human activity systems. Once we develop a model—which is a generalization of this class—we can transform this general model of social systems into a model of online learning. In accordance with Banathy, the second stage lies in the process of internationalization-application: the integration of those concepts, principles, and models into our own thinking and their application in real-life contexts—in systems and situations of interest to us. This process of internalization and application constitutes our journey toward the development of a systems view. The next stage is the actual application. When I talk about systems applications, I am considering the application of systems approaches, models, methodologies, methods, and tools in a specific functional context, that is, a social system involves selecting the approach, model, methodology, methods, tools that are appropriate to the type of systems under consideration. A description of the two stages follows.

Stage 1: Creating a General Systems Model (After Banathy, 1996)

As I indicated previously, Banathy constructed three systems models (or lenses): a systems-environment model, a function-structure model, and a process model, all of which are applicable to understanding and working with online learning as a social system. The process of using the lenses and describing a system provides the first experience of internalization and application of the systems view.

Stage 2: Transforming the General Model Into a Specific Context

At this stage, we transform the general model into the context of a specific social system. This transformation enables us to portray, characterize, and use social-societal entities and systems and work with them in four complementary domains of organizational inquiry. These process domains are as follows:

1. the analysis and description of social systems, by the application of the three models presented above: the systems environment, the functions, and the process models;

2. systems design, conducting a design inquiry with the use of design models, methods, and tools appropriate to social systems and the specific type of system chosen;

3. implementation of the design by systems development and the institutionalization of the new system; and
4. systems management, the management of systems operations, and
   the management of change.

Based on findings at this stage, we can revisit Stage 1 and revise it if
indicated. Then, we move to Stage 2 again, learn from the application, and
proceed in a spiral fashion. The never ending spiral is the method of the
continuing development of systems inquiry (Banathy, 1996). The stages
are illustrated in Figure 5.5.

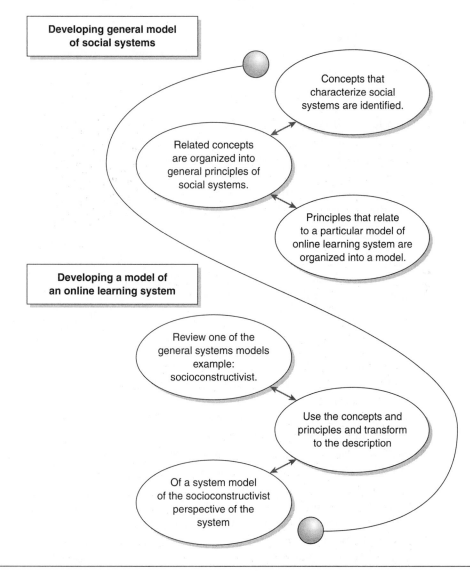

Figure 5.5   The Development of a General Model of an Online Learning System as Social
System

SOURCE: Adapted from Banathy (2000a).

Challenging the Transmission Model of Communication of Online Learning With the Moodle Collaborative Platform

The University of Quebec in Montreal (UQAM) Ongoing Experience

The UQAM joined the open source Moodle community in 2005 and developed several inhouse online learning features and modules through the UQAM Online Learning Platform Committee (UOLPC). This social-constructivist learning platform had been in use in our Applied Community Informatics Laboratory since 2003 on an experimental basis. With my colleagues Albert Lejeune and Gilles Lemire, we began developing several courses in education, communication, technology, and management using the Moodle platform.

The name Moodle was originally coined by Martin Dougiamas as an acronym for modular object dynamic learning environment. It is also a verb found in dictionaries, which means something like a cross between muse and doodle, describing the kind of creative tinkering and emergent systems thinking that is actively and socially developed among Moodle professors, searchers, students, and designers-developers. The goal for us is now to develop communities of practices among those different groups and the international Moodle community to freely share ideas about large scale open space learning design to construct sustainable social capital for the UQAM's communities of Moodlers.

In the summer of 2005, we were asked to be part of the UOLPC as consultants to the communication faculty of UQAM. In respect to the collaborative design philosophy of the open source movement and with the support of a multistakeholders approach, we defined multiple criteria by which to analyze different LMS. The committee chose MOODLE among an impressive amount of solutions available on the proprietary and open source market. The platform has been in use since January 2006 and, during this time, has undergone substantial collaborative design development and extensions in terms of features, tools, resources, virtual learning space, and networks between labs, professors, institutions, and universities in Quebec. It is different in functionality from the commercial learning management systems such as WebCT that we used before the adoption of Moodle. A key finding of our committee review process was that the WebCT platform was being used predominantly as a traditional instructional delivery tool to supplement rather than enable the learning environment, even if the latest version of the platform had many collaborative technologies and applications.

Qualitative survey results indicated that there was a focus on the technological and information processing aspect rather than on the constructivist use of the online learning environment. Most of the pedagogical approaches referred to a teaching culture based on a linear model of communication and transmissive information delivery rather than to a social constructivist learning culture. Across the different experiences of our university, the uses of the platform for collaborative courses and communicative activities were not very advanced. The adoption of the WebCT online environment was largely characterized by the virtual replication of traditional forms of instructional learning design in higher education contexts, hence the predominance of static course Web sites that integrate lecture notes, course plan, project toolkit, PowerPoint's documents, and online videos. The review committee (Fusaro, 2005) recommended the Moodle as the open source Web application in order to encourage the effective integration of online learning environments to support collaborative learning strategies in UQAM.

When our research team discovered Moodle in August 2002, we were surprised to see that at the very beginning of the first usable 1.0 version of the platform, Martin Dougiamas, the founding father, had already written two articles (1998, 1999) claiming that he was inspired to design his Web-based application from constructivist and socioconstructivist theories that point to the importance of collaborative learning activities (Bonk & Cunningham, 1998; Boud & Prosser, 2002) and collaborative learning communities. Dougiamas wrote a case study in 2006 for the joint Information Systems Committee of the Open Source Software Advisory Service explaining the factors responsible for the success of his platform:

> Moodle is a Web-based application that helps people create dynamic sites where learning communities can communicate and collaborate. Such communities may range from a university course or a secondary school class, to a professional association or company doing training. It contains a lot of tools and techniques distilled from the experiences of a huge community of educators to make these processes easy without sacrificing flexibility, and provide a variety of activity modules ranging from fora and chat rooms through quizzes and surveys, to workshops, lessons and assignments. Being open source and free, anyone can install it wherever they like.
>
> Moodle is underpinned by a belief that people learn best when they are together, and the Moodle development community strives to improve the capability of the tool so that it satisfies educational requirements around the world. Within the wider educational community in the UK, Moodle is probably one of the most well-known of all open source software projects and has been extremely influential in both raising the profile of open source software and demonstrating how an open source development can rival proprietary solutions. ("Introduction," para. 1)

The successful dispersion of the Moodle LMS around the world is largely due to its open source architecture and social-constructivist philosophy. This is certainly the point of view of Francis Heylighen, a pioneer in the development of the complex Principia Cybernetica Web site. In a recent article, "Why is Open Access Development so Successful?" (2007), he stated that the explosive development of free or open source information goods contravenes the conventional wisdom that markets and commercial organizations are necessary to efficiently supply products. Heylighen proposed a theoretical explanation for this phenomenon, using concepts from economics and theories of self-organization. Once available on the Internet, information is intrinsically not a scarce good, as it can be replicated virtually without cost. Moreover, freely distributing information is profitable to its creator since it improves the quality of the information and enhances the creator's reputation. This provides a sufficient incentive for people to contribute to open access projects. Unlike traditional organizations, open access communities are open, distributed, and self-organizing. Coordination is achieved through stigmergy: listings of work-in-progress direct potential contributors to the tasks where their contribution is most likely to be fruitful.

In the appropriation of online learning with the open source platform Moodle, stigmergy plays a key role in the distribution of resources and the commitment of users. The concept of stigmergy is used in the modeling of collective intelligence (Susi & Ziemke, 2001) when work (*ergon* in Greek) completed by one agent provides a stimulus stigma that entices other agents to continue the design activities in a collaborative manner. Open access freeware such as Moodle and other stigmergic open source social organizations are self-reinforcing or autocatalytic (Heylighen, 2007; Heylighen & Gershenson, 2003): The more high-quality design resources and material available on the community site, the more people will be attracted to check them out, and thus the more the users-designers are able to enable the site further.

A positive feedback loop explains the explosive growth of most large scale open source projects such as Wikipedia and Linux. Most design activities are typically performed in a distributed, sociocultural, and self-organizing way. The absence of strict planning or the more open character of the projects are largely compensated for the fact that knowledge about the present state of advancement of the project is completely, flexibly, and freely available, allowing anyone to contribute intelligently to anything, at any moment, and potentially anywhere in the world.

In this context, stigmergy is more than blind variation and natural selection of good ideas. The visible traces of the work performed previously function as a social mediating system memorizing and directly or indirectly communicating information for the community. In that way, the mediator coordinates further activities, by directing it toward the design tasks where collective action is most likely to be fruitful in the sense of increasing social capital. This phenomenon requires a shared design workspace accessible to all designers-contributors. The shared memories in most open access platform projects register important task design activities that have already been performed and those that are left to be addressed. The open access development and architecture of the Moodle platform and its social constructivist philosophy profit from the evolutionary dynamic of variation, recombination, and selection of design features. Sociocultural openness attracts a greater number of users-designers and a diversity of active participant designers, augmenting the potential for new insights, and the transdisciplinarity of their ideas that can lead to design of new artifacts. The community informatics design community considers this phenomenon under the concept of metadesign. Fischer (2007), from the Center for Life Long Learning and Design of the University of Colorado, defined metadesign as follows:

> Meta-design is focused on "design for designers": an emerging conceptual framework aimed at defining and creating social and technical infrastructures in which new forms of collaborative design can take place. It extends the traditional notion of system design beyond the original development of a system. It is grounded in the basic assumption that future uses and problems cannot be completely anticipated at design time when a system is developed. Users at times will discover mismatches between their needs and the support that an existing system can provide for them. These mismatches will lead to breakdowns that serve as potential sources of new insights, new knowledge, and new understanding. (p. 4)

Metadesign is relevant to illdefined, wicked design problems (Rittel, 1984) that cannot exclusively be left in the hands of computer professionals because they are not understood well enough to be described in sufficient detail or they cannot be definitively planned. Fischer and Giaccardi (2006) point out that metadesign advocates a shift in focus from finished products or complete solutions to conditions, modular and coconstructed solutions. Socioconstructive metadesign supports social creativity in which all the different stakeholders of a project incrementally acquire ownership of problems and contribute proactively in the new configuration of a system (Boulding, 2004). The experts and reflective practitioners join to become a creative community of active contributors that act as users-designers in collective meaningful activities. Social creativity and the social constructivist approach to online learning needs stigmergy, the kind of energy or synergy facilitated by the division of labor and collective intelligence.

The open source platform Moodle and the community informatics codesign methodology at my institution have enabled a large range of design activities and addressed the development of learning solutions that can cope with complex design problems that emerged in our online learning environment at UQAM. UOLPC communities of online learning developers and contributors collaboratively construct innovative ways of solving problems that have benefited not only our institutional members at UQAM, but also contributors in different universities in the Montreal region and the province of Quebec, Canada, and even in the large scale communities of Moodlers across the world.

The relationship between CSCL and platforms such as Moodle must be considered as a subsystem of the larger university's social practices. The shape of open source CSCL technology does not determine linear social consequences, but if society is indeed codesigned and complex, one must assume that technologies can cause multiple, nonlinear social effects that might even contradict one another (Hofkirchner, 2007). CSCL theories, methodologies, and applications influence universities and online learning in nonlinear ways, just as universities and online learning influence technology in nonlinear ways. The relationship between universities and technology is shaped by complex, nonlinear circular causality in a long-term social design process. Technology has the means, purpose, and task of solving learning challenges and educational problems. Social practices, cultural values, norms, and ethics are thus a manifestation of CSCL in the entire process of its social design and development. However, CSCL technology is not completely subordinate to the social system of education. CSCL technology is ambivalent: At times, it appears to resist our intentions by wholly or partly failing to do what is required of it; at other times, it not only fulfills our expectations but also goes on to do other useful tasks not originally anticipated. CSCL technology represents the potential for the redesign of instructional learning and the implementation of social learning and lifelong learning goals. CSCL goals may correspond to preexisting goals within the activities of our universities; the practical attainment of these goals may, however, cause them to change, at least to some extent (Ulrich, 1983). It is of course also possible that the intended goals may differ from those that can be reached with technological support. In this case, new technology may be developed to meet the requirements, or the requirements may, as it were, be adapted to fit the reality of what is technically possible. Realizable goals, therefore, do not always exist at the start of the process, but may be discovered as options made available by technology (Underhill, 2006). Whether society decides to pursue these goals on the grounds that they are possible is then no longer a question of technology, but rather of social decision making (Hofkirchner, 2007).

In the philosophy of social system design, it is a part–whole relationship that is characteristic of the technology–society relationship at large. The parts contribute to the emergence and maintenance of the whole, but the quality of the whole cannot be reduced to any quality of the parts. The whole exerts a pressure on the parts, but it will fail to wholly anticipate their interaction. Emergent properties arise from the knowing and organizing activities of design. Following Hofkirchner's (2007) recent work, we can say that the same holds for the open source and Web based technology of CSCL. That is to say, the dynamic of self-organizing open source CSCL tools like Moodle are not without influence on the dynamic of the self-organization of our universities, nor does it unfold independently of the university social system and its learning practices. We must observe these phenomena.

The term *information society* denotes a society in which information and communication technologies (ICTs), the Internet, and the computer are widely used. Pessimistic, technophobic, and catastrophic writings proclaim the negative impact of the Internet on society through digitization and virtualization. Contrary to these push approaches, Horkirchner (2007) thought that there are a variety of social-constructivist perspectives that resort to a pull approach and identify certain nontechnological factors as the leading determinants for our knowledge society or for knowledge monopolies, for participation through e-government or for control and surveillance, and for the fun and leisure society or for the manipulated society. Systemism can reveal the onesidedness of these approaches because of their strict deterministic thinking. Systemism turns the perspective of a mutual shaping of technology and society into the only practical, proactive guidance for designing the Internet according to the needs of society, whereas deterministic theories see either no possibility of or no necessity for intervention. Unwillingly or not, they support prevailing approaches that are industry-funded, especially funding social-scientific rationalizations of any information and communication technologies (ICT) application by any method whatsoever. In contrast, integrative ICT assessment and design approaches develop a normative view of technology and society, interpret their object of study as starting point for improving technology and society according to their normative criteria, and use every method promising to shed light on causes and conditions that further or hinder meeting of normative criteria. They feed the assessment of the impact of the Internet back to the design of the Internet. Only this kind of approach can be considered critical, according to Hofkirchner's findings.

We also believe that only a systemic approach can lead to the shaping of the type of online learning we want for the future. We must observe ways of learning, thinking, and knowing that are specific to social system design and the evolution of social practices in different levels of society in their evolutionary phases (Lejeune & Harvey, 2007).

Through the integration of models, ideals, and actions, the individuals and the FOSSVCSD become fully empowered as users-designers of their ongoing evolution. FOSSVCSD serves not only as a metaphor or representation for online learning systems but also as the catalyst of other systems of learning. As mentioned earlier, these range from the individual level, to the team level and communities of practice, to social systems of users-designers, and to large evolutionary ecosystems of Web 4.0. Figure 5.6 portrays how FOSSVCSD serves as the vehicle for the generation of these additional stages. The first level of the evolutionary process of FOSSVCSD is at the individual level. Individual designers are dedicated to learning how to learn and consciously seek to do so in ways which are evolutionary. At the next level, microsocial systems such as virtual teams are formed from various kinds of virtual social structures of designer teams or learning design teams seeking to collaborate and create an emergent subculture of socioconstructivist designers. Social systems of designers that have developed their full evolutionary potential have attained a degree of evolutionary competence that permits them to engage in the creation of greater ecosystems of FOSSVCSD.

Hypothesis for the process of working and constructing the designerly knowing university from socio-cultural practices through design activity of the free open source socioconstructivist virtual community of social designers (FOSSVCSD)

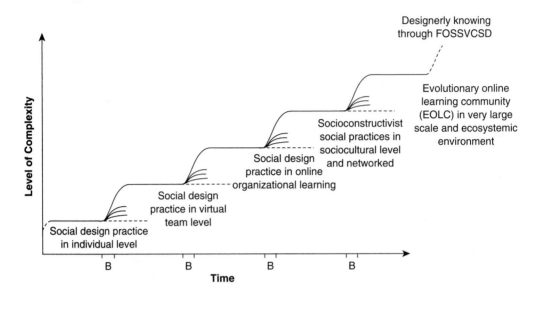

Figure 5.6   The Evolution of Evolutionary Online Learning Community

NOTE: B = Bifurcation.

Evolutionary learning ecosystems (Lazslo, 2001) form groups of people engaged in purposeful FOSSVCSD to form an evolutionary learning community. Such communities can foster the emergence of other systems of learning and online learning. At the level of the evolutionary online learning community (EOLC), people no longer come first—the whole ecosystem comes first. All aspects of the EOLC—psychocognitive and sociocultural to biophysical and process-structural—all are actors with a voice in the creation of evolutionary stigmergy in online learning (Laszlo & Lazlo, 2002). All listen to and create with one another. These EOLC are communities of practice and virtual communities, ones in which people act as stewards of their own futures in synchrony with their dynamic surroundings. Figure 5.7 depicts how EOLC facilitates the emergence of social systems within and beyond its boundaries. Still, we must remain cautious and not rely entirely on the evolution of the social technological Web as shown in Figure 5.7 no matter how interesting it is for building our online education project.

As I just pointed out, we must challenge and mature our understanding of the social practice level in conjunction with the social Web to find new ideas and concepts in online learning. However, in the case of Figures 5.6 and 5.7, we can observe an evolution toward a complex ecosystem. In fact, even if we gain insight into shaping the future of our online learning system through technological models, we need social system principles to

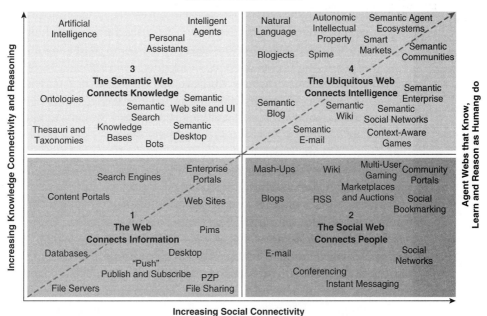

Figure 5.7   Social System Development

plan for development and implementation of our new model and to ensure the attainment of consensus and coparticipation in design to enhance commitment to idealize design so that its realization can be evolutionary, and we continue to imagine the ideal like a horizon forever moving ahead of us (Banathy, 1996; Long & Erhman, 2005). Designerly ways of thinking and communicating are distinct from scientific and other instructional ways of thinking, but they are as powerful as scientific and scholarly methods of inquiry, when applied to socioconstructivist ways of designing and knowing in the open source movement.

Social System Design Thinking and Community Informatics for Future Online Learning: A Research Agenda

Curiously, universities must play a more important role in the knowledge society. With the rapid adoption and growth of free open source platforms and tools, they can expand their traditional roles in research, education and community services (Jantsch, 1976; Jenlink, 2001; Reigeluth, 1999). FOSSVCSDs give them the potential to exploit local design, applications features, and designerly acquired knowledge and social innovations and to spread them to all levels of society. They provide universities with opportunities to change and evolve their business process model, life-long learning, and sustainability. To implement the potential for massive innovation, universities have to reconceptualize education and realize the importance of design practices in all their programs, by taking into account the tremendous power of social networks and open source virtual communities of online learners and designers. Beyond the traditional model of instructional teaching, I believe that the socioconstructivist philosophy of learning (Bruner, 1996; Vygotsky, 1978; Wenger, 1998) in open source social system designing (Fischer, 2006) and designerly knowing (Falin, 2007; Kotro, 2005), coupled with the concepts of social capital (Huysman & Wulf, 2004, 2006), social creativity (Fischer, 2007; Simon, 2005), and community informatics, hold considerable promise for the repositioning of universities in the knowledge society.

Predicting the next advancement in online learning is as difficult as predicting the next big trend or dominant paradigm that the continuing expansion of the Internet will enable in the future. It is the dynamic, flexible, emergent nature of the Web that makes it so unpredictable and challenging for universities and other social systems. But as McKey and Ellis (2007) pointed out, new enabling technologies and communities give rise to new design models, patterns, and principles (functionalities, solutions, applications, practices), which then drive new, unforeseen, invisible, and intangible sociocultural trends. One method to predict sociotechnical change is to develop a prospective mind-set to include concrete and tangible social design principles. This mind-set does not focus on linear change in technologies and functions but considers rich design principles to determine how technologies and usage patterns and functions will evolve in the open source context to satisfy the needs and requirements of our students and professors. This mind-set is the beginning of an extensive networked university of the universal (Harvey & Lemire, 2001). The development of new forms of online learning environment and the efficient use of new CSCL tools and facilities require us, among other tasks, to consider a variety of transdisciplinary research challenges in the field of social system design and community informatics design thinking in our universities. The distributed nature of social system design intelligence in the online learning environment, its modeling and dynamic evaluation for lifelong learning and social creativity, provides an effective and operational framework for the virtual knowledge communities of the next design society where universities must be on the forefront. Accepting this responsibility for the cocreation of new systems of online education means committing ourselves to social system design inquiry and the design of appropriate environments for the next generation to come, immersed in a fast, evolutionary, participative culture. Through open source online learning design, we contribute to create the future of education. And there is no more important project than participating in its creation for the betterment of our universities and society.

Note

1. Designerly knowing is a new concept that explains the nature of design activity, expertise, and evidence for design cognition in education. It was first introduced as designerly ways of knowing by Professor Nigel Cross in 1970 as a particular and essential aspect of human intelligence.

References

Ackoff, R. L., & Emery, F. E. (1972). *On purposeful systems*. Chicago: Aldine-Atherton.

Ama, S. 2006. *Using Moodle to Build Social Capital*. Retrieved December 18, 2007, from http://www.cvc.edu/faculty/articles-opinions/posts/using-Moodle-to-build-social-capital

Anderson, T. (2004). Toward a theory of online learning. In T. Anderson & F. Elloumi (Eds.), *Theory and practice of online learning*. Athabasca, CA: Athabasca University. Retrieved February 17, 2008, from http://cde.athabascau.ca/online_book/index.html

Argyris, C., & Schön, D. (1982). *Reasoning, learning and action*. San Francisco: Jossey-Bass

Banathy, B. H. (1996). *A taste of systemics. Why a system view*. Retrieved from http://www.newciv.org/ISSS_Primer/asem04bb.html

Banathy, B. (2000a). A taste of systemics: Why a system view? In *The Premier Project* [Web]. Retrieved February 13, 2008, from http://www.isss.org/taste.html

Banathy, B. H. (2000b). *Guided evolution of society: A systems view*. New York: Kluwer Academic/Plenum Press.

Banathy, B., & Jenlink, P. A. (2003). *Systems inquiry and its application in education*. Retrieved January 7, 2008, from http://depts.washington.edu/edtech/banathy.pdf

Barab, S. A., Kling, R., & Gray, J. H. (2004). *Designing virtual communities in the service of learning*. Cambridge, UK: University of Cambridge.

Bieber, M., McFall, B., Rice, R. E., & Gurstein, M. (2007). Towards systems design for supporting enabling communities. *Journal of Community Informatics, 3*(1). Retrieved January 4, 2008, from http://ci-journal.net/index.php/ciej/article/view/281/313

Billett, S. (2001). Knowing in practice: re-conceptualising vocational expertise. *Learning and Instruction, 11*(6), 431–452.

Bonk, C. J., & Cunningham, D. J. (1998). Searching for constructivist, learner-centered, and sociocultural components for collaborative educational learning tools. In C. Bonk & K. King (Eds.), *Electronic collaborators: Learner-centered technologies for literacy, apprenticeship, and discourse* (pp. 25–50). Mahwah, NJ: Lawrence Erlbaum.

Boud, D., & Prosser, M. (2002). Key principles for high quality student learning in higher education from a learning perspective. *Educational Media International, 39*(3–4), 238–245.

Boulding, K. E. (2004). General systems theory: The skeleton of science. *E:CO Special Double Issue, 6*(1–2), 127–139. Retrieved December 18, 2007, from http://www.scribd.com/doc/2310135/General-Systems-Theory-The-Skeleton-of-Science-Boulding

Bourgeois, D. T., & Horam, T. A. (2007). A design theory approach to community informatics: Community centered development and action research testing of online social networking prototype. *Journal of Community Informatics, 3*(1). Retrieved February 15, 2008, from http://ci-journal.net/index.php/ciej/article/viewarticle

Bruner, J. (1996). *The culture of education.* Cambridge, MA: Harvard University Press.

Buchanan, R. (2001). *Design Research and the New Learning. Design Issues, 17*(4), 3-23.

Cavallo, D. (2004). Models of growth. Towards fundamental change in learning environments. *BT Technology Journal, 22*(4), 96–112.

Checkland, P. (1981). *Systems thinking, systems practice.* New York: Wiley.

Checkland, P., & Scholes, J. (2001). *Soft systems methodology for action.* New York: Wiley.

Cross, N. (1974). *Redesigning the future.* New York: Wiley.

Cross, N. (1984). *Developments in design methodology.* New York: Wiley.

de Moor, A. (2005, July 22–27). Towards a design theory for community information system. Paper presented at the 11th International Conference on Human-Computer Interaction, Las Vegas, NV.

Dougiamas, M. (1998). *A journey into constructivism.* Retrieved August 7, 2004, from http://dougiamas.com/writing/constructivism.html

Dougiamas, M. (1999). *Moodle—A Web application for building quality online courses.* Retrieved August 7, 2004, from http://Moodle.com

Dougiamas, M. (2006). Moodle: A case study in sustainability. Retrieved February 4, 2008, from the Open Source Software, Advisory Service (JSC OSS WATCH): http://www.oss-watch.ac.uk/resources/cs-Moodle.xml

Dron, J. (2007). Designing the undesignable: Social software and control. *Educational Technology and Society, 10*(3), 60–71.

Engenström, Y. (1987). *Learning by expanding: An activity theoretical approach to developmental research.* Helsinki, Finland: Orienta-Konsultit Oy.

Falin, Y. (2007). *The social dimension in construction of designerly knowing.* Retrieved January 8, 2008, from http://www.nordes.org/data/uploads/papers/133.pdf

Fallman, D. (2003). Design-oriented human-computer interaction. Proceedings of Conference on Human Factors in Computing Systems. *CHI Letters, 5*(1). Retrieved March 27, 2007, from http://citeseer.comp.nus.edu.sg/670190.html

Fischer, G. (2006). Learning in communities: A distributed intelligence perspective. *The Journal of Community Informatics, 2*(2). Retrieved September 17, 2008, from http://www.ci-journal.net/index.php/ciej/article/view/339/245

Fischer, G. (2007, July 18–21). *Designing socio-technical environments in support of meta-design and social creativity.* Paper the Conference on Computer Supported Collaborative Learning presented at Rutgers University, Piscataway, NJ. Retrieved from http://l3d.cs.colorado.edu/~gerhard/ papers/CSCL-2007.pdf

Fischer, G., & Giaccardi, E. (2006). Meta-design: A framework for the future of end user development. In H. Lieberman, F. Paternò, & V. Wulf (Eds.), *End *user development—Empowering people to flexibly employ advanced information and communication technology* (pp. 427–457). Dordrecht, The Netherlands: Kluwer Academic.

Fischer, G., & Konomi, S. (2007). Innovative media in support of distributed intelligence and lifelong learning, *Journal of Computer-Assisted Learning, 23*(4), 338–350.

Fischer, G., Rohde, M., & Wulf, V. (2006). Spiders in the Net: Universities as facilitators of community-based learning. *The Journal of Community Informatics, 2*(2). Retrieved from http://www.ci-journal.net/index.php/ciej/article/viewArticle/337

Forrester, J. W. (1971). Counterintuitive behavior of social systems. *Technology Review, 73*(3), 52–68.

Fox, S. (2002). Studying networked learning: Some Implications from socially situated learning theory and actor network theory. In C. Steeples & C. Jones (Eds.), *Networked learning: Perspectives and issues* (pp. 1–14). New York: Springer.

Frielick, S. (2004). Beyond constructivism: An ecological approach to e-learning. In R. Atkinson, C. McBeath, D. Jonas-Dwyer, & R. Phillips (Eds.), *Beyond the comfort zone: Proceedings of the 21st ASCILITE Conference* (pp. 328–332). Retrieved December 1, 2007, from http://www.ascilite.org.au/conferences/perth04/procs/frielick.html

Fusaro, M. (2005, December 14*). Rapport du Comité Institutionnel sur les plateformes d'apprentissage en ligne* [Institutional committee report on platforms for online learning]. Travaux du Vice–Rectorat aux Services académiques et au Développement technologique, Université du Québec à Montréal. Retrieved from http://www.moodle.uqam.ca/moodleinfo/PDF/Platesformes_UQAM_2005.pdf

Gurstein, M. (2000). *Community informatics: Enabling communities with information and communications technologies.* Hershey, PA: Idea Publishing Group.

Gurstein, M. (2003). Effective use: A community informatics strategy beyond the digital divide. *First Monday.* Retrieved November 12, 2007, from http://www.sdnp.undp.org/egov/papers/effective%20use%20-%20gurstein.pdf

Harvey, P. L. (1995). *Cyberespace et communautique: Appropriation, réseaux, groupes virtuels* [Cyberspace and community informatics: Adaptation, networks, virtual groups]. Québec, Canada: Presses de l'Université Laval/L'Harmattan.

Harvey, P. L. (2005). *La communautique. Un paradigme transdisciplinaire pour l'étude des arts, des sciences et des métiers de la communication médiatisée par ordinateur. Publié dans le collectif communication. Horizons de pratique et de recherche. Sous la direction de Johanne Saint-Charles et Pierre Mongeau* [Community informatics. A transdisciplinary paradigm for the study of arts, sciences and communication trade assisted by computer]. Montreal, Canada: Presses de l'Université du Québec.

Harvey P. L. (2006a*). Design communautique et coopération organisationnelle. Une théorie du design communautique pour les systèmes d'information collaboratifs qui supportent les processus émergents de la connaissance* [Community informatics design and organizational cooperation. A theory of community informatics design for collaborative systems of information supporting the emerging process of knowledge]. In J. M. Penalva (Ed.), *Les rencontres en Intelligence Collective.* Paris: Presses de l'École des Mines de Paris.

Harvey, P. L. (2006b). *Les îlots de vie communauticielles. Topologie situationnelle des communautés de pratique* [Community informatics living clusters. Topology situational of communities of practice]. Dans Proulx, S. , Poissant, L.

et Sénécal, M. Actes du colloque sur les communautés virtuelles, publiés aux Presses de l'Université Laval.

Harvey, P. L., & Lemire, G. (2001). *La Nouvelle éducation. NTIC. Transdisciplinarité et communautique* [The new education, NTIC. Transdisciplinarity and community informatics]. Québec, Canada: Presses de l'Université Laval/L'Harmattan.

Haythornthwaite, C., Bruce, B. C., Andrews, R., Kazmer, M. M., Montague, R. A., & Preston, C. (2007). Theories and models of and for online learning. *First Monday, 12*(8). Retrieved December 23, 2007, from http://firstmonday.org/ issues/issue12_8/haythorn/index.html

Heylighen, F. (2003). The science of self-organization and adaptivity in knowledge management, organizational intelligence and learning, and complexity. In *The Encyclopedia of life support systems.* Oxford, UK: Eolss.

Heylighen, F. (2007). *Why is open access development so successful? Stigmergic organization and the economics of information.* Retrieved February 19, 2008, from http://pespmc1.vub.ac.be/papers/OpenSourceStigmergy.pdf

Heylighen, F. and C. Gershenson (2003). The meaning of self-organization in computing. *IEEE Intelligent Systems, Trends & Controversies—Self-organization and Information Systems,* July/August 2003, pp. 72–75

Hofkirchner, W. (2007). A critical social system view of the Internet [Electronic version]. *Philosophy of the Social Sciences, 37*(4), 471–500. Retrieved January 8, 2008, from http://pos.sagepub.com/cgi/reprint/37/4/471

Huysman, M., & Wulf, V. (2004). *Social capital and information technology.* Cambridge MA: MIT Press.

Huysman, M., & Wulf, V. (2006). IT to support knowledge sharing in communities: Towards a social capital analysis. *Journal on Information Technology, 21*(1), 40 – 51.

Jackson, M. C. (1985). Social systems theory and practice: The need for a critical approach. *International Journal of General Systems, 10,* 135–151.

Jantsch, E. (1976). *Design for evolution.* New York: Braziller.

Jenlink, P. M. (2001). Activity theory and the design of educational systems: Examining the mediational importance of conversation [Electronic version]. *Systems Research and Behavioral Science, 18*(4), 345–359.

Jenlink, P. M., & Reigeluth, C. M. (2000, July 16–22). A guidance system for designing new K–12 educational systems. In J. K. Allen & J. Wilby (Eds.), *The proceedings of the 44th annual conference of the International Society for the Systems Sciences.* Toronto, Canada.

Jenlink, P. M., Reigeluth, C. M., Carr, A. A., & Nelson, L. M. (1998). Guidelines for facilitating systemic change in school districts. *Systems Research and Behavioral Science, 15*(3), 217–233. Retrieved January 7, 2008, from http:// www.indiana.edu/~syschang/decatur/new_members/pdf_documents/gste _systems-research.pdf

Koohang, A., & Harman, K. (2005). Open source: A metaphor for e-learning. *Informing Science Journal, 8,* 75–86.

Kotro, T. (2005). *Hobbyist knowing in product development, desirable objects and passion for sports in Suunto Corporation.* Unpublished dissertation, University of Art and Design, Helsinki, Finland.

Laszlo, A. (2001). The epistemological foundations of evolutionary system design [Electronic version]. *Systems Research and Behavioral Science, 18*(4), 307–321. Retrieved June 8, 2007, from http://www.interscience.wiley.com

Laszlo, A., & Laszlo, K. (2002). *The evolution of evolutionary systems design* [Special issue dedicated to Bela Banathy]. *World Futures, 58*(6–7). Retrieved

November 2007, from http://archive.syntonyquest.org/elcTree/resourcesPDFs/ Evolution_of_ESD.pdf

Lejeune, A. & Harvey, P. L.(2007). L'analyse des systèmes d'activités, l'apprentissage extensif,et le co-Design en communauté: une approche alternative à la réingénierie du système de santé au Québec. Translation: Activities Systems' Analysis, Extensive Learning, and Codesign [Community: An alternative approach to redesigning the health system in Quebec]. In Etienne Cracco, Éditeur, *Revue Gestion 2000, 24,* No Bimestriel 5. Louvain-La-Neuve, Belgique.

Li, M.-F. (2000). *Fostering design culture through cultivating the user/designers design thinking and system thinking.* Paper presented at the National Convention of the Association for Educational Communications and Technology, Denver, CO.

Long P. D. and Ehrman, S. C. (2005). Future of the learning space. Breaking out of the box. In *Educause Review,* July/August 2005, pp. 42–58.

McKey, P., & Ellis, A. (2007). *Three design principles for predicting the future of the Web.* Sydney, Australia: Southern Cross University. Retrieved January 4, 2008, from http://ausweb.scu.edu.au/aw2007/papers/refereed/mckey/paper.html

Mor, Y., Tholander, J., & Holmberg, J. (2005, June). *Designing for cross-cultural web-based knowledge building.* Paper submitted to the 10th Computer Supported Collaborative Learning (CSCL) Conference, Taipei, Taiwan.

Nadler, G. (1981). *The planning and design approach.* New York: Wiley.

Nelson, H. G. (1993). *Design inquiry as an intellectual technology for the design of educational systems.* In C. M. Reigeluth, B. H. Banathy, & J. R. Olson (Eds.), Comprehensive system design: A new education technology (pp. 145–153). Stuttgart, Germany: Springer-Verlag.

Nicolescu, B. (1996). *La transdisciplinarité manifeste:* Collection "transdisciplinarité" [Manifesto of transdisciplinarity]. Monaco: Editions du Rocher.

Norman, S., & Porter, D. (2007). *Designing learning objects for online learning: A topical start up guide to distance education practice and delivery.* Vancouver, BC, Canada: Commonwealth of Learning. Retrieved January 4, 2008, from http://www.col.org/SiteCollectionDocuments/KS2007_Designing-Learning-Objects.pdf>

Owen, C. (2008, Winter). Design thinking: On its nature and use [Electronic version]. *Rotman Magazine,* pp. 26–31. Retrieved February 14, 2008, from http://www.rotman.utoronto.ca/pdf/winter2008.pdf

Pettenatti, M. C., & Cigognini, M. E. (2007). Social networking theories and tools to support connectivist learning activities. *Journal of Web Based Learning and Teaching Technologies, 2*(3), 42-60.

Rasmussen, T. (2003). On distributed society. The history of the Internet as a guide to a sociological understanding of communication and society. In G. Liestol, A. Morrison, & T. Rasmussen (Eds.), *Digital media revisited* (pp. 443–467). Cambridge: MIT Press.

Reigeluth, C. M. (1995). *A conversation on guidelines for the process of facilitating systemic change in education.* Englewood Cliffs, NJ: Educational Technology.

Reigeluth, C. (1999). What is instructional-design theory and how is it changing? In C. Reigeluth (Ed.), *Instructional design theories and models, Volume II,* pp. 5–29. Mahwah, New Jersey: Lawrence Erlbaum Associates.

Reigeluth, C. M., Banathy, B. H., & Olson J. R. (Eds.). (1993). *Comprehensive systems design: A new educational technology.* Stuttgart, Germany: Springer-Verlag.

Rheingold, H. (1993). *The virtual community: Homesteading on electronic frontier.* Reading, MA: Addison-Wesley.

Rittel, H., (1984). Second-generation design methods. In N. Cross (Ed.), *Developments in design methodology* (pp. 317–327). Oxford, UK: Wiley.

Sack,W., Détienne, F., Ducheneaut, N., Burkhardt, J. M., Mahendran, D., & Barcellini, F. (2006). *A methodological framework for socio-cognitive analyses of collaborative design of open source software.* Retrieved May 5, 2007, from http://arxiv.org/ftp/cs/papers/0703/0703009.pdf

Sage, A. (1977). *Methodology for large-scale systems.* New York: McGraw-Hill.

Scardamalia, M., & Bereiter, C. (1994). Computer support for knowledge-building communities. *The Journal of the Learning Sciences, 3*(3), 265–283. Retrieved September 20, 2006, from http://www.informaworld.com/openurl?genre= journal&issn=1050–8406

Senge, P. (1990). *The fifth discipline.* New York: Doubleday.

Siemens, G. (2005). *Learning development cycle: Bridging learning design and modern knowledge needs.* Retrieved March 16, 2007, from http://www .elearnspace.org/Articles/ldc.htm

Smith, J., & Brown, A. (2005*). Building a culture of learning design in the tertiary curriculum.* Retrieved June 2, 2007, from http://www.ascilite.org.au/ conferences/brisbane05/blogs/proceedings/71_Smith.pdf

Stephan, P. F. (2006). *Le design cognitif. Une perspective pour la recherche en design* [Cognitive design. Perspectives for research in design]. Retrieved March 19, 2007, from http://www.peterstephan.org/fileadmin/website/ 05_publikationen/PFS_Le_Design_cognitif.pdf

Susi, T., & Ziemke, T. (2001*).* Social cognition, artefacts, and stigmergy. Cognitive systems research. Retrieved October 6, 2007, from http://www .carleton.ca/iis/TechReports/files/2002–13.pdf

Taylor, J., Rodden, T., Anderson, A., Sharples, M., Luckin, R., Conole, G., et al. (2004). *An e-learning research agenda.* Retrieved November 11, 2007, from http://www .epsrc.ac.uk/ResearchFunding/Programmes/e-Science/eLearningRAgenda .htm

Ulrich, W. (1983). *Critical heuristics of social planning: A new approach to practical philosophy.* Bern, Switzerland: Haupt.

Underhill, A. F. (2006). Theories of learning and their implications for on-line assessment Turkish. *Online Journal of Distance Education-TOJDE, 7*(1). Retrieved October 3, 2007, from http://tojde.anadolu.edu.tr/tojde21/articles/ anthony.htm

Vygotsky, L. S. (1978). *Mind and society: The development of higher psychological process.* Cambridge, MA: Harvard University Press.

Warfield, J. N. (1976). *Societal systems.* New York: Wiley

Warfield, J. N. (1990). *A science of general design: Managing complexity through systems design.* Salinas, CA: Intersystems.

Wenger, E. (1998). *Communities of practice: Learning, meaning and identity.* Cambridge, MA: Cambridge University Press.

Ye,Y., & Fischer, G. (2007). Designing for participation in socio-technical software systems. In C. Stephanidis (Ed.), *Proceedings of 4th International Conference on Universal Access in Human-Computer Interaction* (part 1, pp. 312–321). Heidelberg, Germany: Springer.

Chapter 6

Media Psychology Controls the Mouse That Roars

Bernard Luskin

James Hirsen

The Evolution of Distance Education

Prior to the early 1970s, the primary method of delivering education at the college level was the traditional classroom lecture. Various types of distance learning had existed for some time, but modern advanced media methods began to grow in use with the emergence of the VCR, public broadcasting, and digital formats. For more than a quarter century, closed circuit television was used for distance learning. Correspondence courses, especially in the military, had been offered for more than 60 years; the famous *Sunrise Semester* on television began in 1957, and telecourses driven by community colleges and the adult learning service of PBS pioneered new distance learning formats during the 1970s. The 1980s was a decade of spreadsheet technology; the 1990s, digital gadgets; and now, with advanced technology, psychology has taken center stage because of advanced understanding of human behavior.

Before World War II, higher education was not generally available to most people. Only the wealthiest portion of the population could afford the cost of formal higher education. Economic evolution, fueled by technological advancement following World War II and stimulated by the

GI Bill, had a profound effect on the way higher education was delivered through the last half of the 20th century. In the 1950s, the country's economic base underwent a transformation from an industrial to a technological, service-based commerce. Increasingly, sophisticated training and education became essential elements for the continued viability of the nation. Every business, government, and nonprofit organization became aware of the high degree of skill necessary to be able to manage the vast quantities of available information. The last half of the 20th century was one of great technological progress. As we crossed to the 21st century, we left analog technology behind and began the digital century with a new understanding of learning and media psychology that is now influencing nonclassroom-based learning.

The demographics have also changed dramatically. Only a few decades ago, classrooms in undergraduate colleges and universities were generally filled with unmarried, full-time students between the ages of 18 and 23. Today, the number of both undergraduate and graduate students has grown exponentially, and the profile of students now includes individuals of varying age, employment, and financial status. Creative longevity and lifelong learning have become a 21st century trend, and the movement is worldwide. New definitions of time and money are emerging, and the value of education in offering mobility and opportunity is more and more understood and available.

The Internet Changed Global Learning and the Mouse Began to Roar

The Internet has opened up new possibilities in technology, business, and education in both professional development and lifestyles. It has become a portal into new worlds and possibilities and has changed the way we think and the way we learn. The Web has broken down the barriers of time and space in distance learning, giving distinct advantages in location, scheduling, student diversity, maintenance of current teaching materials, archival capabilities, and cost-effective course development. Learning systems are becoming easier for colleges to use and more appealing and acceptable to students pursuing all types of programs. Learning psychology and media psychology have now become the hot topics of the early 21st century.

It is now widely acknowledged that the Internet has altered the distance learning paradigm with respect to student–teacher and student–student interaction. In many instances, Internet forums afford students who might otherwise be reluctant to participate in classroom discussions the opportunity to more freely express ideas in a medium that provides visual anonymity. World economics are reinforcing this perception, and the sinking dollar makes it a relative bargain for a European or Asian student to pay for an American degree. In addition, the fact that English is the leading language of international communication and commerce and that many individuals can complete programs from their own homes is fueling diversity and growth. Research on distance learning has reinforced that this type of learning opportunity offers equal quality when compared to classroom learning opportunities (Frydenberg, 2007; Saba, 2000). Media in learning, distance, distributed, blended, online, and e-learning have entered the modern lexicon and impediments to their use in higher education are fading apace. There are few critical obstacles.

The market for online education is expanding at a rate of more than 20% a year, with individual Internet-centric universities experiencing even greater growth. The Sloan Foundation reports that approximately 20% of higher education enrollment is now participating in online related education formats (Allen, 2007). In 2008, more than 90% of all colleges now offer some online programs, and venture capital is fueling growth in profit colleges and universities and adding to competition and availability of opportunity (National Center for Education Statistics: http://nces.ed.gov). Both blended and fully online learning opportunities are growing briskly.

This trend is continuing to increase as a result of a perfect storm of the simultaneous factors noted. The decline of the dollar in the United States, in particular, makes the international market significantly more accessible, affordable, and appealing to potential students in other countries. Advances in learning technology, Internet-based social networking, and media and learning psychology are providing more student-friendly forums, while the rising cost of transportation due to fuel inflation is rapidly conditioning society to view learning opportunities that do not require physical presence in a classroom positively. The learning paradigm has changed.

Worldwide Economics Are an Important Personal Propellant

U.S. Census Bureau Population Surveys (Cheeseman Day & Newburger, 2002) report that the lifetime earning of a 4-year college graduate is $2.1 million, but those having master's degrees double their earnings to more than $4.4 million. Yearly earnings for college graduates are greatly increased with the acquisition of additional education. Currently in the United States, college graduates with bachelor's degrees earn about $60,000 a year. However, those holding master's degrees earn an average of $75,000 a year, and those with doctorates more than $100,000 per year (ASEC, 2006). This incentive is widely known, and the second wave GI Bill will have the same effect in the first half of the 21st century that it had in the last half of the 20th century.

At the same time, traditional brick-and-mortar public university–based educational costs are increasing. State–subsidized universities are entangled in bureaucracy, politics, and budgetary problems. Increasingly, the best of these colleges can only accept comparatively limited numbers of students, which satisfies only a fraction of what we now know to be the real demand. It therefore makes sense for federal, state, and local governments to align with universities and support Internet-based education as a way to ease state budget shortfalls that are now being experienced in higher education. Governments in other countries, such as in the United Kingdom, are also currently subsidizing universities that provide online degree programs because of the advantages and cost savings. To remain competitive, the United States is doing the same by establishing legislative eligibility for students to receive student financial aid. Given the rapidly rising price of gasoline, the mouse will roar more intensely as many students move online for economic reasons.

The costs of private and independent universities are out of reach for many students. In addition, there has been a dramatic rise in interest rates for student loans. Various agency reports reveal annual increases from 5% to almost 8%, while need-based student aid availability has dropped almost 10 percentage points in the last 6 years. The average college graduate carries $17,000 in debt, an overwhelming burden for a new graduate (Shedden, 2006). Some students find employment while pursuing an education. Work schedules are frequently compromised due to conflicts with family and school demands. Some employers even view working toward a degree as counterproductive to job commitment and performance. Many employers who have educational reimbursement policies are likely to resent the high educational costs and are increasingly restrictive in the amounts provided and the conditions required for reimbursement.

Fortunately, new technology, computers, and the Internet have greatly enhanced the educational potential of distance learning. Lower overhead costs in teaching online enable significantly lower expenses. Eliminating formal classroom attendance enables greater flexibility. More than reducing expenses, this newfound flexibility provides the time and opportunity to generate new revenue, which is a big factor in future growth. Online education is currently a $16 billion market that is increasing, and experts expect the growth to continue. Due to rising educational costs and recent changes to a U.S. law permitting financial aid to online schools, online programs compete on an equal basis with those of traditional schools. Campus-based brick-and-mortar settings have served well and will continue to serve well. What are happening are growth, diversity, and increased access and opportunity for more people (Allen, 2007).

The Mouse and the Hotspot
Have Changed the Paradigm

Internet-based distance learning has changed the traditional educational model with respect to time and space. Society is highly influenced by media trends. The incoming student body has been brought up in what Jenkins of MIT calls convergence media (Jenkins, 2006). Various platforms that are available to deliver news, entertainment, and information are converging into a new, integrated medium, which no longer follows the traditional notion of a scheduled broadcast or event. Today's generation is sometimes referred to as the on-demand generation because members have been conditioned to receive music, video, movies, and news whenever and wherever they so choose.

Internet-based educational programs are not tied to the time and space specifications of the traditional model but instead can be set up so students are able to access information, interactive modules, multimedia, assignments, lectures, and tests on demand. Obviously, the notion of place has been radically altered by cyberspace, a teaching terrain that allows an instructor and student(s) to be located anywhere on the globe as long as there is computer and Internet access. Internet-based distance learning opens up even more flexibility when it comes to time. When the transmission of educational material to students is simultaneously received, the experience is said to be synchronous. When the transmission of educational material precedes the student or students' receipt of the material, it is said to be asynchronous (Graves, 1997).

Bulletin boards, instant messaging, file transfer Web sites, and e-mails allow educational materials to be distributed and returned. Dedicated Internet teaching programs such as Blackboard, eCollege, Angel, and Moodle allow extensive postings of documents, links, and multimedia resources. Interactive custom Web lessons use programs such as Java for emphasizing certain points. Synchronous videoconference sessions with document and desktop sharing such as Webex or Gotomeeting create a degree of physicality and intimacy that are useful adjuncts to other Internet-based protocols.

The newest mode of distance learning, virtual worlds such as Second Life, completely shatter traditional notions of time and space with the creation of three-dimensional digital forums, which can be utilized with either synchronous classrooms or asynchronous devices and multimedia. Phenomenology is at work here. Psychology is at the center. Learning is more about behavior than about technology, which is simply a vehicle. Nonetheless, virtual worlds allow students to interact with digital objects, which serve to enhance deeper comprehension of the educational material (Bricken & Byrbe, 1994). Student interaction takes the form of a first-person experience as opposed to the detached third-person feeling normally associated with distance learning technologies (Winn, 1993).

The very advantages that distance education offers in terms of scheduling (time) and location (space) also necessitate a greater degree of individual student initiative in order to maintain continuity and comprehension when compared to traditional classroom settings. Motivating students then becomes a paramount consideration in the design and implementation of a distance learning program.

Motivation can be subdivided into two categories: extrinsic motivation in which the activity engaged in by the individual is encouraged by an outcome and intrinsic motivation in which the activity engaged in by the individual is for sheer enjoyment (Davis, Bagozzi, & Warshaw, 1989). Students most effectively learn when they exhibit intrinsic motivation (Ghani & Deshpande, 1994). Students who are intrinsically motivated exhibit greater motivation toward education and display a more intense desire to achieve positive results (Chan & Ahern, 1999).

Flow Theory and Motivation in Online Education

Flow theory is a valuable psychological tool for analyzing student motivation and is particularly helpful in understanding intrinsic motivation within a distance learning setting. Csikszentmihalyi (1990) described flow as a psychological state that reflects the optimal feeling of individuals who exhibit motivation, contentment, and cognitive efficiency. People who experience flow have similar descriptions of the experience; positive affect, time distortion, and effortlessness are common. Athletes and performers describe the experience as being "in the zone" (Ghani & Deshpande, 1994).

The most important variables in flow theory are perceived skill and perceived challenge. When students perceive challenges as greater than their skills, they are likely to experience anxiety. Conversely, when their perceived skills are greater than their perceived challenges, they experience boredom and apathy. Students experience flow when they perceive both their skills and their challenges to be at high levels. Because students engaged in distance learning activities are dealing with greater complexity in the delivery system than traditional students, the more students experience power over technology, the higher the perceived skill. The level of interactivity greatly assists students in high skill perception.

A recent study (Liao, 2006) examined emotional and cognitive responses to distance learning systems. Two models were utilized in the determination of students' flow states. The first model focused on the flow experience with respect to cause and effect when using distance learning systems. The second model focused on the effect of several interactions of student flow experiences. Results from the first model suggest that flow theory works well in a distance learning environment. The second model's results suggest that the interaction between the instructor and learner has a positive relationship with flow experience.

Students engaged in distance learning experience psychological distance. This psychological distance is more significant to students than physical distance in assessing their motivation. Psychological distance can be altered by instructional structure or institutional planning (Moore, 1991). Distance is dead. Experience and new learning methods will create continually improving communities of interest and practice. There is a great deal of research to support the premise that once people know each other, communicating from a distance is very effective (Keegan, 1993).

The notion of psychological distance in distance learning is discussed within the context of the level of interaction between the instructor and student and to a lesser extent, the interaction between a student and another student (Saba, 2000). The term *telepresence* indicates the perceptions of interaction between two or more individuals utilizing media technology that alters the traditional notions of time and space (Buxton, 1993). Transactional presence expands the concept of telepresence to include connectedness, that is, the conviction that an individual is engaged in a reciprocal relationship in the given communication context (Munro, 1998). In part, the cultivation of transactional presence within the online learning environment is an issue of exposure and generational change. Part of the future is simply getting used to it.

The interaction of students in distance education is also dependent upon the comfort level that students possess with regard to particular delivery systems being used in respective programs. The more fluently students interact with a system, the more flow students realize (Hillman, Willis, & Gunawardena, 1994). Our experience is one of great enthusiasm from students working within current early learning management systems such as Blackboard or eCollege. When students in distance learning experience flow, they demonstrate motivation by their continued diligence in assigned tasks, willingness to move into uncharted territory, and manifestations of high levels of satisfaction in the learning process (Novak, Hoffman, & Yung, 1998).

The Mouse Is Breeding

Distance learning is still in the beginning stages. Currently, 90% of traditional universities offer online courses; some offer online degrees. For instance, Boston University, Jones International University, Capella University, Touro University, Walden University, University of Phoenix, University of Maryland, and others now offer regionally accredited bachelor's, master's, and doctoral degrees entirely online.

According to an article in the *Wall Street Journal* (Golden, 2006, p. 1) "online enrollment is skyrocketing." This may or may not be an exaggeration. However, the trends are clear. The University of Phoenix's online division is growing at a reported rate of up to 50% per year. In fact, in the same *Wall Street Journal* article, Brian Mueller, former president of the Apollo Group Inc., which operates the University of Phoenix, predicted that demand for online education will outstrip the supply in 5 years, and there is therefore room for all comers. Many lesser-known, totally online universities are doing as well or better. Walden University in Minnesota grew from 1,200 students in 2001 to 24,000 in 2008.

Because of increased competition for student enrollees, institutions of higher learning are forming consortiums to offer more flexible approaches to degree programs. In addition, business enterprises such as Motorola, Disney, McDonalds, ATT, and an acknowledged array of major corporations are offering courses to their employees to enhance their skills. The corporate university is emerging as a force.

The previous discussion has highlighted many of the reasons for the market growth of online higher education programs. What follows is a brief summary of the primary determinants of this movement.

1. *The value of U.S. degrees abroad.* Possession of a U.S. degree is highly prestigious abroad, and almost half a million international students enroll in U.S. university programs annually. It is estimated that even more foreign students who are desirous of U.S. degrees are unable to come to the U.S. due to financial or September 11th restrictions. However, they could conceivably attend online programs. Demand from students from other areas of the world will continue to accelerate growth for online university degree programs in the United States and Europe.

2. *Higher education and increased earning power.* There is a significant annual salary gap between those holding undergraduate and advanced degrees, which fuels the flames for higher education. The likelihood of such gaps is even greater in foreign countries.

3. *Higher education and career advancement.* In addition to the incentive of increased earning power, higher degrees such as MBAs, the EdD, PsyD, or PhD offer distinct advantages in career advancement.

4. *Adult students and scheduling needs.* It is difficult for working adults to arrange work schedules to attend classes, take exams, and study at traditional schools. Distance learning formats allow students to earn a living while they receive their education. Students also will save time and money as the rising cost of gasoline has become a concern for many commuting to a physical classroom.

We believe there will be continued explosive growth in online education in the coming years. Additional support is provided in a study by Greg Eisenbarth (2004), Director of The Online University Consortium, who made the following points:

- Employers will drive online enrollments, and they are increasingly using the Web to do it. For example, 60% of IBM's existing classroom content has now moved online.

- More working professionals who are interested in, but have been unable to pursue a first or second degree, will migrate online.

- As younger learners have grown up with both computers and the Internet, they fully expect to continue using computers and the Web in the process of learning. Miami High School seniors can now take over 65 classes in art, math, social studies, and physical education through Florida Virtual School via the Internet (Eisenbarth, 2003). Other high schools also follow this high school's example. These students are inclined to later seek higher education and advanced degrees online.

- The short history of the Internet demonstrates that the ubiquity of the Web makes geographic boundaries obsolete and hypergrowth very possible.

The Disadvantages and Requirements Must Be Acknowledged

With all of the positives mentioned, there are many areas where the requirements for Internet-based education are substantial. Greater student initiative is required for distance learning programs. A certain level of technical proficiency and computer equipment is required by students. And for those in remote locations and those with disabilities, there may be obstacles to Internet access.

Moreover, there are still squabbles regarding the availability of student financial aid, litigation regarding the right of individual states to regulate programs, and increasing pressure for oversight in accreditation and accountability. We view accreditation and accountability in both positive and negative terms: positive in terms of oversight and a defensive response by those trying to slow growth. The future of online education is not without complications, but the obstacles continue to diminish.

It is clear that distance learning is central to the new media revolution and is a growth industry and a necessary part of the future of higher education and corporate training. In order for educational institutions to take full advantage of the technological delivery systems of tomorrow, they must be able to motivate students by applying psychological principles developed for the new educational media.

Learning Psychology and Media Psychology Are Central to Progress

The discussion and literature about online learning has been limited in the areas of media psychology and learning psychology. To create the perfect storm now that public resistance is not an obstacle, digital technology is here, education and government are receptive, and the world economy is acting as a booster rocket, there needs to be much more research and teaching about the why as well as the how. Media psychology and learning psychology simply draw on theories in psychology and apply them to media in facilitating learning, or include them as tools enabling learning to take place.

The discussion of theories in psychology that follows is not specific or unique to media or to learning. These are examples of concepts and theories in psychology that must be understood if the e-learning world is to continue to improve. Essentially, the field of psychology is learned one theory at a time. This list is fundamental and important to the future of online learning. It includes the following theories:

- Motivation
- Success and Failure
- Intelligence
- Mastery
- Psycho-Visualization
- Believability
- Color
- Sound
- Cognition
- Positive Addiction

- Attention
- Emotions
- Repetition
- Brain-Based Learning
- Retention
- Semantics
- Personality
- Persuasion
- Control

Media Psychology: New Growth Area

The first blended model of master's and doctoral programs in media psychology was launched by Fielding Graduate University in 2002. PhD and EdD graduates of the media psychology and media studies program at

Fielding are now teaching at other colleges and universities. In addition, the Media Psychology Division of the American Psychology Association is growing and fostering media in learning as a priority. Media psychology has also attracted the attention of the community of family therapists, and media and the family is a growing area of professional attention.

New programs are increasing in number. There are now courses in media psychology in a number of colleges and universities. There is a search for qualified faculty with the component skills to launch these new programs. Educational institutions need faculty and staff who understand higher concepts in the media arts and sciences. The number of positions in media studies and the use of media in e-learning, distributed education, and classroom learning are increasing. Graduate programs are emerging worldwide. Tools of the future are both physical and intellectual. Individuals in all facets of educational leadership and change must now understand how to apply media effects in order to perform successfully in the majority of new and emerging occupational specialties.

This chapter has offered an overview of the e-learning industry, distance education, and new media. The new learning psychologies that are related to media are growing and they are being refined. The specialty needs in media psychology and learning psychology are on center stage. However, it is appropriate to conclude that the future is about access, opportunity, learning how to learn, psychology, and pursuing the perfect storm. The pieces are all now here. All we need to do is put them together.

References

Allen, I. E., & Jeff, S. (2007). *Online nation: Five years of growth in online learning.* Needham, MA: The Sloan Consortium. Retrieved June 30, 2008, from http://sloanconsortium.org/publications/survey/online_nation

Bricken, M., & Byrne, C. M. (1994). Summer students in virtual reality: A pilot study on educational applications of virtual reality technology. In A. Wexelblat (Ed.), *Virtual reality: Applications and explorations* (pp. 199–218). Boston: Academic Press.

Bureau of Labor Statistics & the Census Bureau. (2006). *Current population survey: Annual social and economic supplement.* Retrieved July 12, 2008, from http://pubdb3.census.gov/macro/032007/perinc/new03_001.htm

Buxton, W. A. S. (1993). Telepresence: Integrating shared task and person spaces. In R. M. Baecker (Ed.), *Readings in groupware and computer-supported cooperative work* (pp. 816–822). San Francisco: Morgan Kaufmann.

Chan, T. S., & Ahern, T. C. (1999). Targeting motivation—Adapting flow theory to instructional design. *Journal of Educational Computing Research, 21*(2), 151–163.

Cheeseman Day, J., & Newburger, E. C. (2002). *The big payoff: Educational attainment and synthetic estimates of work-life earnings* (Current Population Report P23-210). Washington, DC: U.S. Census Bureau, U.S. Department of Commerce,

Economics and Statistics Administation. Retrieved July 10, 2008, from http://www.census.gov/prod/2002pubs/p23-210.pdf

Csikszentmihalyi, M. (1990). *Flow: The psychology of optimal experience:* New York: Harper & Row.

Davis, F. D., Bagozzi, R. P., & Warshaw, P. R. (1989). User acceptance of computer technology: A comparison of two theoretical models. *Management Science, 35*(8), 982–1003.

Eisenbarth, G. (2003). The online education market. *On the Horizon, 11*(3), 10.

Eisenbarth, G. (2004). *The online education market: A crossroads for higher education & business.* Retrieved May 14, 2008, from http://www.onlineuc.net/oucarticle.html

Frydenberg, J. (2007). Persistence in university continuing education online classes. *International Review of Research in Open and Distance Learning, 8*(3). Retrieved from http://www.irrodl.org/index.php/irrodl/article/view/375/934

Ghani, J. A., & Deshpande, S. P. (1994). Task characteristics and the experience of optimal flow in human-computer interaction. *The Journal of Psychology, 128*(4), 381–391.

Golden, D. (2006, May 9). Degrees@StateU.edu. *Wall Street Journal,* p. 1.

Graves, W. H. (1997). Free trade in higher education the meta university. *Journal of Asynchronous Learning Networks, 1,* 97–108.

Hillman Daniel, C. A., Willis, D. J., & Gunawardena, C. N. (1994). Learner-interface interaction in distance education: An extension of contemporary models and strategies for practitioners. *The American Journal of Distance Education, 8*(2), 30–42.

Jenkins, H. (2006). *Convergence culture: Where old and new media collide.* New York: New York University Press.

Keegan, D. (1993). *Theoretical principles of distance education.* New York: Routledge.

Liao, L.-F. (2006). A flow theory perspective on learner motivation and behavior in distance education. *Distance Education, 27*(1), 45.

Moore, M. G. (1991). Distance education theory. *The American Journal of Distance Education, 5*(3), 1–6.

Munro, J. S. (1998). *Presence at a distance: The educator–learner relationship in distance learning* (Vol. 16). University Park: Pennsylvania State University.

Novak, T. P., Hoffman, D. L., & Yung, Y. F. (1998, March). *Modeling the structure of the flow experience among Web users.* Abstract for the INFORMS Marketing Science and the Internet Mini-Conference, Cambridge, MA. Retrieved from http://sloan.ucr.edu/blog/uploads/papers/Modeling%20the%20Structure%20of%20the%20Flow%20Experience%20Among%20Web%20Users%20%5BHoffman,%20Novak,%20Yiu-Fai%20Yung%20-%20Dec%201997%5D.pdf

Saba, F. (2000). Research in distance education: A status report. *International Review of Research in Open and Distance Learning, 1*(1), 4.

Shedden, M. (2006, September 21). Students dogged by debt. *Tampa Tribune,* p. 1.

Winn, W. (1993). *A conceptual basis for educational applications of virtual reality* (HITLab Tech Report R-93-9). Seattle: University of Washington, Human Interface Technology Laboratory. Retrieved July 10, 2008, from http://www.hitl.washington.edu/projects/learning_center/winn/winn-R-939.txt

Chapter 7

Globalization in Online Learning

Janet Poley

Article 26: Universal Declaration of Human Rights—December 10, 1948

(1) everyone has the right to education. Education shall be free, at least in the elementary and fundamental stages. Elementary education shall be compulsory. Technical and professional education shall be made generally available and higher education shall be equally accessible to all on the basis of merit.

(2) education shall be directed to the full development of the human personality and to the strengthening of respect for human rights and fundamental freedoms. It shall promote understanding, tolerance and friendship among all nations, racial or religious groups, and shall further the activities of the United Nations in the maintenance of peace.

I personally committed myself to making it a priority, for education is a fundamental human right, set forth in the Universal Declaration of Human Rights and the International Human Rights Covenants, which have force of international law. To pursue the aim of education for all is therefore an obligation for States.

— Koichiro Matsuura, UNESCO Director General, 2000

The Global Environment

Once upon a time, the world was flat. But then sailors and their ships went exploring, and it became round. If one believes Gavin Menzies, it all started in *1421: The Year China Discovered the World* (Menzies, 2003). But even earlier, as far back as 150 BC, globes were imagined and constructed. More recently authors have been writing about *The Death of Distance* (Cairncross, 1997) and once again declaring that *The World is Flat* (Friedman, 2005) or spiky (Florida, 2005) due to the massive deployment of information and communication technology. Although we know that the shape of the earth has not really changed, people's perceptions of it have changed through the magic of technology. In many ways, Cairncross, Friedman, and Florida are right and wrong at the same time. Their books are interesting articulations of today's global environment changing with technological innovation and deployment. The Internet connections rapidly surrounding the globe have, in slightly more than a decade, significantly altered work, relationships, and education.

And still, we have a growing and highly significant digital divide where the "haves" live in a very robust environment with access to learning. Without payment, it is now possible to dip into the expanding body of world knowledge and retrieve whatever is required just in time. The irony is that those who have access to education, those who know a lot, and those who are motivated to learn more continue to benefit more from the information revolution than those who "have not." Knowledge continues to beget knowledge, and the gap grows in ways that are disturbing if one believes that self-actualization, peace, and prosperity are built upon educated populations.

The United States is the single largest e-learning market worldwide with revenues exceeding $17.5 billion in 2007. The world market is expected to exceed $52.6 billion by 2010. The e-learning market is fragmented, including niche players from public and private universities and businesses. The United States is dominant in the corporate e-learning market with over a 60% share, followed by Europe with less than 15% (Global Industry Analysts, n.d.)

Cairncross wrote *The Death of Distance* in 1997, while editor of the *Economist* magazine, predating the Friedman (2005) book by 8 years. There is considerable similarity in her predictions and his 10 flatteners, but critics around the world continue to seriously debate the notion that the playing field is leveling. Countries are cutting taxes; outsourcing grows; English continues to flourish as the language of science, trade, and online education; mobile digital devices proliferate; governments can watch over all, and people can communicate, take classes from anywhere, and collaborate and work virtually. Many cannot yet directly participate in this digital world, but the forces driving toward wider deployment and utilization are everywhere.

At the same time, British historian Niall Ferguson (2004) asked whether globalization might collapse. He wrote in a section of his book *Empire* titled "The Annihilation of Distance" that in the 19th century, British

Empire technologies such as steam-powered ships, the telegraph, mobility of commodities, capital, and people produced euphoria related to the tremendous possibilities until World War I wrecked it all. Ferguson wrote that "it may seem excessively pessimistic to worry that this scenario could somehow repeat itself—that our age of globalization could collapse just as our grandparents' age did" (p. 142). He believes that the possibility of failure today is just as real as it was in 1915 when the Lusitania sunk. With the growing realization that there are tremendous uncertainties and inconvenient truths (David, Bender, Burns, & Guggenheim, 2006) in this round, flat, spiky, complex world, many are not divorcing themselves from globalization but are being reminding that for most people the world is local.

This chapter addresses global trends, challenges, and opportunities in online learning, as well as key areas of interest such as access, learning, business, openness, and innovation. The local learners' perspective and needs are the focus. At the center of the discussion, I rebuke the view of online learning as a means to deliver mass produced education pumped through the Internet to empty vessels anywhere, anytime.

It should be noted that online learning is a misnomer like nearly every other term used to annihilate distance in learning. This chapter includes a discussion of interactive, collaborative learning made possible through the use of wires, fiber, radio signals, and so on—the technology is necessary but far from sufficient to create access to learning. Whether a person chooses to call this type of learning online, distance learning, distributed learning, or just plain learning is irrelevant. Far too much time is and has been spent worrying about what to call this type of learning rather than working on the really important dimensions of broadened access to quality learning resources and opportunities.

The African situation is the most extreme case in point. As a continent of 47 countries, it represents the greatest pent-up demand for education at all levels, has the least Internet access, nearly all of it by satellite, which is costly and far from widely distributed. Although access is growing to institutions of higher education in urban areas in politically stable countries, nearly all rural locations are excluded from the digital education revolution. Cell phone connectivity is growing to populations just now making their first phone calls.

In many countries, literacy remains an issue, and lack of education beyond Grade 6 presents a bottleneck. No wonder interest in educational access to all types at all levels is huge. Connections to the oceanic cables in East and West Africa are first steps in creating changes. Ghana, Tanzania, Mali, and others have been preparing with regulation changes, infrastructure upgrades including overcoming the electrical power problem, and an Internet service provider set-up that will take the Internet to colleges, schools, learning centers, businesses, and eventually homes outside the large cities.

Global Trends in Online Learning

Distance and Access to Education

In 2007, six international scientific journals launched a common call for papers on the theme of distance education and the right of access to education. The participating journals include *The Asian Journal of Distance Education, Distances et Savoirs; European Journal of Open and Distance, International Review of Research in Open and Distance Learning,* and *Open Praxis and the Journal of Asynchronous Learning Networks.* Texts can be found in English, French, Spanish, Hindi, and Portuguese. The need is great, and the problem is recognized, but too few development strategists have recently focused on educational networking as fundamental to place and prosperity worldwide (http://www.distanceandaccesstoeducation.org).

Demographics and Drivers

At the end of 2007, China was ready to overtake the United States as the nation with the most Internet users. The United States had 210 million. China was advancing to 215 million with expected growth of 6 million more each month. China also claims the world's largest number of broadband users with 60% of those on the Internet using broadband. One third of the new broadband users are farmers, where the demand for the service is high. The Chinese Agricultural Broadcasting and Television School calls itself the largest distance education organization in the world, serving 800 million small farmers in a country of 1.4 billion people. Distance education and online learning are of high priority interest, and the concern is significant with respect to the disparity between rural and urban residents. Audiences include the nonliterate to those pursuing certificate programs and university degrees. Many who have graduated from institutions outside China have returned to play leadership roles in science, technology, engineering, and online learning.

Coupled with the tremendous growth in India, the Asian continent is rapidly leading the march to do business through the Internet. In February 2007, Baidu became the leading search engine. Founded in 2000, it is often referred to as the Chinese Google. The name Baidu comes from an old Chinese poem about the persistent pursuit for the ideal. In June of 2008, Baidu.com announced it is preparing to launch its instant messaging application with real-time video chat ("Video chat," 2008). Baidu traffic is growing rapidly as is information and communication technologies (ICT)–based distance learning and e-learning. China has three of the world's mega universities—institutions with over 100,000 students largely using distance education methods. China, India, Malaysia, and Singapore import and export distance learning programs to countries such as Bangladesh, China, Indonesia, and Sri Lanka. Other mega universities, all using some e-learning, are located in Pakistan, Canada, Turkey, India, Korea, United Kingdom, Thailand, and Indonesia. The mega universities were originally traditional media-based correspondence oriented and are—like other educational promoters struggling to modify policies, procedures, practices, and quality assurance—in the new environment.

Counting learners on a global basis is less commonly done than measuring bits, bytes, hits, videos, and other types of Internet measurements that are easy to do. The Alfred P. Sloan Foundation, under the auspices of Program Manager A. Frank Mayadas, has led the way in tracking online learners taking academic courses through U.S. colleges and universities. The 2007 Sloan Consortium (Sloan-C) study *Online Nation: Five Years of Growth in Online Learning* in the United States states that 3.5 million students are taking at least one online course, as reported from 2,500 U.S. colleges and universities. This is a 10% increase over the previous year and the expectation of administrators is that this will continue to grow (Allen & Seaman, 2007).

U.S. courses are primarily in English, programs exist in many subject areas, and new partnerships and relationships, particularly with Mexico, Latin American, and the Caribbean, are growing. Entrepreneurial initiatives in virtual and blended learning come from the private Technologico de Monterrey (ITESM), a well-established and successful provider of educational opportunity using technology throughout Mexico, Latin America, and now in the United States through its growing number of community learning centers. ITESM, or the Tec, has worked with multiple public, private, and business enterprises on a large scale partnering throughout the western hemisphere and Europe!

Its new sister institution, Tec Milenio, is modeled somewhat after the University of Phoenix (the largest private higher education institution in the United States), with its significant and growing number of online courses and programs. It intends to create a large-scale institution with multiple campuses and online programs of high quality and affordability to reach Spanish speakers wherever they may reside geographically. They are also partnering with many public and private partners in education and business.

Master's degree programs are available in nearly all disciplinary areas with bachelor's degree completion and PhD degrees less common. A large number of options online are available for the first 2 years of college. Associate degrees are offered by public community colleges and private sector providers. The private sector providers have particularly targeted minority populations in urban areas where they market expensive programs on an open admissions basis to populations eligible for government assistance. In late 2007, the United States began to investigate the marketing practices and the student loan aspects of a number of these providers.

As of May 2008, there were 1,407,724,920 world Internet users and the top 10 Internet languages were English, Chinese, Spanish, Japanese, French, German, Arabic, Portuguese, Korean, and Italian (Internet World Stats: Usage and Population Statistics, 2008). The National Online Learners

Priorities Report of 2006 (Noel-Levitz, 2006) was conducted with 34,000 students from 78 higher education institutions in the states of Texas, Ohio, Colorado, Arizona, Minnesota, Iowa, Georgia, Florida, Wisconsin, and Virginia. Sixty-eight percent of the online learners were women, and the majority was employed full time while taking a full-time class load. Seventy-seven percent were 25 to 54 years old. Eighty-two percent of the learners were studying primarily online, while the others were engaged in blended learning mostly on campus. The 2006 study did not include race and ethnicity demographics, but the 2005 report (Noel-Levitz, 2005) stated that seventy-four percent of the enrollees were Caucasian, 12% African American, 4% Hispanic, 3% Asian and 7% Other. Many U.S. e-learning providers and the mega universities have large numbers of cross-border students. English-speaking users represented 30.4% of users; Chinese, 16.6% of users; Spanish, 8.7%; and Japanese, 6.7%.

The 2007 report (Noel-Levitz, 2007) showed slightly increasing numbers overall and nearly the same percentage breakdown as the 2006 study discussed above, indicating some stabilization in the market.

The 2007 satisfaction assessment indicated the following as overall strengths of online learning (in order of importance):

- Student assignments are clearly defined in the syllabus.
- Registration is convenient.
- Program requirements are clear and reasonable.
- Instructional materials are appropriate for program content.
- Assessment and evaluation procedures are clear and reasonable.

The top challenges identified by online learning were (in order of importance):

- Instruction is of excellent quality.
- Faculty is responsive to student needs.
- Faculty provides timely feedback about student progress.
- Tuition paid is a worthwhile investment.
- There are sufficient offerings within the program of study.

Overall, 72% of the online learners stated they were satisfied or very satisfied with their experience, and 76% indicated they would probably or definitely reenroll in the program if they were to do it again. Convenience was the primary motivation for enrollment in the program (Noel-Levitz, 2005, 2006, 2007).

There has been little, if any, reporting that breaks down participants in online courses by nationality. This will become increasingly important as new and creative partnerships are developed allowing ease of course sharing, course registration, and tuition payments. Many online classes include participants from other countries, however, as reported by the Organisation for Economic Co-operation and Development (OECD). Observer, higher education is subsidized to greater and lesser degrees across countries, and online learning often is treated differently from campus-based education (OECD, 2006). Only three of the 22 nations among the OECD countries pay more than 30% of their tertiary education: Korea, Japan, and the United States (OECD, 2006).

Australia and New Zealand, big players in online education, actually have rules that prevent universities there from providing subsidized educational services to students from other countries. Australia is an example of a country exporting higher education to learners' home countries through e-learning. The proliferation of both distance education and locally delivered traditional education is demand driven, largely from the rapidly emerging countries of North and Southeast Asia. Increasingly, partnerships are being developed as a more sustainable way to address the educational demand outstripping supply in many countries where learners want degrees from U.S. Australian, and European institutions (Larsen & Vincent-Lancrin, 2002).

Need to Improve Historical and Contextual Research

Michael Moore (2008), editor of the *American Journal of Distance Education,* wrote that too much online learning research lacks scientific rigor and produces findings that are ungeneralizable. He stated that the lack of attention to historical research in the distance learning field is very serious. He noted that so much attention is focused on "mastering and applying fashionable technologies" (p. 67) that little attention is paid to understanding important historical factors and context that would more efficiently inform present programs. Across nationals and cultural boundaries, few may have the background to conduct historical research as compared to case studies and surveys, techniques emphasized to a much greater extent in methodological research preparation today. He noted that in education-related research, perfect control is impossible, and the oft-used case study also has the challenge of studying dynamic situations in flux. Historical studies may have an advantage because the effects of interventions should be observable, post hoc. He states that the rich historical gray literature, fugitive papers, and collections, materials from individuals, institutes, organizations, and agencies from the past three quarters of a century, are nearly unexamined. He suggests that these have particularly rich potential for policy and leadership understanding. Moore's observations are particularly important in the international context as currently comparative studies of online learning are emerging (Moore, 2008).

Rapid Expansion of Study Abroad Programs and Potential for New Online Models

A renewed interest in study abroad programs is emerging and is frequently coupled with online learning components. A number of higher education institutes in China are opening Chinese cultural centers on U.S. university campuses, working out student exchange programs and developing 1 + 1 + 2 agreements where students take blended programs with face-to-face in the home country, face-to-face in the exchange country, and online learning for language culture and courses. A larger number of dual-degree programs with institutions in two countries awarding the degree are anticipated. The Internet makes transparency of the teaching and learning process much greater. Collaborative instructional design, teaching, learning, certification, and dual-degree granting are now possible. However, the "not invented here" and financial aspects of these new approaches are not uniformly seen as positive, but they are occurring, and growth is inevitable.

Students are increasingly demanding ways to connect to underserved areas of the world and relate to other people, places, and culture. Economic globalization, climate change, trade, health and disease, and fear of the negative consequences of not understanding (nuclear war, etc.) require that educational systems change. The intent makes isolation a more deliberate decision than ever before.

In the United States, students' interest in the Middle East has grown rapidly. According to the International Institute for Education, more than 2,500 Americans participated in study abroad programs in the region in 2005 (latest figures available). This is up from 1,000 2 years earlier (Open Doors, 2007). For U.S. students, European countries remain the favored destinations (United Kingdom, Italy, Spain, France, and Germany) with slight increases in student visitors: 1% to 5%. However, Mexico, China, Chile, Argentina, India, South Africa, Brazil, and Ecuador had much larger percentage increases. Although many of the face-to-face programs are short-term in nature, they are leading to previsit online collaborations, during visit online course participation with back home institutions, pre- and postglobal seminars, and now the beginning of new multicountry partnerships and relationships to develop joint alliances in distance education and online learning.

Why Learners Are Opting for Online Learning–Distance Education: A U.S. and U.K. Comparison

SkillsTrain is Europe's leading provider of information technology (IT) skills, and the company has trained over 6 million students in the last 60 years. Located in the United Kingdom, it published a list of the top 10 reasons why those returning to study after an education gap prefer to study at home (distance education) (SkillsTrain, 2008). The reasons are as follows:

1. They want to improve job and career prospects.

2. They cannot afford to give up work.

3. They want to earn more money.

4. They have family commitments.

5. They need the education to qualify for promotion.

6. They want to prove they can do it.

7. They left school without formal qualification.

8. They want to do something useful with their time.

9. They want flexibility of studying on their own time.

10. They feel too old to go back to school.

In the United States, degree.com, a Web site focused on online degree programs and distance learning, had 38% more visitors during April through May 2008 as compared to February through March 2008, after adjusting for seasonal differences. The number one reason for being interested in an online degree was higher gas prices, followed by convenience, parking, scheduling, babysitting, and the costs of classes. In the previous years, convenience has ranked as the number one driver in the United States.

Online Learning: A Vehicle to Educating All?

Tanzania's first president and international statesman, Julius Nyerere, preferred to be addressed as *Mwalimu* (teacher in Kiswahili). Nyerere believed strongly in the importance of both formal and nonformal education as the vehicle for peace, stability, and independence. Nyerere defined education as the development of one's consciousness to think, decide, and act; hence, it should be aimed at improving people's freedom and their control over their own lives and environment:

> The ideas imparted by education, or released through education, should therefore be liberating ideas; the skill acquired by education should be liberating skills. Nothing else can properly be called education. Teaching which induces a slave mentality or a sense of importance is *not education for all.* (Nyerere, 1975, p. 10)

Mbilinyi (2003) argued that Nyerere had it right with respect to education and that Tanzania's education policy today should focus on a strong public education system at all levels, emphasizing access, content, and quality. Historically, Kiswahili was a unifying factor in Tanzania's educational achievements. Mbilinyi noted that privatization and liberalization have resulted in a dual education system with potentially explosive class inequities.

As the Internet and Community Learning Centers become more widely available in African countries such as Tanzania, there is an opportunity to improve learner-centered teacher education to share educational resources with other countries, collaborate in the development of online learning resources, and create greater access and quality. The country's Open University began in 1994, and prior to that, the country had a number of educational initiatives, as noted above: The Institute of Adult Education, Universal Primary Education, Training for Rural Development, and the continuing Education Institute at Sokaine University in Morogoro. Tanzania played a leading role in the World Bank virtual university experiment, and more recent activities focused on teaching and learning over the Internet.

However, online learning is lagging in Tanzania and most other African countries due in large measure to connectivity issues. Moreover, a number of difficult barriers haunt Sub-Saharan Africa as countries reach for the promise of e-learning. The following list applies (Braimoh, 2008):

- unstable power supply;
- greed—distance education institutions sacrificing quality and chasing money;
- high cost of distance education offerings;
- high cost of accessible technology;
- technological illiteracy among learners, even if technology is present;
- rural learners without access to power or technology;
- lack of cultural and context appropriative;
- lack of trained teachers, tutors, and mentors; and
- inadequate learner support.

Open Sesame and Online Learning

Ali Baba was a poor Arab woodcutter who overheard 40 thieves in the woods seeking their stolen treasures from a cave sealed by magic. The secret word to open the cave was "Open O Simsim," or "Open Sesame" in English, and to seal shut, "Close, Simsim" or "Close Sesame." Ali Baba uses the magic words to enter the case and steal some coins leading to the death of his brother Cassim and rescue from the thieves' revenge by the slave girl Morgiana (Ali Baba, n.d.).

In today's online world, the magic word used by all seeking online treasures is open: open education, open source software, open educational resources, open courseware initiative, open platform, and open Wikis. Those who know that an ocelot is a leopard may be surprised to discover that an OSCELOT is an open source community for educational learning objects and tools (oscelot.org). The number of open conferences are too many to count, and July 12, 2008, was the third open source day held in Las Vegas intended for developers, managers, and members of the educational community to learn about OSCELOT.

The term Pachyderm (nmc.org/Pachyderm) has always been used to describe elephants and sometimes rhinos and hippos but now it is an open source multimedia authoring tool that was recently described by *Edutopia*, the magazine of the George Lucas Foundation, as "multimedia authoring for peanuts." Pachyderm offers dedicated multimedia accounts and/or servers to schools, museums, universities, and anyone interested in easy, Web-based multimedia. Source code is open and can be found at Sourceforge (sourceforge.net).

Moodle: Growing Platform of Choice

Moodle (moodle.org) is a free open source software content management system designed to help education create effective online learning communities. Moodle has a large user community with over 400,000 registrants (from) individuals to major universities, speaking 75 languages in 193 countries. The main discussions are held in English, but increasingly, online conversations are held in other languages.

Developers contribute to Moodle, and it is available in a variety of download packages with different levels of stability with additional modules or plug-ins and language packs. Moodle's "Buzz" includes news releases and updates from around the world, and the Moodle community holds international conferences. It is built around a constructionist learning paradigm influenced by Brazilian adult educator Paulo Freire.

Sakai (sakaiproject.org) is an alternative to Moodle as an online collaboration and learning environment. It is used to support teaching and learning, for ad hoc group collaboration, to support for portfolios, and for research collaboration. The Sakai Foundation is dedicated to developing a Sakai community and sustaining its use. Foundation board members come from the United States, Canada, and the United Kingdom, and its users are heavily clustered in the United States and Europe. Commercial affiliates such as IBM, Oracle, Sun, and other less well-known companies are offering support and expertise for the project. The University of

Capetown is working on a version of Sakai called Vula. Sakai partners pay an annual membership fee of $10,000 with discounts and multiple-year memberships available for small institutions for reduced fees.

Open Educational Resources

Increasingly, attention is focused on strategies to make online learning resources more available to all. These open learning resources are growing and are often free to the user and available for them to adopt, adapt, or change as appropriate to the country, culture, and student population. International organizations including UNESCO, the United Nations Food and Agricultural Organization, Instituto Interamericano de Cooperacion para la Agricultura, and others are discussing open standards and technology, interoperability, and requirements for federated services. Although easy to talk about, developing interconnected learning repositories in global federations so that institutions, countries, and regions can share and exchange resources and metadata is a significant challenge. In addition, quality assurance procedures are not yet well developed and agreed upon. Questions related to learning object ownership, use, maintenance, and user fees are only a few of the sticky issues. Considerably, more money has been and likely will continue to be invested in expansion of broadband and wireless networks and thousands of devices to use digital content than in learner-oriented strategies and systems to improve access and learning effectiveness.

Wikis and Wiki Educator

Wiki is originally a Hawaiian word for fast, and a wiki wiki was the name of the shuttle bus running between terminals at the Hawaiian airport. The wiki glossary defines a wiki as a type of Web site that allows visitors to add, remove, and sometimes edit the available content using a simple markup language as a tool for collaborative authoring. The wiki originated in 1995 with the work of Ward Cunningham, developer of the Wiki Wiki Web. He chose the name as an alternative to quick ("Please Read: A Personal Appeal From Wikipedia Founder Jimmy Wales," 2008).

WikiEducator (wikieducator.org) is an evolving community intended for the collaborative planning of educational projects linked with free content. Development of free content on WikiEducator is for e-learning purposes and building open education resources (OERs). The Commonwealth of Learning (COL) launched WikiEducator in 2006. COL has worked with Zambia, Ghana, Nigeria, and Sierra Leone in transforming Canadian math and English learning materials into Wiki format (Wilson & Mackintosh, 2007).

Can Free Open Source Software
Help Developing Countries?

Free and open sources software (FOSS) is viewed by the United Nations Conference on Trade and Development (UNCTAD) as an inseparable component of the global technological ecosystem. UNCTAD argues that FOSS can have positive externalities, making it an important aspect of policy formulation and e-strategy. FOSS is being considered as a strategy between proprietary institutions and the public domain for education, science, and other creative endeavors. FOSS is a dominant force on the Internet, with more than half of Internet servers running an operating system such as GNU/Linux and the open source Apache program handing out Web pages. FOSS is not necessarily free of charge—free means free speech, not gratis. FOSS is also not noncommercial—it is not freeware or software in the public domain. Many large companies are using, developing, and deploying FOSS for profit. Two major entities deal with FOSS: the Free Software Foundation and the Open Source Initiative.

FOSS defines the four freedoms relating to software development and use as follows:

- Freedom 0: Freedom to run a program for any purpose
- Freedom 1: Freedom to study how a program works and adapt to one's own need
- Freedom 2: Freedom to improve the program to help other users
- Freedom 3: Freedom to improve the program and release these improvements to the public so the community benefits

FOSS is distinguished by open source code and free and open licenses. UNCTAD concludes that FOSS presents a significant development opportunity because of the critical role that users can play in determining the need for software products and influencing the overall trajectory of technology evolution. Software innovations can and should come increasingly from developing countries. Developing countries are not implicitly dependent on commoditized, proprietary innovation from the developed worlds. In a FOSS environment, users—be they individuals, governments, or businesses—could push technology development toward applications that specifically address local needs and demands. However, for indigenous demand to be expressed, users need to understand the opportunities they have and the ways in which a digital infrastructure could contribute to their lives.

Given the importance of the FOSS issue and the timeliness of the debate, governments should consider including policy on FOSS as part of their overall e-strategy. Although there are many good reasons to favor FOSS, these should be evaluated on the basis of digital readiness and other factors such as connectivity, human resources, and potential for the development of a local software services sector. From a development perspective, FOSS has a number of advantages. The task for policy makers is to determine whether and how these can be exploited (UNCTAD, 2004).

Derek Keats, a professor at the University of Western Cape in South Africa, stated in March of 2008 that FOSS is as much about democracy as it is about technology. He thinks that being able to rewrite source code gives users a greater sense of ownership. Governments are particularly interested in whether FOSS will save money and increase efficiency. And although it sounds obvious, until African learners have computers and connections to the Internet allowing online participation, FOSS may to many be somewhat irrelevant (Barber, 2008).

Reforming Pedagogy Through Online Learning

COL (col.org) was established by heads of government in 1987 as a way to strengthen higher education in the developing world by making use of the potential of open, distance, and technology enhanced education. Today, the majority of people in the developing the British Commonwealth are under the age of 20, and by 2020, it is predicted that 40% of the global workforce will be knowledge workers who need higher education.

Reform of pedagogy and curricula in online programs and courses is underway throughout the world, and increasingly, the focus is moving away from the technology and delivery mode to improving teaching and learning. Asha Kanwar of COL advised in a speech at Tamil Nadu Open University in January of 2008 that it is critical that faculty change the ways in which they have been teaching by moving to constructivism and connectivism. She noted that many younger students may prefer to be passive and want immediate gratification (sometimes called the fast-food approach to learning), but now the Internet allows faculty to challenge learners by creating interactive opportunities. Instructional design that is learner centered rather than teacher centered is rapidly taking hold, and instructors can no longer dash into class to deliver a lecture from a prior year's notes. Learner-to-learner approaches are being incorporated to improve understanding and scaling of digital course offerings. Collaborative course development, team teaching, and adaptation and translation of freely available materials from professors in other countries are increasing (Kanwar, 2008).

Digitization of books and other library materials, as well as content from course notes, is moving more toward a 3D and video world of learning objects, animations, models, pictures, maps, and other online tools. Simulations, visualizations, laboratory experiments, and collaborative work environments are being developed and tested, although not yet widely deployed. The critical problem of bandwidth "have-nots" on all continents—particularly in rural, remote, and developing locations—remains, and deep concern about widening access to learning resources, courses, and programs is growing. In addition, access is increasingly considered to be a problem, with its roots more in affordability than in technology.

American Distance Education Consortium (ADEC) and Sloan-C Quality Factors and Use of Online Learning as Strategic Asset

In part because the Sloan-C filled a void with its annual online learning quality pillars and annual learning survey, this work has increasingly become the foundation for assessing quality of online learning beyond the U.S. borders. As online learning becomes incorporated into mainstream academic and nonacademic education, it appears that revalidation of what has long been known about quality management, continuous improvement, and teaching excellence and facilitation of learning are occurring.

The Sloan quality factors are (1) access, (2) learning effectiveness, (3) student support, (4) cost effectiveness, and (5) faculty satisfaction. The *Journal of Asynchronous Learning Networks* and a number of resources on quality and best practices with international applicability are available from Sloan-C (sloan-c.org). The ADEC (adec.edu) is a Sloan-C partner. ADEC includes more than 60 state universities and land-grant colleges in the United States and a growing number of internationally affiliated members throughout the western hemisphere. Collaborative efforts are underway with African and Chinese organizations interested in distance education and online learning.

ADEC's goal is to enable, harness, and empower visionary thinking and action using technology to create access to quality learning opportunities anywhere, anytime. Collaboration helps provide the means for meeting needs of ADEC members. Specific strategic initiatives in support of ADEC's goals include the following: (1) global science and education programs; (2) innovation in pedagogy and technology for learning; (3) development of digital infrastructure, including collaborative development of affordable approaches to access and content sharing through standards, tools development, and sharing; (4) development of human capacity through workforce development, shared learning materials, and courses; and (5) disaster planning and response using online learning repositories and other strategies.

ADEC's (adec.edu) guiding principles for teaching and learning are :

1. The learning experience must have a clear purpose with tightly focused outcomes and objectives.

2. Web-based learning designs must consider the nature of content, specific context, desired learning outcomes, and characteristics of

the learner. Learner-centered strategies include modular, stand-alone units that are compatible with short bursts of learning. Learning modules may also be open, flexible, and self-directing.

3. The learner is actively engaged. Active, hands-on, concrete experiences are highly effective. Learning by doing, analogy, and assimilation are increasingly important pedagogical forms. When possible, learning outcomes should relate to real-life experiences through simulation and application.

4. The learning environment makes appropriate use of a variety of media. Various learning styles are best engaged by using a variety of media to achieve learning outcomes. Selection of media may also depend on the nature of content, learning goals, access to technology, and the local learning environment.

5. Learning environments must include problem-based as well as knowledge-based learning. Problem-based learning involves higher order thinking skills such as analysis, synthesis, and evaluation, while knowledge-based learning involves recall, comprehension, and application.

6. Learning experiences should support interaction and the development of communities of interest. Learning is social and sensitive to context. Learning experiences based on interaction and collaboration support learning communities while building a support network to enhance learning outcomes. Multiple interactions, group collaboration, and cooperative learning may provide increased levels of interaction and simulation. The practice of distance learning contributes to the larger social mission of education and training in a democratic society. Changing mental models and constructing new knowledge empowers learners and encourages critical thinking. "Knowledge becomes a function of how the individual creates meaning from his or her experiences; it is not a function of what someone else says is true" (Jonassen, Davidson, Collins, Campbell, & Hagg, 1995).

The following characteristics of quality Web-based teaching and learning are proving to be applicable irrespective of country or culture:

- foster meaning-making and discourse;
- move from knowledge transmission to learner-controlled systems;
- provide for reciprocal teaching;
- are learner centered;
- encourage active participation and knowledge construction;
- promote higher level thinking skills—analysis, synthesis, and evaluation;

- promote active learning;
- allow group collaboration and cooperative learning;
- provide multiple levels of interaction; and
- focus on real world and problem solving.

European Distance and E-Learning Network (EDEN): The Learnovation Initiative

EDEN exists to share knowledge and improve understanding for professionals in distance and e-learning across the whole of Europe and beyond and to promote policy and practice for this field of endeavor. EDEN holds annual conferences and has launched and supports the *European Journal of Open and Distance Learning*.

In March 2008, EDEN joined with nine major European networks concerned with e-learning, lifelong learning, and education to discuss a new vision of innovation in learning that embeds ICT in a comprehensive and future-oriented perspective. This initiative is known as the Learnovation Stakeholders Roundtable. In addition to EDEN, the other networks include The European Association for Distance Learning, the European Foundation for Management Development, the European Federation for Quality in e-Learning, European Learning Industry Group, European Student Union, European University Continuing Education Network, and MENON.

The Learnovation manifesto states that learning and change go together:

> ICT is a pervasive technology that makes innovation happen more quickly but requires all citizens and workers to be adequately skilled. E-Learning is at the meeting point of Lifelong Learning and ICT and is likely to give a great contribution to innovation, but its potential has been underestimated, especially in formal education. (Learnovation Manifesto, February 2008, bullet 3).

Food and Agricultural Organization of the United Nations (FAO): Rural and Remote Audiences

During April and May 2008, FAO initiated an Agricultural Learning Repositories E-conference in order to gather worldwide feedback about learning resources and repositories in agriculture and rural topics, and the importance of and challenges around open resources, and their potential impact on teaching and learning. Results emphasized the need for cross-border collaborative metadata on standards, the problems with too many versions of a learning resource, the wide variety of contexts for which learning resources are developed, defining the users and their needs, the requirements for multiple languages, the few demonstrations of Internet and computer applications for these audiences, the fact that computer-based and online learning materials may not be learner oriented, and the difficulty in interaction and collaboration.

The African Council for Distance Education (ACDE)

The ACDE strives to be a major player in advocacy for open and distance learning in Africa. ACDE is in the early development stage, pushing to establish a permanent secretariat in Nairobi, Kenya. Its goals and objectives are (African Council for Distance Education, n.d.) as follows:

- promote open and distance learning and flexible and continuing education in Africa;
- promote research and training in open and distance learning in Africa;
- contribute to the development of policies essential to the advancement of open and distance learning;
- foster continental and global collaboration in open and distance learning;
- provide a forum where individuals, organizations, and governments can deliberate on policy matters on open and distance learning;
- promote the development of appropriate methods and technologies in education and training relevant to open and distance learning; and
- provide a forum for interaction, sharing, and dissemination of ideas on open and distance learning. ("Goals and Objectives of ACDE")

Priorities include quality assurance, infrastructure development, and establishment of collaborative partnerships.

OECD–Online Learning, a Tool for Capacity Building in Developing Countries

The OECD Open Educational Resources expert meeting held in 2006 expressed concern about the complexity of the open educational resources concept, indicating that Open Educational Resources (OER) could create barriers to understanding if it became too complex. The participants concluded that OER is as much cultural as educational in that it might give an insight into culture—specific methods and approaches to teaching and learning. Senior officials responsible for professional and staff training at 30 national institutes, universities, and bilateral and multilateral development organizations, including the World Bank Group and the International Monetary Fund, issued a statement on July 8, 2008, outlining their consensus on future directions for training and capacity building (World Bank, 2008). The so-called Berlin statement seeks alignment on capacity building and will be significant in future training and development of blended and online learning programs.

1. *Effectiveness—Training in the context of capacity development*

   Training must be integrated with a comprehensive capacity development approach to effectively address capacity gaps in organizations and institutions. Effectiveness of training depends also on trained staff being retained by institutions, so as to strengthen them.

2. *Guidelines for the development of training programs*

   In international training for development, there is a strong need for general directions on training cycle management to guide training institutions worldwide.

3. *Metrics—Indicators and evaluation of training*

   Research is needed on the metrics of training programs to improve monitoring of results and to facilitate learning about what works best in different contexts. Metrics need to be formulated on the basis of general guidelines agreed upon between partner governments and donors. Development Training Institutes (DTIs) must also seek ways to share methodologies and results of training evaluations.

4. *Country Ownership—Strengthening training institutions*

   Promising approaches to strengthen existing national training institutes are as follows: supporting national champions and centers of excellence, and linking them to DTIs; training trainers; making increasing use of national training experts in DTIs' own programs; and providing salary and budget support to improve staff retention rates.

5. *Alignment—Partner country needs assessments*

   DTIs need to align their practices to partner countries' needs assessment systems. All partners need to have a development strategy that includes identifying local institutions and stakeholders to participate in assessments linked to results and clear priorities.

6. *Harmonization—International division of labor*

DTIs agree on the need to improve harmonization of their work to reduce duplication and burdens on partners and to build synergies among themselves.

7. *Collaboration—Joint content development, sharing rosters, didactic approaches, and training formats*

International development training materials developed with public funds should be disseminated as widely as possible. Sharing existing materials or expert rosters would be an effective first step for collaboration.

The International Council for Open and Distance Education (ICDE)

ICDE is recognized by the United Nations (UNESCO) and serves as the Global Umbrella Membership Organization in online, flexible, and blended learning, including e-learning and distance education. ICDE has adopted a new project partially funded by the European Commission called Open Educational Practices and Resources. Open eLearning Content Observatory Services (OLCOS) has published a report *Roadmap 2012* (2007), with recommendations related to open educational resources covering three areas:

- policies, institutional frameworks, and business models;
- open access and open content repositories; and
- laboratories of open educational practices and resources.

The report identifies drivers and exhibitors in each area and is to be used as a discussion stimulus (OLCOS, 2007).

The New Media Consortium and EDUCAUSE Learning Initiative

Along with the open movement, key emerging technologies that will continue to impact and change learning approaches and programs include the following:

- Grassroots video—Video sharing on the Web is mushrooming—cameras and editing packages are easier to use and searching is improved. Video for learning purposes can come from anywhere.

- Collaboration Webs—These will become more refined and perhaps less fragmented. Open programming can allow collaboration, but collaboration is based on relationships and some of today's approaches are not mature.

- Mobile broadband—Cell and local wireless technology will increase Internet availability and increase the opportunity for anywhere teaching and learning. Various physical and network security issues remain problems.

- Social networking is proving very popular with the young, and some predict these networks built around people rather than content will significantly impact online learning in the future.

- Data mashups—Custom applications allow combinations of data from different sources, allowing new ways to view and analyze large amounts of data.

- Collective intelligence—EDUCAUSE predicts that future educational applications will come from today's development of Wikipedia, search patterns, cell phone locations, geocoded photos and other passively obtained data (New Media Consortium & the EDUCAUSE Learning Initiative, 2008).

Conclusion

Valuing the Local and the Peripheral: Recomputing Distance

Brown and Duguid (2000) argued that online learning tempts centralization and overlooks the fact that much of what we learn is remarkably local. Care must be taken so that African students are not once again being taught out-of-context and irrelevant content as in the early days of formal education on the African continent brought by colonial powers. At that time students learned more about Britain, France, Belgium, and other countries than Africa and were propagandized with faulty facts, such as the assumption that African soils are only good for growing crops and commodities but not for building factories and producing goods (Brown & Dugurd, 2000).

Questions about locality of knowledge are far from trivial. Universities need to steer a path between the academy's and technology's centralizing tendencies and the optimistic belief that e-learning will overcome distance in all forms. According to Brown and Dugurd (2000), learners need three things from universities:

1. access to authentic communications of learning, interpretation, exploration, and knowledge creation;

2. resources to help them work with distant and local communities; and

3. widely accepted representations for learning and work.

The Internet has rapidly changed the world of learning and the potential for connecting people everywhere. Online learning allows access to content and educational tools and, if well done, can encourage development of much more detailed and sophisticated understanding of (1) what is near, what is far, and how they relate; (2) what is old, what is new, and what is real; and (3) what is humanizing and what is not. When history is written, will it be said that online learning was an artifact enriching the human spirit, or simply a way of lining elite pockets with riches? The choice is now: Education for all or education not at all.

References

African Council for Distance Education. (n.d.). [About the organization and background information.] Retrieved July 22, 2008, from http://www.acde-africa.org/html/about_ACDE.htm

Ali Baba. (n.d.). In *Wikipedia* [Web]. Retrieved July 22, 2008, from http://en.wikipedia.org/wiki/Ali_Baba

Allen, I. E., & Seaman, J. (2007, October). *Online nation: Five years of growth in online learning.* Needman, MA: The Sloan Consortium. Retrieved July 22, 2008, from http://www.sloan-c.org/publications/survey/pdf/online_nation.pdf

Barber, K. (Writer). (2008, March 21). Experts: Free open source software could help African development. *News Now.* Washington, DC: VOA News. Retrieved January 5, 2008, from http://www.voanews.com/english/archive/2008-03/2008-03-21voa47.cfm

Braimoh, D., & Ohiorenuan Osiki, J. (2008). The impact of technology on accessibility and pedagogy: The right to education in Sub-Saharan Africa [Electronic version]. *Asian Journal of Distance Education,* 6(1), 53–62. Available from http://www.AsianJDE.org

Brown, J. S., & Dugurd, P. (2000). *The social life of information.* Boston: Harvard Business School Press.

Cairncross, F. (1997). *The death of distance.* Boston: Harvard Business School Press.

David, L., Bender, L., Burns, S. Z. (Producers), & Guggenheim, D. (Director). (2006). *An inconvenient truth* [Motion picture]. United States: Paramount Classics & Participant Productions.

Ferguson, N. (2004). The annihilation of distance. In *Empire* (p. 142). New York: Basic Books.

Florida, R. (2005, October). "The world in numbers": The world is spiky. *Atlantic Monthly,* p. 48.

Friedman, T. L. (2005). *The world is flat: A brief history of the twenty-first century.* New York: Farrar, Straus and Giroux.

Global Industry Analysts, (n.d.). World market for eLearning projected to exceed $52.6 billion by 2010, according to new report by Global industry Analysts, Inc. Retrieved July 22, 2008, from http://www.strategyr.com/pressMCP-4107.asp

Internet World Stats: Usage and Population Statistics. (2008). *Internet world users by language: Top 10 languages.* Retrieved July 22, 2008, from http://www.internetworldstats.com/stats7.htm

Jonassen, D., Davidson, M., Collins, M., Campbell, J., & Hagg, B. B. (1995). *Constructivism and computer-mediated communication in distance education.* Retrieved January 6, 2009, from http://www.uni-oldenburg.de/zef/cde/media/readings/jonassen95.pdf

Kanwar, A. (2008, January 3). *Signs of the times: Change or be changed.* Speech presented at the Third Convocation of the Tamil Nadu Open University, Chennai, India. Retrieved July 22, 2008, from http://www.col.org/resources/speeches/2008presentations/Pages/default.aspx

Larsen, K., & Vincent-Lancrin, S. (2002, December). The learning business: Can trade in international education work? *OECD Observer,* pp. 26–28. Retrieved from http://www.oecdobserver.org/news/fullstory.php/aid/872/the_learning _business.html

Learnovation Manifesto (2008, February). Retrieved July 22, 2008, from http://learnovation.files.wordpress.com/2008/02/learnovation_manifesto_feb08.pdf

Matsuura, K. (2000). *Education for all: The unfulfilled promise. 21st century talks session for education for all.* Retrieved January 5, 2009, from http://portal.unesco.org/education/en/ev.php-URL_ID=9019&URL_DO=DO_TOPIC&URL_SECTION=201.html

Mbilinyi, M. (2003). *Equity, justice and transformation in education: The challenge of Mwalimu Julius Nyerere today* (HakiElimu Working Paper Series, 2003. No. 5). Retrieved from January 5, 2009, from http://www.hakielimu.org/hakielimu/documents/document48equity_justice_transformn_edu_en.pdf

Menzies, G. (2003). *1421: The year China discovered the world.* London: Bantam Press.

Moore, M. G. (2008). Where is the historical research. *The American Journal of Distance Education, 22*(2), 67.

The New Media Consortium and the EDUCAUSE Learning Initiative. (2008). *The Horizon report,* 2008 edition. Retrieved July 22, 2008, from http://www.nmc.org/pdf/2008-Horizon-Report.pdf

Noel-Levitz. (2005). *National online learners priorities reports.* Retrieved July 22, 2008, from http://www.noellevitz.com/Papers+and+Research/Papers+and+Reports/overview.htm

Noel-Levitz. (2006). *National online learners priorities reports.* Retrieved July 22, 2008, from http://www.noellevitz.com/Papers+and+Research/Papers+and+Reports/overview.htm

Noel-Levitz. (2007). *National online learners priorities reports.* Retrieved July 22, 2008, from http://www.noellevitz.com/Papers+and+Research/Papers+and+Reports/overview.htm

Nyerere, J. K. (1975). The Arusha declaration teach-in. *Dar Es Salaam: The Information Services,* p. 10.

OECD. (2006, February 6–7). *Notes from expert meeting on open educational resources.* Malmö, Sweden 6-7 February, 2006. Retrieved July 22, 2008, from http://learn.creativecommons.org/wpcontent/uploads/2008/03/malmnotes.pdf

Open Doors. (2007). *American students study abroad at record levels: Up 8.5%.* Retrieved August 12, 2008, from http://www.opendoors.iienetwork.org

Open eLearning Content Observatory Services. (2007). *Open Educational Practices and Resources, OLCOS Roadmap 2012.* Retrieved August 11, 2008, from http://www.icde.org/oslo/icde.nsf/id/A33F0D2CD3C9458CC1257 295004ACA91?OpenDocument

Please read: A personal appeal from Wikipedia founder Jimmy Wales. (2008). Retrieved July 22, 2008, from http://en.wikipedia.org/wiki/Wiki

SkillsTrain (2008, June 13). *Top ten reasons for students opting for home study* [Press release]. Retrieved January 5, 2009, from http://www.prlog.org/ 10080022-top-ten-reasons-for-students-opting-for-home-study.html

United Nations Conference on Trade and Development. (2004, September). *Report of the expert meeting on free and open-source software: Policy and development implications.* Retrieved January 6, 2009, from http://www.unctad .org/en/docs/c3em21d3_en.pdf

Video chat on Baidu's search engine menu. (2008, June 6). *China Tech News.* Retrieved July 22, 2008, from http://www.ChinaTechNews.com/2008/06/06

Wilson, D., & Mackintosh, W. (2007). *College donates learning materials to WikiEducator.* Retrieved July 22, 2008, from http://www.col.org/news/ archives/2007news/Pages/2007-01-college.aspx

World Bank. (2008). Training institutes to align efforts on capacity building in developing countries (News Release No. 2009/014/WBI). Retrieved July 22, 2008, from http://web.worldbank.org/WBSITE/EXTERNAL/TOPICS/ EXTEUCATION/0,,contentMDK:21834604~menuPK:282391~pagePK:6402 0865~piPK:149114~theSitePK:282386,00.html

Chapter 8

Online Learning Research

Yolanda Gayol

This chapter presents key research studies that help to understand the sociology and psychology of cyberspace. Rather than making an effort to present a comprehensive review of the evolution of distance education research, I focus my attention on the dynamics of learning online. The structure of the chapter is as follows. First, I clarify my position within the diversity of concepts and constructs seeking to describe and interpret Internet-mediated learning and research, learning, and education. Second, I briefly present the results of several meta-analyses that provide an eagle-eye view of the status of research in this subfield of education. Third, I address major findings derived from the study of media attributes, which in time have acted as conceptual underpinnings guiding the research in online learning. Fourth, I track a few concepts derived from theory and research that have been associated with the perennially fuzzy notion of quality in online education. Fifth, I present the findings along five research paths: design, teaching, learning, outcomes, and emerging trends. Finally, I close the chapter with a condensed explanation of the way that online learning environments could be portrayed.

The Meaning of Research, Learning, and Education

A report on research about online learning is complicated because of the complexity found in the essence of the terms defining the title of this chapter: learning, online, and research. Specialized literature reporting research in electronic environments uses the concepts of learning and education indistinctly to address radically different processes. Thus, I need to deviate from the route suggested in the title to clarify my position on these concepts before I address the substance of my topic.

Learning refers to the *incidental* or *intentional* appropriation of knowledge, skills, attitudes, and values that keep configuring the individual and social experience. Incidental learning (Brookfield, 1986) is serendipitous; it occurs by the simple fact of being there (dasein; Heidegger, 1962). Except for an impeding disability, any person continuously scans, records, judges, senses, feels, and reacts to immediate or remote environments. Human beings are permanent learners, so incidental learning is a continuous flow. As Freire (1992) put it, we are always in the process of becoming.

Incidental learning articulates a personal biography of the individual through memory sequences, before-after (Kant, 1781/2008). Vygotsky (1926/1992) had already understood that self-awareness is an interrelated process. He defined consciousness as a phenomenon that unifies attention, intention, memory, reasoning, and speech (Vigotsky, 1926/1992). This statement reflects his familiarity with recent findings in the psychology of his time. While "being there," individuals witnessing events related to themselves, others, nature, or media are making meaning of reality through an inner dialogue.

Intentional learning takes advantage of incidental learning to organize targeted learning goals. Although incidental learning is a continuous process, intentional learning is discrete, and it occurs in a spectrum oscillating from autonomous to socially guided. *Autonomous learning* refers to a situation in which the learner is able to keep on task toward the learning goal without receiving systematic help from others; it is a self-directed process. Autonomous learning occurs in a dyad, since it involves the learner and the content. *Guided learning* includes regular support from an instructor or facilitator who acts as a coach to gain new competencies[1]. When an instructor intervenes to support this systematic effort, learning becomes embedded within the educational process. Therefore, learning is the result of participating in such a process. An educational environment is a triad that includes student(s), instructor, and content.

Both intentional learning and education occur in the interaction among individuals working in immediate or remote environments. Consequently, online learning is the result of incidental or intentional knowledge appropriation that occurs in the human–computer (networked) interaction. If a facilitator is involved, then it should not be called online learning, but instead, we should refer to it as online education.

Online learning results from the use of electronic media in synchronous, asynchronous, or combined modes. According to the modality used, it could be characterized as follows:

- course enhancement (face-to-face teaching with some online activities),

- blended or hybrid learning (a certain percentage of the program occurs in a face-to-face mode and the rest online),

- full online courses or programs (no immediacy is required), and

- media combination[2] (media that could be addressed as online and/or mixed-mode distance education).

I observe that the process of learning over the Internet has received multiple designations. Among the most common designations found are virtual classroom (Gayol & Schied, 1997; Hiltz, 1994; Tiffin & Rajansingham, 1995), computer-mediated communication (Berge & Collins, 1995; Wells, 1992), virtual education (Loutchko, Kurbel, & Pakhomov, 2002), Web-mediated education (Abbey, 2000), asynchronous learning (Sloan-C, n.d.), online learning-education (Larreamendy-Joerns & Leinhardt, 2006), distributed education, (Oblinger, Baron, & Hawkins, 2001), cyberspace education (Land & Bayne, 2005), e-learning (Clark & Mayer, 2003), virtual learning environments (Miligan, 1998), learning technologies (Pea et al., 1999), information and communication technologies (ICT) in education (Pelgrum, 2001), and more recently, Web 2.0 and Web 3.0 distance education (Gayol, 2007). The reader will find all these terms used interchangeably because exploring in detail their respective roots and meanings is beyond the aims of this chapter.

The polysemic nature of online learning has resulted from the diversity of communities of practice experimenting with online education. A great diversity of groups are involved in teaching and learning through ICT, and many of them step into the field without prior training. Research in (online, blended enhanced, mixed-mode) learning education is found in K–12 groups, the military, multinational organizations, professional associations, universities and graduate programs, and think tanks all over the world. The task of portraying the findings of all these groups is a prodigious long-term endeavor. The criteria for including or excluding a particular investigation cannot rely solely on the specific delivery mode or community of practice that generated this knowledge because the boundaries are fuzzy. Thus, the following review focuses on the conceptual development of the field and retain the unavoidable conceptual fuzziness.

The third complex term is *research.* The *Cambridge Advanced Learner's Dictionary* (Cambridge University Press, 2008) defines research as "a detailed study of a subject, esp. in order to discover (new) information or reach a (new) understanding." Consequently, a relevant account of online learning research should contain a cohesive body of knowledge that allows the reader to gain a good grasp of how this subfield of education is progressing. If this definition is compared and contrasted with the state of the art in distance education, most studies would not qualify being designated as research. Some meta-analyses provide a good picture of the challenges faced in this regard.

Saba (2000) declared that the theoretical and epistemological frameworks used by researchers while studying online teaching and learning are rarely disclosed, though awareness of researchers about the importance of providing a theoretical framework to their work is growing over time.

Contrarily, Perraton (2000) stated that research in open and distance learning is "often *atheoretical* and predominantly descriptive" ("Abstract," italics added). Bates (2007) worked on a meta-analysis[3] of e-learning publications by European authors between the years 2003 and 2005. He selected 15 print-only journals, 50 online journals, 28 books, and major European Commission e-learning project reports published in this period. All of them had in common a research focus on e-learning. Almost 2,000 articles were selected for review in this study. After having organized his sample, Bates used three criteria to decide how to choose a paper for a more in-depth review. These criteria required that

a. The author(s) had reported actual experience in e-learning.

b. The paper had included some data, either quantitative or qualitative.

c. The study had included some analysis or evaluation of the data.

From the 2,000 papers originally selected, only 300 complied with the aforementioned criteria.

E-learning meant different things to different writers, and sometimes it was not possible to know which kind of e-learning they were referring to (full, blended, course enhanced, mixed mode). Only one third of the selected papers were related to teaching and learning issues, whereas 60% of them focused on technology issues (e.g., tagging learning objects) and 10% percent were concerned with policies and strategies (Bates, 2007). Following Bates' conclusions, it is important to note that (apparently) the research studies continue to rely on a techno-centric view of innovation. The author added that the studies addressing teaching and learning lacked quantitative support. Usually, they presented an overview of the problem followed by qualitative reports. Often, the research conclusions lacked strong evidence (qualitative or quantitative), and no use of large samples was found. Most papers consisted of narrative and anecdotal case studies and were more descriptive than analytical. Based on these findings, a second observation could be made: E-learning lacks a solid empirical foundation since it does not rely on evidence-based interpretations to understand the rapidly changing environment in which students and instructors interact.

Bates (2007) also found a huge number of reports analyzing learning objects and almost nothing about the future of e-learning. Ironically, interdisciplinary networking does not appear to be occurring among the e-learning communities of practice. Rather, authors seem to be working in isolation without talking to each other. Educators and computer scientists work independently and publish in different journals. However, computer scientists produced a greater proportion of the papers and were more likely to have quantitative data. Bates explained that he found very few papers that provided empirical data on the effectiveness of constructivist approaches to e-learning in terms of increased or better learning outcomes.

In another meta-analysis, Berge and Mrozowski (2001) reviewed the studies published from 1990 to 1999 with the intention of defining a research agenda for distance education. They found mainly laundry lists enumerating the topics that, in the view of the various writers, required the attention of researchers. However, they recognized that some authors assigned priorities to the listed issues. Many studies lacked theoretical foundations in both the formulation of the hypotheses and the chosen methodology. Similarly to Bates (2007), Berge and Mrozowski found that the preferred methodology is a qualitative approach. Eighty-four percent of the articles reviewed were case studies, 8% were correlational, and 7% were experimental. As Bates also stated, the research is usually conducted by individual practitioners.

From the perspective of educational technology, Roblyer (2005) declared that we suffer from the "single study syndrome." Roblyer noted with sarcasm that the single agreement attained by this community of practice is that "we need a more organized and persuasive body of evidence on technology's benefits to classroom practice." Roblyer introduced five criteria or pillars to strengthen research in educational technology: the *significance criterion*, the *rationale criterion*, the *design criterion*, the *comprehensive reporting criterion*, and the *cumulative criterion*. The first pillar calls for indicators that demonstrate quality related to achievement, attendance, persistence, and learning because federal funds are tied to the provision of scientific evidence. Similarly to the above-cited authors, the rationale criterion invites researchers to use theory-related research to serve as the foundation of their studies. Pillar three, the design criterion, refers to the use of methodology that captures the impact of the variables studied, either in an objective or naturalistic (hermeneutic) inquiry. The fourth pillar for Roblyer (2005) is the comprehensive reporting criterion. The author emphasizes the need for detail in the research reports to open the possibility of replication. The inclusion of an APA style structured abstract that includes context, goals, conditions, target audience, planning, method, instruments and procedures, analysis, process, results, conclusions, and future research is essential to improve the quality of the research reports. If the structure of the abstract unfolds in the completed study, the results would support the trustworthiness of the reports since they would include the significance criterion, the rationale criterion, the design criterion, and the comprehensive report criterion. Finally, the cumulative criterion (a fifth pillar) calls for continuity in the analysis of issues to open the possibility of exploring cause-effect connections.

Although the studies cited above have an underlying framework of topic frequency, method frequency and theory frequency, this chapter uses historical landmarks as the background thread for tracking conceptual development in e-learning research. I start by focusing on media attributes to further explore the key concepts of design, learning, teaching, and outcomes. This approach positions me toward the transformative power of a technology view and away from techno-centered discussions. In the disparate views (Clark, 1994; McLuhan, 1964) on the transparent-transformative power of technology in education and in society, I lean toward McLuhan's views (Gayol, 1998).

The complexity of the terminology used to report the process of teaching and learning through computer networks has forced me to blur the conceptual differences, epistemic traditions, and communities of practice from which of these terms have emerged. I come from the milieu of distance education; thus, my analysis is made from this tradition.

The Beginnings: Understanding the Power and Complexity of the Electronic Medium

On September 2, 1969, professor Leo Kleinrock, as a team member of the Network Working Group, brought to reality Bush's Memex (1945) and Licklider's intergalactic network (1963), by connecting two computers in the United States. After this successful event, they did the first host-to-host connection between University of California, Los Angeles and the Stanford Research Institute, where Doug Engelbart was in charge of the second node. The University of California Santa Barbara added a third node on November 1st and Ivan Sutherland joined with a fourth node from the University of Utah. These universities were the locus of experimentation of the military group Advanced Research Project Agency (Ceruzzi, 2003). After the Network Working group succeeded, new nodes were added at a rate of one per month. Almost 4 decades later, 3.9 million students in the United States (E. Allen & Seaman, 2008) benefited from this invention by taking courses online.

Parallel to the development of the Internet, Sutherland was working on the creation of virtual reality. The first fully functional virtual[4] environment was tested on January 1, 1970. Rheingold (1991) reported that the project leader, Sutherland, found intimacy in the human computer interaction and called it the sense of presence. Kramarae and Taylor (1993) further described the impression of immersion reported by users working on cyberspace. Baym (1995) explored the effects of having a disembodied experience. Some of these effects are as follows: *Pseudonimity* is the intensification of emotions, misunderstandings, horizontal communication, and linguistic changes. Pseudonimity refers to the concealment of the sociocultural symbols of status attached to the personal appearance, but not immediately available while using textual communication (C. Allen, 1996). Individual identities are reduced to what is declared or shown on the screen, with the possibility of metamorphoses, and reinvention of identities at the users' will. *Intensification of emotions* occurs for the same reason. The reduction and filtering of meanings found in facial expressions and body language lead to frequent misunderstandings and flaming[5] practices. *Linguistic changes* (Wegeriff, 1998) emerged from the need to express emotions (Jones, 1995) and to save time while interacting; this need leads to the creation of new semantic conventions (e.g., LOL = lots of laughter or laugh out loud, TTYL—talk to you later). *Horizontal communication* addresses the enabling capability for allowing users to engage in a dialogue, regardless of the position or hierarchy of the receiver (Walther, 1992). In brief, virtual reality is a simulacrum of reality using visualization to present a synthetic environment with tridimensional appearance. Five attributes characterize this environment: *immersive, interactive, intuitive, illustrative,* and *intensive* (Barilli & Cunha, 2004). As compared to previous generations of distance education (print, audio, satellite), the Internet has the communicative attribute many-to-many—that is, any user can interact with others. The hypertextual attribute of the Internet offers the possibility of rearticulating, writing and editing the content (writerly text) in a distributed manner (Barthes, 1970/1974). Online content induces exploratory behaviors. Nielsen (2006) found that users do not read electronic text, but they scan and jump in the site and intersite to select information. This behavior is important because it has had the consequence of chunking educational materials into small units and helps to understand current findings on the digital native who behaves in a continuous partial attention mode being typified as having the "attention span of a gnat" (Prensky, 2001, p. 4)

The attributes described above have enabled the Internet to transform the nature of teaching and learning. It also transforms the identities of students. The separation between student and instructor is not only geographical and temporal, but also psychological. In this regard, Moore developed the theory of transactional distance, whereby a synergic relationship could be established in educational transactions by finding adequate balance among structure, dialogue, and learner autonomy (Moore & Kearsley, 2004).

The psychological and institutional changes required to deliver efficient online courses were not addressed in the first place. Military trainers and educators considered only the pragmatic side of this new tool. They started using the screen with black background and green letters as the new warehouse of correspondence courses. Early innovators foresaw potential savings if they invested in replacing printed material with electronic text. They thought that if students could gain flexibility through access to the Internet, they would have the advantage of being able to review the learning materials any time, anywhere. Scanners were not available yet, so the content had to be retyped and delivered, but the effort was foreseen as worthy. They no longer had to reprint, store, and deliver documents to multiple locations, which could save months of planning and logistics. The technological transition from correspondence education to electronic storage represented a tremendous institutional effort. However, when the conversion had been done, instructors found that the students were not reading the materials. On top of the serious problems of access, usability, transparency (reliability), and fluency (as defined in modern terms), researchers found that learners and learning were affected by the technological mediation. The advantages of the independence of time and place appeared to be shadowed by the disadvantages of having separated, geographically or temporally, the students from the instructor. Apparently, the dematerialization of experience was taking its toll in online education (Herman, Ardekani, & Ausubel, 1989).

Distance educators inquired about the reasons for this detachment from the electronic content. Obviously, the first barrier was technological performance. It was clear that computer systems were primitive, frail, complex, and scarce.[6] Thus, researchers addressing the complexities of computer networks recommended finding ways for overcoming the last (cognitive) mile—that is, the learning curve of preusers and new users (Bradshaw, 2001). Others invested their efforts in understanding how media attributes (McLuhan, 1964) could help to explain student behaviors. Repeatedly, students reported that technology was cold and not inviting. J. Naisbitt, N. Naisbitt, and Philips (2001) found a way to translate this iterative result by introducing the construct of high tech-high touch, which became very popular. They explained that "High tech is about shortening time . . . is about the demand on the individual to produce more in less time. . . . High touch is about taking time . . . is about process, about allowing time for discovery" (p. 33).

While exploring attrition in online courses, Keller (1987) developed the ARCS model of motivation in which attention, relevance, confidence, and satisfaction were the pillars of retention, but low response rates in interactive forums also have some significance. Monro (1987) pointed to the impact of feedback (instructor–student interaction) through e-mail on quality, as measured by a decrease in faculty workload in marking papers because students can discuss the difficulties found in the readings and receive direct advice from the instructor. Roxanne Hiltz (1994), who coined (and copyrighted) the term *virtual classroom*, observed social anomie among students working in online environments. She reported (along with Turoff) that online education with excessive numbers of students, having long lapses of response time to their inquiries, suffering from information overload, and maintaining impersonal relationships, were factors affecting the development of a sense of community. Other authors found that virtual interaction created communication anxiety. Feenberg (1989) reported that communication anxiety is triggered by the absence of cues usually found in facial expression, body language, and speech intonation. Such cues inform the reaction of others in a given communicative action.

Anxiety is also triggered by the demand of participation in online forums. Even in a well-designed course with responsive professors, educators have problems with lurkers. Lurkers are students who do not interact socially with their peers or the instructor while working in asynchronous discussion forums. Beaudoin (2002) tracked the behaviors of 55 students participating in a fully online course. He defined students with high visibility as those who had posted at least 1,000 words in one of the forums. Low visibility meant not having participated in one of the forums, and no visibility defined students who did not post any message. He reported that 24 of the students in his class (43%) were not participating in the discussion forums. Beaudoin designed a questionnaire to explore the reasons for the lack of visibility. Three out of four respondents declared that "they simply preferred to read what others wrote, or that they had thoughts but others made similar comments before they could post anything themselves" (p. 150).

Research on Design

The design of the interface received great attention when it was clear that a cold environment would not appeal to learners. I have explained that the lack of text formatting in the first correspondence courses over the Internet generated aversion among the learners. However, in only 1 decade, research on the design of e-learning environments has moved from didactic conversation and instructional design to simulation, gaming, and 3-D worlds using MOOS and MUVs.[7]

One of the early attempts to decrease learners' syndrome of isolation and their sense of remoteness was grounded in Holmberg's theory of didactic conversation (1960), later reformulated as the theory of teaching and learning conversations (1999). In the European context of impersonal and formalized use of language prevalent during the early 1960s, Holmberg successfully tested the effects of manifesting warm human relationships and emotional involvement in the printed materials delivered to students. He used and tested widely this construct in the design of correspondence courses at the German distance education institution FernUniversitat (Holmberg, 2001).

In the United States, the institutional emphasis of technology-mediated education became part of the design of instruction. In the book *Web Teaching: A Guide to Designing Interactive Teaching for the World Wide Web*, Brooks (1997) declared, "When one reads literature, it is very clear that the instructional design is what it is important" (p. 20). This relevance emerges from the influence of teaching machines (Pressey, 1927) and programmed instruction and behaviorism (Skinner, 1958), added to the tremendous progress made by psychology during the first half of the 20th century. The development of instructional design (Bloom, 1956; Gagne, 1962; Mager, 1962) made a mark in distance education, surviving the transitions from print to audio, video, and electronic education.

Other factors influencing the preeminence of instructional design derive from the prestige gained by the Open University of Great Britain, established in 1971. Because of its success, other institutions emulated its instructional model, conceptualized by Peters (1967/2001) as the industrial model of education or fordist model. In this model, it is assumed that the most efficient way to produce high quality instruction is through the centralization of tasks, the division of labor, the mechanization, and the mass production of educational materials, as they occur in industry. The assumption was that use of a combination of media and highly specialized experts in content, design, delivery, and evaluation would enrich learning (Wedemeyer & Najem, 1969). The limitations found in the use of the industrial model were the high production costs and the high structure of the design.

The arrival of the Internet supported the transition toward the postfordist model, a more flexible, less structured, and less expert-dependent approach. The postfordist model gained momentum in online learning. Added to the formal adoption of constructivism, it became the most popular mode of designing online courses. The highly structured layout in which all students had to do the same activities was not effective in a writerly[8] (Barthes, 1970/1974), hypertextual medium that enables high exploration, high participation, and instantaneous many-to-many communication (Peters, 2002). Researchers moved forward the discussion of design by focusing in the components of a good design of instruction rather than only addressing the overall fordist or postfordist structure. A prominent place among these components was given to culture.

Culture has been addressed as an important element of instructional design, and some explanations on how the teaching-learning process could be organized have been provided by exploring a diversity of models. Bruner (1960) has argued that modern civilization shapes the way that knowledge is appropriated. He suggests that *enactive, iconic,* and *symbolic* knowledge is the result of modern culture. Enactive representation is learning while doing and includes the integration of prior experience; iconic knowledge refers to the internally visualized processes; symbolic knowledge addresses the verbal and numerical representations. Because cultural differences are not always obvious to course designers, he recommends that planning educational interventions begin with the learner experience so that the cultural nuances become apparent.

Harasim (1993) pointed out the importance of paying attention to the barriers of cross-cultural communication while designing global learning networks. The meaning of colors, symbols, and values between the originating and the receiving sites should be carefully contrasted to avoid problems during the interaction. In Harasim's book, Bellman, Tindimubona, and Arias (1993) reported that the increased awareness of cultural design derives from the experience with BESTNET (Binational English and Spanish Telecommunications Network, which had been established in

1985 by Arias and Bellman; 1987). The authors worked in a 4-month learning experience with 3,000 students from Mexico and the United States. The combination of interviews and content analysis allowed the author to find that "technology greatly augments regular classroom instruction and computer conference induces active participation" (Bellman et al., 1993, p. 242). Similarly, Gunawardena (1995) developed the culturally relevant design model in a review of the international exchanges of students, which generated 125,000 words. In the conclusions of her study, Gunawardena warned that while doing cultural research, the implicit beliefs of American sameness and native points could be a barrier for solid comparative studies. In the same venue, Gayol and Schied (1997) observed the risk of cultural imperialism in the design process while working with an international population of students.

Harasim (1993) found that another important component in the design of online instruction is the use of spatial metaphors. She suggested to hold different activities in different spaces—that is, seminar, library, café—because "they provide familiarity and serve as navigational and cognitive aids, helping to organize interactions and set participants expectations" (p. 30). This finding influenced the transition from unformatted text to differentiated spaces that later evolved into course management systems (CMS, LMS).

Research on Learning

Research on learning is one of the most frequently reviewed topics in distance education. Particularly important are the variables of interactivity, social presence, cognition and e-learning, and learning styles. These variables are regarded as predictors of quality in the specialized literature.

According to the Webster's encyclopedic unabridged dictionary of the English language (Portland House, 1996), interaction is defined as "reciprocal action or influence" (p. 729). Michael G. Moore was one of the first distance educators elaborating on the importance of interaction in distance education. Moore (1989) stated that quality in teaching and learning relies on three types of interaction: learner–content, learner–learner, and learner–teacher. Bernard et al. (2004) distinguished between surface and deep interaction. The second occurs "wherein complex learning is promoted through effective communication." (Bernard et al., 2004, p. 413). Hiltz and Goldman (2005) brought to this discussion the concept collaboratory, first used by William Wulf in 1989. Hiltz and Goldman (2005) suggested adopting it in asynchronous learning networks to understand online collaborative environments.

Karatas (2008) reviewed the research on interaction published in 2003, 2004, and in the first 3 months of 2005. His research includes articles published in three journals: *The American Journal of Distance Education,* the *Quarterly Review of Distance Education,* and *Distance Education.* Using EBSCO Academic Search Premier, the author determined that from the 138 articles published in the three journals, only 25 were focused on interaction during the period reviewed. The sample selected was classified using Lee, Driscoll, and Nelson's (2004) topical system analysis, which includes design related, development related, institutional and operational related, and theory and research related. Karatas (2008) added to this system the combination of topics and found that the types of interaction most frequently addressed in the 25 articles were learner–learner (19 times), learner–instructor (17 times), and learner–content (12 times). He found that no articles were published on the design-related, management-related, or institutional- and operational-related topics. The development related topic, the theory and research topic, and the combined topic each accounted for 8% of the publications. The evaluation-related topic accounted for 52% of the publications (13 articles), which made it the most frequently addressed issue by the researchers publishing in these journals.

Probably drawing from Sutherland (cited by Rheingold, 1991), the construct of social presence became increasingly used in the analysis of online learning. According to Richardson and Swan (2003), social presence theory was developed in communication studies. Social presence is defined as the "degree of salience of the other person in the (mediated) interaction and the consequent salience of the interpersonal relationships. This is interpreted as the degree to which a person is perceived as 'real' in mediated communication" (p. 2).

Gunawardena and Zittle (1997) were among the researchers who introduced the variable of social presence in online learning. They wanted to know the extent to which the medium was modifying learners' perceptions and behaviors in computer-mediated conferencing. They found that social presence could be cultured among teleconference participants, a position different from the view that social presence is largely an attribute of the communication medium. Their research thus demonstrated that social presence is both a factor of the medium and of the communicators and their presence in a sequence of interactions.

In a mixed-mode study designed by Richardson and Swan (2003), 97 individuals were selected among 369 students who completed an online course. The authors confirmed Gunawardena's (1997) hypothesis that links perceived social presence with overall learner satisfaction. The variable of gender correlated positively with learner satisfaction, but other sociodemographic and academic variables (e.g., age, number of credits earned) were not relevant in the perception of presence. Instead, interaction, feedback, peer participation, and acknowledgement were decisive factors in the selection of course activities reported as the most beneficial. The conclusion of this Richardson and Swan's (2003) research is that "interaction among participants is critical in learning and cognitive development"(p. 80). In another study, Swan (2003) further elaborated on the notion of presence using the concept of immediacy. Argyle and Dean (1965) defined intimacy and immediacy as components of social presence. Swan (2003) characterized immediacy as "the perceived psychological distance between communicators" (p. 148). Perceived immediacy occurs in both face-to-face and virtual classrooms. Following Rourke, Anderson, Garrison, and Archer (2001), Swan (2003) reported that there are three kinds of verbal immediacy responses: "*affective responses,* personal expressions of emotion, feelings, beliefs and values; *cohesive responses,* behaviors that build and sustain a sense of group community, and *interactive responses,* behaviors that provide evidence that the other is attending" (p. 150). Swan proposed an equilibrium model in which the expected level of communication, immediacy, and presence in a learning community is attained.

Garrison, Anderson, and Archer (2000) increased the precision of the concept of social presence. They suggested exploring three kinds of presence: cognitive, social, and teaching. Similarly, Garrison and Cleveland-Innes (2005) explained that this precision is required since there is a difference between interaction and presence. Interaction does not involve personal engagement. Cognitive presence refers to "an environment and climate for deep approaches to learning and meaningful educational exchanges" (Garrison & Cleveland-Innes, 2005, p. 144). Social presence refers to the ability to project the social personae into a community. Teaching presence "includes designing and managing learning sequences, providing subject matter expertise, and facilitating active learning" (Rourke et al., 2001). As constructivism (Jonassen, Mayes, & McAleese, 1993) became a mainstream theory in the design of e-learning, the delivery models minimized the role of the instructor. However, Garrison and Cleveland-Innes (2005) explained that teaching presence is important because it sustains the community of inquiry. Social presence builds the community of inquiry by facilitating the development of trust and a sense of belonging. A sense of belonging has been studied in conventional and distance education as the extent to which students fit in a learning community. Garber (2004) explained that "a shared history contributes to the community's sense of identity, and this forges a sense of who belongs to the community and who does not" ("Growing Virtual Learning Communities," para 7). The author continued to explain that "weak ties . . . do not permit the creation of new knowledge through shared experience and social interaction" ("Experiencing Virtual Communities," para 3). Race and ethnicity, for example, affect a student's sense of being included in an institutional environment (Garrison & Cleveland-Innes, 2005). Gilliard (1996) found that African American students felt more distant from the group than Caucasians. Retention is also affected by social presence. Cheng, Lehman, and Armstrong (1991) found that students who work in collaborative environments have much higher completion rates than those learning in isolation. The persistence ratio in their study was 90% versus 22%. The feeling of isolation affects quality and efficacy.

Shin (2003) developed the construct of transactional presence (TP) as a critical predictor of learning achievement, learning satisfaction, and learning persistence. TP is measured using the variables of availability and connectedness. Shin conducted a study at the Korea National Open University to validate the TP construct. She used modified random selection procedure to choose 506 individuals from 2 of the 12 regional study centers existing in the country. The average age of the participants in the study was 34 years old, 71% were females, and they had a median of 2.6 years studying at a distance. There were freshmen (24%), sophomores (34%), juniors (39%), and seniors (3.5%) in the sample. She found that the psychological perception that a student has "on the part of the teacher, the student peers and the institution can be significant predictors of their success in distance learning" (p. 79).

Beyond the inquiries on the students' perceptions and behaviors in online environments the research on how they learn is critical to progress in the field of distance education. The topic of cognition and e-learning has been reviewed by Shih, Feng, and Tsai (2008), who selected 1027 articles published in five major journals in education from 2001 to 2005. These authors explored the *British Journal of Educational Technology; Innovations in Education and Teaching International; Computers and Education; Educational Technology Research and Development;* and *Journal of Computer Assisted Learning.* Seven major topics and other subtopics about cognition and e-learning were selected as recognized by the Social Science Citation Index and Education Resources Information Center (ERIC). The major topics were motivation, information processing, instructional approaches, learning environment, prior knowledge, metacognition, and cognitive psychology. They found 16 articles addressing the topic of cognition and e-learning in the reviewed journals. Using constant comparative analysis, they found that the two most salient topics in the 5-year review were interactive learning environments and collaborative learning. Regarding methodology, they noticed that descriptive studies were used in 75% of the cases. Similarly, over half of the articles (10) used the questionnaire as the primary data collection instrument. The most-cited articles on cognition and e-learning received 18 citation counts. They concluded that the topics of instructional approaches, information processing and motivation "may be perceived as the research foundations of e-learning studies" (p. 962).

Research on thinking styles is another frequently addressed topic in online education. Thinking styles refer to consistent individual preferences to appropriating knowledge, regardless of the content or the student background. Thinking styles can be cognitive styles or learning styles. An early example of cognitive styles is the distinction between field dependence (social) and field independence (self-directed) cited in studies by Witkin and Goodenough (1979) on the communication preferences of students in a learning situation.

Witkin, Moore, Oltman, Goodenough, Friedman, and Owen (1977) developed the concept of field dependence and field independence to understand "the extent in which a person perceives part of field as discrete from the surrounding field as a whole, rather than embedded in the field; the extent to which a person perceives analytically" (p. 7). Field-dependent individuals are perceived as "warm, tactful, considerate, socially outgoing and affectionate. Altogether, field-dependent persons may be characterized as having an 'interpersonal' orientation to the world" (Witkin et al., p. 4). Contrastingly, field-independent (FI) individuals "have an impersonal orientation to the world" (Witkin et al., p. 4). They have been referred as analytical, competitive, individualistic, task oriented, internally referent, intrinsically motivated, hypothesis testing, self structuring, linear, detail oriented and visually perceptive" (Hall, 2000, p. 5). Handal and Herrington (2003) hypothesized that such attributes could increase the success rate of FI students in computer-assisted instruction in which learner interaction is mediated by technology.

Learning styles inform how students respond to a learning environment (Park, 1997). Kolb (1984) developed a vastly used learning style inventory (LSI) that considers four types of learners: *divergers, assimilators, convergers,* and *accomodators*. Divergers examine concrete situations from multiple perspectives, and assimilators have a preference for abstract concepts and theoretical explanations. Convergers value the practicality of ideas, whereas accomodators prefer to learn from hands on experience. Evidence has been found that learning styles influence academic performance. Some research suggests that if an instructor takes the time to adapt the design of the course to the particular learning styles of the students, it is more likely for them to have good academic outcomes and be more satisfied. Sahin (2008) studied the interaction between learner characteristics and learners' perception of satisfaction using Kolb's LSI and Walkers's distance education learning environment instrument. The author adopted Moore and Kearsley's (2004) transactional distance theory as the conceptual framework for the study and suggested to using it as scaffolding for Web design. Gayol (2000) has also recommended using Moore's transactional distance theory as an instructional design framework.

Two hundred seventy-nine Web-based college students from five different courses participated in Sahin's study (2008). He reported that younger males, in comparison to females and older students (>21 years old), prefer abstract conceptualization (AC). He found a positive correlation between authentic learning and active learning among students who prefer AC and found a negative correlation among students with preference for concrete experience (CE). Therefore, AC students may fit better in Web-based courses with low interaction, and CE students may be more satisfied in collaborative learning environments and those that include real-life experiences. Additionally, significant correlations were found between learning styles and gender. Male students favor AC over females and adults over 21 years old. But the author warned that these results "may be specific to the United States" (Sahin, 2008, p.131). The author recommended the inclusion of a variety of learning experiences in Web education to accommodate diverse types of learners. He concluded that the inclusion of simulations, collaborative tasks, and real-life activities could benefit students having CE and AE as their preferred style.

In another context, Dede (2005) did a large-scale study to understand how multi-user virtual environments shape learning styles. He explains that the new research in learning styles explores whether the interplay between storyline, motivation, content, and perceived domain of the environment induces learning. Dede and Palombo (2004) declared that students of the Net generation have a different mind-set and different ways of learning. Neomillennials are fluent in multiple media; they learn collectively, practice active learning, and express themselves in a nonlinear manner. They are also engaged in the coproduction of learning experiences (p. 15).

Similarly, Chen, Toh, and Mohd Fauzy (2005) explored the effects of virtual reality on students with different learning styles using the Kolb inventory (LSI) in a quasi-experimental design. The sample ($n = 184$) was divided into three groups: two were experimental, and one control. The control group ($n = 64$) did not participate in virtual reality. The first experimental group participated in virtual reality with guided exploration ($n = 62$), and the second ($n = 58$) was also immersed in virtual reality, but they lacked guidance. The researchers used a pre–post test and applied ANCOVA to analyze the results. A significant correlation was found between the students' preferred learning styles and a design of instruction responsive to the preferences of the learners. "The assimilator group exposed to VR [virtual reality] (guided exploration) mode obtained a significantly higher score for the VR based test than the assimilator learners exposed to the non VR mode" (p. 131). Similarly, "the accommodator learners exposed to the VR (guided exploration) mode obtained significantly higher gains for the VR-based test" (p. 133). The performance of the assimilators was higher, but not statistically significant. However, those students participating in the virtual reality guided exploration mode benefitted the most, regardless of their learning. This result is explained by the authors stating that a virtual reality mode involves all four learning styles, which may suggest that virtual environments are suited to all kinds of learners.

Research on Teaching

Wilensky (1991) portrayed the theoretical distinction between face-to-face and online learning through the perspective of *instructionism* and *constructionism.* These terms suggest that online learning defines the role of the instructor as a "guide on the side rather than as sage on the stage" (Stinson & Milter, 1996, p. 40). Hult, Dahlgren, Hamilton, and Söderström (2005) declared that instructors have been pushed to having an invisible presence, defined as reluctance to intervene. Sometimes, faculty become lurkers. These authors reviewed 3,700 online postings from eight courses delivered in upper secondary schools in Sweden and held a series of interviews with students, instructors, and educational leaders. They identified the teacher visibility in the courses and compared it with the perception that teachers and students have in diverse course activities. The authors explored the views of students and teachers on the role of instructors. They found that three types of guidance were valued: activity orientation, conference orientation, and validation orientation. The first refers to the tasks "foster[ing the] understanding of the subject matter" (Hult et al., 2005, "Activity Orientation," para. 1). Students reported that their knowledge gains were broader and deeper when they receive this kind of guidance. Conference orientation refers to the conversational mode established through the asynchronous platform. Some teachers took a laid-back position (13% of the postings was the lowest teacher participation rate in a given course). Others were more active than the students (the highest teacher participation rate was 50%).

During the interviews, the students expressed disappointment with teachers not fully engaged and acting as course leaders. Students valued the intervention of faculty. Hult et al. (2005) found that the promotion of learning in an open environment requires an animating or steering presence—not as a controller or instructor, but someone drawing out the goal-directed process. In consonance with these findings, Burge (2008) reported that responsiveness is one of the most important commitments that faculty can make in their teaching, as found in a review of expert knowledge among distinguished distance educators. Regarding teaching presence, T. Anderson, Rourke, Garrison, and Archer (2001) found that it was essential to maintain direction in online environments. Learners working in distance education are often regarded as unique, autonomous, responsible, and highly motivated, but their sociodemographic attributes are shadowed. As this subdiscipline of education expands, more and more attention is given to these variables, with gender one of the most salient.

Gender differences have been found in online communication styles, but some the findings are not conclusive. Burge (1998) warned distance educators to be aware of potential male domination in online discussion forums. Later on, Graddy (2006) reported that previous studies had found "the male discourse as direct, aggressive, competitive, and resistant to influence"(p. 212). Similarly, Graddy called the readers' attention on Lakoff, who considers female language "*as powerless language*" (p. 212). Further, Rovai (2001) stated that there are differences in the communication styles among men and women. Women tend to use a connected voice that is supportive and intimate. Men tend to use an assertive voice, which has an authoritative tone and shows power and independence. Based on those findings, Rovai and Baker (2005) used the classroom community scale (CSS) to explore gender differences among 193 students from 12 online courses in which 83% were women. CSS has two subscales, one to measure learning, and the other, a sense of community. It was found that "on average, females feel more connected to other students, in their courses, they felt more aligned with their own values and educational goals and perceived they learned more than their male peers" (p. 39). Rovai and Baker concluded that women actually differ in their "sense of classroom community and levels of perceived learning" (p. 39). Contrarily, Graddy (2006) found that gender-tied communication styles may vary since other factors come into play. For instance, if the group sets independence as a norm, gender communication styles are diluted. In a review of the discourse of 33 students (16 men and 17 women) using qualifiers (i.e., may, might, probably, I believe) and intensifiers (i.e., never, always, and personal pronouns), no significant "evidence of a 'male crowding-out effect'" was found (p. 211).

D. Anderson and Haddad (2005) studied gender differences in a distance learning sample of 80 women and 29 men using a survey methodology. The authors explored student control over their learning process as a function of both, student concern for others and instructor support. The students' concern for others was analyzed using three constructs: voice, professor support, and deep learning. They found that voice is a strong predictor of perceived (deep) learning in both face-to-face and online courses. Professor support and perception of deep learning had an indirect effect on satisfaction, as they intersect with voice. Women reported deeper learning in online than in face-to-face courses. The debate on the role of gender on online discourses and communication styles continues.

Research on Outcomes

Research on the learnability of media in instructional interventions as compared to conventional education is probably the first question that newcomers to the field raise. This topic is so pervasive that Moore and Kearsley (2004) have advised us to walk away from it. The no-significant-different phenomenon (http://www.nosignificantdifference.org) refers to the comparison of learning outcomes between face-to-face and distance education. Before the advent of the Internet, Schramm (1962) did a meta-analysis based on 400 empirical studies comparing the effects of conventional education with instructional television. He concluded that there was no significant difference between the modes of instruction. Russell (2001) collected 355 research reports published between 1928 and 1998 comparing face-to-face and distance education. The abundance of conclusions equating the quality of learning in both situations led him to adopt the notion of no significant difference in the results of learning, regardless of the medium used.

Probably with the intention of putting this issue to rest, Bernard et al. (2004) reviewed exhaustively the research published between 1985 and 2002, by comparing the effectiveness of different learning modalities. The topics reviewed relate to effective interaction, student achievement, and attitudes and retention in face-to-face and distance learning environments. The authors were also interested in understanding the impact of synchronous and asynchronous delivery modes, the state of the art of methodology, and the implications for further research. This research is one of the strongest studies found in the literature of distance education.

Through the use of major electronic library databases, Bernard et al. (2004) found 2,262 abstracts comparing conventional instruction with distance education. As a standard for selecting a paper, the research team established an 89% rate of interrater agreement and 91% to control the effect size of the reported sample in 321 studies related to achievement outcomes, 262 related to attitude outcomes, and 105 related to retention outcomes. The authors developed a codebook, which included the following categories: (a) outcome features, (b) methodology features, (c) course design, (d) media and delivery, and (e) pedagogy. They ranked the outcomes as low, medium, and high and coded the selected articles independently. Then they compared the results and decided to recode the pedagogical and media features. They controlled the sample size statistically and reviewed a total of 232 studies using multiple regression. The most difficult obstacle was the lack of information. In this regard, they declared that "Overall, nearly 60% of potentially codable study features were found to be missing" (p. 396). Obviously, the relative quality of the research studies reviewed affected the validity of the results. It was reported that among the three measures explored, missing values accounted for 56.5% on achievement, 60.4% on retention, and 52.8% on attitude. They sadly declared that "had the research reports been more complete, we would have been able to offer substantially better quality advice as to what works and what does not work in DE [distance education]" (p. 396). They did conclude that methodology and pedagogy are more important predictors of achievement than type of media.

Attitudes toward technology, subject matter, instructor, and course were found to be important in both synchronous and asynchronous modes, whereas pedagogy was found to be especially important in asynchronous distance education. With regard to retention, they reported several studies comparing distance education and face-to-face instruction at a state level. They found a small significant effect favoring DE conditions. Synchronous distance education had a more positive effect than asynchronous learning. However, all three findings have great variability. "Methodology, pedagogy and media accounted for 62.4% of variation in synchronous DE achievement outcomes and 28.8% of variability in asynchronous DE outcomes" (Bernard et al., 2004, p. 404). The authors were cautious about their recommendations for practice because of the variability and the missing data sets found in the research reports. Still, they suggested conferring preeminence to the quality of course design and pedagogical excellence over the media attributes. The use of active learning and the provision of opportunities for interaction were relevant in the quality of these outcomes. In spite of Moore and Kearsley's (2004) calls to direct attention toward more relevant issues than the no significant difference phenomenon and regardless of Bernard et al.'s (2004) meta-analysis reviewing the validity claims of all the reasonably well designed research studies on this topic, it continues to be a magnet for newcomers. Hopefully, researchers in the field will soon reduce their focus on this overwhelmingly reviewed issue and orient their attention to the design of rigorous studies.

Emerging Trends: E-Research and Web 3.0

A decade after the diffusion of Nielsen's World Wide Web, content-based and platform-based education have been left behind because new ways to manage efficiently the massive volumes of information have emerged. The expansion of personal learning environments using the broadband power available in the developed world via blogs, wikis, e-portfolios, YouTube, MySpace, and serious games calls for more visual, customized learning, networked, and coproduced curricula. Students are increasing their internal locus of control over learning tasks. As we are in the Web 2.0 era, the advent of Web 3.0 has already been announced. Knowledge mining, intelligent agents, social robotics, 3-D learning, and automation of teaching and learning routines are already a reality. Very soon, institutions working in online environments will transition toward an open system model (Gayol, 2008).

Presently, planners and programmers are working on the development of Web 3.0. In the United States, the Semantic Technology Institute International is collaborating with the European Union to attain such a goal. Simon (2005) characterized Web 3.0, the third generation of the World Wide Web, as a network that understands emotion, reason, and meaning because it will have limited rationality. Web 3.0 will work with virtual reality— that is, 3-D learning using avatars, intelligent agents, digital artifacts, and virtual contexts. Teacher agents will track student progress, provide customized resources, disseminate knowledge selectively, and work on routine tasks (T. Anderson & Whitelock, 2004). Mobile devices and serious games will increase their presence in learning. Some research has been done on the socio, cognitive, and affective identities of learners, as shaped by augmented reality (Dede, n.d.; Dede & Palombo, 2004). Dede and Palombo have increased the precision of early insights about the sense of immersion

(Kramarae & Taylor, 1993) by explaining that immersion in virtual reality implies the combination of exo-centric, ego-centric, and bi-centric experiences. They envision the future of virtual 3-D education being structured through codesign and co-instruction of situated learning pedagogies (including participatory simulations and scenario-based learning). They assume that this new structure will imply "unlearning almost unconscious beliefs, assumptions, and values about the nature of teaching, learning, and the academy" (Dede, 2005, p. 16). In the near future, children, teachers, and avatars would work together in international projects (Dede, 2004).

T. Anderson and Kanuka (2003) suggested that e-research is part of the emerging trends: "E-research is both a conceptual guide to the creation of an 'operating philosophy' for research using the Net and a practical guide for educational researchers" (p. 1). E-research refers to a "collaborative and interactive research made possible by the Internet and computational grids" (Applebee & Bannon, 2007, p. 83). It is a complex, interdisciplinary, international, and multisite endeavor performed through shared massive computing capacity. Because e-research operates with different "economic, security and ethical constraints" (T. Anderson & Kanuka, 2003, p. 2), these authors expect that e-researchers will embrace, along with the highly specialized methodology, a research philosophy and an ethical standing. E-research does not refer to the infrastructure required to process large data sets, but it addresses the scaffolding of multipoint collaboration processes and standards settings. An example of participation in e-research would be the maintenance of live international statistics continuously updating online learning growth that could include all the modalities (self-directed, enhanced classroom, blended learners) within all countries and institutions and the current status of students.

E-research is already a reality in other disciplines (e.g., astronomy), but to my knowledge, online educators are not yet taking advantage of the potential of e-research to process large data sets of learning events using computer grids, knowledge mining, artificial intelligence, and semantic networks. In the e-research process, a computer grid connects the computers of the researchers involved, retrieves the information generated from each end user, and processes the data according to the protocols established until the work is done. Problems of interoperability, software performance, and authentication are still challenges to overcome, but the development of new ways of knowing is promising.

Conclusion

The findings reported above provide a portrait of the relation between artifact, interface, learner, teacher, and the learning process. Research on computer-mediated communication has significantly contributed to increasing our understanding of the relations with self, others, and nature in a situation of disembodied experiences and dematerialized contexts. Online educators work in an environment in which iconic, cohesive, and interactive responses take prevalence over the spatial-temporal experience. The distributed nature of learning networks increases access and flexibility and enables participation 24 hours a day, 7 days a week to adults and individuals living in remote locations. Research studies have shed some light on the initial challenges of the visual interface acting as a cold barrier, and the design of instruction favoring the development of a sense of belonging by introducing social presence, cognitive presence, teaching presence, and transactional presence as relevant constructs in online learning environments. We have learned to consider learning styles and gender in the design of online instruction. We are learning to increase the scope of interventions in teaching online learners while embracing students as coproducers of content and designers of instruction in Web 2.0 and 3.0 environments.

Because computer networks induce exploratory behavior, incidental learning should never be ignored in online learning because in doing so, researchers exclude a huge portion of content and learning behaviors of students. All research on learners should report incidental and intentional behaviors. In doing so, the attribution of learnability, frequently assigned to computers and other mobile devices, would be clarified. It is not the teaching act or a particular technology that induces learning, but a good design and the will of students being there, ready to follow and coconstruct an inviting route to learning, that does.

Research in online education is not following the research trends pushing for the use of integrated models, mixed-mode methods, or bricolage (Tobin & Kincheloe, 2006, p. 6). It neither uses solid research frameworks. The need to overcome the single case syndrome and the methodological and theoretical flaws associated with much of our understanding of online education was found as a constant call among researchers. Further, I found little research addressing online learning issues that apply these emerging research practices. Multidisciplinary, multinational collaboration is an inviting door available to e-researchers—a door that online educators should be ready to cross . . . now.

Notes

1. Competency in this entry refers to the set of knowledge, skills, values, and attitudes used to solve a set of complex problems in the professional or knowledge realms.

2. Other media could be printed, audio, video, or mobile in a one-to-one, one-to-many, and many-to-many modes and used in synchronous, asynchronous, or combined frameworks.

3. Glass, McGraw, and Smith (1981) developed the meta-analysis technique of inquiry with the idea of supporting cumulative research.

4. A virtual environment on the flat screen creates the appearance of tri-dimensionality or a cave that induces the same illusion.

5. Flaming refers to emotionally charged communication over the Internet, which conveys hostile messages and behaviors.

6. The notions of word processor, formatting background, World Wide Web, graphic environments, multimedia, or even mouse were still to be developed. The green text was poured as a continuous line that the user had to break down to avoid horizontal lines going far beyond the screen size.

7. MOOS is the acronym for MUD object oriented; MUVs refers to multi-user environments.

8. *Writerly* is a term developed by Roland Barthes that defines the power of readers of electronic texts who cannot only read, but actually edit, write, and transform any given text. It addresses the transition of being a passive receiver to becoming a powerful actor in a discourse community. The growth of the community of bloggers, having voice in media and politics, is representative of the writerly attribute of the Internet.

References

Abbey, B. (2000). *Instructional and cognitive impacts of Web-based education.* Hershey, PA: Idea Group.

Allen, C. L. (1996). *Virtual identities: The social construction of cyber selves.* Unpublished doctoral dissertation, Northwestern University, Evanston, NY.

Allen, E. I., & Seaman, J. (2008). *Staying the course. Online education in the United States, 2008.* Needham, MA: The Sloan Consortium. Retrieved January 10, 2009, from http://www.sloan-c.org/publications/survey/pdf/staying_the _course.pdf

Anderson, D. M., & Haddad, C. J. (2005). Gender, voice and learning in online course environments. *Journal of Asynchronous Learning Networks, 9*(1). Retrieved June 10, 2008, from http://www.sloan-c.org/publications/jaln/index.asp

Anderson, T., & Kanuka, H. (2003). *E-research.* Boston: Pearson Education.

Anderson, T., Rourke, L., Garrison, D. R., & Archer, W. (2001). Assessing teaching presence in a computer conferencing context [Electronic version]. *Journal of Asynchronous Learning Networks, 5*(2), 1–17. Retrieved June 10, 2008, from http://www.aln.org/publications/jaln/v5n2/v5n2_anderson.asp

Anderson, T., & Whitelock, D. (2004, May). The educational semantic Web: Visioning and practicing the future of education. *Journal of Interactive Media in Education,* 1–15.

Applebee, B., & Bannon, D. (2007). E-research—Paradigm shift or propaganda? *Journal of Research and Practice in Information Technology, 39*(2), 82–90.

Argyle, M., & Dean, J. (1965). Eye-contact, distance and affiliation. *Sociometry, 28,* 289–304.

Arias, A., & Bellman, B. (1987). International cooperation through interactive Spanish/English transition telecourses. *Technology and Learning, 1*(2), 6–9.

Barilli, E. C. V. C., & Cunha, G. G. (2004, September 7–10) *Desenvolvimento, aplicação e avaliação de ambiente de aprendizagem baseado em realidade virtual para formação profissional permanente de recursos Humanos a distância, cuja competência exija o desenvolvimento de habilidades motoras: uma proposta de aplicação no campo da saúde* [Development, application and evaluation of a learning environment based on virtual reality for professional training at a distance of human resources whose competency demand the development of motor skills: A proposal for application in the area of health]. Paper presented at the VIII Congress of Distance Education CREAD, MERCOSUL/SUL, Cordoba, Argentina.

Bates, T. (2007, September 14). *The world of research on e-learning: An overview of the contemporary research.* Keynote speech presented at the International Conference Aprenred II, Guadalajara, Mexico, University of Guadalajara.

Barthes, R. (1974). *S/Z: An essay.* New York: Farrar, Straus and Giroux. (Original work published 1970)

Baym, N. (1995). *Technology, open learning and distance education.* London: Routledge.

Beaudoin, M. F. (2002, Summer). Learning or lurking? Tracking the "invisible" online student. *Internet and Higher Education, 5*(2), 147–155.

Bellman, B., Tindimubona, A., & Arias, A., Jr. (1993). Technology transfer in global networking: Capacity building in Africa and Latina America. In L. Harasim (Ed.), *Global networks: Computers and international communication.* Boston: MIT Press.

Berge, Z., & Collins, M. (Eds.). (1995). *Computer-mediated communication and the online classroom.* Cresskill, NJ: Hampton Press.

Berge, Z., & Mrozowski, S. (2001). Review of research in distance education, 1990–1999. *American Journal of Distance Education, 15*(3), 5–19.

Bernard, R. M., Abrami, P. C., Lou, Y., Borokhovski, E., Wade, A., Wonzey, L., et al. (2004). How does distance education compare with classroom instruction? A meta-analysis of the empirical literature. *Review of Educational Research, 74,* 379–439.

Bloom, B. (1956). *Taxonomy of educational objectives: The classification of educational goals: Handbook I.* New York: McKay.

Bradshaw, F. (2001). The new learning curve: Creating online courses. In Indiana University (Ed.), *Sketches of innovators in education: A collection of articles on teaching with technology by Indiana State University faculty and staff* (3rd ed., pp. 11–12). Terre Haute: Indiana State University.

Brookfield, S. D. (1986). *Understanding and facilitating adult learning.* San Francisco: Jossey-Bass.

Brooks, D. W. (1997). *Web teaching: A guide to designing interactive teaching for the World Wide Web.* New York: Plenum.

Bruner, J. S. (1960). *The process of education.* Cambridge, MA: Harvard University Press.

Burge, E. (1998). Gender in distance education. In C. Campbell-Gibson (Ed.), *Distance learners in higher education: Institutional responses for quality outcomes* (pp. 25–45). Madison, WI: Atwood.

Burge, E. (2008). Crafting the future: Pioneer lessons and concerns for today. *Distance Education, 29*(1), 5–17.

Bush, V. (1945, July). As we may think. *The Atlantic Monthly.* Retrieved June 8, 2008, from http://www.theatlantic.com/doc/194507/bush

Cambridge University Press. (2008). *Cambridge advance learner's dictionary.* Retrieved June 28, 2008, from http://dictionary.cambridge.org/define .asp?key=67155&dict=CALD

Ceruzzi, P. (2003). *A history of modern computing.* Boston: MIT Press.

Chen, J. C., Toh, S. C., & Mohd Fauzy, W. I. (2005). Are learning styles relevant to virtual reality? [Electronic version]. *Journal of Research on Technology in Education, 38*(2) 123–141. Retrieved January 10, 2009, from http://www.iste.org/content/

navigationmenu/publicatios/jrte/issues/voume_38/number_2_winter_2005/
_are_learning_styles_relevant_to_virtual_reality_.htm

Cheng, H., Lehman, J., & Armstrong, P. (1991). Comparison of performance and attitude in traditional computer conferencing classes. *The American Journal of Distance Education, 5*(3), 51–64.

Clark, R. E. (1994). Media will never influence learning. *Educational Technology Research & Development, 42*(2), 21–29.

Clark, R., & Mayer, R. (2003). *E-learning and the science of instruction.* New York: Wiley.

Dede, C. (2005). Planning for neomilennial learning styles: Implications for investments in technology and faculty. In D. G. Oblinger & J. L. Oblinger (Eds.), *Educating the Net generation* (pp. 16–22). Boulder, CO: EDUCAUSE. Retrieved January 10, 2009, from http://net/educause/edu/ir/library/pdf/pub7101o.pdf

Dede, C., & Palombo, M. (2004, Summer). Virtual worlds for learning: Exploring the future of the "Alice in Wonderland" interface. *Threshold,* 16–20.

Feenberg, A. (1989). The written world: On the theory and practice of computer conferencing. In R. Mason & A. Kaye (Eds.), *Mindweave.* Oxford, UK: Pergamon.

Freire, P. (1992). *Learning to question: A pedagogy of liberation.* New York: Continuum.

Gagne, R. (1962). Military training and principles of learning. *American Psychologist, 17,* 263–276.

Garber, D. (2004). Technical evaluation report: Growing virtual communities. *The International Review of Research in Open and Distance Learning, 5*(2). Retrieved January 10, 2009, from http://www.irrodl.org/index.php/irrodl/article/view/177/810

Garrison, D. R., Anderson, T., & Archer, W. (2000). Critical inquiry in a text-based environment: Computer conferencing in higher education. *The Internet and Higher Education, 2*(2–3), 87–105.

Garrison, R. D., & Cleveland-Innes, M. (2005). Facilitating cognitive presence in online learning: interaction. *The American Journal of Distance Education, 19*(3), 133–148.

Gayol, Y. (1998). Technological transparency: A myth of virtual education. *Bulletin of Science, Technology & Society, 18*(3), 180–186.

Gayol, Y. (2000). Analyzing the quality in the design of education of international virtual graduate programs: A new model of evaluation. *Indian Journal of Open Learning, 9*(2), 237–249.

Gayol, Y. (2007, September 10). *Web 2.0 & 3.0 in distance education for social change.* Keynote speech presented at the International Conference Aprenred II, Guadalajara, Mexico, University of Guadalajara.

Gayol, Y. (2008, March 2–5). *Web 3.0: What is it and why is it important?* Keynote speech at the Summit of the Alliance for Distance Education of California, Pasadena.

Gayol, Y., & Schied, F. (1997). *Cultural imperialism in the virtual classroom: Critical pedagogy in transnational distance education.* Retrieved June 3, 2008, from http://www.geocities.com/Athens/Olympus/9260/culture.html

Gilliard, M. D. (1996). Racial climate and institutional support factors affecting success in predominantly White institutions: An examination of African-American and white student experiences. *Dissertation Abstracts International, 57*(4), 1515A. (UMI No. 9624618)

Glass, G., McGraw, B., & Smith, M. L. (1981). *Meta-analysis in social research.* Beverly Hills, CA: Sage.

Graddy, D. B. (2006). Gender salience and the use of linguistic qualifiers and intensifiers in online course discussions. *The American Journal of Distance Education, 20*(4), 211–229.

Gunawardena, C. (1995). Social presence theory and implications for interaction and collaborative learning in computer conferencing. *International Journal of Educational Telecommunications, 1*(2–3), 147–166.

Gunawardena, C. N., & Zittle, F. J. (1997). Social presence as a predictor of satisfaction within a computer-mediated conferencing environment. *The American Journal of Distance Education, 11*(3), 8–26.

Hall, J. K. (2000) *Field dependence-independence and computer-based instruction in geography.* Unpublished doctoral dissertation, Virginia Polytechnic Institute and State University.

Handal, B. & Herrington, T. (2003). Re-examining categories of computer-based learning in mathematics education. *Contemporary Issues in Technology and Teacher Education, 3*(3).

Harasim, L. (Ed.). (1993). *Global networks: Computers and international communication.* Boston: MIT Press.

Heidegger, M. (1962). *Being and time.* Boston: Blackwell.

Herman, R., Ardekani, S. A., & Ausubel, J. H. (1989). Dematerialization. In J. H. Ausubel & H. E. Sladovich (Eds.), *Technology and environment* (pp. 50–69). Washington, DC: National Academy Press.

Hiltz, R. (1994). *The virtual classroom: Learning without limits via computer networks.* Norwood, NJ: Ablex.

Hiltz, R., & Goldman, R. (2005). *Learning together online: Research on asynchronous learning networks.* New York: Lawrence Erlbaum.

Holmberg, B. (1960). On the methods of teaching by correspondence. *Lunds Universitet årsskrift. N.F. Adv. 1, 54*(2).

Holmberg, B. (1999). The conversational approach to distance education. *Open Learning, 14*(3), 58–60.

Holmberg, B. (2001). *Distance education in essence.* Studien un Berichte der Arbeitstelle Fernstudienforschung der Carl von Ossietzky Universität Oldenburg, ASF Series No. 4. Oldenburg, Germany: BIS-Verlag.

Hult, A., Dahlgren, E., Hamilton, D., & Sörderström. (2005). Teachers' invisible presence in net-based distance education. *International Review of Research in Open and Distance Learning, 6*(3). Retrieved January 10, 2009, from http://www.irrodl.org/index.php/irrodl/article/view/262/839

Jonassen, D. H., Mayes, J. T., & McAleese, R. (1993). A manifesto for a constructivist approach to technology in higher education. In T. Duffy, D. Jonassen, & J. Lowyck (Eds.), *Designing constructivist learning environments.* Heidelberg, Germany: Springer-Verlag.

Jones, (1995). *Cybersociety: Computer-mediated communication and community.* Thousand Oaks, CA: Sage.

Kant, I. (2007). *Critique of pure reason.* New York: Penguin Classics. (Original work published 1781)

Karatas, S. (2008). Interaction in the Internet based distance learning researches: Results of a trend analysis. *The Turkish Online Journal of Educational Technology, 7*(2), 1–9.

Keller, J. M. (1987). Strategies for stimulating the motivation to learn. *Performance and Instruction, 26*(8), 1–7.

Kolb, D. A. (1984). *Experiential learning.* Englewood Cliffs, NJ: Prentice Hall.

Kramarae, C., & Taylor, J. (1993). Women and men on electronic networks: A conversation or a monologue? In J. Taylor, C. Kramarae, & M. Ebben (Eds.), *Women, information technology and scholarship.* Urbana: University of Illinois.

Land, R., & Bayne, S. (2005). *Education in cyberspace.* New York: Routledge Farmer.

Larreamendy-Joerns, J., & Leinhardt, G. (2006). Going the distance with online education. *Review of Educational Research, 76,* 567–605.

Lee, Y., Driscoll, M. P., & Nelson, D. W. (2004). The past, present and future of research in distance education: Results of a content analysis. *The American Journal of Distance Education, 18*(4), 225–241.

Licklider, J. C. R. (1963, April 23). *Topics for discussion at the forthcoming meeting. Memorandum for: Members and affiliates of the intergalactic computer network.* Retrieved June 10, 2008, from http://www.chick.net/wizards/memo.html

Loutchko, L., Kurbel, K., & Pakhomov, A. (2002, May 1–4). *Production and delivery of multimedia courses for Internet based virtual education.* Workshop presented at the World Congress Networked Learning in a Global Environment: Challenges and Solutions for Virtual Education, Berlin, Germany.

Mager, R. (1962). *Preparing instructional objectives.* San Francisco: Fearont.

McLuhan, M. (1964). *Understanding media: The extensions of man* [sic]. New York: McGraw-Hill.

Milligan, C. (1998, November). *The role of virtual learning environments in the online delivery of staff development* (Report for JISC Technology Applications Programme). Retrieved June 2, 2008, from http://www.jisc.ac.uk/publications/publications/talismanfinalreport.aspx

Monro, D. (1987, November 29–December 3). Quality distance education = computer based feedback + electronic mail. In J. Barret & J. Hedgberg (Eds.), *Using computer intelligently in tertiary education: A collection of papers presented to the Australian Society for Computers in Learning in Tertiary Education* (pp. 147–152). Kengsinton, New South Wales, Australia: ASCLTE.

Moore, M. G. (1989). Three types of transaction. In M. G. Moore & G. C. Clark (Eds.), *Readings on principles of distance education* (pp. 100–105). University Park: Pennsylvania State University.

Moore, M. G., & Kearsley, G. (2004). *Distance education: A systems view.* Belmont, CA: Wadsworth.

Naisbitt, J., Naisbitt, N., & Philips, D. (2001). *High tech/high touch—Technology and our accelerated search for meaning.* London: Brealey.

Nielsen, J. (2006). *F-shaped pattern for reading Web content.* Retrieved June 12, 2008, from http://www.useit.com/alertbox/reading_pattern.html

Oblinger, D. G., Baron, C. A., & Hawkins, B. L. (2001). *Distributed education and its challenges: An overview.* Washington, DC: American Council of Education.

Park, C. (1997, January). Learning style preference of Korean, Mexican, Armenian American and Anglo students in secondary schools. National Association of Secondary School Principals, *NAASP Bulletin, 81*(585), 103–111.

Pea, R. D., Tinker, R., Linn, M., Means, B., Bransford, J., Roschelle, J., et al. (1999). Toward a learning technologies knowledge network. *Educational Technology Research and Development, 47*(2), 19–38.

Pelgrum, W. J. (2001). *Obstacles to the integration of ICT in education: Results from a worldwide educational assessment.* Amsterdam: Elsevier Science.

Perraton, H. (2000). Rethinking the research agenda. *The International Review of Research in Open and Distance Learning, 1*(1) Retrieved June 3, 2008, from http://www.irrodl.org/index.php/irrodl/article/view/5/338

Peters, O. (2001). Distance teaching and industrial production. A comparative interpretation in outline. In D. Ely & T. Plomp (Eds.), *Classic writings on instructional technology* (pp. 239–256). Westport, CT: Libraries Unlimited. (Original work published 1967)

Peters, O. (2002). *La educación a distancia en transición* [Distance education in transition]. Guadalajara, Mexico: Universidad de Guadalajara.

Portland House. (Ed.). (1996). *Webster's encyclopedic unabridged dictionary of the English language.* New York: Author.

Prensky, M. (2001). Digital natives, digital immigrants, part II: Do they really think differently? *On the Horizon, 9*(6), 1–9.

Pressey, S. L. (1927). A machine for automatic teaching of drill material. *School and Society, 25*(645), 549–552.

Rheingold, H. (1991). *Virtual reality.* New York: Summit Books.

Richardson, J. C., & Swan, K. (2003). Examining social presence in online courses in relation to students' perceived learning and satisfaction [Electronic version]. *Journal of Asynchronous Learning Networks, 7*(1), 68–88. Retrieved January 10, 2009, from http://www.sloanc.org/publications/jaln/v7n1_richardson.asp

Roblyer, M. D. (2005). Educational technology research that makes a difference: Series introduction. *Contemporary issues in technology and teacher education, 5*(2). Retrieved June 12, 2008, from http://www.citejournal.org.ezproxy.fielding.edu/v015/iss2/seminal/article1.cfm

Rovai, A. P. (2001). Building classroom community at a distance: A case study. *Educational Technology Research and Development Journal, 49*(4), 35–50.

Rovai, P. A., & Baker, D. J. (2005). Gender differences in online learning. *Quarterly Review of Distance Education, 6*(1), 14–27.

Rourke, L. Anderson, T., Garrison, R. & Archer, W. (1999). Assessing social presence in asynchronous text-based computer conferencing [Electronic version]. *Journal of Distance Education/Revuee de l'enseignement à Distance, 14*(2), 50–71. Retrieved June 10, 2009, from http://www.jofde.ca/index.php/jde/article/view/153/341

Russell, T. L. (2001) *The no significant difference phenomenon* (5th ed.). Montgomery, AL: International Distance Education Certification Center.

Saba, F. (2000). Research on distance education: A status report. *International Review of Research in Open and Distance Learning, 1*(1). Retrieved January 10, 2009, from http://www.irrodl.org.php/irrod/issue/view/6

Sahin, S. (2008). The relationship between student characteristics, including learning styles, and their perceptions and satisfaction in Web-based courses in higher education. *Turkish Online Journal of Distance Education, 9*(1), 123–138.

Schramm, W. (1962, April). Learning from instructional television. *Review of Educational Research, 32,* 156–157.

Shih, M., Feng, J., & Tsai, C. (2008). Research and trends in the field of e learning from 2001 to 2005: A content analysis of cognitive studies in selected journals. *Computers & Education, 51*(2), 955–967.

Shin, N. (2003). Transactional presence as a critical predictor of success in distance learning. *Distance Education, 24*(1), 69–86.

Simon, H. (2005, October 23–28). *Agent-based computational economics and market design.* Presented as part of the Fourth Herbert Simon Lectures at National Chengchi University, Taipei and National Kaosiung University of Applied Sciences, Kaohsiunh. Retrieved June 10, 2008, from http://www .agsm.edu.au/bobm/teaching/Taiwan.html

Skinner, B. F. (1958). Teaching machines. *Science, 128*(3330), 969–977.

Sloan-C. (n.d.). *Sloan-C a consortium of institutions and organizations committed to quality online education.* Reviewed January 10, 2009, from http://www .sloan-c.org/aboutus/index.asp

Stinson, J., & Milter, R. (1996). Problem-based learning in business education: Curriculum design and implementation issues. In L. Wilkerson & W. Gijselaers (Eds.), *Bringing problem-based learning to higher education: Theory and practice: New Directions for Teaching and Learning, No. 68* (pp. 33–42). San Francisco: Jossey-Bass.

Swan, K. (2003). Developing social presence in online course discussions. In S. Naidu (Ed.), *Learning and teaching with technology: Principles and practices.* London: Kogan Page.

Tiffin, J., & Rajansingham, L. (1995). *In search of the virtual classroom: Education in an information society.* New York: Routledge.

Tobin, K., & Kincheloe, J. (Eds.). (2006). *Doing educational research.* Rotterdam, The Netherlands: Sense.

Vygotsky, L. (1992). *Educational psychology.* Boca Raton, FL: St. Lucie Press. (Original work published 1926)

Walther, J. B. (1992). Interpersonal effects in computer mediated interaction. *Communications Research, 19*(1), 52–90.

Wedemeyer, C. A., & Najem, R. (1969). *AIM: From concept to reality: The articulated instructional media program at Wisconsin.* Syracuse, NY: Center for the Study of Liberal Education for Adults.

Wegeriff, R. (1998, March). The social dimension of asynchronous learning networks. *Journal of Asynchronous Learning Networks, 2*(1). Available from http://www.sloan-c.org

Wells, R. (1992). Computer-mediated communication for distance education: An international review of deign, teaching, and institutional issues. *ACSDE Research Monograph* (No. 6). State College: The American Center for the Study of Distance Education, The Pennsylvania State University.

Wilensky, U. (1991). Abstract meditations on the concrete and concrete implications for mathematics education. In I. Harel & S. Papert (Eds.), *Constructionism* (pp. 193–203). Norwood, NJ: Ablex.

Witkin, H. A., & Goodenough, D. R. (1979). Cognitive styles essence and origins. *Psychological Issues* (Monograph No. 51). New York: International Universities Press.

Witkin, H. A., Moore, C. A., Oltman, P. K., Goodenough, D. R., Friedman, F., & Owen, D. R. (1977). *A longitudinal study of the role of cognitive styles in academic evolution during the college years* (GRE Board Research Report GREB No. 76-10R and the National Institute of Mental Health, MH21989). Princeton, NJ: Educational Testing Service.

Uncertain Frontiers

Exploring Ethical Dimensions of Online Learning

Dorothy Agger-Gupta

Chapter 9

The aim of this chapter is to raise awareness of key ethical issues that impact online learning and to promote informed dialogue among educators and students in online learning. I begin with a glimpse at the massively interconnected virtual world of the 21st century and emerging ethical dilemmas concerning online community, authorship, and ownership of online text, identity, privacy, secrecy, power, and dominance. In online learning, Western ethical beliefs need to be reconciled with alternate values of non-Western cultures. Professional ethical principles for online educators need to change. I consider those attributes of information and communication technologies that influence the nature of online living and learning communities. This chapter concludes with a summary of unanswered questions embedded in online learning. Through increased dialogue about ethical dilemmas, we can make more informed choices about the nature of online learning. As Zuboff (1984) remarked in the early days of the digital era, "People have to talk about what they think and why. This kind of interaction introduces new psychological demands and implications for social relationships" (p. 204). Ethics in online learning involves attention to the ultimate implications of our social transformation (Fisher & Wright, 2001; Hobart & Schiffman, 1998).

Sitting in her kitchen in Wisconsin, with her children finally asleep, Linda, an accountant, mother, and graduate student, turns on her computer and enters a unique worldwide learning community that includes colleagues around the world. Tonight, she will read e-mail, check two Web logs on Facebook, view a video from Japan, and have an instant message check-in with her professor who lives in Hawaii. Linda will visit a university research site in Denmark and refer to Wikipedia, an online encyclopedia. She notices that her own professor has contributed material about her topic of social networks and wonders why her university's policy states students cannot cite Wikipedia (Carvin, 2007). Linda logs onto her own university's Web site and retrieves several full-text journal articles and an electronic book. She switches to an online seminar, reviews and comments on the papers of four other students (who live in Holland, Chile, Australia, and California), and posts her scholarly paper on social networks. Linda receives an Internet video call on Skype from a close friend who lives in Rome. She delights in seeing the Italian sunrise.

Linda does a quick check on her son's postings on a social network site, Facebook, and reviews a video her daughter posted on YouTube. After purchasing an online article from a research university's online library on Second Life, Linda relaxes by creating a new flower for her virtual garden in Second Life.

Just as she is about to turn off her computer, Linda receives an e-mail from her California colleague who is upset because a member of their online seminar copied a portion of their text and posted it on a public blog. Linda feels uneasy. Her personal ideas had been copied and posted elsewhere without her consent. As Linda reviews some adjoining postings, she becomes further alarmed because some responses to this blog include strong negative trashing of one of her professors.

Reading further, Linda finds that she herself appears to be the target of some demeaning accusations. Although the words are false, they are emotionally upsetting and frightening. As she turns off her computer, she wonders about the power of online words to cause harm and wonders if she has any rights to protect herself and others from this abusive cyberbulling.

Why Online Learning Ethics?

Early in the 21st century we find ourselves in a worldwide cultural and technological transformation. Millions of people of all ages form online relationships with strangers, discuss issues of interest, and reveal intimate details of their lives on social network sites such as Facebook. They share billions of videos on YouTube; contribute millions of articles on the online encyclopedia, Wikipedia; build fantastic artifacts in virtual communities such as Second Life; and argue politics on Web blogs. Emotional entanglements, intellectual dialogue, frivolity, sexual encounters, bullying, and flaming all thrive in the online environment. Online conversation might be characterized as *prosthetic communication* (Stone, 1995), and online relationships may be more intense than in face-to-face communications.

Online learning challenges the traditional ethical guidelines of Western academia space. Alternate cultural beliefs that impact our relationships in the face-to-face world (Morgan, 1998) become more complex in virtual learning communities. The ways we use our digital technologies may silently nourish electronic colonization among an unaware populace. This chapter raises tough ethical questions on issues facing online educators and encourages informed dialogue (Hongladarom & Ess, 2007).

Ethical Dilemmas in Online Learning

> I bought land in Second Life, built a house, filled it with furniture, bought and razed the adjoining land, lifted my house a hundred meters into the sky. . . . I was befriended by dozens of Second Life residents, several of whom I now know better than my real neighbors. If the world we create together is less lonely and less unpredictable than the one we have now, we'll have made a good start. (Roush, 2007, p. 48)

Freed from classroom walls, online learning welcomes men and women whose educational opportunities had been limited by location, age, disabilities, and economics (Althauser & Matuga, 1998). However, the freedoms in online learning are tempered by new ethical dilemmas.

Online relationships and the conundrum of blurred boundaries between public and private online material fuel new uncertainties. Unresolved legal and ethical issues about online text concern authorship, ownership, and the capacity for unlimited and unseen copying, storing, modification, and dissemination. Complex issues of personal identity, anonymity, and confidentiality bridge the online and in-person worlds.

Academic researchers are beginning to notice virtual communities (Krotoski, 2007; http://socialsim.wordpress.com). Inhabitants of Second Life represent 40 different countries, the majority have college degrees, and nearly one third have PhDs (Fetscherin & Lattemann, 2007). They share personal information, sell professional services, use credit cards to purchase goods, and establish compelling relationships. The 2008 subprime mortgage crisis in the United States had its counterpart in virtual space, where real money is invested, exchanged, and lost (Lang, 2008). Depositors in one virtual bank lost $750,000 in real money through the actions of a competing virtual bank (Sidel, 2008).

Yet, the law and ethical principles are unclear about liability for slander, fraud, or destruction of virtual property (http://ethicalbloggerproject .blogspot.com). Issues of copyright and ownership of intellectual properties are unresolved in virtual environments that bypass national boundaries and have no consistent way to assess ownership, value authorship, or monitor the copying, modifying, storage, and dissemination of information.

Online Learning Communities

Today's online communities are more than computer-mediated social groups (Rheingold, 2000). They are contexts for sharing ideas, learning, and mutual support that may become more relevant to participants than their land-based neighbors, friends, and even families (Grodzinsky & Tavani, 2007; White, 2002). Even in the early years of computer development, Weizenbaum (1976) noted that people seeking counseling preferred to interact with Eliza, a computer program, rather than with an actual counselor. For some, it is easier to develop trust for others in virtual communities than in face-to-face engagements (Kasper-Fuehrer, & Ashkanasy, 2001).

Authorship

In Western academia, copying text without citing the author is plagiarism and violates copyright laws. Even the opposing views of utilitarian ethics and of deontological values share a Platonic sense of the value of the individual and view a creative act as a solo endeavor (Burk, 2007; LeFevre, 1987). Wikipedia, an online encyclopedia with over 7 million entries, violates this Platonic concept and is rejected as an academic resource in Western academic circles (Jaschik, 2007).

However, in many non-Western traditions, copying the words of an expert is a virtue and indicates respect. Confucian thought reveres classical works and respects those who emulate the masters (Burk, 2007).

Personal Identity, Anonymity, and Confidentiality

People feel violated when their online identity is stolen and used by another person (Lawson, 2004). Most social networking sites such as Facebook state that individuals must use their real identity when enrolling. Yet, we are uncertain of the ethical implications when an individual assumes an alternate persona. If others are harmed mentally, emotionally, or professionally through a posting, does it matter if the posting is untruthful or if the author assumed an alternate persona? When a teenager committed suicide after being rejected by an online suitor, there were no laws available to attach liability to the online suitor, who was a neighbor who was using an alternate persona.

Do participants in a public forum have a right to know who comes into the room—or can we allow one-way access where people can read and copy conversations, without giving any trace to the participants that they have been eavesdropping?

What is the impact of anonymous comments, when the identity of one participant is not known by the others? Is it enough to know that participants who are using pseudonyms are members of the university? Or must their identities be revealed before they are allowed access to public forums? Does the identity of a whistle-blower need to be disclosed? What if anonymity is being used to cover up abusive behavior for which one does not want to be accountable? Can institutional policy allow anonymity, but prohibit abusive and illegal discourse online (Moor, 2000b)?

The autonomous self is seen by many to disappear in the online world, replaced by a mosaic of multiple selves (Kolko, 2000)—or by a meta-self cocreated by several participants engaged in online discourse (Turkle, 2000). When people assume multiple online personas, "slippages often occur in places where persona and self merge, where the multiple personae join to comprise what the individual thinks of as his or her authentic self" (Turkle, 2000, p. 132).

Some online contexts, such as Web logs (blogs), tend to support the off-line identity of the author. In contexts that offer rich descriptions of environments and activities, gender tends to be reflected in what is noted about off-line lives as well as how the authors describe themselves (van Doorn, van Zoonen, & Wyatt, 2007). Research on women in online fan communities reveals that the embodied self does not disappear in the online environment. Rather, there is an extension of the real-life identity where attributes such as class and gender were "extended into cyberspace rather than left behind" (Bury, 2005, p. 210). Although it might take time for these facets to be obvious, much of a person's identity becomes known through language, grammar, and topics of discourse.

Privacy, Secrecy, and Confidentiality

The online environment raises new questions about the importance of privacy to identity and self. When we display multiple personas online, we go outside of the socially constructed boundaries that guide our real-world relationships. People who enact alternate online personas are sometimes shocked when others respond to the exposed persona, often feeling angry, vulnerable, and personally violated (Palloff & Pratt, 1999). It is often easy to reveal intimate secrets online. Sexually explicit material thrives. In online research, Witmer (1997) found that the majority of respondents were not concerned about privacy as they interacted on unmoderated, sexually explicit newsgroups. "Respondents tended to feel personally and technologically secure in their CMC (computer-mediated communication) and felt that they had little or nothing to lose if their activities were discovered by unintended others" (p. 11).

In a computerized society, we have limited ability to control our own information or to know if others access it. Our rights are based in a control-restricted access theory of privacy that allows access to information based on needs and relevance (Moor, 2000a). Those who have the authority to determine needs and relevance have power over others.

Information on individual purchases, library and video rentals, medical records, real estate transactions, telephone numbers, and online dialogue are gathered and stored, creating intimate personal profiles, usually without our awareness or authorization. Information can be gathered and used to generate new information, on a scale unimaginable prior to the advent of computers. Providers of Internet services may store private e-mails and instant messages without notifying those who use the service.

Secrecy involves the power to control the flow of information (Bok, 1979). As advocates of freedom on the Internet argue that secrecy is anathema to true democracy, others fiercely defend their rights to keep secret information from becoming publicly accessible.

Confidentiality is the ability to set and preserve boundaries around secret information (Bok, 1989). In education, confidentiality is protected by law and policy. We rarely question codes of confidentiality as they are supposed to preserve the secrecy of students' records, grievances filed against faculty, administrators' salaries, and private online seminars. Yet, in the online world, the power to impose confidentiality may be abused and used to keep relevant information secret, hidden from those who would otherwise have rights to it. "One name for professional confidentiality has been the 'professional secret.' Such secrecy is sometimes mistakenly confused with privacy; yet it can concern many matters in no way private, but that someone wishes to keep from the knowledge of third parties" (Bok, 1989, p. 119).

Instances of secrecy and confidentiality often appear so innocuous that they are accepted without question. Access to the information is controlled by those with administrative, technical, or other forms of power. There is rarely a challenge to the power or right to keep information secret. Online seminars are closed to nonparticipants. Faculty evaluations, student information, and administrative dialogue are all kept confidential.

The ability to maintain personal secrets and the choices over when and with whom to reveal secrets may be fundamental to our sense of professional identity. But the power to control secrets, to maintain confidentiality, can become the power to conceal wrongdoings. "These risks are great when control over secrecy is combined with personal unscrupulousness; greater still when it is joined to unusual political or other power and to special privileges of secrecy such as those granted to professionals; and greatest of all when it is in the hands of government leaders" (Bok, 1989, p. 282).

Power and Dominance

Power differences that exist in the off-line world are often carried forward into the online world by determining the dominant discourses

(Murdock & Golding, 2004). To counter power differentials, fragmentation and isolation, and homogenization, critical theorists who focus on the online public sphere are promoting a vision of online public dialogue that "moves beyond a consensus model of democracy. . . . towards a more radical, contestationary understanding" that supports and promotes "counter-discourse and discursive contestation" (Dahlberg, 2007, p. 842).

The dominance of English in online learning may serve to promote elitism and is often perceived as a form of colonialism. In a study of online communication among Egyptian professionals, English appeared to be used as the language of the elite, while Arabic was used for less prestigious dialogue (Warschauer, El Said, & Sohry, 2002). One study found that English-Cantonese bi-lingual participants in synchronous real-time dialogue created a unique online language that serves "to achieve both specific interactional purposes and to articulate a dual cultural identity" (Fung & Carter, 2007, p. 345).

Cyberbullying

Cyberbullying occurs when individuals repeatedly harass, demean, intimidate, insult, defame, discriminate, or otherwise cause intentional harm to others in the online environment (Patchin & Hinduja, 2006). The often deep-seated harm caused by bullying in the physical environment may be equally devastating in the online, e-mail, instant messaging, and mobile phone environment where anonymity can hide the identity of the perpetrator and the harm can occur in secrecy (Fogg & Eckles, 2007; Shariff, 2008a). Victims often hide the abuse (Hinduja & Patchin, 2005b), while perpetrators often claim that their actions are done "in fun" and may improve the strength of their victims (Hinduja & Patchin, 2005a). The damage inflicted by cyberbullying extends into the face-to-face world, fueling delinquency and impacting the lives of both offenders and their victims (Hinduja & Patchin, 2008a, 2008b). As public awareness and anger has emerged over widely publicized cases of cyberbullying leading to personal damage and even suicides, legal systems and educational policies in many countries are trying to reconcile rights of free speech and privacy with those of safety and antidefamation (http://shariff-research.mcgill.ca/cyberbullying; Shariff, 2008a, 2008b). Universities are disciplining cases of cyberbullying ("U of M Students Disciplined," 2008) and sponsoring research to better understand cyberbullying both within and beyond school and university systems (Li, 2007a, 2007b; Murphy, 2007). Web sites such as www.cyberbullying.ca, http://www.uwindsor.ca/cyberbully, and www.stopcyberbullying.org offer research, guidance, and support to students, parents, educators, and policy makers.

Academic Ethics

Traditional Western Academic Ethics

Codes of ethics are sets of rules that often lead to paradoxical dilemmas. Codes such as "do no harm" and "protect privacy" can be difficult to follow when protecting the privacy of one person can cause harm to another person. When ethical rules conflict, ethical theories provide a system of underlying beliefs that provide the rationale for ethical choices (Newman & Brown, 1996). Traditional Western models of ethics all assume a face-to-face linear world in which we can use logic to assess the inherent ethics of an action or use assess the probable consequences of an action.

Relativism ethics claims that there are no universal truths, but that the rightness or wrongness of an act depends upon the context, culture, and unique circumstances of the act itself (Johnson, 1985). *Deontological theories* are based on the theoretical rightness of the action itself irrespective of the situation, while *consequentialism* claims that the rightness or wrongness of an action can be determined by the consequences of the action itself irrespective of the situation (Johnson, 1985).

Pragmatic sensibility is based in the ideas of two American philosophers, John Dewey and William James. It recognizes that different people have different experiences that influence their beliefs, yet share an obligation to act to make the world a better place, even as we know that "better place" is an unreachable ideal (Dewey, 1984, p. 218). It has three core concepts: *transiency, pluralism,* and *meliorism.* Transiency supports the sanctity of individuals (McDermott, 1986, p. 122), while pluralism acknowledges that knowing is based in unique experiences that produce multiple views of what should and should not be done. "Most of our difficulties emerge from misunderstanding, condescension and arrogance, none of which are salutary for building a genuine moral community throughout the world" (McDermott, 1986, p. 125). The third concept is meliorism in which "we effect no ultimate solutions, yet strive to make things better" (McDermott, 1986, p. 126).

Differences also emerge in the nature of the values that underpin these belief systems. *Utilitarianism,* which bases rightness on maximizing total happiness, ranges from individual happiness to considering the happiness of all peoples both living and of future generations (Smart, 1986). *Contractualism* is based on informed agreement: "An act is wrong if its performance under the circumstances would be disallowed by any system of rules for the general regulation of behavior which no one could reasonably reject as a basis for informed, unforced general agreement" (Scanlon, 1986, p. 43). *Existential ethics* may be viewed as an approach that forces people to go beyond their social roles, taking responsibility for their own lives, "striving to be clear-sighted about the implications of our involvements, and acknowledging our indebtedness to the wider community" (Guignon, 1986, p. 88).

Alternate Views of Ethics

The ever expanding virtual space opens up new opportunities to challenge traditional ethics (Hine, 2005; Kitchin, 2003). Our attention to ethical issues often ends when we are satisfied that we have addressed the needs of those near to us (Bauman, 1993). In online learning environments, our close connections extend around the world and include people we never meet face-to-face. Even in its early days, computer technology "introduced actions of such a novel scale . . . that the framework of former ethics could no longer contain them" (Jonas, 1974, pp. 7–8).

Madge (2007) promotes a *fluid ethics* in which ethics is a process "weaving its web through a constant process of reiterative dialogue . . . that will in practice produce more ethical researchers and more ethical research than any set of formalized codes" (p. 667).

Narrative logic values a shared understanding of the potential consequences of an action. It is based on the understanding that comes from telling stories of anticipated outcomes—and listening to the stories of others. Narrative logic is particularly well suited for online environments in which people share learning experiences while living and working in different locations with diverse cultures. "While logic is good for describing what is, narrative is good for exploring what could be and for figuring out what should be" (Artz, 2000, p. 77).

The Status of Information

Information is often considered to be a means to an end and technology merely a vehicle to achieve those ends. In this view, the information itself has no moral status. Wetlesen (1999) ascribes four levels of moral status. At the highest level are moral persons who can think and make decisions, next are self-conscious beings such as dogs, then sentient beings such as fish, and finally, striving entities such as microorganisms.

Moral status can also be ascribed to nonsentient entities such as certain forms of information that serve as "irreplaceable and constitutive parts of someone's practical identity" (Soraker, 2007, p. 15). In certain situations, the destruction or modification of information that was essential to an individual's identity could have ethical implications.

Non-Western Cultural Beliefs and Ethical Values

Jake, a professor in North America, is facilitating an online seminar that includes learners from Cambodia, China, Japan, and Nigeria as well as from North America. The learners were asked to post papers on workplace democratization and to critique each other's papers. As Jake reviewed the postings, he noticed that some learners had posted papers that were copied verbatim from a leading textbook. He failed both papers. Other students posted comments that only stated "very good" and gave no critique. Jake posted a response saying that these comments were insufficient. The final paper was on a totally different topic. Jake posted, "If you didn't understand the assignment you should have asked." In all of his comments, Jake used their informal nickname.

Jake's comments confused and upset the students. Those who had copied the text believed they were honoring the expert and that they did not have enough expertise to write their own words. Those students who did not critique the work of others believed that it would be impolite to do so. The student who did not understand the original assignment believed it was morally wrong for a student to question a teacher.

Each student's actions were ethically consistent with their own culture. They had not yet learned the Western ways of approaching issues of authorship, critique, and questioning. But they will. "The developed world's paradigms of utilitarian and deontological informational control are rapidly overgrowing other indigenous models . . . to the extent that these models are promulgated by legal instruments, the imposition of the developed worlds models is deliberate and calculated" (Burk, 2007, p. 105).

There are cultural differences in perspectives on what is personal what is public. Information that is personal in the West, such as one's wealth or health, may be viewed as community information elsewhere. Similarly, the informal use of nicknames may be considered public in the West—and highly personal in other countries (Burk, 2007).

Little is known about the impact of differences in online learning and whether people feel more or less comfortable and understood when they are not judged by their appearance or speech (Mallen, Vogel, & Rochlen, 2005). Research on the experiences of people with disabilities found that miscommunication often occurs in the online environment. "Managing this methodological challenge required a meticulous attention to detail where additional questions and clarification were offered to reduce ambiguity and improve specificity" (Bowker & Tuffin, 2004, p. 237).

Some researchers have found that the democratization of information serves to narrow the dialogue. "Information is exchanged among like-minded people, where there may be little incentive to verify truth claims or question traditional modes of practice" (Harshman, Gilsinan, Fisher, & Yaeger, 2005, p. 235). Others assert that people who engage in online dialogue tend to join groups of like-minded people, thereby increasing the fragmentation of people into homogenous groups based on existing beliefs (Sunstein, 2005). However, Stromer-Galley (2003) found that online interactions serve to increase dialogue among people with differences.

Newman and Brown (1996), in addressing the ethical conflicts inherent in situations that embody differing ethical belief systems, proposed a guiding framework for ethical decision making that is based on Kitchener's

(1984) ethical principles: "respecting autonomy, avoiding undue harm, doing good, being fair, and being faithful" (Newman & Brown, 1996, p. 5).

When a paper is posted on a Web site, the paper is assumed to be owned by the person who wrote it—and full acknowledgement must be given for every use of the content and ideas in the paper. To copy the words of another, without authorization and acknowledgement, is condemned as plagiarism in all of Western academia. Collaborative papers are suspect because they do not clarify who contributed which piece. The structure of Western education is based on separation of people into categories. "As they educated themselves in self-government, the European bourgeoisie succeeded in excluding the non-literate, the non-affluent, and the non-male" (Habermas, 1989, p. 51).

Ethical issues that are difficult to unravel within a Western perspective are further blurred when viewed from multiple cultural lenses. As online domains cross national, cultural, and social borders, irreconcilable legal and ethical differences emerge on issues such as the dominance of English, what is public and what is private, ownership of online identities and text, and individual versus community rights. It is easy for a wide variety of voices and views to be posted on the Internet. There is an ethical challenge in ensuring that there is space for listening, not just for promoting one's own views (Downing, 2003).

Public or Private? Who Owns the Online Text of Conversation?

During an online seminar using an asynchronous forum, students and faculty develop a new theoretical model. Several months later, the professor publishes a journal article, claiming ownership of the theory that emerged during the chat dialogue.

An online, synchronous chat among students delves into personal issues as participants share facts and emotions about their personal, professional, and social lives. A few years later, a member of this seminar publishes articles that include some of these stories.

The university develops a process for enabling multilanguage dialogue on its forums. It chooses to maintain ownership of this process. In spite of the university's order, the students who developed the process are disseminating the details of the process on the Web and are encouraging educators in underdeveloped countries to copy and use this process to better access Web-based conversations that are conducted in English.

Who owns online conversations on forums? Our traditions of intellectual ownership seem increasingly irrelevant to online communication. The tensions inherent in the issues of ownership of intellectual property in the United States originated from the dual purpose of the U.S. copyright acts that are designed to both serve the public through promoting science and the useful arts and to protect the rights of authors (Goodwin, 2000). This foundation for considering ownership is called into question in an era of global networks, flowing information, and online collaboration.

Current ethical and legal codes do not reflect the complex nature of conversations in online forums. "Although an online forum may be accessible to the public, the activities engaged there might be confidential to the participants. Public access does not guarantee public disclosure" (Bowker & Tuffin, 2004, p. 231).

Creativity and innovation are not viewed as social acts in our laws, even though the creative process may be seen as occurring in multiple modalities from a sole creator through a collective process (LeFevre, 1987). Collaboratively developed intellectual property is troublesome to Western notions of ownership as property laws of ownership still seek definitive linkages between the product and specific owners of the product. When the value of products comes from use, including copying and modification, Western perspectives on ownership are no longer viable (Johnson, 1985, 2000).

Of special interest to the online learning environment are the challenges of real-time MUDs, Multi-user domains, and MOOs, Object-oriented MUDs. In these online spaces, people converse in real time, assuming a variety of personas. They participate in collaborative learning, storytelling, and community, building. The foundation of our notions of ownership—that of a distinct self as a solo creator—is challenged by this real-time environment. This Western notion of an autonomous self is superseded in the MUD environment, where multiple personas interact to create new realities. Ownership of material is collaboratively regulated (Kolko, 2000; MediaMOO, 1997).

When people converse using real-time text and collaborate using computer-mediated communication, it is difficult to categorize the text, as it often entails a hybrid of speech and writing (Kolko, 2000). The difficulties in determining authorship, property and even text in computer-mediated conversations require more relevant laws than currently exist associated with copyrights (Post, 1996). "It is precisely the interweaving of selves that occurs in MOO environments that makes the question of intellectual property a thorny one" (Kolko, 2000, pp. 259–260).

Countries exert control and censorship over online texts. Civil liberties groups, such as the Electronic Frontier Foundation (http://www.eff.org), note that existing laws in the United States on ownership of text were written for traditional journalists, and it is uncertain how they apply to online authors . The Center for Democracy & Technology (http://www.cdt.org) has petitioned the U.S. Federal Election Commission to protect individual freedom of online speech . In 2007, China forbade access to Wikipedia. "We can all hope for the day when no country prevents its citizens from learning from, and contributing to, this free, collaborative, online source of information" ("Jimmy Wales, Founder of Wikipedia, Speaks at the Commonwealth Club," 2007, p. 2). The U.S. Supreme Court has ruled that Internet speech is entitled to First Amendment protection but gave conflicting opinions as to whether the discourse is written or spoken (Kolko, 2000).

Professional Ethics of Educators

Professional ethics assume that professional roles matter (MediaMOO, 1997). When one assumes the role of a professional, the codes of ethics established for that profession matter, going beyond that of an individual (Johnson, 1985). Professional ethics provide explicit guidance for people engaged in similar professional roles. The professions could be centers for creative, reflexive debates on issues of importance to international education (Madge, 2007).

People in professions have unique powers. "It is because professionals have this power to affect the world, that imposing obligations on them to behave in certain ways is justified" (Johnson, 1985, p. 25). "Clinical pragmatic ethics" focuses on doing what one's profession has trained one to do (Lowenberg & Dolgoff, 1988). Most professionals tend to rely on their intuition, past experience, conventional behavior among colleagues, and professional codes of ethics as the basis for ethical decisions (Newman & Brown, 1996), with little reflection or debate on ethics beyond support for good intentions.

The online professional educator faces unique ethical challenges that include a reexamination of the role of professional identity in the democratization of expertise (Harshman et al., 2005). Professors have the power to shape the virtual world to match their own ethical codes, and students may be more apt to trust a person who is presented as an expert in the online environment. "The result is a virtual vicious circle" (Harshman et al., 2005, p. 235).

Professional codes of ethics in educational institutions often delineate the responsibilities of professors to defend their own freedoms while upholding the freedoms of others, to respect the dignity of others, to respect the rights of others to express diverse opinions, to support intellectual freedom and honesty, and to create a learning environment for students that supports learning and equity in the student–teacher relationship (Sterling College, 2000).

Ethical guidelines may be difficult to follow. Sumison (2000), in a reflective log of her initial year as a college professor, found that the professional code of ethics that she was required to sign was insufficient and soon became messy in its ambiguity. She developed a bounded form of an ethics of caring that included a measure of being present in the moment, to balance the nurturing with professional accountability. "Embracing presence as a pedagogical practice . . . holds potential for enacting a commitment to caring as a foundation of professional practice without perpetuating the disadvantages associated with women's traditional nurturing roles" (Sumison, 2000, p. 167).

The Ethical Obligation for Competence in Online Teaching

The Society for Teaching and Learning in Higher Education developed ethical principles for teachers that begin with the ethical value of competence in content and pedagogy (Dahl, 2006, p. 2). In online learning, pedagogical competence requires technological competence. Although today's students are fluent in a digital world of blogs, virtual 3-D spaces, instant messaging, Internet phone, and video, many teachers remain unable—or unwilling—to develop the technological competence to make use of these opportunities. "As students' impatience with their instructors' technological obtuseness increases, college and universities need to have some honest and open discussions about their ethical obligations to meet technology-related instructional needs and interests" (McLeod, 2007, p. 38).

Ethical Obligations of the Online Researcher

When conducting research in the online environment with interactive media such as e-mail, extra care is needed to avoid deception and to address power differences when there is no longer face-to-face contact between the researcher and the participants (Olivero & Lunt, 2004).

Some see the collecting of synchronous or asynchronous text from a private dialogue as similar to video or audio recording. It requires the preauthorization of the person(s) being recorded (Mallen et al., 2005). When conducting research via e-mail or online forums, the text that is gathered as data need to be treated as respectfully as video or audio data. Although it is simple to copy and distribute, text from online sources is not transferable among researchers unless prior informed consent has been given (Krishnamurthy, 2004). Just as in other research contexts, the online researcher needs to respect the online authors' ownership of their words. Further, they need to honor the participants' interpretation of privacy and copyright entitlement even when it differs from their own (Roberts, Smith, & Pollock, 2004).

Because of the uncertain ethical and legal boundaries between public and private online text, online ethics requires researchers to treat all publicly available documents as private and obtain explicit permission for the use of any text in an online forum. Although there is an implicit understanding that material posted online is recorded digitally, authors who post material on forums do not expect to be subjects of research (Clark, 2004).

There is an ethical controversy over the actions of a research team from Harvard and the University of California, Los Angeles—studying the postings on Facebook of 1,700 college juniors who do not know they are subjects of their research (Rosenbloom, 2007). It is easy and may appear harmless for researchers to lurk in online spaces, by assuming a role of an active participant in a forum, blog, or other virtual space. However, there are ethical consequences for the researcher who takes advantage of the ease of entry into an online community. Communities in online as well as face-to-face environments are built on trust that members will be following the same rule set (Hosmer, 1995). When researchers violate that trust, there is the potential to disrupt the community and the value the community has had with its individual members (Eysenbach & Till, 2001).

Institutional Responsibilities

Frankena (1986) suggested three ethical questions that an institution needs to address: "1) What should our laws require, forbid or permit? 2) What should our positive social morality require, forbid, or permit? and 3) what should be the rules and ideals of other social institutions?" (p. 314). Issues of personal ethics are outside of the purview of the institution. The challenge for online communities is to differentiate what should and should not be permitted within the institution while still supporting the rights of individuals to assert their own ethical beliefs.

When professors share information about a student using any form of electronic media, the student has a right to access that information. When two students discuss a professor on e-mail, the professor has no similar right. The professor has rights only when the student posts false and damaging information about a professor, in a forum that is more broadly accessible by members of the learning community (Carlson, 2001). In a 2001 act by the U.S. Supreme Court, it let stand a 2001 ruling by the U.S. Court of Appeals for the Fourth Circuit, in Richmond, Virginia, that supported a university administration's right to prohibit employees, including faculty, from viewing sexually explicit material on the Internet without the approval of their supervisors (Foster, 2001).

Each institution is responsible for establishing its own core intellectual property policy. Within the institution, this policy extends to ownership of a distance learning course, the rights of faculty and students within that course or seminar, access rights to the seminar, potential liability for the institution and the faculty associated with the course, and accreditation and international policy implications as the participants are located globally.

Ethics and Digital Technologies

No uniform, causal relation stands out between the technologies of information and the ages they demarcate . . . technology exists in dynamic interplay with culture, shaping and being shaped by it. Thus, in some instances, technology may foster new forms of information, while in others, it is fostered by them. (Hobart & Schiffman, 1998, p. 5)

Technology is often considered a means to an end, with a particular emphasis on tools that have been developed in recent history. It can be viewed in a much broader context as ways and means of achieving a goal and can therefore encompass practices such as language and psychotherapy as well as traditional notions of tools, equipment, and electronics (Hobart & Schiffman, 1998; Hofkirchner, 1999).

There are two dominant ways of viewing the relationship between technology and culture. In one, technological determinism, technology develops on its own, influencing and changing cultures and societies. An alternative view is that of social construction where those who have the power to control the technologies control the direction of human change (Turkle, 1984). The relationship between culture and technology may also be viewed as a dialectic in which they are different yet depend upon each other and together form an inseparable relationship (Herdin, Hofkirchner, & Maier-Rabler, 2007).

Digital Culture

In the 21st century, another variation of culture appears to be emerging, made possible by digital technologies. People from different geographic and national cultures meet in online communities and cocreate a unique culture that is based in mutual interests and exists independent of other forms of affiliation (Herdin et al., 2007). Welsch (1999) describes the formation of transcultures among people who may share a profession that separates them from others.

This confluence of technologies is not ethically neutral. It is embedded with the values and intentions of those who fund, design, develop, manage, and use them. Together, we are as the gods of antiquity, creating the rules for new worlds—sometimes with serious intent and at other times, with playful abandonment. The discipline of computer ethics has a rich, if brief, history stemming from a need to develop ethical foundations for the human dilemmas made possible by new technologies. Much of the field of computer ethics is inductive, derived from case studies (Floridi, 1998), written by people who understand the social engineering aspects of technology.

The development of the computer by Turing and von Neuman concerned the power of logic and the thrill of play. They yoked logic to electronic circuitry, creating power from information as well as early versions of poker-based game theory and computer chess. "And both toyed with the computer as a plaything in its own right. Their interest reveals deeper, more culturally rich levels of play, which connect the determinism of the computer's symbols and operations to the sensory world of experience" (Hobart & Schiffman, 1998, p. 204).

Logical Malleability, Invisibility, and Subsumption

The penetration of the computer into homes and offices in the second half of the 20th century introduced several key ethical issues that are part of the nature of computer technology: *logical malleability, invisibility,* and *subsumption.* As computers are engrained as necessities in our society, these ethical dimensions remain powerful, silent, influences in our lives.

Logical malleability refers to the fundamental task and ability of computers—to take inputs, shape the inputs with a set of programmer-defined logics, and create an output. We become the gods, creating the rules of the game. There is no logic that is right or wrong. There is only the set of directions that is established within the computer's internal connections. In the early days of the computer, human programmers created these rule sets. Computers have evolved in complexity to where these rule sets may be designed to continuously evolve into new rule sets. Programmers establish the nature of computer applications, by choosing the forms of logic to use to select, filter, and manipulate data and then to store, transfer, and selectively distribute information according to any schema of format, media, and audience (Kling, 1974; Moor, 1989, 2000b).

The power of logical malleability is that we rarely question data that appear on computer screens because the logic remains invisible to us. We have come to depend upon computer-generated information—to do otherwise is no longer an option. The malleable logic that controls the computer's systems is within the purview of the programmer and invisible to both sponsor and user of the system. As a society, we are way past the time when we could question this instrumental reasoning of the computer (Weizenbaum, 1976). Knowingly, or unknowingly, we fully accept it as part of ourselves.

Subsumption occurs as one set of logical components is subsumed into subsequent components. The decisions that are made early in the development of a program continue forward as the initial program becomes a subset of larger programs. Some of our most prominent technologically related disasters, such as the Challenger, are directly attributable to the subsumption of faulty decisions into larger, ultimately disastrous decisions (Gleason, 2000). The ethical questions become increasingly complex. Who is responsible when faulty choices are made that then become part of larger decisions? We are left with contaminated choices that are not directly traceable to the originators.

Invisibility is present when people interact with computers without being aware of the underlying software logic that determines what appears on the screen. Computer-generated information has a potential for delusion that accompanies the freedoms of online learning. In the mid 1960s, Joseph Weizenbaum, a professor of computer science at MIT, authored a software program, ELIZA, that analyzed text and presented replies that appeared to maintain a conversation, mimicking a Rogerian therapist.

Weizenbaum was trying to demonstrate that language could only be understood in contextual frameworks. He was shocked when people became emotionally involved with computer, believing that the machine was actually understanding them (Weizenbaum, 1976).

The power of unnoticed surveillance is omnipresent, available to everyone who has access to electronic text. Software developed and marketed by Ari-Pekka Hameri creates self-organizing maps to illustrate the communication dynamics among individuals. It reveals the closeness with which people work together and graphically illustrates differences in self-discipline and creativity ("The Big Picture," 2001, p. 75).

As our current technologies are just the initial steps toward a more intimately surveyed future, our comfortable ways of understanding privacy may no longer be relevant. Colleges are finding that the benefits of wireless communication—immediate, unfiltered access from any space within the reaches of the wireless network—also create problems of privacy, security, and unauthorized surveillance as the networks are easily penetrated, with the penetration remaining undetectable with our current technologies (Olsen, 2000).

The Persuasive Power of Computer-Generated Script

O most ingenious Theuth, the parent or inventor of an art is not always the best judge of the utility or inutility of his own inventions to the users of them. And in this instance, you who are the father of letters, from a paternal love of your own children have been led to attribute to them a quality which they cannot have; for this discovery of yours will create forgetfulness in the learners' souls, because they will not use their memories; they will trust to the external written characters and not remember of themselves. (Socrates, as cited in Plato, 5th century BC)

The power of persuasion in online learning is a critical ethical issue. The impact of an immediate, global audience is to generate more controversy, speculation, and dialogue with varying degrees of validity and reliability. In summer of 2000, two anthropology professors received page proofs of a book that alleged serious misconduct by two prominent scientists. The professors sent e-mail messages to colleagues, intending to open a forum for dialogue about this issue, prior to the book's publication. The news spread rapidly, inflaming worldwide dialogue, charges, and countercharges. The author revised some of the book in response to the issues that were raised. "Fierce and inconclusive debates on e-mail lists are nothing new in academe, of course. But in this case, reports, research memos, and press releases sent by email and posted on Web sites became the primary source of scholarly grist. While academics wondered, 'can this be true?' Internet-savvy scholars fed that hunger for information" (Miller, 2001, p. A14).

The social psychology of persuasion suggests several human tendencies that matter: reciprocation (if you give me something, I feel obliged to give you what you are asking for), the need to appear to be consistent (if I agreed to a similar request earlier, I want to be seen as consistent and am more likely to comply), social validation (we comply with requests when we know that others have already complied), liking (we support the requests that come from people we like), authority (we follow those we presume have authority), and scarcity (the more unique something is perceived to be, the more we tend to value it). These values seem to reflect the key components in effective persuasion (Cialdini, 2001). In the case of the response to the e-mail message regarding the anthropologists' research, these factors came into play in an explosive manner. People responded to the unexpected information. As scholars, they needed to appear consistent. The flood of e-mail responses created an impression of a massive social response.

Dialogue and Engagement

> Concerning society in the year 2000. . . . the most remarkable predictions concern the transformation of educational methods and the problem of human reproduction. Knowledge will be accumulated in 'electronic banks' and transmitted directly to the human nervous system by means of coded electronic messages . . . What is needed will pass directly from the machine to the brain without going through consciousness. (Ellul, 1964, p. 432)

There is no pretension here that ethical dilemmas dominate our thinking. We are so deeply engaged in the development of our new forms of online learning that it is difficult to justify taking time out to consider the ethical implications—no matter how profound—of our choices in creating our learning environments. And yet, the ethical dilemmas persist, ever the more powerful through their subtle and unobtrusive manner. As our nature is more intertwined with the reasoning of our computers and technologies, we have less opportunity to engage in dialogue and debate about the ethical implications of our acquiescence to an unplanned future (Ellul, 1964; Weizenbaum, 1976).

The stuff of information is created by our human mind, influenced by our collective technologies, and has a unique meaning in each era and culture. Beginning with the joining of the oral world with the literate world, the participative nature of information was established. Technologies have always impacted the nature of society itself (Hobart & Schiffman, 1998). Learners who feel connected to their online learning communities develop a powerful sense of virtual proximity that enables socialization and collaboration (Haythornthwaite, Kazmer, Robins, & Shoemaker, 2000). We can only glimpse at the ways in which our new technologies will be impacting learning in the years to come (Fisher & Wright, 2001).

These ethical dilemmas require thoughtful and open debate and dialogue. There is no attempt here to propose simple frameworks for resolving difficult dilemmas. Any such a framework is mired in its own assumptions and values. "A system of moral philosophy put to such uses (for hard choices) is like a magician's hat—almost anything can be pulled out of it, wafted about, let fly" (Bok, 1979, p. 57).

There are no simple answers. But there are questions to ponder, choices to be made, rules to be established and new games to be played in this new frontier. The ethical dilemmas of the face-to-face world persist and are often more complex in our emerging virtual worlds (Johnson, 1997). With engagement and dialogue, we can promote a world whose ethics promote sharing, listening, and caring for each other in the online and face-to-face worlds.

References

Althauser, R., & Matuga, J. M. (1998). On the pedagogy of electronic instruction. In C. J. Bonk & K. S. King (Eds.), *Electronic collaborators: Learner-centered technologies for literacy, apprenticeship and discourse* (pp. 183–208). Mahwah, NJ: Lawrence Erlbaum.

Artz, J. M. (2000). Narrative vs. logical reasoning in computer ethics. In R. M. Baird, R. Ramsower, & S. E. Rosenbaum (Eds.), *Cyberethics: Social & moral issues in the computer age* (pp. 73–79). Amherst, NY: Prometheus Books.

Bauman, Z. (1993). *Postmodern ethics.* Oxford, UK: Blackwell.

The big picture. (2001, January 6). *Economist, 358,* 75.

Bok, S. (1979). *Lying: Moral choice in public and private life.* New York: Vantage Books.

Bok, S. (1989). *Secrets: On the ethics of concealment and revelation.* New York: Vantage Books.

Bowker, N., & Tuffin, K. (2004). Using the online medium for discursive research about people with disabilities. *Social Science Computer Review, 22,* 228–241.

Burk, D. L. (2007). Privacy and property in the global datasphere. In S. Hongladarom, S. Ess, & C. Ess (Eds.), *Information technology ethics: Cultural perspectives* (pp. 94–107). Hershey, PA: Idea Group Reference.

Bury, R. (2005). *Cyberspaces of their own: Female fandoms online.* New York: Peter Lang.

Carlson, S. (2001). North Dakota professor sues former student and a Web site over allegations in an article. *The Chronicle of Higher Education, XLVII,* A33.

Carvin, A. (2007, February 14). Wikipedia receives a citation. *Learning.now.* Retrieved January 27, 2008, from http://www.pbs.org/teachers/learning.now/2007/02/wikipedia_receives_a_citation_1.html

Cialdini, R. B. (2001). The science of persuasion. *Scientific American, 284*(2), 76–81.

Clark, D. (2004). What if you meet face to face? A case study in virtual/material research ethics. In E. A. Buchanan (Ed.), *Readings in virtual research and ethics: Issues and controversies* (pp. 247–261). Hershey, PA: Information Science.

Dahl, J. (2006). Ethical principles and faculty development. *Distance Education Report, 10*(2), 5–8.

Dahlberg, L. (2007). Rethinking the fragmentation of the cyberpublic: From consensus to contestation. *New Media & Society, 9*(5), 827–847.

Dewey, J. (1984). *The quest for certainty: The later works* (Vol. 4). Carbondale: Southern Illinois University Press.

Downing, J. D. H. (2003). Audiences and readers of alternative media: The absent lure of the virtually unknown. *Media, Culture, & Society, 25,* 625–645.

Ellul, J. (1964). *The technological society* (J. Wilkenson, Trans.). New York: Vintage Books.

Eysenbach, G., & Till, J. E. (2001). Ethical issues in qualitative research on Internet communities. *British Medical Journal, 333*(7321), 1103–1105.

Fetscherin, M., & Lattemann, C. (2007). *User acceptance of virtual worlds: An explorative study about Second Life.* Retrieved February 1, 2008, from Second Life Research Team Web site: http://www.fetscherin.com/UserAcceptance VirtualWorlds.htm

Fisher, D. R., & Wright, L. M. (2001). On utopias and dystopias: Toward an understanding of the discourse surrounding the Internet. *Journal of Computer-Mediated Communication, 6*(2), 13. Retrieved January 28, 2009, from http://jcmc.indiana.edu/vol6/issue2/fisher.html

Floridi, L. (1998, March 25–27). *Information ethics: On the philosophical foundation of computer ethics.* Paper presented at the ETHICOMP98: The fourth international conference on ethical issues of information technology, Erasmus University, the Netherlands.

Foster, A. (2001). Supreme Court rebuffs professors' challenge to a Virginia law on Internet use. *The Chronicle of Higher Education, XLVII,* A31.

Frankena, W. K. (1986). Moral philosophy and the future. In J. P. DeMarco & R. M. Fox (Eds.), *New directions in ethics: The challenge of applied ethics* (pp. 299–318). London: Routledge & Kegan Paul.

Fogg, B. J., & Eckles, D. (Eds.). (2007). *Mobile persuasion: 20 perspectives on the future of behavior change.* Stanford, CA: Stanford Captology Media.

Fung, L., & Carter, R. (2007). New varieties, new creativities: ICQ and English-Cantonese e-discourse. *Language and Literature, 16*(4), 345–366.

Gleason, D. H. (2000). Subsumtion ethics. In R. M. Baird, R. Ramsower, & S. E. Rosenbaum (Eds.), *Cyberethics: Social & moral issues in the computer age* (pp. 56–72). Amherst, NY: Prometheus Books.

Goodwin, M. (Ed.). (2000). *Wild, wild web.* Amherst, NY: Prometheus Books.

Grodzinsky, F. S., & Tavani, H. T. (2007). Online communities, democratic ideals, and the digital divide. In S. Hongladarom, S. Ess, & C. Ess (Eds.), *Information technology ethics: Cultural perspectives* (pp. 20–30). Hershey, PA: Idea Group Reference.

Guignon, C. (1986). Existentialist ethics. In J. P. DeMarco & R. M. Fox (Eds.), *New directions in ethics: The challenge of applied ethics* (pp. 73–91). London: Routledge & Kegan Paul.

Habermas, J. (1989). *The structural transformation of the public sphere.* Cambridge, UK: Polity.

Harshman, E. M., Gilsinan, J. F., Fisher, J. E., & Yaeger, F. C. (2005). Professional ethics in a virtual world: The impact of the Internet on traditional notions of professionalism. *Journal of Business Ethics, 58,* 227–236.

Haythornthwaite, C., Kazmer, M. M., Robins, J., & Shoemaker, S. (2000). Community development among distance learners: temporal and technological dimensions [Electronic version]. *Journal of Computer-Mediated Communication, 6*(1), 30. Retrieved January 28, 2009, from http://jcmc.indiana .edu/vol6/issue1/haythornthwaite.html

Herdin, T., Hofkirchner, W., & Maier-Rabler, U. (2007). Culture and technology: A mutual-shaping approach. In S. Hongladarom, S. Ess, & C. Ess (Eds.), *Information technology ethics: Cultural perspectives* (pp. 54–67). Hershey, PA: Idea Group Reference.

Hinduja, S., & Patchin, J. (2005a). *Research summary: Cyberbullying offending.* Retrieved May 1, 2008, from http://www.cyberbullying.us/cyberbullying _offending.pdf

Hinduja, S., & Patchin, J. (2005b). *Research summary: Cyberbullying victimization.* Retrieved May 1, 2008, from http://www.cyberbullying.us/cyberbullying _victimization.pdf

Hinduja, S., & Patchin, J. (2008a). Cyberbullying: An exploratory analysis of factors related to offending and victimization. *Deviant Behavior, 29*(2), 1–29.

Hinduja, S., & Patchin, J. (2008b). Offline consequences of online victimization: School violence and delinquency. *Journal of School Violence, 6*(3), 89–112.

Hine, C. (2005). Virtual methods and the sociology of cyber-social-scientific knowledge. In C. Hine (Ed.), *Virtual methods: Issues in social research on the internet* (pp. 1–13). Oxford, UK: Berg.

Hobart, M. E., & Schiffman, Z. S. (1998). *Information ages: Literacy, numeracy and the computer revolution.* Baltimore: Johns Hopkins University Press.

Hofkirchner, W. (1999). Does electronic networking entail a new stage of cultural evolution? In P. Fleissner & J. C. Nyiri (Eds.), *Cyberspace: A new battlefield for human interests? Philosophy of culture and the politics of electronic networking* (Vol. II, pp. 3–22). Innsbruck, Austria: Studienverlag.

Hongladarom, S., & Ess, C. (Eds.). (2007). *Information technology ethics: Cultural perspectives.* Hershey, PA: Idea Group Reference.

Hosmer, L. (1995). Trust: The connection link between organizational theory and philosophical ethics. *Academy of Management Review, 20,* 379–403.

Jaschik, S. (2007). A stand against Wikipedia. *Inside Higher Ed.* Retrieved February 1, 2008, from http://www.insidehighered.com/news/2007/01/26/wiki

Jimmy Wales, founder of Wikipedia, speaks at the Commonwealth Club. (2008). *The Bay Area Intellectual.* Retrieved February 1, 2008, from http://www .thebayareaintellect.com/jimmy-wales-founder-of-wikipedia-speaks-at-common-wealth-club

Johnson, D. (1985). *Computer ethics.* Englewood Cliffs, NJ: Prentice Hall.

Johnson, D. (1997). Ethics online. *Communications of the ACM, 40*(1), 60–65.

Johnson, D. (2000). Should computer programs be owned? In R. M. Baird, R. Ramsower, & S. E. Rosenbaum (Eds.), *Cyberethics: Social & moral issues in the computer age* (pp. 222–235). Amherst, NY: Prometheus Books.

Jonas, H. (1974). *Philosophical essays: From ancient creed to technological man.* Englewood Cliffs, NJ: Prentice Hall.

Kasper-Fuehrer, E. C., & Ashkanasy, N. M. (2001). Communicating trustworthiness and building trust in interorganizational virtual organizations. *Journal of Management, 27*(3), 235–54.

Kitchener, K. S. (1984). Intuition, critical evaluation and ethical principles: The foundation for ethical decisions in counselling psychology. *The Counseling Psychologist, 12*(3), 43–56.

Kitchin, H. A.(2003). The tri-council policy statement and research in cyberspace: Research ethics, the Internet, and revising a "living document." *Journal of Academic Ethics, 1,* 397–418.

Kling, R. (1974). Computers and social power. *Computers & Society, 5*(3), 6–11.

Kolko, B. E. (2000). Intellectual property in synchronous and collaborative virtual space. In R. M. Baird, R. Ramsower, & S. E. Rosenbaum (Eds.), *Cyberethics: Social & moral issues in the computer age* (pp. 257–281). Amherst, NY: Prometheus Books.

Krotoski, A. (2007). Whither the (market and academic) research in Second Life? *Social Sim.* Retrieved January 27, 2008, from http://socialsim.wordpress.com/2007/11/14/whither-the-market-and-academic-research-in-second-life

Krishnamurthy, S. (2004). The ethics of conducting e-mail surveys. In E. A. Buchanan (Ed.), *Readings in virtual research and ethics: Issues and controversies.* (pp. 114–121). Hershey, PA: Information Science.

Lang, G. (2008, January 23). *Banking crisis (also) in Second Life.* Retrieved February 1, 2008, from Second Life Research: http://secondliferesearch.blogspot.com

Lawson, D. (2004). Blurring the boundaries: Ethical considerations in online research. In E. A. Buchanan (Ed.), *Readings in virtual research and ethics: Issues and controversies* (pp. 80–100). Hershey, PA: Information Science.

LeFevre, K. B. (1987). *Invention as a social act.* Carbondale: Southern Illinois University Press.

Li, Q. (2007a). Bullying in the new playground: A research into cyberbullying and cyber victimization. *Australasian Journal of Educational Technology, 23*(4), 435–454.

Li, Q. (2007b). New bottle but old wine: A research on cyberbullying in schools. *Computers and Human Behavior, 23*(4), 1777–1791.

Lowenberg, F., & Dolgoff, R. (1988). *Ethical decisions for social work practice* (3rd ed.). Itasca, IL: F. E. Peacock.

Madge, C. (2007). Developing a geographers' agenda for online research ethics. *Progress in Human Geography, 31*(5), 654–674.

Mallen, M. J., Vogel, D. L., & Rochlen, A. B. (2005). The practical aspects of online counseling: Ethics, training, technology, and competency. *The Counseling Psychologist, 33*(6), 776–818.

McDermott, J. J. (1986). Pragmatic sensibility: the morality of experience. In J. P. DeMarco & R. M. Fox (Eds.), *New directions in ethics: The challenge of applied ethics* (pp. 113–134). London: Routledge & Kegan Paul.

McLeod, S. (2007). Our ethical obligation. *Technology & Learning, 28*(1), 38.

MediaMOO. (1997). *MediaMoo symposium: The ethics of research in virtual communities.* Retrieved October 6, 2000, from http://www.cc.gatech.edu/~asb/mediamoo/ethics-symposium-97.html

Miller, D. W. (2001). Academic scandal in the Internet age: When a furor broke out in anthropology, e-mail was more powerful than peer review. *The Chronicle of Higher Education, XLVII,* A14–A17.

Moor, J. H. (1989). How to invade and protect privacy with computers. In C. C. Gould (Ed.), *The information Web* (pp. 61–62). Boulder, CO: Westview Press.

Moor, J. H. (2000a). Moor: Toward a theory of privacy. In R. M. Baird, R. Ramsower, & S. E. Rosenbaum (Eds.), *Cyberethics: Social & moral issues in the computer age* (pp. 200–212). Amherst, NY: Prometheus Books.

Moor, J. H. (2000b). What is computer ethics? In R. M. Baird (Ed.), *Cyberethics: Social and moral issues in the computer age* (pp. 23–33). Amherst, NY: Prometheus Books.

Morgan, E. (1998). *Navigating cross-cultural ethics: What global managers do right to keep from going wrong.* Boston: Butterworth Heinemann.

Murdock, G., & Golding, P. (2004). Dismantling the digital divide: Rethinking the dynamics of participation and exclusion. In A. Calabrese & C. Sparks (Eds.), *Towards a political economy of culture: Capitalism and communication in the Twenty-first century* (pp. 244–60). Lanham, MD: Rowman & Littlefield.

Murphy, M. (2007). Funding allows experts to gang up on cyber-bullying, *McGill Reporter, 39*(11). Retrieved May 1, 2008, from http://www.mcgill.ca/reporter/39/11/shariff

Newman, D. L., & Brown, R. D. (1996). *Applied ethics for program evaluation.* Thousand Oaks, CA: Sage.

Olivero, N., & Lunt, P. (2004). When the ethic is functional to the method: The case of e-mail qualitative interviews. In E. A. Buchanan (Ed.), *Readings in virtual research and ethics: Issues and controversies* (pp. 101–113). Hershey, PA: Information Science.

Olsen, F. (2000). The wireless revolution. *The Chronicle of Higher Education, 47*(7), 59–60, 62, 64.

Palloff, R. M., & Pratt, K. (1999). *Building learning communities in cyberspace: Effective strategies for the online classroom.* San Francisco: Jossey-Bass.

Patchin, J. W., & Hinduja, S. (2006). Bullies move beyond the schoolyard: A preliminary look at cyberbullying. *Youth Violence and Juvenile Justice, 4*(2), 148–169.

Plato. (5th century BC). *The phaedrus.* Retrieved January 28, 2009, from http://www.units.muohio.edu/technologyandhumanities/plato.htm

Post, D. (1996). "Clarifying" the law of cyberspace. *American Lawyer, 18*(3), 115.

Rheingold, H. (2000). *The virtual community: Homesteading on the electronic frontier* (Rev. ed.). Cambridge: MIT Press.

Roberts, L., Smith, L., & Pollock, C. (2004). Conducting ethical research online: Respect for individuals, identities, and the ownership of words. In E. A. Buchanan (Ed.), *Readings in virtual research and ethics: Issues and controversies* (pp. 156–173). Hershey, PA: Information Science.

Rosenbloom, S. (2007, December 17). On Facebook, scholars link up with data. *The New York Times.* Retrieved February 1, 2008, from http://www.nytimes.com/2007/12/17/style/17facebook.html?_r=1&pagewanted=1&ref=education&oref=slogin

Roush, W. (2007). Second Earth. *Technology Review, 110*(4), 38–48.

Scanlon, T. M. (1986). A contractualist alternative. In J. P. DeMarco & R. M. Fox (Eds.), *New directions in ethics: The challenge of applied ethics* (pp. 42–57). London: Routledge & Kegan Paul.

Schweizer, K., Paechter, M., & Weidenmann, B. (2001). A field study on distance education and communication: experiences of a virtual tutor. *Journal of Computer-Mediated Communication, 6*(2), 16. Retrieved February 3, 2008, from http://jcmc.indiana.edu/vol6/issue2/schweizer.html

Shariff, S. (2008a). *Confronting cyber-bullying: What schools need to know to control misconduct and avoid legal consequences.* Cambridge, MA: Cambridge University Press.

Shariff, S. (2008b). *Cyber-bullying: Issues and solutions for the school, the classroom and the home.* London: Routledge.

Sidel, R. (2008, February 1). Cheer up, Ben: Your economy isn't as bad as this one: In the make-believe world of 'Second Life,' banks are really collapsing. *Wall Street Journal.* Retrieved February 1, 2008, from http://online.wsj.com/article/SB120104351064608025.html?mod=hpp_us_inside_today

Smart, J. J. C. (1986). Utilitarianism and its applications. In J. P. DeMarco & R. M. Fox (Eds.), *New directions in ethics: The challenge of applied ethics* (pp. 24–41). London: Routledge & Kegan Paul.

Soraker, J. H. (2007). The moral status of information and information technologies: A relational theory of moral status. In S. Hongladarom, S. Ess, & C. Ess (Eds.), *Information technology ethics: Cultural perspectives* (pp. 1–19). Hershey, PA: Idea Group Reference.

Sterling College. (2000). *Sterling College's code of professional ethics.* Retrieved February 3, 2008, from http://www.sterling.edu/campus/acadaffr/code.cfm

Stone, A. R. (1995). *The war of desire and technology at the close of the mechanical age.* Cambridge: MIT Press.

Stromer-Galley, J. (2003). Diversity of political conversation on the Internet: Users' perspectives. *Journal of Computer-Mediated Communication, 8*(3). Retrieved January 28, 2009, from http://jcmc.indiana.edu/vol8/issue3/stromergalley.html

Sunstein, C. (2005). *Why societies need dissent.* Cambridge, MA: Harvard University Press.

Sumison, J. (2000). Caring and empowerment: A teacher educator's reflection on an ethical dilemma. *Teaching in Higher Education, 5*(3), 167.

Turkle, S. (1984). *The second self: Computers and the human spirit.* New York: Simon & Schuster.

Turkle, S. (2000). Who am we? In R. M. Baird, R. Ramsower, & S. E. Rosenbaum (Eds.), *Cyberethics: Social & moral issues in the computer age* (pp. 129–141). Amherst, NY: Prometheus Books.

U of M students disciplined for cyberbullying. (2008, January 31). *Globe and Mail.* Retrieved May 1, 2008, from http://www.theglobeandmail.com/servlet/story/RTGAM.20080131.wgtfacebully0131/BNStory/Technology/home

van Doorn, N., van Zoonen, L., & Wyatt, S. (2007). Writing from experience: Presentations of gender identity on weblogs. *European Journal of Women's Studies, 14*, 143–159.

Warschauer, M., El Said, G., & Sohry, A. (2002). Language choice online: Globalization and identity in Egypt. *Journal of Computer Mediated Communication, 7*(4). Retrieved January 31, 2008, from http://jcmc.indiana.edu/vol7/issue4/warschauer.html

Weizenbaum, J. (1976). *Computer power and human reason: From judgment to calculation.* New York: W. H. Freeman.

Welsch, W. (1999). Transculturality—The puzzling form of cultures today. In M. Featherstone & S. Lash (Eds.), *Spaces of culture: City, nation, world* (pp. 194–213). London: Sage.

Wetlesen, J. (1999). The moral status of beings who are not persons: A casuistic argument. *Environmental Values, 8*, 287–323.

White, M. (2002). Regulating research: The problem of theorizing research in LambdaMoo. *Ethics and Information Technology, 4*(1), 55–70.

Witmer, D. (1997). Risky business: Why people feel safe in sexually explicit on-line communication [Electronic edition]. *Journal of Computer-Mediated Communication, 2*(4), 16. Retrieved January 28, 2009, from http://jcmc.indiana .edu/vol2/issue4/witmer2.html

Zuboff, S. (1984). *In the age of the smart machine: The future of work and power.* New York: Basic Books.

Part II

Implementation of Online Learning

Section A. Programs and Courses

Revisiting the Design and Delivery of an Interactive Online Graduate Program

Chapter 10

Judith Stevens-Long

Charles Crowell

In 1997, Fielding Graduate University created one of the first online graduate degree programs in the United States, a master's degree in organizational design and effectiveness. Although the name has changed over the last decade—it is now called organizational management and development—the basic design and the delivery system are essentially the same, and many of the observations and recommendations that we made in our 2002 paper on which this chapter is based have been supported by research, most of which has appeared in the last 5 years.

The growth of online education over the past 10 years has been spectacular. Although estimates vary, one conservative guess places the number of online learners at over 3 million (Sprague, Maddux, Ferdig, & Albion, 2007). The latest Sloan Consortium report (Simonson, 2006) indicated that 40% to 60% of schools with traditional courses also offer online courses and programs, enrolling about two and a half million learners.

Moreover, 56% of institutions indicated to Sloan that online instruction was critical to their long-term plans.

Recently, the image of e-learning as a technology that relies on the use of shrink-wrapped (i.e., digitized) lectures and learning objects has been supplanted by work on team-based virtual learning, virtual community, and presence in online environments. This is, from our point of view, good news. In 2002 (Stevens-Long & Crowell), we argued for a new educational pedagogy based on small, interactive group and problem-based instruction. At the core of our ideas was the notion that complex inquiry can be supported and enhanced if (a) a form of dialogical and highly responsive inquiry is established among all the learners and (b) instructor and learner are considered colearners.

At that time, the notion that this form of inquiry would include peer-to-peer interaction was implicit in our design, but we have recently written about peer-to-peer interaction more explicitly (Stevens-Long & McClintock, 2008). We believe that learner-centered pedagogy is critical to the success of online learning and that interpersonal interaction and peer-to-peer collaboration should be the cornerstone of the virtual classroom.

Porush (2005) summarized the Sloan-C Quality Framework for a successful Internet learning environment that recommends an active, constructivist, andragogic, and agentive approach. These have been foundational qualities in the learning model at Fielding Graduate University from its inception. Beginning with Malcolm Knowles (Knowles & Associates, 1984), a founding faculty member in the School of Human and Organization Development at Fielding, andragogy has been the basis of our learning model. As articulated by Knowles, andragogy emphasizes self-directed learning and the integration of life, work, and education. Over time, we have added a greater emphasis on dialogue and collaborative strategies (Schapiro, 2003).

The online environment at Fielding is congruent with the general learning model. The weight of the model falls on the learners' needs and goals, and the process is wrapped around problems rather than subjects, inquiry rather than answers, and collaboration rather than competition. Learners are expected to reflect on their own experience and work as well as reflect on the work of their classroom peers. Instructors are expected to adapt to student needs, motivate students to stay on task, provide meaningful examples, direct the leading edge of online discussion, and facilitate communication. Research has linked learner satisfaction with this kind of partnership between instructor and learner (Young, 2006). We believe that interaction amongst learners as well as interaction between learners and the instructor allows for the cocreation of a real interactive space, a phenomenon we have been calling copresence (Stevens-Long & McClintock, 2008).

Copresence is the experience that someone is engaged with another in the online learning environment. It is a subtle experience, not easily defined, but it can be built in the online environment through collaborative learning practices and an appreciation of the life of the group. It is a combination of a more commonly discussed variable, instructor presence, and the experience of peer-to-peer interaction.

In our experience, peer-to-peer interaction promotes cognitive engagement in the online classroom. Online students, particularly older adults, prefer a deeper level of engagement and demonstrate deeper levels of motivation in the electronic classroom (Richardson & Newby, 2006). Evidence for the link between peer-to-peer interaction and performance is offered by research that shows a connection between interaction and performance on written assignments, if not multiple choice examinations (Picciano, 2002). Very recently, Ho and Swan (2007) showed that the quality of participation in online discussions is predictive of overall grades in the course.

At the time of this writing, there is fairly widespread agreement that faculty–student interaction makes a critical difference in whether learners are satisfied with their online classrooms. Recent research in management education has greatly contributed to our understanding of how online learning works. As Arbaugh and Stelzer (2003, p. 23) put it, "There is more to delivering Web-based courses than building a series of Web pages and handing them off to students." Today, there is clear support for the proposition that a sense of interpersonal community built on peer-to-peer interactions can contribute to learner satisfaction (Gunawardena & Zittle, 1997; Richardson & Swan, 2003; Shea, Swan, & Pickett, 2003). However, the impact of peer-to-peer interactions on learner performance (versus satisfaction) has been difficult to assess since the demand for and structuring of these interactions varies across subject matter, programs, and institutions.

At Fielding, we have developed a quite specific method for structuring peer-to-peer interaction. Learners are expected to read and reply to each other's work. After posting their own work in response to an assignment, learners also post a written reply in response to the points, ideas, and conclusions offered in the work of other members of their small group. In effect, a recursive dialogue is established about each assignment. The dialogue occurs not only between the instructor and the learner, but among the learners as well. The resulting multilayered dialogue is enriched by both the thinking and the experience of all members of the group.

This kind of small-group discussion has been the cornerstone of our practice for over 10 years, and new research has demonstrated the effectiveness of this practice. In particular, the research literature from management education (Stevens-Long & McClintock, 2008) has shown that learners find small-group discussions help them overcome feelings of isolation and increase not only their satisfaction with the course, but also the level of learning they believe they have achieved. In our classrooms, membership in the small groups is stable over the lifetime of the course, and part of the grade in the course is dependent upon the level of participation learners exhibit in these groups. These aspects of our practice have been demonstrated to have a positive relationship to learner satisfaction (Dixson, Khulhorst, & Reiff, 2006; Picciano, 2002; Shea, Swan, et al., 2003).

There has been some research on what elements of interaction, at least interaction between instructor and students, facilitate learner satisfaction. In this work, much attention has been focused on the construct of instructor presence. Short, Williams, and Christie (1976) first used the term social presence to refer to the degree to which the medium is experienced as sociable, warm, sensitive, or personal, which creates the impression that the person communicating is real. Lombard and Ditton (1997) wrote about presence as "an illusion that a mediated experience is not mediated" (p. 1).

Instructor presence appears to be created by a variety of specific instructor behaviors including the presentation of content and questions, attempts to focus on or to summarize student discussion, confirmation of understandings, diagnosis of misperceptions, injection of knowledge, and response to technical concerns (Shea, Swan, et al., 2003; Swan, 2002). Instructor presence has also been discussed in terms of instructor immediacy behaviors (Arbaugh & Stelzer, 2003). Based on work by Mehrabian (1971), immediacy behaviors include using personal examples and humor, providing and inviting feedback, and addressing students by name.

At Fielding, we have also drawn on the literature that describes the experience of presence in novel or foreign environments (Fontaine, 2002). Fontaine writes about novelty and unpredictability as key precipitants of presence. The optimal mix of surprise, predictability, and drama is required. The exchange of small talk, metacommunications about the course, attempts to build culture through the exploration of group process, offers of support, encouragement, and perspective are all part of building community through collaboration. This can be as simple as beginning a post with a remark about the weather.

Like peer-to-peer interaction, teaching presence is associated with learner satisfaction and perceived learning (Bangert, 2006; Shea, Pickett, & Pelz, 2003; Young, 2006). In one recent provocative study (Dixson et al., 2006), researchers reported that peer-to-peer interactions, especially those offering orientation and information, had a significant impact on the level of learner performance. However, nothing that the instructor posted appeared to affect the quality of the learner's work product. These authors believe that instructor effects are probably created indirectly, through careful design and planning. Although these data are based on a very small sample and may turn out to be anomalous, there is ample evidence that learners clearly prefer well-planned courses. "When interactive activities are carefully planned, they lead not only to greater learning, but they also enhance motivation" (Young, 2006, p. 67). We believe that these activities permit the group to create a sense of copresence.

Adult learners are also likely to demand that the instructor offer flexibility in the timing of assignments, provide meaningful examples, motivate students to stay on task, and facilitate the group discussion well (Young, 2006). Careful planning begins with the structure of the learning environment and proceeds through the design of assignments and discussions and the provision of timely feedback. In the next section, we outline how planning the use of virtual space can be the first step in structuring the learning environment.

Designing the Space

In our experience, the architecture of the learning space can support the development of copresence. Developments in conferencing software over the last decade have made it possible to engage in a truly interactive way on the World Wide Web. At Fielding, we have been using SiteScape by AltaVista for our online classroom needs because it offers a user-friendly interface, a breadth of conferencing and document features, and supports sophisticated small-group inquiry. There are now any number of conferencing software programs that offer comparable functionality.

When using SiteScape, learners enter a Web page environment that identifies both "Topics" and "Replies." Generally, faculty use "Topics" to identify and to list assignments over the course of a quarter. Usually, the syllabus for the entire course is available on the forum, and each of the assignments is listed as a topic from the first day of the course, which allows students to proceed to future assignments if necessary. This offers flexibility for those who anticipate family or job pressures or who find they need to travel during the course.

Learners post their responses to each assignment as a "Reply" to the "Topic" and peer-to-peer discussion appears as a series of replies to each of the assignments. In this fashion, both a structured chronology of "Topics" and a threaded hierarchy of nested replies is created. A typical string might look as follows:

TOPIC #1: TODAY'S ASSIGNMENT

Reply 1.1: Learner A's paper

Reply 1.1.1 Learner B's response to Learner A's paper

Reply 1.1.1.1 Instructor's response to Learner B's comment

Reply 1.1.2: Learner C's response to Learner A's paper

Reply 1.1.2.1: Learner A's question about Learner C's response

Reply 1.1.2.2: Learner B's comment on Learner C's response

Reply 1.1.3: Learner D's response to Learner A's paper

Instructors often choose to use one of the "Topics" to create a space for informal discussion. It may be designated as the café. Under this topic, continuing conversation about an assignment or a reading may go on throughout the term without cluttering up the classroom. The café may also be used for discussion of problems that come up outside of a particular assignment. Learners may post a problem from their work environments in the café or make social conversation. Guest faculty or administrators may interact with learners in the café or special hyperlinks may be posted to Web sites that may be useful for some of the learners but are not required by the course. SiteScape also allows for the creation of special folders at the top of the classroom page where additional resources may be posted.

Instructors may also designate a "Topic" as an office space in which they answer the usual office hours questions about assignments, grades, and the like. Another topic may serve as a space for discussing process issues. That is, the structure of the course or the assignments or the problems people are having giving or receiving feedback may be brought up in this space without disrupting the threads of conversation about particular assignments. Information on conflict management might, for example, be posted in this space. Part of the role of the instructor in a Fielding online classroom is to help learners manage their online personae and the disputes that arise when learners try to collaborate online (Palloff & Pratt, 2005).

The structure may seem elaborate but is actually created and maintained. Careful architecture has the advantage of creating a "there" in cyberspace with all the advantages of the spaces available in the traditional instructional setting—the classroom, the café, the hallway can all be available. We even offer an auditorium space for our master's students called "Community Hall," which is just another virtual classroom, but one to which all learners from all classes belong. Learners are required to check in on the "Community Hall" regularly. All syllabi for new courses are posted in the hall, new faculty are introduced there, and learners are surveyed about their curricular needs.

Over time, the variety and depth of learner–instructor and learner–learner participation build a sense of shared community. As Hudson (2002) described it, such classrooms are composed of "a distributed many-threaded dialogue constructed as a process of self-organized discovery" (p. 213). There is a shift from hierarchy to a flat, decentralized format that is more flexible and actually permits faster changes than the more traditional classroom. The need to create copresence may seem daunting, especially to the beginning learner or instructor who may feel overwhelmed by the possibilities for interaction. It is here that a grasp of group process can make an important contribution to online andragogy.

Three sets of principles have guided our efforts to manage the life of an online group over the past decade. These are the principles of group process, the principles of adult education, and the principles of human development. The work we have done is most clearly applicable to the education, training, and development of adults, but we also believe that most of what we have learned can be translated into educational design for secondary school learners.

Principles of Group Process

It is our belief that copresence and community are most efficiently created when participants, and particularly instructors, learn to facilitate the life of the group rather than respond at the individual level. For this reason, a consideration of the group process literature, and especially the work of Bion (1959), is a key element in our model of online andragogy. In an extension of Bion's thinking, Stevens-Long (1994) has argued that most groups can be understood in terms of two dimensions: boundary and role structure. Boundary refers to the limits of membership and the degree to which information flows into the group from the outside while role refers to the extent to which member duties are specified and hierarchically arranged. In most traditional classroom setting, roles are hierarchically structured. The teacher delivers knowledge through lecture or the design and interpretation of experiential learning. He or she has objectives, and students are to meet them through changes in their verbal or nonverbal behavior. The boundary of the group is physical. One belongs because one is on the roster, and no one else may enter the group without the permission of the instructor. In the online classroom, it is difficult if not impossible to replicate the norms of face-to-face instruction.

Online, the instructor becomes the facilitator of the learning of the group. First and most importantly, he or she must model acceptable communication and behavioral norms and demonstrate that risk taking is safe in the small-group environment. The facilitator is expected to demonstrate his or her presence and work to create a sense of community and to manage group processes.

If this sounds overwhelming for the facilitator, an appreciation of the literature on the group-as-a-whole or the group mind is a useful guide to optimal work habits for instructors (Wells, 1985). The instructor, as a group facilitator, is well advised to direct the efforts of the group-as-a-whole toward understanding the materials rather than constantly responding to every individual posting. Facilitators need not give feedback to every learner on every assignment. It can be assumed that mature students are capable of recognizing outstanding work by their peers and also of recognizing the errors and learning difficulties of others. The facilitator attends to the understanding that the group as a whole is developing.

In each small group, the facilitator posts a commentary after group members have responded to each other's assignments. In this commentary, he or she may summarize where the group stands in regard to the content or point out the ways in which the group has mastered the ideas or where the group has missed a point. He or she may refer to points made by individual students (or points missed by individuals), ask for clarification from the group, help the group make a course correction in regard to understanding, or create a segue for the group from one assignment to the next. The commentary may include an example or a case study that is brought to mind by the group discussion or point to additional resources that might be helpful in light of the work of the group.

Responding at the group level is a way of doing what Marks, Sibley, and Arbaugh (2005) referred to as responding holistically, but it is difficult for facilitators to learn to stay at the level of the group. Groups typically exert great pressure on the leader to do the work of the group. In the group process literature, there is much talk of role suction (Horowitz, 1985), and the facilitator will often experience an undertow pulling for responses to individual postings. In the long run, however, responding to the group rather than to the individual assists in the development of copresence and promotes community while keeping the workload at a reasonable level.

Responding to the group level has long been associated with learning in psychotherapeutic settings. There is every reason to believe it can be as effective in supporting the cognitive development of mature students as it is in supporting their emotional development. It is the job of the facilitator to present a model of reflective, articulate thinking and to demonstrate the kinds of affective disclosure that are appropriate and helpful. He or she must also model the form and content of feedback and the level of support and collaboration that is required for the work of the group.

The electronic environment offers a number of process challenges that are linked to particular competencies. Certainly, there are technical competencies that learners develop as a function of using the computer as their primary learning space. They have to become accustomed to dealing with problems of interface, with electronic infrastructures that are not always optimal. They must find the way through the Internet to school, and most of the courses require some roaming and research on the Web. In addition, they must function in novel social ways that are completely, uncompromisingly explicit. The subtle, nonverbal cues that grease the wheels of daily interaction are not available, and learners must compensate for that. This compensation involves the explicit setting of new norms and the development of new social competencies.

New Norms and Behaviors

When group process is portrayed in terms of stage development, it is common to describe the first stage as one devoted to norming—that is, to the development of the rules of engagement that will govern the processes of the group. Rarely do norms arise through conscious dialogue. Groups struggle over authority, timeliness, and task versus process orientation. We have found in developing online classroom and team environments that bringing a discussion of norms into conscious dialogue is critical to the quality of subsequent work. For instance, if groups discuss how they might respond to member absence prior to the posting of assignments, later workflow is less likely to become disrupted when one member fails to post in a timely manner. Training and preparation, particularly time spent face-to-face prior to the initiation of the project or course, is best spent establishing and clarifying the norms and expectations for online participation.

It might well be argued that if conscious norms were set in any workplace, groups would prove more productive and less conflicted. For instance, if all teams spent a few minutes talking about how to give and receive feedback, members might find feedback easier to provide and to manage. However, in virtual teams, it is doubly important since many of the physical and nonverbal cues that promote discussion of group process will be missing subsequent to the training or orientation. Furthermore, the norms and behaviors ordinarily expected at work or in class are different than those required by the virtual environment.

For some, the norms we advocate will require the development of new competencies, particularly since all of the work must be accomplished in writing. The asynchronous classroom eliminates some face-to-face norms that are frequently violated (e.g., keeping a straight face while someone is speaking or showing up at the same time as everyone else), but it offers its own unique challenges and benefits. In face-to-face or phone conference orientations, we highlight the following norms:

- Participants must meet requirements for minimal frequency of log-on. In most of our courses, the requirement is a minimum of two times every 7 to 10 days. Some standard must be chosen for time (Greenwich Mean Time, PST, etc.) so that everyone knows when a day ends and begins.

- Learners are expected to compose work off-line and send it as an attachment from a word-processing document or cut and paste it into the study group's workspace. Generally, attachments are required for longer documents, so spelling and grammar checks can be executed. This requirement is related to the more abstract, but related norms of thoughtful articulation and reflectivity noted below. Good writing and editing has been shown to increase the number of responses other learners make to a posting as well as to a final grade (Ho & Swan, 2007).

- It is critical to make both deadlines and breaks explicit and to set clear expectations about what will happen if learners fail to adhere to the schedule. In a dialogic environment, late work can cause the whole class to fall behind schedule and group coherence to deteriorate. Although occasional work-arounds are possible, making many exceptions creates chaos for the whole class and erodes critical norms. Students should be encouraged to work ahead if they anticipate problems meeting deadlines. Instructors should consider deducting points or half-grades from late assignments.

- A premium is placed on thoughtful articulation. Participants need to spend extra time reflecting on and reviewing their work. In this medium, all communication becomes a permanent, public record, and participants are held strictly accountable for their words in ways that do not happen clearly in face-to-face environments.

- Immediate reactions, particularly to feedback on one's own work, are discouraged. Swift responses are unnecessary and largely inappropriate, given the premium placed above on thoughtfulness.

- Affective disclosure is encouraged. Since the medium does not offer ordinary cues to social orientation, participants must learn to indicate emotional tone: tentativeness-certainty, anxiety, investment, motivation, and the like. Although emoticons have come into regular use (☺) along with creative use of punctuation (????!!!!), capitalization, fonts, and hyperlinks, we advocate that team members take a moment to reflect on their emotional and intellectual stance and to articulate the breadth and depth of their response and the emotions associated with it ("I'm not sure this is the best way to express this idea, but here goes . . ."). Parenthetical commentary ("Is this too abstract?") helps the receiver interpret and respond to the message in ways most likely to support the work without long process-related digressions. In addition, the ability to express these emotional and state-of-mind commentaries can facilitate greater depth in the dialogue. For instance, learners may feel safer floating novel ideas if they use parenthetical commentary ("We don't mean to imply that this type of writing is simple. It is often a new competency, and therefore, the orientation, training, and course development materials as well as the facilitator need to articulate its advantages and to support its appearance").

- Lecturing is discouraged, from both the instructor and the learner. All participants, including the instructor, are considered colearners and may direct each other to resources or post short papers, but posting lectures is discouraged in favor of integrated facilitation and feedback that addresses the ongoing dialogue.

- Postings should be substantial. "Atta boy" or "good work" responses simply make it harder to follow a thread. These kinds of social communication contribute to the cohesion of the group (Dixson et al., 2006), but they should be added to deeper commentary or posted as a title only and clearly marked "nnto" (no need to open).

- Agreements that support equity should be made prior to beginning the work. Explicit norms that require all members to read all documents and respond to them (or to a specified subset of them) support the equity balancing effect of the medium.

- Methods for making decisions should be clear to all members. If there is to be a collaborative project, how will members reach agreement—by consensus or vote? Will complete agreement be required for consensus? By what date must members lodge their objections?

- Notice of absence must be posted. Members are encouraged to explain absences, offer revised contributions in light of their absence, and make return dates explicitly so that assistance can be given if possible or the group can come to a conclusion in the absence of a member. Failure to define and adhere to explicit norms here can result in rapid deterioration of group cohesion and significant declines in qualitative outcomes. We advocate that work be completed on schedule and decisions not be reopened when missing members return. Proceeding with members in absentia powerfully reinforces the norms of participation and equity balancing.

- Provisions for a safety net should be discussed and articulated at the outset of any inquiry. What happens if the conferencing software system or the Web server crashes? What is the responsibility of members for backing up their own work?

Obviously, the characteristics of good instructors in the online environment are both similar to and different from traditional faculty. One needs, of course, to possess content expertise and the ability to engage student interest. At Fielding, we also look for faculty who can respect and use the work and life experience of mature learners in a collaborative relationship. In addition, the instructor has to be able to construct a presence online and be willing to cope with the everyday exigencies of the environment. Instructors have to be able to take advantage of real events and address the real problems learners experience in the medium. We have found that few instructors really know whether they are going to be comfortable and satisfied in the medium until they have some experience. Some come to realize that the rewards they find in teaching are quite dependent upon face-to-face contact with the learners. Some cannot create a strong presence online. Some are too present, interfering with student participation and reflection and overwhelming themselves with the need to respond to every post. Finding the right fit between instructor, medium, and the goals of the program becomes a complex problem. We have instituted internships and probationary periods during which that fit is tested. Immediate, long-term commitments on the part of either the institution or the instructor can be counterproductive in a novel environment.

Finding the right faculty and the right pedagogy is a challenge. For this reason, writers and faculty working in this field often envision re-creating the face-to-face classroom at a distance. Streaming video and voice-to-voice protocol for the computer are already accepted technologies. The only obstacle to replicating face-to-face contexts appears to be the cost and, perhaps, the accessibility for learners with older computers or less efficient connections to the Internet.

Human Development

We would now like to pose an argument for the unique developmental properties of a non-face-to-face computer-mediated education. As Anderson (1997) has argued in *The Future of the Self* or as Gergen (1990) suggested in *The Saturated Self,* cyberspace makes it possible to construct one's identity in a uniquely conscious way. In chat rooms around the globe, people use gender ambiguous names, switch genders altogether, rewrite their own histories, and adopt fabricated identities. These phenomena create an opportunity to experience the world as a socially constructed space where sex, race, manner, status, and so on determine how others respond.

In normal development, the growth of identity is primarily an unconscious process. Online experience allows that process to become more explicit for some adolescents and adults. In a similar way, learners participating in a collaborative online environment appear to become more conscious of the ways in which knowledge is socially constructed. In an online classroom, they offer various interpretations of the same materials to each other. They are required to read and comment not only on the text but also on the meaning others draw from the text in a systematic way. All learners must put themselves forward, not just the highly verbal or the brightest.

Furthermore, since all interactions are written, learners have the opportunity to participate in more thoughtful ways than is possible "on your feet" in traditional classroom discussions. They are given time to reflect upon and interpret the remarks of others. Everything they post in the classroom remains posted for the entire term. Other learners and the instructor are able to review entire discussions or to look at the remarks of any contributor again. Our experience has been that classroom discussions are much more reflective under these conditions than in the ordinary face-to-face setting, and systematic research has supported this view (Dixson et al., 2006; Shea, Swan, et al., 2003).

Finally, in cyberspace, everyone's voice is equally loud. Everyone speaks without interruption. What impresses others is the quality of the idea itself or the way it is communicated rather than frequency or volume. Voices that are ordinarily underrepresented in face-to-face discussion are as frequent as those that are used for speaking up. In fact, since all are required to participate equally, underrepresented voices may take on special value because they have not been heard before. New ideas receive more attention in online classrooms and constitute part of what people experience as quality (Ho & Swan, 2007). Dominant interpretations can be challenged. We have certainly seen that the voices of learners working and living in Europe or Asia or Africa make unique contributions to courses originating in North America, contributions that are readily recognized by the group.

If we begin to replicate face-to-face online, we run the risk of losing all of this rich collaboration in favor of the expert paradigm. The one who lectures is seen as the source of knowledge while the other participants are seen as the absorbers. In many computer-mediated video environments, one raises an electronic hand in order to ask a question or make a comment. The lecturer calls on the learner who has raised his or her hand, and the old paradigm is replicated in cyberspace.

Asynchronous collaborative dialogue presents so much greater opportunity for making the day-to-day applications that anchor knowledge in the concrete world. Learners are able to test their insights, bring the results back to the group, reevaluate the learning, and retest it. Each learner can speak as long and as often as he or she wishes. A conversation regarding a particular problem or application can be continued over very long periods through the use of the café configuration. Learners can come back to a discussion that may have taken place a month earlier and reevaluate it in light of new data.

The facilitator must keep in mind that learners are acquiring much more than a knowledge of the materials at hand. They are also learning how to construct themselves and communicate in a new setting, how to give feedback and take it, how to collaborate, and how to design the very structure of their own learning. We encourage learners to comment on the design of the course and the assignment as the course goes along. Their feedback is taken seriously, not only at the level of the classroom but also at the level of the program. The online environment offers unique opportunities for the kind of access that supports a learning organization as well as an academic program.

Most learners at the graduate level come to the task with what Piaget (1972) has described as formal operations. They are able to think scientifically, historically, and philosophically and to evaluate the truth of proposition from several points of view. It is partly the task of graduate educators to scaffold a learner's education in such a way that one's thinking moves from formal to postformal operations. Postformal operations include the ability to compare systems of relationships and to engage in fuzzy logic.

According to Torbert (1993), postformal adult education should embrace capacities for empirical, operational learning; for abstract, hypothetical learning; and for subjective self-knowledge. It must provide the opportunity to coordinate thought, action, and outcomes. It must invite learners to improve not only their analytic competence but also their competence as professionals. It should encourage the cycle of feedback and support new initiatives. A postformal education is designed to encourage and support systems thinking (Commons, Armon, Richards, & Schrader, 1989). We believe that online education provides an unprecedented opportunity to meet the requirements of a postconventional education.

References

Anderson, W. A. (1997). *The future of the self: Inventing the postmodern person.* New York: Jeremy P. Tarcher/Putnum.

Arbaugh, J. B., & Stelzer, L. (2003). Learning and teaching on the Web: What do we know? In C. Wankel & R. De Fillippi (Eds.), *Educating managers with tomorrow's technologies: A volume in research in management education and development.* Greenwich, CT: Information Age.

Bangert, A. (2006). Identifying factors underlying the quality of online teaching effectiveness: An exploratory study. *Journal of Computing in Higher Education, 17*(2), 79–99.

Bion, W. F. (1959). *Experiences in groups.* New York: Basic Books.

Commons, M. L., Armon, C., Richards, F. A., & Schrader, D. E. (with Farrell, E. W., Tappan, M. B., & Bauer, N. F.). (1989). A multidomain study of adult development. *Adult development: Vol. 1. Comparisons and applications of adolescent and adult development* (pp. 334–360). New York: Praeger.

Dixson, M., Kuhlhorst, M., & Reiff, A. (2006). Creating effective online discussions: Optimal instructor and student roles. *Journal of Asychronous Learning Networks, 10*(4), 15–28.

Fontaine, G. (2002). Presence in "teleland." In K. E. Rudestam & J. Schoenholtz-Read (Eds.), *Handbook of online learning* (pp. 31–52). Thousand Oaks, CA: Sage.

Gergen, K. (1990). *The saturated self: Dilemmas of identity in contemporary life.* New York: Basic Books.

Gunawardena, C., & Zittle, F. (1997). Social presence as a predictor of satisfaction with a computer mediated conferencing environment. *American Journal of Distance Education, 11,* 8–26.

Ho, C. H., & Swan, K. (2007). Evaluating online conversation in an asynchronous learning environment: An application of Grice's cooperative principle. *Internet and Higher Education, 10,* 3–14.

Horowitz, L. (1985). Projective identification in dyads and groups. In A. D. Colman & M. H. Geller (Eds.), *Group relations reader* (Vol. 3). Washington, DC: A.K. Rice.

Hudson, B. (2002). Critical dialogue online: Personas, covenants, and candlepower. In K. E. Rudestam & J. Schoenholtz-Read (Eds.), *Handbook of online learning* (pp. 29–53). Thousand Oaks, CA: Sage.

Knowles, M. A., & Associates. (1984). *Andragogy in action.* San Francisco: Jossey-Bass.

Lombard, M., & Ditton, T. (1997). At the heart of it all: The concept of telepresence. *Journal of Computer-Mediated communication, 3*(2), 1–39.

Marks, R. B., Sibley, S. D., & Arbaugh, J. B. (2005). A structural equation of predictors for effective online learning. *Journal of Management Education, 29*(4), 531–563.

Mehrabian, A. (1971). *Silent messages.* Belmont, CA: Wadworth.

Palloff, R., & Pratt, K. (2005). *Collaborating online: Learning together in community.* San Francisco: Jossey-Bass.

Piaget, J. (1972). Intellectual evolution from adolescence to adulthood. *Human Development, 15*(1), 1–12.

Picciano, A. G. (2002). Beyond student perceptions: Issues of interaction, presence and performance in an online course. *Journal of Asynchronous Learning Networks, 6*(1). Retrieved January 7, 2009, from http://www.aln.org/pubications/jaln/v6n1/v6n1/_picciano.asp

Porush, D. (2005). Toward a universal learning environment: A vignette from the future. In J. C. Moore (Ed.), *Elements of a quality online education: Engaging communities: Wisdom from the Sloan Consortium* (pp. 191–202). Needham, MA: The Sloan Consortium.

Richardson, J. C., & Newby, T. (2006). The role of students' cognitive engagement in online learning. *American Journal of Distance Education, 20*(1), 23–37.

Richardson, J. C., & Swan, K. (2003). Examining social presence in online courses in relation to students' perceived learning and satisfaction. *Journal of Asynchronous Learning Networks, 7*(1), 68–88.

Schapiro, S. A. (2003). From andragogy to collaborative critical pedagogy. *Journal of Transformative Education, 1*(2), 150–166.

Shea, P., Pickett, A., & Pelz, W. (2003). A follow-up of reaching presence in the SUNY Learning Network. *Journal of Asynchronous Learning Networks, 7*(2), 61–80.

Shea, P., Swan, K., & Pickett, A. (2003). Teaching presence and the establishment of community in online learning environments. In J. C. Moore (Ed.), *Elements of quality online education: Engaging communities. Wisdom from the Sloan Consortium* (pp. 33–66). Needham, MA: The Sloan Consortium.

Short, J., Williams, E, & Christie, B. (1976). *The social psychology of telecommuiations.* New York: Wiley.

Simonson, J. (2006). Growing by degrees: Latest report from the Sloan Consortium. *Quarterly Review of Distance Education, 7*(2), vii–viii.

Sprague, D., Maddux, C., Ferdig, R., & Albion, P. (2007). Online education: Issues and research questions. *Journal of Technical and Teacher Education, 15*(2), 157–167.

Stevens-Long, J. (1994). The application of decision-making theory and theories of adult development to diagnosis and intervention in group process. In *Proceedings of the International Society for the Psycho-Analytic Study of Organizations, June 3–5* (pp. 203–229). Chicago: International Society for the Psychoanalytic Study of Organizations.

Stevens-Long, J., & Crowell, C. (2002). The design and delivery of interactive online graduate education. In K. Rudestam & J. Schoenholz-Read (Eds.), *The handbook of online learning* (pp. 151–171). Thousand Oaks, CA: Sage.

Stevens-Long, J., & McClintock, C. (2008). Co-presence and group process in online management education. In C. Wankel & R. De Fillippi (Eds.), *University and corporate innovations in lifelong learning: A volume in research in management education and development* (pp. 15–33). Charlotte, NC: Information Age.

Swan, K. (2002). Building learning communities in online courses: The importance of interaction. *Education, Communication and Information, 2*(1), 23–49.

Torbert, W. (1993). Cultivating postformal adult development: Higher stages and contrasting interventions. In M. Miller & S. Cook-Greuter (Eds.), *Transcendence and mature thought in adulthood* (pp. 181–204). Boston: Rowman & Littlefield.

Wells, L., Jr. (1985). The groups-as-a-whole perspective and its theoretical roots. In A. D. Colman & M. H. Geller (Eds.), *Group relations reader* (Vol. 2). Washington, DC: A. K. Rice.

Young, S. (2006). Student views of effective online teaching in higher education. *American Journal of Distance Education, 20*(2), 65–77.

Chapter 11

Candlepower

The Intimate Flow of Online Collaborative Learning

Barclay Hudson

Candlepower: The Phenomenon

Back in 1997, when Fielding Graduate University was launching its new online program for graduate study in human and organizational development, some of us had some serious doubts about distance learning. But the first experience of teaching online was a revelation. Contrary to expectation, the minimalist format of pure text was far from the flat and impersonal medium we expected. It was strangely engaging, almost like staring into a fireplace or listening to campfire stories. Somehow, the limited field of a computer screen seems to actually strengthen the focus of concentration and the power of imagination, just as conversation can deepen over candlelight. I think of this as the candlepower of online collaborative dialogue.

Candlepower is shorthand for a surprising quality of online dialogue—the intimacy it creates among participants. Even in a forum with a dozen participants, posting a message can feel as if there is only one other person involved. The mind's eye narrows the audience to a particular other, like a face seen across a candlelit table, with the rest of the space in shadows.

Perhaps this should not be such a surprise. Wives of ARPANET (Advanced Research Projects Agency Network) builders in the early 1970s used to log on late at night and talk among themselves at scattered university sites, never meeting face-to-face but deeply engaged in discussion that touched on their personal lives. That suggests, at least, that intimacy is not dependent on having the latest in sophisticated software features. And even in the early days of computers, it was obvious that people could become addicted to the screen, concentrating for hours, in a kind of out-of-body experience.

But exactly how this happens and how it relates to learning is not all that obvious. Early 20th century correspondence courses were mostly a postal-service exchange of books and assignments and exams shuttled back and forth between student and anonymous graders—no hint of intimacy there. A century later, we have digital technology—indeed a culture of connected, 24-hours, 7-days-a-week, all-things-all-people (Waters, 2006), but the text message networks that give cohesion to social groups seem largely devoid of thought or content, functioning almost at the level of bird calls: "I am here, I am plugged in—therefore I exist, I belong."

Candlepower builds on this sense of comfort with digital technology and the sense of belonging found in virtual communities—increasingly so with each generation. But in a higher education context, candlepower takes that foundation of trust and applies it to learning—critical thinking, questioning of assumptions, collaborative inquiry, and pressing for alternative ways to frame issues through different lenses, such as through action implications, cross-cultural perspectives, and questions of social justice. Different from the kind of dialogue found in most self-organized virtual communities, candlepower is not oriented around confirmation, but around questioning, experimenting, learning, and seeing something different. It opens room for experimentation with language—testing of different voices—but it also brings attention to care with language and digging for what lies behind words.

Still, it is the trust and willingness for risk taking that makes all this possible. As Brown (1998) put it,

> There is a type of intimacy achievable between students and teachers in this medium that is quite extraordinary. . . . I believe this intimacy results from a sense of shared control and responsibility, commitment to collaboration and dialogue, and increased willingness to take risks in communications with other online. . . . The text-based forum network also forces one to make one's thoughts very explicit. . . . As one administrator put it: "in an online environment, words matter. . . . Words are everything." (p. 3)

People's feelings can be hurt (more easily online), so more time and effort are put into explaining meanings and supplying detailed contextual background to enhance mutual understanding. Thus, writers get to know one another intimately.

The Quality of Candlelight Dialogue: A Dinner With Andre

Louis Malle directed a film that came out in 1981, *My Dinner With Andre*, about two men having a conversation at a restaurant. Nothing happens—they just talk—yet the film is remarkably powerful and engaging. As Roger Ebert said, in his retrospect nearly 2 decades later (1999),

> How wonderfully odd this movie is, there is nothing else like it. It should be unwatchable, and yet those who love it return time and again, enchanted. . . . As in all conversations, the tide of energy flows back and forth, . . . almost impossible to nail down. . . . Someone asked me the other day if I could name a movie that was entirely devoid of clichés. I thought for a moment, and then answered, *My Dinner With Andre.*

One of the film's characters, played by Wallace Shawn, comes out with a passionate defense of the scientific method as an answer to the ignorance and superstition that characterizes the middle ages (and still permeates much of our own culture). His friend, played by Andre Gregory, does not argue back, but responds in a different frame: Science is fine, but not helpful in times when people are starving for new visions and ideas and questing for transcendence even though there is precious little of that to find. It is a vernacular conversation worth volumes of academic prose on issues of epistemology and communication and the social construction of experience.

Ebert made an interesting point in his 1999 review that reveals why the film was so powerful, and that also says something about online learning when it is done well. Despite its very tight frame of events, Ebert says, this is a film "with more action than *Raiders of the Lost Ark.* What *My Dinner With Andre* exploits is the well-known ability of the mind to picture a story as it is being told" (para. 12).

The images that come to the mind's eye in this movie are not what is literally seen on the screen, but painted with the spoken word: Andre talks about his travels to Tibet and the Sahara, to rural England and a Polish forest in moonlight, but the camera never leaves the table. It is the audience who takes these trips, through the strength of their own imagination.

Even today, bloggers refer to this film, both for the surprising power of its minimalism and for its specific themes of making human connections across widely divergent ways of thinking. One blog (PaulasHouseofToast, 2005) looked at the film from the standpoint of photography and poetry, describing how the two men's conversation evokes

> a network of centers, like the monasteries in the dark ages, that would keep the cultural fires burning in a dark time. That would preserve art, science, and philosophy against a rising tide of ignorance, appetite, and violence; that would stave off clashing fundamentalisms. . . . There are such outposts of light, of course. There always are. Small ones, large ones, compromised ones, improvised ones. Some mainstream, some marginal. Some as small as a moment. . . . There is nothing outside this moment, outside this cultivated hollow. (PaulasHouseofToast, 2005)

There is a candlelamp on the table that centers this movie's conversation. The larger context of the scene remains blurred—passing waiters, vague noises of other conversations and dish clatter, shadows, other lives and possibilities. The context nourishes the conversation, but it does not intrude or substitute for it, or get in the way. The shadows and background murmurs allow things to be said and perceived in subtleties that would simply be washed away in the brightness of a fluorescent classroom or in the charmless functionalism of a cafeteria.

Online learning can be like that, in its best moments, and it does not get better than that. This chapter is about describing what happens with candlepower and why it is so different from traditional distance learning with its command-and-control approach to teaching and its klieg lights of deconstructive analysis. In some respects, it means getting out of the way—learning not to teach but instead to plant seeds of conversations that let people find their own voices.

Enter Chaos

It turns out that a fairly good explanation of candlepower can be found in chaos theory and its cousin, complexity theory—which together pose an alternative to the command-and-control model. Those theories describe processes that are self-feeding, nonlinear in their direction of evolution, and marked by spontaneous transitions through tipping points or phase changes in the way they behave. They deal with the notion of emergence in the sense of creating behaviors that cannot be predicted from the sum of their parts, and they address the process of self-organized systems, which create patterns and resource pools and movements that are not guided by blueprints or outside guidance.

The next section of this chapter looks at complexity-chaos theory in more detail, but to summarize what has been said so far, I use the term candlepower to describe the surprising intensity, personal depth, and intimacy that can arise in an online forum. In essence, one is working in the dark, with attention highly focused—and people highly engaged—within a small patch of light where the narrative takes place. In asynchronous dialogue, words linger, thoughts are not interrupted, and errors of spontaneity are forgiven by the chance for rewrite. There is a departure from business as usual, a sense of risk taking, and a quality of speaking off the record in exploring ways to get outside the box. The very limitations of a purely text-based forum—its inability to command instant feedback, or to touch all the senses, and or to replicate traditional classroom pedagogies—far from being a drawback, turn out to be a great advantage.

From Complexity Theory:
Explaining the Unpredictable

Since about 1970, educational programs and digital technology have paired up as coevolving systems capable of mutual adaptation and shared benefits. But the two systems are fundamentally different in the way they adapt, and coevolution can be difficult. Complexity theory captures many aspects of chaos theory as well, and I refer to both theories collectively as KT from here on. Together, they provide some useful guidelines about what kinds of strategies work.

The Internet itself is a classic example of a self-organized system, as described by KT. It behaves unpredictably, evolves without blueprints, abruptly shifts its behavior, thrives on opportunism, and nourishes itself by a mix of evolving predatory and symbiotic relationships with other systems in its environment. Since the emergence of open-source software development, collaborative efforts (as opposed to top-down, command-and-control design programs) have become a more central feature of innovation and progress (Rosenberg, 2007). KT and the open source movement have grown in parallel, both evolving from a quirky band of mavericks doing battle with mainstream thinking, to a fully accepted way of thinking and doing business.

Universities are a fertile spawning ground for open source approaches, dating back to the 1960s, with their participation in ARPANET, the parent of today's Internet. But they have had much more trouble embracing a KT approach to teaching and learning. Universities tend to be driven by ancient standards of performance, with narrow behavioral degrees of freedom, a tendency to be self-referential rather than tuned to outside opportunities, and with functions that are highly compartmentalized.

Nevertheless, this resistance to change may be dissolving in ways that can be revealed and also nourished through reference to KT. One feature of KT is its focus on a particular zone called *the edge of chaos*, a narrow region of activity that maintains a fine balance between stability and change, creativity and continuity, order and disorder. It thus serves as a possible model for coevolution between educational institutions and Web-based learning.

A good metaphor for KT as applied to organizational evolution is the double helix structure of genetic material. The base pairs that form the twisting ladder rungs of the DNA molecule provide a code of almost endless variety, capable of evolving from one generation to another, shutting themselves on and off in the course of a given lifetime, and exchanging bits of information (and functional capacity) between organisms in real time, especially under conditions of stress. But the most remarkable feature of DNA is not creative adaptability, but its extraordinary stability and the remarkable simplicity of its spiraling handrails—the sugar phosphate backbone of the molecule, which organizes the base-pair genetic code. It is this minimalist-design backbone that preserves the continuity of that code intact over literally several billion years, faithfully transmitting hundreds of thousands of messages from one generation to the next. It is the perfect design for edge of chaos phenomena—stable enough to persist, learn, and pass the lessons on but flexible enough to adopt the lessons evolved by others, to explore and adapt to new circumstances, and to contribute and benefit from emerging symbiotic ecologies, governed by nothing but a spontaneous commonwealth of the unexpected and unpredictable.

In another 100 years, the very idea of learning in silent, passive rows before a droning instructor will probably seem very strange. That bizarre practice will be swept away, just as the Wright brothers' plane at Kitty Hawk gave way to the Mars landings in the last century. Or as Morse code gave way to the Internet, or as animal husbandry evolved from goat breeding to the direct manipulation of DNA itself.

Education, surely, is next in line for big changes. Not long ago, armies marched into battle shoulder to shoulder, the front ranks falling to the bullets, but most reaching their objective—a matter of acceptable losses. Similarly, in education, ranks of students have been trained to sit in passive and stoic ranks before the withering hail of words from the front of the classroom; many students never reach the learning objective, but the losses have always seemed acceptable. Internet technology will hopefully change that. Some day soon, education will be a dispersed, Internet-embedded process, less like a one-room schoolhouse than a British university degree program—no fixed classes, but simply a richness of intellectual wealth to feed a self-designed study program fed by the world's great libraries and one-on-one discussions with virtual Nobel laureates.

KT has sometimes been described as the science of surprise (Casti, 1994; see also Bass, 1999; CALResCo: http://www.calresco.org/index.htm; Gleick, 1987; Griffin & Stacey, 2005; N. Hall, 1992; Lewin, 1993; McClure, 1998; Mitleton-Kelly, 2003; Stacey, 1992; Uhl-Bien & Marion, 2007, 2008; Wheatley, 1999). Some pertinent concepts of KT are briefly described below, with special attention to the particular conditions that lie at the edge of chaos (Kauffman, 1995; Lewin, 1993; Waldrop, 1992)—conditions which are particularly favorable not only to creativity and change but also to the mutual adjustment of coupled systems that are on the cusp of being either antagonistic or symbiotic. For purposes of integrating the Web with the classroom, the edge of chaos defines a narrowly bounded "sweet spot" for the symbiosis of two very different animals.

A Brief Tour of Chaos

In KT, chaos has a meaning quite different from its popular connotations of confusion, anarchy, and randomness. On the contrary, the most compelling models of chaos are based on rigorously deterministic processes, often generated by simple mathematical formulas. Yet, the outcomes are surprising in a number of ways, and they have major implications for management of change and for understanding the ways that change inherently defies management. Some specifics are as follows:

a. *Nonlinearity.* KT addresses the nature of change in nonlinear systems, involving small changes that feed on themselves, sometimes resulting in massive changes. A familiar example is the butterfly effect, whereby a whisper of air movement in one part of the globe can create growing eddies that are self-reinforcing and end up as a hurricane somewhere else.

b. *Deterministic unpredictability.* Not only do infinitesimal variations become magnified and lead to unpredictably divergent outcomes, but also there can also be shifts in the very nature of the engines that drive change. This can reflect the nature of scaling up (through bifurcation points) or the nature of phase shifts, seen for example in the transformation of water to ice or vapor or the shifting gate of a horse from trot to canter. These shifts also arise through resonance between independent subsystems that begin to interact loosely, eventually behaving like a single organism. One of the most important KT concepts that applies here is emergence—which refers to the unpredictable, but coherent, patterns of new behavior that arise from interactions among a system's members. This might be described as a kind of sociological version of Heisenberg's uncertainty principle—an insistence that behaviors that cannot be anticipated from the sum of the parts.

c. *Open systems and closely coupled systems: Evolution as a pas de deux.* Finally, no system operates in isolation but responds to its environment. Just as beavers build dams to create ponds, systems can create their own environment and make use of it to accelerate the path of their own evolution, bringing into play various other phenomena depicted by KT, under such headings as lock in, fitness environments, closely coupled systems, autocatalysis, and autopoiesis. Many of these processes are already at work in the evolving interface between education and the Web.

All these elements lead to the phenomenon of self-organizing systems. The Internet itself is a classic example of a self-organized system (Coveney & Highfield, 1995, pp. 269–70, 338–39). These basic, naturally occurring structures described in KT are far from obvious, not only because they transcend (and lie unseen beneath) the separate academic disciplines but also because the whole idea of self-organizing systems is based on order for free, as Kauffman (1995, p. 71) put it. This is a notion that flies in the face of the older notion of entropy, whereby only human planning and intervention can bring order to a world that would otherwise—left to its own devices—fall into decay and disarray.

KT initially met up with severe resistance in every discipline where it had independently emerged—in physics and biology, math, economics, anthropology, psychology, and business management—but it has steadily overcome objections and has proved to be more than simply a nice metaphor. In fact, some the leading theorists in the field have applied computer-based KT models to stock market predicting—models that have proven very successful indeed, with funding from some of the world's largest investment banks (Bass, 1999).

Despite skeptics, KT keeps demonstrating itself in the phenomenon of self-organization, not only for groups and learning processes but especially in the hard sciences of biology and the self-assembly of chemicals into living organizations. Until recently, this self-assembly process (swimming against the tide of entropy) has been described in the billion-year evolution of life from simple cells to larger assemblies. But we are beginning to find that this process can happen spontaneously in a very short time frame. In a recent experiment, for example, a fairly ordinary inkjet printer was used to position living mammalian cells onto a surface in patterned layers, along with a bath of chemicals that cells normally use to communicate with each other. A couple of surprising things quickly emerged: first, cells survived quite well the inkjet stresses—both the heat and severe forces of acceleration (up to 1,000 G). Secondly, the cells show an unexpected ability to work collectively and use their chemical bath to build structures and membranes, creating an enclosing environment that enhances their survival (Webb, 2008, pp. 56–57).

Some 90% of the cells shot by the inkjet survive; not a bad success rate. Not even bad if we applied that standard to successful classes we have taught. Adult learning groups, like cells, probably have a deep hidden reservoir of ways to survive, self-organize, and use resources collectively to create an environment that supports their own integrity and identity. As most high school teachers can attest, groups find ways of establishing their identity and behaving in ways completely unprompted by teacher intentions, often in ways that work at cross-purposes to educational objectives. But for adults in an online learning environment, this hidden resourcefulness of the group—reflected in the basic principles of complexity theory—is probably better aligned with learning and is more reliable as an alternative to traditional command-and-control teaching.

Midcareer adults are not only more motivated and focused but also more skilled in working with people outside their own social circle; less infused with dysfunctional hormones; more sensitive to group processes; and less preoccupied with a struggle for identity in opposition to parents, rival cliques, or teachers. In short, more likely to find ways of self-organizing collectively, based on group trust and self-trust, and more likely to find delight in a "dinner with Andre."

Edge of Chaos as the Evolutionary Sweet Spot

As Kauffman (1995, p. 26) put it, the edge of chaos is "a compromise between order and surprise," a place that allows both spontaneous evolution and continuity that builds on past successes. In the context of biological networks, Kauffman found these edge-of-chaos conditions as the place where networks "appear best able to coordinate complex activity and best able to evolve as well" (p. 26). Moreover, these conditions allow coevolution of partner systems: A predatory relationship can evolve toward a symbiotic one, provided there is both stability enough for each partner to learn and adapt, yet also sufficiently flexible to handle mutual adjustment (p. 27).

Kauffman's (1995) research demonstrates that there is a narrow band of criticality at work here. To coevolve, the relationship must be neither too tightly coupled, which suppresses evolution, nor too loosely coupled, which makes them uselessly unresponsive to each other (pp. 86–94). At just the right level of connectedness, each small change cascades into other changes, in a process of mutual adaptation. Once started, the process can take off very quickly—a phenomenon seen in the fits and starts of evolutionary divergence, in mathematical models of complexity events (at bifurcation points), and even in historical processes that we have witnessed, such as the fall of the Berlin Wall and the surge of interest in science in American schools after Sputnik during the 1960s.

A chief lesson of KT may be the need to let go of strategic blueprints and to work instead on reinforcement of small beginnings that seem to be wafting in the right direction, waiting to become hurricanes.

KT (Chaos–Complexity Theory) at Fielding

We look now at more specific ways that the KT paradigm applies to online learning, in the experience of the organizational management and development (OMD) master's degree program at Fielding Graduate University. As it happens, the OMD program at Fielding offers a seminar in KT applied to leadership, group processes, organizational design for change, and management of turbulence in the context of globalization (a class taught by the author of this chapter).

The OMD program is conducted almost entirely online, with students from around the globe. Some of the lessons of experience include the superior value of loosely coupled dialogue, involving asynchronous rather than real-time interactions—a learning mode that seems optimal for working at the edge of chaos. This program, now in its 12th year, was designed from scratch to work specifically for learning through the Internet. Intensive face-to-face sessions take place at the beginning of the 20-month program and again halfway through the process (when final projects get underway). Otherwise, assignments consist of seminars involving students and faculty ranging from Belgium to Hong Kong and from South Africa to Alaska. Fielding operates this dialogue in a completely asynchronous mode, not in real time, but with each person posting and responding in a flexible window to accommodate widely varying time zones as well as personal work schedules (the majority of these students being midcareer adults).

Often, the first instinct of distance learners is to want more contact, and the normal impulse is to use real-time media—a telephone conference call, a chat room, a time-specific event—to restore the sense of doing something together. But based on experience at Fielding program, this could be a mistake. There are other temptations, too—to incorporate multimedia for supplementing text with sounds, visuals, and other document enhancements. But here, too, less is more. The power of a text lies partly in the starkness of words, without distractions. The focus on pure text means lends itself to seeing the subtext and to sensing the writer's feelings and intentions and context behind the words. As in black-and-white photography, attention is more focused and undistracted, demanding greater intentionality.

I want to draw a couple of conclusions at this point. First, the positive assessment of asynchronous learning devices, however subjective, may have a more objective basis in the notion of edge of chaos conditions for creative coevolution. The speaker and listener (writer and reader) have a sense of immediate connectedness, timed to their own situation and context, yet they are loosely coupled in a way that is quite different from traditional classroom practices, where each member of the audience must be on the same page at the same moment, in lock-step according to a lesson plan.

Second, the shifting of the center of gravity of the dialogue—from instructor to self-organized topics and issues generated by the learner—has a deeper resonance with the intellectual movement now beginning to emerge under the heading of decentralized intelligence and the open source movement. In part, this movement reflects the shift of expertise and authority from top-down, centralized institutions to highly dispersed groups and individuals. In part, it reflects deliberate strategies to make institutions more responsive to the variety of real-world conditions and their increasing pace of change. As Shelley Hamilton (OMD alumni, November 29, 1999, e-mail) noted,

> Information can be centralized because it is just quantitatively categorized bits of data. But knowledge needs to be decentralized because it is the experiential interpretation of that information, and experience is relationship based—thus decentralized. This notion of "decentralized intelligence" is making an appearance in the literature of strategic planning and human resources training programs in application to cutting edge business and public sector organizations alike. Even the U.S. Army has committed to a radical shift away from older ideas of centralized command, control, and

intelligence. Here, the issue becomes one of managing massive amounts of information and resisting the temptation to over-control it. The competitive advantage is nullified when you try to run decisions up and down the chain of command. [Everyone has] real-time information on what is going on around them . . . [so] once the commander's intent is understood, decisions must be devolved to the lowest possible level to allow these frontline soldiers to exploit the opportunities that develop." (as cited in Pascale, Millemann, & Gioja, 1997, p. 134)

In this new era, leaders are trained to learn to live with the ambiguity and discomfort of leading from a different place by refusing to provide all the answers to the troops. Instead, they allow a stressful vacuum of answers to develop until the troops learn that they must provide the answers themselves as well as learn the commitment to implement them.

Emergence of the Third Voice

An important element of candlepower is the emergence of a third voice—a quality of conversation that is emergent in exactly the sense used by complexity theory: it cannot be produced on command, and it is more than the sum of its parts—more than any one person's ideas in a conversation and more than the separate ideas of everyone contributing. It is almost as if people in this kind of conversation become channels for the unspoken voices of others, through a special kind of listening.

There is a tradition of hermeneutic inquiry that aims at engaging this third voice, rooted in upward epistemology. Specifically, Heidegger thought that hermeneutic understanding was not aimed at reexperiencing another's experience, but rather held the power to grasp one's own possibilities for being in the world through engagement with others. In this way, conversation becomes a space where individuals have the possibility of creating a third voice, one in which subject–other becomes subject–subject and then intersubjective in which the conversation itself becomes a part of collective being (Gadamer, 1976, p. 23). As Gadamer (1976) put it, "In every true conversation each person opens himself/herself to the other, truly accepts his/her point of view as valid and transposes himself into the other to such an extent that he understands not the particular individual but what he says" (p. 385). Conversation is alive and is the opening to greater understanding and knowledge. In this moving, changing relationship, a reflective moment of understanding emerges (K. Rogers & Hudson, 2007).

So how do we go about finding this third voice in online conversations? What can we do to strike a match to light this phenomenon of candlepower? That is the focus of this chapter's next section.

Embracing the Shadows:
Listening for Mystery and Surprise

To embrace candlepower, to invoke and experience what it has to offer, we also have to embrace its context of shadows, with a willingness to work with uncertainty and ambiguity and with multiple frames of reference and lenses. The aim is not just deconstructive analysis but also is listening deeply to what is there in the unexpected.

KT provides a useful window on the emergence of trust—using the word *complexity* in the rigorous KT sense described earlier. It is a process that cannot be forced or predicted, but it emerges from a series of feedback loops, driving the system, usually in a series of nonlinear steps, from one phase of behavior to another. Trust is not an entity in itself, but (in KT parlance) a strange attractor.

In the language of group dynamics, a little trust leads to some information sharing, then more trust, in a dynamic spiral (Butler, 1999, pp. 219–220; C. Rogers & Roethlisberger, 1952, pp. 47–48). Rogers's research on small groups showed that the decisive element for trust is the conscious act of suspending judgment about others as people and instead to seek understanding from the other's point of view. That shift "can be initiated by one party, without waiting for the other to be ready" or "by a neutral third person, provided he can gain a minimum of cooperation from one of the parties" (Rogers & Roethlisberger, 1952, p. 47). Then,

> The dropping of some defensiveness by one party leads to further dropping of defensiveness by the other party . . . [until] communication tends to be pointed toward solving a problem rather than toward attacking a person or group . . . These defensive distortions drop away with astonishing speed as people find that the only intent is to understand, not to judge. (Rogers & Roethlisberger, 1952, p. 48)

Sampson (1993) saw this embracing of differences as a process of celebrating the other. Bakhtin (1990) elaborated on this by asking,

> In what way would it enrich the event if I merged with the other, and instead of one there would be now only one? And what would I myself gain by the other's merging with me? If he did, he would see and know no more than what I see and know myself. . . . Let him rather remain outside of me, for in that position he can see and know what I myself do not see and do not know from my own place, and he can essentially enrich the event of my own life. (p. 87)

In his essay, "Shakespeare and the Listener," White (1986), posed the question: If I say I had a good conversation with X today, what does that mean? It means we each pulled the other into a new idea or feeling or understanding that would not have been possible without the other. It means a personal experience with an unexpected outcome, discovering something together. But it starts with the power of listening:

> What we *hear* is what enables us to *speak*. . . . It is the listening function which is, far from being passive, of prime creative importance in determining the direction and future course of a conversational interaction. (p. 125)

Indeed, dialogue, at its best, is not constrained by the initial "givens" or guided by managers of critical dialogue as a technique, but instead opens doors to the kind of learning where information consists of surprise. Claude Shannon, one of the founders of information theory while working at Bell Labs in the 1940s, defines information in terms of uncertainty about the next message to be received. This is counterintuitive, but the higher the uncertainty or surprise, the greater the new information or surprise value contributed by the communication (Coffman, 1997; Shannon & Weaver, 1998). Communication that brings out nothing unexpected can only confirm what we already know, deepening of the ruts of unquestioned thought habits. These habits can become constraining, as Coffman points out, not only in terms of what we perceive, but in defining the circumference of our being. With too much order, predictability, and stasis, "we have no window left in our lives for information to intrude—to stir things up and make us doubt, challenge, practice, fail, and learn again" (Coffman,1997, para. 20). We need messages that provide us with the raw materials to grow and evolve, and for that, they need to surprise us out of compliance.

From the standpoint of scientific discovery, this calls for a willingness to suspend assumptions and certainties and to maintain a spirit of inquiry (Marquart, 1996). In Feynman's (1988) view, the essence of science is the willingness and freedom to doubt, which was "born out of a struggle against authority in the early days of science" (p. 245). Scientific progress comes from a "satisfactory philosophy of ignorance" that recognizes "the openness of possibilities. . . . If we want to solve a problem that we have never solved before, we must leave the door to the unknown ajar" (pp. 247–248).

Feynman (1998, p. 47) maintained that one of the great heritages of Western civilization is "the scientific spirit of adventure"—the adventure into the unknown, an unknown that must be recognized as unknown in order to be explored, the demand that the unanswerable mysteries of the universe remain unanswered, the attitude that all is uncertain. To summarize it: humility of the intellect.

Feynman (1998) saw in that humility the very basis of effective discourse and the basis of democracy itself. "The writers of the Constitution knew of the value of doubt," which provided an "openness of possibility" so that uncertainty is seen as an opportunity for people, some day, to find another way beyond our own powers to imagine" (pp. 49–50). "We have plenty of time to solve the problems. The only way that we will make a mistake is that . . . impetuously we will decide we know the answer" (p. 57).

But aside from critical skepticism as a foundation of science, there is the element of mystery. Feynman's (1998) philosophy of ignorance, as he called it, provides a door to the experience of mysteries, which is for him a "particular type of religious experience" available to serious scientists; a good scientist, he maintains, will see that "the imagination of nature is far, far greater than the imagination of man. . . . [We] turn over each new stone to find unimagined strangeness leading on to more wonderful questions and mysteries—certainly a grand adventure" (1998, pp. 242–243).

Lessing (1973) made a similar point about the power of the written word derived from its unresolved quality. There is a power in ambiguity, which leaves a continuing open dialogue between writer and reader, even if the text is from a book of a long departed author. For Lessing (1973),

> a book is alive and potent and fructifying and able to promote thought and discussion *only* when its plan and shape and intention are not understood, because that moment of seeing the plan and shape and intention is also the moment where there isn't anything more to be got out of it. (p. 22)

If the purpose of dialogue is to find meaning, then the goal is not the arrival at a fixed point of understanding, but the sustaining of a process. Meaning is not static, but exists only within the process of its own development. Berger and Mohr (1982) put it this way:

> Without an unfolding, there is no meaning; meaning is a response, not only to the known, but also the unknown; meaning and mystery are inseparable and neither can exist without the passing of time. (p.15)

This is reflected, too, in the thought: "Zen teaches nothing; it merely enables us to wake up and become aware" (Suzuki, as cited in Cleary, 1995, p. xi).

The Art of Candlepower

This section is aimed at being practical, with a look at some elements that might be described as fuels for candlepowered conversations. One is the special nature of *asynchronous* collaboration. Another is the effect of *storytelling*, an important part of which consists of listening for the third voice beyond two people in a conversation. Finally, there are the elements of *trust* in the group and just as important, of *self-trust*, which is always an emergent quality, a work in progress.

The Asynchronous Moment

Asynchronous dialogue allows uninterrupted pauses and silence and shadow space for thoughts to come to the surface, as if simultaneously authored by speaker and listener. This helps create a sense of reciprocity and cooperation, based on collaboration rather than on competition, and of social skills apart from academic ones. This is very different from the real-time jostling of ideas in a chat room. Instead, asynchronous dialogue allows learners (both students and faculty) time for reflection, resulting in more thoughtful replies (Stevens-Long, 1999, p. 14).

As part of a flowing dialogue, asynchronous postings let one draft comments quickly and spontaneously, with the juices flowing, which keeps one's intuition and personal context in play. This kind of instinctive, even impulsive expression, is a vital quality of candlepower. But in asynchronous mode, one can do this with more self-trust and lack of inhibition, without self-censorship or immediate need to define where ideas are leading. One can write and then set his or her reply aside for a while and come back to it with fresh eyes and a second round of reflection: "How might this be perceived apart from my intentions? How would it seem in another cultural context? How might this be misconstrued?"

Asynchronous conversations have a paradoxical quality to them—a sense that "someone is always listening" (Pratt, 1996, p. 116) and that the dialogue is maintained independent of normal time and space constraints. They also allow for individual differences in the way people like to communicate—even the person who says, "I am an expert procrastinator and am able to practice my skills at my leisure" (Pratt, 1996, p. 116).

Something not so obvious about asynchronous work in a group is that it seems to narrow the focus into a dialogue between just two people, in the present moment. Asynchronous dialogue can feel like an off-the-record, closed-door conversation. The effect of asynchronous online dialogue is to focus on a particular person as audience. One's own words arise from a kind of continued listening to the words of that person, regardless of when they were actually posted. A thoughtful person might feel, "I am a slow thinker, but online that problem goes away. I don't have to be good at repartee: it feels like the other person is always there, waiting, and I can use my strengths of cognition and mulling" (Paraphrase of a student comment reported by Pratt, 1996, p. 116). One reason Internet conversations *feel* safe is that one's side of the conversation is literally taking place on his or her own turf—at home or wherever one's computer happens to reside. One can reach out anytime one wishes, working around the time-space dictates of work, family, and other obligations. Like a small, candlelit table at a restaurant, asynchronous communication creates a time and space of one's own choosing.

Asynchronous Cadence and Pace: An American Disadvantage

One student talks about asynchronous forum as a place for "critical inquiry" that can "keep the deep water still and clear" (E. Franklin, personal communication, 1999). Another referred to the "wonderful starkness of just pure thought" (Rubin, personal communication, 2000). Asynchronous dialogue brings into play the spaces and messages of silence in a way that is often lost on Americans. As Ruch (1989) pointed out in his cross-cultural study of communication styles, "In many cultures, silence is used very effectively in the course of conversation; Americans, on the other hand, rush to fill silence, talking when they should wait patiently" (p. 28).

Americans have a tendency to interrupt others in the middle of a thought—it shows interest and enthusiasm and collaboration in the joint development of ideas. But this habit can greatly annoy Europeans (as Fielding faculty based in Europe sometimes remind us), and it comes across as rudeness in many other cultures. But it can also handicap Americans because it causes them to miss most of the message. Pascale and Athos (1981) made a similar assessment:

> Americans listen in an evaluative way, accepting or rejecting ideas pre-sented, which leads to fatigue and listening shortcuts so that they absorb only about 30 percent of the message. [In contrast] The Japanese practice "less-ego listening": . . . They hold "principle" in abeyance, regard them-selves as one among others in the situation, and thus achieve easy accom-modation with the circumstances of the meeting. This situational ethic enables the Japanese to air different views without falling into a duel of personalities. (pp. 130–131)

In a more local context (for American educators at least), the council format of Indian meetings has received considerable attention as a basis for school discussion, being less formalistic than traditional debate for-mats and giving more opportunity for everyone to speak without inter-ruption. A salient feature of the council is the rule not to interrupt the speaker. To European-origin Americans, the phrase "I have spoken" sounds pompous, but it is simply the speaker's way of saying, "Well, that's all I wanted to say. Your turn now, and I will give my full attention to your own thoughts. Take your time." This is different from typical chat room conversation, where multiple voices are simultaneously in play, somewhat disjointed and unfocused, but always impinging on the social construction of the conversation.

Americans may have another disadvantage here. The skill of seeing behind the message based on the sender's personality and intent is a skill that does not come naturally to our culture. E. Hall's (1977) studies indicate that Americans (along with most Northern Europeans) fall into the category of a low-content culture, meaning that it places great confidence in *words* for conveying information but discounts the broader context of a message—who it came from and under what circumstances. Online dialogue helps to reintroduce those high-context elements, allowing greater attention to the subtext of the other person's words and situation, in a way less possible in the give and take of a real-time discussion.

Trompenaars (1994) agreed with Hall's assessment, based on his own research on cross-cultural differences. Trompenaars uses the terms *diffuse-specific* for high-low-context cultures, but his point is the same. Americans have trouble dealing with the whole person in their business dealings, but focus on a particular role segment. Americans can be relaxed, garrulous, and friendly in part because they are relating on a thin "public layer" that is "not a very big commitment. You 'know' the other person for limited purposes only" (p. 80). On other layers, Americans are comfortable with not telling, not asking, and skimming over any implicit layers of subtext.

A Possible Asynchronous Advantage: The Power of Sensory Deprivation

Online forums are highly limited in many respects: They do not touch all the senses, and they cannot command immediate responses. But that can be an advantage. Other senses, drawing on the powers of experience and the imagination, may come to the surface and take over. Once on a field trip, I injured both eyes, which were bandaged during my plane trip home. The temporary state of blindness brought an unexpected awareness of things usually beyond my normal perceptions—the slope and texture of floors, the heat from surfaces that were sunlit, the sense of distance to walls and ceilings from sound echoes, the awareness of smells, the inflections and accents and feelings behind spoken words.

Perhaps people have a similar range of sensitivities about the subtext of other peoples' written words, but they are distracted from that awareness by the preemptive strength of visual clues in face-to-face conversation or in vocal inflections on the telephone. In academic and business contexts, too, conventional syntax and jargon tends to mask the personalization of language. But asynchronous online dialogue provides more freedom to add subtext and more time to absorb it.

There are many studies about the high percent of communication that is nonverbal (93%, according to Mehrabian, 1981, p. 44), with the majority of information transmitted through visual clues such as body language, facial expression, and vocal inflection. Perhaps, however, these numbers may be misleading. Many of those nonverbal cues may fact stem not from visual or auditory inflections but from subtleties in the use of language that most people are barely aware of using or hearing. These subtexts come closer to the surface through the vernacular mode of online dialogue— with its mix of spontaneity and thoughtfulness—in words usually directed to a particular person but that tap into the shared meanings evolving within a small group.

In the absence of other signals, one's attention shifts to a richer interpretation of cues within the written text, by going deeper into the layers of meaning behind words. This does not require formal training in communication skills, but it does call for the full exercise of people's innate capacities for listening and responding.

Online asynchronous dialogue reestablishes the possibility of working more effectively and sensitively at the level of subtext. Research on perception suggests that our sense of vision gives us power to discriminate among more than 7 million colors and 300,000 tones (Geldard, 1953, p. 53). But until now, the emphasis of schooling has been on low context subject matters, where subject matters are diced into objective, unambiguous bricks of information, separate from the personalities of the people who discovered or validated those facts. Online critical dialogue reconnects the word with the speaker by focusing the candlelight of dialogue on subtext, without the distraction of other sensory inputs.

Farr (1991) pointed out that, paradoxically, another person's physical presence can lead to a psychological distancing. The other person becomes an object, he argued, "because the skin is such a compelling boundary from a visual perspective" (p. 253). Regardless how much information may be missed or misinterpreted in the words of a conversation, an even stronger effect of confusion and uneasiness stems from the physical presence and unconscious signals between two conversants. Body language and facial expression send powerful messages, all the more powerful because the messages are usually unconscious.

If we take this evidence at face value, then we have an interesting result: Far from diminishing the power and accuracy of messages, the asynchronous online format of dialogue that strips away visual images has the effect of purifying and strengthening the transmission of information and meaning, in effect by eliminating the extraneous confusion of unconscious, random, and inaccurate signals that are sent by one's physical presence. Again, there is a dramatic improvement in the ratio of signal to noise.

Storytelling

Forty years ago, business schools discovered the importance of learning through case studies, calling on learners to integrate disparate forms of information and multiple levels of interpretation. Case studies engage students higher up in Bloom's taxonomy of critical thinking skills (Anderson & Sosniak, 1994), moving from pure description and memorization to analysis and synthesis and ultimately to evaluation and application.

Storytelling provides this same coherence between teller and listener, concept and context, and problem presentation and problem-solving action. It also attains comprehension through the conduits of visual imagery, contextual setting, and movement. It is analogous to seeing the movie as motivation for reading the book.

Storytelling has special application to online learning. A story begins with something gone awry. Enter a cast of characters, a narrator (or chorus), a crisis, a resolution, a coda. In contrast, traditional education imparts knowledge in a format as different as one can get: rules, principles, logical, self-evident facts, tools for manipulation—devoid of tension, surprise, human emotion and imperfections, or the satisfying drama of coming to terms with mystery (Bruner, 2002; Denning, 2001; Gold, 1997).

Alumni from the Fielding OMD program have expressed the feeling that adult learners (like their colleagues at Fielding) can make good use of "integrative learning (drawing on experience) and learning through conversations and story-telling" (Coleen Douglas, e-mail, October 19, 2002). Douglas goes on to say,

> This is how Fielding works, and was a key to its success for me. I do think that conversations and story-telling are the way most people learn things in the world. Applying those methods to graduate school was great.

Paige Marrs (e-mail, October, 19, 2002) made a similar point:

> What has worked for me as a 2nd term student: use of stories and examples— less words, more impact. If I could suggest one thing only [about teaching online] it would be to teach the profs to teach by story . . . and teach them to teach students to communicate in stories. IMHO, it is by far, the most powerful method of teaching and learning information, one that I'm trying to learn on my own. I'm not suggesting this as the only or even the primary method of learning/teaching, but I think we'd all be better leaders, teachers, guides, managers, consultants if we learned to do this.

Good conversations almost always seem to entail storytelling. Fielding faculty member Dottie Agger-Gupta (conversation, April 2, 2002) pointed to a recent study of how best practices are compiled and exchanged in organizations sush as IBM and NASA. Those organizations have discovered that proven ideas do not "stick" with listeners unless they are conveyed as a form of storytelling. War stories put things in a context of significant consequences. The information is provided in a coherence of parts, and in a sequence that listeners can absorb as a whole, each part relating to the one before. Best practices are understood in terms of not just the desired outcomes, but the context for action—the what, why, and who of how things happen. They establish a shared framework for collaboration. And they give credibility and acceptance to some basic requirements of real-world learning that are usually absent from expert advice and classroom learning—the need for trial and error, false leads, failures, surprises, and unpredictable contingencies of success (Agger-Gupta, Peters, & Singer, 2002, part 3, p. 10).

What NASA and IBM have found is that storytelling keeps people engaged over time because the story continues to evolve, both among tellers and listeners. Listeners themselves become interpreters and retellers, by drawing on their own experiences and personal speaking styles—their own inner voices.

Something important is added, too, in the retelling—a personally shared context of workplace experience, life issues, current events. This back-and-forth style of listening, absorbing, retelling, adding, and evolving ideas constitutes the conversational form of learning. It is collaborative, it draws on objective facts and personal interpretation, it evolves over time, it engages people actively, and it entails an innate motivation of group discovery. At the same time that it solves a particular problem, it also increases a group's understanding of the how things work, while also adding to the personal skill of each person actively engaged in the conversation (Agger-Gupta, Interview, April 4, 2002).

Stories often serve as the foundation for defining organizational culture and can be incorporated into programs to orient, assimilate, and align new employees into organizations that emphasize a clear sense of purpose and core values (Schein, 1992, pp. 79–82; Walsh, 2001). Peter Senge and others, in *The Fifth Discipline* (1994, p. 354), talked about "purpose stories" used to enhance organizational vision and vision meaningful shared goals. Pearce (1995, p. 106) and Simmons (2001, pp. 31, 123) pointed to the effectiveness of storytelling's ability to grip attention beyond rational exhortation through devices such intuition and emotion, counterintuitive surprises, brevity, sensory details, use of natural language, and the engagement of human characters.

Storytelling Online Through Personas

Use of personas for critical dialogue is an exercise in role-playing. A persona is sometimes defined as a dramatic, fictional, or historical character. But real people, too, carry around various personas within them, some intentional, some unconscious, and occasionally in conflict. An adult student, especially, has a keen appreciation of carrying around several roles at once, with multiple involvements as student, team partner, family member, economic provider, boss, employee, and colleague.

Personas can give voice to opinions and perspectives that are otherwise silenced. Both students and faculty can take these character roles, sometimes in prestructured ways, other times spontaneously. There are several variations, including the use of left-column voices. Their effect is to establish a constructive tone for dialogue—a lightened mood for dealing with serious issues, by allowing alternative views to be expressed in a way that feels separated from person-to-person attack and defense.

The identity of a persona is usually best if sketched out in a sentence or two, requiring little advance preparation or pedagogical baggage. They draw out student creativity on a minimalist stage, by avoiding elaborate construction of scenarios. In my own courses, I have asked students to take on the voice of a persona (usually an assigned character), to critique readings, each other's postings, or to explore different facets of a concept or organizational practice, from the standpoint of different stakeholders, cultures, or personality types. Or an assignment might be presented in the context of a vaguely defined country, say, Galitia, into which the group has been parachuted at the beginning of the course. One persona might be given the role of Khaldun, the Galitian Minister of Culture; another Rinzai, the CEO of a multinational corporation based in that county; Tallala, a rural cooperatives agent with a concern for preserving viable traditional economies and social structures; or Arafar, an investigative journalist and intellectual. Again, both the personas and the setting are described at the outset only in the barest terms, the rest being left for students to develop in ways that best address their own issues.

Students can take it from there with little other guidance. Occasional reminders may be needed to keep people from adding unnecessary detail and local color to a persona or host country setting; a simple sketch is sufficient as a frame for substantive issues. In the final round of such an exercise, students usually revert to their own voice, but sometimes stay in voice of a persona that has proved strong in articulating an issue.

As a way of providing feedback, persona voices allow students to express critical ideas more forcefully and clearly, without apologies, and with less fear that the recipient will take the criticism as an ad hominem attack. Speaking through a persona lets one give (and take) criticism, with a more overt understanding of differences between the parties engaged. Effective criticism (and effective feedback) needs to be based on a mutual understanding of these differences, and the personas help bring them into play on an explicit and conscious basis.

Role-playing makes use of what Mills (1959) called "the sociological imagination," an approach that stresses the interplay between history and biography, relating "the most impersonal and remote transformations" of the world at large to "the most intimate features of the human self—the relation between social structural changes defining public issues at large, and personal troubles within" (pp. 2–12). This contrasts with traditional forms of criticism that tend to separate ideas from their social context and history, based on a somewhat outdated view of objectivity that posits a neutral analyst separated from what is being observed.

Use of personas draws attention to the importance and power of language and specifically to the possibility of choosing different voices to open up different issues. Whereas most academic writing encourages a neutral language (discourages the subjective voice beginning with "I"), the use of personas encourages ideas to be expressed in a more consciously acknowledged subjectivity, using a tone of voice that serves an aware intent. It reveals that each of us carries inside a repertoire of voices, each attuned to a particular role and attitude—but most of them preempted by academic formalism.

This personalized voicing of individual differences, can end up creating a stronger sense of solidarity within the group (Bates, 1999). I suspect that comes from breaking down the unspoken concern of many groups: "Do I belong? Am I up to the standard? Am I going to put my foot in my mouth?"

Putting oneself in another's shoes can be unexpectedly self-revealing, tapping into thoughts and feelings from outside the normal academic subject matter. As one student said, "It is amazing how much you can learn about yourself when you're pretending to be someone else" (Caesar-Beaubien, Fielding forum posting, December 2, 1997). Another student reflected,

> I discovered a nasty little surprise about me. When I took on the persona of Tallala, I could easily imagine her. . . . But Makjubar meant nothing to me. I couldn't feel him, understand what he was interested in or comfortably speak for him. I couldn't relate. This really got me thinking about my inter-action with real people. Do I sub-consciously give value to some and not to others because of my ability to *relate* to them? Do I bring that to my inter-actions within my organizations? . . . This course has been different than I expected, and I really struggled with the personas. But that struggle may have been the part . . . that provided the greatest insight. (Post, Darnell, Fielding forum posting, April, 27, 1999)

These remarks illustrate the importance of Bakhtin's insights into the importance of confrontation among different language frameworks—or "heteroglossia"; as Bakhtin saw it,

> utterances acquire meaning only in dialogue, which is always situated in a social-cultural context where a multiplicity of different languages intersect (political, technical literary, interpersonal, etc.). From this *emerges a conception of personhood where we author ourselves in dialogue with others and subject to the reinterpretations they give us.* (Bakhurst, 2005, p. 78, italics added)

The same happens at a more conscious level in exposures to other national cultures. As Hampden-Turner (1993) put it,

> We talk about culture shock, but the shock may be strongest from seeing exposed and explicit and accepted and powerful in others what is sup-pressed or tacit or unconscious—but nevertheless deeply part of—our own culture. The shock of looking into a mirror after a life of no mirrors. (p. 2)

Personas help people to engage a playful element in social criticism, not just making it more fun but also more creative and less likely to set up defensive responses. Some of the best persona responses start with a preface that reminds everyone of this half-serious, half-playful context. For example, one student began his critique with the comment that

> Folks, please go into this with your sense of humor intact and forgiveness in your hearts. It took me a while to begin thinking like this Arafar character, but when I got into it, well, he just took over, before I even knew what was happening. My voice changed, my ears got pointy and my fangs came out. There was no stopping it. HE wrote the commentary you are about to read. . . . I'll be myself again next week when we get into the de-briefing comments, but until then, watch out for Arafar. He's scary, and I truly hate this character. P.S. to Karen: Arafar thinks you're American. I tried to tell him you were Canadian, but there's no reasoning with this guy. (Joel Zimmerman's Fielding forum posting, October 14, 1997)

How easily do students adapt to the role of an assigned persona? I have not done any systematic evaluation of this, but my impression is that only 1 or 2 out of 10 students in a group will feel somewhat uncomfortable with role-playing in the first round, but even that resistance is usually gone by the end of an 11-week course. As one student posted in the online Cafe:

> Julia, You asked how it was to write in persona. Very strange! Tallala has taken this task to heart, while I seem to be along for the ride. I see the humor in Khaldun's comments, but Tallala takes it all so seriously. Could this be sanctioned schizophrenia? It will be interesting to see how Tallala evolves. (Post-Darnell, Fielding forum posting, March 14, 1999)

Storytelling Online: Using Principles of Improvizational Theater

Personas tap into the spirit of improvisational theater, which employs specific techniques for making the other guy look good and seeing with big eyes. The phrase used by D. Johnson's (1998) thesis captures well the phenomenon of working with personas, and it also brings out this important aspect of candlepower—*The Power of Not Knowing What Comes Next.*

Improvisational theater—the subject of D. Johnson's thesis (1998)—is an intriguing model for collaborative learning and also for organizational management and development. Traditionally, we mold our action around predefined goals and paths to get there, under the tight control of managers and leaders. But it might be otherwise. There might be an entirely different source of guidance to be found in that hermeneutic third voice, which arises out of conversations, where listening becomes stronger than insistent defense of an argument. Improv theater does not appear very often in lists of best practices or efficiency measures for traditional teaching. Nevertheless, it may serve as a good metaphor, and even a good mind-set, for making the transition from instructor-centered, text-driven teaching toward more creative, dialogue-based group-facilitated learning. It is worth noting here some of the basic improv techniques that D. Johnson's (1998) thesis proposed as tools for organizational (and learning group) collaboration:

- offering, accepting, and advancing;
- no blocking, no wimping;
- seeing the world with big eyes;
- making the other guy look good;
- storytelling; and
- point of concentration.

Intensive listening and response is always an invitation to mystery, leading to surprise and unforeseeable outcomes. Improvization produces the same unpredictable, unscripted, and powerfully creative process that comes out of critical dialogue when a group takes off on its own path (D. Johnson, 1998; Spolin, 1999). To be sure, even improvisation has its own techniques and conventions, but it cannot have the self-consciousness of a facilitator-managed process. Instead, in the parlance of complexity theory, it follows the model of a self-organized system (Kauffman, 1995; Wheatley, 1999).

So in the end, the best model for group learning may not be the traditional lesson plan, where everything is set out predictably in advance under the tight control of the instructor. Instead, the best model for group learning might be improvisational theater.

There are actually a number of techniques that apply to this aim of listening for other voices. The hermeneutic third voice is third because it grows out of real people's conversations, tapping into personal or shared experiences. Yet, these conversations, in the frame of candlepower, give rise to creative, unpredictable ideas that seem to draw on a hidden intelligence beyond the sum of ideas that each person brings to a conversation. I will mention two practical techniques that can be brought to bear, starting first with De Bono's (1985) six thinking hats and then left-column voices.

De Bono's (1985) *Six Thinking Hats* is a particular version of role-playing that seems to work well online. This approach has evolved through decades of use both in business and school settings. It is based on De Bono's (1968) earlier work on lateral thinking is but recast in a simple format that makes it easy for participants to recognize different mind-sets that can be brought to problem solving by assigning each group member to put on one or another color hat in sequence (De Bono, 1985):

White—calls for information known or needed

Red—feelings, hunches, intuition

Yellow—values, benefits, why something might work

Black—devil's advocate, why something might not work

Green—creative possibilities

Blue—managing the thinking process (facilitation)

Left-column voices can be used independently of personas, but it seems to work just as well—and often more forcefully—within a role-playing exercise. Left-column thinking is one of the methods used by David Bohm's Dialogues Group in Britain (Bohm, 1996; Bohm, Factor, & Garrett, 1991) and is described by Argyris (1999, pp. 61–63) as "the left- and right-hand column case method." The left-column exercise is also presented in *The Fifth Discipline Fieldbook* by Senge, Kleiner, Roberts, Ross, and Smith (1994, pp. 246–252). The starting point is the notion that in every conversation or group, there are things that people express openly, while other thoughts and feelings are withheld. The function of a left-column exercise is to provide a safe way—a sanctioned peephole—to reveal what is hidden.

The technique is very straightforward: one simply draws a line down the center of a blank page, and in the right column, one writes what one would normally say in a conversation. In the left-column, one enters what one might be thinking, but normally keeps to oneself. Some online forums do not provide an easy way to write in two columns, so left-column voices can be simply given a prefix or a bracket, interjected among normal right-column remarks:

> Perhaps our countries are not so different, if one compares our slums with yours, or our suburbs or universities or nightclubs.[LCV: I wonder if Barclay will think my comment is insensitive—I see a lot of books on his Suggested Readings list that take a Third World perspective. But I think we're doing some kind of "noble savage" number with the ethnic personas, projecting all our human wisdom and spirit onto the Third World and assigning all human greed to the Americans.]

> Interesting point—do you have a book or web source I can use to go deeper? [LCV: I'm disturbed by your reaction: you seem to be really defensive about transnational enterprise and bitter about "ignorant management consultants." Strong stuff. What's happening?]

Why are people willing to express their hidden thoughts openly in this kind of exercise? Partly, it seems, because the rules of the game are stated clearly, and the risks of self-revelation are shared by everyone on the same basis. Another factor is the playful element at work: People can reveal their own thoughts but in a voice that is different from the academic, formal tone of the right-hand column. The left column is expressed in a vernacular that has an off-the-record quality, not meant to be judged but listened to carefully and valued for its authenticity as opposed to its conformity with accepted norms.

Left-column voices inject a conscious form of dialectical thinking—the direct questioning of one statement with its hidden opposite—which is one of the major foundations of critical analysis. As McWhinney (1992) put it, dialectical thinking is a process that comes from "getting people to let go of one truth to explore another" (pp. 169–171). Letting personas loose in the forum helps support one of the distinctive features of adult education, which is a break from the notion of an academic hierarchy, with one voice—the instructor's—at the top. With personas, the voice of authority dissolves into multiple voices, often giving contradictory advice, requiring the student to exercise the important art of polarity management (B. Johnson, 1992). This awareness of contradiction and contradictory voices is a form of stereoscopic vision (Senge et al., 1994)— which is also an important basis for critical dialogue aimed at shared exploration rather than criticism geared to attack and defense.

Group Trust

All of the techniques just mentioned require a form of group trust that is not given much attention in traditional classrooms. In fact, the techniques have the quality of not just assuming but also of building trust, which is more important to collaborative learning than almost any other factor. It is what allows a group to let go of expectations about being led by the instructor and turns the group's attention to the task of its own self-organization. And self-organization, as we have already seen, is probably the most productive concept from KT theory for its applications to groups, leadership, and learning.

Pascale et al. (1997, pp. 133–135) talked of this shift in terms of "leadership from a different place," and the transition is almost always very awkward for everyone, taking both teachers and students out of their comfort zone. It calls for "a shift of mind-set, a resocialization . . . a great resolve . . . to resist the temptation to provide the answers. The solutions, and the commitment to deliver on them, must come from the ranks" (Pascale et al., 1997, p. 135). For this transition to happen, teachers need to help students tolerate the inevitable buildup of anxiety, and maintain the pressure until students see that "*they* are going to have to make things happen" so that leaders within the group "step forward and begin to engage in leaderlike acts" (Pascale et al., 1997, p. 134).

A key point here is that it does not feel right at all, in the beginning, either for students or teachers. The change feels uncomfortably forced, until the results allow the process of be embraced. "We are all much more likely to act our way into a new way of thinking than to think our way into a new way of acting" (Pascale et al., 1997, p. 135).

One thing that can greatly help this transition is to shift attention from individual student needs to the needs of the group as a collective. Stevens-Long, one of the principle architects of the OMD program, had this to say (Interview, Santa Barbara, February 28, 2003):

> To be effective, you can't just think about each student in isolation when you're commenting on work. The group is the source of the dynamics, and that's where the 80 percent of results come from. If you're just thinking about one person, you're reverting to an old model of education as a private tutorial. What you need to figure out is what the group mind is saying. Then you pose the right question to the group mind. This isn't obvious. In fact, it's an epiphany that you need to reach to be effective.

Kjell Rudestam, another of the OMD founding faculty (Interview, April 9, 2002), stated that

> It's useful to be aware of making comments to one person, but always looking for ways to generalize those lessons for the whole group. It's a little like group therapy, where you talk to one person but there's a meta-message to the others. . . . Taking comments from one person to the whole group is important, because if people see it's a group issue and not just a personal problem, then the group can begin to work on themselves. The wisdom of a group can be very powerful, and students can take the main load of a course through its own self-direction.

At first, for many students, this feels like being cast adrift and a bit abandoned by those in charge. But Bennis and Biederman (1997, pp. 11, 28) talk about collegial tribes whose strength of focus and autonomy thrives on a context of partial isolation: "Every Great Group is an island—but an island with a bridge to the mainland" (p. 206).

Leni Wildflower, OMD faculty (Interview, March 15, 2002), made a similar point:

> Something important for effectiveness—and being efficient, too—the group has to get into a rhythm. It's like a symphony, a single entity. People know when they're playing together, and then they don't have to feel their way around, they just get into it, without hesitation. And suddenly you're going a lot faster into stuff, and a lot deeper.

Peter Park (Fielding faculty, Interview, Santa Monica, February 4, 2002):

> Sometimes I'll help start a discussion and then "leave the room," to make it clear that the ways of going deeper have to come from them. Some students

are uncomfortable with that at first, until they figure out that if they're going to be really engaged in the learning, they have to take charge of it for themselves.

Jonathan Darby, Oxford University (Telephone conversation, March 21, 2003), put it succinctly: "We are trying to apply too much of our intelligence and not enough of our students' intelligence."

But facilitating calls for careful attention and continual traces of "presence," as pointed out by Annmarie Rubin, OMD alumni (e-mail, January 27, 2003): "In my experience, the most common pitfall is when a prof thinks that because students are teaching each other he or she does not need to be present. But if they are not present, students seem to instinctively know that. Yet, facilitating is so different from teaching. As Lao Tzu says,

A leader is best when people barely know that he exists . . .

But of a good leader, who talks little,

When his work is done, his aim fulfilled,

They will all say, "Amazing, we did this ourselves"

—From the *Tao Te Ching*, chap. 17

Self-Trust

I want to conclude this section with a hypothesis suggested by a host of anecdotes: My guess is that trust in the group revolves around self-trust by group members, or at least a core of them who can serve as models for taking risks and being authentic to their own voices.

The theme of self-trust was broached earlier in the chapter—the idea that to come into one's own and contribute one's own best work, one needs to cultivate a bit of Feynman's (1998) insistence on a satisfactory philosophy of ignorance, Lessing's (1973) sense of embracing the shadows of unresolved or unresolvable questions, and B. Johnson's (1998) improv theater approach, calling on the power of not knowing what comes next.

Arriving at self-trust may happen once in a lifetime, either before, during, or after participation in a degree program—or for many people, never. Unlike best practices and theories of group processes, self-trust revolves around the intrinsic value of what makes each person distinct rather than what makes them typical or conforming to group expectations or instructors' expectations. It is the gift of offering something unexpected that makes self-trust powerful and what makes it ultimately valuable for groups and learning processes at places like Fielding.

Conclusion

Rich, group-based, self-organized learning does not come with a warranty. Not every candlelit experience is transformative or successful in evoking the third voice. Things can also go wrong. For a teacher, the role of nourishing self-organization often takes more attention and better management skills than command-and-control instruction.

The job of teacher becomes less a matter of managing the flow of information in and out, and more a task of sensing whether the group is effective in organizing its own work: seeing when it is getting off track or dysfunctional; sensing when the challenges become so stressful that learning stops and then stepping in to redefine immediate tasks; and seeing how each group is different, how each brings different solutions, or frames problems in different ways. In short, this kind of teaching is not an algorithm, to be run by formulas, but a continual process of evolving one's own personal best practices—none of which can guarantee consistent results.

It is in the nature of candlepower that the conversations that prove most important are the ones that were not in anyone's mind when they came together. It is like the stories that get told on return from a journey—the experiences that linger as important and memorable for their very absence from the travel sales brochure.

Still, there are ways to increase the likelihood of outcomes we value and as complexity theory shows us, the factors leading to emergence of new behaviors tend to be remarkably simple. Most of these factors have been mentioned already in this chapter, and I conclude here with a brief summary of those that can help us move ahead or recover from the risks of self-organized learning when things get too far over on the other side of the edge of chaos.

- *Attention to basics, and keeping it simple.* One can create self-organized learning by setting up a structure for it and then being clear to oneself and one's students, that one is going to step out of their way. One is going to be present and responsive, but not the one to take initiative or lead them on. This takes extra attention from faculty, not less.

- *Seeking the edge of chaos.* Almost every good conversation has a simple theme and usually a graphic metaphor, a story, but also an element of mystery that keeps people listening for more. Sometimes these can be built into tasks, but often they appear in students' sidebar conversations. Some of the most productive threads of dialogue—future thesis projects, paper topics, fruitful metaphors and anecdotes—come out of forum cafés where people gravitate for informal exchange and revert to being themselves (not just their scholar persona). This is often a good context for candlepower: People feel safer about taking risks and following ideas wherever they lead (improv theater), without tasks or deadlines. If a conversation gets too chaotic and unproductive in this kind of candlelight scene, no problem—the dialogue thread just runs out.

- *Awareness of butterfly effects.* A basic principle of chaos theory is that small, random events can build on themselves very quickly—the flap of a butterfly's wings spiraling into a hurricane. For any given dialogue thread, there is no telling where it is going to end up, yet it is often possible to sense very quickly whether the energy is positive or negative and to inject elements to reinforce or dampen or redirect the flow. One thing especially worth listening for is that hermeneutic third voice that emerges in a good conversation, not from a single person's ideas but from two or more postings. Here, faculty can help see underlying patterns and suggest (perhaps through questions) what they might signify, beyond the original elements. Again, this takes fairly consistent scanning of what is going on and providing inputs that are simple, not elaborate.

- *Ultimate objectives.* If things slide off the edge of optimally balanced chaos and structure, it is worth standing back a moment to think about priorities: Is the immediate goal to get assignments in on time? Or dispel anxiety? Or is the most important thing to reinforce the group's capacity for self-organization, self-trust, self-determination, by giving them ways to redefine their own tasks and boundaries? If that last is ultimately most important (and I think it is), there are ways to work at it, described earlier in the chapter: Hand out De Bono's six hats or specific personas to reframe the assignment (or the confusions). Divide people into smaller groups for less impersonal, more self-tailored and self-determined ways of handling the situation. Invite people to use left column voices to get hidden issues out on the table.

Or for others more willing to embrace the shadows, ask people to trade confusions instead of expertise about how to proceed, in the spirit of improv, or even theater of the absurd. At some point in this process, leaders will often emerge, expressing their own priority to get back on task, to draw clearer boundaries, and suggesting ways for the group to do this. Adults can be very resourceful about doing just that, if they know they are trusted to carry the ball. The moment of realizing that they have been handed the ball can be an important turning point. So important a lesson, in fact, that it carries over to life management, not just turning in an assignment. And so important that it is usually worth taking the risk of them dropping the ball, instead of keeping it to yourself as happens in traditional pedagogy—the teaching of children.

Ask students what they remember from their graduate work. If the question is raised in an academic setting, they mention theories, authors, concepts. But in a setting of life-beyond-school, they talk about moods, people, incidents, exasperations, stories, and turning points triggered by conversations.

This is the stuff of candlepower: conversations among people thousands of miles apart, working toward a collective voice, and struggling to self-organize around elusive capabilities that often emerge in unpredictable, unplanned ways. Like having a dinner with Andre, the scope and richness of the excursion comes from an uncluttered minimalism, not only a setting of shadows and mystery but also a place of safety and trust, to allow improvisation, critical thinking, humor, voices of personas, and a third voice that is not the instructor's or any member of the group, but one that emerges from collective thoughts.

Who would have known, 20 years ago, that computer-mediated learning could be like this? But as it turns out, astonishingly, this is the intimate flow of online collaborative learning when we risk letting go of the way we usually teach in a classroom—when we put the lectern into storage, turn off the fluorescent lights, and light candles.

References

Agger-Gupta, D., Peters, I., & Singer, P. (2002). *Excellence in HR: Best practices for learning and development.* Report for Baxter Healthcare Corp., Fielding Graduate University, Santa Barbara, CA.

Anderson, L. W., & Sosniak, L. A. (1994). *Bloom's taxonomy: A forty-year retrospective.* Chicago: University of Chicago Press.

Argyris, C. (1999). *The learning organization* (2nd ed.). Malden, MA: Blackwell.

Bakhtin, M. M. (1990). *Art and answerability.* Austin: University of Texas Press.

Bakhurst, D. (2005). Bakhtin. In T. Honderich (Ed.), *The Oxford companion to philosophy* (2nd ed., p. 78). Oxford, UK: Oxford University Press.

Bass, T. A. (1999). *The predictors.* New York: Henry Holt.

Bates, B. (1999). *Mining meaning with the power of paradox: How differences enhance spirituality and community.* Unpublished master's thesis, The Fielding Institute.

Bennis, W., & Biederman, P. W. (1997). *Organizing genius: The secrets of creative collaboration.* Reading, MA: Addison-Wesley.

Berger, J. and Mohr, J. (1982). *Another way of feeling.* London: Writers and Readers Publishing Co-Op.

Bohm, D. (1996). *On dialogue* (L. Nichol, Ed.). New York: Routledge.

Bohm, D, Factor, D. & Garrett, P. (1991). *Dialogue: A proposal.* Gloucester, UK: Hawthorn Cottage. Retrieved February 2001 from http://world.std.com/~lo/bohm/0000.html

Brown, B. M. (1998). *Digital classrooms: Some myths about developing new educational programs using the Internet.* Unpublished manuscript, San Jose State University.

Bruner, J. S. (2002). *Making stories: Law, literature, life.* New York: Farrar, Straus and Giroux.

Butler, J. K., Jr. (1999). Trust expectations, information sharing, climate of trust, and negotiation effectiveness and efficiency. *Group and Organization Management, 24*(2), 217–238.

Casti, J. (1994). *Complexification: Explaining a paradoxical world through the science of surprise.* New York: HarperCollins.

Cleary T. (1995). *Zen essence: The science of freedom* (C. Thomas, Ed. & Trans.). Boston: Shambhala.

Coffman, B. S. (1997). Weak signal research, Part II: Information theory. Retrieved September 24, 2008, from http://www.mgtaylor.com/mgtaylor/jotm/winter97/infotheory

Coveney, P., & Highfield, R. (1995). *Frontiers of complexity.* New York: Faucett Columbine.

De Bono, E. (1968). *New think.* New York: Avon.

De Bono, E. (1985). *Six thinking hats.* Middlesex, UK: Harmondsworth.

Denning, S. (2001). *The springboard—How storytelling ignites action in knowledge-era organizations.* Woburn, MA: Butterworth-Heinemann.

Ebert, R. (1999, June 13). My Dinner With Andre: A retrospective film review. [Review of the motion picture *My Dinner With Andre*]. *Chicago SunTimes.* Retrieved January 31, 2008, from http://rogerebert.suntimes.com/apps/pbcs.dll/article?AID=/19990613/REVIEWS08/906130301/1023

Farr, R. (1991). Bodies and voices in dialogue. In I. Marková & K. Foppa (Eds.), *Asymmetries in dialogue* (pp. 241–258). Hemel Hempstead, Hertfordshire, UK: Harvester Wheatsheaf.

Feynman, R. P. (1988). *What do you care what other people think?* New York: W. W. Norton & Company.

Feynman, R. P. (1998). *The meaning of it all.* Reading, MA: Addison-Wesley.

Franklin, E. (1999). *Executive revolution: Transforming leaders to transform the organization.* Unpublished master's thesis, Fielding Graduate University.

Gadamer, H.-G. (19761977). *Philosophical hermeneutics* (D. E. Linge, Ed. & Trans.). Los Angeles: University of California Press.

Geldard, F. A. (1953). *The human senses.* New York: Wiley.

Gleick, J. (1987). *Chaos: Making a new science.* New York: Viking.

Gold, J. (1997). Learning and story-telling: The next stage in the journey for the learning organization. *Journal of Workplace Learning, 9*(4), 133–141.

Griffin, D., & Stacey, R. (Eds.). (2005). *Complexity perspective on researching organizations: Taking experience seriously.* New York: Routledge.

Hall, E. T. (1977). *Beyond culture.* Garden City, NJ: Doubleday.

Hall, N. (Ed.). (1992). *The new scientist guide to chaos.* London: Penguin Books.

Hampden-Turner, C. (1993). *Seven cultures of capitalism.* New York: Doubleday.

Johnson, B. (1992). *Polarity management: Identifying and managing unsolvable problems.* Amherst, MA: HRD Press.

Johnson, D. (1998). *The power of not knowing what comes next.* Unpublished master's thesis, The Fielding Institute.

Kauffman, S. (1995). *At home in the universe: The search for laws of self-organization and complexity.* New York: Oxford University Press.

Lessing, D. (1973). *The golden notebook.* London: Granada.

Lewin, R. (1993). *Complexity: Life at the edge of chaos.* London: J. M. Dent.

Marquart, M. (1996). *Building the learning organization.* New York: McGraw-Hill.

McClure, B. A. (1998). *Putting a new spin on groups: The science of chaos.* Mahwah, NJ: Lawrence Erlbaum.

McWhinney, W. (1992). *Paths of change: Strategic choices for organizations and society.* Newbury Park, CA: Sage.

Mehrabian, A. (1981). *Silent messages* (2nd ed.). Belmont, CA: Wadsworth.

Mills, C. W. (1959). *The sociological imagination.* New York: Oxford University Press.

Mitleton-Kelly, E. (Ed.). (2003). *Complex systems and evolutionary perspectives on organisations: The application of complexity theory to organizations.* Amsterdam: Pergamon.

Pascale, R. T., & Athos, A. G. (1981). *The art of Japanese management.* New York: Simon & Schuster.

Pascale, R., Milleman, M., & Gioja, L. (1997). Changing the way we change: How leaders at Sears, Shell, and the U.S. Army transformed attitudes and behavior—and made the changes stick. *Harvard Business Review, 75*(6), 126–139.

PaulasHouseofToast. (2005). Blog posted 12/28/05. Retrieved January 7, 2009, from http://paulashouseoftoast.blogspot.com/2005_12_01_paulashouseoftoast_archive.html

Pearce, T. (1995). *Leading out loud: The authentic speaker, the credible leader.* San Francisco: Jossey-Bass.

Pratt, H. K. (1996). *The electronic personality.* Unpublished doctorate dissertation, The Fielding Graduate University.

Rogers, C. R., & Roethlisberger, F. J. (1952). Barriers and gateways to communication, *Harvard Business Review* (Reprint No. 52408). In *Business classics: Fifteen key concepts for managerial success* (pp. 44–50). Cambridge, MA: Harvard Business School Publishing Company.

Rogers, K. S., & Hudson, B. (2007). *Action research for environmental stewardship: "Upward epistemology" and other lessons learned.* Manuscript submitted for publication.

Rosenberg, S. (2007). *Dreaming in code: Two dozen programmers, three years, 4,732 bugs, and one quest for transcendent software.* New York: Crown.

Ruch, W. V. (1989). *International handbook of corporate communication.* Jefferson, NC: McFarland.

Sampson, E. E. (1993). *Celebrating the other: A dialogical account of human nature.* San Francisco: Westview.

Schein, E. H. (1992). *Organizational culture and leadership* (2nd ed.). San Francisco: Jossey-Bass.

Schreiber, D. A. (1998) Organizational technology and its impact on distance training. *In Distance training: How innovative organizations are using technology to maximize learning and meet business objectives,* ed. D. A. Schreiber and Z. L. Berge, p. 3–18. San Francisco: Jossey-Bass.

Senge, P. M. (1990). *The fifth discipline: The art and practice of the learning organization.* New York: Currency Doubleday.

Senge, P. M., Kleiner, A., Roberts, C., Ross, R., & Smith, B. (1994). *The fifth discipline fieldbook: Strategies and tools for building a learning organization.* New York: Currency Doubleday.

Shannon, C. E., & Weaver, W. (1998). *The mathematical theory of communication.* Urbana: University of Illinois Press.

Simmons, A. (2001). *The story factor: inspiration, influence and persuasion through the art of storytelling.* Cambridge, MA: Perseus.

Spolin, V. (1999). *Improvisation for the theatre* (3rd ed.). Evanston, IL: Northwestern University Press.

Stacey, R. D. (1992). *Managing the unknowable: Strategic boundaries between order and chaos in organizations.* San Francisco: Jossey-Bass.

Stevens-Long, J. (1999). *The design and delivery of interactive on-line graduate education.* Unpublished manuscript, The Fielding Graduate University.

Trompenaars, F. (1994). *Riding the waves of culture: Understanding diversity in global business.* Chicago: Irwin.

Uhl-Bien, M., & Marion, R. (Eds.). (2007). *The Leadership Quarterly* [Special issue on leadership and complexity], *18*(4).

Uhl-Bien, M., & Marion, R. (Eds.). (2008). *Complexity leadership: Part 1. Conceptual foundations.* Charlotte, NC: Information Age.

Waldrop, M. M. (1992). *Complexity: The emerging science at the edge of order and chaos.* New York: Touchstone.

Walsh, A. M. (2001*). Anterior fusion: Storytelling in new employee orientation.* Unpublished thesis, The Fielding Graduate Institute.

Waters, R. (2006). Plugged into it all. In B. I. Koerner (Ed.), *The best technology writing of 2006* (pp. 156–168). Ann Arbor: University of Michigan Press.

Webb, S. (2008). Life in print: Cell by cell, ink-jet printing builds living tissues. *Science News, 173*(4), 56–60.

Wheatley, M. J. (1999). *Leadership and the new science: Discovering order in a chaotic world* (2nd ed.). San Francisco: Berrett-Koehler.

White, R. S. (1986). Shakespeare and the listener. In G. McGregor & R. S. White (Eds.), *The art of listening* (pp. 124–151). London: Croom Helm.

Chapter 12

Designing and Developing Web-Based Intelligent Tutoring Systems

A Step-by-Step Approach With Practical Applications

Kay Wijekumar

Web-based distance learning environments use course management systems, portals, and custom designed Web-pages to deliver instructional-learning modules to students at their convenience. There is an abundance of research on the needs for learning environments such as course management systems, the use of interactive communication tools such as bulletin boards, and online learning activities. Recent advances in the form of the Web 2.0 and virtual reality environments such as Second Life, games, and podcasting add more possibilities to available technologies for learning. Brown (2007) summarized the contributions of the Web 2.0 to course management systems and suggested that social networking, collective decision making, and blogging types of applications should be incorporated into the current Web 1.0-based course management systems. Bradford, Porciello, Balkon, and Backus (2006) summarized the pros and cons of using the Blackboard course management system. They present seven principles on how Blackboard improves learning by highlighting increased communication between the professor and students, cooperation among students, immediate feedback, and acknowledgement of diverse ways of learning among students. This chapter presents an innovative advance to Web-based distance learning not discussed in the recent literature—intelligent tutoring systems (ITSs).

E-learning environments are at a crossroads. They can continue to expand the use of course management systems that provide the standard plate of offerings (i.e., notes, assignments, quizzes, multiple-choice tests, discussion boards, and chat rooms), or they can create interactive learning environments that provide modeling, engaging activities, assessment of student performance, and immediate feedback using intelligent tutoring technologies. Even though intelligent tutoring environments have been highly effective (Meyer & Wijekumar, 2007), they have not been widely incorporated into e-learning environments because of the perceived complexities of designing and delivering the technologies, interactions, assessments, and feedback in Web-based distributed environments-platforms. The current crop of course management systems and any proposed advances (Brown, 2007) can all benefit from the in-depth analysis and design techniques presented in this chapter.

We have streamlined the creation of intelligent tutoring technologies to four basic steps: modeling, practice, assessment, and feedback. Each step is supported by research on metacognition, motivation, memory, and multimedia learning, hence the name of the model—4M. The model was used to create Intelligent Tutoring for the Structure Strategy, a Web-based ITS designed to teach K–12 school students a reading strategy called the structure strategy (e.g., Meyer et al., 2002; Meyer & Poon, 2004).

The four-step process was then applied to another project to create an intelligent discussion forum for an undergraduate information science class. Additionally, this chapter presents examples of how the approach can be applied to other undergraduate and graduate classes through the example of a writing tutor construction. Based on these experiences and relevant extant research (Anderson, Corbett, Koedinger, & Pelletier, 1995; Baylor, 2001a, 2001b; Craig, Gholson, & Driscoll, 2002; Graesser et al., 1999; Magliano et al., 2005; Mayer, 2001; Mayer, Dow, & Mayer, 2003; Song, Hu, Olney, & Graesser, 2004; Wijekumar & Meyer, 2006), we have compiled a series of steps to achieve success in creating powerful e-learning environments using intelligent tutoring. Our approach was developed using distributed computing architectures that have object-oriented modules. These modules allow a programmer to reuse them in many different courses. For example, a discussion forum module can easily be adapted to different courses in different domains. The discussion forums used in anthropology classes can use the same framework for sociology classes. Our approach allows for easy development, modifications, and transfer of the modules to multiple-computer platforms such as Windows or Macintosh as well as to different subject domains.

This chapter presents the step-by-step 4M model of creating ITTs that can be applied to many domains and learning environments (i.e., K–12, undergraduate, graduate, and corporate training). We begin with an overview of ITSs, which includes supporting theories of metacognition, motivation, multimedia learning, and research on ITSs effectiveness. We then present our four-step 4M model and provide examples of how we applied each step of the model for our project (including the technologies used) and how others can adapt the model to e-learning environments for universities or other higher learning environments. Finally, we present challenges and solutions in applying the model at each step.

ITSs

ITSs provide powerful learning environments that can model expert performance, provide interactive activities for students to perform, assess student performance, and provide immediate feedback mimicking human tutors and their role in helping students learn (Anderson et al., 1995; Azevedo, 2002). They also can use multimedia capabilities, feedback, and adaptive lessons to motivate students and improve transfer of problem-solving skills. The definition of ITSs can include learning environments that incorporate machine learning algorithms. For example, as the computer interacts with each new user, the system will learn how to adapt to that type of learner and incorporate that into its vocabulary of interactions. There is also another class of learning environments very similar to ITSs referred to as *cognitive tutors* that apply similar techniques to interacting with learners without the machine learning component. This chapter does not differentiate between the two because the approach requires similar practical techniques to implement.

ITSs and cognitive tutors have been created for algebra (Anderson et al., 1995; Koedinger, Aleven, & Heffernan, 2003), biology (Moreno, 2001; Moreno, Mayer, Spires, & Lester, 2001), reading (e.g., McNamara, Levinstein, & Boonthum, 2004; Salomon, Globerson, & Guterman, 1989; Wijekumar & Meyer, 2006), physics (Graesser et al., 1999), teacher education (Baylor, 2001a), and counseling (Johnson, 2001). Even though each application has different approaches, domains, and works on a different platform, they all have a common theme of modeling expert performance to students, providing interactive activities, scaffolding the learner in achieving his or her goals, and providing feedback. Major supporting research themes for these developments have come from four areas: multimedia learning, motivation, metacognition, and memory structures. Next, we describe these research themes.

Supporting Research: Multimedia, Motivation, Metacognition, and Memory

Multimedia

Multimedia learning environments are powerful when we heed the research on what makes them effective. Mayer (2001) compiled a collection of valuable research studies that can guide the use of multimedia in learning environments. They include the following:

- Students' perceptual channels should not be overloaded with too much text or unrelated graphics (Mayer, 2001; Mayer & Moreno, 2003).

- Students in multimedia environments attend to listening and text better than multiple text windows that compete for their attention (Mayer, 2001).

- Unnecessary or peripherally related graphics may divert the attention of learners. Harp and Mayer (1998) referred to this as the seductive details.

Specifically in hypertext environments, Jacobson, Maouri, Mishra, and Kolar (1995) and McKeague (1996) have shown that when students are faced with selecting which Web pages to visit or learning in environments with choices, many students lack the metacognitive skills to know what they do not know. As a result, students in linear hypertext conditions where they have to read all the information (instead of choosing which options to read), perform better on recall and transfer measures.

Based on these research studies, we can conclude that multimedia in intelligent tutoring environments must do the following:

1. *Reduce unwanted graphics.* Many environments provide animated cartoon characters or pictures of peripherally related information that may distract the learner from the focus of the learning module.

2. *Include narrations in addition to graphical images.* This reduces the overload of the visual channel of input to the brain and helps distribute the information transmission to the visual and auditory channels. For example, showing a working engine with a narration that describes the parts and how they operate will help students more than if they have to split their attention between viewing the animation and reading a text description of the animation.

3. *Increase scaffolding for learners to encourage the development of metacognitive skills and limit unproductive jumping around in hypertext environments.* This means that students should be given different

types of feedback by the tutor and that feedback should depend on the activity, student responses, and how critical the errors or misunderstanding may be.

4. *Provide interactivity that can engage the students.* Interactivity should use real-life problems and case studies, which allows students to be actively engaged in understanding the problem, identifying solutions, and implementing the solutions. The interaction tasks should include realistic artifacts such as the tools necessary to solve the problem.

Motivation

Research on motivation and feedback shows that students' engagement is enhanced with the use of authentic texts, choice of reading passages, encouraging feedback, and ways for students to track their achievement (Alexander & Jetton, 2000). Based on this research, we can suggest that motivation in intelligent tutoring environments must provide the following:

1. *Choices for learners.* It is important that students have choices in tasks to perform and/or real-life problems that make the problem meaningful to the learner.

2. *Feedback that is informative and supportive.* Encouraging students' attempts and providing substantive help on how they can correct any errors.

3. *Tools that allow students to track their progress.* For example, an advance organizer that outlines the learning module or a slide bar that shows how much they have completed in the full module.

4. *Authentic texts and activities that are age appropriate.* Real-life problem-solving activities and reading materials and supporting artifacts that help with setting the context for learning. For example, if students are required to analyze data about poverty and school outcomes, they should have a spreadsheet or data analysis tool built into the problem-solving task to accomplish the goal.

Metacognition

Research on metacognition shows that students can be trained to improve their metacognitive skills using scaffolding, modeling, and practice tasks that allow them to abstract the processes and apply them in transfer situations (Heffernan, 2001). Based on this research, we can suggest that intelligent learning environments should provide:

1. *Scaffolding.* As stated earlier, scaffolding requires the tutor to understand what students know and what they do not know. Scaffolding

is an interaction between the tutor and student to guide the student to varying degrees of intervention depending on the needs of the student. The scaffolds should eventually be removed, thereby allowing the learners to apply their knowledge independently.

2. *Modeling of expert behavior.* From the beginning of time, apprenticeship has been the foremost method to transmit knowledge from one generation to another. Students learn by observing and practicing skills that are presented by their teachers. Therefore, it is important for an intelligent tutoring system to model expert behavior to learners to show them how the task needs to be completed.

3. *Problem-solving tasks that can support the transfer of skills to similar and different situations* (low-road versus high-road transfer) (Salomon & Perkins, 1989). The problem-solving tasks should be realistic and vary in degrees of difficulty as well as context. If students are learning about Newton's Laws of Motion, they need to know that the laws can be applied to automobile crash tests as well as exertion of athletes.

Memory

Research on problem-solving schemas and text comprehension shows that learners create schemas for situations and experiences (Gick, 1986). Existing schemata are adapted and modified as new experiences emerge. Creating effective schemata requires practice. Schema need to be flexible and readily available to apply in new problem-solving situations (Salomon & Perkins, 1989). Some of the recommendations for achieving these goals include the following:

1. *Provide learning and transfer tasks that allow the creation of flexible schemata.* Through a variety of activities and scaffolding by the tutor, students can be shown how their knowledge and skills can be abstracted to be useful in many different situations.

2. *Support the creation of schemata using prompts and focused help.* The modeling and scaffolding in an intelligent tutoring system should point out the critical concepts as well as how different applications of the concepts are similar and different. Supporting the creation of schemata can also include Ausubel's advanced organizers and carefully explaining how the expert model is solving the problems.

3. *Model how experts would view and solve the problem.* Similar to the previous descriptions, not only is modeling critical for learners to see how the ideal problem-solving process works, but also students should be instructed on what the expert model focuses on and how they abstract their knowledge and apply it.

The designs of many of the intelligent tutoring environments presented earlier include the 14 features reported here. These elements contribute to the effectiveness of ITSs showing significant improvement in learning (Meyer & Wijekumar, 2007). This and other research on the effectiveness of ITSs in learning environments are described next.

Research on ITSs

Research focused on ITSs shows that ITSs are very effective in learning environments (e.g., Anderson et al., 1995; Magliano et al., 2005; Meyer & Wijekumar, 2007). ITS is a field of research with great promise in reaching new audiences, maintaining consistency, motivating learners, providing immediate feedback, and delivering effective tutoring (Anderson et al., 1995; Heffernan, 2001). Research has shown that these agent tutors are believable (Moreno, 2001), improve performance by at least one standard deviation compared to human tutors (Cohen, Kulik, & Kulik, 1982), and are useful to convey feedback through their facial mannerisms (Graesser, Person, & Magliano, 1995; Link, Kreuz, Graesser, & The Tutoring Research Group, 2001). ITSs provide consistent tutoring and are able to adapt to a learner's performance and can work one-on-one with students.

Some ITSs also use animated pedagogical agents that provide a human-like tutor to help the students (Baylor, 2001a, 2001b; Craig et al., 2002; Graesser et al., 1999; Meyer & Wijekumar, 2007; Moreno & Mayer, 2007). Students find that agent-based tutoring systems are useful and attend to their advice (Baylor, 2001a). The facial expressions and narration provided by the animated tutors have been effective in motivating students in learning environments (Craig et al., 2002).

We have combined the research on multimedia, memory, metacognition, multimedia, and ITSs to create our 4M model.

4M Model: Four Steps to Creating ITSs

Creating ITSs for most domains can be accomplished using our four step 4M model. Figure 12.1 shows the four steps: modeling, practice, assessment, and feedback, intermingled with the supporting research themes to create a powerful learning environment. Next, I describe each step of the method showing the data collection tools (what we did and how it can be adapted to a new environment), analysis and coding schemes, design tools and technologies, challenges, and solutions for each step.

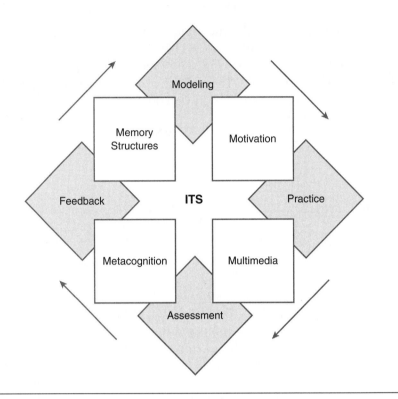

Figure 12.1   4M Model Cornerstones and Focus

Task 1: Modeling

Modeling is the first task in the 4M model. Three steps are required to create the framework for presenting expert modeling to students. The first step is the data collection component. Experts, students, and teachers are interviewed to collect data on how teachers teach and how students best learn the strategies, skills, and knowledge to be taught in the e-learning environment. Cognitive task analysis using think-aloud data is also collected to catalog the interactions that take place in the learning environment. Student performance on tasks as well as stumbling blocks and best practices are also collected.

The second step is to code the cognitive task analysis data, identify the steps to achieving each learning goal, and create a storyboard for the learning module.

The third step is to compare available technologies with the types of interactions that are outlined on the storyboard. The technology delivery choices include text, images, narration, video, software agents, and so on.

ITSs Approach to Modeling

In creating ITSs, we interviewed fifth-grade teachers, students, and researchers who had conducted extensive research on the structure strategy, including the research team that completed the initial static Web-page based lessons (Meyer et al., 2002). After the design decisions were made to create approximately 12 lessons for each text structure, we conducted cognitive task analysis with tutor–student modeling of interactions as well as think-aloud teacher modeling of lessons.

Based on the data collected and reviewed, we decided to use a human-like software agent (I.T.) with a real human voice to model the tutor behaviors. The storyboard was completed for each lesson showing the narrated sections, the student tasks, the assessment schemes for the student responses, and the feedback to the students.

Tools for Development of Modeling

Three tools were used to construct the interface and infrastructure for the ITS system, and they are specified below:

1. The animated software agent was created using Caligari TrueSpace. Since the faces provided by TrueSpace were not very realistic, we hired a graphic designer who created the necessary humanlike head in jpeg format and created the grid of the face that TrueSpace needs to render the animations. The advantage to using a product like TrueSpace was that it allowed us to save the rendered animations in a Flash or AVI format. These formats are easily viewed by Web browsers and therefore afforded us easy compatibility to almost all browsers (with the Flash player) and were not operating system dependent (Mac OS versus Windows).

    The software agent I.T. could have used synthesized computer voices or real voices. Based on research we had conducted, we chose the real human voice. All narrations, feedback, and interactions were recorded by a young adult in .WAV format. The files were then converted to an MP3 format and compressed. Once the file was merged into TrueSpace for rendering into .AVI format we compressed the files again to make them easier to load even if Internet connections had lower bandwidth.

2. Flash and Flash Remoting were used to create the Web pages. The system was designed to look like a book (see Figure 12.2, p. 311) and provided an eye-catching but smooth design. The animations were all related to the content and flashing the words that were important. There were no unrelated graphics on the pages, and the pages were organized with the left side of the book presenting the content

to the students and the right side of the book showing the animated tutor, I.T. The right side of the page was also reserved for all student responses and navigation buttons.

Since our Flash files had to communicate with a central database (SQLServer) we had to create connections to a client-server infrastructure using .NET. This was accomplished using an application called Flash remoting.

3. Because we wanted to create an application that could be easily accessed using any browser on the WWW and an object oriented development system that could easily be modified, we chose a client server platform called .NET. (Please note that the decision on using .NET from Microsoft versus J2EE from Sun Microsystems was a difficult one. Both have pros and cons and require expertise in overcoming challenges.)

The ITS started with the Flash interface that was loaded into a browser. As soon as any interaction started (i.e., student logging in), the .NET framework program written in C# took control. The C# program was the intermediary in all the communication between the browser-client front end and the internal systems such as the database (SQL Server) and operating systems (Windows 2003 server).

Applying ITSs—Modeling in Advanced E-Learning Environments

To create the perfect modeling situation for any e-learning environment the following steps are required:

1. *Cognitive task analysis.* Two types of data should be collected. First, if a designer were creating an ITS for teaching college-level writing, the first task would be to collect data through video and audio tapes of an expert writer performing a writing task. Data should be collected using many different types of writing tasks such as scientific writing and story writing. Second, expert tutors of writing should also be observed in their tutoring tasks with students. Please note that the expert tutor may or may not be the expert writer.

2. *Analyzing and coding possible interactions* (with emphasis on those interactions where students have difficulties). The data collected through video- and audiotapes of the expert models and tutor–tutee interactions should be carefully transcribed and analyzed. The sources for these data can be graduate tutors who conduct tutorials for undergraduate students. The interactions can be coded as rules that follow the model-practice-assess-feedback cycle. The source of modeling samples, instructions that support the modeling, practice

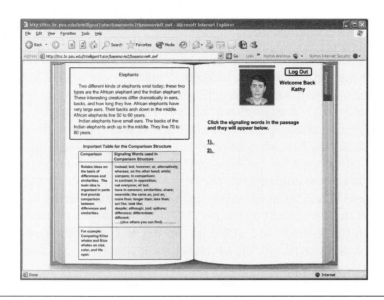

Figure 12.2   Booklike ITSs Interface That Minimizes Unnecessary Graphics

tasks for the student, assessment of the student's responses, and feedback from the system should use the collected data. For example, if a student makes a spelling error, the designer should note how the expert tutor handled the error. If the expert tutor focused initially on the organization of the writing and ignored the spelling error, then the ITS should follow that route of scaffolding as well.

3. *Storyboarding.* Storyboarding requires the designer to create lessons that use the data collected through the cognitive task analysis and the careful review of the modeling and interactions. Sources for modeling can be video- and/or audiotaped lectures that may be available or tutorial sessions for undergraduate classes. PowerPoint presentations can also serve as an organizer for the lesson storyboard. Finally, interviews with the professor and students on points that are emphasized in a regular class lecture or problems that they have observed in the learning process may also be used. The tutor–tutee dialogue can also serve as a strong foundation to build scaffolding feedback, hints, and prompts to guide the learners (based on how they are performing).

Challenges and Solutions in Modeling

The first major challenge in performing this step is the time required to conduct extensive cognitive task analysis and interviews. However, the final results will not only be greatly enhanced, but also the modules that are storyboarded and created can be used in many different courses within the same domain and by the same professor. For example, any modeling of metacognitive skill usage can be inserted into other courses. One solution to the challenge can be the reuse of videotaped lectures and materials already used in the regular classroom. Professors are a great source of information about domain-specific information, on what students know, how they learn, and what types of hints and scaffolds are helpful.

The second challenge is that most teachers and students are eager to perform at their best when being videotaped, which makes it difficult to collect information on the slips and mistakes that students make. One great source of information for the design of ITSs was the computer logs that maintained all the responses that students posted during an earlier research study reported by Meyer et al. (2002). This source of information (with all the "not-so-good" responses posted by the students) was completely coded and used in the Latent Semantic Indexing (LSI) assessment scheme described later.

The third challenge is the wide variety of computer applications to create the animations and interactions. Whatever the chosen solution, the decision must be made on the effective delivery of the content and should not be based on the glitz and glamour of creating animations. So once the decision to use some application such as Flash is made, the designer must control the urge to place unrelated or peripherally related graphics or animations in the learning environment. As noted earlier, cleaner and consistent learning environments are better for learning than those that are complicated by lots of unrelated graphics or animations and many windows of text. Overloading the perceptual channels of the learner should be minimized.

Task 2: Practice

The second task in the 4M model is practice. Practice is the term used here to describe the interactions that take place between the student and the learning environment. Similar to the first task of modeling, it requires data collection, creation of a learning objective—practice task matrix—and, finally, technology solutions.

Data sources for the creation of practice tasks include interviews with the professors, students (the audience), and other domain and motivation experts. Artifacts such as laboratory notebooks, classroom activities, and examinations are also part of the data collection.

The analysis of the collected data requires the creation of a complete matrix of learning objectives and the most appropriate task to accomplish that goal. Table 12.1 shows a sample of some of the learning goals and tasks we used. Once this matrix is created, the activities can be designed. These activities can range from students clicking on different parts of a diagram or multiple-choice answers to complex simulations that require

Table 12.1   Matrix of Learning Objectives and Practice Tasks

Learning Objective	Activity-Task to Promote Learning
Recall signaling words for text structures	Click on the signaling words in passage
Analysis of passage to find most important ideas	Write main idea or create a concept map using the text structure as the organizer
Use text structure to organize memory	Write complete recall of passage using the structure pattern

students to modify settings and conduct research (hypothesis, analysis, synthesis, and higher-order problem solving).

It is important to make the technology choices after these design steps are completed so that the focus is on the learning objectives and practice tasks and not on the glitz that can be introduced with technologies. We also need to push the technologies to adapt to the learning environments instead of using a one-size-fits-all approach.

ITSs Approach to Practice Tasks

The audience for ITSs was fifth- and seventh-grade students. After observing students who had used computers frequently and those that did not, we decided to reduce the amount of typing required. Nine activities were created to engage the learners in learning the structure strategy for reading comprehension. They included the following:

1. Writing the name of the structure based on how the main ideas of an article were organized and any signaling words emphasizing this organization. For example, if students found the signaling word *differences* they would write *comparison* for the name of the structure.

2. Clicking on signaling words (with an available key to signaling words and an expandable signaling word table within ITSs for each structure). The key for each structure was a laminated learning aid provided for each of the five structures when the structure was initially introduced to the student and added to a key ring available for consultation during the lessons. It became a part of the program after discovering in an earlier study (Meyer et al., 2002) the difficulty fifth-grade students had in comparing information on two windows on a computer (i.e., a text in one window and signaling words in another).

3. Writing main ideas for the text passages they read

4. Writing a complete recall of all the ideas they could remember from the article

5. Filling in a tree diagram showing the organization of the main ideas of an article (i.e., ideas compared, a problem and its corresponding solution, a cause and its consequences, etc.)

6. Clicking on multiple-choice answers for questions

7. Creating their own titles for passages

8. Creating their own passages given signaling words and some general themes

9. Correcting other students' work and writing main ideas or recalls as provided to them by I.T

Tools for Development of Practice Tasks

Two tools were used to construct the interactions for the ITS. They are described next.

First, Flash with action scripts was used to construct the interaction boxes and graphics. Responses from students were collected using text boxes, mouse clicks, and filling in the blanks on structure diagrams (similar to concept maps). Each input from the user was uniquely coded with a lesson and question number and was stored in the database. The information was also passed onto the next assessment step.

Second, an SQL server database was used to track each activity, response, progress, and the number of tries for the lesson question. Thus, each lesson and question had information about what type of question it was (for assessment purposes) and what type of response the student should be given at each try for that question. This allowed us to easily track activities and student performance over time.

Applying ITS—Practice Tasks in Advanced E-Learning Environments

To create the perfect practice situation for any advanced e-learning environment the following steps are required. The examples presented earlier about creating an ITS for a college-level writing course module is continued here.

1. *Interviews and observations with teachers-expert tutors of writing and students learning how to write.* The data collected during the cognitive task analysis should be reviewed carefully for the examples presented by the tutors, the exchanges of information during that task, and how the tutor scaffolded the learning of the student. A writing

course can consist of a focus on planning, outlining, writing, revising, and editing. If the expert writer and expert writing tutor used a particular writing prompt, then the ITS should include that prompt as the beginning of the student's practice task.

2. *Creating a matrix of learning objectives and practice tasks that can achieve those objectives.* The matrix for the ITS writing module should include the planning, outlining, writing, revising, and editing tasks showcased by the expert writers. Each segment of the task should then be designed as a subtask of the greater task of writing the full essay. Once the subtasks are defined the designers should identify the types of activities that will help the student learn it and the ITS to assess their performance. During each step in the subtask, the designer must select from the video- and/or audiotaped segments the most appropriate feedback to give to the student.

3. *Implementing the practice tasks with the chosen technologies.* The practice task can be presented in a Web page or through a Flash animation. Ideally, the student will be asked to write how he or she will complete the plan to write the essay. If the student performs poorly on the task, then the ITS should replay the expert model's planning phase video followed by directed prompts on how to plan the writing. The assessment can be coded as rules through a programming language or in a database.

The sources for the practice tasks can be video- and/or audiotapes of student–tutor interactions, previous course activities, laboratory manuals, textbook exercises, quizzes, and exams.

Challenges and Solutions

The first major challenge in creating interactions is to make sure they are motivating. We consulted with motivation experts who gave us advice on the types of lesson choices that students in Grades 5 through 7 would like. We pilot tested the ITS with students in the same age group and obtained information about what they liked to read (sports, music, popular figures, and games). We also introduced some games at milestones during the progression of lesson. For example, after the completion of the comparison structure (12 lessons), the students were given a game to play that allowed them to follow a dragon to find signaling words in a castle.

When applying the 4M model for undergraduate or graduate students, it is important to adapt the motivational components to their age group and to pilot test the systems with undergraduate or graduate students. These older students will need to track their progress similarly to younger learners.

The second challenge is to make sure that students follow instructions and do not "game" the system. We found that some students knew how to game the system by just clicking on anything or writing nonsense answers such as repeated 1's. We maintained a complete log of student interactions and notified the students that the system kept track of their responses. We also coded some checks into the assessment program to check for students gaming the system (Wijekumar, Meyer, Fergerson, & Wagoner, 2006). We checked for multiple characters, blank responses, and nonsense responses (using the *Urban Dictionary*) and changed the system so that the students were not allowed to move on until they corrected their work. Undergraduate and graduate students are less likely to game the system, but they can do it. It is even more important to track student progress with these students so that we do not propagate gaming.

The third challenge is to coordinate all the necessary animations, responses, and tasks associated with the practice task. For example, the students in ITSs were required to read a passage thoroughly and then press the "finished reading" button. When they pressed the button, the passage disappeared and the recall page was presented to the students. Some students tried to copy and paste the passage from page to page, so we programmed the Flash files to prohibit the highlighting of text. We also had issues where students would log out in the middle of the recall question and then forget what they had read. So when the students logged out in the middle of the recall, we reset the page back to the reading passage to accommodate their need to reread the passage.

Undergraduate and graduate students may be able to process more information in a shorter time frame requiring less system management of their time on task. However, research with undergraduates performed by McKeague (1996) does show that they are likely to skip reading in hypertext environments, resulting in poor knowledge construction.

The fourth challenge is designing tasks that can encourage students to improve their task performance. For example, after observing that some students did not pay attention to the details in the passages they read, we incorporated a task where students graded another person's answers. This placed the students in the role of graders and motivated them to remember the details of the passage.

Undergraduate and graduate students are most likely to engage in a task that has the most utility to them. So it becomes very important to focus on the real-world tasks that students need to solve and use them as examples in the design of the tasks.

Task 3: Assessment

Assessment is the third task in the 4M model. To create the assessment framework we have to expand the practice task versus learning objective table (Table 12.1 described earlier) to include the assessment methods and identify the approach to parsing and segmenting the student input. The types of practice tasks can range from simple exact match of answers (such as multiple-choice questions) to complex recall of text in paragraphs. The updated table should include the correct answers where there can be an exact match. For the complex text passages, the system requires additional parsing of the responses, checking spelling, segmenting the responses, searching for key words, and matching against a more complex system such as the LSI. LSI is a text matching algorithm that allows designers to check similarities of texts for purposes of grading essays and natural language processing (Landauer, Laham, & Foltz, 2000).

ITSs Approach to Assessment

Since the ITSs program is designed to teach a reading comprehension strategy, our focus was articles—144 texts. Text was presented to students to read, and students wrote responses back to the system for their interaction tasks. The database entries for each practice task identified what type of task it was (simple exact match or full text strings). If the practice task was clicking on signaling words, then we matched it against the correct answer in the database.

For complex text strings (paragraphs), we parsed the response (using delimiters like blank spaces and periods). The words were checked against a spell checker, and modifications were made to the words. A recursive parse tree was created for all the passages by the lesson designer. The more important words in the passage—signaling words, details, and the main idea of the passage—were coded into this parse tree. The system traversed the parse tree to match the words in the student responses. It scored the students' responses based on whether there was a match or not.

If a word was not found in the parse tree, we searched through a synonym checker that was custom made for the ITSs passages. This allowed for student responses to be different than the original passage but still be constrained the checking to the same meaning and context.

Finally, the entire text string was passed to a LSI engine to check if any previous responses were similar to this one. The LSI text space was loaded with all the responses from students in the previous study done by Meyer et al. (2002). Each response had an identifying code and a corresponding set of scores in the database. The scores were main idea, details, structure, and signaling words and had been manually created by trained scorers. If a student in the current ITS posted a response that matched 80% of an existing string in LSI, then we retrieved the response ID of the original passage and scores associated with that posting and used it as part of the assessment.

Finally, as each student response was scored these new student responses were added into the LSI text space. The scores were the best of the parse tree method as well as the LSI method.

Tools for Development of Assessment

Four tools were used in constructing the assessment scheme. First, a database was used to maintain the parse tree (key words) and that practice task IDs. We also used the database to maintain the scores for each response.

Second, we used the ApplePie parser initially to segment the student input. We then created a customized product to create the same functionality using a C# program.

Third, we included an open-source spell checker. The spell checker dictionary was updated with the words that were part of our text base. Since the spell checker gives recommendations for substitutions (like the spell checker on a word-processing program), we had to create a customized interface using C# to pick the most appropriate substitution for our text base. This required that the spell checker's recommendations for corrections be compared to our passage keywords as well as the synonym checker to make sure we substituted the most relevant word.

Finally, LSI can be obtained for development purposes from open source sites. We installed the version from Telecordia on a Sun Solaris 9 system with an interface to our .NET infrastructure. We connected the Sun machine to the Windows 2003 server directly and used sockets to transfer the information back and forth.

Applying ITS—Assessment in Advanced E-Learning Environments

The assessment scheme for any e-learning environment can make or break the system. Capturing the teachable moments during the student interaction is critical for ITSs. This means that teachers and designers must invest a great deal of time in documenting the types of data useful in finding those teachable moments and then figure out how to use them. This brings us back to the original steps conducted during the modeling exercises:

1. *Cognitive task analysis of tutor–tutee interactions (focusing on the teachable moments, documenting what was said, what the tutor asked the student, how the tutor adapted her tutoring for the response, and how the tutor figured out that the student was having a particular difficulty.* These are a sample of inquires that must be answered to create good assessment schemes.

2. *Identifying the types of responses that the student is providing.* In the college-level writing example presented earlier, the designer of the ITS would focus on how the tutor motivated different types of learners and during different stages of the learning process. An early simple error may be ignored, but a misunderstanding of what is required

in the planning requires critical intervention. As described earlier, the ITS may replay the expert model's planning process and then present an outline of how the student should plan writing again.

3. *Creating rules for when and how to invoke the appropriate responses.* The analysis of the tutor–tutee interaction can be the source of the programmed rules. Basically, the system will use a series of if–then rules. For example,

> IF *student answer* to PlanQuestion < 5
>
> THEN *replay* ModelPlanVideo

4. *Coding the rules into a database* (this can be done within the programs or using a database; ITSS uses a database driven rules engine).

The sources for the assessment scheme can be video- and/or audiotaped tutoring sessions or segments of lectures where professors are working directly with students on problem solving. Professors can also create grading schemes and highlight important concepts and processes for the practice task. The ideal response(s) to the question should also be created in consultation with the professor. Finally, the data collected must include information on where students have difficulties and how the tutor should respond in those conditions. Since there will be a larger volume of information on these difficulties, special emphasis should be placed on collecting and coding them carefully.

Challenges and Solutions in Assessment

As stated earlier, assessment can make or break the system's success. There are four challenges in implementing good assessment.

First, identifying all the possible responses that students may give is a daunting task. The system's intelligence comes from its ability to learn from each interaction and adapt to the learner. The designers should create many sample situations using task analysis, interviews, and observations of students. Then the system should have the ability to use all previous interaction histories to adapt to new situations. In higher education settings, there are more sources of tutor–tutee interactions available. For example, graduate students conducting tutorial sessions can be a source for retrieving such dialogue.

Second, the student responses, especially for text information, can vary based on the spelling, meaning, and context. Natural language processing systems continue to advance with the introduction of many tools that parse, segment, match, and relate words and their usage. Designers should keep updating their systems with the addition of these types of tools. Creating a system using a distributed architecture allows designers the flexibility of adding additional modules as they become available. In undergraduate and graduate settings, students may write advanced texts and the systems need to accommodate that higher level of writing.

Third, ideally, assessment should include multiple probes (data sources about the student's performance such as the time it took to respond, classroom situation, previous history on tasks, current task performance, and correctness of response) and multiple assessments (such as the parse tree and LSI combined approach). These are very complex to implement and designers have to weigh the pros and cons of using each method and whether the data can actually be collected. For example, in a real tutoring environment, the tutor will observe that the student appears tired or sleepy; in a computer-tutoring environment, such affective information cannot be collected easily. The solution to this challenge would be to collect as much information as possible that can be useful in invoking the assessment rules.

Task 4: Feedback

The final task of the 4M model is feedback. The feedback presented to the student can motivate, encourage, pump for more information, support, scaffold, and acknowledge the student's work. Similar to the first three tasks, interviews with expert tutors and professors can provide details about the types of feedback given to the students. Observations of tutor–tutee interactions and student performance can provide information about the student responses to the feedback.

Feedback can be direct or indirect. Direct feedback is a tutor telling the student what to do or saying "great work." Indirect feedback in the computer environment can be multimedia responses like a chime to tell students that they did well.

ITSs Approach to Feedback

Our approach was to create specific feedback in each lesson storyboard. As a result, each practice task had feedback that was generated by the expert tutors. There were also general feedback messages such as "Super Job" for students who had completed the task with a score of 80% or better on the first try. These were the direct feedback examples.

The book interface designed for ITSs provided three indirect feedback methods. The first was the tabs of the book (one for each of the five text structures) that filled incrementally with color as the student completed each lesson about a particular structure. Also, there were fireworks when the student completed the lesson successfully and moved on to the next lesson. This provided a gauge for students to see their progress on the lessons.

The second indirect feedback method was the pop-up windows that provided hints about missing words or important words.

Finally, the system always had a welcome message with the student's name appearing in the book. This made the system appear customized for the student. This was a motivational component that made the students feel comfortable in using the system. When the students made good progress on the lessons, "Intelligent" preceded their names (i.e., "Intelligent Jamie"), making their names similar to I.T.'s name–Intelligent Tutor. This encouraged students to keep working hard and was another indirect feedback method.

Tools for Development of Feedback

The tools we used include Flash, the database, and prerecorded animations. As described earlier, all animations and responses were created using TrueSpace and Flash movies. The database stored the responses and the conditions under which the rules were invoked.

Applying ITS—Feedback in Advanced E-Learning Environments

Feedback in any learning environment serves as a motivational, tracking, encouraging, and helpful tool. In e-learning environments, the feedback has a large role to play since there is little synchronous interaction between the professor and student.

The sources for the feedback can be video- and/or audiotaped tutoring sessions, interviews with professors and students, and artifacts reviewed from previous courses. A focus when collecting and analyzing these data should be the teachable moments, the types of questions that tutors ask, the types of responses that students give, and how the tutor adapts to the student's performance.

Once the data have been collected a set of rules must be created on where and when to invoke the rules. This requires the design and collection of multiple probes during the practice tasks. For example, if one wants to know whether students are happy, then one can ask the question before they do their practice task. If one wants to know if students are confused, one can add a set of categories that students can click on after completing the task. This probe can ask how they felt about their response. These additional probes provide more information about how students feel that can be used to provide tailored feedback to the students.

One student in the ITSs program said that he would like I.T. (the intelligent tutor) to help him with other homework problems. This student also said that he would have enjoyed "talking" to I.T. about other topics. These types of interactions can be built into the system to collect information that can help in improving the feedback to the student.

Challenges and Solutions in Feedback

The first challenge in providing good feedback is collecting the source data from tutor–tutee dialogue or interviews with expert tutors, professors, and students.

The second challenge is collecting data from the student interaction with the system that provides insight into what the student is feeling and thinking. This is very difficult to accomplish and technologies such as heart rate monitoring are not feasible to include at this time. A currently feasible solution can be to ask students to provide the response and then click on a task bar to report how they feel about the response.

The third challenge is customizing the feedback for the learner's needs. Once the student has submitted a response and the system has assessed the performance, the rules engine should find the most appropriate feedback for that student. This is also a complex process. Designers must start with the simplest rules and adapt the system as more data are collected over time.

The fourth challenge is providing indirect feedback such as the multimedia examples described earlier. Careful thought into the age of the learners and the types of practice tasks they are performing, blended with the available multimedia options, can provide motivational tools. A smiley face icon presented to students when their answer is correct can be highly effective in motivating learners and giving them indirect feedback that the tutor is happy with their performance.

In summary, our approach has many important facets applicable to developing high-quality ITSs. The following are highlights of the facets that are critical to the success of the projects:

1. Model the problem-solving task to help learners see how to solve the problem.

2. Narrate information and animate agents that can engage students, reduce cognitive load, and not overload any one sensory channel.

3. Engage learners by using choice of tasks, realistic problems, and activities.

4. Scaffold the development of good problem schemata by using hints, varieties of tasks, and appropriate feedback.

5. Minimize the use of unrelated graphics, animations, and activities so that learners may focus on the learning environment.

6. Assess student performance using multiple constructs.

7. Provide constructive feedback based on expert tutor–tutee interactions.

8. Encourage metacognitive skill development by using practice tasks with modeling and scaffolds to guide students.

9. Guide the students in managing their learning, especially on reading and comprehending information in hypertext environments.

Conclusion

By using the research reviewed, the 4M model, and applications presented above, intelligent tutoring technologies can be introduced to a wide variety of e-learning environments. The focus of designers and professors should be on modeling, practice, assessment, and feedback. Each task should be influenced by the existing research on multimedia, metacognition, memory, and motivation.

The ITSs development and research are funded by the U.S. Department of Education, Institute of Education Sciences, and the Claude Worthington Benedum Foundation of Pittsburgh, Pennsylvania.

More information on the ITSs project is available at http://itss.br .psu.edu.

References

Alexander, P. A., & Jetton, T. L. (2000). Learning from text: A multidimensional and developmental perspective. In M. L. Kamil, P. B. Mosenthal, P. D. Pearson, & R. Barr (Eds.), *Handbook of reading research* (Vol. 3, pp. 285–310). Mahwah, NJ: Lawrence Erlbaum.

Anderson, J. R., Corbett, A. T., Koedinger, K. R., & Pelletier, R. (1995). Cognitive tutors: Lessons learned. *The Journal of the Learning Sciences, 4*(2), 167–207.

Azevedo, R. (2002). Beyond intelligent tutoring systems: Using computers as metacognitive tools to enhance learning? *Instructional Science, 30,* 31–45.

Baylor, A. (2001a, August). Cognitive requirements for agent-based learning environments. In T. Okamoto, R. Hartley, Kinshuk, & J. Klus (Eds.), *Proceedings of the IEEE International Conference on Advanced Learning Technologies: Issues, Achievements, and Challenges* (pp. 462–464). Washington, DC: IEEE Computer Society.

Baylor, A. (2001b, October). *Effects of MIMICing instructional theory with MIMIC.* Presentation at the AECT International Conference, Atlanta, GA.

Bradford, P., Porciello, M., Balkon, N., & Backus, D. (2006). Blackboard learning system: The be all and end all in educational instruction? *Journal of Educational Technology Systems, 35*(3), 301–314.

Brown, M. (2007). Mashing up the once and future CMS. *EDUCAUSE Review, 42*(2), 8–9.

Cohen, P. A., Kulik, J. A., & Kulik, C. C. (1982). Education outcomes of tutoring: A meta-analysis of findings. *American Educational Research Journal, 19,* 237–248.

Craig, S. D., Gholson, B., & Driscoll, D. M. (2002). Animated pedagogical agents in multimedia educational environments: Effects of agent properties, picture features, and redundancy. *Journal of Educational Psychology, 94*(2), 428–434.

Gick, M. L. (1986). Problem solving strategies. *Educational Psychologist: Learning strategies* [Special issue], *21*(1–2), 99–120.

Graesser, A. C., Person, N. K., & Magliano, J. P. (1995). Collaborative dialogue patterns in naturalistic one-to-one tutoring. *Applied Cognitive Psychology, 9,* 1–28.

Graesser, A., Wiemer-Hastings, P., Wiemer-Hastings, K., Harter, D., Person, N., & The Tutoring Research Group. (1999). Using latent semantic analysis to evaluate the contributions of students in AutoTutor. *Interactive Learning Environments, 8,* 129–148.

Harp, S. F., & Mayer, R. E. (1998). How seductive details do their damage: A theory of cognitive interest in science learning. *Journal of Educational Psychology, 90*(3), 414–435.

Heffernan, N. T. (2001). Intelligent tutoring systems have forgotten the tutor: Adding a cognitive model of human tutors. *Carnegie Mellon University Research Paper, 179,* ill.

Jacobson, M. J., Maouri, C., Mishra, P., & Kolar, C. (1995). Learning with hypertext learning environments: Theory, design, and research. *Journal of Educational Multimedia and Hypermedia, 4*(4), 321–364.

Johnson, W. (2001, August). Animated pedagogical agents for education training and edutainment. In T. Okamoto, R. Hartley, Kinshuk, & J. Klus (Eds.), *Proceedings of the IEEE International Conference on Advanced Learning Technologies: Issues, Achievements, and Challenges* (p. 501). Washington, DC: IEEE Computer Society.

Koedinger, K. R., Aleven, V., & Heffernan, N. (2003). Toward a rapid development environment for Cognitive Tutors. In U. Hoppe, F. Verdejo, & J. Kay (Eds.), *Artificial intelligence in education: Shaping the future of learning through intelligent technologies, proceedings of AI-ED 2003* (pp. 455–457). Amsterdam: IOS Press.

Landauer, T. K., Laham, D., & Foltz, P. W. (2000). The intelligent essay assessor. *IEEE Intelligent Systems 15*(5), 27–31.

Link, K. E., Kreuz, R. J., Graesser, A. C., & The Tutoring Research Group. (2001). Factors that influence the perception of feedback delivered by a pedagogical agent. *International Journal of Speech Technology, 4,* 145–153.

Magliano, J. P., Todaro, S., Millis, K., Wiemer-Hastings, K., Kim, H. J., & McNamara, D. S. (2005). Changes in reading strategies as a function of reading training: A comparison of live and computerized training. *Journal of Educational Computing Research, 32*(2), 185–208.

Mayer, R. E. (2001). *Multimedia learning.* Cambridge, UK: Cambridge University Press.

Mayer, R. E., Dow, G. T., & Mayer, S. (2003). Multimedia learning in an interactive self-explaining environment: What works in the design of agent-based microworlds? *Journal of Educational Psychology, 95*(4), 806–813.

Mayer, R. E., & Moreno, R. (2003). Nine ways to reduce cognitive load in multimedia learning. *Educational Psychologist, 38,* 43–52.

McKeague, C. A. (1996). *Effects of hypertext structure and reading activity on novices' learning from text.* Unpublished doctoral dissertation, Pennsylvania State University.

McNamara, D. S., Levinstein, I. B., & Boonthum, C. (2004). iSTART: Interactive strategy trainer for active reading and thinking. *Behavioral Research Methods, Instruments, and Computers, 36,* 222–233.

Meyer, B. J. F., Middlemiss, W., Theodorou, E., S., Brezinski, K. L., McDougall, J., & Bartlett, B. J. (2002). Older adults tutoring fifth-grade children in the structure strategy via the Internet. *Journal of Educational Psychology, 94*(3), 486–519.

Meyer, B. J. F., & Poon, L. W. (2004). Effects of structure strategy training and signaling on recall of text. In R. B. Ruddell & N. J. Unrau (Eds.), *Theoretical models and processes of reading* (5th ed., pp. 810–851). Newark, DE: International Reading Association.

Meyer, B. J. F., & Wijekumar, K. (2007). A Web-based tutoring system for the structure strategy: Theoretical background, design, and findings. In D. S. McNamara (Ed.), *Reading comprehension strategies: Theories, interventions, and technologies* (pp. 347–375). Mahwah, NJ: Lawrence Erlbaum.

Moreno, R. (2001, August). Contributions to learning in an agent-based multimedia environment: A methods-media distinction. In T. Okamoto, R. Hartley, Kinshuk, & J. Klus (Eds.), *Proceedings of the IEEE International Conference on Advanced Learning Technologies: Issues, achievements, and challenges* (pp. 464–466). Washington, DC: IEEE Computer Society.

Moreno, R., & Mayer, R. E. (2007). Interactive multimodal learning environments: Special issue on interactive learning environments: Contemporary issues and trends. *Educational Psychology Review: Interactive learning environments: Contemporary issues and trends* [Special issue], *19*(3), 309–326.

Moreno, R., Mayer, R. E., Spires, H. A., & Lester, J. C. (2001). The case for social agency in computer-based teaching: Do students learn more deeply when they interact with animated pedagogical agents? *Cognition and Instruction, 19*(2), 177–213.

Salomon, G., Globerson, T., & Guterman, E. (1989). The computer as a zone of proximal development: Internalizing reading-related metacognitions from a reading partner. *Journal of Educational Psychology, 81*(4), 620–627.

Salomon, G., & Perkins, D. N. (1989). Rocky roads to transfer: Rethinking mechanisms for a neglected phenomenon. *Educational Psychologist, 24*(2), 113–142.

Song, K., Hu, X., Olney, A., & Graesser, A. C. (2004). A framework of synthesizing tutoring conversation capability with Web-based distance education courseware. *Computers & Education, 42*, 375–388.

Wijekumar, K. & Meyer, B. J. F. (2006). Design and pilot of a web-based intelligent tutoring system to improve reading comprehension in middle school students. *International Journal of Technology in Teaching and Learning, 2*(1), p 36–49.

Wijekumar, K., Meyer, B. J. F., Ferguson, L., & Wagoner, D. (2006). Technology affordnaces: The "real-story" in research with K-12 and undergraduate learners. *British Journal of Educational Technology: Technology Effects* [Special issue], *37*, 191–209.

Synthesizing Higher Education and Corporate Learning Strategies

Bruce LaRue

Stephanie Galindo

In fact, the acquisition and distribution of formal knowledge may come to occupy the place in the politics of the knowledge society which the acquisition and distribution of property and income have occupied in our politics over the two or three centuries that we have come to call the Age of Capitalism.

—Peter Drucker (1994a)

The conceptual foundations underpinning this chapter are based on doctoral research and consulting activities conducted by Bruce LaRue in consultation with diverse multinational organizations representing network technology, forest products, commercial airlines, wireless telecommunications, financial services, surgical products, chemical manufacturing, management consulting, and the U.S. Department of Defense. Although the organizations span various levels of technological complexity and their workers function at various levels of professional competence, each organization relies increasingly on the use of network technologies to conduct routine business affairs across cultural and national borders, and each faces similar challenges in addressing the need for increased skill and knowledge requirements of its dispersed workforce. Each is also facing heightened levels of competition and rapid change due in large measure to economic forces propelled by the burgeoning use of information and communication technologies, leading to what has become known as the knowledge economy.

This chapter also draws upon Stephanie Galindo's experience in higher education administration, curriculum management, and instructional design. Both authors have designed programming for midcareer graduate students from major global organizations who are conducting their studies through an online learning environment. These students seek to design models for managing vision and change in highly complex organizational contexts in international and multinational settings as diverse as Iceland, Mexico, Canada, and Qatar. Other students focus on themes such as integrity, loyalty, trust, and faith, leveraging their impact in the organizational environment.

We argue in this chapter that knowledge work[1] is predicated on a significantly heightened level of epistemological development and theoretical reasoning capacity wherein otherwise tacit systems of inference, inductive, and deductive schemata are made explicit as a basis of communication and coordinated action within and between knowledge-intensive organizational environments. This characterization of the geographically dispersed knowledge worker forms the basis for a model of networked learning that integrates selective aspects of higher education and corporate training with emerging forms of social networking technologies.

"According to U.S. News & World Report in 1994, knowledge workers in North America outnumber all other workers by a four-to-one margin" (Haag, Cummings, McCubbrey, Pinsonneault, & Donovan, 2006, p. 4). Given the progression of economic trends that promote outsourcing and automation of workers and work processes deemed peripheral to the core competence of contemporary organizations, it is likely the proportion of knowledge work, and the share of economic productivity this work contributes to society, will continue to rise (see Appendix A).

According to the Bureau of Labor Statistics (BLS, 2007), "The long-term shift from goods-producing to service-providing employment is expected to continue," and the high-flex networked firm appears to be a natural consequence of this shift from a manufacturing to a service economy. Unlike products, services cannot be stockpiled during an economic downturn; hence, firms are increasingly flexing their workforce. Information and communication technologies have, in turn, given rise to various forms of networked organizations characterized by highly flexible relationships among organizational subunits, among multiple core firms, and among these firms and their suppliers, contractors, and workers. Furthermore, advances in technology, together with an efficient global transportation infrastructure, have meant that these new flexible relationships increasingly occur with few constraints of space and time.

Revisiting the Role of the University

From the standpoint of the knowledge worker, contradictions are surfacing with alarming rapidity between the reality encountered in the college classroom and the reality encountered in the workplace. These contradictions are no more apparent than when the knowledge worker, motivated by wrenching changes in the workplace, makes the pilgrimage to the university for further education. Here it appears (perhaps deliberately) that little has changed for hundreds of years, and the harsh reality of the workplace that originally compelled their journey does not appear to be an imperative for the traditional university.

Public policy debates about crises in higher education have been framed largely in terms of the need for increased access. In fact, more than 2,500 higher education institutions in one study cited improved access as their top reason for offering online courses and programs (Allen & Seaman, 2007, p. 2). Yet, we argue that traditional pedagogical principles associated with the university may be ill suited to the learning needs of an increasingly sophisticated and mobile workforce. The integrated use of information and communication technologies has given rise to new organizational forms that appear unrecognizable from their predecessors. Handy (1996a, 1996b, 2000) referred to the basic structure of these new organizational hybrids as the "shamrock" firm, characterized by a small core of essential executives and workers surrounded by outside contractors and part-time help. The growth in the use of part-time adjunct faculty suggests a similar evolutionary process in higher education.

When discussing flexible workplace and learning models one must also consider that "today, over 35 million people in North America telecommute, and that figure is expected to grow by 20 percent over the next several years" (Haag et al., 2006, p. 7). One example of the need for a change might be the paradox of conflicting timelines, priorities of higher education, and modern knowledge work. At the university, research and development of solutions can take many years, yet "a healthy organization is one that is effective and efficient in the short and the long run" (Adizes, 2004, p. 42).

Although the rise of new for-profit higher education models may indicate that the traditional university model is not meeting the current challenge of continuous knowledge worker development, at the same time these for-profits may be, paradoxically, sacrificing critical intellectual contributions that are able to evolve from the traditional university system. It is important to recognize that "most institutions that plan to offer online education are now doing so," and "future growth in online enrollments will most likely come from those institutions that are currently the most engaged" (Allen & Seaman, 2007, p. 2).

According to the Sloan Consortium (Allen & Seaman, 2007), few new institutions are likely to emerge to fill the widening vacuum developing between traditional higher education and the demands of today's knowledge-intensive workplace.[2] Therefore, we argue that the quality and character of programming offered is likely to be where real evolution must take place. Programs will need to adequately balance the long- and short-term objectives of the workforce to blend academic rigor with workplace relevance.

Synthesizing Corporate and Higher Education Learning Strategies

The rise of the flexible network firm also has implications for the education of workers. According to the Business and Higher Education Forum (BHEF) position paper on *Public Accountability for Student Learning in Higher Education* (BHEF, 2004, p. 11), an increasing number of Americans will be going to college through 2015, boosting enrollment by 2.5 million students. The enrollment of older, working adults is expected to grow. Further, over 40% of the online student population is in graduate programming.[3]

The flexible firm also carries far-reaching implications for the manner in which we conceive of learning, education, and training. Whereas skills connote specific abilities that can be readily imparted to the individual in preparation for prespecified organizational needs and objectives, flexibility implies something quite different. Flexibility connotes the embodiment of a quality or characteristic rather than a specific, definable, even codifiable content of knowledge or ability. Formal education and training, although certainly important, may not be well suited to preparing workers for nonroutine, context-dependent occurrences that increasingly characterize today's rapidly changing work environment. The flexing corporate structure is likely to also impact the traditional communication hierarchy, as "need to know" may be redefined to facilitate strategic thinking at deeper levels within the organization, greater connectivity within the internal and external operating environment, and recognition of value added and the potential for bottom line repercussions throughout the operation (LaRue, Childs, & Larson, 2006).

As firms react to competitors from home and abroad and respond to local demographic changes internally caused by declining birthrates and retirement of the baby boom generation, the form that this advanced education should take remains in question. One of the four primary concerns stated by BHEF (2004) is the educational sector's ability to respond to the corporate need for sophisticated and skilled workers. It emphasized that "the economic and social vitality of our country depends upon the future success of our postsecondary educational system. Accomplishing this agenda will require not just preserving past successes, but also building new models for the future" (p. 1). It further stated that "a number of economic, demographic, and labor force trends are shaping this discussion, which will persist long after the political mood shifts. From these trends, a national agenda for higher education is emerging" (p. 1).

Yet, the different ideological assumptions rigorously defended by business and higher education are so profound that they have been described as a chasm to be spanned. According to the BHEF (2004), closing the degree attainment gap could add as much as $230 billion to the national wealth, but employers are looking for something more:

> A combination of skills and knowledge, including proficiency in leadership, teamwork, problem solving, analytical, critical thinking, communication, and writing skills. They want employees who have the skills to succeed in a global, multicultural environment. They also place a premium on colleagues who are proficient at multitasking and able to upgrade their skills continuously. (p. 10)

The BHEF discussion is focused on the outcomes of the baccalaureate degree rather than graduate-level curriculum, by identifying a need to develop strategic and critical thinking skills early in educational process. However, continuing and professional education is increasingly demanded by students and is a primary objective of the U.S. higher education institutions providing online offerings.[4]

Based on the need for increased quality and responsiveness of accelerated learning programs, it may be worthwhile for larger corporations to consider designing their own advance educational programming. One potential disadvantage to this approach is the lack of transferable university credentials. If university credentials are not required, the model we outline in the sections that follow will work equally well for in-house corporate training and development programs. With this thought in mind, we now return to the particular learning requirements of knowledge workers and the extent to which these requirements are being addressed through existing means.

Knowledge Work and the Professions in Historical Perspective

It appears that many of the qualities and characteristics that increasingly define educational processes for workers in today's high-flex organizations were previously the carefully guarded domain of a minority of elite specialists in craftsman's guilds and apprenticeship programs. These programs typically required years of study—and a combination of theory and practice to excel. It is perhaps no accident that the burgeoning new pro-fessional class shares one important characteristic with knowledge work-ers: the increasing amount of formal schooling combined with practical experience they require. We argue that it is the rising prominence of the knowledge worker that poses the greatest challenge to those institutions charged with preparing this new breed of professional for sustained social and economic engagement.

As Drucker (1994b) pointed out, for approximately the last 200 years in the West, to be an educated person meant that one shared a common stock of knowledge or what the Germans called *Allgemeine Bildung,* a term known later by the English and 19th-century Americans as the liberal arts. In the shadow of the hard sciences, this form of knowledge fell into severe disrepute, as both the German and the Anglo-American liberal arts had no utility or practical application whatsoever.

Since the time of ancient Greece, the question about what constitutes verifiable knowledge and truth has been at the heart of the Western philosophical tradition and has become the sole pursuit of the branch of philosophy known as epistemology. Plato's Socrates, more than 2,500 years ago, refused to refer to applicable knowledge as knowledge at all but instead referred to it as *techne,* or mere skill.

The modern reincarnation of the controversy over what constitutes verifiable truth (or, for our purposes, knowledge) is perhaps best portrayed in the classic debate between the Continental rationalists and the British empiricists represented by René Descartes and John Locke, respectively. Whereas rationalism holds that verifiable knowledge is arrived at through deduction from irreducible axioms, concepts, or laws, empiricism holds that knowledge is arrived at through induction based on sense perception.

The present discussion over legitimate forms of knowledge is most often referred to in terms of theory and practice. These two terms, which arguably should be hyphenated, instead appear as an irreconcilable dichotomy of two concepts that seem to be as far removed from one another as the ivory tower is from the shop floor. Reframing the classic debate about verifiable knowledge, the late Donald Schön (1983, 1987) saw profoundly negative consequences for professionals brought about by the hallowed distinctions between theory and practice. Professionals, he believed, are typically different from other workers in that they do not learn technical rules that are then unilaterally applied. Instead, they must learn to think like lawyers, architects, or doctors: Learning takes place under conditions of surprise, anomaly, and nonroutine circumstances that require heightened awareness, experimentation, and determination of the underlying nature of a problem. "The situations of practice are not problems to be solved, but problematic situations characterized by uncertainty, disorder, and indeterminacy" (Schön, 1983, p. 15). Such situations often require critical reflection and careful epistemological analysis of taken-for-granted assumptions and beliefs that may underlie one's approach to the problem.

This ability to think like a professional is very close to the qualities required of workers in today's high-flex workplace. However, the development of such qualities appears, in some important respects, incompatible with the preparation that one receives in the modern university.

> In the varied topography of professional practice, there is a high, hard ground overlooking a swamp. On the high ground, manageable problems lend themselves to solution through the application of research-based theory and technique. In the swampy lowland, messy, confusing problems defy technical solution. The irony of this situation is that the problems of the high ground tend to be relatively unimportant to individuals or society at large, however great their technical interest may be, while in the swamp lie the problems of greatest human concern. The practitioner must choose. Shall he remain on the high ground where he can solve relatively unimportant problems according to prevailing standards of rigor, or shall he descend to the swamp of important problems and non-rigorous inquiry? (Schön, 1987, p. 3)

Schön (1987) saw this dilemma of what he terms *rigor versus relevance* arising from two related sources: "first, the prevailing idea of rigorous academic knowledge, based on technical rationality, and second, awareness of indeterminate, swampy zones of practice that lie beyond its canons" (p. 3). Technical rationality, he held, has its origins in a positivist epistemology that finds its roots in the very foundations of the modern research university. According to this view, a practitioner is ideally an instrumental problem solver, trained in the application of particular techniques "derived from systematic, preferably scientific knowledge" (p. 4).

To further complicate this situation, as more and more workers reach retirement age, those with the ability to conceptualize and think strategically may be at a loss with regard to how to pass this type of insight on to their traditionally trained subordinates. According to the BLS (2007),

> Professional and related occupations are projected to be one of the two fastest growing major occupational groups, and are expected to add more jobs than any other major occupational group, about 5 million, by 2016. However, the majority of job openings are expected to come from more than 6 million replacements.

Research demonstrates that U.S. schools have been quick to embrace distance learning systems primarily as a means for increasing student access (Allen & Seaman, 2007, p. 2) to the otherwise traditional classroom. We posit that many schools and corporations may have embraced this increased access model of distance learning without testing and evaluating the epistemological and pedagogical underpinnings of the learning and knowledge transfer model embodied in this approach. According to the BHEF (2004, p. 22), "Too often, 'productivity' is seen as a way to cut costs, rather than a way to protect and improve quality."

Rather than focusing primarily on increasing access to higher education, we argue that we must also incorporate the need for improvisational, intellectual bootstrapping and strategic thinking in our workforce into our higher education model. Brown and Duguid (2002) also offered serious reservations about mainstreaming programs that focus on increasing numbers of students without preserving and expanding on the university's core competencies, especially those that will provide access to and full engagement in what they call *communities of practice*, or what Hamel (2007) referred to in the contemporary workplace as *communities of purpose*. Formulating a new middle ground on this age-old debate, we argue that the learning needs of knowledge workers can best be met today through integrating information and communication technologies in authentic learning scenarios tied to the core competencies of organizations and universities.

We agree that higher education, taken as an entire system, has certain core competencies that must be not only preserved but also expanded and improved on if today's knowledge worker is to be adequately served. Equally important are the development of effective feedback systems between the domains of higher education and the arenas of practice in which workers apply their knowledge. The model of networked learning explored in this chapter directly addresses these crucial and highly interdependent issues. Let us now examine the respective core competencies of both domains in closer detail.

To develop closer relationships between the university and modern organizations, we look at an important historical precedent—that is, although through one lens the university and the modern business organization may hold divergent ideological assumptions, a slightly different lens may reveal a highly complementary relationship enabled through modern technology.

Mumford, in *The City in History* (1961), described the university's original role in the development of society as an exalted form of the craftsman's guild, professional schools for the study of law, medicine, and theology. It was precisely its detachment from the standards of the market and politics that permitted the university to perform its important function. It may now be important for universities to reevaluate the balance of both areas of detachment and engagement. In the last century, universities have often been perceived as exercising their power in the political arena as gatekeepers for knowledge. This has given rise to questions of higher purpose and academic freedom, as well as the role of the university as a bastion of knowledge.

In the university, the pursuit of knowledge was elevated into an enduring structure which did not depend for its continuance upon any single group of priests, scholars, or texts. The system of knowledge was more important than the thing known. In the university, the functions of cultural storage, dissemination and interchange, and creative addition—perhaps the three most essential functions of the city—were adequately performed. The very independence of the university from the standards of the market and the city fostered the special sort of authority it exercised: the sanction of verifiable truth. Too often, the major contributions to knowledge, from Newton to Einstein, from Gilbert to Faraday, have been made outside the university's walls. Nevertheless, the enlargement and transmission of the intellectual heritage would have been inconceivable, on the scale actually achieved since the thirteenth century, without the agency of the university. (Mumford, 1961, pp. 275–276)

We build here on Mumford's (1961) description of the university as an institution founded for the "enlargement and transmission of the intellectual heritage" to manage "the functions of cultural storage, dissemination, interchange, and creative addition." However, we challenge the role of the university as the sole means of sanctioning verifiable truth in that this function must also be seen in light of the need for knowledge that can be applied in practice to improve the effectiveness of the modern workplace and to provide continuous development of knowledge workers.

Looking at theory and practice in simplified terms, the former has generally been viewed (often disparagingly) as the domain of academia, whereas the "swampy zones of practice" are the realm of the professions. Perhaps the problem lies in inadequate feedback loops that would allow the function of "enlargement and transmission," "dissemination and interchange, and creative addition" to more adequately and immediately inform the realms of practice and vice versa (Eastman & Mallach, 1998).

In addition, viewing modern organizations as an important social variant of complex adaptive systems (Middleton-Kelley, 2003; Stacey, 2007) indicates a growing sophistication of interaction between organizations and their environments. This leads to the need for "enabling infrastructures," "the socio-cultural and technical conditions that facilitate the emergence of new ways of organizing, allowing the new patterns of relationships and ways of working to emerge" (Middleton-Kelley, 2003, p. 14).

Brown and Duguid (1995, 2002) held that the university must be viewed as a system that is also evolving due to a changing environment. They felt that core competencies arise from the unique relationship that universities create among pedagogy, credentials, and communities of practice and that the core must be recognized and preserved as part of any system reform effort. To preserve these core competencies while also expanding access to the university for nontraditional students, they espouse a system called open learning. This system includes the development of social, institutional, and technological arrangements in support of the following key criteria: access to authentic communities of learning, interpretation, exploration, and knowledge creation; resources to help them work with both distant and local communities; and widely accepted representations for learning and work (2002, p. 232).

A central theme in Brown and Duguid's (1995, 2002) conception of open learning is the university's responsibility for knowledge generation, conferring of credentials, and engagement in communities of practice to be extended to the distant arenas in which learning takes place. For Brown and Duguid, the central competency of the university is the community of practice. Students learn "what it takes to join a particular community. In so doing, they may progress from learning 'about' to learning 'to be,' from, that is, learning about a group of different communities toward learning to be a member of one" (2002, p. 220).

Without full engagement in communities of practice, a phenomenon not unlike traditional apprenticeships, Brown and Duguid (2002) maintain that knowledge generation and credentials are rendered dubious at best. With this in mind, they hold suspect any reformulation of the university based solely on more efficient means of delivery. This includes many conceptions of distance learning to the degree that these preclude the development of, and active engagement in, authentic communities of practice.

Universities that attempt to create a community of practice often ask students to engage in their own workplace or to develop personal access to another professional environment for experimentation or research purposes. We argue that while it is appropriate to expect students to conceptualize and conduct research, it may be inappropriate at times to expect them to experiment using their own professional environment as a staging ground, essentially putting their jobs and personal network on the line as an academic burden. Either way, we feel that the university should take responsibility for developing authentic communities of practice that provide access to cutting edge thought, studies, experts, and activities in the field. The student would be provided with opportunities to develop expert relationships through the university resources and would be encouraged to build upon that knowledge by developing applications that may be appropriate for the professional environment, whether action is taken in that particular context or not. This connectivity would engage the energetic fellowship currently emerging from Web-based social networks. Applications would be grounded in, and verified, by supporting research. This would facilitate the development of both theory and practice, supporting the university's core competencies on one hand, and providing an opportunity for the application of informed professionally based studies where ever viable.

In modern corporate and military settings (LaRue & Ivany, 2005), the expectation to impact the immediate professional environment is paramount and has the effect of developing action leaders and action learning teams (ALTs) able to assess, develop, apply, and refine plans within the action context:

> Action-learning teams are charged with developing specialized capabilities to close process gaps or generate new capacity. [They] tend to be cross-functional and cross-organizational, drawing together individuals with specialized knowledge to collaborate on the development and application of new forms of knowledge. The ALT process is designed to enhance current leadership development initiatives. The knowledge workers and executives who remain in the core of today's firms require significant development to keep up with the increasing pace of change, heightened competition from emerging economies, technological complexity, succession planning, and shifting demographics. (LaRue, 2006)[5]

In the following section, we outline a model that attempts to integrate the core competencies of the university with the swampy zones of practice where workers apply their knowledge.

The 4-Plex Model of Networked Learning

Although the following model finds its theoretical basis in the preceding arguments, the model also emerged as a result of the our work with graduate students performing their studies in a networked learning environment and applying their knowledge in a wide variety of public and private sector organizations and in national contexts. In addition, while not operating under the auspices of a university system, we have also used these principles in executive and organization development initiatives in a variety of settings. The major objectives of the 4-plex model of networked learning are as follows:

1. Provide the infrastructure for an expanded community of practice with authentic engagement that transcends boundaries of distance, particular organizations and rigid disciplinary domains.

2. Offer ready and timely access to an arena for systematic theoretical inquiry and discourse based on the mechanisms of cultural storage, dissemination, interchange, and creative addition.

3. Provide transferable credentials as well as a ready means for keeping these credentials current.

4. Carry out the preceding functions in a manner consistent with the geographic, time, and developmental demands of adult professionals-knowledge workers.

In the decade of work and thought following the original observations, and in the years following the publication of the first edition of this text, we can say that the model appears to be on solid ground. The following diagram (Figure 13.1) will illustrate the model graphically as an aid to understanding its functionality.

The four main components of this model—question, theory, validate, and reflection—are arranged in a circular matrix designed to indicate a nonlinear movement through each respective domain. The question and validate (or vertical) dimension of the diagram is intended to represent the practice domain, and the reflection and theory (or horizontal) dimension is intended to represent the academic domain. That these two domains are joined by a common axis indicates a unification of the two fields, and their distinct quadrants represent their relative autonomy and distinct character. This aspect of the model is intended to directly address the need for the relevance of academic study to the arenas where workers apply their knowledge. In reverse, one cannot sacrifice rigor lest relevance become suspect. The various dimensions of the model have the following distinct purpose and function:

Question and Validate Dimension: The Practice Domain

The vertical axis, or the swampy zones of practice wherein problematic situations are encountered, is where questions arise, as do processes for evaluating the effectiveness of potential solutions. This dimension is

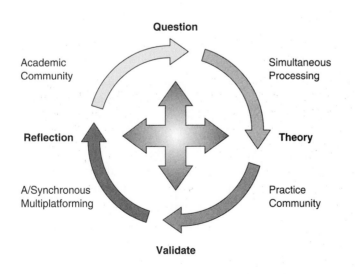

Figure 13.1   The 4-Plex Model of Networked Learning[6]

designed to provide grounding for theory and a basis for evaluating the relevance of learning through its direct application in the workplace. This axis provides authenticity and relevance.

Reflection and Theory: The Academic Dimension

The horizontal dimension offers an arena for informing questions derived in the practice domain with literature and academic research, potentially operable information that may provide foundational structure and sustainability to solutions. It is also a domain of abstracted or decontextualized thought and reflection that affords the chance to examine the problem from multiple critical perspectives, including prior studies in parallel fields. Reflection also refers to evaluation of outcomes, where intellectual and practical feedback is sought with academic rigor. Theory also refers to theoretical reasoning based on the development of cognitive and epistemological competencies required for knowledge work.

Simultaneous Processing

All domains are accessible from all other points in the matrix at all times. Each domain can be used separately or simultaneously in both distant and local arenas. Both academic and practice arenas can be engaged simultaneously through appropriate technologies so that problems encountered at work can be reflected on in the academic environment and vice versa. This dimension of the model is designed to tighten and strengthen feedback loops between academia and complex modern work environments.

A/Synchronous Multiplatforming

Work at any point (or among points) of the matrix can be accomplished by using any appropriate technological media in both synchronous and asynchronous modes. User-friendly media include various collaborative network platforms, phone, videoconferencing, and e-mail accessed wherever and whenever circumstances, time, and geographic proximity warrant. This dimension of the model is designed to address the need for greater mobility and flexibility in workforce learning through the leveraging of appropriate technologies.[7]

Academic Community

This dimension refers to ready access to academic resources and realms of intellectual capital, not only research libraries, networks, databases, journals, and books, but also individuals and groups with academic and practical expertise. These communities of scholars, practitioners, and researchers are engaged through college courses, degree programs, on and off campus activities and support services. This dimension of the model is designed to explicitly conceive of the university as an infrastructure for expanded communities of practice that extends beyond traditional practice arenas to encompass various academic disciplines, economic sectors, and social forums. It is expected that the academic community can be engaged by a variety of means, both on and off campus, locally and through virtual linkages. This aspect of the model is also intended to address the need for increased mobility and the flexible time constraints of knowledge workers.

Synthesizing Learning Strategies

The rapid pace and highly volatile character of organizational environments today do not lend themselves easily to reflection or to informing actions through relevant theory embodied in academic or professional research. The decentralized American educational system presents a similar context; its ability to connect with evolving realms of practice is limited to all but the most specific circumstances. The result is that many organizations and educational institutions inadvertently find themselves in the unenviable position of reinventing the wheel as they confront problematic issues that have been the subject of academic inquiry or practical integration elsewhere. Students and knowledge workers must each be able to obtain the skills for locating and judging the relevance of research as it applies to their particular situations. They must also become adept at making contributions to existing knowledge that reach a broader community.

Practice Community

The practice community refers to colleagues and team members within organizations and also includes professional networks outside of the organization, including those in academia. This dimension of the model is intended to address the workers' need for full engagement in professional networks as an integral component of their learning and developmental process. This dimension also addresses the need for learning accomplished outside the educational institution to be more relevant to the practice domain.[8]

Example of the 4-Plex Model in Action

The central organizing principle of the model assumes that network technologies are, first and foremost, enablers of simultaneous functioning within all domains represented in the matrix. For example, a student who is also a member of an organization identifies a complex problem (or question) in his or her organization and attempts to generate a solution through dialogue with colleagues (reflection and practice community) through use of a/synchronous multiplatforming. Assuming that solutions are not forthcoming, dialogue concerning the problem extends to the Internet discussion groups, outreach to experts, a conversation with peers, or a conference hosted by a professional association (professional networks[9]).

As a participant in a university program, the problem can be addressed with peers in a course related to the subject. The student draws from the expertise of faculty and student peers, as well as expert liaisons facilitated by the school (reflection and academic community), those who work in other industries and may have dealt with similar problems, or who, through the course of dialogue, may be able to help reframe the problem and identify actionable concepts.

The individual discovers a body of literature on the subject (theory) that can help him or her to understand the problem in a broader and more systemic context (theoretical reasoning) and studies in parallel fields that may have practical relevance. This process may, in turn, lead to a reframing of the problem as it is informed by relevant literature and further reflection with professional colleagues, academic experts and peers.

It is this action-learning context that can bring authenticity to learning, and bring learning to life with a balance of relevance and rigor in the learning forum (LaRue et al., 2006). "Action Research is used when the research is expected to be responsive to situation or when circumstances require flexibility and organizational change must take place quickly or holistically. Action Research is a powerful methodology for large-scale change and transformation along with knowledge creation" (Madhu, 2006, p. 179).

Defining what now appears to be a suitable solution, the student writes a proposal (submitted for credit in the academic community) that is informed by a broad array of resources and experts. The plan may be implemented on a pilot basis in the student's professional environment or evaluated through the community of practice facilitated by the university, and the next iteration of the cycle begins. One or several cycles might present a longitudinal study with suggestions for ongoing evolution.

Existing theory may be insufficient to describe the problematic phenomena, providing the student with an ideal opportunity to add to the body of literature on the subject through further research in cross-disciplinary literature, theory building (grounded theory), validation or data collection using qualitative or quantitative methods, and reflection informed by an expansive array of colleagues and peers.

A central point of this model is that learning, enabled by the use of appropriate technologies, is now capable of occurring in both local and distant arenas simultaneously, with virtually seamless feedback between the domains of academia and practice. Network technologies are not viewed as mechanisms of delivery; instead, they are viewed as more or less transparent tools for dialogue and outreach, participatory action, documentation, and research. The core competencies of academia and business are also preserved, by maintaining their respective autonomy while informing one another in a seamless flow of questioning, theorizing, validating, and reflecting, thereby reconceptualizing the relationship among theory, learning, and practice.

APPENDIX: HIGHER EDUCATION AND THE NEW PROFESSIONAL CLASS

Projected changes in the composition of the labor force during the decade from 2006 to 2016 were released in December 2007 by the BLS. This report provides evidence that attention must be paid to the continuing education and training of an active workforce, which includes higher education practitioners themselves.

The BLS (2007) estimated that the labor force will grow by 15.6 million jobs in the next decade, most of which will be in services rather than goods-producing industries. There will be an additional 12.6 to 12.8 million workers, representing a 10% increase, slightly less than the previous decades: 1996 to 2006 at 11% and 14% from 1986 to 1996.

Public and private educational services will add 1.4 million new jobs through 2016. "Rising student enrollments at all levels of education will create demand for educational services" (BLS, 2007).

- Employment in professional, scientific, and technical services will add 2.1 million new jobs by 2016.

- The professional and business services supersector of the labor industry will add over 4 million new jobs by 2016.

- Employment in the information and management sectors specifically are expected to add 482,000 jobs.

Together, these sectors account for close to half of the overall increase in jobs in the coming decade. Education will play an important role within key occupations:

- For 15 of the 30 fastest growing occupations, a bachelor's or higher degree is the most significant source of postsecondary education or training.

- On-the-job training and work experience are the most significant source of postsecondary education or training for 24 of the 30 occupations projected to have the most total job openings due to growth and net replacements. (BLS, 2007)

Employment and total job openings by category of postsecondary education are also cited. Twelve to 13 percent of occupations will continue to require a bachelor's degree for employment. Four percent will require the bachelor's degree and work experience, and almost 9% will require a master's, doctorate, or other first professional degree. About 52% of these occupations will also require moderate or short-term on the job training, and another 7% will require long-term training.

Synthesizing Learning Strategies

The average age of workers is also increasing according to the BLS (2007): "As the baby boomers continue to age, the 55 to 64 age group will increase by 30.3 % or 9.5 million persons, more than any other group." As previously discussed, different levels of training and education are likely to be required to replace expertise in industry, as compared to the expansion of traditional sectors.

> Professional and related occupations are projected to be one of the two fastest growing major occupational groups, and are expected to add more jobs than any other major occupational group, about 5 million, by 2016. However, the majority of job openings are expected to come from more than 6 million replacements. (BLS, 2007)

In sum, these statistics indicate that to obtain the jobs in the fastest-growing, highest-wage sectors of the economy during the coming decade, it is imperative that increasingly older, mid-career workers are provided with authentic multidimensional models for education and professional training.

Notes

1. The *knowledge worker*, a term coined by Peter Drucker in 1959, is an individual who works primarily with information or one who develops and uses knowledge in the workplace, such as individuals who create, research, develop, and invent in many contexts—throughout the arts and sciences, and particularly those in technology management. Technology is a term that has come to mean innovation and change or modification processes within an environment and the various forms of acquisition, integration, management, communication, and dissemination of information.

2. All U.S. higher education institutions in the United States were classified by the Sloan Consortium (Allen & Seaman, 2007) based on their adoption of, and strategic view of, online education. Fifty-three percent were identified as integrating online learning into their long term strategic plan. Five percent of schools see the value and may implement. Forty-one percent of the schools surveyed were categorized as not interested or not strategic. These results indicated to the authors that new institutions with online programming are unlikely to emerge. Therefore, those schools that currently offer online programming are the institutions

where overarching objectives will need to evolve to meet the needs of the workforce. The schools were divided into five categories:

Not Interested: These schools neither have nor are interested in offering online learning. They do not see it as part of their long-term strategy due to questions of legitimacy and value added. This category includes about 800 smaller institutions, or 18% of the total number of postsecondary degree granting institutions in the United States, handling about 5.5% of higher education enrollments.

Not Strategic: These schools offer some online programming but do not see it as an important part of their long-term strategy. This category includes about 1000 schools, or 23%, hosting 27% of enrollments.

Not Yet Engaged: A small group of institutions (5%) sees online learning as critical to long-term strategy but have not yet engaged due to perceived cost for development and delivery of programming, and other factors.

Engaged: This category includes about 800 (18%) institutions that currently have online offerings and believe they are critical to long-term strategy. However, they may not have included online learning in their formal strategic plan. These schools represent 23% of all enrollments.

Fully Engaged: About 1500 schools (35%) have fully integrated online learning into their formal long-term plan. Most offer online degree programs (69%) in addition to a variety of course offerings. They host 43% of all students in the United States, and 73% of all online students. Ninety-four percent of these schools believe that students will continue to demand online programming in increasing numbers.

3. "Online enrollments have continued to grow at rates far in excess of the total higher education student population, albeit at slower rates than for previous years" (Allen & Seamen, 2007, p. 1). About 40% of the online student population is in graduate programming, with 73% of online students at 35% of U.S. schools (Allen & Seaman, 2007, pp. 1, 7, 10).

4. According to The Sloan Consortium analysis (Allen & Seaman, 2007, p. 1), continuing and professional education is a primary objective of the institutions providing online offerings overall. A percentage of chief academic officers (67–72.7%) surveyed at higher education institutions in the United States agree that online graduate-level programming and enrollment will continue to rise (p. 12). At schools with a positive outlook toward this type of programming (58% of all degree-granting postsecondary schools in the United States), the overwhelming majority anticipate increased graduate programming online (84–85.7%) and increased student demand (86–93.5%).

5. For an example of action learning teams (ALTs) in practical scenarios, reference LaRue and Ivany (2005). Retired Major General Robert Ivany, former president of the U.S. Army War College, explored the application of action learning in national defense scenarios in this article and in the book, *Leading Organizations from the Inside Out* (LaRue et al., 2006).

6. Thanks to Charles Handy for his wheel of learning, the question, theory, test, and reflect elements of this model arranged in circular clockwise configuration (Handy, 1996a; 2000). We updated the model with the term *validation* rather than *testing* because we feel that a variety of learning processes may be engaged at this stage. The Kolb learning cycle, consisting of reflection, conceptualization, experimentation, and experience, also shares some resemblance to the 4-plex model. However, the integration of the four components of network technologies, academic and practice communities, the principle of simultaneous processing, and the

addition of nonlinear sequencing among the various components all are unique to the 4-plex model.

7. The learning environments considered in this study are based on intense dialogue among course participants and professors. Students were routinely required to analyze problematic organizational issues in light of relevant theory, and vice versa, as an integral part of their formal assignments. These assignments then became the subject of structured course dialogue and feedback, wherein participants would offer supportive yet critical evaluations of one another's assignments under the guidance and facilitation of faculty. The level of theoretical discourse resulted not only from discussion of specific organizational theories presented in course materials, but also from demands on students to explicate their otherwise tacit knowledge as a basis of their communicative competence (Chandon, 2000).

Theoretical discourse also emerged as a result of students challenging the premises and inferences underlying extant theory in their field of inquiry when such theory failed to provide sufficient explanatory capability. Such discourse based on an examination of the premises and systems of inference underlying theory represents a qualitative shift in the developmental level of students, for example, from Kegan's (1994) third- to fourth-order level of consciousness. This is also a fundamental component of what Zuboff (1988) refers to as "intellective skill" (p. 95).

8. As students engaged in theoretical discourse and dialogue around problematic organizational issues, they would then routinely apply their new and deepened understanding in their work contexts. Often, this would result in changes in these contexts, which in turn became the basis of further reflection within the course forum in a process of multiple iterations (Chandon, 2000). This entire process occurred more or less seamlessly as students engaged in both activities simultaneously through access to the course forum from work, from home, or while traveling abroad.

In comparison, interactive technologies used in K–12 classrooms, where hardware access is often limited, have developed curricula to inspire collaborative outreach with global knowledge centers and their experts, as well as various approaches to learning styles, with a level of reflection and conscientiousness that is not always emulated in mainstream university curriculum design or corporate learning environments. In the K–12 environment, instructor training strategies may focus on the creation of authentic student experiences to enhance learning outcomes (Shelly, Cashman, Gunter, & Gunter, 2004). Rather than only using case studies and simulations, there is, ideally, actual engagement in real-world activities through expert contacts facilitated by the school. K–12 classrooms seek to make use of technology as a creative means for bringing information to life, for creating connectivity rather than as a point of student access to data, or school access to increasing student numbers. This once again touches on the need for university reflection on parameters selected for engagement with (and detachment from) various environments impacting the university system.

9. The importance of this element of the model has already been given substantial attention in this chapter. Adult students engaged in professional endeavors increasingly desire knowledge that is relevant to their immediate professional endeavors. They also tend to make significant and routine use of formal and informal networks of colleagues both within and outside of their current organizations as an integral component of their learning process.

Within the networked learning environment examined here, students routinely commented on how invaluable the dialogue with their peers from industries all over the world has been in their learning process (see, e.g., Chandon, 2000, p. 172).

References

Adizes, I. (2004). *A new paradigm for management: The ideal executive: Why you cannot be one and what to do about it.* Santa Barbara, CA: Adizes Institute.

Allen, I. E., & Seaman, J. (2007, October). *Online nation: Five years of growth in online learning.* Needham, MA: The Sloan Consortium.

Brown, J. S., & Duguid, P. (1995). *Universities in the digital age.* Palo Alto, CA: Xerox Corporation. Retrieved January 30, 1998, from http://www.parc.xerox.com/ops/ members/brown/index.html

Brown, J. S., & Duguid, P. (2002). *The social life of information* (2nd ed.). Boston: Harvard Business School Press.

Bureau of Labor Statistics. (2007). *BLS releases new 2006–2016 employment projections.* Retrieved January 10, 2008, from http://www.bls.gov/news.release/ecopro.nr0.htm

Business and Higher Education Forum. (2004). *Public accountability for student learning in higher education: Issues and options.* Washington, DC: American Council on Education.

Chandon, W. (2000). *Virtual community praxis.* Unpublished doctoral dissertation, Fielding Graduate University.

Drucker, P. (1994a). The age of social transformation [Electronic version]. *The Atlantic Monthly, 274*(5), 53–80. Retrieved January 7, 2009, from http://www.theatlantic.com/politics/ecbig/soctrans.htm

Drucker, P. (1994b, May 4). *Knowledge work and knowledge society: The social transformations of this century.* The 1994 Edwin L. Godkin Lecture presented at the John F. Kennedy School of Government, Harvard University, Cambridge, MA. Retrieved January 7, 2009, from http://www.iop.harvard.edu/Multimedia-Center/All-Videos/Knowledge-Work-And-Knowledge-Society-The-Social-Transformations-Of-This-Century2

Eastman, D., & Mallach, E. (1998, May). *Four modes of organizational network usage: An information modality framework for organizational assessment and choice management.* Paper presented at the International Information Resources Management Association Conference, Boston.

Haag, S., Cummings, M., McCubbrey, D., Pinsonneault, A., & Donovan, R. (2006). The information age in which you live: Changing the face of business. In *Management information systems for the information age* (3rd Canadian ed.). Canada: McGraw-Hill Ryerson. Retrieved January 10, 2008, from http://highered.mcgrawhill.com/sites/dl/free/0070955697/361072/Haag3ceCh01_new.pdf

Hamel, G. (2007). *The future of management.* Boston: Harvard Business School Press.

Handy, C. (1996a). *Beyond certainty: The changing worlds of organizations.* Boston: Harvard Business School Press.

Handy, C. (1996b). The numbers. In P. Myers (Ed.), *Knowledge management and organizational design* (pp. 167–178). London: Butterworth-Heinemann.

Handy, C. (2000). *21 ideas for managers: Practical wisdom for managing your company and yourself.* San Francisco: Jossey-Bass.

Kegan, R. (1994). *In over our heads: The mental demands of modern life.* Cambridge, MA: Harvard University Press.

LaRue, B. (2006, October). Developing action leaders: Tie rewards to outcomes. *Executive Excellence,* 9.

LaRue, B., Childs, P., & Larson, K. (2006). *Leading organizations from the inside out: Unleashing the collaborative genius of action-learning teams.* Hoboken, NJ: Wiley.

LaRue, B., & Ivany, R. (2005, December). Transform your culture: Do it using action learning teams. *Executive Excellence,* pp. 2–3.

Madhu R. K. (2006). *Total quality management as a basis for organizational transformation of Indian railways—A study in action research.* Unpublished thesis, Southern Cross University.

Middleton-Kelley, E. (2003). *Ten principles of complexity & enabling infrastructures: Complex systems and evolutionary perspectives on organisations: The application of complexity theory to organisations.* London: Elsevier. Retrieved January 20, 2008, from http://www.psych.lse.ac.uk/complexity/Papers/Ch2final.pdf

Mumford, L. (1961). *The city in history: Its origins, its transformations, and its prospects.* New York: Harcourt Brace Jovanovich.

Schön, D. (1983). *The reflective practitioner.* New York: Basic Books.

Schön, D. (1987). *Educating the reflective practitioner: Toward a new design for teaching and learning in the professions.* San Francisco: Jossey-Bass.

Shelly, G., Cashman, T., Gunter, R., & Gunter, G. (2004). *Teachers discovering computers: Integrating technology in the classroom* (3rd ed.). Boston: Thomson Course Technology.

Stacey, R. D. (2007). *Strategic management and organisational dynamics: The challenge of complexity* (5th ed.). Harlow, UK: Prentice Hall.

Zuboff, S. (1988). *In the age of the smart machine: The future of work and power.* New York: Basic Books.

Chapter 14

Teaching Action Research at a Distance

Jenny Edwards

Sue Marquis Gordon

We have both found teaching action research (AR) through distributed methods to be one of the highlights of our teaching careers. Students have also reported that their learnings from our work with them have served to greatly advance them as scholar-practitioners. According to Taylor and Pettit (2007), "To lead effective action for social change, practitioners are challenged to learn new skills and competencies, to develop their capacities for critical reflection on action, and also to learn how to learn" (p. 232). These goals are all served by learning about and conducting AR.

In this chapter, we focus on the ways that different institutions have met the challenges of teaching AR at a distance by highlighting key programmatic components of distance learning courses recently studied. The examples vary in the technology used, length of the course or courses, the number and type of students involved, and in the emphasis on actually carrying out research. Because the details of courses for most of the examples are relatively sparse, at the end of the examples, we present a more explicit description of teaching AR based on our experiences at Fielding Graduate University. Before discussing the courses, however, we talk about what AR is and how it differs from other research, how teaching AR differs from teaching other types of research, how teaching AR at a distance differs from teaching other virtual courses, and three models for teaching AR at a distance. The chapter ends with recommendations for virtual AR instructors.

How AR Differs From Other Types of Research

According to Greenwood and Levin (1998), AR is "social research carried out by a team encompassing a professional action researcher and members of an organization or community seeking to improve their situation" (p. 4). Sankaran, Hase, Dick, and Davies (2007) suggested that rather than being "a set of techniques or an approach to doing rigorous and relevant research," AR "is a way of thinking; an attitude" (p. 295). They stated that AR is "real science. It involves being able to test, in real-time situations, the assumptions derived from the previous AR cycle" (Sankaran et al., 2007, p. 295). According to Sankaran et al.,

> AR seems . . . to approximate what we do as humans most days of our lives from cradle to grave. We experiment with the world, we gather information and experiment some more. We even pass our findings on to others and, if the receivers of this wisdom have any sense, they check it against their own reality. Learning is much deeper than a change in behavior. (p. 296)

No single definition of AR is repeatedly quoted; however, most definitions of AR include the involvement of practitioners, the solution of a practical problem that leads to the betterment of the individuals involved, collaboration, and research—systematic use of data gathering tools, procedures, and analysis. Reflection by the individual(s) undertaking the research, if not stated directly, is implied (Arhar, Holly, & Kasten, 2001; Glanz, 1998; Greenwood & Levin, 1998; Reason & Bradbury, 2001; Stringer, 1999). In contrast to traditional research methods, in order for AR to be successful, the researcher is required to actively engage in group interaction.[1] The quality of this engagement can dramatically influence all stages of the research, including the direction it takes, the methods used, the participation achieved, and the nature and distribution of the findings.

How Teaching AR Differs From Teaching Other Types of Research

Since AR differs from other types of research, it follows that instructors need to adopt different methods for teaching it. In addition to paying attention to group process, McNicoll (1999) identified five other issues that instructors face in teaching action-oriented research, as opposed to other research courses:

1. the need to adopt a new research perspective,

2. the tension between grading and modeling,

3. the realization that ethical considerations sometimes hide social control elements,

4. the limitation of the time frame, and

5. the tension between research and action. (p. 53)

Taylor and Pettit (2007), developers of the Master of Arts in Participation, Power and Social Change program at the University of Sussex that uses AR as a focus, posed additional questions that challenged those teaching AR:

> What skills, awareness, understandings and ways of working do such change agents need, and how can these be learned in ways that are dynamic, enduring and internalized? How can we help learners bridge the worlds of experience and theory, integrate their personal reflection with critical analysis and action, and draw from the strengths of diverse traditions of participatory learning? (p. 234)

For all these reasons, teaching AR is different from many other topics in that students not only need to learn the subject matter but also to acquire the skills necessary to collaboratively carry out research that results in change. This requirement makes the teaching of AR multifocused. Students need to learn and utilize content knowledge, research skills, and group interaction skills. Theoretically, it would be possible to teach any one of these foci independently; however, pedagogy and andragogy indicate that combining them is most productive in that students learn best when they are applying what they are learning (Dewey, 1916; Knowles, 1980). As Sankaran et al. (2007) confirmed, AR cannot be taught "in the same didactic way as other research methodologies . . . because while the theory of AR sounds simple, it takes some practice to do it well, given its complexity and applied nature. . . . AR is learnt not only through theory but by observing and interacting with others who are doing AR as well as through practice" (p. 303).

How Teaching AR at a Distance Differs From Teaching Other Courses at a Distance

The challenge of a multipronged approach to teaching AR is increased in a virtual learning environment where individuals do not have regular opportunities to interact. Instead of relying on regular classroom interactions where it is easy to share work and informal encounters and meetings on campus are a matter of course, opportunities for online or phone synchronous interaction must be scheduled to fit varied living and work schedules, as well as time zones. The time limitation issue for teaching AR mentioned above by McNicoll (1999) is increased because time for communication must be structured to heighten learning in relatively short periods of interaction.

Other complicating factors are the lack of eye contact and visible body language, which inhibit social presence (Tu & McIsaac, 2002). Feelings of isolation can hinder individuals' motivation to participate, inhibiting not only individual engagement but also the synergy of the group as a whole, which is needed to model and teach the collaboration required of AR. The technology can also be problematic: As Hudson (2002) epitomized in his chapter, "The Jungle Syndrome: Some Perils and Pleasures of Learning Without Walls," students often become lost in the technology of online courses. Consequently, special attention needs to be taken to provide the extensive support that students need so that the technology is facilitative rather than a hindrance.

Strategies for Teaching AR at a Distance

A number of strategies exist for teaching AR at a distance. Larreamendy-Joerns and Leinhardt (2006) suggested that there are three online models: "the presentational view, the performance-tutoring view, and the epistemic-engagement view" (p. 567). In the presentational view, instructors teach AR online by creating presentations on the topic to post on the Web. In the performance-tutoring view, instructors develop Web-based programs for tutoring students in conducting AR studies. Most of the examples that we found in the literature use the "epistemic-engagement view" (p. 567) in which students and faculty engage in discussion and dialogue about AR and their studies. In this model, students "are given opportunities for participatory practice and, as competencies develop, they seek and obtain supporting skills and concepts. Thus, from the very onset of learning, the learner engages in questioning, makes connections, draws inferences, and validates knowledge" (p. 590).

The models for teaching AR at a distance basically fall into three categories or some variation of them. In Model I, instructors teach students about how to conduct AR. Students read literature on AR and research methodology, write about it, and discuss it. This can be done through a combination of classroom and online contact, or it can be done completely online. Students can also design AR studies to conduct in the future in this model. Model II includes instruction in how to conduct AR and how to design studies. In addition, students conduct the AR studies that they design. In Model III, students learn about AR. Then they conduct AR studies as a group, with all of the members of the group working collaboratively on one AR study. We discuss these models below and present some of the courses that have been offered in each.

Model I: Group Collaboration Followed by Independent Study

This section includes two examples. In this model, students are able to learn about AR and perhaps even design a study. They do not conduct the study, however. This model can generally be completed in a semester or whatever length of time fits the schedule of the institution.

AR and Evaluation Online (AREOL)

Sankaran et al. (2007) wrote about a free, Web-based AR program called AR and Evaluation Online (AREOL), which is a service of Southern Cross University in Australia. Its Web site, http://www.scu.edu.au/schools/gcm/ar/areol/areolhome.html, offers 14 weeks of assignments. Students have a list of references, and participants can comment on the references as they are reading. Students can either go through the program week by week, or they can complete the course at their leisure. They may access the course free of charge or take it for credit. Participants are asked to share their experiences online. In addition, they are able to join e-mail lists of other students who share their interests, such as those who are new to AR, those who are practitioners, those who work in academic settings, those who are writing their dissertations, and those who are advising students on their dissertations.

Students in the course receive an introduction to the field of AR, learn about the importance of reflection and the importance of the participation of stakeholders, experience the importance of rigor, learn about the process, and discuss AR as a way to evaluate programs (Sankaran et al., 2007). Students complete three assignments. First, they compare AR with other ways of doing research. Next, they compare several AR methodologies with each other. Finally, they discuss strategies that they will use for designing an AR study and for gathering and analyzing the data. Students need to justify why their methods for collecting data are consistent with their goals. They also need to integrate both theory and practice. Consistent with AR methodology, the developers revise the course based on the course evaluations that the students complete.

AR Course at the University of Tennessee, Knoxville

Peters and Gray (2007) described an AR course that has been offered since 1996 in which students either met for 3 hours a week for 14 weeks during a semester, or they met for 5 weeks in the summer with 2 weekly meetings, each lasting 4 hours. Students engaged in discussion and dialogue, and faculty members provided occasional lectures. Students spent the bulk of their time preparing AR proposals. Half of the time was spent on reflection, and the other half of the time was spent on research methods.

In this model, the faculty members used a combination of face-to-face meetings and online methods (Peters & Gray, 2007). Students engaged in discussion during class time, and they posted responses on the Blackboard course management system. They also posted their reflections on what they experienced in class. Students' postings served as a springboard for further discussions. Although the faculty members began the course providing feedback, students moved toward providing feedback to their peers.

Students used the systematic cyclic planning model, DATA-DATA, that can be repeated as needed (Peters & Gray, 2007). In this eight-step model, students first used the DATA1 model, consisting of D = Describe, A = Analyze, T = Theorize, A = Act, to reflect on the situation. In the second part, or DATA2, also consisting of D = Design, A = Analyze, T = Theorize, and A = Act, they designed their study. According to Peters and Gray, the model is "a systematic approach to planning and conducting AR projects. Because the steps are cyclic, they can be repeated as many times as needed" (p. 321). Half of the students in the class posted material each class session. Then students who posted received feedback from other students about what they wrote. They then revised their work and reposted it for further critique until each student had posted a final research proposal.

Peters and Gray (2007) learned that students had difficulty switching from a traditional research paradigm to an AR paradigm. In addition, students were often reluctant to examine their frameworks. During the process of dialogue, students were able to clarify their thinking about the concern that they were addressing in the AR process. Students also had difficulty stepping out of their situation and describing the problem without judging it. As well, students tended to not see themselves as theorists. According to Peters and Gray, "Students consistently report that their course experience was enhanced by their interactions with peers . . . and attribute much of their success to this feature of the course" (p. 327). This is important because the authors also pointed out that a faculty member alone would not be able to successfully guide all of the students in developing a proposal for an AR study.

Model II: Students Learning About AR, Designing AR Studies, and Gathering and Analyzing Data

In Model II, students learn about AR, design AR studies, and conduct their studies. Faculty members are available to guide the students and answer questions. Students share their discoveries and learning with each other both online and on conference calls. They support each other, both intellectually and emotionally, throughout the process of conducting AR.

A benefit of using Model II is that students are able to conduct AR in their particular area of interest. They are able to gather data and work on their own in order to discover knowledge that is relevant and useful for them. Another benefit of using this model is that faculty can work individually with each student, as well as with the group as a whole. Also, students will be able to publish their own work under their own names. In addition, students who work in diverse organizations are able to conduct research that will benefit those with whom they work.

College of St. Scholastica in Duluth, Minnesota

At the College of St. Scholastica, Aune (2002) reported that students took three courses in AR at the end of their master's program. Approximately 45 students were enrolled in the AR courses at one time. In Introduction to Action Research, students learned about AR and its importance. Students wrote the initial problem statement, which needed to be approved for them to begin the proposal. After that, they wrote the proposal, including the literature review. When that had been approved, they wrote about the methodology that they were planning on using. In the second course, Conducting Action Research, they gathered their data, analyzed it, and wrote a draft of the findings. In the third course, students presented their findings to their colleagues in the program. In these courses, students worked individually with faculty by e-mail and phone. In addition, they used asynchronous online discussion groups to communicate with each other. Faculty provided feedback using redline editing in the Microsoft Word program.

While students were collecting their data, faculty members did not generally have contact with them (Aune, 2002). They requested that students send monthly reports telling them what they had done in collecting data, any challenges that they might have encountered, how they had solved those challenges, what they were planning to do before writing the draft of the findings, what types of assistance they needed, what types of assistance they had, and what questions they had.

When students communicated through an asynchronous online discussion group, they were able to share their successes, ask questions, and collaborate with each other (Aune, 2002). Although each student was conducting a different study, the students seemed to enjoy the sense of support that they gained from participating in the online discussions. A faculty member suggested that the collaboration and social contacts that students gained through participating in an online discussion group almost appeared to be more important than the knowledge that they were gaining. He observed that students sent e-mails to each other outside of the online discussion group and supported each other in their personal lives, as well as in their studies and AR projects.

Aune (2002) reported that students said that the project was the most memorable and best experience of their master's program. Students indicated that their relationship with the faculty members was vitally important in their ability to move forward in the program. They talked about the importance of faculty respecting their ideas, caring about them, and taking their needs into consideration. They valued being cared for as persons and wanted to be seen as people—as more than just their papers. In addition, they valued learning about inquiring, and they reported that their learning in this area helped them to become even better teachers. They were able to take the skills and processes that they had learned into their professional lives, for the benefit of students in years to come. They learned to reflect on their practice and intended to continue doing AR in their classrooms. In addition, students said that they shared their research findings with others at their schools, including principals, faculty, students, and school boards. As a result, others saw them as leaders and placed them in positions of leadership in their schools and districts.

AR in Rural Australia

Maxwell, Reid, McLoughlin, Clarke, and Nicholls (2001) described a yearlong online AR course for teachers in rural Australia that combined classroom and online work. During the first semester, students in their last year at the university met in classes and posted their reflections on what they read online. They also wrote responses to other students' postings. During their classes, they discussed what they posted. The focus of the first semester was on learning about the AR process. During the second semester, students conducted AR studies as they were completing their 10-week internships in rural schools. The authors emphasized the importance of the Internet for rural areas.

Students who participated in their AR study saw a benefit in reading online what other students wrote about what they read. The students also were grateful for the opportunity to read material and think about it, and they valued having the opportunity to learn about AR (Maxwell et al., 2001).

Model III: Students and Faculty Collaborating to Conduct an AR Study

Another strategy for teaching AR at a distance is for faculty to work collaboratively with students in conducting AR so that all of the members of the group are working together on one study. In the first example below, students work together. In the second example, both faculty and students collaborate in conducting an AR study. Some of the advantages of this model are that multiple people are sharing the responsibilities, they are learning to collaborate, and they are able to engage in dialogue throughout the process of conducting the study.

AR for Teachers in Rural Schools

Alexander (2003), a faculty member at the University of Idaho, was approached by teachers who were teaching in a rural school in Idaho to develop a course in AR that they could access through the Internet. During this 2-month long course, the instructor visited the teachers two thirds of the way through. He assigned their readings based on their expressed needs in order to provide them with a foundation of knowledge on which to build. Then he led them through identifying a topic, conducting a review of the literature, determining research methods to use, gathering data, analyzing the data, drawing conclusions, and writing a paper for publication. The teachers decided to work collaboratively on one topic.

Alexander (2003) found that as a result of completing the course, "the teachers [had] the tools and skills necessary to become agents of inquiry and change" (p. 323). He also noted that when teachers in a rural school were able to participate in a distance course on learning to conduct AR, "the interaction created by participation in the Internet course reduced the teacher's feelings of both personal and professional isolation and enhanced their ability to improve their practice despite geographic limitations" (p. 328). In addition, Alexander found that the instructor who conducted the course in AR, as well as the teachers who participated, gained new learnings.

Collaborative Interactive Group AR (CIGAR)

In Saurino and Saurino's (2003) study, elementary and secondary preservice teachers and two university faculty members worked together to collect and analyze data to improve their practice. The authors coined the acronym, CIGAR, to represent "collaborative interactive group action research" (p. 6). Saurino and Saurino depicted their approach in a figure with three concentric circles. AR was the outer circle, collaborative AR was the next circle toward the center, and collaborative interactive group AR was the bull's-eye.

Students and faculty met once a week for 10 weeks using video teleconferencing technology. When the group first came together, they decided on a research question for which they could all gather data as the students were doing their student teaching assignments. They gathered the data while they were teaching, and they discussed their CIGAR project during the last 20 to 30 minutes of their video teleconference. During this time, they asked questions, discussed problems, reflected, brainstormed, and sought to answer the research question that they had posed (Saurino & Saurino, 2003).

A major goal was for students to learn AR techniques that they could continue using. Another goal was for them to have the opportunity to discuss various aspects of their student teaching programs. First, the students gathered data about the existing situation with regard to the research question that they were asking (Saurino & Saurino, 2003). Then, they took action to change the situation. Finally, they gathered data on the changes, and they reflected on what they had done.

In course evaluations, students said that they felt distracted by the technology. Even so, they enjoyed hearing about what other student teachers were doing and interacting with them. Saurino and Saurino (2003) found that both students and faculty benefit from gaining knowledge and going through the process.

Outcomes of Courses

The authors of the examples of learning AR at a distance just presented found that students benefited from their experiences. Student knowledge of AR was not directly measured, although two authors indicated knowledge gains (Alexander, 2003; Saurino & Saurino, 2003). Statements of improved practice and esteem by colleagues (Aune, 2002) would indicate that virtual learners gained the knowledge and skills anticipated. Most of the authors commented that students found the student-to-student interaction especially valuable (Alexander, 2003; Aune, 2002; Peters & Gray, 2007; Saurino & Saurino, 2003). In the Educational Leadership and Change Program at Fielding Graduate University, we also have seen these outcomes from teaching AR in a virtual environment. In order to provide the reader with a deeper understanding of what goes into a virtual AR course and how the course materials and content can stimulate positive results, we next present one of our courses in some depth.

Fielding Graduate University

Our course started with a group collaborating in order to learn course content, with the participants, as a group, going through every chapter of Reason and Bradbury's (2006) *Handbook of Action Research: A Concise Paperback Edition* and then working independently on their own research interest. We chose this example of learning AR at a distance for several reasons. From the perspective of the students, the material in the handbook provided them with the content they needed to become acquainted with the broad parameters of AR and its history, to appreciate the breadth of AR applications, and to appreciate the variety of research and other skills required. Second, the division of the course enabled students to work together on material that was new and/or may have been difficult for them. At the same time, it enabled nontraditional students with a wide range of jobs to focus on research that was of concern to them professionally. Also, the course was structured so that in addition to learning traditional research skills such as interviewing and questionnaire design, students learned and practiced working collaboratively. The advantages for instructors who might want to use this model are that the course focuses on readily available texts and materials, the approach can be used in online formats with varying structures, and the model can be readily adapted to be more or less intense and/or could be divided into more than one course.

The goals of the course were three-pronged: content, research competencies, and interaction competencies. These goals, along with the students' anticipated knowledge and skills, follow.

Content objectives:

- To understand what AR is, its history, major issues, and relationship to research in general
- To identify research traditions, authors, and issues of importance to research generally, and to AR specifically
- To understand the principles of research design

Research competencies:

- To identify major research in one's field through reading original sources
- To critically review research articles and reports
- To conceive and plan action-oriented research
- To become skilled in one research approach
- To practice ethical principles of research

Interaction competencies:

- To be receptive to multiple perspectives
- To demonstrate respect for one's dialogue partners
- To participate in critical dialogue and discussion
- To participate in ongoing self-reflection

In the School of Educational Leadership at Fielding Graduate University, Action-Oriented Research is a graduate-level course worth 10 credits. The course is divided into three sections, including an overview, an in-depth study, and an application, each of which is considered to be a substantial undertaking. For the overview, the eight doctoral students worked as a group to understand AR by reading the *Handbook of Action Research: A Concise Paperback Edition* (Reason & Bradbury, 2006). In addition, students supplemented the handbook with a basic text in research methods of each person's choosing. The electronic tools that we used included e-mail, bulletin boards, threaded and nonthreaded discussions, and the posting and appending of documents. Part of the work was asynchronous. Students were expected to read every chapter, but two students were assigned to report on each chapter. Every 2 weeks, each student posted a summary of a chapter in sufficient detail that others could understand the authors' major theses, points of interest to the reader, comparisons to other chapters, and any questions they might have. Each student was required to make two additional postings in which he or she compared and/or contrasted what was in the chapter(s) with other students' postings and/or impressions of their own from all of the week's chapters.

Every 2 weeks, we met by phone for 2 hours, during which time we discussed the chapters assigned for the week and/or related questions that the instructor or group members had raised. Students were expected to be active, thoughtful participants in conference call discussions. Prior to the first conference call, all the participants had bought into the nature and format of the course and had started to introduce themselves to each other in a coffeehouse set-up in the class site on our electronic environment, called FELIX. We spent part of our first conference call confirming the nature and responsibilities called for in the group work, discussing the structure of the electronic environment, and covering how to post, online manners, and ethics. The assignment for the session was the introductory chapter of the handbook (Reason & Bradbury, 2006) and the chapter(s) of the students' methods texts that focused on the nature of scientific inquiry. Thus, we started off with a reading in common, as well as a reading of different authors. This set the tone for multiple perspectives around a shared scholarly topic.

To ensure that students developed the ability to critically review research literature for part of the in-depth portion of the course, each student chose two AR studies in his or her area of interest to critique for the group. In order to provide a framework for students to evaluate their studies, we read and discussed the American Education Research Association's publication *Standards for Reporting on Empirical Social Science Research* (available at www.aera.net).

In the third part of the course, the applied, students were expected to develop an AR study and design an instrument to gather data. Given the time constraints of gaining Institutional Review Board approval and most likely approval from their own organizations, carrying out a study was not a requirement. Rather, students were expected to go through several levels of pretesting so that their instrument would be available when they were ready to conduct their study.

A student's specific research goal determined the research skill development focus for the in-depth section, as each student was required to become an expert in designing and implementing the methodology selected for his or her project. For example, an individual who planned to conduct a survey had to learn best practices in how to construct, present, and implement a survey. Students were urged to select their studies early in the course, so they would have something of interest to them in the back of their minds as they read through the handbook (Reason & Bradbury, 2006). In our discussions, this hook appeared to make the reading more relevant, as students often referred to the project they were going to do when discussing an assigned chapter. Peters and Gray (2007) also suggested that instructors should ground students' learning in areas with which they are familiar. Students worked independently on their projects and gained the competency necessary to carry out the project. Some shared this work with the group, and in many cases, they discussed aspects of their work with individual classmates.

Participants

The eight group members included men and women with varied racial-ethnic backgrounds, ages, professions, and time zones. They came with varying levels of research expertise. Some of the members had worked together before, while others were new acquaintances.

Outcomes

Participation in the phone conversations was excellent, and the students consistently met their posting obligations. Although we listed the desired content, research, and collaboration objectives, because of the synergy the model created, examples of the students' accomplishments often fell across the criteria. This, nevertheless, demonstrated that students gained the information and skills targeted in all three categories.

The handbook (Reason & Bradbury, 2006) starts with what the authors call "Groundings," or theories and epistemologies that underlie AR. The next section, "Practices," includes different approaches to conducting AR. "Exemplars" is next, followed by "Skills." After the first session on some of the chapters from "Groundings," the students' struggle with the material made it clear that they needed to understand AR in a different way before they could absorb the opening chapters. McNicoll (1999) and Peters and Gray (2007) also found that students may need to have extra time to understand AR and the differences between it and other types of research. To accommodate this need, we changed the order of readings to focus on the examples of AR. An audible sigh of relief from the group led to an "ah ha" because with "Exemplars" under their belt, the students gained a sufficient understanding of applications in order to return to the conceptual material. Once that happened, the course took off, and students' reflections began to show engagement, as evidenced by the student who remarked, "I never really realized it, but I have been doing AR at some level for the past 20+ years" (G. Kurita, personal communication, March 2, 2007).

Students, paired to read each chapter, began to experiment with ways to post their writing summaries. Some of the strategies included posting two separate summaries, dividing the chapter, or sharing different perspectives. As one student reported, "We discussed how to present a summary and decided to each do our own. We ended up with two very different perspectives. I addressed my summary from a more reflective standpoint and he from a more political standpoint" (N. Zalas, personal communication, March 3, 2007).

Moller, Prestera, Harvey, Downs-Keller, and McCausland (2002) discussed the online facilitator's roles as a "guide, mentor, catalyst, coach, assessment-giver, and resource provider" (p. 56). The instructor fulfilled all of these roles at various points. One of the remarkable outcomes from this model, though, was how few sessions it took for the participants themselves to start filling many of these roles.

Members of the group established a productive, effective learning community by reaching outside of the parameters of the assignment to seek new information and greater understanding. Their suggestions added links to sources, which provided different perspectives about the projects discussed and basic background material to heighten their understanding of the chapters. One of the students wrote,

> As I began reading this chapter (on a study in Tanzania), I realized that there were some things I wanted/needed to review in order to assist me in understanding the setting and the importance of the work. Here are a few of the words, phrases, locations, and people at which I chose to take "a second look." All are mentioned in this chapter (study). (C. Holt, personal communication, May 6, 2007)

> With the supportive environment that the group created, students felt safe to raise and answer questions. An example is the interaction between a student who wanted to know whether AR was a method or approach. A colleague answered I have done quite a bit of reading about action research. One early observation was that trying to pin down a definition for it is not easy. I found some, to be sure, but many seemed vague and written in a way that would refrain from ruffling research feathers. I found the word "method" in about the same number of definitions as I found the word "approach." I have almost concluded that the use of either of the words depends on who is defining action research. It appears that those who are strong advocates of action research tend to use "method." Those "on the fence" or those who are critical of action research prefer to call it an "approach." (C. Holt, personal communication, February 27, 2007)

From these few examples, it may be seen that the virtual environment did not impede and, in fact, may have increased the students' understanding of AR and their group interaction skills. Not yet clear is how their research skills developed.

Originally, the group interaction was designed to stop when the chapters in the handbook (Reason & Bradbury, 2006) had been covered; however, at the students' request, the telephone meetings were extended in order to enable them to share their criticisms of the research articles and some of their independent work. Students posted their criticisms, often appending the articles themselves for others to read. To facilitate the group, one student volunteered to develop a reporting template that she crafted from the *Standards for Reporting on Empirical Social Science Research in AERA Publications* (http://aera.net/opportunities/?id=1850), which the instructor had sent to the group for discussion earlier. Her template facilitated methodological critique and cross-article comparisons. Because the group included individuals from the field of health care and from different levels of education, their choice of articles both increased participants' knowledge of research design and expanded their horizons with regard to the breadth of AR applications.

Discussion of students' research projects was also very informative. For example, one student presented a PowerPoint presentation that contained key information about survey development, which was especially appreciated by the students who were not focusing on surveys. This student then searched for Web sites that host online survey services and settled on one for reasons that she explained to the group. She proceeded to go through two pretests of her survey in which group members could participate. In addition, she creatively added a trailer survey to be answered by a special group of pretesters from whom she solicited detailed comments to improve her survey.

Because the students knew the investment that their colleagues had in their research, the group as a whole seemed interested in the instructor's online comments regarding everyone's instruments. In teaching situations with less student-to-student awareness, students typically do not seek to benefit from comments on each other's work.

Our online discussions ended with the advent of summer and diverse vacation plans. In addition, some students completed their individual assignments more rapidly than others. All of the students expressed a great desire to celebrate their work together at our annual conference. Other commitments kept one student away, but the camaraderie led to a festive dinner. Several months after the group work was over, one of the members e-mailed the others to say that she missed the group and asked how they were doing. That one student's response, "I am really suffering from 'AR Group KA Withdrawal'" (C. Holt, personal communication, September 8, 2007) is indicative of the bonds and synergy developed.

Was this model of learning AR at a distance successful in meeting its content, research, and interaction goals? Based on the work turned in, the instructor answered with a resounding "yes." While multiple factors may be responsible, it is likely that the opportunity to learn AR online helped students such as the one who stated at the beginning of the course, "Research is something that I have always been fascinated with but . . . have felt left out on the periphery for a number of reasons" (L. Saxxon, personal communication, February 14, 2007). Based on the following comments many months later, we leave it to the reader to decide whether this student provides evidence of meeting the course goals:

> In the Action Research KA, after many-a-week of going back and forth, I think we finally have a workable interview instrument that we can use for our African clients. My goodness, I found myself right smack in the middle of about eight people all offering input on the structure of the instrument. The poor consultant who initially started the process has been a perfect "Saint" and has shown a great deal of patience with the whole group. As a result, there is uniform buy-in on the part of all team members, and we have come as close as we are capable of in terms of having a decent model to share with other agencies who have similar interests. It has truly been like pulling teeth! (L. Saxxon, personal communication, January 6, 2008)

The student reported that the interview will be translated into four different languages and that the Department of Public Health would assist with the survey.

What Helped Make This Virtual Learning Experience Valuable?

Several aspects of the structure of the course helped make it a success. First, the expectations of the group aspect of the course were discussed and then spelled out in detail in a contract between the students and faculty, which all members of the group accepted. Second, before engaging in online interaction, we discussed both the technological aspects of FELIX and the rules of engagement so that when the intellectual discussion started, students could concentrate on content and not on technological issues. Expectations of online behavior were clear. One way we facilitated this was to create a virtual "coffeehouse" where informal discussion would be encouraged without taking the threaded discussion off track. The coffeehouse provided a good way for students to introduce themselves, as well as to practice using the learning platform prior to the first formal assignment.

Another helpful aspect of the structure was that the instructor asked the students which chapters of the handbook (Reason & Bradbury, 2006) were their first, second, and third preferences and, as far as possible, honored their requests. This meant that while much of the material was new to them, it was in an appealing context. At the same time, in making the assignments, the instructor strove to pair students so that each person worked with as many other students as possible. To develop their chapter postings, student pairs became telephone buddies. Their behind-the-scene conversations, which necessarily focused on content and on process, nevertheless provided time for individuals to get to know each other. These interactions enabled the students to become familiar with each other, which increased their comfort level in discussing academic issues in a group and encouraged an intimacy within the group as a whole. In turn, the members' loyalty to each other encouraged them to maintain time commitments and give priority to the coursework.

Recommendations for Teaching AR at a Distance

Teaching AR at a distance is a complex undertaking. The approaches in this chapter range from a self-paced free tutorial (Sankaran et al., 2007), to a required course in a graduate curriculum (Aune, 2002), to courses for rural teachers (Alexander, 2003; Maxwell et al., 2001). The instructors used a variety of technology, including video teleconferencing (Saurino & Saurino, 2003), Internet, e-mail, and conference calls. Some included face-to-face meetings, and others did not. In some courses, students conducted AR projects, while in other courses, they did not. With such varied circumstances, and little or no research comparing the components of different approaches to facilitate the development of AR competency, it is too early to specify best practices. Nevertheless, some evidence is beginning to build from the studies reviewed and from related readings that enable us to make recommendations for faculty who are planning to teach AR at a distance. The recommendations are grouped into the areas of planning the course, instructing students in processes, relating with students, instructing students in content, and managing the course.

Planning the Course

- Pay prime attention to the content, structure, and processes that will enhance interaction among course participants. Numerous authors have written about the academic and social-emotional benefits that classmates place on student-to-student interaction (e.g., Alexander, 2003; Aune, 2002).

- Ensure that the structure and technology of the course fit the participants. For example, if conference calls are used, smaller groups of students tend to work better than larger groups so that each person is able to express his or her ideas (Gordon, Edwards, & Hollie-Major, 2006). When too many people are on a conference call, some tend to dominate, and others tend not to speak up. Consider the number of students that an individual faculty member can support (Peters & Gray, 2007).

- Ensure that the guidelines for the AR course that are available online match the syllabus and other printed materials (Aune, 2002).

Sometimes, faculty may revise one set of guidelines and neglect to revise other guidelines. This is especially critical because students cannot ask questions of the faculty in class. It might be a long time before faculty and/or students discover the discrepancies.

- When planning the course, find the balance between providing structure for students and encouraging them to work in a self-directed manner (Taylor & Pettit, 2007). Also, find the balance between teaching content to students and providing them with the environment in which they can reflect, explore, and discover.

- Decide on strategies for providing students with feedback (Aune, 2002). When faculty members give feedback to students over the phone, they do not have a record of it. Faculty members in Aune's (2002) study used the Track Changes function in Microsoft Word to provide a written record of their comments.

- Realize that working in an online environment will require more time for students to complete their assignments, discuss procedures and content, and so one than working face-to-face (Gordon et al., 2006; Taylor & Pettit, 2007). Adjust the timeline for the project accordingly.

- Be aware that working collaboratively with students in conducting an AR project will greatly add to faculty workload, and plan accordingly (Gordon et al., 2006; Taylor & Pettit, 2007).

- If students are going to post items online and then respond to what other students post, set one deadline for students to post their items and another deadline for students to respond to the postings (Maxwell et al., 2001). That will allow the students who are responding to the postings to do a thoughtful job of reading and reflecting on the postings.

- Be aware that due to the nature of AR, a project could extend beyond a semester or quarter, requiring additional work on the part of faculty and students (Gordon et al., 2006).

- When working with educators, be aware of optimum times for them to collect data (Aune, 2002). Teachers generally prefer not to collect data at the beginning or end of the school year. The month of December is generally quite busy for teachers, as are the months in which they are testing students. Aune's (2002) students had other situations arise that delayed their ability to collect data. They encountered a flu epidemic, they needed to allow time for teachers to implement an innovation, and they needed to allow time for the intervention to impact student test scores.

- Be aware that you may need to provide students with fairly quick feedback if they need to begin their studies at a certain time during the school year (Aune, 2002).

Instructing Students in Processes

- Set clear guidelines for participating in the AR study so that when students decide to become involved, they will know what to expect.

- Thoroughly instruct students in the use of the online environment for participating in threaded discussions. McEwen (2002) observed that the quality of online communication was directly related to the quality of products that students produced.

- Teach students how to find literature in a distance environment that is credible (Aune, 2002). Since students may not have university libraries readily available, they need to know how to find online literature that they can trust.

- Provide students with models of papers that they can follow online (Aune, 2002). Since students are working on their own, they need to know what teachers consider to be acceptable papers.

Relating With Students

- Take time at the beginning of the project for students and faculty to form relationships with each other and learn about each other (Pauleen, 2003). Taylor and Pettit (2007) emphasized that "it is . . . important to recognize that learning has both an individual and a collective dimension" (p. 238). They continued, saying, "If we believe that people can take ownership of learning for intentional social change, and that reflection on experience is a vital component of learning, then it follows that sharing of experience should facilitate the generation of knowledge" (p. 239). Maxwell et al. (2001) reported that one sixth of the postings (out of 75 postings by six students) were about support from critical friends. The critical friends included teachers, interns, and the unit coordinator. Two thirds of the postings were made by interns, and one third were made by the unit coordinator.

- Position yourself as a colleague who is also learning, and realize that you will need to perform various roles. According to Peters and Gray (2007), "The teacher is also a learner and should position himself or herself as a co-learner with students as well as serve as facilitator, sometimes lecturer, and coach" (p. 327).

- Be helpful, attentive, available, flexible, and understanding of student needs. Aune (2002) found that student satisfaction and successful completion of the AR course were directly related to the extent to which faculty did these things.

- Provide encouraging feedback to students, and state feedback positively rather than negatively (Aune, 2002). Tell students the changes that you would like for them to make on their papers rather than emphasize what is wrong with their papers.

Instructing Students in Content

- Relate the content to student interests. According to Peters and Gray (2007), students "will benefit most if their learning experience is grounded in their own practices or other aspects of their lives" (p. 327).

- Realize that students may take longer to grasp the concept of AR than they do when learning other types of research (McNicoll, 1997; Sankaran et al., 2007).

Managing the Course

- When working with a larger group, students could first plan on meeting in smaller groups to perform tasks before coming together with the larger group (Gordon et al., 2006).

- Be prepared to demonstrate flexibility and a willingness to adjust timelines for the project, as other situations may interfere with the project (Aune, 2002; Burke & Cummins, 2002; Gordon et al., 2006). Be willing to adjust to the needs and schedules of the students (Aune, 2002; Sankaran et al., 2007). According to Aune, students generally choose to attend distance learning programs because they have many responsibilities and demands.

- Plan conference calls around the schedules of students, and realize that students may not always be able to meet deadlines (Aune, 2002).

- Ensure the smooth flow of communication among members of the AR team. Chen (2004) discovered that people participating online in teams did not have as clear an understanding of goals as members of teams participating face-to-face. As a result, it is even more important for faculty to ensure that all participants understand the goals, and that communication flows smoothly.

- Encourage students to be realistic when they are determining when to begin and end their studies (Aune, 2002).

- Develop a method to ensure that all students are reading the assignments and learning the material. In order to make sure that students were reading the textbook, a faculty member in Aune's (2002) study created questions related to the textbook and invited students to respond to the questions based on the research they were conducting. They also needed to post a reply to at least one other student's posting. Through this process, many students discovered commonalities in their interests and supported each other through the process.

Notes

1. First person AR, which focuses on individual practice reflection (Reason & Bradbury, 2006), may not require the collaboration to the same extent as second and third person AR; however, some collaboration is necessary, and it is useful for the growth of knowledge for reflective practitioners to know how to extend AR beyond themselves.

References

Alexander, G. C. (2003). Reaching out to rural schools: University-practitioner linkage through the Internet. *Journal of Technology and Teacher Education, 11*(2), 321–330.

Arhar, J. M., Holly, M. L., & Kasten, W. C. (2001). *Action research for teachers: Traveling the yellow brick road.* Upper Saddle River, NJ: Prentice Hall.

Aune, B. (2002). Teaching action research via distance. *Journal of Technology and Teacher Education, 10*(4), 461–79.

Burke, L. A., & Cummins, M. K. (2002). Using undergraduate student–faculty collaborative research projects to personalize teaching. *College Teaching, 50*(4), 129–133.

Chen, F. (2004). Using collaborative technology to facilitate face-to-face and sitributed team interactions. *Dissertation Abstracts International, 65*(09), 3455. (UMI No. AAT 3145052)

Dewey, J. (1916). *Democracy and education.* New York: Macmillan.

Glanz, J. (1998). *Action research: An educational leaders' guide to school improvement.* Norwood, MA: Christopher-Gordon.

Gordon, S. M., Edwards, J. L., & Hollie-Major, R. D. (2006). *Benefits and issues arising from a virtual collaborative student-alumni-faculty action research project.* Paper presented at the American Educational Research Association, San Francisco.

Greenwood, D. J., & Levin, M. (1998). *Introduction to action research: Social research for social change.* Thousand Oaks, CA: Sage.

Hudson, B. (2002). The jungle syndrome: Some perils and pleasures of learning without walls. In K. E. Rudestam & J. Schoenholtz-Read (Eds.), *Handbook of online learning* (pp. 185–220). Thousand Oaks, CA: Sage.

Knowles, M. A. (1980). *The modern practice of adult education from pedagogy to andragogy.* New York: Cambridge University Press.

Larreamendy-Joerns, J., & Leinhardt, G. (2006). Going the distance with online education. *Review of Educational Research, 76,* 567–605.

Maxwell, T. W., Reid, J., McLoughlin, C., Clarke, C., & Nicholls, R. (2001). *Online support for action research in a teacher education internship in rural Australia.* Paper presented at the annual conference of Providing Quality Education and Training for Rural Australians, SPERA National Conference Proceedings, Sagga Wagga, New South Wales, Australia.

McEwen, L. (2002). Exploring assessment of on-line collaboration in distance education: An action research study. *Dissertation Abstracts International, 40*(06), 1359. (UMI No. AAT MQ68364)

McNicoll, P. (1999). Issues in teaching participatory action research. *Journal of Social Work Education, 35*(1), 51–62.

Moller, L., Prestera, G., Harvey, D., Downs-Keller, M., & McCausland, J. (2002). Creating an organic knowledge-building environment within an asynchronous distributed learning context. *Quarterly Review of Distance Education, 3*(1), 47–58.

Pauleen, D. J. (2003). An inductively derived model of leader-initiated relationship building with virtual team members. *Journal of Management Information Systems, 20*(3), 22–256.

Peters, J. M., & Gray, A. (2007). Teaching and learning in a model-based action research course. *Action Research, 5*(3), 319–331.

Reason, P., & Bradbury, H. (Eds.). (2006). *The handbook of action research: Concise paperback edition.* London: Sage.

Sankaran, S., Hase, S., Dick, B., & Davies, A. (2007). Singing different tunes from the same song sheet: Four perspectives of teaching the doing of action research. *Action Research, 5*(3), 293–305.

Saurino, D. R., & Saurino, P. L. (2003, April). *Expanding the use of collaborative interactive group action research through distance technology.* Paper presented at the annual meeting of the American Educational Research Association, Chicago.

Stringer, E. T. (1999). *Action research* (2nd ed.). Thousand Oaks, CA: Sage.

Taylor, P., & Pettit, J. (2007). Learning and teaching participation through action research: Experiences from an innovative masters programme. *Action Research, 5*(3), 231–247.

Tu, C., & McIsaac, M. (2002). The relationship of social presence and interaction in online classes. *American Journal of Distance Education, 16*(3), 131–150.

Part II

Implementation of Online Learning

Section B. Faculty and Students

Beyond the Looking Glass

Chapter 15

What Faculty and Students Need to Be Successful Online

Rena M. Palloff

Keith Pratt

> *Oh, Kitty, how nice it would be if we could only get through into looking-glass house! I'm sure it's got, oh! such beautiful things in it! Let's pretend there's a way of getting through into it somehow, Kitty. Let's pretend the glass has got all soft like gauze, so that we can get through. Why, it's turning into a sort of mist now. I declare! It'll be easy enough to get through.*
>
> —Carroll, 1871, p. 181

Those in higher education are seeing the move to online distance education as both a blessing and a curse. Many administrators view it as a way to increase flagging enrollments and extend the reach of the institution, or in simple terms, as an easy way to maximize profits and attract new students. Many students view online courses as a more convenient way to go to school and even sometimes, mistakenly, as an easier way to earn credit. Faculty given the responsibility to develop and teach online courses, however, might not see online education in such a positive light.

There is a significant number of faculty who are sincerely interested in online education and its possibilities. Early enthusiasts explored alternative ways of teaching in this environment and became champions for this form of teaching and learning, encouraging others to join them in new and exciting ways of delivering courses. However, some faculty have been told that they must develop and teach online classes. They are being given no choice in the matter and are reluctantly entering the online environment. Many feel lost, not even sure where to begin. Others have heard that the key to success is content; simply migrate the content that has been taught in the face-to-face classroom into the online classroom and all will be well. Others learn how to use the software that is designed to teach the course and think that this is all they need to know to move successfully to the online environment. Yet, others simply set up a course and then virtually walk away, leaving students to fend for themselves with little guidance or direction.

The result of these false assumptions is the development of courses that are poorly conceived and lack interactivity, taught by faculty who are frustrated by their inability to get students involved. A likely outcome is low enrollment or attrition from online courses and programs. Unfortunately, faculty are rarely provided with training in the pedagogical skills they need to teach online. A 2002 survey of faculty who teach in various disciplines and are located throughout the United States yielded results that appear to be the norm of faculty experience, as 75% indicated that they had received approximately 30 hours of technical training in the course management system they would be using; however, only one third reported receiving any pedagogical training. A subset of surveyed faculty were interviewed and described the difficulties they were having engaging students in online discussion and their perceived need for pedagogical training (Pankowski, 2004). Given that White and Weight (2000) noted that teaching techniques that work in the face-to-face classroom may not work online and that faculty are asking for additional support for effective teaching, it is clear that pedagogical training is lacking. Milam, Voorhees, and Bedard-Voorhees (2004) noted that "The online paradigm holds that learning itself may be different in the online environment" (p. 74). Consequently, not only do faculty need training to be effective in the online delivery of courses and means by which to successful support students in their online learning efforts, students also need assistance in knowing how to effectively learn in an online classroom. Based on these statistics regarding training or the lack thereof, it is no wonder that research into retention in online courses shows upward of 50% dropout rates (Carr, 2000) and that many faculty view online learning as a poor and inferior stepchild of higher education. Akridge, DeMay, Braunlich, Collura, and Sheahan (2002) suggested that student retention online is dependent on three factors: selecting the right students for the right program, using a highly learner-focused delivery model, and engaging learners at a personal level. Hebert (2006) discovered that the responsiveness of faculty to perceived student needs helps to increase persistence in online courses and creates a greater degree of satisfaction with the learning process. This is an essential component of what it takes to teach online, and yet, if faculty are only receiving technical training before they embark on teaching their first online course, how would they know how to do this?

In this chapter, we do not intend to deliver a message of gloom and doom. We believe that if faculty are trained in pedagogical methods that lend themselves to the online environment and if students are effectively oriented to online work, then the result can be highly interactive courses that lead to successful achievement of learning objectives and a sense of satisfaction on the part of faculty and students alike. This chapter explores some of the ways in which faculty and student development can be accomplished to achieve these goals.

Working With Faculty to Develop a New Pedagogy

> In another moment, Alice was through the glass and had jumped lightly down into the looking-glass room. . . . Then she began looking about and noticed that what could be seen from the old room was quite common and uninteresting, but that all the rest was as different as possible. . . . "They don't keep this room so tidy as the other," Alice thought to herself. (Carroll, 1871, pp. 183–184)

Teaching online requires faculty to move beyond traditional models of teaching and to adopt what may be new practices that facilitate student learning. Some faculty resist this notion, however, thinking that it must be possible somehow to retain the lecture-discussion model of teaching in the online medium and the use of tests and quizzes for assessment of student performance. Unlike the face-to-face classroom, where such methods may be successful, in online distance education a lecture simply becomes another article that students need to read, and the use of online tests and quizzes increase concerns about cheating and plagiarism. Although the advent of streaming audio and video applications has made it possible for instructors to deliver lectures to students who have the technology to receive them, students, when asked where they derived the most benefit from an online class, have noted that they often bypassed online lecture material and went directly to the discussion board, where they were able to interact with the instructor and their peers about the subject matter (Feenberg, 1999; Palloff & Pratt, 2001, 2005, 2007). Thus, in online learning, attention needs to be paid to promoting interactivity and the development of a sense of community within the student group to achieve successful learning outcomes. Eom (2006) further noted that when students receive individual attention from instructors in an online course in the form of e-mail messages and feedback on work and assignments, their satisfaction with the course increases as does achievement of learning outcomes, again emphasizing that instructor presence is critical to the online learning process. Interaction between students and between instructor and student are the keys to success in the online classroom.

Even the most seasoned faculty in the face-to-face classroom, however, might not intuitively know how to build interactive courses online. The skills involved in delivering a course using interactive facilitative means—which we term *electronic pedagogy*—can be taught, but these skills are often overlooked when faculty are trained to teach online. Questions that need to be addressed as faculty learn about online teaching are as follows: What does it really mean to be a "guide on the side" or a "learning facilitator" rather than an instructor? How does an instructor successfully make the transition required to teach an online course so that students become empowered learners and take charge of the learning process? Is it possible to develop every instructor into a good online instructor? How can institutions discern the difference between those who will do well online and those who will not, be they faculty or students? Not all faculty are suited for the online environment, and academic institutions are making some serious mistakes when they make their decisions about who should teach. Choices about who should teach online are often based on faulty criteria; it is usually either someone who is considered a content expert or someone who is deemed entertaining in the face-to-face classroom who is chosen. Brookfield (1995) noted that often the most popular faculty, who get the best course evaluations, are the ones who are able to entertain. Being entertaining does not translate so well online, where one's personality is reduced to text on a screen. Focusing on faculty who are content experts may present a problem. Although they may know their subject matter well, they might not have, or might not have been taught, the facilitative skills required for online teaching.

Personality characteristics of successful online faculty may differ from those of successful classroom faculty. Research by one of the authors reveals that it is the introverted student who does particularly well online (Pratt, 1996). We believe that this finding generally applies to introverted instructors as well. In the online environment, facial and body language cues are removed from communication. The introvert, who can be inhibited by these cues in face-to-face communication, generally appears far more extroverted online and frequently becomes quite verbal and interactive. The ability to take time, reflect, and present himself or herself through text serves the introvert well. Self-consciousness diminishes when the instructor is out from under the physical scrutiny of students. On the other hand, the extrovert, who generally establishes presence quickly through verbal and social connection, may have more difficulty in the text-based online environment. Taking time to reflect is not the forte of the extrovert, who tends to process ideas out loud at the time they occur. The responses received help the extrovert to formulate and refine his or her ideas. Consequently, the asynchronous online environment, with its absence of immediate feedback, can be frustrating to the extrovert.

It is more comfortable for an introvert to spend time thinking about information before responding to it. It is more difficult—but not impossible—for extroverts to interact this way, perhaps because they have less need to.

Extroverts tend to feel more comfortable processing verbally and in the company of others (Palloff & Pratt, 2007, p. 29). Consequently, it can be assumed that the instructor who might not be an entertainer in the face-to-face classroom, yet who has subject matter expertise, is flexible, and is open to the development of a more collaborative way of teaching, may be the better candidate to develop and deliver online courses.

The ability to present oneself well in text, known as the creation of social presence, has been receiving significant research attention and is now considered a critical factor in community building in online classes. Both instructors and students need to be able to present themselves as real people in the online classroom. This ability is positively linked to student satisfaction with online learning as well as successful achievement of learning outcomes (Garrison, Anderson, & Archer, 2003; Gunawardena & Zittle, 1997; Picciano, 2002; Rovai & Barnum, 2003). Picciano (2002) asserted that "Students who feel they are part of a group or 'present' in a community will, in fact, wish to participate actively in group and community activities" (p. 24). Participation and interaction online equates with successful course outcome.

In addition to the ability to develop social presence, we have found that successful online instructors are willing to give up a fair degree of control in the teaching and learning process. They are able to empower their learners and build a learning community. In other words, they are learner-focused instructors. Huba and Freed (2000) noted that in a learner-centered paradigm, students construct knowledge by gathering and synthesizing information together by using inquiry, communication, critical thinking, and problem solving. The instructor's role is to facilitate the process and instructors and students together assess learning. An instructor who is willing to use collaborative, active learning techniques and ideas, and who allows for personal interaction, brings in real-life examples, and builds reflective practice into teaching, is a good candidate for teaching online. The open and flexible instructor needs support, however, to make the transition to the online classroom successful. This support rests in training and mentoring.

Training to Support the Transition

Faculty cannot be expected to know intuitively how to design and deliver an effective online course. Although courses and programs about the use of technology in education are emerging, and attendance at conferences on the topic continues to grow markedly, faculty have not been fully exposed to the techniques and methods needed to make online work successful. In fact, the study reported by Pankowski (2004) noted that only 56% of faculty who teach online have taken an online course themselves. Pankowski observed that "It is very difficult to teach in a medium in which one has never experienced learning" ("Faculty as Students," para. 1).

Current course management applications make it easy for faculty to simply transfer material to a course site. The lure to do this is complicated by the fact that institutions, which may view online distance learning as their lifesaver during times of on-campus declining enrollment, are now registering such large numbers of students in online classes that the burden on faculty is enormous. As a result, institutions are increasingly hiring faculty only as facilitators and leaving the responsibility for course development to a team that may or may not include the faculty member who will be teaching the course. Consequently, faculty may be asked to facilitate a course they did not develop and do so with a large group of students.

However, training faculty to help them get started and to support their ongoing teaching online does help. When that training is delivered online, using the course management system in which they will be teaching, faculty have the opportunity to experience the online environment as both a student and an instructor, serving to increase their effectiveness. In an online training course, the best practices involved in online teaching can be demonstrated. The best practices relate to the activities of teaching and learning and not to the technology itself. The course should be long enough so that faculty can be encouraged to develop the skeleton of a course or even one lesson that other participants can critique. The facilitator of the training should model good techniques for building a learning community within the course and for empowering the participating faculty to explore both the medium and the material. We have found that, in online training, it is best to include faculty who will imminently teach their first online course. Faculty who are about to teach online are highly motivated to learn good techniques for doing so. Faculty who are simply interested but who will not immediately be using the training might not participate to the same degree. When the group is made up of those who will be teaching online immediately and those who are simply interested, those who will not be teaching online in the immediate future do not feel as compelled to comply with participation expectations for the course. They may drop out and create frustration for those who stay with the training and who depend on the group to learn how the online learning process works.

Pankowski (2004) also noted that the faculty interviewed in her study cited the need for mentoring to support the transition to online teaching. In our own experience, creating a mentoring relationship through the pairing of faculty who are more experienced online with those who are just starting helps to break down barriers and provides real concrete examples of what works and what does not. Those in Pankowski's study felt that without the support of a more experienced colleague to guide them, they would most likely discontinue their involvement with online teaching beyond their first course. Using a mentoring approach to the training of online instructors can help determine who will succeed and who might not be well suited to teaching online. Mandernach, Donnelli, Dailey, and Schulte (2005) shared the very extensive mentoring model used by Park University in Missouri. In this model, all instructors who teach online first go through faculty training for online teaching and then are assigned a peer faculty mentor who monitors their performance in an online course. In the Park University model, the mentor not only observes the online teaching of the new online instructor but also conducts five formative reviews of teaching performance during the first term. This very intensive model may not be appropriate to all universities, but a mentoring approach can be quite useful in faculty development by allowing the new instructor a peer to consult with and who can make suggestions to improve practice while the course is in progress.

The University of Central Florida has established a comprehensive faculty development program that addresses four key areas of readiness: the institution, faculty, courses, and learners. The areas can be used to generate the following checklist to help institutions and faculty evaluate which aspects of their program or courses need attention.

Institutional Readiness:

- The course or program is a good fit with the institution's character and mission.
- There is a good fit with learner characteristics of the institution.
- There is a clearly articulated mission and strategic plan.
- There is demonstrated faculty interest.
- There is a robust campus infrastructure to support courses and programs.
- There is leadership for the initiative.
- There is a commitment to faculty support.
- There is a commitment to course and program support.
- There is a commitment to learner support.
- There is a commitment to assessment.

Faculty Readiness:
- A willingness to learn
- A willingness to surrender some control over class design and teaching style
- An ability to collaborate with peers

- A willingness to change the traditional faculty role
- An ability to build a support system
- Patience with technology
- An ability to learn from others course readiness
- A demonstrated faculty understanding of the technology in use
- A demonstrated understanding of the pedagogy required for online teaching
- A demonstrated understanding of the logistics of the course production process

Learner Readiness:

- Determined through informed self-selection
- An ability to take responsibility for one's own learning
- An access plan (i.e., has access to a computer and software at home or has a plan for accessing them) for taking the course
- An awareness of one's own learning style
- Technical skill
- An ability to build a support system
- An ability to deal with the uncertainties of using technology to take courses (Truman-Davis, Futch, Thompson, & Yonekura, 2000)

The following are some final reflections on a professional development course. It was conducted over 4 weeks and focused on the development of an effective learning community within the context of an online course. The group was composed of 35 faculty members, instructional designers, and student affairs personnel, all of whom wanted to understand and experience the impact of online learning on the students with whom they worked. The group members were given reading assignments about online teaching and learning. Then they were asked to engage with one another and to reflect on the concepts presented. They were asked to commit to participate in the discussion at least twice weekly during the 4-week course. They were also encouraged, through the discussion questions, to apply the concepts discussed with concrete examples from their own work. Representative faculty participants described their training experiences by providing anonymous feedback about online courses in the following ways:

> I found this course to be an intensive online experience as my regular workload was increasing. I found myself working overtime in the normal workweek digesting information and responding to the academic content, as well as the personal contact, while trying to participate in the course to learn

from my colleagues. I was able to experience firsthand a possible online experience for our new online education program at the college and to extrapolate, albeit slowly, some of the issues raised in the postings to my ever-changing workplace.

Participating in a college committee involving faculty and administrators involved in online education, I felt I could give a student perspective [on] the institution's online education program. Personally, I was excited and pleased to learn some new technical skills. I found myself having new respect for these students as they work with me and I try to interpret the requirements, rules, [and] culture of this new medium with them.

I enjoyed my experience with this online course. Although I was not able to participate in the discussion threads very much these last 2 weeks, I have learned from the experience. As I work with students who are taking or planning to take an online class, I will be better able to advise them [regarding] time commitments, strong self-motivation, realistic expectations, etc. While I learned from the experience without necessarily jumping into every discussion, I'm not being graded. :-) The students do need to be concerned with what is expected of them in terms of participation. It has been enjoyable to begin learning about this new learning environment! Overwhelming. Confusing. And yet enlightening. I think I have learned that what sometimes may seem like a well-structured experience on my end may not be so from the perspective of my students. Ultimately, they as a group need to organize their environment in a way that makes most sense to them.

I have learned that online learning takes a lot of time, but I enjoy writing and reading the writing of others. . . . I've learned what it might feel like to be a new online student who was anxious about where and how to post assignments.

I realize if students are frustrated in the beginning of the class, it might affect their performance in the class. . . . I've also learned how important it is for online teachers to find other online teachers to share their teaching experiences with and the need for us to find, explore, update, and do research in this field.

The reflections of these instructors indicate that significant learning came out of their experience of being students online. The experience will likely assist them in developing and facilitating courses that are more responsive to the needs of learners. The faculty have seen what it is like from the other side of the looking glass. This is invaluable learning—learning that is difficult to convey in face-to-face training.

Developing New Techniques

Bates (2000) noted that in institutions where best practices in the implementation of technology are followed, faculty development focuses on teaching and learning and not on the technology itself. There is little doubt that faculty are in need of developing skills in computer literacy before they can move into teaching online. However, as we have been emphasizing, the focus in faculty development should be on pedagogical methods and not on the software in use.

When presented with instructional design principles that promote interactive delivery appropriate to online teaching, faculty will often ask, "Where is the lecture?" An appropriate response to this question is presented by Lytle, Lytle, Lenhart, and Skrotsky (1999), who stated, "Lectures are important and certainly numerous in higher education, but are not necessarily any more valuable in the learning process than any other learning tool" (p. 58).

Incorporated into faculty training and development, then, should be concrete ways in which content can be presented without the use of lectures. Some of the techniques can include the following:

- Creating Web pages that contain no more than one screen of text and graphics

- Collaborative small-group assignments, such as jigsaw assignments where students contribute pieces to the whole of a topic or problem

- Research assignments asking students to seek out and present additional resources available on the Internet and in books and journals

- Simulations that mimic real-life work applications of the material discussed, such as asking a group to become a work team to develop a proposal on a given topic to be submitted to a fictitious company

- Asking students to become experts on a topic within the scope of the course and to then present that topic to their peers

- Asynchronous discussion of the topics within the scope of the course material being studied

- Fishbowl discussions where one group of students presents and discusses a topic while the other students observe, journal, reflect, and comment on their reflections at the end of the discussion

- Papers posted to the course site and peer-reviewed

- Limited use of audio and video clips

- WebQuests, which are Internet-based scavenger hunts requiring that students find pieces of information related to a topic

- Use of Web 2.0 technologies, such as wikis (collaboratively created Web pages) and blogs (Web logs or journals) to encourage collaborative assignment completion (Palloff & Pratt, 2007)

What is important is to encourage and support faculty in thinking outside the box in terms of developing creative ways to present course content and to assess student performance, while keeping in mind the technology to which students are likely to have access.

Yet, another critical factor in faculty training is to help them develop sensitivity to student needs and expectations as they enter the online environment. Just as faculty struggled in their online faculty development course to understand how online learning works and what is expected, students will not intuitively know how to function in an online course. In addition, learning online poses new challenges to students who previously have been exposed to traditional learning models. We now turn our attention to what it takes to assist students in becoming effective online learners and how faculty can help them with the process.

Learning to Learn Online

> There was a book lying near Alice on the table, and while she sat watching . . . she turned over the leaves to find some part that she could read, "for it's all in some language I don't know," she said to herself. . . . "Why, it's a looking-glass book, of course! And if I hold it up to the glass, the words will all go the right way again." (Carroll, 1871, p. 190)

Students are, for the most part, unaware of the demands that online learning will place on them as learners. They generally enter an online class with traditional learning expectations—that is, that the instructor will teach and they will learn from the material the instructor provides. They do not know that the instructor is less visible in the learning process and that the instructor role is one of facilitator rather than of traditional teacher or lecturer. They also have not been told that the online learning process is less structured and demands significantly more input from them as learners to make it successful. Consequently, it is important that the instructor convey this information to students prior to beginning an online course. Many times, difficulties emerge when students have differing sets of expectations from the course and the instructor and little or no attempt is made to clarify expectations at the outset.

Students generally enter an online program with the expectation that a course will be more attuned to their needs as learners. This may mean that the course is more convenient for them due to distance or work and family demands. Or it may mean that they do not like large classroom situations and prefer the potential for increased instructor–student interaction.

Because students enter online programs and courses with expectations that might not match the realities of online learning, some institutions are creating online courses to teach students about online learning, and some are even mandating that students complete an introductory course before embarking on other online classes. The newer course management systems have been created with this in mind—before a student can access his or her online course, an orientation module must be successfully completed. Once done, access is granted by the system. Some institutions incorporate mandatory face-to-face orientations to online programs and courses, involving both computer training and training in what it means to learn online and how to be an effective online student. This tends to be the orientation method of choice for high school programs moving into online course delivery and is easy to accomplish since the students are all within the geographic reach of the school. The assumption behind all of these approaches is the same: to maximize the educational potential for both the online classroom and online students. We must pay attention to teaching our teachers how to teach and teaching our learners how to learn when teaching and learning are virtual.

As with faculty training, conducting student training online allows students to experience online learning before they take an actual course. Regardless of the means by which the training is conducted, the following should be included in a student orientation to online learning:

- The basics of logging onto the Internet, including the use of a browser, accessing the course site, using course management software, saving and printing material found online, basic Internet searching, and e-mail

- Understanding what is required to become a successful online learner, including time requirements and time management

- The differences between a face-to-face course and an online course, including the role of the instructor and the roles of students as well as expectations about how students will be evaluated

- Interaction between the instructor and students and among students

- How to give feedback to other students

- Appropriate interaction and communication, including the rules of netiquette

- How to get help when it is needed (Palloff & Pratt, 2001, pp. 123–124)

Providing an orientation course might not resolve all of the issues for students as they make the transition to the online classroom. But it certainly can help to provide a clearer understanding of the differences in the type of educational experience they are about to undertake and can help to clarify expectations.

Following up with a written guide to online work, whether in hard copy, e-mailed to each student, or placed on the institution's Web site, can help to reinforce this learning. When concerns or complaints regarding expectations arise, students can then be referred back to the guidelines that are readily available to them to help them understand the online teaching and learning methods and processes.

If the institution cannot provide student training about how to learn, then suggestions for how to learn online become the responsibility of the faculty who are delivering courses. Ways in which faculty can orient students include the following:

- Hold a face-to-face, hands-on orientation, if possible, to show students the course site and discuss online learning.

- Provide an orientation to the course on the course site or as a first discussion item.

- Provide students with a list of frequently asked questions and responses to those questions.

- Place basic information about how to navigate the course site on the welcome screen or course home page.

- Send an e-mail message to each student enrolled in the course containing orientation information. (Palloff & Pratt, 2001, p. 43)

Regardless of how student orientation occurs, it needs to be considered an important element in the development of the course. Unfortunately, it is often overlooked. Including this information in faculty training, especially if faculty have the ability to participate in their own online courses, can create an awareness of just how important student orientation is.

Changing Roles and Relationships

Alice watched the White King as he slowly struggled up from bar to bar, till at last she said, "Why, you'll be hours and hours getting to the table at that rate. I'd far better help you, hadn't I?" . . . So Alice picked him up very gently and lifted him across. (Carroll, 1871, p. 188)

One final issue that faculty and student development should touch on is the changing nature of faculty–student relationships created by the more facilitative methods used in online teaching. The student enrolled in higher education today, whether online or in traditional institutions, is less likely to be the 18- to 21-year-old seeking a onetime educational experience. Instead, today's student is likely to be an adult returning to school to obtain the knowledge and skills needed to compete and advance in the workforce. The 2006 National Online Learners Priority Report produced by Noel-Levitz noted that only 19% of online learners are younger than age 24. When asked to rank reasons for enrollment in an online program, convenience came out on top, coupled with concern about work schedule and the need for flexibility. The adult student, therefore, is more likely to be a lifelong learner embarking on the beginning of what may be a learning process that results in the pursuit of multiple degrees, courses, or certifications (Bates, 2000). The Noel-Levitz report further indicated that the adult learners surveyed found that responsiveness of both the instructor and institution were challenges to their satisfaction with online learning.

Although their previous educational experiences have been traditional—meaning that the instructor is the expert with knowledge and wisdom to impart and that the student has only to receive—the lifelong learner is looking to enter a partnership that results in the achievement of specified learning objectives. The partnership that these students seek is not only with an instructor but also with student colleagues and with an academic institution that understands and tries to meet their needs. Today's high school students going on to college are much more oriented and tied to technology than in the past. They spend as significant amount of their time interacting with technology on social networking sites, such as MySpace, engaging in instant messenger conversations with their friends, or text messaging using a cell phone. With the increasing availability of online high school courses, these students are also entering college with an understanding of how online courses work and a demand to be able to continue their involvement with this form of education.

As a result, there is a movement occurring in the academic world; academic institutions need to be increasingly responsive to those they serve, resulting in a shift from the traditional faculty-centered institution to a learner-focused one. The student is seen as a customer whose needs for technologically-based education must be met. In this context, the relationship between faculty and students will change as well.

In the online classroom, the most effective means of achieving learning outcomes is the use of active learning and collaborative techniques that encourage students to become empowered learners. The fully engaged, active learner is likely to bring new demands to the learning situation. The online environment can be a great equalizer, and the online classroom can become the place where faculty and students partner to achieve learning objectives through interactive, self-empowering means (Harasim, Hiltz, Teles, & Turoff, 1996; Palloff & Pratt, 2001, 2003, 2005, 2007). Bates (2000) noted that

> Modern learning theory sees learning as an individual quest for meaning and relevance. Once learning moves beyond the recall of facts, principles, or correct procedures and into the area of creativity, problem solving, analysis, or evaluation (the very skills needed in the workplace in a knowledge-based economy, not to mention in life in general), learners need the opportunity to communicate with one another as well as with their teachers. This, of course, includes the opportunity to question, challenge, and discuss issues. (pp. 13–14)

Recent studies of the online learning environment have noted that a feeling community and connection among learners and instructor contribute positively to learner satisfaction (Gunawardena & Zittle, 1997; Picciano, 2002; Rovai & Barnum, 2004). Beyond learner satisfaction, however, incorporating collaboration into online courses enhances the achievement of learning outcomes and reduces the potential for learner isolation online (Palloff & Pratt, 2005). By learning together in a learning community, students have the opportunity to extend and deepen their learning experience, test out new ideas with a supportive group, and receive critical and constructive feedback, thus helping to increase their critical thinking abilities. The likelihood of successfully achieving course learning outcomes and competencies increases significantly through collaborative engagement. The ways in which collaboration can be used online are limitless—an instructor might create a game for students to play collaboratively, provide case studies for students to discuss or ask them to submit their own, go on a WebQuest as a team, or participate in a group role-play. Anything that will serve the outcomes of a course will work—creativity and imagination are the keys.

Rather than be threatened by the shift in the faculty–student relationship and the use of collaboration online, faculty can be challenged by the change and embrace it. Faculty, too, are lifelong learners. Even if an activity is a failure, we learn from that failure and that learning informs and enhances our teaching the next time around. In this way, our students become our partners in course design and delivery. The changing relationship between faculty and students serves to expand the network through which faculty can learn and increases the realm of possibilities in techniques for delivering online education. We always believe, as we enter a new online course, that we have as much to learn from our students as they do from us, and we find this to be an exciting element of our online work that we welcome.

Life on the Other Side of the Looking Glass

> "Your Red Majesty shouldn't purr so loud," Alice said, rubbing her eyes and addressing the kitten respectfully, yet with some severity. "You woke me out of oh! such a nice dream! And you've been along with me, Kitty—all through the looking-glass world. Did you know it, dear?" (Carroll, 1871, p. 341)

When faculty and students are provided with good training and support for online teaching and learning, the likely outcome is excitement about new ways of teaching and learning. There is enthusiasm about the meeting of learning objectives in deep and meaningful ways. When courses are designed and delivered with interactivity in mind, a shift occurs as learners become more empowered and discover that the learning in an online course comes from other students and not solely from interaction with the instructor. Ways in which students can collaborate with one another are built into courses and more authentic means of assessing student performance accompany those activities. Self-reflection and critical thinking become important components of assessment. In fact, when courses progress well, the instructor often learns as much from his or her students as students learn from the instructor.

The reflection of one of our students at the end of an online course provided as anonymous feedback on course evaluations demonstrates this shift:

> I wanted to take another opportunity to thank each of you for your participation in this course. I remember when I first joined the program . . . [other students] talked about the importance [that] their colleagues played in their success in the program. I had no idea of the significance of those statements, or the degree to which they were true, until I experienced it for myself. Thank you all for this tremendous contribution to my development. —Jane

Jane's reflection is the type we hope to see at the end of a course. It gives us an indication that the planning and delivery of the course was effective not only in achieving learning objectives but also in moving students toward what we consider to be real learning—a shared creation of meaning and knowledge.

When instructors and students are able to reap the benefits of a well designed online course, the end result is excitement about what is possible in the online realm and about the new relationships that are developed between instructor and student; among students; and among instructor, students, and knowledge creation. The resultant excitement about learning helps to stimulate new creative approaches to online teaching and demonstrates that there is, in fact, the possibility that life beyond the looking glass is not a dream, but a reality with great potential.

References

Akridge, J., DeMay, L., Braunlich, L., Collura, M., & Sheahan, M. (2002). Retaining adult learners in a high-stress distance education learning environment: The Purdue University executive MBA in agribusiness. *Motivating & educating adult learners online*, pp. 62–71. Retrieved from http://www.geteducated.com/images/pdfs/journalmotivateretain.pdf

Bates, A. W. (2000). *Managing technological change*. San Francisco: Jossey-Bass.

Brookfield, S. (1995). *Becoming a critically reflective teacher*. San Francisco: Jossey-Bass.

Carr, S. (2000, February 11). As distance education comes of age, the challenge is keeping the students. *The Chronicle of Higher Education*, p. A39. Retrieved from http://chronicle.com/free/v46/i23/23a00101.htm

Carroll, L. (1871). *Through the looking glass, and what Alice found there*. New York: Macmillan.

Eom, S. (2006, July 5–7). The role of the instructors as a determinant of students' satisfaction in university online education. In *Proceedings of the Sixth International IEEE Conference on Advanced Learning Technologies* (pp. 985–988). Washington, DC: IEEE Computer Society.

Feenberg, A. (1999, September-October). No frills in the virtual classroom. *Academe*, pp. 26–31.

Garrison, D., Anderson, T., & Archer, W. (2003). A theory of critical inquiry in online distance education. In M. G. Moore & W. G. Anderson (Eds.), *Handbook of distance education* (pp. 113–127). Mahwah, NJ: Lawrence Erlbaum.

Gunawardena, C. N., & Zittle, F. (1997). Social presence as a predictor of satisfaction within a computer mediated conferencing environment. *American Journal of Distance Education, 11*(3), 8–25.

Harasim, L., Hiltz, S. R., Teles, L., & Turoff, M. (1996). *Learning networks.* Cambridge, MA: MIT Press.

Herbert, M. (2006). Staying the course: A study in online student satisfaction and retention. *Online Journal of Distance Learning Administration, 9*(4). Available from http://www.westga.edu/~distance/ojdla

Huba, M. E., & Freed, J. (2000). *Learner-centered assessment on college campuses: Shifting the focus from teaching to learning.* Needham Heights, MA: Allyn & Bacon.

Lytle, S., Lytle, V., Lenhart, K., & Skrotsky, L. (1999, November-December). Large scale deployment of technology-enhanced courses. *Syllabus,* 57–59.

Mandernach, B. J., Donnelli, E., Dailey, A., & Schulte, M. (2005). A faculty evaluation model for online instructors: Mentoring and evaluation in the online classroom. *Online Journal of Distance Education Administration, 8*(3), 5–6.

Milam, J., Voorhees, R., & Bedard-Voorhees, A. (2004). Assessment of online education: Policies, practices, and recommendations. *New Directions for Community Colleges, 126,* 73–85.

Noel-Levitz. (2006). *National online learners priorities report.* Retrieved from https://www.noellevitz.com/Papers+and+Research/Papers+and+Reports/ResearchLibrary/2006+National+Satisfaction+Report.htm

Palloff, R. M., & Pratt, K. (2001). *Lessons from the cyberspace classroom: The realities of online teaching.* San Francisco: Jossey-Bass.

Palloff, R. M., & Pratt, K. (2003). *The virtual student: A profile and guide.* San Francisco: Jossey-Bass.

Palloff, R. M., & Pratt, K. (2005). *Collaborating online: Learning together in community.* San Francisco: Jossey-Bass.

Palloff, R. M., & Pratt, K. (2007). *Building online learning: Effective strategies for the online classroom.* San Francisco: Jossey-Bass.

Pankowski, P. (2004, September). Faculty training for online teaching. *T.H.E. Journal.* Retrieved from http://thejournal.com/articles/16956

Picciano, A. (2002). Beyond student perceptions: Issues of interaction, presence, and performance in an online course. *Journal of Asychronous Learning Networks, 6*(1), 21–40.

Pratt, K. (1996). *The electronic personality.* Unpublished doctoral dissertation, The Fielding Graduate Institute.

Rovai, A. P., & Barnum, K. T. (2004). On-line course effectiveness: An analysis of student interactions and perceptions of learning. *Journal of Distance Learning, 18*(1), 57–73.

Truman-Davis, B., Futch, L., Thompson, K., & Yonekura, F. (2000). Support for online teaching and learning. *EDUCAUSE Quarterly, 2,* 44–51.

White, K., & Weight, B. (2000). *The online teaching guide.* Needham Heights, MA: Allyn & Bacon.

Chapter 16

Teaching Professionals to Be Effective Online Facilitators and Instructors

Lessons From Hard-Won Experience

Leni Wildflower

W e have centuries of accumulated understanding of how a physical learning environment might be structured, how to arrange the furniture and establish the norms of behavior appropriate to a lecture, a seminar, a Socratic dialogue. Online teaching requires a new set of conventions. The virtual environment has been constructed and modified during the course of a single generation and is subject to further upheaval.

During the course of my own professional life, technology and the Web have revolutionized distance learning. We have discovered that, far from being merely a poor substitute for the real thing, the online environment has huge potential benefits. It tends to democratize the learning experience, diminish differences of culture and confidence and attractiveness, and challenge the glib volubility of some and the silence of others. It promotes an increased capacity for critical thinking, by requiring students to hear points of view other than their own and to respond to them thoughtfully in writing. For the student, there is the potential for an increased ability to view one's personal or professional experience systemically and to place oneself in relation to that experience. Perhaps most surprisingly, online dialogue can acquire thoughtfulness and depth not often experienced elsewhere (Clark, 2000, p. 603).

The transparency of the medium often allows for a greater level of intimacy and emotional empathy than occurs in the physical classroom.

> Throughout the course, I experienced new insights about myself and about online learning through the many contributions of the active group. This was a rich source of learning . . . Members of the group emerged to support the group process in a variety of ways—with technical assistance, positive feedback, references to related materials and resources, etc. (C. Wilocox, online student, end-of-term online feedback, 2006)

> As each issue came to the surface, questions were asked and fears were shared. I found myself saying "amen"—discovering that students could feel the same way I do. This new empathy is the greatest lesson I will take away from this [online] seminar. Being able to better understand the concerns of those taking an online class is such a valuable lesson. (H. Brainbridge, online student, end-of-term online feedback, 2007)

It would be a mistake, however, to conclude that all technological developments must be beneficial. Just as interactive learning in the physical classroom might be encouraged by skilful use of a chalkboard and stifled by too many PowerPoint presentations, in an online environment, not every advance should be embraced uncritically. A chat room with a video link, for example, would seem to recreate most closely the conditions of the physical classroom. Instant response with all the visual cues of face-to-face interaction might make a system of asynchronous posting sound as antiquated as a snail mail correspondence course. But for the subtle ecology of the successful online classroom to thrive, technology must be subordinated to the needs of education. Asynchronous dialogue, detached from vocal and visual elements, seems to have a particular educational value, placing the emphasis on a reflective exchange of ideas. These benefits are unlikely to occur, however, if online education is approached reluctantly or without a thorough understanding of its particular strengths and challenges.

A recent study produced by the Babson Survey Research group for the Sloan Consortium on online education in the United States (Allen & Seaman, 2006) reported this finding: "The factor which was cited most often by academic leaders of every institutional size and type" as a barrier to widespread adoption of online learning was that "students need more discipline to succeed in online courses. In itself, this is a curious statement. It seems to place the blame for the failure of online education—actual or anticipated—on the students. Their lack of discipline is the problem. Taken out of context, it could be a statement in support of online learning.

Could it be a bad thing that it demands more discipline of the student? But offered as an argument against the virtual classroom, it strongly suggests that the design and delivery of many online programs are not skillful enough to keep students engaged and motivated.

An imaginatively designed online environment can quickly convert participants to the possibilities of the medium.

> As a doctoral student, class forums were designed for purely informational exchanges. Since I took this online dialogue course, I have come to understand that I have cheated myself by not engaging more online. (E. Williams, online student, end-of-term online feedback, 2007)

The online teaching I have been engaged in at Fielding is constructed on the basis of software that is unobtrusive and easy to master and of pedagogy that is eloquent in design. What are the elements that make our online courses successful? This chapter offers some answers.

Creating a Framework for Optimal Online Learning

In the absence of face-to-face contact, the design of an online program becomes a critical factor in the successful creation of a learning environment. As an instructor, you encounter the students without the familiar visual clues of gesture and facial expression and the aural indicators of tone and attitude. In communicating with them, you, like them, are limited to words. This makes it even more important to avoid ambiguity and uncertainty about expectations. Success online requires that a structure be designed to articulate clearly what you want to accomplish, how team members or students should behave, the goals of the learning experience, and the pace and attitude with which team members should move through the program.

Software

Begin with the right software. If you want to create discussion, you do not need too many options. Software that pushes itself to the foreground is a distraction. Too many bells and whistles will please the technophiles, dismay the technophobes, and tend to distract everyone from reflective discussion.

You will need to be able to divide the virtual classroom—the main workspace—into folders containing different modules or topics. Provide also a social place within the program—you might call it the café or lounge—where team members can chat more personally. Additional folders can be created, as required, to allow faculty and students to post articles on related topics. If some students are keen to pursue a tangential topic, or develop a discussion further than the time constraints of the course allow, move that thread into a separate space.

The essential requirement is that topics can bifurcate into threads of dialogue and that the instructor and the participants can respond both to other individuals and to the group as a whole.

Designing Courses or Programs That Promote Optimal Participation

It is not always easy for students to feel that they are the architects of their own learning. But the online forum is an ideal place to promote this concept. If the minimal requirements for the course involve responding to each other and to the group as whole, and the instructor maintains a light touch, the students have the experience of determining, individually and collectively, the quality of the discussion, and the learning becomes truly collaborative. Exercises can be set up in various ways to promote optimal participation. For example, (1) students organize to write collective papers, (2) students are encouraged to collectively determine the guidelines they want the course to function by, and (3) students take turns introducing each new topic, or facilitating the discussion, or summarizing what has been said.

Creating Clear Norms and Boundaries

It is crucial to define clear norms for online behavior and boundaries that allow the team to move through the course as a unit.

> Make it clear that everyone is expected to participate actively, since learning is largely dependent on participation. You might wish to specify, for example, that students are expected to log on to the classroom a minimum of two times per module, though they are encouraged to check in more frequently, and that they should respond to at least one other team member's work during each module, in addition to completing their own assignments. (Wildflower, 2006, p. 14)

For each module, describe what team members should discuss, what reading they need to do, and when their postings are due. There should be due dates for responses to papers as well as for the papers themselves. Assignment due dates for all required postings should be clearly outlined in the course syllabus, and these deadlines should be adhered to. Emphasize that the failure of an individual student to post an assignment on time will hamper the entire class in its progress.

It should not be possible for a student to go back and post papers or responses after the class has moved onto a new topic. Once an assignment is finished, the team moves on to the next assignment, and the previous one is closed off or shunted into a specialized folder. This keeps participants to deadlines and keeps the pace of the team moving. Participants need to negotiate with the instructor on the best way to make up missed work.

Be explicit about what is expected of the student and how success is to be measured. If the course is to be graded, what is the method of grading and what are the criteria? A degree of structure is likely to enhance any kind of educational course. In the online environment, it becomes particularly crucial. The absence of norms and boundaries can have dramatic consequences. A student in one of my classes in online facilitation reported the following experience:

> When I first started teaching online [in 1998], I thought it would be great to have facilitated discussions. I provided virtually no guidelines, boundaries, expectations, etc. What a mess. I had students complaining about other students' postings. Other students shut down completely. I'm sure that many dropped the course as a result of the discussions. I accept full responsibility for what happened. I had no idea what I was doing, and as a result, caused more harm than good. (student quoted in Wildflower, 2006 p. 16).

Although it may seem counterintuitive, the clearer the boundaries in an online setting, the more freedom you create for the participants to move through the course, and the easier it is for the student to respond creatively in the moment.

Confidentiality

Create an atmosphere where confidentiality is respected. Students need reassurance that what is said online will be read only by an agreed list of people and will not be quoted outside the classroom.

Many of our students at Fielding combine study with work, and some of our courses are custom designed for executive teams and other groups in employment at management level. The need for confidentiality, in these contexts, can be of practical importance. It can also raise more challenging questions. In the process of interweaving theory and experience, participants might wish to introduce sensitive workplace issues, references to competition, problems with coworkers, and so on. Who is allowed access to the online dialogue—bosses, family members, coworkers, friends? This needs to be negotiated and agreed at the outset. Questions regarding confidentiality might include the following: What do you need from your teammates to feel comfortable participating in this course?

How do you feel about your boss being a member of the team? How do you feel about senior management observing? Are there issues around power, punishment, and/or performance that might impact team participation (Wildflower, 2006, p. 16)?

Facilitating Dialogue

The role as instructor-facilitator is to synthesize the discussion by drawing together disparate threads, to refocus the group by reigning in digressions, and to encourage a deeper exploration of the topic—and to do all this with a light touch so that the class has space for its self-organizing potential to develop. This concept of andragogy fits nicely into the online collaborative model.

Manage the dialogue in a way that encourages participants to own the process of learning. Where possible, shift the responsibility of learning from yourself as instructor to the students. Wait for the other members of the class to respond to a question posted by a student.

As my colleague Judy Stevens-Long puts it, your job is to "rock in and out of the group . . . and avoid being sucked into an individual in the group, or the group as a whole. You have to think in terms of Senge's 'leverage points.' You have to know where to put the fulcrum" (Stevens-Long, as quoted in Wildflower, 2006, p. 7).

> I think the instructor modeled generosity at the beginning and was able to weave in an out rhythmically, quietly but very effectively. Through her style of facilitation, I was able to integrate a model for myself that fits with my sense of self. (H. Whitford, online student, end-of-term online feedback, 2006)

A posting of yours that responds to an individual student should be addressed to the whole class. You might also respond in a single posting to a number of different students, finding instructive contrasts and common threads. Observations that lead to questions for everyone's consideration are particularly effective. In the absence of a more specific question, a simple request for any thoughts keeps the space open for continuing dialogue. Yours should not be the last word.

Vary feedback responses to include thoughtful praise, critical analysis, and your professional experience as it relates to the theoretical material presented and alternative interpretations. Ask questions to deepen or broaden the dialogue, modeling skills of critical thinking. Aim always to support the students' sense of self-efficacy. You want the dialogue to move forward and remain focused, but it is better to ask a provocative or challenging question than to attempt to force the pace or direction.

Assigning group work can be a powerful way of giving up control. Divide the class into subgroups of manageable size and ask each group to write a group paper, or ask the class to divide itself, negotiating the grouping through online discussion. In some classes, I first assign a short individual case study and then divide the class into groups according to similarity of topic and ask each group to collaborate on a paper exploring that area in more detail.

As with any teaching, simply knowing the subject matter is not enough. Extraordinary teachers inspire students, model skills of critical thinking, foster collaboration, and encourage students to reach beyond what they perceive as their normal boundaries. All of these qualities can be demonstrated by an online teacher. The form is radically different, but the end result is the same.

Establishing an Online Presence

Be present in the round. To the extent that you feel comfortable doing so, let students know something about who you are outside the virtual classroom.

Your presence online is shaped by more than the content of your postings. Your tone and register are also important. Whatever your natural character, in online work it is helpful to cultivate a personality that is emotive, open, and supportive. You might experience this as an exaggerated form of your regular self. Remember, you have only words with which to convey who you are. Being expressive and generous in your postings will ease anxiety among the students and model positive behavior for others to emulate.

Without being inauthentic, it is helpful to adopt an informal register. Try to recreate online the kind of conversational tone you would use naturally in a face-to-face classroom discussion.

The unfamiliar rhythms of the virtual environment can induce unease in experienced teachers who have learned their craft in physical classrooms. There is sometimes an urge to step in prematurely to correct misconceptions, to offer conclusions, and to mentor confused students. Holding back, containing your anxiety as an instructor when the discussion seems to be floating beyond your intellectual zone, and knowing which question to pose and when to pose it—these are nuanced skills that extraordinary online teachers reach over time. To quote Judy Stevens-Long again, this is "an epiphany that you need [to have experienced] to be effective" (quoted in Wildflower, p. 7, 2002).

On the other hand, any sustained period of silence online will be experienced by your students as absence. It is better to check in frequently with short postings than to wait to construct more elaborate, substantial, or articulate pieces. A good facilitator checks on the progress of the class every day and appears online frequently. It has been my experience that students want to know that you are watching their progress. Any posting that acknowledges, however briefly, what has been taking place in the dialogue is affirming, reassuring, and encourages feedback. Some examples include the following:

> Each week, I insert a posting I call a "mid-week stir." It is a question, a thought, a musing—and always a request for a response from students. (F. Campone, recorded faculty discussion, 2008)

> I track which student I am responding to each week and make sure that I rotate my responses among the students. I use my response as an opportunity to engage at both a specific level (responding to the student) and at a general level (a comment about the subject matter in general). (L. Wildflower, recorded faculty discussion, 2008)

When providing a negative comment, preface it with what you find positive in the student's posting. Common mistakes made by inexperienced instructors are to provide too much personal support and not enough intellectual feedback—or to veer in the opposite direction and provide too much intellectual material without the accompanying supportive comments. The absence of balancing cues of gesture and vocal tone can make these contrasts appear starker. Instructors who are too emotionally supportive online can be perceived by students as nonintellectual. Instructors who provide plenty of smart postings, but not a lot of support, might come across as unfeeling or arrogant. Here, as in other aspects of online facilitation, balance is everything.

> I started teaching online like I would in a classroom, posting lectures at various points in the course. I was getting no responses from what had previously been successful lectures. As I became more skilful online, I realized that I needed to fold these lectures into the ongoing dialogue and post them in a context of my own experience or as a response to their dialogue or questions. (K. Rogers, recorded faculty discussion, 2008)

Encouraging Supportive Feedback Among the Students

As in any professional collaboration, you as the instructor are modeling norms in the form of feedback. In a dialogue framework, the aim is to support one another in both professional and personal development and to deliver remarks that are both sensitive and substantive (Spitzer, 2001, p. 165). The deepest online learning takes place through relationship. Your team will move through the online program together. Students should be reminded that to be effective online participants they should post responses that reflect positive emotional tone as well as intellectual content.

Critical feedback online tends to carry a heavier impact than when delivered face-to-face and may sound colder and harsher than intended. Negative comments cannot be tempered with kind gestures or tonal inflections, and it is harder to place them in a larger context of supportive conversation. One result is that students and faculty sometimes shy away from controversy. Helping to create an expectation of sympathy and support, while encouraging argument and challenging individuals to stretch themselves, may be one of the most demanding skills of an online teacher.

Students who feel that they have received inappropriate feedback should be advised to wait a day before responding. The feedback might be unjust or it might have been misinterpreted. Either way, a response posted in the heat of the moment might serve only to inflame the situation. Remind the students that one of the beauties of the asynchronous learning environment is the increased opportunity for reflection.

It is good idea, at some stage in the process, to involve students in a discussion on how they want to be treated online. You might ask them what, in their view, constitutes a helpful posting and how personal disagreements online should be mediated. Give them the opportunity to report adverse experiences with e-mail or online exchanges that might have made them wary of the medium. This can all be accomplished in a space separate from the regular curriculum, such as the lounge or café or in a folder designed for the purpose.

Interestingly, when Fielding first introduced online teaching, participants shared more unpleasant experiences working online. They also expressed far more anxiety about expressing themselves in an online environment. These days, reports of unpleasant online experiences are rare.

At some stage, you might find it helpful to post some guidelines on critical feedback. For example, when giving critical feedback:

1. Respond to the posting with respect, tact, and generosity.

2. Try to make substantial observations that will assist the work of the other student to develop and the class to progress.

3. Frame your observation as part of an ongoing dialogue.

4. Be specific, identifying the sentence or idea to which you are responding.

5. Ask questions prompted by the posting.

And when receiving critical feedback:

1. Remember that anyone who comments critically on your posting pays you the compliment of taking it seriously.

2. Be receptive to criticism. This will encourage your fellow students to be honest with you.

3. Challenge yourself to take something of benefit from any negative comment, however off the mark it seems.

4. Read critical comments with detachment, remembering that some readers are more insightful and more in tune with your intentions than others.

5. Question your readers on their comments with the same tact, respect, and generosity that you expect from them. (Wildflower, 2004b)

Managing Conflict

Intellectual conflict, free of hurtful personal content, promotes a more probing analysis of an issue and engages the students. Critical discourse often depends on participants expressing conflicting points of view. In fact, you might find you need to encourage students to take a stand on an issue or to argue a position that conflicts with their own. Be sure to let a group diverge—to explore and understand each other's differing opinions thoroughly—before attempting to steer them toward agreement and common understanding.

Conflict of a more personal kind is often found in any group dynamic and is not necessarily bad. The more common danger is that politeness will discourage real critical dialogue. And because of the nature of the online environment, deeper conflict can be harder to detect, showing up as nonparticipation. In my experience, when boundaries and norms are clear, conflict rarely occurs. But misunderstandings do happen and need to be managed skillfully.

When conflict arises online, acknowledge it immediately, and invite participants to explore it within the safety of the virtual classroom. When you are confronted with one disruptive person creating conflict, by being verbally aggressive or sarcastic, for example, be prompt in giving feedback to this individual to emphasize the boundaries and expectations of the course (Wildflower, p. 23, 2004a).

> There was one student in particular I had to be very direct with: While I appreciate that you are passionate about your ideas, it is not appropriate to require that your fellow students to agree with them. In this community, every opinion is equally valid, whether or not you agree with it. (L. Wildflower, recorded faculty discussion, 2006)

In rare cases, when you judge that the situation cannot be resolved online, you might have to exclude the individual from the group. You can continue dialogue via e-mail, if meeting face-to-face is not an option. But the longer a hostile individual stays in a group environment, the more difficult it becomes to continue the work of the group. After the person has been removed, it is critical to go back in and process what has happened with the other participants, reassuring them that they are not responsible for the problem and inviting them to contact the excluded student individually if they wish.

Sustaining Motivation

Motivation among the students will vary according to factors over which you have very little control. One of the most common symptoms of low motivation in an online course is silence. This can be disconcerting. It helps to be sensitive to these fluctuations and to acknowledge them online.

There are rhythms of high and low performance that can be anticipated. For the individual student, particularly one who is unfamiliar with online learning, there is a learning period. The early weeks can be frustrating and stressful. Encourage inexperienced students to check in online once a day—not necessarily to post, but to keep abreast of what other students are posting so as not get overwhelmed. It can be debilitating for students to log on and find 60 new responses to wade through. Reassure them that it will become easier as they adjust to the process.

Expect the group to establish its own collective rhythm. It has been my experience that most classes begin with a fairly high level of energy that peaks halfway or two thirds through the course. Then there seems to be a drop-off in participation, caused by exhaustion or an accumulation of conflicting demands, then a resurgence during the last couple of weeks.

There might be any number of reasons for a student's motivation to wane, and your response will vary accordingly. With experience, you can anticipate the more common problems and design the course with these in mind.

> I sometimes have to play a cheerleading role: Okay all. We are coming down the home stretch. Hang in there. Only two more weeks to go. And remember to provide feedback to everyone's paper. Your responses to what they have written are critical to everyone's learning and growth in this course. (A. Withers, recorded faculty discussion, 2008)

For the student who misses the kind of interactive support available in more traditional learning environments, the demands of the course might seem worryingly nebulous. Such students might feel overwhelmed by the demands on them to initiate involvement. Make sure that the course runs for a manageable length of time, probably 12 weeks or less, that the material is broken up into modules, and that within each module there are measurable units of achievement.

Some students will struggle with the challenges of the technology. If possible, begin with a face-to-face or telephone orientation where participants are trained on the software, and allow participants early access to the site so they can practice before the program begins. Keep daily contact in the opening days of the course. Be available to participants who need quick replies to requests for help with the technicalities of posting (Moshinskie, 200, p. 228).

Students might find the course conflicting with other demands in their lives. Be clear up front about the minimum amount of time needed to fulfill the demands of the program. At the same time, acknowledge that the participants have lives or jobs and that unforeseen crises can occur. Make it possible, in the design of the program, for a participant to disappear from time to time and still meet the requirements.

Students trying to dovetail their online studies with the demands of corporate employment might find their involvement insufficiently supported at work. If this problem is shared by a group of participants, you might try conducting pseudo-synchronous sessions. Used sparingly, the pseudo-synchronous format can accelerate discussion and boost involvement, while making a minimal demand on the participants' time.

> In one company where I was doing online training, and having difficulty getting employee participation, I created one hour discussions. We were all online at the same time. I would pose a question for discussion every fifteen minutes or so. Some questions were pre-planned, others flowed from the discussion as it evolved. The process created a learning environment that was energetic and kept the employees involved. (L. Wildflower, recorded faculty discussion, 2008)

Record Keeping and Organization

Although as an instructor I primarily respond to the group as a whole, I also aim to respond to at least one individual during each week-long module. I keep track of which students I have responded to so that I can make sure I have focused on each participant at least once during the term.

As in face-to-face teaching, if you are teaching the same course or program more than once, you notice that some of the same questions come up. If you write a thoughtful response to a student's question, save it. The chances are good that the question will come up again, and with slight morphing, you can insert your saved posting into the new term's discussion. Along these lines, I have created minipapers, which I post in a separate folder. These papers have come directly from questions asked repeatedly over the years. Titles include "An Overview of the History of Leadership Theories," "Some Thoughts on New Skills Needed for

Leadership," "An Annotated Bibliography on Mentoring," and "Thoughts on Using CBT Versus Principles of Humanistic Psychology in Coaching."

An extension of this idea is to have faculty build an online repository of useful postings. In my program, Evidence Based Coaching Certificate, we have a faculty forum where teachers share clever postings and minilectures. They are encouraged to use each other's material, giving credit to the original author. Everybody benefits if the faculty works collaboratively. Strong teaching material can be recycled, adapted, and improved; unnecessary duplication of work is avoided; and less experienced teachers can lean on their colleagues and learn in the process.

Creating Blended Models

Increasingly, for many academic and training institutions, combining some face-to-face or conference call teaching with online instruction has become the preferred model. Often, face-to-face or conference call instruction is used at the beginning of the program to orient the students and to build community. Some programs provide a midcourse or an ending-graduation face-to-face session.

> I loved this course, and especially liked that we had telephone training sessions at the beginning and end of the program. The session at the beginning gave us 'food' for discussion online. And the session at the end helped wrap up the program. Excellent job. (L. Jones, online student, end-of-term online feedback, 2008)

Two years ago Fielding Graduate University launched its Evidence Based Coaching Certificate program. Designing the program posed several issues. We knew that we wanted the bulk of the academic work to occur online, but we also wanted accreditation from the International Coach Federation (ICF). This meant that we needed to create a program that used face-to-face and telephone training as well as online work in order to meet the number of training hours required by the ICF. We settled on a yearlong program that would include three 12-week online courses, four face-to-face training sessions, and about 30 hours of telephone training.

At the design stage, this blend of media caused us some concern. Traditionally, blended programs focus on the heart of the program delivery face-to-face, while online is used for follow-up discussion and the transmission of material (Masie, 2001, p. 58)

The received wisdom when I began online teaching was that any face or voice contact ran the risk of diminishing the degree of participation and the level of engagement in online work. Our master's program actively discourages participants from phoning or e-mailing each other outside of the online forum, and partly for this reason, we create space in the forum for personal discussion.

In this new coaching certificate program, we were faced with the need to supplement online education with more immediate methods. Not only did ICF require it, but we also felt that, unlike academic study, the practical skills training necessary in a coaching course would be most effectively achieved face-to-face, with phone sessions as an additional requirement because our students are dispersed. So with some trepidation, we organized the program as a full blend of these three different media.

To our surprise, we have found that participation in the online section of the coaching course is as vibrant and intense as in the online master's program. In fact, it remains a constant and thriving element of the program. The fact that students are in touch with each other by phone, sometimes on a weekly basis, and meet at frequent intervals throughout the year seems not to detract from the quality of their online dialogue.

I suspect that there are several reasons for this. No doubt external incentives play a part. We make it clear to the students that certification will not be granted unless all three modes of teaching in the program— online, face-to-face, and telephone—are satisfactory completed. We also award, for each online course, four units of graduate-level academic credit, which can be used toward fulfillment of a master's or a doctorate. And we recognize in our grading the level and quality of online participation.

The division of the program into discrete areas also has a positive effect. Face-to-face training focuses on fundamental coaching skills. The telephone work is for regular practice and specific issues in coaching: designing appropriate assessments, asking powerful questions, coaching for change, giving appropriate feedback, knowing when to refer coaching clients to a professional counselor or therapist, and so on. In their online work, participants study theoretical material on coaching and material drawn from related disciplines and discuss the application of coaching theory to case studies. These clearly marked distinctions allow the online dialogue to maintain its own separate character. We feel that the study of the theoretical underpinnings of coaching, which is where the specifically academic excitement of this course resides, can best be accomplished through online participation.

As essential feature is that the students continue to encounter each other as a cohort, though in different groupings and configurations, in all three strands of the course. Whereas private contact through phone and e-mail would tend to dissipate the energy of the virtual classroom, these face-to-face and telephone elements, where the vibrancy of the group experience is maintained, are more likely to reinforce the collaborative nature of the online work.

Furthermore, it is in the online environment that these students, who are all adults, many of them in midlife, can be most truly self-directed in their learning and make use of their rich professional experiences in discussing new ideas.

Selecting and Training Online Instructors

Making decisions about faculty is not easy in any training or academic institutions. The Babson Survey suggests that there are experienced face-to-face teachers who find the online environment uncongenial or for whom it isn't a good fit. But there others who fail to shine in traditional face-to-face teaching and prove exceptional in the online environment.

In my experience, the only way of determining if a teacher is suited for online work is to make sure that he or she engages as a participant in an online seminar. An ideal choice of seminar might be one designed specifically to teach educators about the process of online facilitation. If this type of course is not available, I ask a prospective faculty member to participate as a student in the overview course of my blended coaching program. Because the online environment is unique, it is critical that prospective faculty engage in the medium, in whatever way possible, prior to being hired as instructors.

> As an educator, this course on online facilitation taught me important concepts that I am currently applying in my own work regarding boundaries, roles, and the many advantages and few potential disadvantages of the virtual learning environment. (S. Siphon, online student, end-of-term online feedback, 2007)

After participating in an online course, new instructors either become mentor instructors, helping out in an existing online course or they coteach with a seasoned instructor. In my experience, skillful online facilitation is a sophisticated art, which often involves a learning curve of at least one term.

New Challenges for Faculty

One of the greatest difficulties in helping faculty switch from face-to-face to online is the clash between more traditional modes of instruction and mentoring and the pedagogy of collaborative learning. For many, the instructor's perception of his or her role is to instruct. In an online environment, traditional methods will only go so far. Creating an online collaborative learning environment both sustains participation and adopts a more progressive mode of learning. But it can be difficult for some instructors to hold back long enough to allow the students to think through an issue or problem. The urge to correct and inform is deep. In addition to getting low student participation, faculty who overteach in this manner in online classes tend to burn out quickly. They often report that online teaching is more frustrating than face-to-face classroom work.

Another difficulty encountered with online teachers is the tendency by some to set up the course online and then to show up infrequently, or not at all. With motivated students, minimal presence online on the part of the instructor may not be glaringly obvious. But this situation puts the entire burden of generating dialogue on the students. Like students, online faculty need to be held accountable for showing up online a minimum of several times a week and for both broadening and deepening the online discussion.

Finally, a common difficulty is getting online faculty to understand and apply skillful online procedures. A faculty member might create an online forum that is difficult or confusing to navigate, post in random places, or post in a self-indulgent manner. All these practices make for unskillful online instruction and a less than satisfying online experience for the student.

But while some teachers may feel inhibited or frustrated by the online environment, in my experience, there are many who feel liberated by it and find the process of facilitating collaborative learning online as fulfilling as it challenging.

Conclusion

Success in this environment depends on a range of variables, including user-friendly software, clear norms for discussion and feedback, and the participation of students who are sufficiently at ease with the technology and willing to take some responsibility for their own learning. The quality of the experience depends, above all, on the nuanced skills of the inspirational online teacher.

References

Allen, E. L., & Seaman, J. (2006). *Making the grade: Online education in the United States, 2006.* Needham, MA: Sloan Consortium.

Clark, D. (2000). Psychological myths in e-learning. *Medical Teacher, 24*(6), 598–604.

Masie, E. (2001). Blended learning: The magic is in the mix. In A. Rosett (Ed.), *The ASTD e-learning handbook* (pp. 58–63). New York: McGraw-Hill.

Moshinskie, J. (2001). How to keep e-learners from e-scaping. In A. Rosett (Ed.), *The ASTD e-learning handbook* (pp. 218–233). New York: McGraw-Hill.

Spitzer, D. (2001). Don't forget the high-touch with the high-tech in distance learning. In A. Rosett (Ed.), *The ASTD e-learning handbook* (pp. 165–174). New York: McGraw-Hill.

Wildflower, L. (2002). *Online training workbook: School of HOD.* Santa Barbara, CA: The Fielding Graduate University.

Wildflower, L. (2004a). *Relationships in distance learning.* In J. V. Boettcher, L. Justice, K. Schenk, & P. L. Rogers (Eds.), *Encyclopedia of distance learning.* Thousand Oaks, CA: Sage.

Wildflower, L. (2004b). *Providing appropriate feedback.* In J. V. Boettcher, L. Justice, K. Schenk, & P. L. Rogers (Eds.), *Encyclopedia of distance learning.* Thousand Oaks, CA: Sage.

Wildflower, L. (2006). *Becoming an effective online facilitator, team leader, and coach.* Santa Barbara, CA: The Fielding Graduate University.

Part II

Implementation of Online Learning

Section C. Administration and Support

Leadership and Management of Online Learning Environments in Universities

Chapter 17

Anna DiStefano

Judy Witt

The demands of leadership are humbling—full of challenge and possibility. When leading a dispersed or distance learning environment in a university setting, the challenge grows exponentially (Shelton & Saltsman, 2005). Online learning options increase students' and faculty members' flexibility to live outside the geographic area of a main campus. Dispersed students require rethinking curriculum delivery, learning assessment, support services, and campus life. Dispersed faculty members require a broad rethinking of organizational leadership and administrative strategies as well as a significantly increased focus on clear and consistent communication. Faculty issues include governance and institutional decision making, faculty workload, technical and pedagogical training and development, access to technological support, and compensation. Campus administrators are challenged to guide their increasingly complex organizations by building on what they already know about leadership and administration principles and adapting those principles to online environments.

Based on our combined 35 years of experience leading dispersed and distance learning programs as well as insights from research-based administrative models such as the distance learning administrative operational model (Compora, 2003), we explore key areas essential to successful program operations. These factors include alignment of mission and vision, program planning and institutional capacity, administrative structures, accreditation, academic governance and faculty roles and support, educational effectiveness, marketing, student recruitment and success, and partnerships and strategic alliances.

Alignment of Mission and Vision

With regard to online initiatives, the most significant consideration for leadership and management is the initiative's fit with the university's historic mission (Rowley & Sherman, 2001). For many, if not most, institutions, delivering educational programs online is a departure from business as usual. Such is the nature of major innovations! Nevertheless, the enormity of the change will be greater for some higher education institutions than others. The specific discontinuities that an institution faces between its past and this aspect of its future will place different demands on leadership and management activities.

Leaders must be prepared to ask and answer the fundamental question of motivation as the first step in evaluating opportunities—that is, what motivates this college or university to develop an online program? To better serve a constituency to which it is historically committed? To reach groups of learners whom it has not served at all or very well? To create more effective and relevant curricula? To make better use of faculty expertise? To maximize budgetary allocations? Leaders must demonstrate that they have grappled with these key questions no matter the exact formulation of the questions and no matter how imperfect the answers. They must be able to articulate answers in favor of the initiative. Transparency of this kind will be essential when there are challenges from faculty or staff who are confused or threatened by new directions and responsibilities. Resources need to be allocated to build infrastructure in-line with online program's purpose. Articulating that purpose clearly for constituencies and seeking their input is practically important as well as strategically valuable. In their study examining six areas of planning and implementation of online programs (vision, curriculum, faculty training and support, student services, student training and support, and policies) at 108 community colleges in California, Levy and Beaulieu (2003) found it essential for comprehensive planning to address procedures, governance, and resources.

For example, if a university is seeking to broaden its reach beyond its historic service to traditional age students, it must consider the relevance of its mission to older adults as well as the capacity of its infrastructure to develop online programs to meet the needs of adult students. Or if a college has a unique academic program and wants to expand it to an online environment to a broader base of national or international students, it must evaluate and adapt its infrastructure to support learners of different cultures and in different time zones. We have found the issue of time and culture particularly relevant to planning and development. In their ongoing work to assess barriers to implementing online programs, Cho and Berge (2002) have found that clear, consistent, and centralized policy making and administrative structures are essential to implement quality distance education programs.

As the guardians of institutional mission, the university board of trustees needs to ensure that online learning initiatives are an integrated part of degree and nondegree programs designed to achieve institutional purposes. The board must demonstrate to the leadership, faculty, staff, and students that it is aware of the implications of significant online endeavors, particularly when limited budget resources may be directed to online environments.

As keepers of the curriculum, the faculty challenges itself to seek more and better vehicles for supporting student learning. Faculty must neither jump on the bandwagon of the latest technological fad, nor should they resist incorporating new means to help their students reach their learning goals. Support for faculty development is critical in this assessment both of curriculum and teaching effectiveness.

As architects of the academic enterprise, administrative leaders and managers align resources, structures, processes, and people to sustain an environment in which learners can flourish. It is these leaders and managers who must consider reasonable timelines, implications for workload, technical resources, and accreditation requirements.

With this generally stated set of responsibilities in mind, we turn next to more detailed consideration of specific areas of importance to leaders and managers: program planning, organizational capacity, technological capacity, administrative structures, relationships with accreditors, faculty models and governance, faculty development and evaluation, and assessment of educational effectiveness.

Program Planning and Institutional Capacity

Planning in one way or another assesses both the needs of the external environment and internal capabilities to meet those needs. Questions to assess the external environment include the following:

- Has market research confirmed the existence of a group of students who are interested in learning about this subject manner in an online format?

- What are the vehicles and costs for reaching that market?
- How much are students in that market niche willing to pay for this academic program in an online format?
- What is the expected timeline for students in the identified market to make decisions about enrollment?

Questions to assess the internal capacity include the following:

- What are student expectations about faculty resources and staff support?
- Is there sufficient demand and inclination to admit students more than once a year? For how many years?
- Is the market already well populated by other institutions?
- Is the field so new that work must be undertaken just to familiarize potential students with the possibilities?
- Does the new online venture have the support and approval of the host academic unit?
- If the creation of a new unit is required, has that process been properly vetted?
- Have university-wide academic bodies given their approval?
- Has administrative staff been thoroughly consulted about programmatic needs?
- Have staff needs been financially provided for?
- Does the admissions process include an assessment of the fit of students for this kind of learning program?
- Has the financial aid office been given sufficient time to seek necessary approvals?
- Does the library have appropriate resources to support faculty and students?

Note that many of the above issues seem generic to new program development, and some in fact are. However, especially for institutions with little experience in online learning, answers that have worked for campus-based programs cannot be assumed to work in the new environment.

Colleges and universities cannot leave it to online program champions to answer these questions. The role of the champions is to advocate for the initiative and to gather whatever information they can to help inform faculty colleagues and administrative managers. One task of leadership is to anticipate innovations such as online learning and to provide sufficient exposure to faculty and staff of their opportunities and demands before they are asked to consider specific new initiatives. Institutional leaders are then in a better position to assess the adequacy of questions asked and the quality of answers provided before investing in a new program—or not. Inevitably, there will be concerns. It is the rare academic institution and online initiative where all the stars are perfectly aligned. The risks of both action and inaction must be assessed.

In addition to focusing on the above questions, capacity issues are significant and can stretch leaders and their institutions to the limit if careful planning does not occur.

Organizational Capacity

The capacity of the organization encompasses not only the resources it can bring to bear on a project, but also the level of its knowledge and experience with key facets of the venture. Michael Grahame Moore, editor of *The American Journal of Distance Education,* has recommended Schreiber's (1998) description of developmental stages of an enterprise helpful in understanding an organization's capacity and maturity in delivering programs online (Moore, 2006). These stages begin with sporadic distance learning courses or events occurring at the university and progress to the last stage in which the technological infrastructure, policies, and practices required by online programs are fully institutionalized. This institutionalization represents the maturity of the online program. Problems for universities often occur when they try to move beyond their organizational core capacity and competencies too quickly (Berge, 2002, 2007).

Often, a difficult tension emerges between starting slowly and learning as one goes and the need to put in place scalable structures and well-articulated processes. Paradoxically, one or more small pilot programs can stretch organizational capacity as much as one, huge, fast-growing program. What is probably most important is the organization's capacity to learn from its experience and to make needed changes in an orderly way. The one area where this is the least true is technological capacity, where financial investments in hardware, software, and people are usually of such a magnitude that changing course can be fatal.

Technological Capacity

The scope of technological challenges for leadership and management extend far beyond the adoption of a learning management system, although it would be a huge mistake to underestimate those costs in terms of time, money, and training. Technological capacity includes matters of financial investment, curricular design, faculty and staff training, and administrative services.

University leaders must provide for and rely on the analysis and advice of technological experts who appreciate the central purposes of higher education and who are sensitive to the specific issues related to the new program. Furthermore, leaders are obligated to help such experts understand the specific characteristics that this specific college or university values most highly in the educational process. If small, interactive educational experiences have been the hallmark of a college's life, then the technology adopted must facilitate these experiences. If the integration of theory and practice is what is distinctive about this university, then the technology adopted must facilitate those goals. It may be tempting to adopt the most popular technological platforms, but it would be far preferable to pursue the best match between the specific institution's educational values and various platform capabilities as well as the specific content and process needs of the new program.

There is the nontrivial matter of cost of implementation and continual updating. The need for ongoing financial investment has led many institutional leaders to consider the option of outsourcing. This is a major decision in and of itself. We believe there that there is no right solution, and all solutions will cost money. Resource deliberations involve the highest levels of institutional leadership given their implications for financial management and fund development. Further questions will need to be raised:

- What are the implications for the use of the endowment or institutional reserves or for the priorities of the development staff?

- How do the technological needs of online programs relate to their other technological needs of this college or university? For example, is a greater priority the need for a better student records system?

- Does the sustainability of the institution require prior attention to the online environment supporting prospective students or donors?

- How will the institution access the expertise it needs to address legal and regulatory policy and procedure requirements, for example, services to those with disabilities, copyright law, intellectual property, or confidentiality requirements?

In all but the richest institutions, there will not be sufficient funds in any short period of years to fund all these needs. Some of them can likely be staged and sequenced to allow for the launch of online ventures; otherwise, some online ventures will need to be tabled until some of them are satisfactorily resolved.

Administrative Structures

More attention must be given to designing the optimum administrative structures for the online or dispersed educational environment. The administrative structure can contribute greatly to both success or failure of any given online venture. Paolucci and Gambescia (2007) reviewed the current structures in use at 239 universities across the United States for their online, distance, and distributed programs. They identified six general administrative structures currently emerging: (1) academic department, (2) continuing education-professional studies unit, (3) distance education unit, (4) consortium, (5) alliance, and (6) outsource. They found that 90% of the schools were using an internally based administrative arrangement in which either an academic department, a professional studies unit, or a distance education unit administered the programs. Only 10% were using an externally based administrative structure in which the programs were part of a consortium, alliance, or were outsourced. Although there is a major debate in the field about the administration of online structures, the majority of colleges and universities continue to maintain control of the programs within their own academic departments.

Using a case study research design, Compora (2003) gathered data from six selected colleges and universities in Ohio for the purpose of reviewing their practices in distance learning. He found little consistency in policies and a lack of consistency of operationalizing those that did exist. These findings prompted him to propose a nine-step model to address the major administrative needs of online learning programs—the distance education administrative operative model. This model addresses (1) assessment; (2) budget; (3) coordination of all institutional efforts and with other entities; (4) delivery models; (5) evaluation; (6) faculty involvement and training; (7) generation of a mission statement; (8) hierarchical approval system for establishing academic content, learning outcomes, and budget; and (9) implementation of support systems. This is an excellent example of a model that could be followed to make the most of the capacity of the online learning environment. Haphazard introduction and implementation of online programs lead only to squandering of this powerful learning environment.

Accreditation

The regulations of federal and some state governments as well as the standards of regional and specialized accrediting bodies influence higher education's forays into online learning initiatives. These regulations and standards continue to evolve, and they must be taken into account as institutions create new programs. Some governmental and specialized accrediting bodies remain skeptical, if not openly hostile, to online education. That is a reality that is best addressed through political and educational strategies rather than avoidance of necessary approvals or the futile submission of proposals for which there is no reasonable expectation of success.

College and university leaders must evaluate how proposals for online initiatives fit in with their history with an accrediting body. It is foolish to think that accreditors will not remember that an institution has had persistent problems with technological capacity or with inadequate faculty resources. Or, perhaps, accreditors will wonder how the resources that are directed to these online ventures will impact other areas that they have previously identified as needing institutional attention. Higher education leaders must insist that accrediting body requirements and processes be taken seriously and addressed as part of the program's development. They risk dire consequences for their institutions if they do otherwise.

Finally in this area, given the level of inexperience that some institutions may have with online initiatives and the imprecision of market research and program planning, institutional administrators are asked to provide for realistic and legitimate teach-out plans. Such plans should be more than offering students the opportunity to enroll in campus-based programs. There are likely negative financial consequences associated with teach-out options, and they must be incorporated into financial forecasts.

Academic Governance and Faculty Role and Support

A major issue in higher education today concerns the role of faculty in activities from curriculum development to institutional governance. These concerns focus on two of the three historical expectations of faculty work—that is, teaching and service. Although research and scholarship in the academy remain largely unquestioned, institutional leaders struggle with how to keep up with the need to support such activity while at the same time making space for the kinds of pedagogical innovations offered by online education.

It is more and more common for colleges and universities to consider the unbundling of faculty responsibilities for the teaching-learning process. These efforts are partly motivated by the desire to reduce compensation costs. Other motivations include a wish to remain agile institutionally in responding to the changing demands and expectations of society and employers, or the desire to make better use of professional-practitioner expertise. Still another stimulus is a response to critics of the tenure system that may seem to protect those faculty members who do not feel accountable for what their students learn.

The confluence of these factors has led many institutions to outsource the development of online curricula to instructional designers or a few full-time faculty members and to then hire a cadre of contingent faculty to deliver these prepackaged courses. Although such an approach may make sense in a few circumstances or as a short-term strategy to launch a new program, we believe the benefits are outweighed by the nonmonetary costs. When faculty loses ownership of the curriculum, the value and vitality of their role are diminished. That price is paid by their students who trade the promise of quality for the guarantee of predictability. This argument is not in support of tenure but rather for the centrality of faculty responsibility for the articulation of learning outcomes and the facilitation of student learning to achieve those outcomes. With responsibility comes the opportunity for shared governance and the requirement for meaningful faculty evaluation and development.

Shared governance is at one and the same time both a quaint tradition of the academy and also a manifestation of its progressive and democratic propensity. Online learning initiatives and faculty roles within them are in no way antithetical to shared governance models. Whether faculty have tenure or are on multiyear contracts, whether they are full-time or part-time, they can have a meaningful role in institutional decision making. Indeed, since online learning is first and foremost about learning, whose decision should it be? How this involvement is structured will vary, of course, based on institutional culture and goals.

Concomitant with faculty prerogative for academic decision making is faculty responsibility and accountability for its own development and evaluation. Institutional leaders must build an atmosphere of trust and support such that faculty feel acknowledged and rewarded not only for their strengths but also for being willing to address their online teaching limitations. Developing competence in the facilitation of learning in online environments is noticeably an arena where most faculty members need assistance. It is still too new a learning environment and one that changes too quickly for academic leaders to assume requisite and up-to-date competence. Leadership must be willing to invest in faculty learning in both technical and pedagogical domains. It is too often the case that higher education leaders invest great amounts of institutional capital that is then underutilized by most users. At least at this point in our society's familiarity with technological tools, leaders and managers cannot assume that the best use of such tools, especially by faculty and administrators, is intuitive or uncomplicated. It takes the leadership of an institution to convince such persons of the value of training, and it requires the skill of competent administrators to design programs that deliver useful and relevant information that leads to greater competence and confidence.

Intertwined with the need to support faculty is the need for meaningful and collaborative evaluation. Academic administrators have the responsibility for articulating expectations as unambiguously as possible, for creating environments where they are readily attainable, and then for designing faculty evaluative processes that are fair and results-oriented. Student evaluations of faculty work are part of most assessment processes, but the better evaluation processes go far beyond the collection of student ratings. In particular, the online environment provides unusually rich documentation of course design and delivery. Evaluation of student work products, interactions with students, and quality of resources used can be extensively documented. Management can create systems for both collecting and aggregating performance indicators as well as providing for their external review in light of best online teaching practices. Such assessment of faculty effectiveness feeds directly into the assessment of educational effectiveness of online initiatives.

Educational Effectiveness

We return full circle to the matter of program goals and learning outcomes. One of the advantages of new ventures such as online learning in education today is that their planning has involved statements of intended outcomes and their alignment with both institutional outcomes and program course requirements—that is, course activities and objectives. It is important that these activities be integrated to the fullest extent possible with ongoing institutionwide procedures, for example, periodic program review.

In addition to asking to what extent actual student learning outcomes match intended outcomes, retention and graduation rates are also valuable indicators of effectiveness. Such data are important to examine for all of education, but in particular for online learning. There is still much to be learned about what kinds of online learning environments work best for which students and what could be modified to make them more effective for others.

Harroff and Valentine (2006) explored quality dimensions of Web-based adult education describing six dimensions of program quality in the quality of

1. instruction,

2. administrative recognition and support,

3. advisement,

4. technical support,

5. advance information to potential students, and

6. course evaluation procedures.

These criteria may be used as a clear framework for evaluation of effectiveness on university, department, and programmatic levels. Our discussion of effectiveness leads us to turn now to the student services dimension of leadership and management of online programs focusing developmentally on entry, engagement, and completion.

Marketing, Student Recruitment, and Success

Student recruitment, retention, and completion are the heart of our work as educators and emerged as major challenges in the early days of online learning environments (Morris, Wu, & Finnegan, 2005). Marketing and student support services are essential and may seem particularly challenged in the online environment; thus, it is even more important that student success is viewed as everyone's responsibility at the institution, and the leadership must provide a consistent model by focusing attention on student success continuously. A well-organized administrative structure is essential to providing effective student support (Cho & Berge, 2002). In fact, gaps in service for students taking online courses lead to student feelings of isolation, frustration and alienation (Shelton & Saltsman, 2005, p. 83). This is a significant risk for online students because of perceived lack of access to a campus and its services.

It is important to conduct a student service assessment to evaluate student needs and to develop a plan of action to make each service available and accessible. For most institutions, several adaptations to traditional services will need to be made to serve the online learners. These will include marketing and admissions, academic advising, academic support, financial aid, the business office operations, records, registrar, and student life. To highlight the areas needing the most attention in online learning environments, we discuss students' entry and engagement.

Entry

Entry begins with marketing and advertising. Marketing plans and implementation must clearly align with the institution's brand and identity. Consistent messages are essential. These must be provided through multiple recruitment channels that will potentially include direct marketing, print and online advertising, newsletters, Web sites, and so on. An effective marketing mix is critical to recruiting students well matched with the institution's online environments. Additionally, public relations and publicity efforts must align for recruitment to be effective and cost efficient. As long as alignment is carefully monitored, marketing of online programs can also be outsourced in various ways. Two examples are 1) hiring a marketing firm to conduct the complete marketing operation and 2) utilizing a lead-generation company to generate leads to which the university admissions office responds.

Student finances, financial aid, and locus of control have been identified to predict dropout and completion rates with a high rate of accuracy in distance learning environments (Morris, Wu, & Finnegan, 2005). Recent changes in financial aid have opened online environments to more financial aid eligibility and will greatly enhance opportunities for students. The same financial aid services must be available to both campus-based and online students. This will take careful planning and perhaps an adjustment in staffing in the financial aid office. Web sites must be established with links to information needed both from the university and the federal financial aid centers. Telephone and online helpdesks will be needed for students to access information that they would usually go to the financial aid office to access.

For online students, the records office must provide online registration for online courses. The business office and financial operations must make payment online easy. Although most universities now have these functions available online, some do not. Administrators should make these functions a priority as ease of registration and payment are essential for the student who may live a sizable distance from campus.

With regard to locus of control (i.e., the source of personal motivation), we emphasize the recruitment work of finding the proper fit. However, high-quality, personal, and well-organized orientation programs may also be a key intervention. Orientations to online work generally take one of two forms: course orientation and program orientation. In the course orientation model, the student is given actual course materials usually in a step-by-step fashion. This would include an orientation to the online environment in which the class will be taught and to the specifics of the requirements. The second option, the program orientation, is a separate course or experience specifically designed to orient students to online work. Fielding Graduate University utilizes this second option in all of its degree and certificate programs. For example, the Organization Management & Development online master's program offers orientation (OMD 600) through an online seminar that introduces students to the program's practices, learning model, and technology. Students learn to use the Fielding system to navigate, post, and complete assignments that consist of tutorials, practical exercises, and dialogue with other students and faculty facilitators. Students usually spend from 10 to 45 minutes per day responding to brief assignments and students and faculty online posts. OMD 600 is a required seminar and is offered on a noncredit basis.

Whichever type of orientation a university chooses, a thorough high quality orientation program is essential to online learning and should include an assessment of a student's experience and online abilities as well as previous academic preparation and technical competencies (Shelton & Saltsman, 2003). Buchanan (1999) argued that preassessment helps to ensure the quality of the academic program. Assessment should not generally be used to eliminate students from programs, but to identify support needs. In our opinion, using assessment to eliminate students at the outset would only be recommended if the assessment process has such strong face validity that it is clear to the applicant or student that they are unsuitable for online learning. Even so, the elimination of students should ideally include recommendations for skill building or other academic options.

Preentry variables that may help distinguish students who will complete online learning successfully have been identified as prior educational experience and prior computer training (Dupin-Bryant, 2004). Care should be taken to ensure that students both have access to the needed technology and are able to use it. Technological support such as helpdesks and online training options are important on entry and during a student's enrollment. In addition, orientation programs should engage the student with the university community. Online students need to feel as much a part of the larger institution as the face-to-face students do. At Fielding, we use a combination of online and face-to-face orientations in our doctoral programs. Most assessment, technical, and informational aspects of the programs are accomplished online prior to the face-to-face sessions. This leaves the face-to-face environment for creating professional learning relationships with faculty and other students, experiencing the University culture, and building the motivation and commitment to full engagement with and completion of the program.

Engagement

The instructional methods used in online learning are critical. Learning in the distance environment cannot be passive (Palloff & Pratt, 2007, p. 5). Teacher presence and learner engagement have continuously been identified as major factors in success. Administration should take care in training faculty in both the use of software and the pedagogy of teaching online, which differs significantly from teaching face-to-face. The practice is not the same and training is needed for faculty members. Thus, faculty support is essential.

Faculty members teaching online need basic training in online teaching and learning. An accessible helpdesk is as essential to faculty as it is to students. Faculty must be rewarded for working online through recognition practices (monetary and nonmonetary) and workload equivalencies. Workload adjustments may need to be considered. Many faculty members report that teaching online takes more time and concentrated effort than face-to-face teaching. Recent research, however, is beginning to call that into question and is suggesting that the difference may be more related to the nature and pacing of class assignments than the amount of time or effort (Hislop & Ellis, 2004); the assignments are more frequent and are spread across the week rather than being contained and time-bound as is a traditional class.

In addition to faculty development, faculty must be highly motivated to teach online because it takes constant and consistent attention. Teaching online requires a personal style that is engaging and may best be described as serving as a facilitator or coach. Faculty who do well teaching online are those who enjoy interacting and challenging individual students as well as the class as a whole. In addition, regular time must be set aside to respond to the online work of students as well as to their questions and dialogue. This takes a certain commitment and temperament as an instructor. Attention to these issues must be addressed by the administration and rewarded.

The quality of advisement and accessibility of university services has been identified as one of the major barriers to online student success (Cho & Berge, 2002). Each institution will need to build into its online courses and programs early warning systems for academic issues and provide tutoring and academic support when needed. Although these systems and interventions may parallel those offered to campus-based students, they obviously need to employ the strategies used in course delivery.

Enhancements made to student services on behalf of students in online classes and programs are clearly critical. At the same time, sometimes, supporting student success can also mean entering into partnerships and alliances with other organizations to multiply the resources available to students.

Partnerships and Strategic Alliances

Going it alone is simply not an option today for most institutions. This is especially true as we move to more online operations and instructional models. The complexity of the marketplace, infrastructure needs, and financial options often demand collaborations and partnerships. Such partnerships take on many forms; we will address two types—institutional and programmatic—as they relate to the online environment. Matthews (2002) has described three emerging types of institutional alliances and partnerships in online learning environments: consortia or collaborative, contracted or brokered, and virtual universities.

Consortia or Collaborative

Consortia for online services are in this category, as are agreements to share various institutional resources. Typically, traditional institutions form consortia to join together, pooling their resources to provide distance education, usually on a statewide or regional basis. The nature of the administration and operations of each program varies; however, there always exists a strong, formal relationship among the organizations involved. These alliances and partnerships may be especially helpful as an institution moves more and more online and students and faculty become more and more dispersed. Examples run the gamut and vary in the base for the affiliation. Here are some examples:

- Academic or professional affiliations:
  - The Child Development Training Consortium is designed to deliver specialized instruction in one academic area. See http://www.childdevelopment.org/cs/cdtc/print/htdocs/about.htm
- Like-minded, ideological or pedagogical-androgogical affiliations:
  - Consortium for Innovative Environments in Learning. See http://www.cielearn.org/index.htm
  - Online Consortium of Independent Colleges and Universities. See http://www.ocicu.org
- State and regional affiliations:
  - Connecticut Distance Learning Consortium. See http://www.ctdlc.org/About/index.html
  - SUNY Learning Network. See http://sln.suny.edu/index.html

In all of these arrangements, institutions of higher learning have joined together to provide a virtual learning environment and online courses and degrees via cooperative programming. However, the authority for awarding academic units and degrees rests with the individual institutions.

Contracted or Brokered Agreements

Matthews (2002) defined these as arrangements where the contracted agent actually awards credits and the degree. Although this type of outsourcing is much less common, Howell, Williams, and Lindsay's (2003) seminal meta-analysis of the literature on the current and future directions of distance education found that outsourcing and related partnerships are on the increase. Although full outsourcing of academic programs may run afoul of accrediting agencies, many institutions have turned over much of the administrative and operational duties to outside organizations and are able to stay within accreditation guidelines.

Virtual Universities

Some states and groups of states have collaborated to create distinct virtual universities. Thirteen members of the Western Governors Association created Western Governors University (See http://www.wgu.edu/index.asp). Although virtual universities are a major area of growth in higher education today, we do not discuss them in-depth.

Programmatic alliances and partnerships are usually more focused on an academic area and involve sharing of expertise, curriculum, faculty, or marketplace sectors. Particularly in the online marketplace, universities may agree to share content. Such agreements add resources, speed implementation of new programs, and multiply expertise.

Online and dispersed programs are now beginning to implement creative collaborations across institutional types to build education or professional development pipelines similar to the 2 + 2 programs common in the 1990s linking community colleges with 4-year institutions. Today, such programs exist and are flourishing across all academic levels including graduate education. They fall into three categories:

1. *Feeder or articulation programs and partnerships.* This involves working with other higher education institutions that offer programs that bear academic credit) and articulating them through the programs of each institution such that students can progress from one institution to the other seamlessly. Graduates of one institution's program automatically receive advanced standing or an agreed-upon number of credits at the other institution as they matriculate.

2. *Building from professional development directly into degree programs.* This involves working with various kinds of professional organizations to build on their professional development activities and to offer at least some of these activities together with the home institution for credit that could be applied to degree programs.

3. *Building a consortium between and among professional organizations and colleges/universities.* Programs do this to offer academic credit, certificates, or specialist options as stepping-stones toward degree programs.

For example, at Fielding Graduate University, a master's program in media psychology and social change has been initiated involving a partnership between the University of California, Los Angeles (UCLA), Extension and the Fielding School of Psychology under the consortium model. Students enroll initially at UCLA for the first 12 units of the program. At that point, they receive a graduate academic certificate and may choose to either stop their study or seamlessly enroll at Fielding to complete their master's degree. Other programs offer types of dual enrollment or other creative solutions to maximize resources and enrollments at both institutions. Creating a network of feeders through such programs is one way to both position an institution in the online marketplace and to assure sustainability by enlisting partner institutions to multiply the marketing impact and effectiveness.

Partnerships and collaborations may also be developed with professional organizations. This is particularly useful for online programs because the online environment allows for international connections and easy links to and from Web sites enhancing marketing, creditability and access for all concerned. Such associations usually take the form of offering an approved certification; agreements to market services, courses, or degrees to organization members; and development of research projects or research training sites or other win–win situations for both the professional organization and the university. Corporations and community based nonprofits also offer similar options for universities to explore.

Keys to Locating Partners

In locating partners, institutions must take the initiative. We go back to a question raised earlier: "Why are we (this particular college or university) doing this?" Decide what is needed and look for key organizations that may be able to provide it. A critical factor in seeking a partnership is to be clear on the purpose and what each institution will gain from the relationship. It is just as important to know what the institution needs as it is to know what the institution has to offer. This may include expertise, positioning, market share, online platform, consortium membership, funding resources and relationships, and so on.

The questions each institution will ask itself will vary and many surveys on readiness for selecting institutional partnerships are available (Duin, Baer, & Starke-Mayerring, 2001, pp. 61–66). As an orientation to the quest for suitable partnerships and strategic alliances, we offer the following common evaluative questions:

1. Mission, vision, and values issues

    a. Are the values of the potential partner congruent?

    b. Is the mission of the potential partner compatible?

    c. Does the potential partnership contribute to the realization of the institution's vision, mission, and strategic goals?

2. Accreditation issues

    a. Does the partnership jeopardize in any way the institution's accreditation status?

    b. Does the potential partnership enhance the institution's ability to seek special credentialing or certifications?

3. Program and service issues

    a. Does the potential partnership add to the institution's academic offerings or expertise?

    b. Does the potential partnership add to the institutions online teaching and learning operations or expertise?

4. Resource issues

    a. Does the potential partnership enhance the institution's funds development efforts?

    b. What additional resources will it take to develop, launch, and maintain the partnership, and how will those funds be obtained?

    c. What is the opportunity cost for the institution, and is it worth the potential financial gain or other gain from the partnership?

    d. What is the level of anticipated financial return or saving and over what period of time?

5. Public relations and marketing issues

    a. Would the relationship with the potential partner enhance the institution's reputation and prestige?

    b. How does the partnership address a market need?

Remember that most strategic alliances and partnerships will either be with other service providers or be with clients to whom the institution provides the services and educational options or both.

Forging Relationships and Agreements

Once potential partners are identified, the real work begins. The next step involves negotiating each entity's commitments and responsibilities as well as the financial model. Clarity here is essential. Forging partnerships is a process of discovery and disclosure. Readiness begins with establishing communication, trust, and support (Duin et al., 2001, p. 68). Negotiations can be challenging, but by following basic principles all parties can get their needs met and forge agreements that work. Fisher and Ury (1991) offered some of the best strategies for negotiation that we have found based on principles, interests, and outcomes for mutual gain.

Conclusion

Leading higher education institutions generally and online environments in particular is at once both exhilarating and exhausting. A review of the verbs we have used—for example, rethinking, adapting, communicating, evaluating, questioning, grappling, designing, developing, investing, learning, collaborating, and so on—reveals the skills of grasping what is already in front of us and imagining what could be there as well or instead. Online education is shaped by what we already believe about learning and by our own capacity to engage in it. Successful leaders must be knowledgeable about planning, governance, accreditation, technology, finances, evaluation, collaboration, and more. Most of all, they must have a passion for supporting faculty as facilitators of student learning, wherever and however that occurs.

References

Berge, Z. L. (2002). Obstacles to distance training and education in corporate organizations. *Journal of Workplace Learning, 14*(5), 182–189.

Berge, Z. L. (2007). Training in the corporate sector. In M. G. Moore (Ed.), *Handbook of distance education* (2nd ed., pp. 515–531). Mahwah, NJ: Lawrence Erlbaum.

Buchanan, E. A. (1999). Assessment measures: Pre-test for successful distance teaching and learning? *Online Journal of Distance Learning Administration, 3*(1). Retrieved February 25, 2007, from http://www.westga.edu/~distance/buchanan24

Cho, S. K., & Berge, Z. L. (2002). Overcoming barriers to distance training and education. *USDLA Journal, 16*(1). Retrieved February 18, 2008, from http://www.usdla.org/html/journal/JAN02_Issue/article01.html

Compora, D. P. (2003). Current trends in distance education: An administrative model. *Online Journal of Distance Learning Administration, 6*(2). Retrieved February 18, 2008, http://www.westga.edu/~distance/ojdla/summer62/compora62.html

Duin, A. H., Baer, L. L., & Starke-Mayerring, D. (2001). *Partnering in the learning marketspace.* San Francisco: Jossey-Bass.

Dupin-Bryant, P. (2004). Pre-entry variables related =o retention in online distance education. *American Journal of Distance Education, 18*(4), 99–206.

Fisher, R., & Ury, W. (1991). *Getting to yes: Negotiating agreement without giving in.* New York: Penguin Books.

Harroff, P. A., & Valentine, T. (2006). Dimensions of program quality in Web-based adult education. *American Journal of Distance Education, 20*(1), 7–22.

Hislop, G. W., & Ellis, H. J. C. (2004). A study of faculty effort in online teaching. *The Internet and Higher Education, 7*(1), 15–31.

Howell, S., Williams, B. P., & Lindsay, N. K. (2003). Thirty-two trends affecting distance education: An informed foundation for strategic planning. *Online Journal of Distance learning Administration, 6*(3). Retrieved January 11, 2009, from http://www.westga.edu/~distance/ojdla/fall63/howell63.html

Levy, S., & Beaulieu, R. (2003). Online distance learning among the California Community Colleges: Looking at the planning and implementation. *American Journal of Distance Education, 17*(4), 207–220.

Matthews, D. (2002). Distance education: What is it? Utilization of distance education in the United States. In R. Discenza, C. Howard, & K. Schenk (Eds.), *The design & management of effective distance learning programs* (pp. 1–20). Hershey, PA: City Idea Group.

Moore, M. G. (2006). Stages of organizational capacity. *American Journal of Distance Education, 20*(4), 91–193.

Morris, L. V., Wu, S., & Finnegan, C. L. (2005). Predicting retention in online general education courses. *American Journal of Distance Education, 19*(1), 3–36.

Palloff, R. M., & Pratt, K. (2007). *Building online learning communities* (2nd ed.). San Francisco: Jossey-Bass.

Paolucci, R., & Gambescia, S. (2007). Current administrative Structures used for online degree program offerings in higher education. *Online Journal of Distance Learning Administration, 10*(3). Retrieved February 25, 2007, from http://www.westga.edu/~distance/ojdla/fall103/gambescia103.htm

Rowley, D. J., & Sherman, H. (2001). *From strategy to change implementing the plan in higher education.* San Francisco: Jossey-Bass.

Shelton, K., & Saltsman, G. (2005). *An administrator's guide to online education.* Greenwich, CT: IAP-Information Age.

Chapter 18

Accrediting Online Institutions and Programs

Quality Assurance or Bureaucratic Hurdle?

Ralph Wolff

ccreditation is critical to initiating new online institutions and pro-grams. Not only can accreditation provide access to financial aid for students, but also it can ensure recognition of credits and degrees within and outside the United States. In an increasingly global market, U.S. accreditation can be seen as a mark of quality and as a competitive advantage (Ewell, 2008). Once obtained, accreditation must be maintained, and accrediting agencies give special scrutiny to online programs and institutions. Yet, there are many different accrediting agencies, and each has its own set of standards and procedures that can be a maze of rules to the uninitiated. Learning to navigate the requirements of accreditation might seem bureaucratic at first, but once understood (and embraced), the requirements of accreditation can be a useful force for quality assurance and improvement.

Accreditation itself is a product of institutional needs at the turn of the 20th century when the growth in the number of high schools and colleges led to the institutions themselves establishing processes for identifying measures of quality for recognition of graduates. Given the typical limits of travel at that time, regional associations formed to review institutions to assure one another of their quality. Out of these regional associations began the New England and North Central Associations of Schools and Colleges. These regional groupings have now expanded to six regions covering the United States, whose geographical configuration is more a historical accident than the result of intentional planning. Accrediting functions of online institutions and programs are carried out by a total of seven higher education accrediting commissions since the Western region has separate commissions for junior-community and senior colleges.[1] Although each commission has adopted its own accrediting standards and procedures, there is a common underlying framework of quality that applies to all regions, as described below. The jurisdiction of regional accrediting agencies typically is based on the state in which the institution is incorporated and extends to all activities of the institution, even if it serves students who live beyond the boundaries of the region. This is important for online institutions and programs since they typically extend beyond the boundaries of any particular jurisdiction. Indeed, it might be argued that as online instruction becomes ever more popular at all institutions, its boundaryless character renders regional accreditation obsolete. (Ewell, 2008) Nonetheless, the structure of accreditation is likely to stay the same for the foreseeable future, and online accreditation will continue to be reviewed in this context.

For new online institutions, the state of incorporation will determine the regional accrediting agency that will have jurisdiction over its distance education programs. In the past, some regions were considered more (or less) hospitable to innovative or online education. Now all of the regional agencies accredit online degree programs, and nearly all accredit completely online institutions. As further described below, the regionals have adopted a common set of principles and best practices regarding online programs and institutions to avoid region shopping.

A more recent phenomenon is the development and growth of national and specialized accrediting agencies. National accrediting agencies accredit institutions no matter where incorporated and typically evaluate vocational and technical institutions. Three national accrediting agencies evaluate online learning institutions and programs: the Distance Education and Training Council, the Accrediting Commission of Independent Colleges and Schools, and the Accrediting Commission of Careers Schools and Colleges of Technology. Increasingly, institutions accredited by these agencies are moving toward higher level degrees.

Accreditation by regional and national agencies is granted at the institutional level, not program level, and all programs of the institution are covered within the scope of accreditation. Specialized accrediting agencies focus on programs within a single discipline or disciplinary area, such as psychology, medicine, law, and so on. Specialized accreditation has become increasingly important for professional recognition of degrees and graduates, and in some fields, it is a prerequisite for licensure. In the past 25 years, there has been a significant increase in the number of specialized accreditors, now numbering over one hundred. Notwithstanding their increasing importance, there is still a wide variation among specialized agencies regarding distance education. Some are open to such programs and institutions, while others (e.g., law) do not permit accreditation of online programs or institutions at this point.

The focus of this chapter is on the standards and processes of regional accreditation, though the intent is to be of use for practitioners of online learning. It is important to understand the rules and procedures of one's specific accrediting agency since most agencies have their own standards and procedures for online programs. At the same time, there is enough commonality in the approaches of regional accrediting agencies to review general principles and practices in this chapter. This chapter is intended to highlight problems associated with gaining accreditation of online programs and institutions and to offer ways to address them.

Practice Tip: It is important to identify the specific accreditation agency or agencies that a particular program or institution would need to work with for accreditation. In large institutions, accreditation matters are often handled by administrators and often too little is known about regional accrediting agency standards, policies, and procedures by deans and faculty who might develop such programs. Such ignorance can cause significant trouble since failure to follow agency rules for even the offering of a single program can lead to an institutional sanction and can jeopardize the entire institution's accreditation. It is the responsibility of each institution to learn the agency's rules, policies, and procedures before starting an online program.

What to do. (1) Identify which accrediting agency's rules are applicable and review the agency's standards, policies, and procedures. This may require searching the agency's Web site for information on distance education. (2) Contact the agency for further information. Although agencies are organized differently, all have someone who can answer questions about the rules applying to distance education. Although this may sound simple, it is remarkable how infrequently the resources of accrediting agencies are tapped at the early stages of program development or accreditation. (3) Once you have a general idea of the rules and procedures of the agency and have studied them, get to know your institution's accrediting agency liaison. Several accrediting agencies assign a staff member for each institution, while others might have a specified staff member assigned to address substantive change issues relating to distance education. These staff members can answer specific questions, assist with document preparation, organize site reviews, and often have the ability to conduct staff reviews of programs. It can only help to have agency staff understand the particulars of your program or institution and help you walk through what may seem a labyrinth of reviews.

In the early years of distance education, there was considerable skepticism whether the quality of online programs or institutions would be comparable to on-campus programs with face-to-face instruction. Largely such concerns arose from unfavorable views by traditional academics of correspondence programs. With the advent of the Internet and improved technology—such as widespread access to broadband and software support—such concerns have diminished but have not been eliminated altogether. There remains considerable concern within Congress that the quality of distance education programs be monitored and assured, especially in the management of rapid growth.

To address these quality issues, and the challenges of providing financial aid to students in such programs, Congress authorized the Department of Education to undertake a demonstration program, working with distance education institutional cohorts, whereby the provision of aid and the quality of these programs would be monitored. The department issued three reports to Congress on this project in 2001, 2005, and 2006. In working with both regional and national accreditation agencies, and evaluators, the department found that "there was a remarkable consistency in how they evaluated distance education programs, and in what they considered to be the most important indicators, in spite of the differences in the accrediting organization's standards and means of addressing distance education" (Department of Education, Office of Postsecondary Education [USDE], 2006, p. 2). As further described below, the department found that there were no significant issues preventing moving forward in assuring the quality of distance education.

Rules Governing Accrediting Agencies

Under the Higher Education Act (HEA), accrediting agencies need to be recognized by a process of periodic review by the USDE. Once an agency is recognized by USDE, students in institutions accredited by the agency are eligible for financial aid under Title IV. With each reauthorization of the HEA, Congress imposes new requirements or areas of emphasis. This, in turn, leads to the development of an even more extensive set of regulations by USDE to implement the HEA. Congress has just adopted and the president has signed significant revisions to the HEA, and several new provisions affecting online education have been adopted. The USDE will initiate proceedings in early 2009 for developing and adopting further regulations to implement the new statutory provisions. There has been considerable caution on the part of Congress over the development of online programs and institutions, reflected in both statutory and regulatory provisions specifically relating to online education. Key issues include the following.

Scope of authority. Part of each accrediting agency's recognition by USDE is a determination of its scope of authority. Typically, this has meant the geographical boundaries of the agency or the type of programs it accredits. The USDE has adopted regulations requiring each accrediting agency to be reviewed specifically for online programs and institutions in order for such accreditation to be included in the agency's scope of authority. Under these rules, each agency must be reviewed and approved by the USDE before it is recognized to accredit distance education programs and institutions. All of the regional accrediting agencies have received approval within their scope of authority, though their procedures are reviewed each time the agency comes up for its major recognition review, which occurs within a maximum of 5 years. Each national and specialized accrediting agency also needs to go through this process, which can cause considerable delay and additional review by the USDE. The Higher Education Reauthorization Act would remove this restriction and allow all recognized agencies to extend their accreditation to online programs and institutions without prior approval and to have this authority reviewed at the time of their 5-year recognition continuation review.

Separate standards for online education. Over the past several years, considerable debate has occurred about whether a separate set of accreditation standards should be required for online education. Accrediting agencies have maintained that their standards apply equally effectively to online as well as to classroom-based education and that separate standards would be unworkable. This is especially true as more and more hybrid programs are offered combining classroom and online instruction. So far, this position has prevailed and the newly adopted HEA codifies that separate standards are not required. Nonetheless, in the USDE review of the scope of authority of accrediting agencies, the USDE has required at least one agency, the Senior College Commission of the Western Association, to develop special protocols for the review of online education and demonstrate it is implementing these protocols (Western Association of Schools and Colleges [WASC], 2008).

Substantive change for any change in modality. USDE regulations regarding substantive change have a significant impact on accrediting agencies and online programs. Once a new programmatic or institutional change is identified as a substantive change, the accrediting agency must review and approve it before it is initiated. Failure to do so could jeopardize the entire institution's accreditation. USDE regulations identify a number of areas of substantive change, including one that affects online education: "The addition of courses or programs that represent a significant departure, in either content or method of delivery, from those that were offered when the agency last evaluated the institution" (20 U.S.C. §1099b). This change in the method of delivery regulation has led all accrediting agencies to identify the first or subsequent offerings of online programs to be a substantive change requiring prior review and approval. Each accrediting agency, as a result, has developed specific criteria for prior review and approval of online programs.

Most agencies rely upon a definition that only programs where 50% or more of a degree is offered online will trigger the substantive change process. Thus, individual courses offered online would not constitute a substantive change, unless they added up to 50% or more of a degree or were being offered as the early portion of a full degree program. As described below, substantive change reviews cover a wide range of topics to ensure that new programs are well planned, that students will receive adequate support services, that faculty are well trained, and so on. Moreover, each commission has its own structure for reviewing and approving substantive changes. Several have separate substantive change review committees, composed of commissioners, and/or institutional representatives. Others permit staff reviews for certain types of changes. Depending on the structure of review, processing an application for substantive change may take weeks or many months. At some agencies, the review is focused on institutional characteristics overseeing the development and quality of distance education programs, whereas at other agencies, the focus is on individual program approvals.

Practice Tip: Each accrediting agency has its own criteria for what constitutes a substantive change. Regardless whether the agency requires prior approval of each or reviews only the first or first two programs, online programs must be included in the comprehensive institutional evaluation conducted by the agency.

What to do. One of the first things to do is to conduct an inventory of online programs offered at the institution, including those that are offered in combination with classroom learning. It is surprising the number of times an institution learns that 50% or more of a degree is being offered online without having obtained prior approval by the accrediting agency or sometimes even by the central administration. A few online courses can, over time, accrete to 50% or more of a program without anyone recognizing that this has triggered the need for approval. When the same program is offered online as offered on campus, institutional policy or practice may not call for a separate internal prior review process. Nonetheless, such programs will often trigger an accrediting agency review, and the dean or other responsible administrator may not be aware of the need for separate approval of such a change in modality. If any programs are found that have not received approval and needed to, then the accrediting agency is to be notified so a review can be undertaken. Failure to do so could lead to an institutional sanction. It is important to understand how to prepare a substantive change request and how to prepare programs for review during a site visit. Both are discussed further below. Additionally, it is important to learn the lead time required to develop, submit, and obtain approval for a new online program since a common mistake is to submit the application too late for implementing the program at the desired time.

Rapid growth. Under existing regulations, accrediting agencies are required to monitor rapid growth of programs and enrollments as part of their substantive change processes. As a consequence, agencies are expected to require institutions to seek prior approval before a major expansion of distance education (or off-campus) programs. Each agency has different procedures for monitoring such growth. The concern is that rapid growth can lead to diminished quality and accountability.

Practice Tip: Institutions that are contemplating a significant development or increase of online programs will need to work with their accrediting agency to determine how such an increase will be addressed by the agency, and then monitored. Even institutions that have secured institutional approval to develop online programs should verify that a significant increase would be approved by the agency without additional reporting since this is a federal requirement.

Common Principles Governing Accreditation of Online Programs

In 2001, the Council of Regional Accrediting Commissions (C-RAC) developed a set of common guidelines for online programs adopted by all seven accrediting agencies: a "Statement of Best Practices for Electronically Offered Degree and Certificate Programs." This statement is found on each agency's Web site. These best practices are used as guidelines and support materials for institutions and teams and supplement each agency's separate criteria for substantive change and standards of accreditation.

There are a number of key principles underlying the C-RAC statement. These include a strong emphasis on the institution to design, develop, and implement online programs meeting the same standards of quality and integrity as with other programs offered by other modalities of instruction at the institution. This responsibility includes assuring that there is a coherent and substantive curriculum, that student needs are met to ensure their academic success, and that online programs provide for a community of learning where it is possible for students to interact with faculty and their fellow students and where the institution assumes responsibility to periodically assess its online offerings to ensure quality and to make improvements.

The accrediting agencies have attempted to communicate with this statement that, fundamentally, the assurance of quality of online programs rests primarily with each institution and not its accreditor. And it is the responsibility of the institution to ensure that the quality and integrity of online programs is the same as for any program offered by the institution.

The guidelines and best practice statements were developed at a time when accreditors were dealing with an ever-increasing number of online programs and institutions. C-RAC has made a commitment to update and revise these statements by 2010 to reflect more current needs.

Key Areas of Consideration for Accreditation Reviews

Whether for a substantive change review of a single program, or the review of all programs for an institutional accreditation visit, there are a number of common issues institutions will need to address. These are similar across all accrediting regions.

Relationship to mission. One of the first questions to be asked of the first several online programs is whether the new programs fit within the stated and operational mission of the institution. An institution may be committed to serve learners in diverse locations by diverse means. Where online learning is a major component of the institution, the mission statement itself should address online learning explicitly. Expected as well is a clear alignment of the type of student to be served by online learning, the content areas to be offered, and the relationship of online programs to existing programs of the institution. Some examples where alignment with mission would be problematic, drawn from actual cases: A small regional institution with an MBA program focusing on local business development wishes to offer an online international business program to graduate students in China. It has not offered any international programs before and has only offered classroom-based courses, with no experimentation with any online courses. In another situation, a primarily residential undergraduate institution centered on a full-time faculty, wishes to offer a graduate online program in a field outside of the expertise of its full-time faculty. To do so, it plans to rely exclusively on adjunct faculty. In both cases, the proposed online programs fall outside the mission of the institution and appear, on their face, to be ventures to gain new students more than extending the mission through a new modality.

The issue in such cases is whether new programs fall within the scope of the institution's mission, and from that operational mission, the institution has demonstrated the capacity to offer and oversee the proposed program. A good example is a large university with a long history of service on- and off-campus to traditional-age and adult learners. It wishes to offer several of its on-campus programs online and, in preparation for doing so, offers several pilot courses to test its online software, faculty orientation, and student ability to work online. In addition, the institution conducts an extensive needs analysis to assure itself that the need would extend beyond the first one or two cohorts of students.

If the institution offers only a few online programs, there may not be explicit reference in its mission statement to such programs but it would be expected to find explicit reference to them in planning documents, budgets, faculty development activities, and so on (USDE, 2006).

Practice Tip: If an institution is planning to move significantly into online education, it needs to review and revise its mission statement to reflect the change. Moreover, there should be consideration of the impact of the change on the current mission and on existing programs. The result may be a change in the mission statement. But much more is implicated in a change in mission—it involves the institution's understanding of itself, priorities, allocation of resources, and culture.

Linkage to institutional planning. Institutional planning efforts should be driven by the mission and vision of the institution. Online programs, in addition to being linked to the mission of the institution, similarly need to be linked to the institution's strategic and academic plans. Do these programs arise from careful planning, or are they isolated efforts by an individual program or school?

A key element for any planning process is identification of the characteristics of the students who the institution can best serve. This is especially true for distance education programs. Has the institution conducted an effective analysis of the needs, the types of students to be served, and aligned the program(s) to be offered for these students? Is there ongoing assessment of the effectiveness of the institution's plans with respect to distance education? Does the institution have the capacity to address growth in the programs offered? Has this been factored into planning?

Practice Tip: Institutions typically have multiple planning efforts underway: strategic and academic planning, enrollment management planning, technology planning, library planning, student service planning, and so on. As institutions move more fully into online learning, there is need to ensure that support for online learning is a consistent element to each dimension of planning and is integrated to support these programs. All too often, online programs are seen as a source of enrollment growth and revenue generation without addressing the need to support such growth throughout the institution. Those involved in these planning efforts need to be oriented to the special needs of online students and to the impact online programs and students will have on all aspects of institutional services. It is also helpful to review institutional plans to see if online learning is, in fact, included at an appropriate level of attention and detail. A good practice is to ensure that planning guidelines include attention to online programs as a structured element of any planning process.

Establishment of program needs. A needs analysis enables the institution to assure itself and the accrediting agency that the proposed program is likely to be successful and sustainable. Too often, need is established by informal surveys, expressions of interest from current students, and unanalyzed data on population or industry growth in the field of study of the proposed program, all of which lead to overoptimistic projections of initial and continuing enrollments. One of the most frequent reasons cited for denial of initial program proposals at the Senior College Commission of WASC is the failure to establish an effective needs analysis for the program and its projected enrollment over time. And experience has shown that frequently, enrollment projects are highly optimistic for online programs, which results in a longer start-up period than anticipated.

Practice Tip: Those developing a new program should review the existing and projected market for the new program in terms of current and future student demographics, availability of alternative or competing programs, the distinctive characteristics of the proposed program to fill a market need, the ability of students to meet the financial obligations of the program, and the ability of the discipline or profession to absorb the projected number of graduates from the proposed program. Such an analysis should be required by the institution as much as the accrediting agency to ensure that the investment of institutional funds will lead to successful implementation and continuation of the program.

Approval processes for proposed programs. Another concern frequently found in the review of online programs relates to the processes by which the program was developed and approved. Each institution needs to have a formal process for the review and approval of online programs. This process needs to reflect an awareness of the distinctive characteristics of online learning and to mirror in many respects the kind of review that an accrediting agency would apply. For example, there are instances where an institution takes a preexisting program and moves it online. Since it is an existing program, many institutions do not have a distinct review and approval process, and the program may be initiated without significant internal review. From an institutional standpoint, the degree and/or program has been approved, so all that is involved is moving it online, which is entrusted to the program director or school dean. There also have been instances, applying this reasoning, where a dean may offer an online program without first seeking even institutional approval, let alone accrediting agency review.

From the accrediting agency standpoint, however, there are important issues of faculty orientation and training to offer online courses, the need for significant revision to syllabi, the provision of support services to students, and so on, further described below, that need to be reviewed. Institutions need to ensure its internal processes include review of these issues, as well as others, before committing to offering the program in its name. The same is true even for completely online issues—is there an internal review and approval process for new programs that ensures that the issues raised in this chapter are met? Even if the institution has been granted authority to initiate online programs without prior review and approval of the agency, such an internal process is important to ensure the ongoing quality of online offerings.

Practice Tip: One of the first things to be done when reviewing online programs is to undertake an inventory of offerings by the institution. Have they all gone through the institution's own approval process? Have they all been properly reported and if needed, approved, by the appropriate accrediting agency? In addition, the substantive change criteria of most regional accrediting agencies cover a broad range of topics that many institutions have adopted for their own internal review process. Many institutions have also created a structure where all new online programs are reviewed through an institution-wide committee to ensure consistency of quality standards after there has been departmental- and/or school-level approval.

Curriculum development and oversight. There are many different types of online programs—those designed from the ground up for online learners, those extending an existing program into a distance education format, hybrid programs that combine online and site-based learning, and more. It is essential that there is a deliberate review of both the curriculum and the format for delivery best designed to suit the needs of learners and the field of study. Faculty need to have primary influence over these issues, especially those with previous experience with online learning. Course syllabi need to be tailored to the online format. Decisions need to be made regarding the nature and frequency of synchronous and asynchronous interactions. How will student—faculty and student—student interactions during the course be managed? For example, will such interactions be open and transparent to the class, will they be initiated by faculty-generated prompts or a general discussion, and will they be monitored and commented on? Curriculum planning for online learning is not the same as traditional classroom-based learning, and both faculty and administrators need to be sensitive to and respond to the differences to ensure program quality and effectiveness.

Another issue regarding curricula for online programs is the level of expectation for online learners—are they comparable to similar (campus-based or other) programs of the institution? Are there sufficient points of evaluation to ensure high levels of student performance? Are courses offered in such a way to enable students to complete their programs in a timely way? Are provisions made for students who may need to stop out for a period and then reenter the program? For cohort-based programs, are there clear indicators of how students who miss one or more courses may be able to continue without serious impact on their programs? All too frequently, these questions have not been fully addressed in programs presented for accrediting review.

Practice Tip: As institutions move more into online programming, it can be helpful to develop a comprehensive guide or checklist for online curriculum development for any program or department to use. Such a guide should identify the key issues or questions that all programs need to address and should specify those common elements that are expected of any program offered by the institution (e.g., a common course management software system, a common calendar, a common expectation of faculty–student interactions, syllabi requirements, and so on). Such guides can assist those new to online program development, assure consistency across the institution, and prepare programs for internal and external reviews. Some institutions pilot new curricula or new delivery designs before instituting a full program with these new elements. Pilot testing courses can be a way of determining market as well as faculty readiness.

Faculty qualifications and preparation for online instruction and workload expectations. Faculty qualifications for classroom-based instruction do not automatically carry over to an online environment. Those steeped in a lecture format, even if brilliantly done, will not easily be able to transfer those skills into online courses. Online learning requires a fundamental rethinking of the course—from learning outcomes, course assignments, pedagogy, student assignments, student projects, assessment of work, and so on. Although faculty credentials in the subject area are important, it is also expected that faculty prepared to offer courses in the online format. This requires orientation, support, and often significant course redesign. All too frequently in the review of online programs, course syllabi for an online program are unchanged from those used in a classroom setting. This reflects a fundamental misunderstanding of what is required to deliver high quality programs in an online setting by both administrators and faculty.

Most institutions have now established technology support centers for faculty, but few require faculty to go through training before offering courses. Online institutions do so far more frequently than classroom-based institutions. Regrettably, the presumption that all faculty can teach in all formats is not always borne out in practice.

Experience also has shown that the workload associated with developing and implementing an online course, particularly in the start-up phase, is far beyond the course preparation required for a classroom-based course. This has a significant impact on faculty load. Institutions vary in providing release time for online course preparation, though it is preferred if possible. During the course, there is typically far more interaction with students than in a traditional course and far higher expectations for immediate response. Some institutions, for example, require or strongly encourage that all student interactions and course assignments be responded to within specified time frames. In the case of one online institution, faculty are expected to respond to all inquiries, e-mails, or requests for support or assistance within 24 hours and to evaluate and provide feedback to all required student papers and assignments within 72 hours.

Practice Tip: Clear expectations need to be established regarding faculty workload for online courses, as well as limits on class size in light of the higher volume of student–faculty interactions. As indicated above, faculty need opportunities for support in managing online courses as well as opportunities to discuss online teaching methods with their colleagues. This is also true for adjunct faculty involved in online learning. There also is a need for a monitoring system to ensure that expectations for response times are met.

Student learning outcomes, assessment, and program evaluation. All accrediting agencies have now made the identification and assessment of student learning outcomes a central focus of accreditation. Although this is expected for all programs, it is all the more essential for online learning. There is a big difference between identifying what the course will cover and what students are expected to learn. Thus, it is important that learning outcomes are established and aligned at the program and course levels. Many programs now use curricular maps where program learning outcomes are identified and courses are mapped to those outcomes at the initial, intermediate, and advanced levels to ensure that outcomes are actually addressed in the curriculum and moved to the advanced level expected of graduates. For established programs, curricular mapping typically results in findings by the faculty that not all program outcomes are addressed sufficiently.

In addition, curricular mapping provides a way to review course syllabi to assess learning outcomes for the course, their linkage to the program's learning outcomes, the assignments given, and course assessments to determine they are effectively aligned. Such analyses frequently identify areas where assignments and evaluation methods (e.g., tests, papers) do not align with the stated course or program outcomes.

Online programs also need a clear plan of assessment, where methods of assessment, timelines for collection of data, and linkage to program review are established. Online courses typically have more available artifacts for assessment since all student interactions are typically maintained in an archive for each course, including student assignments, papers, test results, threaded and unthreaded conversations, and so on. Often, the volume of information available can be overwhelming, so a clear strategy and timeline for assessment, and sampling of student work products, is needed to establish a comprehensive plan of assessment. Nearly all online programs administer end of course evaluations regarding course content and instruction. Such self-report information is important, but most accrediting agencies now expect that there is periodic assessment of student work to ensure that learning outcomes are being achieved across the curriculum at levels of performance expected of graduates from the program. Typically, newly initiated programs will conduct reviews after 1, 3, and 5 years to allow for formative and a more summative assessment of the effectiveness of the program in meetings its goals and outcomes.

Most institutions also conduct periodic program reviews, typically every 5 years, to ensure program currency, adequacy of resources, and effectiveness. Online programs need to be included in program reviews, and such periodic reviews can provide the basis for comparisons with classroom-based programs or provide a more comprehensive evaluation, often aggregating the multiple forms of evidence collected annually.

In the Western region, one of the most frequent reasons for not accepting proposals for new online programs has been the lack of an effective, comprehensive assessment program.

Practice Tip: Assessment plans should involve multiple measures, combining survey self-reports, reviews of capstone projects, assembly of student portfolios of work over time, and, if possible, student reflection on their work. A timeline for collection, analysis, and faculty discussion of the evidence should be established. For example, certain data might be collected annually, some biennially and some every 5 years. This allows for followup plans to be established and their effectiveness assessed within a reasonable time frame. To engage in such reviews, faculty involved with online courses, just as classroom faculty, need to be supported in the development of assessment methods, in analysis of the data and evidence collected, and in the interpretation of quantitative and qualitative data. A comprehensive assessment plan and timeline allow faculty, staff, and students to make meaning of the data, to close the loop from analysis to generating action steps for improvement, and then to assess the effectiveness of the action plan.

Admissions requirements and student preparation for online learning. Although institutions are responsible for identifying admissions requirements for all programs, this responsibility is all the more important for online programs since misunderstandings may easily arise. It is especially important for admissions requirements and prerequisites for success in the program to be clear and direct. What hardware and software is needed to participate in the program? What is the level of computer proficiency required? How will the institution verify that the students possess these skills? Are there means for students without such skills to be trained or supported? If not, are they excluded from the program. Is English-language proficiency clearly stated and established? This is important as the number of international students increases.

In addition to the technical capacities needed, is there a clear statement of expectations of student work and engagement to succeed in the program? Most students in their first online courses do not realize the extra work involved, the need to log on almost daily, and the expectations for heavy student engagement throughout the course. Many students find the convenience of online courses appealing, but then cannot meet the expectations for frequent engagement. A clear statement of the time commitments involved to succeed in the program is critically important to ensure student success.

Practice Tip: Institutions need to determine, in advance, whether the level of computer proficiency required for success in the course is a prerequisite or will be developed in special programs. Some institutions offer a boot camp at the beginning of the online program to ensure that all students have the required computer proficiency and to assist students to learn how to navigate the course management system and other software that will be used throughout the program. Boot camps or orientation sessions also provide an opportunity for students to meet their faculty and fellow students, learn what support services are available, and identify realistic time requirements for the program. With or without a boot camp, is there a self-assessment for students to determine their readiness for the program?

Also needed is training for how to use library and support resources available throughout the program. Older students may not have had the information literacy training and support of younger students today, and each institution offers its own procedures for accessing resources online.

Authentication of students and student work. One issue that has arisen in the most recent HEA is the need for institutions to find ways to verify that students enrolled in the program are actually performing the work. No means have been specified how this is to be done, but it reflects the concern that virtual environments can lead to fraud and abuse. Many institutions administer proctored exams in specified locations for online programs; others rely on the heavy interactions between students and faculty and assume that only the enrolled student would engage in such frequent interactions. A variety of new technologies are being developed, such as fingerprint reading, Web viewing of students taking tests, or biometric verification (Foster, 2008). Ironically, no such authentication process is required for site-based courses where the opportunity for fraud in large classes can also be great. With the ready availability of student work for sale on the Internet, the issue is equally important for all programs, regardless of delivery modality.

Practice Tip: Institutions need to develop means for ensuring that the student who registers for the course is the one who produces the work for which credit and a degree are provided. Notwithstanding the success of online learning and its rapid growth, questions remain about the potential for fraud, and institutions should be prepared to address this issue.

Availability of support services. Once students are admitted and enrolled, it is vital they are aware of and able to access a full array of support services. This starts with registration and financial aid, tuition payment, and other business elements of the program. These should be seamless to the student. Perhaps most important is the ready availability of technical support so that students are able to have any issue dealt with in a timely way. Most institutions maintain help desks to assist students with technical issues regarding hardware and software. One of the most frequent student complaints is that such help desks, if not available 24 hours every day, are not accessible to students when they need it most—at unusual hours or in different time zones. Given time differences, it is also important for all institutional support service offices to be prepared to support online learners, with clear and convenient hours and with clear information for students for such issues as program and course registration, financial aid, business office, advising, transcript services, and the like. Where such offices have traditionally provided services only in person, staff members need special training for supporting online learners.

Practice Tip: Staff and faculty should receive special training on how to meet student and institutional expectations and be monitored to ensure that this commitment to students is met. At the boot camp described above, institutions often allow for student services personnel to interact with students to ensure that their program is set up to avoid disruptions. One of the most important areas to assess throughout the program is the availability and effectiveness of support services.

Recruitment promises and management of student expectations. Institutions need to pay careful attention to how online programs are described and what students can expect upon completion of the program. For professional programs, is licensure possible? Given the widespread distribution of students in online programs, it is essential that prospective and current students be given correct and complete information about what their program will prepare them for, whether career counseling and assistance with job placement will be provided, and information on jurisdictional requirements and the relevance of the degree to particular career paths. Especially in the health and counseling professions, graduation from a program accredited by a particular specialized agency may be required to obtain a job. There have been lawsuits filed challenging representations made to students prior to enrollment about their capacity to obtain employment upon completion of the program. Although they have been related to classroom-based programs, the issue is equally relevant to online programs.

Practice Tip: Institutions should have an annual review program of its written recruitment materials and program description, as well as meet with personnel to discuss oral representations made by staff before and during the program to ensure they are accurate, current, and understood by students as intended by the institution. Students can hear promises or assurances when none may be intended. Such a review should also include ongoing sampling of students to ensure they understand what services and licensure requirements exist, what the program can provide, and that they are receiving accurate and adequate counseling in the program.

Assessment of learning outcomes and program evaluation. All accrediting agencies require that institutions establish clear and appropriate learning outcomes for each degree program. The regional accrediting agencies have combined to issue a statement indicating that assessing student learning is central to the accrediting process and is expected within institutions to determine institutional effectiveness and program quality (Council of Regional Accrediting Commissions [CRAC], 2003). Other accrediting agencies have similarly adopted requirements for assessment of student learning. Thus, online institutions and programs can anticipate that assessment will be central to their review.

Once online programs are established and operational, the institution is responsible for determining effective means of assessing these outcomes beyond individual course grades. A plan for assessment is expected as part of a substantive change review prior to the initiation of the program. Assessment data are expected to be collected, analyzed, and acted upon as part of review of program and institutional quality. Online programs have a rich array of artifacts on which a review of quality and the achievement of student learning outcomes can be conducted, including individual student work and archived contributions of each student to synchronous and asynchronous postings. The volume of these data can be overwhelming, however. Programs need to create regular methods for sampling or aggregating the data sources to determine if program outcomes are being achieved at a level appropriate for the degree award. Program assessment should occur at regular intervals, such as 1, 3, and 5 years after initiation, and every 3 to 5 years thereafter, depending on the length of the program. Such interim assessments can provide midprogram corrections based on systematic feedback from students, faculty, and staff and from reviews of student work.

In addition, assessment efforts for online programs need to be aligned with institutional assessment plans and periodic program review processes. Doing so can provide a basis for comparison when the same program is offered on campus. Sometimes, however, program review processes overlook online programs, particularly when the same program is offered on campus, and the on-campus program receives the primary (or exclusive) focus. It is important to establish clear criteria for including online programs and identifying criteria for their review.

Indeed, the effectiveness and quality criteria often established for online programs can be used to assess and improve quality in classroom-based programs.

Practice Tip: Each program has multiple outcomes: some cognitive, some behavioral, and some practice oriented. It will be important to first ensure that all desired outcomes are part of the curriculum and are reinforced at initial through advanced levels. As described above, this is often done through curricular mapping and should be regularly completed. At the same time, not all outcomes can be measured or evaluated at the same time. To do so would overwhelm any program. Nor can a single assessment method provide a complete and comprehensive basis for ensuring achievement of all of the program's outcomes. Thus, each program needs to develop a set of assessment tools and a timetable for implementing them. Many modes of assessment are available to programs and institutions and can be applied readily to the online context. Student and faculty surveys, test results, analyses of samples of student work in several courses or in the same course over several offerings, analyses of students' contributions, and so on can be used. Multiple modalities of assessment can yield a more comprehensive picture of student achievement. One of the greatest virtues of assessment is that it provides a basis for faculty to identify their level of expectation in reviewing student work and determining what is good enough for graduates of the program. Calibration exercises, based on assessing actual student work, have proved to be a powerful device for clarifying and making more consistent faculty expectations and standards.

Retention and graduation rates. Over the past several years, retention and graduation rates for all of higher education have become increasingly important (U.S. Department of Education, 2006). Accrediting agencies are increasingly requiring, or at least encouraging, institutions to track graduation rates for all programs, including online programs. The Senior College Commission of WASC has recently made the analysis of retention and graduation rates a required focus for all comprehensive accreditation reviews and is requiring that such data be disaggregated and made public (WASC, 2008, Standards 1 & 2). Retention in online programs is part of the challenge faced by all institutions.

Online programs can be designed as a course or as cohort based. Special issues arise with cohort-based programs. On the positive side, cohort-based programs can provide a support and peer learning community for students over the length of the program. Such support can keep students motivated and improve the quality of their work. Under what conditions may a student miss a course or drop out for a limited period and still return to the cohort? And for those who cannot rejoin the cohort, how will they be able to complete their program?

Practice Tip: It is important for online programs to track success separately in retaining students and graduating them in a timely manner. To do so requires a complete commitment to student success and to collecting data on a regular basis. Not all institutions have such data readily and regularly available. Thus, there will be a need to work with the registrar's office and the institutional research unit to determine how this information can be made available. Early warning systems are also needed, allowing for problems to be identified and for responses to be developed to student needs before they become of such magnitude that the student has to withdraw from the program.

Institutional and program sustainability. As indicated earlier, in designing an online institution or program, there is a need to provide a realistic basis for meeting enrollment and financial projections. Budgets are typically created that identify only the direct costs of online activities—such as assigned faculty time, course management software, and so on. The total cost of online programs, however, is greater, especially as each of the elements described in this chapter are costed out. What is the capacity of the institution or program to sustain the program over time and to ensure and improve quality? Are resources available for faculty to develop courses online and receive adequate training for online learning? All too often, institutions allocate faculty time as an overload, allowing faculty to increase their salaries. Over time, however, if the program (or institution) grows, there is need for a core of full-time faculty. The same is true for support services and staff. There is a point where the current carrying capacity is overloaded and new systems and personnel are needed. Are these factors calculated?

Practice Tip: It is important to develop contingency budgets—what would happen if enrollment projections are not met? Or if they are exceeded? Is the budget linked to planning?

Preparing for an Accreditation Site Visit

All of the above criteria are necessary elements for getting a new institution or program approved. Special considerations obtain when the institution or program is to be reviewed in a formal site visit.

Preparation of the online institutional or program report. For online institutions, the self study report will necessarily address all of these factors and incorporate the institution's analysis of evidence of effectiveness. For online programs, however, there is need to determine if a special report or section of the self study needs to be devoted to online programs. This needs to be determined in advance and, if so, the criteria for such a special report or section. Regardless whether such a report is required, if the institution offers a significant number of online programs, it is recommended that the institution undertake an overview of the effectiveness of their online programs on its own. Are there lessons to be learned in reviewing, and comparing, one program to another? Are there special actions that can or should be replicated in other programs?

Given that there is so much evidence readily available for team review in online program archives, there is a tendency for institutions to invite the team to review the archives directly. Although this may be done for the purposes of verification, it is the responsibility of the institution or program to review and analyze the considerable mass of information and evidence it has available, by using methods described above, and to provide the team the results of its analysis and its recommendations for improvement. The primary purpose of the evaluation team is verification of the institution's or program's findings, not an independent investigation with the team drawing its own conclusions from the limited time spent reviewing materials.

Selection of site visitors. At the present time, most accrediting agencies have a limited number of experienced site visitors with extensive online experience (Ewell, 2008). As a result, it is important to work with the accrediting agency to ensure the selection of evaluators who will be able to understand the institution and/or online programs. It is far easier to do so before evaluators are selected by discussing the special attributes of the institution or programs with the person at the accrediting agency making the team selection. All accrediting agencies provide opportunity to challenge a team member for cause, but it is not always easy or possible to establish cause, such as bias or a conflict of interest. What is wanted are those understanding quality within the framework of online education.

Development of a visit protocol. Conducting an evaluation of an online institution or program differs from a traditional site-based review. Although key administrators and faculty can typically be interviewed, much of the actual visit needs to be done online. Typically, evaluators observe an online threaded conversation or chat, interact with students online, and review archives of previous online activities. At the Senior College Commission of WASC, for all visits, not just to online institutions or programs, a confidential e-mail account is established on an independent server (with a Yahoo or Google account), and the institution broadcasts an e-mail to all faculty, staff, and students a request for comments about the institution and their experience. Positive comments and areas for improvement are requested, and special attention is paid to gaining feedback from online and off-campus students. This process can be adapted to any review of an online institution or program outside the WASC region, providing an opportunity for anyone to comment. In the past 2 years of implementing this process, teams have been able to gain a far wider range of views than would be possible from a limited set of interviews.

By conducting virtual interviews and archive reviews, the site visit takes on a different form. It can be more of a capstone experience rather than a fact-gathering one, digging deeper and following up on issues arising from the online review. Use of this process may also provide the basis for shortening site visits, with more work done online by teams.

Putting It All Together: Will It Make a Difference?

One of the questions most frequently asked of accrediting agencies is whether there is a bias against online education. Experience has shown that online institutions have been accredited in all regions, and nearly all institutions today have online programs leading to a certificate or degree. These programs have been reviewed and approved or accredited. Thus, the record of most accrediting agencies is one of acceptance of online education. There is no structural bias against online education. Online education offers unique opportunities to reach whole new constituencies, thereby enabling many institutions to achieve their missions more effectively. The emphasis on learning centeredness that is required in effective online learning also has the potential for improving the quality of traditional class-based education.

As online education becomes more widespread and institutions acquire and demonstrate capacity to mount and maintain high quality programs, less and less regulation of these programs will likely occur. Accrediting agencies will need to find ways to regularize their reviews of online programs, even while meeting federal requirements. Institutions have a corresponding responsibility to undertake internally effective processes for the development of new online programs and then for their review and improvement. Together, accreditors and institutions can demonstrate the quality and effectiveness of online education and assure Congress and the public of the quality and integrity of these programs.

APPENDIX

Each of the regional accrediting associations maintains a Web site where key documents relating to online learning and substantive change can be found:

The Middle States Commission on Higher Education: http://www.msache.org

The New England Association of Schools and Colleges, Commission on Institutions of Higher Education: http://www.neasc.org

The North Central Association of Colleges, The Higher Learning Commission: http://www.ncacihe.org/index.php?option=com_frontpage&Itemid=113

The Northwest Commission on Colleges and Universities: http://www.nwccu.org

The Southern Association of Colleges and Schools, Commission on Colleges: http://www.sacscoc.org

The Western Association of Schools and Colleges, Accrediting Commission for Community and Junior Colleges: http://www.accjc.org

The Western Association of Schools and Colleges, Commission on Senior Colleges and Universities: http://www.wascsenior.org

Notes

1. The New England Association Commission on Institutions of Higher Education, the Middle States Commission on Higher Education, the Higher Learning Commission of the North Central Association, the Southern Association Commission on Colleges, the Western Association Accrediting Commission for Community and Junior Colleges, the Accrediting Commission for Senior Colleges, and Universities of the Western Association, and the Northwest Commission of Colleges and Universities.

References

Council of Regional Accrediting Commissions. (2001). *Best practices for electronically offered degree and certificate programs.* Retrieved from http://cihe .neasc.org/downloads/POLICIES/Pp90_Best_Practices_for_Elect._Off ._Degree_Cert._Prog.pdf

Council of Regional Accrediting Commissions. (2003). *Statement of mutual responsibilities for student learning outcomes: Accreditation, institutions and programs.* Retrieved from http://www.msche.org/publications/Regnls l050208135331.pdf

Ewell, P. T (2008). *U.S. accreditation and the future of quality assurance.* Washington, DC: Council for Higher Education Accreditation.

Foster, A. (2008, July 25). New systems keep a close eye on online students at home. *The Chronicle of Higher Education.* Retrieved August 10, 2008, from http://chronicle.com/weekly/v54/i46/46a00103.htm

U.S. Department of Education. (2006a). *A test of leadership: Charting the future of U.S. higher education.* Washington, DC: Author. Retrieved from http://www.ed .gov/about/bdscomm/list/hiedfuture/reports/final-report.pdf

U.S. Department of Education, Office of Postsecondary Education. (2006b). *Evidence of quality in distance education programs drawn from interviews with the accreditation community.* Retrieved August 10, 2008, from http://www.ysu .edu/accreditation/Resources/Accreditation-Evidence-of-Quality-in- DE-Programs.pdf

Western Association of Schools and Colleges, Accrediting Commission for Senior Colleges and Universities. (2008). *Protocol for the review of distance education programs.* Retrieved August 10, 2008, from http://www.wascsenior.org/ document_library

Chapter 19

Virtual Libraries in Online Learning

Stefan Kramer

The information resources and services provided by a library are as important to the online learner as they are to the traditional learner. Indeed, because the online learner—as opposed to the traditional learner, who may find a familiar environment and perhaps even reassurance and comfort in the surroundings of a campus library—can more easily come to feel disconnected from his or her fellow students, instructors, and institution, the design and provision of library services and resources for online learners can require even more care and planning than those in the traditional physical library. To online learners, the absence of any physical library at their institution, or the impracticality or inability to visit it if one does exist, can become daunting when it comes to questions such as "How do I get this book I need for my course?" or "Can you help me with conducting this search for articles on my subject?" or "Where can I look at dissertations or theses written by previous students of this institution?" Wondering how and of whom to ask these questions and when an answer might come back can add to the various frustrations an online student may already be experiencing while studying at home, be it toward the completion of one course or a complete degree. Much of that also holds true for faculty members, be it in their role as instructor and mentor of their students or as researchers.

In consideration of the obligations and challenges that academic institutions face in developing and maintaining appropriate library resources and services for their online students and faculty, the Association of College & Research Libraries has created, and repeatedly refined over now more than 4 decades, the *Guidelines for Distance Learning Library Services* (Association of College & Research Libraries, 2004). The introduction stated unequivocally,

Library resources and services in institutions of higher education must meet the needs of all their faculty, students, and academic support personnel, regardless of where they are located. . . . The principle applies to individuals on a main campus, off campus, in distance learning or regional campus programs, or in the absence of a campus at all.

Although they were written for higher education, the guidelines can also provide useful direction to other educational and corporate organizations that need to serve the information needs of online learners. They stated that

The originating institution is responsible for providing or securing convenient, direct physical and electronic access to library materials for distance learning programs equivalent to those provided in traditional settings and in sufficient quality, depth, number, scope, currentness, and formats to:

1. meet the students' needs in fulfilling course assignments (e.g., required and supplemental readings and research papers) and enrich the academic programs;

2. meet teaching and research needs;

3. facilitate the acquisition of lifelong learning skills. (Association of College & Research Libraries, 2004)

The following sections outline the attributes and components of library services for online learning, beginning with what they might actually be called.

Terminology: Virtual, Digital, or Online Libraries?

The question of what to call nontraditional libraries without walls that serve online learners inevitably arises. Virtual, digital, and online libraries are commonly used terms, sometimes regarded as interchangeable, yet it can reduce confusion to choose just one for the discussion. Rather than argue the semantics of each label to select the right one, it may be more useful to consider what it might encompass and to choose one as most appropriate for the discussion at hand.

- Digital emphasizes that a library's information resources or holdings are in electronic format, which will be important to online learners but really does not address the service and staffing aspects of the library. As long as human librarians and library support staff serve the online learner, regardless of the format and delivery of the library's resources, the digital label would seem to not accommodate their part in the library very well, but be overly library-content-centric.

- Online reflects that resources, holdings, and/or services of the library are reachable via a computer network—nowadays, largely synonymous with the Internet, or in corporate settings, an intranet. This is narrower than digital with regard to information resources in that it may exclude other off-line electronic formats such as CDs or DVDs that may not (yet) be suitable for online delivery or access be it for reasons of licensing, technology, or both. It is broader than digital concerning services and staffing, reflecting how services and resources are made available—online—by library staff via the network.

- Virtual can express that all—or as many as possible and desirable of—the services and resources that libraries typically provide are made available to the online learner, but simply outside of the brick-and-mortar environment of the traditional library building. In being agnostic to how the resources and holdings of the library are stored or delivered or what part of the services are delivered or made available online versus by other means, this label seems to be have the broadest possible application to the discussion.

Other uses and definitions of electronic, virtual, digital, and online in the library context abound. For example, quite different from the above: "the 'virtual library' is not a library as such, but rather a site on the Internet representing a collection of links or electronic metadata available for individual digital and nondigital items which are usually distributed among an indistinguishable number of Web sites produced by heterogeneous institutions" (Rusch-Feja, 2001, p. 8811). In this chapter, however, what might alternatingly be referred to as a library with any of those labels, depending on the exact context, will consistently be termed virtual library.

Reference Services

Online learners, be it in academic or other educational settings, will come up with many of the same kinds of—what librarians have come to call reference—questions that have been asked in and of libraries for centuries. They are, in ascending order of complexity, the following:

- How and/or where do I find this particular article or conference paper or book or dissertation or . . .—the *known-item search*, where the research has already revealed a particular work that is needed, and the question is now how to obtain the actual document.

- How/where do I find something useful on this particular subject—an exploratory or cursory search in a given area of inquiry, perhaps to support an assertion or to choose or get started on a research subject. These questions can be surprisingly difficult for librarians to address, for the learner may not state—and not yet know—whether the something might be an introductory text to a subject area, a bibliography or literature review, an article or paper containing the latest possible research, or any other kind of work, which really depends on where the research is supposed to go from here. This question can be the beginning of an ongoing consultation for which the most appropriate communication mode(s) of those described further below must be chosen for the virtual library to be effective for the learner.

- How and/or where do I find (as close as possible to) everything on this particular subject—the less frequent kind of question that comes up when, for instance, a doctoral student writes a dissertation or an adult learner incorporates research in a narrowly defined area into project work for his or her employer. This is one of the stages in the pursuit of research where an online learner may feel particularly isolated, trying to enter considerable scholarly depths from the confines of his or her own home or office. In this author's experience with students, both the timely and substantial support from the librarians of the virtual library and the online community of faculty and fellow students that their institution should provide can become most important to their ongoing success at this point.

The partially counteracting effects of curiosity, practicality, time constraints, and effort on the side of the online learner will frequently lead to the hybrid outcome of finding answers between something and everything, regardless of the original intent.

Chat, Instant Messaging, and Other Virtual Reference Methods

In the absence of the reference desk, at which a student in a traditional library might seek assistance in person, libraries (both traditional and certainly virtual ones) increasingly offer real-time online communication methods to support their users—that is, virtual reference services. These services can use a combination of chat, instant messaging, and other technologies. Chat refers to the exchange of short text messages by two parties (such as librarian and virtual library user), typically using computers; it can be entirely Web-based or can utilize software geared toward Internet-based real-time communication, such as Windows Messenger, Colloquy, or Skype. Instant messaging not only can be regarded as synonymous with chat but also can describe more specifically a short-text exchange method available for devices more portable than computers, such as mobile phones and PDAs, using services such as Yahoo Messenger, AIM, or Google Talk. These communication methods are particularly suitable for getting an online learner pointed in the right direction when using the virtual library—answering questions about the availability of resources or services and helping with known-item searches or exploratory searches. Unless both librarian and online learner have a good deal of time (in one session), patience, and experience in using these communication methods, they may be less suitable to support in-depth subject searches.

Searching can be better accomplished, possibly in multiple successive virtual reference sessions, using software that adds cobrowsing to chat and/or voiceover-Internet Protocol (VoIP). VoIP allows the audio communication to take place via the computer over the Internet, eliminating the need for a regular telephone connection. Cobrowsing refers to the librarian and the virtual library user viewing the same Web site together from their respective computer screens so that they can jointly conduct and discuss an online search. Software that enables this more extensive virtual reference method includes QuestionPoint, GoToAssist, and Docutek VRLplus. It should be noted, however, that with the expanded capabilities of such software comes additional complexity, increasing the chance for technical problems or shortcomings on the virtual library user's or the librarian's side or with any of the systems between them. In addition, longer cobrowsing sessions can be more mentally demanding on virtual library user and/or librarian, as either or both find themselves in a more interactive virtual environment than they may be accustomed to. Also, questions posed via virtual reference may grow during the reference interview in an iterative back-and-forth of chat—which can be good if it leads to clarification or refinement of the question or not good if it is due to undesired topic drift not kept in check by either online learner or librarian.

Virtual reference, then, is most suited to the types of information-seeking support that are best handled in real-time, synchronous communication. It can only take place when a librarian is actually available to staff this service, and other communication methods, described below, may be better for different purposes. "In the successful implementations, virtual reference finds its place in the entire suite of reference services. It isn't the only service, sometimes not even the busiest one, but it fills an important, unique niche" (Tenopir, 2004, p. 42). In this author's experience, while infrequently used, it can make a major difference to an online student who feels quite stuck in research or has problems using a particular online resource's interface. Library administrators, even in traditional libraries, may want to carefully assess the trade-offs, benefits, and library user perspectives for virtual reference services. This has been done at the University of Arizona vis-à-vis traditional reference desk work (Bracke, Brewer, & Huff-Eibl, 2007), at San Jose State University and San Jose Public Library along with e-mail reference and online instruction evaluation (Gilbert, Mengxiong, & Matoush, 2006), and at Pennsylvania State University regarding instruction as part of virtual reference (Moyo, 2006). In implementing virtual reference services, including transitions to different platforms or software, librarians need to carefully consider how the confidentiality of each communication and the users' identities can be adequately protected (Reference and User Services Association, 2004).

E-Mail Reference

Reference via e-mail has advantages and disadvantages compared to the real-time online reference models discussed above. Advantages include the following:

- Questions can be received by the library at any time, even when it is not staffed.

- Virtual library users can receive answers when they are not at their computer and can retrieve and read them later.

- As a more mature technology, e-mail may be more comfortable and familiar for (especially older) students, faculty, and librarians than virtual reference tools. For librarians, it avoids having to possibly juggle answering multiple questions at the same time—as can happen in the real-time virtual reference environment, leading to possible decreased answer quality.

- The librarian can take time to reflect on the reference question, explore resources and search strategies to suggest to the online learner and to formulate a response with selectively chosen citations, hyperlinks, and/or screen snapshots.

- Library users (students or faculty members) can take time to reflect on the answer received to their reference question, try out suggested techniques and information resources, and then possibly formulate a further refined or different question to send back to the library.

- Reference answers given via e-mail can be easily stored and searched and therefore can be easily consulted by librarians answering future reference questions. Access to the e-mail message store of prior reference questions and answers needs to be appropriately restricted to ensure the confidentiality of the reference transactions.

- The limit on message length that the real-time, synchronous environment imposes both on writing and on reading text is not a factor. However, questions sent via e-mail are not necessarily longer than those submitted through virtual reference services—a study of its own virtual reference service at one Australian university found that "Reference enquiries via email have an average total word length of 57 words compared to 162 words in chat" (Lee, 2004, p. 100).

Disadvantages of e-mail compared to virtual reference include the following:

- It can take longer, perhaps much longer, than necessary for the virtual library user to get a response to what may be a simple question.

- The question-and-answer back-and-forth of the reference interview between librarian and library user can take far longer to the degree of becoming very problematic if either party is unable to retrieve or recall prior message exchanges. If the virtual library can arrange for a message exchange in an online discussion forum that can be appropriately access-restricted (to only the library user and the librarians) to maintain its confidentiality, this may be an alternative to exchanging messages via e-mail.

- It offers no equivalent of the cobrowsing component found in more advanced virtual reference tools and therefore cannot match the personable, interactive experience of traditional in-library reference services.

- Having it available as the only method for communication about library questions can make students feel more isolated both in their learning experience and from the institution at which they are enrolled.

In the virtual library, any single reference transaction need not be conducted by either virtual reference or e-mail alone; it can begin with one method and then go on to another. As Carter (2002) advised fellow virtual reference librarians,

> We may think that because a patron is using chat, it is her preferred way of asking us that question—but that need not be the case. More probably, it is the first method that she found for getting in contact with the library. Do not be afraid to take note of her email address, let her know that you'll do some searching and then email what you find. You're really not doing her any favors by keeping her waiting in the chat client while you spend 20 minutes tracking something down.

Conversely, a reference question may arrive via e-mail, but the receiving librarian may invite the sender to a virtual reference session if the instant back-and-forth of the chat exchange or a cobrowsing activity will make answering the question considerably easier or faster.

Reference via Phone

With the availability of virtual and e-mail reference services, is there still a need for virtual libraries also to offer reference services over the phone? Arguably, yes—for situations where the library user who has a question is not at a computer, has a technical problem with a computer or Internet connectivity that does not allow him or her to utilize e-mail or virtual reference, or has a matter that is simply best discussed person-to-person. However, since not all calls to the virtual library are necessarily at the level of a reference question requiring a librarian's expertise or may not even be a matter for the library but rather another department, incoming phone calls may best be routed first to paraprofessional or help-triage staff. An analysis by one librarian at the University of Oklahoma of telephone calls handled at the reference desk revealed that "40 percent . . . of the . . . telephone calls answered . . . at the reference desk simply needed to be transferred to another number, department, person, or location" and that two thirds of the telephone calls "answered while working at the reference desk could have been handled by a student assistant, paraprofessional, or other library staff" (McCain, 2007, p. 14). However, each (virtual) library will need to gauge its own unique experiences and user needs when planning or reassessing reference assistance via the telephone.

Self-Help (FAQs, Question-and-Answer Systems)

Many inquiries to a virtual library will be recurring, requiring just about the same answer each time. Systems containing such frequently asked questions, along with their answers, have come to be known as FAQs since the earlier days of the Internet. The development of FAQs by virtual libraries can reduce the staff time needed to respond to such repetitive questions—either by preempting the question being posed by the online learner or faculty member because he or she found it and the answer in the FAQ or by making the response quicker and easier to send, as well as shorter, namely as a link or pointer to the particular question and answer in the FAQ. Virtual library users can benefit from the availability of FAQs since they may be able to find a needed answer immediately, without having to contact the library. FAQs can also, judiciously, be populated with information that the librarians feel their virtual library users should be aware of, even when it is not the answer to an FAQ, in order to give that information more exposure. FAQs need to be conscientiously maintained so that the answers do not become outdated and so that the questions remain in synch with the information needs of the virtual library's users. FAQ implementers also need to consider whether the questions and answers should be publicly accessible, accessible only to their own institution's users, or a blend of both, depending on their subject matter or confidentiality of content.

FAQs may not be solely institution specific, but subject oriented, and in that case, collaborative maintenance of a FAQ by multiple institutions can make sense, particularly when local target audience and resource considerations can still be accommodated. For example, the University of Pennsylvania Library developed a business research FAQ that later became adopted at several other academic research libraries (University of Pennsylvania Library, 2004).

Instructional Services

Most virtual libraries supporting online learning will want to offer some form of instruction in order to make their users more efficient and effective in utilizing the available information resources for their research and learning. The degree and form of library-specific instruction may vary considerably between types of institutions; it could be minimal or nonexistent in professional or corporate training settings and extensive in higher education institutions. The *Guidelines for Distance Learning Library Services* mentioned at the beginning of this chapter state as one of the essential services "a program of library user instruction designed to instill independent and effective information literacy skills while specifically meeting the learner-support needs of the distance learning community" (Association of College & Research Libraries, 2004). However, the focus on information literacy in autonomous instruction is not without controversy; as Stanley Wilder (2005) put it, "Information literacy is . . . harmful because it encourages librarians to teach ways to deal with the complexity of information retrieval, rather than to try to reduce that complexity" (p. B13).

Web-Based Instruction

In online learning, both self-guided tutorials and courses or seminars led by librarians are typically Web based. Few students may relish learning about effective library usage for its own sake; library instruction should therefore be clearly linked to positive outcomes in the student's online learning experience. When creating Web-based tutorials that students can complete at their own pace—which may be of particular appeal to many online learners—librarians may consider using software specifically geared toward creating such material, such as ReadyGo, ToolBook Assistant, or Adobe Authorware (Mirsky, 2007), while keeping in mind that an online tutorial can and possibly should have, unlike an instructional text written for the print medium, a nonlinear structure. At Baruch College, City University of New York, librarians based their tutorial development on possible sequences of events, or "scripts" (Bailin & Pena, 2007). As with any instructional activity, assessment plays an important role in creating and restructuring online tutorials. It benefits the tutorials and generates student feedback that leads to improvements to the library's Web site (Lindsay, Cummings, & Johnson, 2006).

Instruction in search strategies and the use of the virtual library and other information resources via online courses or seminars can take different forms:

- Asynchronous—the instructing librarian posts guides, lessons, and exercises on a regular (e.g., weekly) basis, and online learners respond to those or each others' postings on their own schedule, though within a given time frame. Platforms enabling such an instructional format include Sakai, SiteScape, and Blackboard. Advantages of this format include the online learner having, hopefully, time to digest and practice advice received on search strategies and to explore suggested resources and not being tied to a specific date and time when this must be done.

- Synchronous—the instructing librarian and learners meet online at set dates and times to go over potentially useful information resources and strategies for selecting and utilizing them and to incorporate the results in their work. Platforms for this instructional format include WebEx, Adobe Acrobat Connect, and Citrix GoToMeeting. Desirable features for online meetings include cobrowsing (as found in more advanced virtual reference, discussed above), VoIP and/or synchronized conference calling communication, and text chat. Advantages of this format include the librarian being able to demonstrate online searching in immediate response to learners' questions, a sense of spontaneity and common exploration of virtual library and other information resources, and, more generally, possibly a stronger sense of learning community by being together at the same time, if only online.

- A blend of the two above—for example, the librarian could post a lesson with exercises in an asynchronous discussion forum and students could share their findings and questions in a subsequent online meeting.

In-Person Instruction

The notion of instruction where online learners and librarians meet face-to-face may seem to contradict online learning, but it can be a feature of distributed learning models that combine online interaction with occasional on-campus, residential, or other meet-in-person events. It can offer many of the advantages of the synchronous online meetings described above, but with an even stronger sense of community building and without the potential problems of technology (namely, the online meeting platform of choice) getting in the way of the learning process. However, if students need to have a lot of other in-person interaction with faculty, fellow students, and possibly administrators during the course of such limited-time in-person events, especially if those are fairly infrequent, the guideline for virtual library instruction in these settings may be to keep it as long as necessary, but as short as possible. Some or much of the content of in-person instruction may be portable to synchronous online instruction, and delivered with success, but the time and effort required for that should not be underestimated (Blakeslee & Johnson, 2002).

Content of Virtual Libraries

If the printed books, periodicals, and other materials in its collection are the essence of a physical library, then the content (along with its organization and accessibility) it makes available to its users is the core of the virtual library. This content will likely—depending to a considerable degree on what level and subjects of online learning it supports—be composed of the following: electronic journals; individual journal articles in digital format; e-books; dissertations, theses, conference papers, and other forms of gray literature; digitally stored images, audio, and/or video; numeric data sets and/or statistical analysis results of such; and/or other types of content. For online learning, this content will be desirable to be available online as much and as early as possible, but some of it may still require, or be of better quality via, storage and dissemination by CD-ROMs, DVD-ROMs, or local-wide area network installations. Examples include motion pictures as well as databases of texts or numeric data that can only be accessed with software found on the same optical disc or network drive, where the restrictions may be of a technical and/or licensing nature.

Aggregator Databases: Full Text and Abstracting-Indexing

Databases that contain subject indexing of the literature in a field, and often also abstracts of documents, have been in existence for several decades and were accessed through dial-up online information services such as DIALOG and BRS, and/or CD-ROM before there was an Internet. ABI/Inform, covering business, management, and related areas, for example, dates back to the early 1970s. Such databases have proved increasingly important to literature research as the number of publications in many fields has grown rapidly. Databases that add the full text of documents to their indexing and abstracting have been another boon to researchers. Databases that thus bring together full-text coverage of articles, conference papers, technical reports, and so on from a number of different publishers and sources—through an often complex relationship between these databases' vendors and the primary-content publishers (Chambers & So, 2004) of journals, books, and so on—are called *aggregators.* That is also the term often used for the vendors of such databases. Examples of aggregator databases, which may focus on a narrow subject range or be quite broad in coverage, include GenderWatch by ProQuest, LexisNexis Academic, and OmniFile Full Text by H. W. Wilson. There are also online full-text databases containing articles from multiple journals, but only from one publisher or from a small group of closely associated publishers. Examples include SpringerLink, the SAGE Full-Text Collections, and PsycARTICLES. Such databases are often accessible through a library-initiated institutional subscription via different online database platforms, such as CSA Illumina, EBSCOhost, or OVID. To reduce administrative overhead associated with maintaining database subscriptions and to make online literature searching as much of a one-stop shopping experience as possible for their users, virtual libraries may seek to provide access to as many different aggregator databases as possible through as few different online database platforms as possible. However, specific contents or functionalities of some databases, such as a particular index and how users can browse or search it, may be implemented better on one platform than another, and pricing for the same database to the same subscribing virtual library can vary from one vendor or platform to another, so those selecting aggregrator databases for a virtual library to subscribe to need to balance these conflicting factors.

As an alternative to requiring online learners and researchers to run the same search in each appropriate online database platform separately, with the syntax modified as necessary for each platform, it is possible for a virtual library to license and deploy federated searching tools. Those allow end users to enter a single search query that then gets relayed to different databases on different platforms and returns and displays the matching results. However, federated searching products can require a considerable amount of configuration to work with the databases the library subscribes to, may not be able to reach nearly all of those databases, and may take a considerable time to execute the entered search against all reachable database and then return, de-duplicate, and sort the results for presentation to the user. Examples of federated searching products include WebFeat, MetaLib by ExLibris, and 360 Search by Serials Solutions.

An advantage of subscribing to aggregator databases to virtual libraries is that they can thereby offer their users access to a large amount of content through relatively few different subscriptions they have to maintain and through relatively few interfaces their users have to become accustomed to. A disadvantage of relying solely on aggregator databases is that the virtual library has little control over which journals' or publishers' article content will become or remain available through those databases. The library may lose access to content that it, and its users, wanted. For example, in 2001, the Harvard Business Review became exclusively available via EBSCOhost, withdrawing from all other aggregators (Krumenaker, 2001). The library may also end up paying for added content it does not want, as a database vendor signs up new content providers that may not provide the same quality or subject focus of material that had characterized the database thus far.

Electronic Journals

Electronic journals follow more or less the traditional periodical subscription model in libraries. The virtual library subscribes to one or more journals in electronic format (possibly in addition to print format) and thereby gains access to forthcoming issues of those journals via the online service designated by the publisher. Access to back issues may be included in the subscription or may come at additional cost. The access service may be operated directly by the publisher or outsourced to a third party. Examples of online e-journal services include Elsevier ScienceDirect, SAGE Journals Online, and Blackwell Synergy. A major advantage over gaining access to journal articles via aggregator databases is that with the e-journal subscription, the virtual library typically secures the right to perpetual access to the e-journal issues covered by the subscription— similar to a print journal subscription, where the library gains ownership of a copy of a journal issue to keep in its collection. In the e-journal environment, however, the virtual library generally accesses content directly on the publisher's online e-journal service—which raises the question of what happens to access when a publisher goes out of business or is acquired by another or when the online e-journal service experiences protracted technical problems. Digital preservation efforts such as LOCKSS and Portico seek to address these issues (Schneider, 2007).

Articles in electronic journals and aggregator databases are increasingly easy to reach from nonfull-text resources, such as indexing-abstracting databases through the OpenURL protocol (Van de Sompel & Beit-Arie, 2001), which allows for the linking of a record about an article to different possible sources for obtaining the actual article.

Electronic Books

The availability of entire books in electronic format (e-books) is a considerably more recent development than electronic availability of periodical articles, which occurred well before the dawn of the World Wide Web. E-books may rarely be read in their entirety online, which makes the e-book format probably more suitable to reference works from which researchers will generally glean smaller parts, such as handbooks, encyclopedias, and dictionaries. Access models for e-books vary. One of the pioneers of e-book provision, NetLibrary, emulated the traditional access model for print books—a library would purchase an e-book title, which would be accessed on the NetLibrary Web site, but only by one reader at a time, unless the library bought multiple copies of that title. By contrast, ebrary started out with licensing access to a growing database of e-book content to libraries on a subscription basis, similar to the model of aggregator databases of journal articles; later, ebrary added the option of allowing libraries to buy perpetual access to selected titles. Although scholarly journal titles have become widely available in electronic format, far fewer book titles are found in e-book format, and the functions of linking between and searching across e-books on different vendors' platforms are not as developed as they are for journal articles. However, virtual libraries will want to investigate e-book services for their users; this includes raising awareness among users that e-books are, in fact, available to them (Milliot, 2007).

Other Content Types: Numeric Data, Images, Video, Sound, and So On

Although texts in various forms have long been in the collections of libraries, virtual libraries may also seek to acquire, license, or (if freely available) link to other types of content for their users, depending on research needs and curricula. This could include the following:

- Collections of digitized images, video, or audio, such as the ARTstor digital library of artwork images, Theatre in Video (Alexander Press), American Memory (Library of Congress), the *Vanderbilt University TV News Archive,* and the Naxos Music Library.

- Numeric data sets, such as listed in the online catalog of University of Wisconsin-Madison's Data and Information Services Center or in Yale University's StatCat and available via institutional membership in the Inter-university Consortium for Political and Social Research (ICPSR) or the Roper Center for Public Opinion Research. Unlike published statistics, which represent the outcome of already conducted analyses of gathered data, available data sets containing the actual data collected during research studies afford online learners the opportunity to formulate and answer new questions of already conducted research. Examples of widely used data sets (in the social sciences) include the General Social Survey (by NORC, University of Chicago), the American Community Survey (by the U.S. Bureau of the Census), and the American National Election Studies (by Stanford University and the University of Michigan).

Whether for aggregator databases, e-journals, e-books, or other types of content, virtual libraries will want to implement a system for tracking the usage that the online resources they subscribe to or acquire actually get from their users in order to inform decisions about renewals or expansions of such subscriptions and purchases. Such a system could do the following:

- Access statistics gathered by the virtual library itself, which has the advantage of easy access to those statistics and easy comparability across different vendors' resources, possibly along with being able to analyze usage per user in addition to usage per resource (Kramer, 2007).

- Access statistics retrieved from, or delivered by, the vendors that provide the online resources the virtual library subscribes to. Being able to straightforwardly retrieve such statistics from the vendors, and having those statistics be comparable among different vendors resources, promises to become easier for virtual libraries with the developments of Project COUNTER (Counting Online Usage of Networked Electronic Resources) and SUSHI, the Standardized Usage

Statistics Harvesting Initiative (Needleman, 2006). However, the focus of those developments has been on e-journal access statistics.

- A combination of the two above.

Institution-appropriate evaluation criteria then need to be applied together with the gathered usage statistics. For example, librarians could divide the annual subscription cost of a resource by the number of times it has been accessed by the institution's online learners and faculty during the past 12 months to calculate a cost per use. This considered together with centrality of an information resource to the curriculum or faculty members' foci of research, or with the unique and important content a resource provides researchers and online learners, can then inform whether to renew a subscription to an online resource.

Delivering Content the Virtual Library Does Not Have

Although the content of a majority of current scholarly journal issues, and an increasing number of older journal issues, is becoming available electronically, few virtual libraries will be able to subscribe to enough aggregator databases and electronic journals to ensure that every article their users might ever need is thus directly and immediately available to them. With book content, both availability and accessibility in electronic format (as e-books) are less developed than for journals, so the chances that a needed book or book chapter will be available online are considerably smaller, though that situation may be improving with mass book digitization efforts such as Google Book Search, Microsoft Live Search Books, and the Open Content Alliance. Therefore, virtual libraries need to offer their users ways for obtaining readings that the library itself does not have.

Interlibrary Loan

For obtaining entire books or published theses or dissertations in print, the often desirable alternative to purchasing them—or the only method, if they are no longer available to buy—for the online learner is to borrow them from another library, through interlibrary loan. In the United States, the underlying processes are guided by the *Interlibrary Loan Code for the United States* (Reference and User Services Association, 2001). For online learners, important questions to ask are whether the virtual library of their institution can arrange for books obtained via interlibrary loan to be sent directly from the lending library to their home or office or whether the book must first go to their own institution's library and then be sent to them from there, which will likely take longer, and what the return process will be. Online learners may also want to explore the interlibrary loan offerings of their local public library.

Document Delivery

Unlike interlibrary loan, which arranges for the lending and borrowing of materials, document delivery provides copies of journal articles, book chapters, conference papers, and similar shorter publications for the recipient to keep. Document delivery is often provided in libraries by the same department that handles interlibrary loan requests. It is also offered by commercial providers. It is an important service for virtual libraries to (arrange to) offer their users particularly for articles from older issues of magazines, journals, newsletters, newspapers, and so on, which may only be available in print format, as well as for articles or chapters from any periodical or book that the virtual library does not have access to. Organizations that offer document delivery services directly to end users include the University of California, Los Angeles Library (Fee-Based Document Delivery for Non-UCLA Users), the British Library Document Supply Service, and MITS at the University of Michigan. Virtual library managers and document requestors alike should be aware that document suppliers generally add copyright clearance fees—which may vary considerably between publications and are paid to the publisher—to their charge for obtaining and providing the document. In some cases, the combination of all the charges for delivery of a single article can be so high that it is cheaper to purchase the back issue containing the article directly from the publisher, if still available, though that may take longer. Virtual libraries and their users should also seek a document delivery service that can provide electronic copies of documents from print sources for fast and convenient delivery via the Internet, as opposed to delivery only via fax or mail.

Linking Virtual Libraries to Online Learning

The online learning environment offers both challenges and opportunities for making the resources and services of the virtual library relevant and accessible to the learner. Librarians can identify, ideally in collaboration with instructors, information resources that will or may be useful or even required for the students to use, and provide links to them from the online learning platform the institution has chosen, such as Blackboard (Dygert & Moeller, 2007), Sakai, or WebCT. These links may go to aggregator databases or other content collections with materials generally in the same subject area as an online course, to selected electronic journal titles regarded as important for the subject area of instruction or inquiry, or to specific articles, e-books, or other works that are recommended or required reading. Linking technologies, which can be proprietary or based on standards (OpenURL and Digital Object Identifiers—DOIs) make it increasingly easy to create links from an online course or discussion forum to a specific journal article (Langston & Tyler, 2004). Librarians should also seek to place links to the virtual library's reference and instruction services into the online learning environment.

Electronic Course Reserves

Linking to online information needed by learners during an online course or seminar is not always feasible—for instance, a required reading may not be available through the resources the virtual library subscribes to, or it is available only on a platform that does not allow for the establishment of links directly to a specific article, or a required or recommended work is not yet available in electronic format at all and needs to be scanned first. In this case, electronic course reserve (i.e., e-reserve) solutions can provide the needed alternative access. Here, digital or digitized copies of articles or other works (often selected and provided by instructors) are placed on an internal server typically managed by the virtual library, and made available to the online learners (Brinkman, Lavallee-Welch, & Paul, 2004). Copyright issues need to be carefully considered, including ensuring that any requisite copyright clearance costs are paid to the publisher and that the article is made available only to the participants of a particular instructional event (online class or seminar), only for the duration of that event, and only after readers have been authenticated as enrolled participants in the event. E-reserves have become a point of contention regarding copyright law application between publishers and libraries (Albanese, 2007). Both for reasons of the copyright complexities and costs of making readings available as e-reserves, virtual libraries should generally first investigate the possibilities for directly linking to online content, which major database aggregators (Bickford, 2004) as well as e-journal providers offer.

Models for Obtaining
Access to Online Information

From the payment model perspective, virtual libraries have several possible options for securing access to the information resources needed by their students, researchers, and instructors. For any one particular work (e.g., a book or journal title), there may only be one, but increasingly, multiple options are becoming available, and librarians have to consider which one is best for any usage scenario.

Access by Subscription or Purchase

Entering into a subscription agreement with a vendor or publisher is the most common method by which virtual libraries secure access to aggregator databases and electronic journals. For electronic books and some other types of e-content, either subscription or outright purchase may be possible, depending on the content provider and the material. When considering new subscriptions, and sometimes even when renewing subscriptions, librarians need to carefully consider, and sometimes negotiate with the provider, the passages of the licensing agreement that require them or their users to undertake, or refrain from undertaking, certain activities. For example, librarians should be on the lookout for clauses that effectively require them to police end users' utilization of content or that ask them to waive rights that the copyright law of their country explicitly grants them.

Access by Pay-Per-View

Inevitably, there will be information resources (journal articles, dissertations, books, etc.) that cannot be anticipated to be needed often or urgently enough to warrant a just-in-case subscription or purchase by the virtual library. When such a resource is sought by an online learner, instructor, or researcher, interlibrary loan or document delivery are the services traditionally used to meet the information need. However, both of those methods take time, typically on the order of days to weeks. At least for periodical articles, pay-per-view access provides a sometimes costly (single articles from scholarly journals can easily cost tens of dollars) but fast alternative: the article can be downloaded immediately after credit card payment (Fadel, 2006). Publishers, having discovered and developed this revenue stream, partly in competition with document delivery services, increasingly make searching and viewing citations and abstracts of their journal articles, which once required subscription to an online database, freely available, so that researchers will easily be able to find an article, the full text of which they may then be willing to pay for.

The advantage of this development to online learners and researchers is that they can now search major article databases that their virtual library may not even subscribe to, even though they would have to pay to retrieve immediately an article of interest thus found; examples include Elsevier's ScienceDirect, Springer-Verlag's SpringerLink, and the American Psychological Association's PsycARTICLES Direct. There are also hybrid models that do not require paying for each full-text article, but also do not require a long-term subscription commitment. For example, the American Medical Association offers individual online article purchases from journals it publishes, as well as buying online access to all articles from one or more journals for a period of 24 hours.

A disadvantage of this development is that, particularly during serendipitous online browsing outside of their virtual library's Web site, online learners and researchers may happen upon an article available for pay-per-view and purchase access to it, although their virtual library may already have a database or e-journal subscription that includes that same article, so it would be available at no further cost to them. To avoid this, virtual libraries need to make it as easy as possible for their users to determine whether or not full-text articles from the periodical in question are available to them, in other words, to conduct known-item searches for articles. Because it would be very time-consuming, if not impossible, for a virtual library to create a straightforward list of which periodical titles in their various databases and e-journal hosting services provide full-text article coverage for which periods, various vendors have developed for-fee services showing exactly that for any given virtual library collection. Examples include EBSCO A-to-Z, Serials Solutions' 360 Core, and SwetsWise Title Bank.

Free Access

The traditional model for published scholarly content to become available to researchers required the individual or their library to purchase or subscribe to the containers of that content—books, journals, an so on—from the centuries where print was the only available medium into the present. However, the World Wide Web, which has greatly reduced the cost of distributing scholarly content, has enabled alternatives to the reader pays model. The content of popular and professional magazines, once only available on paper for purchase or subscription, is increasingly available online at no charge, supported by advertising. Scholarly research is also becoming increasingly available online for free through open access made possible by various models (Willinsky, 2003), be it in journals or through the growing number of institutional and subject repositories (Scholarly Publishing and Academic Resources Coalition, 2007). Even though the information resources themselves are free, virtual libraries play an important role in enabling their discovery for online learners, through the organization of resource lists and research guides on their Web sites.

Future Directions of Virtual Libraries

Virtual libraries have benefited greatly from the technological development of recent years, particularly the advances of the Internet, in what they allowed them to offer in terms of content and service delivery. The future holds potential for still further improvements:

- How electronic books are sold, packaged, accessed, searched, navigated, and read may become somewhat more standardized, for the benefit of virtual libraries and their users. Librarians are now particularly concerned with the long-term preservation of e-books, which lack the equivalent of efforts for e-journal content such as LOCKSS and Portico; this should be a shared concern for publishers.

- Federated searching has not met librarians' or users' expectations for one-stop shopping in searching and finding articles across a variety of e-journal platforms and aggregator databases to the point of being sometimes regarded as detrimental to the research process (Warren, 2007). The developers of federated searching systems, in cooperation with those of e-journal and database platforms, still have an opportunity to make them useful to online learners and researchers by making them faster, more reliable, more intuitive, and possibly capable of reaching into online content other than journal articles, such as e-books.

- Digital content that remains off-line and must be accessed on local computers or networks, or from CD-ROMs or DVD-ROMs, will hopefully become a thing of the past as Internet bandwidth restrictions, copy protection issues, and single versus multiple user licensing matters become resolved so that the Internet becomes the universal content delivery and access channel.

As the open access movement gains momentum and academic and other research institutions increasingly realize that their own communities' intellectual output needs better long-term management for preservation and access, institutional repositories gain in potential importance. Although the final product of research has traditionally been disseminated and preserved through the traditional publishing channels in the form of books and journal articles, and libraries then acquiring those publications, the intermediary products are often at high risk of becoming lost, destroyed, or for all practical purposes nonfindable: namely, data sets, interview transcripts, survey instruments, laboratory notes, photos, audio and video recordings, and so forth. Institutional repositories can become the container that makes and keeps these intermediary products available—ideally together with the final products. Virtual libraries are becoming planners and caretakers of such repositories, working with faculty members, graduate students, and other creators of research results to ensure that their papers, articles, dissertations, data sets, online learning modules, and so on find a secure and accessible home. This long-term process involves legal, procedural, policy, technical, and service aspects (Horrell, 2008).

The future holds exciting possibilities for the development and deployment of new and better information resources and services; as important as they have become in and to the online learning environment, virtual libraries have truly only begun to reach their full potential in serving and enhancing it.

References

Albanese, A. R. (2007). Down with e-reserves. *Library Journal, 132*(16), 36–38.

Association of College & Research Libraries. (2004). *Guidelines for distance learning library services.* Retrieved December 26, 2007, from http://www.ala.org/ala/mgrps/divs/acrl/standards/guidelinesdistancelearning.cfm

Bailin, A., & Pena, A. (2007). Online library tutorials, narratives, and scripts. *The Journal of Academic Librarianship, 33*(1), 106–117.

Bickford, D. (2004). Using direct linking capabilities in aggregated databases for e-reserves. *Journal of Library Administration, 41*(1/2), 31–45.

Blakeslee, S., & Johnson, K. (2002). Using HorizonLive to deliver library instruction to distance and online students. *Reference Services Review, 30*(4), 324–329.

Bracke, M. S., Brewer, M., & Huff-Eibl, R. (2007). Finding information in a new landscape: Developing new service and staffing models for mediated information services. *College & Research Libraries, 68*(3), 248–267.

Brinkman, C. S., Lavallee-Welch, C., & Paul, M. T. (2004). From pilot to program: Developing an e-reserves service. *Kentucky Libraries, 68*(2), 9–13.

Carter, D. S. (2002). Hurry up and wait: Observations and tips about the practice of chat reference. *The Reference Librarian, 38*(79/80), 113–120.

Chambers, M. B., & So, S. (2004). Full-text aggregator database vendors and journal publishers: A study of a complex relationship. *Serials Review, 30*(3), 183–193.

Dygert, C., & Moeller, P. (2007). Linking the library and campus course management system. *The Serials Librarian, 52*(3/4), 305–309.

Fadel, S. (2006). The pay-per-view trend. *Online, 30*(6), 39–42.

Gilbert, L. M., Mengxiong, L., & Matoush, T. (2006). Assessing digital reference and online instructional services in an integrated public/university library. *The Reference Librarian, 46*(95/96), 149–172.

Horrell, J. L. (2008). Converting and preserving the scholarly record: An overview. *Library Resources & Technical Services, 52*(1), 27–32.

Kramer, S. (2007). *Pattern of online library resource usage per user in a distributed graduate education environment.* Retrieved December 28, 2007, from http://dlist.sir.arizona.edu/1876

Krumenaker, L. (2001). A tempest in a librarian's teapot: EBSCO, ProQuest, gale exclusive, and unique titles [Electronic version]. *Searcher, 7*(9).

Langston, M., & Tyler, J. (2004). Linking to journal articles in an online teaching environment: The persistent link, DOI, and OpenURL. *The Internet and Higher Education, 7*(1), 51–58.

Lee, I. J. (2004). Do virtual reference librarians dream of digital reference questions? A qualitative and quantitative analysis of email and chat reference. *Australian Academic & Research Libraries, 35*(2), 95–110.

Lindsay, E. B., Cummings, L., & Johnson, C. M. (2006). If you build it, will they learn? Assessing online information literacy tutorials. *College & Research Libraries, 67*(5), 429–445.

McCain, C. (2007). Telephone calls received at an academic library's reference desk: A new analysis. *The Reference Librarian, 47*(2), 5–16.

Milliot, J. (2007). E-books need visibility. *Publishers Weekly, 254*(28), 16.

Mirsky, S. (2007). ReadyGo delivers an online tutorial. *Computers in Libraries, 27*(8), 6–8, 54–56.

Moyo, L. M. (2006). Virtual reference services and instruction: An assessment. *The Reference Librarian, 46*(95/96), 213–230.

Needleman, M. H. (2006). The NISO standardized usage statistics harvesting initiative (SUSHI). *Serials Review, 32*(3), 216–217.

Reference and User Services Association. (2001). *Interlibrary loan code for the United States.* Retrieved January /11, 2009, from http://www.ala.org/ala/mgrps/divs/rusa/archive/protools/referenceguide/interlibrary.cfm

Reference and User Services Association. (2004). *Guidelines for implementing and maintaining virtual reference services.* Retrieved January 11, 2009, from http://www.ala.org/ala/mgrps/divs/rusa/archive/protools/referenceguide/virtrefguidelines.cfm

Rusch-Feja, D. D. (2001). Libraries: Digital, electronic, and hybrid. In N. J. Smelser & P. B. Baltes (Eds.), *International encyclopedia of the social & behavioral sciences* (pp. 8810–8814). Oxford, UK: Pergamon Press.

Schneider, K. G. (2007). Lots of librarians can keep stuff safe. *Library Journal, 132*(13), 30–31.

Scholarly Publishing and Academic Resources Coalition. (2007). *Repository resources.* Retrieved January 20, 2008, from http://www.arl.org/sparc/repositories

Tenopir, C. (2004). Chat's positive side. *Library Journal, 129*(20), 42.

University of Pennsylvania Library. (2004). *Penn library FAQ.* Retrieved January 21, 2008, from http://datafarm.library.upenn.edu/pennlibraryfaq/faqmain.htm

Van de Sompel, H. & Beit-Arie, O. (2001). Open linking in the scholarly information environment using the OpenURL framework [Electronic version]. *D-Lib Magazine, 7*(3).

Warren, D. (2007). Lost in translation: The reality of federated searching. *Australian Academic & Research Libraries, 38*(4), 258–269.

Wilder, S. (2005). Information literacy makes all the wrong assumptions. *Chronicle of Higher Education, 51*(18), B13.

Willinsky, J. (2003). The nine flavours of open access scholarly publishing. *Journal of Postgraduate Medicine, 49*(3), 263–267.

Index

About the Editors

Kjell Erik Rudestam is Associate Dean of Academic Affairs in the School of Psychology at Fielding Graduate University. He was also a founding faculty member of Fielding's Master's Program in Organizational Design and Effectiveness. Prior to his affiliation with Fielding, he was a Professor of Psychology at York University in Toronto. He holds a PhD in psychology (clinical) from the University of Oregon and an honorary doctorate from the Professional School of Psychology. He is coeditor (with Judith Schoenholtz-Read) of the *Handbook of Online Learning* (1st edition) and coeditor of the *Encyclopedia of Distributed Education*, as well as the author of seven books, including two Sage research publications (*Surviving Your Dissertation* [3rd edition] and *Your Statistical Consultant*, both with Rae Newton), and numerous published articles in the areas of clinical psychology (psychotherapy and change processes and suicide), research methodology, and online pedagogy. Dr. Rudestam is a Fellow of the American Psychological Association (Division 12) and a Diplomate of the American Board of Examiners in Professional Psychology (clinical).

Judith Schoenholtz-Read is the Director of the Respecialization in Clinical Psychology Program and faculty in the School of Psychology at the Fielding Graduate Institute. She received her EdD from the Department of Counseling Psychology at the University of British Columbia (UBC) and served as a coordinator of an intensive group treatment center at the UBC Health Sciences Centre Hospital. She is coeditor (with Kjell Rudestam) of the *Handbook of Online Learning* (1st edition) and has been studying retention in distance learning and online environments for the past 12 years. She has written about clinical training online (with Dean Janoff) and has published articles on topics related to gender and psychotherapy. She was secretary of Division 49 of the American Psychological Association (group psychology and psychotherapy) and is a fellow of the American Group Psychotherapy Association and of the Canadian Group Psychotherapy Association.

About the Contributors

Dorothy Agger-Gupta is a professor and Associate Dean in the doctoral program in the School of Human and Organization Development at Fielding Graduate University. She received her PhD from the School of Management at the University of Massachusetts, Amherst. Her research interests include social networking and online games, ethics in virtual living, escalation and negotiation, and phenomenographic research. She has extensive experience as a systems developer and is an artist.

Grace Chun has an undergraduate degree in Economic Law from Southwest Nationality University (Chengdu, Sichuan, China) and an MA degree in Communication from the University of Hawaii at Manoa. She has worked as both an apprentice lawyer and as an international school teacher in China. Her professional interests include leadership, coaching, intercultural communication and training, and online learning in education and geographically dispersed teams.

Charles Crowell is Associate Professor of Management and the Director of Entrepreneurship at Southern Vermont College. At Southern Vermont College, he designed and leads an innovative entrepreneurship and management program called Build the Enterprise (BTE), which emphasizes inquiry and practice in knowledge management topics, sustainable enterprise activities, and working in global environments. BTE is the first degree program in the U.S. to integrate learning applications of the Kindle 2 into all of its coursework. His current projects at South Vermont include developing both its online programs and eMobile educational applications. He is also the President of the Institute for Virtual Inquiry.

Anna DiStefano has served as the Provost for Fielding Graduate University since August, 1996. She received her EdD and her MEd both in Counseling, from Boston University. She was awarded an American Council of Education Fellowship (1987–1988). Her specialized areas of interest are planning and leadership in higher education, especially distributed education, feminism, public schooling, moral development, and conflict resolution. Her most recent publications include a special issue of *American Behavioral Scientist* titled "Researching Across Difference" (coedited with Jody Veroff) and the *Encyclopedia of Distributed Learning* (coedited with Kjell E. Rudestam and Robert Silverman).

Jenny Edwards is on the faculty of the doctoral program in Educational Leadership and Change for Fielding Graduate University. She has been working in the field of education for 35 years. She obtained her PhD in Human and Organizational Systems from Fielding Institute in 1993. She has done extensive research in the field of Cognitive Coaching[SM]. She served as Project Director and Principal Investigator for a 3-year, $3 million grant that she coauthored from the U.S. Department of Education. She investigated the effects of Cognitive Coaching[SM], Nonverbal Classroom Management, and monthly dialogue groups on teacher efficacy, conceptual development, learner-centeredness, empowerment, and other related areas. She has presented seminars in 11 countries in French, Spanish, Italian, and English on multiple topics.

Gary Fontaine is a professor in the School of Communications at the University of Hawaii at Manoa and an adjunct faculty the Master's Program in Organization Management and Development at the Fielding Graduate University. He obtained his PhD in social psychology from the University of Western Australia. His professional focus is on persons, teams, and organizations as they encounter the challenges of novel and rapidly changing ecologies characterized by new people, places, cultures, and technologies. He has applied this focus to contexts such as global assignments in business and government, diverse and rapidly changing workplaces and communities at home, geographically dispersed teams, and online learning. His most recent emphases have been on coaching teams and leaders and on self-organization and swarm intelligence models of globalization in multinational enterprises.

Stephanie Galindo is Administrator and Student Dean for an online graduate program focused on managing change and complexity. She has specialized in mentoring and retention strategies to offset early attrition, and has designed and cotaught preparatory courses for ABD students. She has an Advanced Certificate in Educational Management from the University of Leicester and a Master's of Education Degree from American Intercontinental University. She has professional certificates in visual communications from the University of California at Santa Barbara and another in hospitality management. Ms. Galindo holds a utility patent and has worked to streamline operations in OEM manufacturing, publishing, and health care venues.

Yolanda Gayol is a faculty mentor in the doctoral program at the School of Educational Leadership and Change at Fielding Graduate University. She earned an EdD in adult-distance education at Pennsylvania State University. She has worked as a distance education specialist at the World Bank, the Inter-American Development Bank and NASA Goddard Space Flight Center.

She has been Program Director in the Master of Distance of Distance Education at the University of Maryland University College (UMUC). She has been an international consultant and keynote speaker in Latin America and Europe. Dr. Gayol has been funded to conduct research on digital fluency of citizens, government officials, science teachers, faculty, and graduate students. Presently, she is studying how critical pedagogy can impact Second Life regarding teaching, learning and acting as a public intellectual.

Sue Marquis Gordon received her PhD in sociology from the University of Chicago. Currently, she is a member of the faculty of the Educational Leadership and Change Program at Fielding Graduate University where her research interests are mentoring and learning at a distance. Prior to Fielding, at the Educational Developmental Center (EDC), she was Principal Investigator and Director of a number of grants focusing on the placement of children with special needs in general education classrooms.

Pierre-Léonard Harvey is a professor in the Department of Social and Public Communication on the Faculty of Communication at the University of Quebec in Montreal, where he is also the Director of the Community Informatics Laboratory. He is one of the founding member of the Hexagram Institute for Research and Creation in Media Arts and Technologies, which is a partnership between four universities: Concordia, UQAM, McGill, and University of Montreal. He is also Director of the Program in Research and Cultural Animation in UQAM. He obtained his PhD from the Department of Sociology at the University of Montreal and a Master's Degree in Social Psychology from the University Louis-Pasteur in Strasbourg, France. He is the author of several published articles and books on virtual communities, community informatics design, e-learning, and collaborative work environment. He is the team leader of an International group of researchers working on the project COL@B, which is a new research collaboratory focusing on organizational communication and storytelling, knowledge-based economy, social system design, telework, electronic commerce, virtual communities, and online learning.

James Hirsen is a *New York Times* best-selling author, commentator, media analyst, and educator. He has taught Media/Entertainment Law and Ethics in the journalism school of Biola University for six years and at Trinity Law School for fifteen years. He holds a JD, magna cum laude, from Northrop University and MA in Media Psychology from Fielding Graduate University. Hirsen is admitted to practice in the California and Washington, D.C. Bar Associations as well as the U.S. Supreme Court and the U.S. Court of International Trade. He has made several appearances as a friend of the court in the U.S. Supreme Court.

Barclay Hudson has been a founding faculty member of several innovative programs including the Graduate Program in Urban Planning at UCLA, the Center for Regenerative Studies at Cal Poly Pomona, and the Master's Program in Organization Management and Development (OMD) at the

Fielding Graduate University. He received his EdD from Harvard University and has worked with the Harvard Center for Education and Development, the Harvard Office of Programmed Instruction, and the Harvard Economic Research Project, where he participated in forecasting studies under Nobel laureate Wassily Leontief. His overseas consulting on educational and economic development has included Chile, Costa Rica, Bangladesh, and Tunisia—mainly with the Ford Foundation, Harvard, and the United Nations. He has also worked in the fields of environmental science (UCLA) and human rights, particularly for the rights to water.

Shelley K. Hughes has been Director of the Fielding Graduate Institute's online academic environment since 1997. She oversees the development of Fielding's Learning and Community Support system that includes a portal, as well as collaborative forum software, structured learning environments, and Web content. She is coauthor, with Jeremy Shapiro, of "Information Literacy as a Liberal Art" (*EDUCOM Review*, 1996). Her background in counseling psychology informs her work with adults around the use of technology. Current interests include the intersection of social behavior with technology, information management, and usability.

Stefan Kramer received his Master's in Librarianship from the University of Washington in 1993 and worked in Internet user services for the Northwest Academic Computing Consortium and the University of Washington. From 1999 to January 2007, he was Director of Library Services at Fielding Graduate University, where he developed online library resources and services. He is presently the Social Science Data Librarian at Yale University.

Bruce LaRue is President of Applied Development Services, Inc., a consultancy specializing in executive and organization development. As a consultant and professor, Bruce works with managers and executives in aerospace, the U.S. Department of Defense, wireless telecommunications, network technologies, pharmaceuticals, petrochemicals, financial services, municipal government, and the nonprofit sector. Dr. LaRue is a Founding Faculty Member of the Adizes Graduate School, and his publications are used in graduate schools and organizations worldwide.

Bernard Luskin is CEO/Provost and a professor at Touro University Worldwide. Luskin has also been Chancellor/President and CEO at Jones International University, Orange Coast College, and Coastline College. He is founding director of the Media Psychology program at Fielding Graduate University, where he was Executive Vice President. Luskin is author of nine books and has been awarded two Emmys for documentary films. In industry, Luskin was president of Philips Interactive Media, Philips Education and Reference Publishing, Jones Education Networks, Mind Extension University, and Knowledge TV. He has served on the faculty at Claremont Graduate University, UCLA, California State University, and The University of Oxford. A leader in media and distance education, Luskin received distinguished leadership awards from the UCLA Doctoral Alumni Association, California State University, the Irish Government, and the European Union.

Robin Mason is a professor of Educational Technology at the Open University, where she has designed, tutored and directed the Master's Programme in Online and Distance Education. Her academic interests include open educational content, e-learning, distributed learning in developing countries, and Web 2.0 tools. She currently holds two European Union grants on the use of open educational content with developing countries. Recently she has published two books: *Key Concepts in Elearning* (with Professor Rennie) and *Educational Uses of EPortfolios* (with L. Steffani and C. Pegler).

Rena M. Palloff is a mentoring faculty member in the Educational Leadership and Change Doctoral Program as well as a faculty member of the Master's of Organizational Management and Development and the Director of the Teaching in the Virtual Classroom Graduate Certificate Program at Fielding Graduate University. Rena also holds an academic position at Capella University in the School of Human Services. She and Keith Pratt are managing partners of Crossroads Consulting Group and the authors of the Frandson award-winning book, *Building Learning Communities in Cyberspace,* published in 1999. They have since written 5 additional books on the topic of online learning. Their most recent, *Assessing the Online Learner,* was released in November 2008. Dr. Palloff earned a Master's Degree in Organizational Development and a PhD in Human and Organizational Systems from Fielding Graduate University.

Janet Poley is CEO and President of the American Distance Education Consortium (ADEC). She develops collaborative distance education initiatives and conducts research and education programs related to technology access and applications with more than 60 land-grant university members and international affiliates. She is in the International Adult and Continuing Education Hall of Fame and on its Board of Directors, a Board member and Treasurer of Sloan-C, on the NASULGC Committee on Partnerships between African and U.S. Universities, a member of the Creighton University Health Sciences Distance Education Advisory Board, and a member of the Board of Advisors for Zamorano University in Honduras. Dr. Poley received the Mildred B. and Charles A. Wedemeyer Award for Outstanding Practitioner in Distance Education in 2000. She is a professor in the College of Journalism and the Institute of Agricultural and Natural Resources at the University of Nebraska–Lincoln. Dr. Poley is the author of a number of journal articles, book chapters, and presentations on information technology and distance learning and is currently authoring a book titled *Building an Inclusive Future for Learning: A Practical Guide for Campuses and Communities.*

Keith Pratt has previously served as the Dean of Distance Learning and Educational Technology at Northwest Arkansas Community College. He also served as a Senior Project Manager for Datatel, Inc. He retired from the Air Force after 22 years as a Computer Systems Engineer and worked with many organizations such as the National Security Agency, Department of the Navy, Department of the Army, and the Coast Guard. Dr. Pratt teaches in the Graduate School at Colorado State University Global in both the Business and Online Teaching and Learning program. He is currently the Lead Mentor for the Faculty Development Training program at Northcentral University. Dr. Pratt has coauthored seven books, the first of which won the Frandson Award for most significant contribution to Adult Continuing Education Literature. He holds an MA and PhD in Human and Organizational Systems from the Fielding Graduate University and an MS in Human Resource Management and Development from Chapman University. Dr. Pratt also has an Honorary Doctorate in Economics from Moscow State University, Russia.

Frank Rennie is Professor of Sustainable Rural Development at the UHI Millennium Institute in the Highlands and Islands of Scotland and is the Head of Research and Post Graduate Development at Lews Castle College, UHI. He is the Course Leader for the MSc in Managing Sustainable Rural Development at the UHI. His research interests lie in the general areas of rural and community development, especially in community-based approaches to integrated sustainable development. His recent work has been on new approaches to online education and distributed learning with rural communities and individuals, particularly Open Access and Open Content resources. He has been an advisor to several government committees and is a Fellow of a number of learned societies. Dr. Rennie has published a wide range of resources related to rural issues, including over 20 books, most recently *Elearning: the Key Concepts* (with Robin Mason) and *E-learning and Social Networking Handbook*.

Jeremy J. Shapiro is a faculty member in the PhD Program in Human and Organization Development and Senior Consultant on Academic Information Projects at Fielding Graduate University. His PhD, in the history of ideas, is from Brandeis University. With a background in critical social theory and computer science, and with experience as an information systems professional, his current research interests are computer simulation as a social and historical phenomenon, the impact of Internet technologies on identity and embodied experience, nonhierarchical classification systems for information and knowledge, and information literacy, and he has published or presented papers on these topics. He is a coauthor of *Mindful Inquiry in Social Research* (Sage, 1998) and of *Computers for Social Change and Community Organizing* (Hayworth Press, 1991).

Judith Stevens-Long is an Associate Dean of the PhD Program in Human and Organization Development at the Fielding Graduate Institute. She was codirector and founder of the Organization Design and Effectiveness Program at Fielding. She received her PhD in developmental psychology from the University of California, Los Angeles. She has written several textbooks on human development, including four editions of *Adult Life: Developmental Processes,* and numerous articles on personality development, theories and paradigms in adult development, group process, and the role of empathy in human development.

Kay Wijekumar is Associate Professor in the College of Information Sciences and Technology at Pennsylvania State University Beaver. She obtained her MS in Computer Science from the University of Pittsburgh and a PhD in Instructional Systems from Pennsylvania State University. Her expertise includes serving as a Senior Consultant at Accenture Corporation and more recently as a researcher concentrating on the effectiveness of learning technologies. She is a co-Principle Investigator for the Odyssey Math randomized control trial being conducted by the Regional Educational Laboratory-Mid-Atlantic and also Principle Investigator for the efficacy trial on the Intelligent Tutoring System for the Structure Strategy (ITSS) software. Her professional focus is geared to understanding the effects of computer learning environments and whether we can improve their effectiveness.

Leni Wildflower is the Director of the Evidence Based Coaching certificate programs at Fielding Graduate University. She studied at the University of California at Berkeley, the University of Hawaii, and obtained her PhD. from Fielding Graduate University in Human and Organizational Development. As Director of the coaching certificates, her interests include both online teaching in the application of evidence based theories to coaching strategies and developing coaching competence through face-to-face skills training. Dr. Wildflower has worked for over 30 years as a coach, consultant, and educator. Fielding University's coaching program's manual, edited by Dr. Wildflower, *Origins and Applications of Evidence Based Coaching* is being revised for publication in 2009.

Judy Witt has served as Dean of the School of Educational Leadership and Change at Fielding Graduate University since June, 1998. She received her PhD from Fielding Graduate University and her MS in Special Education from Portland State University. She was also was a principle of the consulting firm The Hobbs Group, assisting many higher education institutions in organizational development as well as the development of new degree programs. Her specialized areas of interest are leadership and innovation in higher education, especially distributed education; adult learning; student services; and organizational development. Her most recent publications include coauthored articles with Fielding Faculty Four Arrows *An Indigenous Perspective on Women in*

Leadership: A Case Study in Higher Education and *Collaborative action Learning* and *Leadership: A Feminist/Indigenous Model for Higher Education.*

Ralph Wolff was appointed President and Executive Director of the Senior College Commission of the Western Association of Schools and Colleges in 1996. WASC serves 160 institutions in California, Hawaii, and the Pacific Basin. He led WASC to a multi-stage learning-centered approach. For this work, he was selected as the recipient of the 2008 Virginia B. Smith Innovative Leadership Award. In 2007, he was appointed by Secretary of Education Spellings to serve as a negotiator for negotiated rulemaking proceedings on accreditation. He is an elected Fellow of Meridian International, a global think tank, and the World Academy of Art and Science. He writes and speaks extensively on the changing character of accountability. Prior to joining the Commission staff, Mr. Wolff was on the law faculty of the University of Dayton Law School. Previously, he was a founder of the Antioch School of Law, the first law school expressly designed to prepare lawyers to serve in public interest. He also served as Associate Provost of Antioch College and Dean of the Graduate School of Education.

Supporting researchers
for more than 40 years

Research methods have always been at the core of SAGE's publishing program. Founder Sara Miller McCune published SAGE's first methods book, *Public Policy Evaluation*, in 1970. Soon after, she launched the *Quantitative Applications in the Social Sciences* series—affectionately known as the "little green books."

Always at the forefront of developing and supporting new approaches in methods, SAGE published early groundbreaking texts and journals in the fields of qualitative methods and evaluation.

Today, more than 40 years and two million little green books later, SAGE continues to push the boundaries with a growing list of more than 1,200 research methods books, journals, and reference works across the social, behavioral, and health sciences. Its imprints—Pine Forge Press, home of innovative textbooks in sociology, and Corwin, publisher of PreK–12 resources for teachers and administrators—broaden SAGE's range of offerings in methods. SAGE further extended its impact in 2008 when it acquired CQ Press and its best-selling and highly respected political science research methods list.

From qualitative, quantitative, and mixed methods to evaluation, SAGE is the essential resource for academics and practitioners looking for the latest methods by leading scholars.

For more information, visit **www.sagepub.com**.